THE YEAR'S WORK 1995

The Year's Work in Critical and Cultural Theory 5

Edited by
KATE McGOWAN

Advisory Editors

STEVEN CONNOR (Birkbeck College, London)
TERRY EAGLETON (St Catherine's College, Oxford)
LAWRENCE GROSSBERG (University of North Carolina,
Chapel Hill)
STUART HALL (The Open University)
LINDA HUTCHEON (University of Toronto)
FREDRIC JAMESON (Duke University)
CHRISTOPHER NORRIS (University of Wales, Cardiff)
ELAINE SHOWALTER (Princeton University)
ALAN SINFIELD (University of Sussex)
STAN SMITH (University of Dundee)
PATRICIA WAUGH (University of Durham)

Published for
THE ENGLISH ASSOCIATION

by
 **BLACKWELL** *Publishers*

Copyright © The English Association 1998

First published 1998

2 4 6 8 10 9 7 5 3 1

Blackwell Publishers Ltd
108 Cowley Road
Oxford OX4 1JF
UK

Blackwell Publishers Inc.
350 Main Street
Malden, Massachusetts 02148
USA

British Library Cataloguing in Publication Data
A CIP catalogue record for this book is available from the British Library.

Library of Congress data has been applied for

ISBN 0–631–20896–8 (hbk)

Typeset in 9 on 10pt Times by Forewords, Oxford, and
Longworth Editorial Services, Oxford.
Printed in Great Britain by MPG Ltd, Bodmin, Cornwall

This book is printed on acid-free paper

Preface

The Year's Work in Critical and Cultural Theory is a companion volume to *The Year's Work in English Studies*, also published for the English Association by Blackwell Publishers. It provides a narrative bibliography of work in the field of critical and cultural theory, recording significant debates and issues of interest in a broad field of research in the humanities and social sciences. This volume covers books and journal articles published in 1995, and will be of interest to scholars working in many areas of literary and cultural studies as well as in media and visual arts, and law and policy.

Now in its fifth year of publication, *The Year's Work in Critical and Cultural Theory* has grown significantly from the time of its inception in 1991. This year the volume consists of twenty-one chapters, including five new chapters in the following areas: 'Postmodernism', 'Science, Technology and Culture', 'Cultural Policy', 'Law and Culture' and 'Australian Pacific Cultural Theory'. These additions reflect the volume's continuing commitment to expanding the range and the scope of work developing in the field of cultural studies and theory, as well as to encouraging contributions from scholars working in critical and cultural theory outside of the British Isles. This commitment to development will continue in future volumes and the range of chapters offered will expand accordingly. While every effort is made to consider the expansion of the volume in the direction of new and developing areas of critical and cultural theory, suggestions and proposals will always be welcomed by the Editor.

Regrettably, we are unable this year to include what have been regular chapters on 'Intertextuality', 'Art History and Visual Cultural Studies' and 'Theories of Reading and Reception'. However, all three of these chapters will return in the next volume with comprehensive reviews of work in respective fields, covering publications from 1996 as well as 1997.

Readers will note that the volume is again divided into two sections – Part I: Critical Theory, and Part II: Culture and Communications. Though arbitrary, this division is intended once again to emphasize a commitment to developing work in areas of cultural concern which may not necessarily be encompassed in the traditional canon of poststructuralist critical theory. This is a feature which will remain in place in future volumes.

No bibliography of this kind can claim to be complete in its review of new publications. Authors, publishers and editors are therefore invited to submit review copies of journals, books and articles for inclusion in future volumes. Items for review should be addressed to The Secretary, The English Association, The University of Leicester, University Road, Leicester LE1 7RH.

Kate McGowan
The Manchester Metropolitan University

The English Association

This bibliography is an English Association publication. It is available through membership of the Association; non-members can purchase it through any good bookshop.

The object of the English Association is to promote the knowledge and appreciation of the English language and its literatures.

The Association pursues these aims by creating opportunities of co-operation among all those interested in English; by furthering the recognition of English as essential in education; by discussing methods of English teaching; by holding lectures, conferences, and other meetings; by publishing a journal, books and leaflets; and by forming local branches overseas and at home.

Publications

The Year's Work in English Studies. An annual evaluative bibliography. Published by Blackwell Publishers, Oxford and Malden, MA.

The Year's Work in Critical and Cultural Theory. The first issue of this new critical theory volume appeared in 1994. Published by Blackwell Publishers, Oxford and Malden, MA.

Essays and Studies. An annual volume of essays by various scholars assembled by the collector covering usually a wide range of subjects and authors from the medieval to the modern. Published by Boydell and Brewer, Woodbridge, Suffolk.

English. The journal of the Association, *English*, is published three times a year by the English Association.

Use of English. This journal is published three times a year by the English Association.

English 4–11. This journal is published three times a year.

Benefits of Membership

Institutional Membership
Full members receive copies of *The Year's Work in English Studies*, *Essays and Studies*, *English* (three issues) and three *News-Letters*.

Ordinary Membership covers *English* (three issues) and three *News-Letters*.

Schools Membership covers one copy of each issue of *English*, one copy of the *Use of English*, one copy of *Essays and Studies*, three *News-Letters*, and preferential booking for Sixth-Form Conference places.

Individual Membership
Individuals take out basic membership, which entitles them to buy all regular publications of the English Association at a discounted price and three *News-Letters*.

For further details write to The Secretary, The English Association, The University of Leicester, University Road, Leicester LE1 7RH.

Contents

Part I

Critical Theory

Critical Theory: General

DAVID AMIGONI

This chapter has six sections: 1. Defining the Literary: Literature, the Institution and Philosophy; 2. Listening and Discerning Readers: Counselling, Christianity and Theory; 3. Marxism and Literary History; 4. After Foucault; 5. Structuralism Revisited: Mimologics; 6. Reference Works.

1. Defining the Literary: Literature, the Institution and Philosophy

The work of the late Bill Readings on 'The University without Culture' (see the essay of this title, *New Literary History* 26:iii.465–92) asks what happens to literary pedagogy when the postmodern 'university of excellence' no longer defines itself in terms of its service to the national culture and opts instead to reassure its customers, again and again, how good it is at being good (see Readings's 'Dwelling in the Ruins', *Oxford Literary Review* 17.17–28, and Timothy Clark's editorial to this issue entitled 'The University in Ruins').

This raises again the question of literature's relations to culture and whether the languages of literature and culture are resurgent rhetorics or dying discourses. This year's work has seen renewed debate over locating and reading the literary, and the terms in which its significance should be affirmed, institutionally or otherwise. Well-established but polarized positions in this debate – materialist criticism against deconstruction – were marked out in *Textual Practice* (now under the editorship of Alan Sinfield). Isobel Armstrong's 'Textual Harassment: The Ideology of Close Reading' (9:iii.401–20) draws attention to the fact that 'close reading', once taken to be the pedagogic guardian of the literary and its poetic canon as defined by the New Critics, is sixty years old. Armstrong is not convinced that close reading is ready for retirement. Instead, taking Stanley Fish's sexualized and erotic defence of close reading as a starting point (Clarendon Lecture 1993), she suggests that 'the task of a new definition of close reading is to rethink the power of affect, feeling and emotion in a *cognitive* space'. Armstrong breaks down the thought/feeling binary through a reading of Levinas, but her theoretical quarry is Voloshinov's emphasis on material struggle, and this enables her to read Wordsworth's 'Tintern Abbey' as a mode of 'thinking' which examines and creates categories of knowledge through a rigorous transferential struggle for the sign.

Alternatively John Hillis Miller's 'History, Narrative and Responsibility:

Speech Acts in *The Aspern Papers*' (9:ii.243–67) argues for a fundamental distinction between speech acts as defined by Austin, and speech acts as conceptualized by Derrida and de Man. Claiming that an historical event cannot be known through narration, and taking James's *The Aspern Papers* as the text which performs this insight, Hillis Miller argues, following Derrida and de Man, for a conception of the speech act as performative which emphasizes the non-phenomenal and non-knowable aspects of literature, philosophy and action. It is precisely in this indeterminate space that 'history' is made and an ethics of reading takes shape; and it is through reading texts such as *The Aspern Papers* that readers become aware of the incalculable effects of the speech act on the future, and the responsibilities bound up in reproducing speech acts. Hillis Miller returns to the speech act in his essay 'The University of Dissensus' (*Oxford Literary Review* 17. 121–43) in which he claims that this speech act-oriented ethics of reading alone evades a troubling complicity with the institutional nihilism of the 'excellence'-fixated postmodern university. Furthermore, Hillis Miller makes the controversial claim that cultural studies's 'constructionist' models of reading and representation are complicit with the postmodern university's new politics.

For others in this debate, it is a matter of tenaciously affirming the specificity of the literary. Simon Dentith reacts to a personally troubling institutional curricular review by means of a theoretically inclined plea for an acknowledgement of literature's unique sense of historicity and otherness ('Teaching Theory Again', *English* 44:178.71–8). Roger Shattock's trenchantly anti-theoretical 'Nineteen Theses on Literature' (*Essays in Criticism* XLV:iii.193–8) declares that 'in order to affirm literature in its full humanist sense, let us eschew the tendentious, freestanding word, *text*'. Both Shattock and Dentith resist the instrumentalist presumption of some other discourse's mastery over literature.

This connects them to Mark Edmundson's *Literature Against Philosophy*, which argues that since Plato's banishing of the poets from the republic philosophy has been opposed to literature. For Edmundson this takes the form of literature's 'disenfranchisement'. Critical theory has continued to operate in a similar vein, and yet Edmundson is keen to stress that even the so-called 'foundations' of literary criticism are faulty. Edmundson argues that if Plato undermined the literary, then so too has the tradition inaugurated by Aristotle's formalism; a tradition of structuralist practice which Edmundson finds productively deconstructed in the work of Derrida. This is not, as Edmundson is right to stress, an anti-theoretical tract.

Edmundson argues that formalisms and structuralisms need to be deconstructed because they bring literary utterances 'under the control of concepts and so assume a godlike detachment and power'. In part, then, Edmundson is a suspicious interpreter (and he acknowledges that Foucault's project has touched the book). However, his suspicion is principally directed at the rhetorics which enable critical theories to disenfranchise art and claim authority for their own neo-Platonic and neo-Aristotelian operations. The central figure here – in a double sense – is de Manian 'blindness and insight', itself a Coleridgean legacy which critics who 'feel they have passed beyond de Man' still unconsciously practise (so Edmundson, simultaneously a fellow-travelling Freudian, is not above utilizing the figure for himself). For Edmundson, the operations of blindness and insight operate most problematically in New Historicist criticism, and he critically analyses recent classics by Marjorie Levinson (on the repressions in 'Tintern Abbey') and Marlon Ross. As the target critics suggest, Romanticism is the field upon which Edmundson builds what amounts to an anti-historicist defence of poetry. Edmundson asks why it should be such a matter of conscience to account for poetry in terms of origins – repressed or otherwise – and his point is that philosophy and history should recognize their limits and acknowledge those points where Wordsworthian poetry – for example 'Intimations of Immortality' – resists explanation. Edmundson performs this central point with the aid of lucid and sympathetic readings of Derrida, Barthes and Foucault, and concludes with an analysis of the work of Harold Bloom. It appears that the early Bloom holds for Edmundson the promise of a poetic criticism; yet it is precisely Bloom's most famous work, *The Anxiety of Influence*, which, Edmundson argues, is not about poetry at all, but instead the operations of professional, literary-critical anxiety.

Edmundson's book is elegant and insightful, but I did wonder, when told that Bob Dylan's music was 'one of the major artistic accomplishments of this century', if Edmundson was a neo-Ricksian dressed in Foucault's clothes. Moreover, his naive musings on the possibility of institutional openness – 'open up the Ph.D. process a little, allowing anyone who could write a good book of literary criticism, and could speak well about major works, to join our number . . . . give a few poet-philosophers a chance' – could benefit from a critical encounter with Bourdieu.

The 'workaday world of meaning production' haunts Paul H. Fry's *A Defence of Poetry* and its account of the 'ostensive moment' which defines literature, placing it temporarily – but only temporarily – beyond this world and its processes. For Fry, the ostensive moment is neither historical nor linguistic, nor, properly speaking, semiotic: instead 'as a sign of the preconceptual . . . . [it] is merely indicial, disclosing neither the purpose nor the structure of existence but only existence itself'. Fry insists that the scope of his argument about the disclosure of 'non-significance' is modest, and it is for this reason that much of his book is conducted in the negative – carefully delineating what the ostensive moment is not, even though its disclosure is dependent upon the interconnections between genre, structure and history. There are many parallels between Fry's book and Edmundson's. In common with Edmundson, Fry's book is punctuated by exemplary re-readings of Romantic poetry – particularly the work of Wordsworth, Keats and Byron. And Fry too has written a book which, whilst sceptical about the claims of the New Historicism (the example is McGann's well-known essay on Keats), conducts itself via a deep and sophisticated engagement with the theoretical writings of Adorno, Heidegger, Bachelard, Lyotard and Blanchot. However, whereas Edmundson seeks to address the current state of the literary institution and academy, Fry pursues a different direction. Indeed, Fry's path is consciously pitted against the pedagogics of Gerald Graff – 'teach the conflicts' – which Fry contends 'is now inspiring the closest thing to a teaching revolution in [the US] since Brooks and Warren'. In its place Fry proposes, in alliance with Lyotard and Blanchot, that we come to terms with the ostensive moment as a panhistorical anthropological gesture which, paradoxically, thinks the non-human as only human beings can do. Clearly Fry's invocation of Blanchot in defining this anthropological gesture helps him to a more critically acute solution than Cameron Laux finds in the traditionally humanistic 'anthropological turn' taken by Tzvetan Todorov's later work, which is analysed in 'Mapping the Other: On Anthropology and Literature's Limits' (*Paragraph* 18:ii.194–209).

The work of Maurice Blanchot is one of Fry's supportive reference points, but as Michael Holland points out in *The Blanchot Reader*, Blanchot remains a shadowy significance – this despite an increasing awareness of Blanchot's importance to Derrida, Foucault and Levinas, and the fact that the majority of Blanchot's works are now translated into English. According to Holland, Blanchot's enigmatic status is not merely due to Blanchot's own ascetic refusal to self-disclose, but indeed owes something to commentators' insistence on Blanchot's apparent unworldliness and ahistoricism. Holland's collection of Blanchot's writings aims to revise this impression. In addition to reproducing writings which clearly define the terms in which Blanchot has conducted dialogues with Barthes ('The Pursuit of the Zero Point', 1953), Levinas (over Judaism and the Other in 'The Indestructible', 1962), and Derrida ('Thanks (be given) to Jacques Derrida', 1990), Holland's selection traces the trajectory of Blanchot's career as a writer from the 1940s to the 1990s. Holland's selection and his commentary advances an argument which seeks to return Blanchot to history. Holland argues that Blanchot's exit from worldliness – evident in his literary criticism from the late 1930s and 1940s – was a response to the crisis of the Nazi Occupation of France. Holland makes the similar case for Blanchot's renewed enagagement with politics in the historically specific moments of 1958 and 1968.

If one follows Holland's line on Blanchot, then the support that Blanchot offers to Paul Fry's thesis on ostension and non-significance in *A Defence of Poetry* is perhaps in need of qualification. Whilst in these essays Blanchot often affirms the need 'to bring literature to that point of absence where it disappears', and even whilst his turn away from literature and towards philosophy after 1958 marked, as Holland argues, the extent to which 'philosophy . . . had become] the guardian of "language" as a whole', and the means by which language could be silenced and a responsibility to the Other shown, Blanchot does not fall into 'the extreme form of anti-intellectualism' which Fry claims for his own project. Indeed, Blanchot's thoughtful and complex argument in the 1984 essay on the role of the intellectual, the Dreyfus affair, anti-Semitism and Lyotard ('Intellectuals under Scrutiny: An Outline for Thought') heightens one's sense of the extent to which Fry's project is modest in its purview.

2. Listening and Discerning Readers: Counselling, Christianity and Theory

It is instructive to look at Ben Knights's *The Listening Reader* to gain a sense of the extent to which the paradigms of linguistics and literary theory have started to impact upon professions and practices which owe their first allegiance to the social sciences as traditionally constituted. Knights has aimed his practice-oriented book at persons in the business of listening: counsellors, psychotherapists, probation officers, the clergy. In many ways Knights's book represents an extension of the New Critical/Leavisite close reading pedagogy into new areas, and, indeed, the book is aware of its lineage in this regard. In a book which is non-specialist it is the embeddedness of the paradigms of literary-theoretical argument which is really striking: in advancing a non-mimetic, constitutive theory of art and language (reading *Brighton Rock* will not help probation officers to get into the mind of a young offender), Knights advances a Bakhtinian/Vygotskian account of the centrality of symbolization whilst at the same time acknowledging but defending his practice against a Foucauldian critique of the confession industry.

The longest-serving confessors face a crisis of authority: is it viable, after Saussure and structuralism, to listen for the sacred Word of God? As John Schad points out, in his contribution to *The Discerning Reader: Christian Perspectives on Literature and Theory*, when Roland Barthes unfixed meaning and killed off the author in 1968, he claimed to have refused God as well (Schad suggests that this is to settle matters prematurely). If Derridean deconstruction seemed to have fatally undermined the authority of the Graeco-Christian logos, then there remained a powerful engagement with the implications of the Judaic textual tradition (see for instance Maurice Blanchot's essay 'Being Jewish' in Holland's collection). However, the editors and the contributors to the *Discerning Reader* – all of whom are committed Christians – seek to enter into a sympathetic and enagaged dialogue with the major claims and paradigms of literary theory which may once have appeared irreconcilable with Christianity. The editors, who have aimed the volume principally at a student audience, have divided the volume into a section on 'theory' and a section on 'texts', and within this division there are, for example, lucid and accessible attempts to think through the relationship between Christianity and feminism, and Christianity and deconstruction. These essays – by Elisabeth Jay and Elizabeth Clark on feminism, Kevin Mills and John Schad on deconstruction – provide successful examples of the volume's aim to present Christian commentaries on theoretical perspectives and then to develop a reading of particular texts (Atwood's *The Handmaid's Tale*, Pynchon's *The Crying of Lot 49*). The editors – and the contributors, who have clearly read one another's work – have done a good job in producing a volume which, by and large, actually reads as a book. As contributions to the elaboration of theoretical discourse some essays work better than others: it is hard to place Donald G. Marshall's thoughtful and original essay on the self and interpretive communities in the same league as Donald T. Williams's rather pedestrian and dated essay on Christian poetics.

Yet overall the success of *The Discerning Reader* as a source for staging a debate on theoretical approaches to the reading of sacred and other texts is clear when compared to John D. Moores's *Wrestling with Rationality in Paul*. Moores's highly specialized work (which must constitute a bold step in biblical studies), presents a semiotic approach to Romans 1–8 and the enthymematic (quasi-syllogistic) mode of rhetoric which Paul employs to generate such obscure results. Moores takes his semiotic theory and taxonomy from Umberto Eco, and interestingly he rejects the consignment of Paul's slippery discourse to the domain of the aesthetic (Matthew Arnold's preferred route in the nineteenth century), arguing instead that the 'fuzziness' of concepts in the Pauline ideolect is not incompatible with systematic analysis by means of a calculus for measuring 'fuzziness' (which is to be distinguished from polysemy). The calculus would seem to be Moores's way of reconciling semiotics with Enlightenment styles of reasoning. Yet for all its erudition and close textual and linguistic argument – and these are considerable – Moores's thesis is less successful in staging a sense of debate between contrasting philosophies of textuality than Kevin Mills's essay on 'Words and Presences' in *The Discerning Reader*. Whilst Moores relegates the fireworks of theoretical contrasts to scholarly endnotes, Mills wants us to be aware of the differences in the process of meaning generation envisaged respectively by Saussurean semiotics and Ricoeur's theory of the sentence and discourse.

3. Marxism and Literary History

In 1986 John Frow published *Marxism and Literary History* which sought to recast the protocols of Marxist literary history in terms of linguistic pragmatism, a Foucauldian account of power and a Bakhtinian practice of intertextual reading. Classic Marxist historical materialism was unsettled by the operation, but that was Frow's aim. At least Frow considered Marxism to be of sufficient importance to merit this kind of attention. In Marshall Brown's edited collection *The Uses of Literary History*, literary history no longer appears to have any uses for historical materialism in that no single contributor defines his or her methodological – and political – position as Marxist. The historicizing methodologies and politics of feminism, queer theory, postcolonialism and psychoanalysis are represented, and Virgil Nemoianu and Annabel Patterson (Patterson writes a Miltonic rejoinder to Stanley Fish's polemic against free speech) conduct arguments from avowedly liberal positions (Nemoianu contends that liberalism is the genuinely significant ideological terrain of the 1990s). Marshall Brown stresses in his introduction that the volume constitutes a 'clash of voices' illuminating the variety of approaches to literary history, so it is a pity that a specifically Marxist voice was not invited to participate.

The volume, which is an expanded version of the spring 1993 relaunch of *Modern Language Quarterly*, contains essays by Marjorie Perloff, Jerome McGann and Geoffrey Hartman. The essay by McGann is a little disappointing in that it states a familar position and acts as a 'trailer' to work which has already appeared (and the essay by Jonathan Arac is a 'work in progress' statement). Hartman presents new work on public memory via a consideration of Toni Morrison's *Beloved* and the Holocaust. Perloff spends a good deal of time critiquing a conference paper in advancing her general point which is that 'we need to proceed more inductively'. This is a concern expressed elsewhere, notably by Lawrence Lipking, who identifies some of the dangers that have arisen from the loosening of the borders which traditionally defined the content of literary history, and the rules of evidence that selected materials for its construction. The New Historicism is the culprit here, but the postcolonial work of Rukmini Bhaya Nair (on Kipling and Tagore) is touched by its methods. Bhaya Nair is, however, troubled by her essay's need to provide so much by way of diectic reference, which she sees as symptomatic of the problems of the (Western) audience and its knowledge-base which confront the postcolonial critic.

If *The Uses of Literary History* leaves the reader with a sense that Marxism has reached the end of the critical road, Terry Eagleton and Drew Milne have produced a valuable reader in *Marxist Literary Theory*, which presents a representative account of the emergence, development and continuing relevance of Marxist aesthetics. The volume contains writings by Marx and Engels, as well as generous selections from the different traditions of European Marxism: Soviet (Lenin, Trotsky) and Western (Lukács, Adorno) tendencies are represented. Surprisingly there is no Gramsci, but the interesting and underexposed work of Galvano Della Volpe (similar in some ways to Voloshinov and an influence on Franco Moretti) is included to represent the Italian tradition. Even British Euro-sceptic Marxism (Caudwell, Alick West) is included. In addition there are essays by Brecht, Barthes (on Brecht), Benjamin and Sartre; and from the 1970s Althusser, Macherey and Balibar, Goldmann, Williams and Eagleton himself. The work of Aijaz Ahmed from the 1980s usefully weaves a Marxist emphasis on the global unity produced by the struggle between capital and labour with a nuanced, postcolonial insistence on specificity, and is juxtaposed against an extract from Jameson ('On Interpretation' from *The Political Unconscious*), whose Hegelian totalizing Ahmed thoughtfully (and fraternally) critiques.

These texts are framed by two introductory essays. Eagleton's introduction seeks to contest the notion that the dismantling of the Berlin Wall marked the demise of Marxism, arguing instead that it was 'the quickening contradictions' evident after the oil crisis of 1973-4 which fatally undermined the complex Marxist culture which had grown up in the West. Culture is the key word in Eagleton's discussion, 'at once absolutely vital and secondary' which explains why, for Eagleton, cultural materialism is the most comprehensive and best adjusted critical methodology. Indeed, Eagleton performs for Marxist criticism what Harold Abrams did for literary criticism in *The Mirror and the Lamp*; that is to say he constructs a typology of theoretical orientations: anthropological, political, ideological and economic (cultural materialism is a species of the economic orientation). It is a pity that these useful distinctions do not play a more significant role in actually organizing and cross-referring between the texts in the reader.

In the second introduction, Drew Milne contributes a challenging and original essay on the problem of reading Marx, and how Marx himself operated as a reader. Drawing upon Foucault's notion of Marx as a 'founder of discursivity', Milne argues that in many respects the 'founding' texts of Marxist aesthetics, where Marx addresses art itself, are not good illustrations of Marx's most rigorous forms of close reading and analytic practice (evidenced in *Capital*). However, again, these valuable insights are not really brought to bear on either the selections of primary materials, or the editorial notes introducing the texts (informative and full though these are).

In the introductory notes to the Lukács text ('The Ideology of Modernism') that appears in *Marxist Literary Theory*, it is pointed out that Lukács's failure to appreciate Modernism, once derided, is being reassesed now that Lukács might appear to be 'prefiguring critiques of the ideology of postmodernism of the kind offered by Jameson'. This takes a different line to the one advanced by Stuart Sim in his 1994 book on Lukács, which sought, among other things, to reconcile Lukács with postmodern theory (see 'General Chapter 1994'). This confirms the fact that Lukács is being reassessed from a number of angles, and Arpád Kadarkay's *The Lukács Reader* is another contribution to this process. In seeking to project a revisionary image of a figure 'very much at the centre of European thought' Kadarkay's selection from Lukács's corpus – much of it not previously published in English – plays down Lukács's Marxism, and his explicit contribution to literary history. Only one of the four sections comprising the book is devoted to 'Philosophy and Politics' (and this contains Lukács's essay on 'Class Consciousness' [1920] from *History and Class Consciousness*, and essays on Nietzschian and Heideggerian 'irrationalisms' from the depths of the Cold War). 'The Ideology of Modernism' (1963) also appears in Kadarkay's selection, but it is placed alongside a pre-Marxist essay from 1910 entitled 'Aesthetic Culture' which, whilst containing statements which could be said to prefigure a Marxist critique of postmodernism – 'aesthetic culture confines the potential effect of art to the surface' – also places Lukács's preoccupations in a broader context of philosophies of existentialism and discourses of self-fashioning. Indeed, Kadarkay's opening section is devoted to four so-called early 'Autobiographical' texts which the Marxist Lukács sought to 'bury'. What emerges from these texts – essays, letters and journals – is a philosophical laboratory in which the struggle to self-fashion through readings of figures from the continental philosophical tradition is explored. These texts cast a fascinating light on the origins of Lukács's later Marxist discourses on class consciousness with their emphasis on proletarian 'self-criticism' and the struggle of the proletariat against 'itself', its own internal structures and values.

4. After Foucault

In writing his autobiographical experiments the young Lukács was trying on masks representing powerful philosophical precursors. But whereas Lukács came permanently to wear the mask of the Marxist intellectual, Daniel T. O'Hara must keep changing masks in a succession of parodic moves. If one seeks to know the state of the left in the American academy then O'Hara's *Radical Parody: American Culture and Critical Agency after Foucault* seems to offer some indicators. O'Hara seeks to speak from and for the left, which is evident from the indignation he expresses at the way in which the neo-pragmatist Stanley Fish has been constructed as spokesperson for the left by the US media in its desire to 'explain' the culture wars and the political correctness debate. And it is clear from the concluding chapter, which is an endorsement of the recent work of Frank Lentricchia, that O'Hara is committed to a radical, historical, ethical and socially – indeed class – oriented literary criticism which, like Lentricchia's, is aware of its own historicity, and which, again like Lentricchia's, is critical of new historicism, neo-pragmatism and essentialist feminism. Yet O'Hara cannot identify with Lentricchia in any naive sense because first he must read Lentricchia for the masks he assumes in constructing his complex critical acts; these masks include Lentricchia's favoured critical precursors (Kenneth Burke) and the masks of those poets (Pound, Stevens) whose writings he reads.

For O'Hara significant critical agency in American culture is only possible when it is acknowledged, first, that masks are being worn in the process of producing selves; and, second, that parodic self-reflexiveness is displayed. (O'Hara's problem with the media-friendly Fish is that he seems to acquiesce to the part that television has 'scripted' for him.) For O'Hara the fact that we come 'after Foucault' should enhance our realization of these possibilities, given that Foucault wore multiple masks and was a radical parodist *par excellence.* In one of his central chapters, O'Hara reads 'What is an Author?' as a radical parody of Nietzsche's egotistical *Ecce Homo*, and for O'Hara the act of writing criticism involves the necessary parodying of others' critical styles before the 'ideal' critical mask can be donned. For O'Hara criticism is a complex imaginative act, and he decries readings which simply 'prove' authorial complicity in some or other ideology. In a sense, then, O'Hara seeks to advance an argument which is not dissimilar from Mark Edmundson's (see 1 above), though O'Hara's emphasis is on the imaginative richness of criticism. However, I did wonder whether he convincingly demonstrated this in some of the moments from Lentricchia which he approvingly cites, and which seemed to me to be rather ordinary.

John Pizer's *Towards a Theory of Radical Origin*, a complex, dense and challenging account of the concept of 'origin' in modern German thought, devotes a chapter to Foucault's reception of Nietzsche in the essay 'Nietzsche, Genealogy, History'. Foucault is a key figure for Pizer in the sense that his anti-linear genealogical practice exemplifies poststructuralism's critique of the rhetoric of 'origin' as a myth of originary presence and univocality, totality and teleology. However, for Pizer, Foucault – in seeking to align his own practice as a genealogist with his precursor – misreads the stresses attached to Nietzsche's apparently opposed concepts of 'emergence', in which forces clash and compete (*Enstehung*), and 'origin' as univocal continuity (*Ursprung*). In an argument which focuses closely on internal semantics and intellectual contexts, Pizer contends that for Nietzsche *Ursprung* itself signifies 'the interstice where competing moral forces emerge, struggle, disappear and dominate' and thus 'provides the foundation for a geneaology of morals'. According to Pizer, the concept of origin or *Ursprung* has always, in the modern German tradition at least, sought to articulate indeterminacy, rupture and fragmentation.

This is an important move in Pizer's thesis, for it opens up a space in which to read for and recuperate such a theory of *radical* origin in the writings of Benjamin, Adorno, Rozenweig and Heidegger. Pizer draws the reader's attention to the often acute differences between the theorists he examines. Above all, however, he is concerned to correct what he contends are imbalanced misreadings of Benjamin and Heidegger perpetrated by deconstructionists and poststructuralists. Consequently he draws out Benjamin's attachment to the theologically generated concept of the fragmented totality; and in Heidegger's philosophy of origins the unexpected presence of a proto-Foucauldian practice of genealogical thinking. Pizer's account of the wider significance of his project – he sees his return to a measure of foundationalism as a potential corrective to irrational nationalisms and the vacuum left by the collapse of socialism in Eastern Europe – remains sketchy at best. But, he concludes, re-reading *Ursprungphilosophie* in terms of a theory of radical origin makes us confront and re-read the scene of poststructuralism's origins. Such a purpose also informs Daphna Erdinast-Vulcan's 'Bakhtin's homesickness' which, in reading Bakhtin's neglected philosophical works from the 1920s, challenges the carnivalesque-intertextualist version of poststructuralist Bakhtin powerfully but selectively established by Julia Kristeva's highly influential *Desire in Language* (*Textual Practice* 9:ii.223–42). Such work urges us to reconceptualize what we think we mean by saying that we come 'after Foucault', or post structuralism.

'What then might we *do* with his philosophy, to what new uses might it yet be put?' is the post-Foucault question posed by John Rajchman in *Michel Foucault: J'Accuse* (*New Formations* 25:summer), which collects papers presented at the 1994 London Conference which marked the tenth anniversary of Foucault's death. Not every contributor looks forward: David Macey situates Foucault in the tradition of French political protest and activism institutionalized in the title of Zola's open letter to the state – 'J'Accuse'. Having situated Foucault in this tradition of intellectual activism reaching back to Voltaire, Macey goes on to problematize Foucault's pronouncement on the death of the universal oppositional intellectual; a function which, paradoxically, Macey argues, Foucault came to occupy in French social life. In writing an essay on the possibility of the philosophical life, James Miller – Foucault's other prominent English-language biographer from 1993 – contributes an essay which reinforces the major theme of the volume: the question of selfhood and subjectivity. The essay traces Foucault's late interest in the philosophical life, and Miller speculates on how such an integrated life might be fashioned. Indeed the essays by Alan D. Schrift and Sue Golding (and latterly Wendy Wheeler) focus on late (*History of Sexuality*) Foucault and the ramifications of his work for contemporary theorists such as Judith Butler. In one of her typically poised and questioning pieces – Baudrillard's injunction to 'Forget Foucault' is turned into a question ('Forget Foucault?) – Kate Soper suggests that postmodern feminism's embrace of Foucault carries political dangers in its wake. Especially worrying for Soper is Foucault's return to classical ethics and what she sees as the politically myopic focus on modes of male self-regulation: it is here, she claims, that Foucault is in danger of forgetting himself, or at least the radicalism of his early researches. Robert Young, extending his work on the history of colonial discourse, focuses on the problem of Foucault's silence on the operations of colonial power. Young argues that an analysis of racism as a form of biopower which emerged from modern sexual discourse was, in fact, taking shape in *The History of Sexuality* (the unpublished volume six was to be entitled 'Populations and Races'). But Young also looks back to that moment of *The Order of Things* when, despite Foucault's protestations to the contrary, structural analysis touched his methods. Interestingly, Young mounts something of a postcolonial defence of structuralism which, he argues, 'at a theoretical level . . . was developed as part of the post war process of cultural decolonization, disputing the cultural hierarchy of racialism, and turning the critical ethnography that had been developed for the analysis of non-western cultures onto the culture of the West itself'.

5. Structuralism Revisited: Mimologics

Robert Young prefaces his discussion of structuralism by acknowledging that these days few students of theory can find a good word to say about it. One might worry, then, that the newly published English translation of Gerard Genette's *Mimologiques: Voyage en Cratylie*, published for the first time back in 1976, has arrived at a moment when its intellectual currency appears debased. As Gerald Prince points out in his foreword, *Mimologics*, a study of the Cratylean tradition in the intellectual history of the West, needs to be seen in the context of Genette's researches into structuralist poetics which include the influential *Narrative Discourse, Figures* (I, II and III) and *Palimpsests*. Fans of *Narrative Discourse* will not be disappointed by Genette's taxonomic skill in differentiating between and classifying division upon subdivision of mimological thought. However, in 1976 Genette was clearly sensitive to the deconstructive strains and tensions playing upon structuralist discipline, though not in the seemingly obvious ways. The inclusion of a diagram prompts the comment 'I do not intend to downplay the . . . strained and mythical aspect of this overly neat symmetry, probably inspired by the demon of taxonomy and the rage for structural diagrams.' But this is not defensiveness; rather, it is playfulness and the translator, Thais E. Morgan, has gone to considerable labours to reproduce this voice throughout the volume. As Morgan points out in her extensive introductory essay, 'Invitation to Cratylusland', *Mimologics* is an experiment in intellectual history, a voyage in search of the different cultural manifestations of a myth of origin.

Genette's voyage begins with a reading of the source of this myth, Plato's *Cratylus*. Genette's reading draws out the philosophical complexity constructing this myth of language as mimesis, and he is concerned to show the way in which the myth prefigures the tradition of mimologism in all its variety. Central to Genette's argument is that mimological arguments about the acoustic basis of language in the process of naming things are always much more subtle and sceptical of their own conditions of possibility than has been supposed. As Genette points out, the *Cratylus* is a debate within an apparently monolingual culture between three positions: the extreme mimologism of Cratylus, the proto-Saussurean conventionalism of Hermogenes, and Socrates' refinement of the two. For Genette, Socrates' position acknowledges the impossibilities in the Cratylean account of the purity underpinning the relationship between sound, words and things. Genette describes Socrates' consequent attitude as 'secondary mimologism', which acknowledges that language is a flawed and arbitrary system where words do not always imitate things, and thus in need of reform precisely to make it ideally mimetic.

Accordingly Genette traces quests which desire the ideal reformation of a flawed language. His investigations take him through Enlightenment philosophies of the origin of language and into the very different theoretical world of nineteenth-century philology and beyond. In his account of nineteenth-century comparative philology Genette is on very similar territory to Foucault in *The Order of Things*. Indeed, he agrees with Foucault's analysis of the shift from an interest in nouns to verbs as the 'core' of language, and the consequent inscription of spontaneous human subjectivity and action in the roots of language. Genette is alert here to the threat that this poses to the mimological tradition, as language, defined now by grammar, is tacitly held to be no longer motivated by objective imitative properties. At the same time, however, Genette's analysis acknowledges ideology and power as sources which subtly reinvigorate previously submerged facets of the Cratylean myth at the moment when its secondary mimologism seemed to have lost its hold. We can make a link back to Robert Young's postcolonial 'recovery' of structuralist method at this point: for Genette's structuralism is flexible enough to allow him to argue that Ernst Renan's account of the Semitic family of languages in terms of its 'lack' of grammar draws its racism, or incapacity to recognize the other in terms which are not Indo-European, from the illusory assumption of monolinguism which underpins Plato's *Cratylus*.

Genette's quest does not stop here, and he shows how a modern, poetically complex and culturally alienated form of seondary mimologism is crafted by Mallarmé, and thus further parallels with Foucault's claim in *The Order of Things* about the emergence of 'literature' in the late nineteenth century are invited. This is a fascinating and enormously subtle work of history and theory – as well as a living document in the history of theory – and Thais Morgan has done important and difficult work (translating between the onomatopoeic fantasies of different languages) in bringing *Mimologics* to English readers.

6. Reference Works

The entry for Genette in Michael Payne's *Dictionary of Cultural and Critical Theory* seems to bear out Gerald Prince's observation that *Mimologiques* has been somewhat overlooked in that it does not get a mention. *Mimologiques* is, however, mentioned briefly in the entry for Genette in Stuart Sim's *A–Z Guide to Modern Literary and Cultural Theorists*. Given the different aims and ambitions of these volumes, this is not a fair basis for criticizing Payne's *Dictionary*, which is a wide-ranging publication in which brief accounts of theorists' works and their significance is one commitment amongst many; others include entries on terminology ('the name of the father', 'writerly and readerly texts'), and interpretive essays on fields from 'philosophy of science' and 'women's studies' to Renaissance and Victorian studies which seek to delineate the impact of theory upon these fields. Sim's *A–Z Guide* is, on the other hand, exclusively concerned with a biographical and *oeuvre*-based account of one hundred theorists which includes accounts of Marx, Nietzsche and Freud. Payne's contributors have been asked to take a line on the topic they are writing on, and so, in familar polemical fashion, Christopher Norris is of the view that the *lisible/scriptible* distinction 'gave rise to some problems fairly typical of the heady rhetoric which characterized that period of endlessly deferred textual "revolutions that as yet have no model" '. Norris is in the unusual position of being both a contributor to and the subject of an entry in the *Dictionary*. Norris is also the subject of an entry in the *A–Z Guide* and, in common with all other entries, there is biography, exposition of his works, assessment of his significance, a bibliographical guide and suggested further readings. Payne's introductory chapter is a lengthy survey essay on some versions of cultural and critical theory; Sim's introductory remarks about the field are more brief, and he is more concerned to guide readers in how to use the book that follows. Both books have useful cross-referencing systems, though Payne's *Dictionary* is also furnished with a very comprehensive bibliography.

Both the *Dictionary* and the *A–Z Guide* are held together by the collective efforts of academics at single institutions (Bucknell University, USA, and Sunderland, UK), though neither is simply an 'in-house' work, and both have contributions from significant scholars from elsewehere: Steven Connor, for instance, on postmodernism in the *Dictionary*; and Antony Easthope on Freud and Belsey in the *A–Z Guide*. It is fitting to conclude with the observation that the late Raman Selden, a vastly skilful expositor and elucidator of abstruse theoretical discourse, is a presence in both works; Payne dedicates the *Dictionary* to his memory, as the project was initially proposed by Selden.

Many of the contributors to the *A–Z Guide* belong, we are told, to a research centre dedicated to Selden's memory at the University of Sunderland, the institution at which Selden was working when he died, tragically early, in 1991.

Books Reviewed

Barratt, David, Roger Pooley and Leland Ryken, eds. *The Discerning Reader: Christian Perspectives on Literature and Theory*. Apollos (UK) and Baker Books (USA). pp. 320. £10.99, $19.99. ISBN 0 85111 445 8 (UK), 0 8010 2085 9.

Brown, Marshall, ed. *The Uses of Literary History*. Duke University Press. pp. x, 316. hb £47.50, pb £15.99. ISBN 0 8223 1704 4, 0 8223 1714 1.

Eagleton, Terry, and Drew Milne, eds. *Marxist Literary Theory: A Reader*. Blackwell. pp. 446. hb £45.00, pb £14.99. ISBN 0 631 18579 8, 0 631 18581 X.

Edmundson, Mark. *Literature Against Philosophy: Plato to Derrida*. Cambridge University Press. pp. xii, 243. hb £35.00, pb £13.95. ISBN 0 521 41093 2, 0 521 48532 0.

Fry, Paul H. *A Defence of Poetry: Reflections on the Occasion of Writing*. Stanford University Press. pp. 255. hb £35.00, pb £11.95. ISBN 0 8047 2452 0, ISBN 0 8047 2531 4.

Genette, Gerard. *Mimologics (Mimologiques: Voyage en Cratylie)*. University of Nebraska Press. Stages series. Translated from the French by Thais E. Morgan with a foreword by Gerald Prince. pp.lxvi, 446. hb £62.00, pb £23.95. ISBN 0 8032 7044 5, 0 8032 2129 0.

Holland, Michael, ed. *The Blanchot Reader*. Blackwell. pp. ix, 329. hb £40.00, pb £13.99. ISBN 0 631 19083 X, 0 631 19084 8.

Kadarkay, Arpád, ed. *The Lukács Reader*. Blackwell. pp. ix, 292. hb £40.00, pb £13.99. ISBN 1 55786 570 1, 1 55786 571 X.

Knights, Ben. *The Listening Reader: Fiction and Poetry for Counsellors and Psychotherapists*. Jessica Kingsley. pp. 166. pb £14.95. ISBN 1 85302 266 7.

Moores, John D. *Wrestling with Rationality in Paul*. Society for New Testament Studies Monograph 82. Cambridge University Press. pp. xvi, 210. hb £32.50. ISBN 0 521 47223 7.

O'Hara, Daniel T. *Radical Parody: American Culture and Critical Agency after Foucault*. The Social Foundations of Aesthetic Forms. Columbia University Press. pp. xvi, 311. pb £12.50. ISBN 0 231 07693 2.

Payne, Michael, ed. *A Dictionary of Cultural and Critical Theory*. Blackwell. pp. xii, 644. hb £65.00. ISBN 0 631 17197 5.

Pizer, John. *Towards a Theory of Radical Origin: Essays on Modern German Thought*. Modern German Culture and Literature. University of Nebraska Press. pp. xi, 215. hb £38.00. ISBN 0 8032 3711 1.

Sim, Stuart, ed. *The A–Z Guide to Modern Literary and Cultural Theorists*. Prentice Hall–Harvester Wheatsheaf. pp. xiv, 432. pb £10.95. ISBN 0 13 355553 4.

2

Semiotics

ADRIAN PAGE

The justification for a compendium of information on semiotics as vast as Winfried Nöth's *A Handbook of Semiotics* is that the subject itself has proliferated at such a rate that it now needs a reference work of this magnitude. The test of a work that presents itself as a handbook is most probably to see whether it is able to fill the lacunae in one's own knowledge and provide structures through which it is possible to discover new directions in research. A handbook of this encyclopaedic kind can act both as a guide to basic concepts for the beginner, and as a source of new initiatives for the experienced researcher. The concept of a *handbook* signifies that the history of the subject is not attempted here and that, instead, a semiotic approach has been taken to the organization of the material.

As with a previous example of a guide to the territory, *New Vocabularies in Film Semiotics: Structuralism, Post-Structuralism and Beyond* edited by Robert Stam et al. (see *YWCCT* 3), the concept of a topographical survey, however, is not an appropriate metaphor. Nöth adopts the approach of building up the subject by accretions of information. The introduction sketches the history of the issues since the Greeks and then briefly accounts for the influence of the major theorists of the twentieth century: Peirce, Saussure, Morris, Hjelmslev and Jakobson. There is also reference to other major figures such as Thomas Sebeok and lesser-known historical figures such as Richard Gatschenberger. The subject is, therefore, quite comprehensively treated in historical terms, but then the volume returns to concepts which were dealt with by the major figures and sketches the development of theory. Thus the following chapter begins with the concept of the sign and explores varying methods of conceptualizing this term. Other issues such as sense and reference follow in a chapter which broadens the historical base by providing a complementary conceptual history. This gives the author the opportunity to cross-reference to leading figures when there is an interesting issue to which they have made an important contribution. This avoids the problem of chapters which attempt to summarize a vast contribution in insufficient space.

The volume progresses by examining the fundamental concepts of the discipline, such as codes, the language-based semiotic systems and the later developments of Russian Formalism, Barthes, Greimas and Kristeva. In the following section there are guides to the principal theories of the text, non-verbal communication, and visual and aesthetic communication. Comprehensive coverage is achieved by revisiting the territory in waves to incorporate major and lesser-known figures in a conceptual trawl when they may not have featured in the history. There is extensive bibliographical referencing which enables the reader to trace the major contributions of leading semioticians and the growing number of disciplines which have arisen from semiotics. Thus zoopragmatics, the study of how animals communicate, can be traced without difficulty.

This is an invaluable companion for anyone who wishes to take the subject seriously, but it inevitably betrays the acknowledged difficulty of mapping a path through a dense jungle. The tensions within semiotics over its status as a discipline, a science or a method, for example, have to be represented in a comprehensive approach and sometimes may become too complex. The section on myth inevitably acknowledges Barthes, but accuses him of the naive assumption that there is a 'primary level of meaning onto which myth is grafted'. Although Barthes is also credited with withdrawing this theoretical approach, it is not made clear that he also called for 'changing the object itself', or destroying the mythic power of the sign by re-examining the function of the signifier, rather than its relation to the signified. The absence of a reference to what Eco called 'semiotic guerrilla warfare' makes this a fairly conservative account of the intellectual origins of the subject, rather than a summary of the more exciting developments, but this is none the less a very valuable reference work. Nöth's *Handbook* was first published in 1990 and has not been revised to include all major publications since, such as Stam's *New Vocabularies* which is cited above. A companion to this work is C. Liungman's 'comprehensive encyclopaedia' of Western signs in all aspects of culture. *Thought Signs: The Semiotics of Symbols – Western Ideograms* attempts a guide to the social significance of all Western symbols from those used in advertising to those found on subway walls. This reference work invites the reader to identify four characteristics of the symbol whose meaning they want to explore and on this basis enables the reader to locate its social significance. There is a strange mixture here of the familiar and the enlightening as some symbols are traced to unexpected origins and others are somewhat predictably catalogued. This enterprise, however, is a manifestation of the semiotic fascination with classificatory systems which are increasingly challenged in critical thought.

Nöth and other authors of reference works, however, do not pause to reflect on the ideological repercussions of semioticians such as Peirce, whose pragmatism seems to be undergoing something of a revival. In *The Semiotic Self* (1994) Norbert Wiley attempts to forge a theory of human nature which is inspired by Peirce's statement that 'man is a sign'. By merging the theories of George Herbert Mead and Peirce, Wiley aims to produce a theory which explains the self as a semiotic system and completes the programme of intellectual enquiry which the early American pragmatists set themselves. Whereas Peirce saw the self as a dialogue between an *I* in the present and a *you* in the future, Mead regarded the self as a dialogue between an *I* in the present and a *me* in the past. Wiley merges these theories into a triadic structure which incorporates all three positions and conforms to Peirce's sign–interpretant–object model, and thereby establishes a foundation for the Peircean doctrine of the semiotic self. The model enables the author to analyse statements which appear to be dialogues between a former identity and oneself now. It is also possible to converse with a future self. Wiley argues that literary criticism, for example, often makes these kinds of assumptions. The notion of the self as a kind of inner conversation between three terms resembling the Freudian triptych is what, for Wiley, guarantees the relative autonomy of the self. Attempts to reduce the self to simpler factors must fail on this model because the actual identity of individuals inheres in the unique relationship between these three internal elements which is maintained by a dynamic, reflexive, internal conversation. Wiley argues that this model, which challenges the attempts in, for example, cybernetics, to reduce the human self to cybernetic factors, is fundamental to American liberalism which is structured to preserve the rights of the individual. Wiley's work is complemented by the work of Vincent Colapietro, whose book entitled *Peirce's Doctrine of Signs* also appears this year and extends the ideas of his previous publication, *Peirce's Approach to the Self* (1989). In the same vein as Wiley, Colapietro sees the self as an internal dialogue between the elements of identity which can be distinguished in time. In an interesting article on 'Authorial Audiences in Shakespeare's *A Midsummer Night's Dream* (*Semiotica* 106:i/ii) Sunhee Kim Gertz draws attention to the way in which Shakespeare's play demands a form of audience attention which is, perhaps, an example of 'meta-reflexivity' of the kind that Wiley attributes to the semiotic self. When, for example, Lysander says the famous line that 'the course of true love never did run smooth', he is drawing attention to a literary tradition in the performance text. Gertz finds many other examples of such moments when the dramatic text and performance text appear to be temporarily confused. At moments when, for example, Bottom is literally transformed into an ass, the allusion to classical descriptions of lovers as asses is enacted before the audience, who are compelled to judge. The meaning of the play lies not just in responses but in the ability to reflect on those responses in the context of the dramatic action.

In the same volume of *Semiotica*, in a paper entitled 'Changing Individuals in Narrative: Science, Philosophy, Literature', however, Uri Margolin points out that in fictional contexts we are prepared to accept that we are dealing with the same individual even though this would be regarded as ridiculous in scientific and philosophical contexts. He undoubtedly reminds us that genre determines the degree of freedom in interpretation which we readers assume.

It may be that the radical scepticism of the postmodern era has encouraged certain thinkers to turn to semiotics as the only obvious alternative to fragmentation and the lack of meaning. Klaus Bruhn Jensen in *The Social Semiotics of Mass Communication* argues for a return to Peircean pragmatism as an antidote to the excesses of poststructuralism. This is the culmination of the project which the author mentioned in Jensen and Jankowski eds (1991) *A Handbook of Qualitative Methodologies for Mass Communication Research*. Jensen maintains that pragmatism is the theory which enables us to mediate between the meaning of media texts and their effects. He quotes a maxim from Peirce which states that our conception of its effects amounts to our total conception of the object which causes them. Thus the media can be seen as an example of the social practice of semiosis which engages in producing signs and creating effects. A sophisticated version of reception theory, therefore, can account for the semiotic effects of the media. Since we think in signs, and signs have a socially defined meaning, the institutions which create signs also contribute to 'new forms of interaction between the private and public spheres'. Habermas and Giddens are invoked to support the claim that the personal and the social are intimately linked. It is argued that we know a great deal about the demographics of audiences, but little about their strategies for interpreting media semiotics. A truly social semiotics, in Jensen's view, would explain the social origins of signs which we use to think with. The apparent denial of the self in pragmatism is compensated for by the fact that audience feedback can create a two-way process of semiotic interaction. The Peircean triad of object, sign and interpretant can be applied to mass communications with the medium as the sign, and the audience as the interpretant.

For Peirce, however, the fundamental approach appears to identify the interpretant or the mental conception formed by the audience with the meaning of the text. Jensen reveals the weak point of pragmatism when he cites an example of an elderly lady who made a bizarre interpretation of a televised funeral. He is obliged to say that this was really a case of misperception rather than aberrant decoding, since the reading was too bizarre to be entertained. This reintroduces a notion of legitimate and non-legitimate readings of texts which the theory of effects-as-meaning cannot allow. A useful distinction which pragmatists might do well to consider is that which Umberto Eco makes between the *use* and the *interpretation* of texts (see *Semiotics* in *YWCCT* 2).

In *Postmodern Semiotics: Material Culture and the Forms of Postmodern Life*, M. Gottdiener also proposes an alternative to postmodern fragmentation by constructing a theory of semiotics on a Peircean basis. Gottdiener is one of many writers who divide semiotic theory somewhat simply. Saussurean semiology is held to be a fundamental origin of the attack on meaning which leads to deconstructionism and a fascination with representation in literary studies. On the other hand, in cultural studies, Gottdiener maintains that the influence of Baudrillard has meant that the hyperreal and the simulacrum have also created a similar concern with representation in other studies. Peirce is adopted because his notion of the interpretant enables the real object to be linked with its form of representation, whereas in other theories there is no such link with the real. Hence material culture does not *represent* something, instead, it is the irreducible form which ideology takes when it is expressed. Gottdiener offers case-studies of cultural phenomena such as Disneyland, shopping malls and fashion, and attempts to demonstrate that the postmodern reduction of meaning to a play of signifiers is not valid and denies the potential of countercultures. Alex Haley's novel *Roots* is cited as a means of resistance through the rediscovery of 'lost signifieds' which enable a people to recover a buried history. Although this theory is undoubtedly useful evidence in the struggle to prove that individuals are not necessarily dominated by the disconcerting influence of mass culture, it is not what many readers would describe as a thorough-going materialist approach. Like many theories of resistance through popular culture, it is difficult to see how resistance is not itself idealized as a free creative response that is not subject to social power structures with a material basis.

Jensen's theory is dissociated from the earlier book *Social Semiotics* (1988) by Hodge and Kress. Jensen maintains that they argue for a narrow notion of text semiotics which involves the social but does not derive from it. Volosinov is quoted with approval as an early example of a semiosis which is, by its very nature, social. The underlying structure of Jensen's approach, however, is based on the functioning of media systems, or 'network models'. A general theory of semiotics might have to be extended beyond this particular set of structures. In a chapter in her own collection of essays, *Bakhtin in Contexts*, Amy Mandelker elaborates on a new paradigm for semiotics which emanates from Russian Formalism and is championed by Bakhtin.

Bakhtin originated the term 'logosphere' in order to import an organic metaphor into the realm of semiotics and this has inspired contemporary Russian thought. The logosphere is a conception of semiotics not as a codified set of rules, but as a natural process of growth, decay and change which constantly regenerates itself in the form of a dialogue. It is developed from the concept of the 'biosphere' in Russian geological sciences. The concept of semiosis as a dialogue is shared with the disciples of Peirce, but in the emerging Russian concept of the semiosphere – a development of Bakhtin's notion by Lotman – the dialogue which generates semiotic meaning is between the left and right hemispheres of the brain. The organicist metaphors introduce a very flexible range of models for conceiving of the exchanges of semiosis in society but, as Mandelker points out, they are also open to appropriation by male interests. The notion of semiosis as fecundity is open to gender-biased interpretation but, according to Mandelker, it may yet liberate semiotics from the prison-house of theory. The chapter opens up some rather surprising new dimensions of the debate, yet it does not explain just how Bakhtin's social model of communication and the return to a romantic-sounding organicism can easily coexist.

James Elkins, in an article entitled 'Marks, Traces. *Traits*, Contours, Orli and Splendores: Non-Semiotic Elements in Pictures' (*Critical Enquiry* 21:iv.822–60) adds another voice to the growing body of thinkers who are denying that there is a specifically visual semiotics which can be construed on the model of linguistics. In his study of the ontology of the mark, Elkins uses ideas such as Derrida's concept of the 'trace' to distinguish marks in paintings from the signs of language, and draws attention to their unique status. The search for new paradigms in semiotics is continued in the new musicology, which seeks to read music as a series of signs with a cultural and ideological meaning.

Robert Samuels's *Mahler's Sixth Symphony: A Study in Musical Semiotics* acknowledges the fundamental problem of this enterprise in that the 'reader' of music has to create both the signifiers and their meaning in the same process. Thus there is a problem about the level of objective analysis which can be undertaken prior to musical interpretation, and Samuels sensibly maintains that the so-called neutral level is a *construct* of the analyst. The only realistic position, therefore, is that the varying cultural codes which analysts bring to music and their resultant effect on analysis will have to be acknowledged. Samuels outlines the classic dilemmas for the musicologist with considerable clarity. The Peircean triad can be used as a model of infinite semiosis, but if this is accepted, then music becomes nothing other than pure form, an endlessly self-referring structure with no capacity to signify outside itself. Samuels therefore turns to Eco's book *A Theory of Semiotics* (1977) to propose an appropriate compromise. The s-codes of the musical text, such as references to standard musical genres, are objective, but actual readings are generated by the interaction between the listener's s-code and that of the text, in what Wlad Godzich calls, 'intra-s-code semiosis'. This method, therefore, enables the listener to exercise freedom in interpretation, yet to do so only through a disciplined procedure. The strategy shows the pragmatists an alternative methodology.

Mahler is considered particularly suitable for such a study since Adorno's monograph on the composer in 1960, which identified meaningful devices in Mahler such as the 'breakthrough' and the 'fulfilment'. The current study, however, proposes means for arriving at such categories in a more systematic manner than Adorno.

This absorbing study demands a great deal of musical knowledge, but the reader will find that the theoretical issues are minutely examined and the difficulties expressed above are encountered. How, for example, can we decide whether a quotation from a dance genre is being used ironically to complete a parody of a symphony? The discussion of resolution and closure in thematic elements of the music is related to literature and gendered notions of suicide. The author considers the work to be an example of feminine musical narrative because it expresses the struggle for individuality within formal conventions. Suicide could been seen as both a means of escape for women and also an established fate. Samuels's subtle reading describes how the score reflects this. This study demonstrates that a semiotic analysis can be both acutely sensitive to a cultural phenomenon and yet not confined purely by the terms of linguistics. It can only be hoped that more such studies will follow.

Books Reviewed

Gottdiener, M. *Postmodern Semiotics: Material Culture and the Forms of Postmodern Life.* Blackwell. pp. 262. hb £50.00. ISBN 0 631 19215 8.

Jensen, Klaus Bruhn. *The Social Semiotics of Mass Communication.* Sage. pp. 228. £13.95. ISBN 0 8039 7810 3.

Liungman, C. *Thought Signs: The Semiotics of Symbols – Western Ideograms.* IOS Press. pp. 660. £34.00. ISBN 0 95199 197 5.

Mandelker, Amy, ed. *Bakhtin in Contexts: Across the Disciplines (Rethinking Theory).* Northwestern University Press. pp. 273. $16.95. ISBN 0 81011 269 8.

Nöth, Winfried. *A Handbook of Semiotics.* Indiana University Press. pp. 576. £23.50. ISBN 0 253 20959 5.

Samuels, Robert. *Mahler's Sixth Symphony: A Study in Musical Semiotics.* Cambridge University Press. pp. 175. £30.00. ISBN 0 521 48166 X.

Wiley, Norbert. *The Semiotic Self.* Polity Press (1994) pp. 250. £12.95. ISBN 0 7456 1503 1.

3

Psychoanalysis

VICKY LEBEAU

When does psychoanalysis become impossible? The question is central to a book that can be read as a delayed response to Jeffrey Masson's assault on psychoanalysis a decade ago in *Freud: The Assault on Truth* (Faber, 1984). Staking his claim to speak for the women and children 'betrayed' by Freud's supposed renunciation of the seduction theory, Masson has been a key figure in the debates concerning repressed memory therapy and false memory syndrome, debates from which psychoanalysis has been largely, and perhaps curiously, absent other than as an object of accusation. *The New Informants: Betrayal of Confidentiality in Psychoanalysis and Psychotherapy* – described by its co-authors, Christopher Bollas, a practising analyst, and David Sundelson, an appellate lawyer, as a 'call to arms' for a profession increasingly undermined by the 'incursion into clinical space of third-party interests' – is a powerful response to a sometimes overwhelming consensus that psychoanalysis can have nothing to say now on the issues of sexual abuse, memory and fantasy.

The immediate, or most pressing, 'third-party interests' at issue for Bollas and Sundelson are the reporting laws, proliferating in the United States and of increasing importance in Europe, which require professionals, among them psychotherapists and psychoanalysts, to disclose to the relevant authorities confidential statements made by their clients concerning sexual abuse and violent behaviour. The authors are adamant: 'Psychoanalysis cannot function if the patient does not have complete confidence that what he says to his psychoanalyst is privileged'; the method of free association, the kind of truth or knowledge it produces, depends on the patient's trust that 'the clinician will not take him at his word, but will instead regard the expression of thought as the means to liberate unconscious ideas, memories, and feelings that contribute to his mental suffering and disturbed relations'. Break that trust, insist that the speech and the listening which takes place through psychoanalytic practice be transferred into a legal or social workspace and you destroy psychoanalysis:

> the practising psychoanalyst's blank screen is littered with legal scriptures that demand various forms of compliance. As he listens to certain sexual disclosures, what appears on the screen is not the unconscious significations of such mental contents but the flashing red lights of the police car that may have to be called to the door. So, too, with aggressive contents; during some reports

the analyst will find himself gazing not at the patient's inner world but at the Tarasoff patrol.

It should be said that Bollas and Sundelson are only too aware that their arguments are controversial in the context of what they describe as a cultural preoccupation with child molestation and sex crime – and here 'preoccupation' bears the weight of Bollas's analysis of a way of being 'Preoccupied unto Death' in his *Cracking Up* (also published this year and discussed below). Controversial, too, for a profession so often, and sometimes violently, divided within itself by disagreements about the relations between, for example, psychoanalysis and psychotherapy, the superiority of one training over another, the ethics governing the analyst–analysand contract. In the final chapter of the book, 'Restoring Privilege', Bollas and Sundelson sketch a way forward for psychoanalysis as an 'independent discipline and profession that generates its own standard of ethics', whatever the prior, sometimes conflictual, loyalties – as psychiatrists, lawyers, social workers – of those who have trained as psychoanalysts. In other words, what psychoanalysis wants is the privilege of confidentiality accorded to priests, to lawyers, to journalists. Only in this way, it seems, can it continue to 'confer freedom through the democratic function of free speech'.

Even such a brief summary is enough to show that *The New Informants* touches on questions which go beyond its apparent professional remit. Read it alongside Richard Ofshe and Ethan Watters's *Making Monsters: False Memories, Psychotherapy and Sexual Hysteria*, for example, and the clash (as well as the sometimes unexpected correspondences) between the two is intriguing. *Making Monsters* is another call to arms, this time against what is described in the preface to the English edition of the book as an 'outbreak of tainted psychotherapy' which America has been enduring for over a decade: 'We hope that the availability of *Making Monsters* in Britain will make a contribution to the speedy rejection of recovered memory practice and thereby prevent some of the needless suffering we have witnessed in America.' The theory and sometimes disconcerting practice of recovered memory therapy is at issue throughout: *Making Monsters* is an exposé and an accusation which casts the recovered memory movement in the role of hysteric, producing ever more fantastic, ever more fanatical, accounts of sexual and satanic abuse of adults and children. The chapters read like X-files, uncovering the effects of a form of therapy that has produced an 'epidemic' of multiple personality disorder, instigated an FBI inquiry into the existence of 'murderous satanic cults' (with links to the CIA), and generated the therapeutic, legal and televisual destruction of individuals and their luckless families:

> Patients can begin the therapy with no memories of abuse and finish with the belief that they suffered endless horrible molestations or rapes – often by their parents.
> . . . the epidemic of repressed memories 'discovered' daily in therapy settings prove not that our society is exploding with the most vicious sort of child molesters and satanists, but rather that therapists – if they are possessed with a predisposition to uncover memories of abuse – can unintentionally spark and then build false beliefs in a patient's mind.

The practice, as described here, stages the very abuse it is supposed to be recovering:

> Believing it therapeutic, therapists encourage abreactions – where the patient, often in hypnotic trance, 'relives' the imagined abuses and in doing so supposedly punctures and drains the psychological abscess that has formed around the repressed memory. . . . The power of the therapists' suggestions is so great that some patients can develop observable physiological reactions, often in the form of welts or rashes.

Ofshe and Watters build a compelling case against the recovered memory movement, not least because there is increasing disquiet concerning the status of the scenes experienced by subjects under hypnosis. Ofshe and Watters share some ground, for example, with a deconstructive reading of the epidemic of multiple personality disorder in America as the effect, rather than discovery, of a therapy which relies on hypnosis. At issue for Ofshe and Watters, however – and this despite their cogent use of theories of narrative – is not a poststructuralist understanding of the subject but a scientific method to which psychoanalytic psychotherapy, along with the recovered memory movement, has little, if any, right to make a claim. In the concluding chapter of *Making Monsters*, that method is offered as something like a defence against the catalogue of abuses just detailed and, in particular, against a Freudian theory, or lack of one, of memory and repression. The accusation is familiar (another version of Masson) but generalized here into one against psychotherapy and psychoanalysis as such. In fact, by the end of the book, it seems that there is no place for a talking cure which works with the pressures of fantasy, or trauma, on speech. We are left with a clearly adaptive model of psychotherapy concerned only with those aspects of psychical pain or functioning which fall outside of the 'biomedical intervention via drug or gene therapy'. In what is left of the 'talk-therapy portion of the industry' in this model, 'patient and therapist endeavor to do nothing more or less than improve the patient's ability to function in the world by identifying troubling behavior and coping patterns and considering ways to improve them'.

After the fury of satanic ritual, cannibalism, rape and murder unleashed by the recovered memory movement, this reads like a quiet prospect, but it is no less disconcerting. What goes missing here is a question that might have concerned the Freud who is so summarily dismissed – and that remains urgent for Bollas and Sundelson. Even if we were to accept that many of the memories uncovered during hypnosis are 'false' (that is, not representations of real events); that the narcissistic preoccupation encouraged by the therapeutic dyad can encourage a type of *folie à deux* in which suggestion can become more or less mutual; that some therapists are so 'possessed' – Ofshe and Watters's word – by the desire to uncover memories of abuse that they induce said memories in their clients, we are still left with the question of why these memories take the forms they do? And why do these memories-scenes of sexual and satanic abuse (or, more rarely, of abduction and abuse by aliens) have such an overwhelming cultural purchase? Why do we want to tell the story of living in a family, the story of childhood, as one of more or less grotesque abuse?

These questions take us back to Bollas and Sundelson's account of a 'national preoccupation' with child molestation and sex crime, a preoccupation itself sustained by 'powerful, intertwined beliefs about sexuality, children, and punishment'. In particular, the fourth chapter of *The New Informants*, 'Creating Informants', is keen to ask why the abused child becomes such a powerful point of identification for 'tens of thousands of Americans [who] also saw the hidden abused child within the self'. The answers proffered are tentative, and sometimes surprising: the 'mass social decision to abandon children to empty homes' (the latch-key child); the experience of the Vietnam War in which 'the country sent its young men to senseless deaths': two 'events' which produce, in this analysis, an unconscious identification with the missed child who must not be left, who must be saved. This is, at least, to bring the recovered therapy movement – or, more generally, a burgeoning therapeutic industry – into connection with the culture that sustains it, to suggest that the recovered memory movement has uncovered something: not memories, perhaps, but something else. And, notably, that connection between psycho-analysis and the cultures in which it takes place comes to the fore when psychoanalysis is in need of defence – from inside and outside of the profession – in order to survive as a practice: 'We believe that degradation of the psychoanalytical situation would not have occurred to the same extent if the public had a greater understanding of what psychoanalysis is and how it must function.'

Bollas's *Cracking Up: The Work of Unconscious Experience* is also published this year, elaborating his reflections on the work of unconscious and dreaming experience and giving a texture to a set of critical concepts familiar from the work of Freud. 'Communications of the Unconscious', for example, returns to Freud's suggestion that one unconscious can communicate with another without detouring through consciousness. Bollas catches at that suggestion, putting it in the context of both therapeutic intervention and metapsychology:

> The analyst's conscious grasp of the patient's latent ideas is often as unconsciously determined as the patient's own associations. Unconscious communication always takes place between two minds that process one another according to the dream work. So the movement which constitutes the specific *workings* of the unconscious will not be available to consciousness, although specific mental contents may be.

What emerges here, and right through the book, is the way in which a Romantic aesthetic informs Bollas's conceptualization of the creative unconscious, its labour and its play. Analytic listening focuses on the fragment, becoming a form of driftwork – 'an idea, an image, a word falls out of the blue' – which tolerates confusion and not knowing (the patient's and the analyst's) for as long as it takes to make a provisional sense of the material brought into the analytic space. Essential here is Bollas's notion of 'unconscious freedom' which expresses itself in a 'freewheeling manner' which is *idiomatic* to the patient – and which risks being lost in states of preoccupation. At the same time, we are invited to consider the influence of a 'death work' – something which mediates between the death drive and the dream work? – as a process, or loss of process, that can bring unconscious freedom to a halt: the patient can 'live out a self-destructive pattern that conscipt[s] all forms of desire into the armies of negation. Death work can destroy the unconsciousness of the unconscious.'

Perhaps of most immediate interest to cultural studies is 'The Structure of Evil', a lengthy essay on the figure of the serial killer as a genocidal being. Bollas brings a psychoanalytic framework to bear on a form of murder which could also be described as a form of (European and American) preoccupation, if the various media have anything at all to tell us about what our dreams, or nightmares, are. But his concern is not only with the killer who lives inside an unconscious structure that gives him a 'sense of his own evil' but with our attempts to 'think about a process to which the word "evil" is assigned': 'As we shall see, there is a clear structure to evil, not only a series of stages in its deployment but a psychic logic that raises profound anxieties no doubt hindering the task of *thinking* about it'. Such hindrance might itself explain some of the 'preoccupation unto death' with the figure of the serial, or pathological, killer, cast here as a '*killed* self' who 'seems to go on "living" by transforming other selves into similarly killed ones, establishing a companionship of the dead'. From the point of view of the stories we tell ourselves as potential victims, the key aspect of such a way of being and killing is that it 'may strike unexpectedly, with no warning . . . whatever we know about him does not help us find him before he appears out of the blue and strikes again'. At the same time, we know where he comes from – the mark, perhaps, of Bollas's psychoanalysis? – because it is a 'nowhere' to which we all have some access:

> We know this place. Even if it is beyond our perception, we know it exists. It is the place of the split-off unknown, where actions with unanticipated consequences originate, where sudden destructiveness against or from the self arises, a zone of darkness that weaves in and out of selves, preserving darkness and nowhere in the midst of vibrant mental life and human relations.

Staying with the 'pathways' between psychoanalysis and culture, Anthony Elliott and Stephen Frosh's edited collection *Psychoanalysis in Contexts* is offered as a 'comprehensive overview of the central issues and debates in contemporary psychoanalytic theory'. The book is divided into three sections – 'Subjectivity and Intersubjectivity', 'The Dynamics of Difference' and 'Modern Conditions, Psychoanalytic Controversies' – and represents the views of a range of well-known psychoanalysts and cultural critics. In 'Transitional Thinking: Paths between Psychoanalysis and Modern Culture', Elliott and Frosh provide a useful editorial introduction to the diverse essays included here, essays which it is worth just listing in so far as they suggest the content and scope of the book. In 'Logic, Imagination, Reflection', Cornelius Castoriadis reflects on Freud's contribution to our understanding of the work of the imagination, and, in particular, on the possibility that what distinguishes 'man' is not logic but imagination, 'more precisely, unbridled imagination, defunctionalized imagination'. Anthony Elliott, in 'The Affirmation of Primary Repression Rethought', takes up the question of representation and subjectivity through Freud's notoriously difficult writings on unconscious representation. Both Peter Dews, 'The Crisis of Oedipal Identity: The Early Lacan and the Frankfurt School', and David Macey, 'On the Subject of

Lacan', contribute to the critical apparatus which surrounds Lacan's thinking. Dews's perhaps surprising starting-point is the suggestion that 'we do not find it surprising enough that the thought of Jacques Lacan should have come to function as a major point of reference for feminist theory', a suggestion which is tested briefly against the work of Jacqueline Rose. Dews is concerned to reinstate the historical context, or crisis, which underlies Lacan's phallocentric symbolic, and he offers a reading of Lacan's early *Les complexes familiaux* (1938) in support of his contention that we must 'introduce a dimension of historicity into even the most fundamental psychoanalytic categories'. Macey's concern is with the philosophical context, and texture, of Lacan's *oeuvre* – though he, too, is keen to point out that feminists have to 'confront the problem that Lacan habitually speaks of a human subject that exists as a universal and prior to any gender determination'. And 'feminism' is represented here largely by Nancy J. Chodorow, 'Individuality and Difference in how Women and Men Love' – a title which is overturned in the opening paragraphs of the chapter: 'I claim, against generalization, that women and men love in as many ways as there are women and men'; by Jessica Benjamin, 'Sameness and Difference: Toward an "Over-Inclusive" Theory of Gender Development' – which asks a question about the beyond of the Oedipus complex through a reconsideration of the concepts of identification and difference; and by Janet Sayers, 'Consuming Male Fantasy: Psychoanalysis Retold', an essay which illustrates the 'relevance of Lacan and post-Lacanian theory' through the discussion of four cases of women's eating disorders. Madelon Sprengnether's 'Mourning Freud' also returns to Oedipus and his patriarchal/fraternal legacy to psychoanalysis, a legacy which shows up through the speculative question which generates the essay: what if 'a woman had created the founding concepts that underlie psychoanalytic theory'? Focusing, usefully, on Lacan's 'The Meaning of the Phallus', Stephen Frosh's 'Masculine Mastery and Fantasy' returns to both Oedipus and Lacan, complicating a tendency within psychoanalytic critical theory to make masculinity the 'simple' or self-evident term.

In the final section of the book, the Kleinian analyst Hanna Segal furthers her attempts to construct a dialogue between psychoanalysis and 'socio-political phenomena' against the resistance she perceives from the 'experts' in the field. 'From Hiroshima to the Gulf War and After: A Psychoanalytic Perspective' combines an argument for the need for psychoanalysts to engage in social critique with an excavation of the psychological motivations, the fantasies, at work in what she describes as the 'nuclear mentality'. Joel Kovel's 'On Racism and Psychoanalysis' takes up the issue of racism as an 'affliction of the modern psyche' in its quest to 'split' peoples according to a notion of race, a splitting which Kovel connects to a certain impoverishment of psychical life: 'it is worth considering whether the emergence of racism is related to the stripping down of the western psyche and the reduction of its own interiority and ambivalence'. Finally, in 'Lacan, Klein and Politics: The Positive and Negative in Psychoanalytic Thought', Michael Rustin makes links between two strands of psychoanalytic thinking sometimes assumed to be at odds with one another. A brief historical survey of the different spheres of influence enjoyed by Kleinian and Lacanian theory in British culture since the 1960s is used to introduce a reading of some of the most influential attempts to construct a 'psychopolitics' through the work of Jacques Lacan – a psychopolitics which has focused largely on culture as something like an ideological fantasy covering over the death drive – before looking at the 'positive' potential of the object relations tradition in British psychoanalysis: the Kleinians, Wilfred Bion.

Also useful for its survey of the early reception of psychoanalysis in Britain is R. D. Hinshelwood's 'Psychoanalysis in Britain: Points of Cultural Access, 1893–1918', published in the *International Journal of Psychoanalysis* this year (135–51). Divided into seven sections, the essay is a bibliographical delight: (i) the interest in hysteria from the Society of Psychical Research; (ii) the interest in psychoanalysis as a support of radical attitudes to sexual freedom (Havelock Ellis); (iii) a turn to psychoanalysis as a reaction against the pessimism of British psychiatry, from *c.*1905; (iv) the attempts by Rivers, and others, to create an empirical psychology (1910–15); (v) the application of psychoanalysis to the novel, and, more generally, the creative process, from around 1913; (vi) attention from progressive groups to Freud's theories of child development; and (vii) a philosophical interest (for example, Bertrand Russell) in the implications of Freud's theory of the unconscious. Also of historical interest in this issue is Ilse Grubrich-Simitis's ' "No greater, richer, more mysterious subject (. . .) than the life of the mind": An Early Exchange of Letters between Freud and Einstein' (115–22): the first translation and publication in English, together with a brief commentary, of a correspondence between Einstein and Freud in 1929, three years before the famous exchange known as 'Why War?'

Of interest in the context of critical debates about the relation between fantasy, memory and real events is the journal's publication of papers from the 39th International Psychoanalytical Association Congress on: 'Psychic Reality: Its Impact on the Analyst and on the Patient Today'. The main theme of the Congress is divided into three parts, and the papers collected here address various aspects: 'Psychic Reality and Clinical Technique', 'Psychic Reality: Theoretical Concepts' and 'Psychic Reality and the Life Cycle'. Drawing on Freud, together with the work of Jean Laplanche and Jacques Lacan – and, perhaps, with an eye on the debates concerning false memory syndrome – in 'Misunderstanding and Psychic Truths' (9–13), Haydée Faimberg points out that the concept of psychic reality was introduced by Freud to distinguish, or to negotiate, between memories of abuse and fantasies or wishes that had *real effects*. While psychoanalysis may still aim to construct something like the historical truth of the analysand's experience, 'reality' is put into parenthesis, including the reality of family life and parental relations, so that both can emerge in the form of 'psychic objects'. Similarly, in 'Psychic Realities and Unconscious Belief' (19–23), Ronald Britton casts the psychoanalyst, like the ego itself, as a 'frontier creature', mediating the boundaries between belief and knowledge. Also worth noting is Antonie Ladan's 'A Silenced Indian: More on the Secret Fantasy of Being an Exception' (77–89), which draws attention to the slide between unconscious fantasy and unconscious ideology, defined as 'an elaborate story from our childhood which is extremely persistent and organizes our psychic reality throughout our lives'. In the case history examined here, the ideology of being an 'exception' is worked through the figure of a 'silent, stoical Indian who had no contact with anyone, no desire for anyone, no need for anyone and was always on his guard because of his assumption that someone was out to kill him'. Such an ideological fantasy cries out to be read alongside not only, say, Edward Said's *Orientalism*, but also – given Ladan's tracing of an intergenerational history to this fantasy – Nicolas Abraham and Maria Torok's elaboration of transgenerational haunting (*The Shell and the Kernel* 1994).

Jean Walton's decisive reading of masquerade in 'Re-Placing Race in (White) Psychoanalytic Discourse: Founding Narratives of Feminism' (*Critical Inquiry* 21.775–804) is also concerned with what could be described as the work of ideological fantasy in psychoanalysis. Drawing attention to a critical silence concerning the fantasy of being attacked by a black man embedded in Joan Riviere's influential 'Womanliness as a Masquerade', first published in the *International Journal of Psychoanalysis* in 1929, Walton traces the racialized aggression structuring Riviere's conception of femininity, suggesting that the 'enduring fascination' of the masquerade for white feminist theory can be understood in terms of the 'permission' given by Riviere's text to 'invoke, only to ignore, the cultural constructions of race that inform it'. That permission is, in turn, implicitly connected to the 'curious' lack of interest in race shown by the other analysts discussed here, including Ernest Jones (notably, his response to Bronislaw Malinowski's attack on the ethnocentrism of psychoanalysis) and Melanie Klein: 'In the same year that Riviere published her essay on female masquerade, friend and colleague Melanie Klein developed her theory of "reparation" in an essay that is, for our purposes, just as striking for its evocation and then dismissal of a racialized figuration in the fantasy life of a female subject.' In this case, it is the figure of a 'naked negress' that haunts Klein's theory of reparation; in Riviere's essay, the body of a black man, cast as rapist-thief, is threatened with a 'justice' that Walton considers in the 'violently racialized context' of the American South (where the patient spent her childhood) in the late nineteenth century.

As Walton suggests, that context has been more or less occluded in the different feminist, and postcolonial, appropriations of Riviere's theory of the masquerade, an occlusion which is all the more striking when Riviere's text is put into dialogue with Frantz Fanon's *Black Skin, White Masks*, first published in its English translation in 1967. Turning to Fanon's account of the role of black men in white women's masochistic fantasies of rape, Walton points to the correspondence between what Riviere and Fanon have to say about the white woman's negotiation of the feminine Oedipus complex through a fantasy of racialized violence – a correspondence which prompts a question about the disparity between the welcome extended to Riviere's analysis of femininity and the critical unease generated by Fanon's analyses of sexuality and sexual difference. Walton's primary concern here, however, is to make the point that even 'when racial difference forms the *content* of the fantasy life of a white female subject . . . it is *not* apparently a constitutive component of the psychoanalytic interpretation of the analyst'. Thus she suggests that 'Apparently it makes no difference in Riviere's account that the "man" in question here is black, that culturally sanctioned fantasies in which a white woman is sexually attacked by a black man form a significant component of dominant white racist hegemony in the United States.'

It could be said that on the evidence discussed by Walton, it does, in fact, make all the difference to Riviere that what her patient describes to her is a fantasy of being attacked by a black man, a difference which Walton touches on in her questioning hint as to how our understanding of Riviere might be altered if 'we were to see her as sharing in the . . . white fantasy of racialized sexuality'. But Riviere's subsequent scrambling of her patient's material through 'Womanliness as a Masquerade' – a scrambling which deforms her psychoanalysis at the same time as it exposes her participation in her patient's fantasy life – tends, I think, to be occluded by Walton's decision to read Riviere through Lacan's theory of the phallus. The logic of the phallus – who has it, who is it? – tends to confine the powerful re-reading of Riviere that is also taking place here and, in particular, to slide over the way in which the pressures of racial fantasy on Riviere's text itself reduce psychoanalysis to a miming (masquerade?) of interpretation: to the reproduction, rather than a psycho-analysis, of the formation of racial fantasy.

Lacan is also central to one of the most frightening, or disconcerting, essays published this year: Ellie Ragland's 'Causes of Illness and the Human Body', included in her collection *Essays on the Pleasures of Death: From Freud to Lacan*. While Ragland here covers the ground which has become a site of contest between psychoanalysis and philosophy (Lacan's theories of nar-cissism, the ego and the subject, for example) and psychoanalysis and feminism (two chapters, '"Foreclosure," or the Origin of the Psychoses' and 'The Paternal Metaphor' take up the notorious phallus–penis issue), she is writing from a more clinical, or 'psychoanalytic', perspective on Lacan's return to Freud. And it is the clinical point of view which comes through her analysis of causes of illness, reinflecting some more or less familiar Lacanianisms through the lens of physical health/illness:

> Do people choose their illness? – No, their illness chooses them insofar as they stay attached to their negative *jouissance*. Does the health-care system perpetuate illness? – Yes, to the degree that mental and physical health-care does not take account of this 'truth': that the cause whose effect of disease in the human body goes beyond biological life. . . . The most radical thesis I wish to advance here is that the body may sicken in childhood or in later life as a result of the powerful role insignia play in pushing individuals to establish the identifications they then use to fill up a palpable void within being, knowledge, and body.

Well aware of the contentiousness of what she is saying, Ragland turns away neither from the possibility that psychosomatic illness, at its limit, may represent an unconscious choice for death, nor from the dangers inherent in a psychoanalytic interpretation of psychosomatic illness in terms of family plots: 'Any analyst who points out to an analysand *the true elementary kinship structures* in the heart of the family may even put a patient's life at risk.'

Though there may be a type of Lacanian fundamentalism at work in this book, what Ragland is saying recalls Joyce McDougall's *Theatres of the Body: A Psychoanalytical Approach to Psychosomatic Illness* (Free Association Books, 1989). McDougall's exploration of the connections between 'psyche' and 'soma' are continued this year with the publication of her *The Many Faces of Eros: A Psychoanalytic Exploration of Human Sexuality*. 'Human sexuality', McDougall declares in the opening lines of the book, 'is inherently traumatic', and the chapters which follow weave a complex set of questions and wonderings about the conflicts and solutions offered to that trauma. Most compelling about McDougall's presentation here, as elsewhere, is her use of clinical material to suggest the movement, or the process, of psychoanalytic interpretation, a presentation which starts to nuance one dominant critical approach to psychoanalysis as a deadening hermeneutic, drawing a range of diverse historical and cultural material back into an Oedipal framework which cannot contain it. No doubt that framework is crucial to McDougall in her exploration of – to take a random sample of chapters – 'The Female Analyst and the Female Analysand', 'The Smell Self and the Skin Self', 'Neoneeds and Addictive Sexualities' and 'Sexual Deviation and Psychic Survival'. At the same time her attention to the transference and countertransference processes at work not only between analyst and analysand but within psychoanalysis itself tends towards a questioning of psychoanalytic dogma; or, as she puts it in 'Beyond Psychoanalytic Sects in Search of a New Paradigm', *Is not our leading perversion, then, the belief that we hold the key to the truth?*'

One defence against dogma is a sense of the diversity of psychoanalytic writing and experience, and several publications this year make such diversity more available. *Essential Papers on Masochism*, edited by Margaret Hanly, really is essential for current critical interest in the theory and practice of masochism. Hanly has collected, in one volume, the well-known, though not all so easily available, 'classic' texts by Freud, Helene Deutsch ('The Significance of Masochism in the Mental Life of Women'), Marie Bonaparte ('Some Biophysical Aspects of Sado-Masochism'), Otto Fenichel ('The Clinical Aspect of the Need for Punishment') and 'Jacques' (*sic*: this should be Jean) Laplanche ('Aggressiveness and Sadomasochism'). Less familiar essays include: Anna Freud's 'Beating Fantasies and Daydreams', first published in 1922, intriguing as a response to her father's theories of feminine masochism; Joan Riviere's 'A Contribution to the Analysis of Negative Therapeutic Reaction', which reminds us that Riviere wrote essays other than 'Womanliness as a Masquerade'; Janine Chasseguet-Smirgel's 'Auto-Sadism, Eating Disorders, and Femininity'; and Betty Joseph's recent 'Addiction to Near-Death'. Hanly's introduction facilitates a theoretical and historical reading of the familiar and not-so-familiar contributions to the *Essential Papers*, as do three introductory essays: Sacha Nacht's '*Le Masochisme*, Introduction' (1965), Rudolph M. Loewenstein's 'A Contribution to the Psychoanalytic Theory of Masochism' (1957) and Victor N. Smirnoff's 'The Masochistic Contract' (1969).

Also worth noting for its broadening of our notions of what constitutes 'psychoanalysis' is the republication of the classic *Psychoanalytic Pioneers*, first published in 1965 and reissued this year with a new introduction by Samuel Eisenstein. Edited by Franz Alexander, Samuel Eisenstein and Martin Grotjahn, the collection tells the history of psychoanalysis through introductory profiles, and short bibliographies, of forty-two of its 'most eminent teachers, thinkers, and clinicians', excluding Freud but including (to name those who will be most familiar outside of psychoanalysis): Karl Abraham, Sándor Ferenczi, Otto Rank, Ernest Jones, Victor Tausk, Ella Freeman Sharpe, Helene and Felix Deutsch, August Aichhorn, Melanie Klein, Otto Fenichel, Karen Horney, Edward Glover, Anna Freud and Erik H. Erikson. Two final essays, by Edward Glover and John A. P. Millet, offer some crucial historical insights into the different reception of psychoanalysis in Britain and the United States, a reception which seems to be so very much at issue for contemporary discussions of psychoanalysis.

With that reception in mind, a fascinating reading of Freud comes through Ann Douglas's *Terrible Honesty: Mongrel Manhattan in the 1920s*. Freud, in particular his 'élite pessimism', appears here as an 'influence' on the 'soul of a generation' that made New York the capital of American culture in the 1920s. Douglas has fused any number of sources to produce a very readable, sympathetic and trenchant account of Freud's troubled relation to things American: his dependence on American money in his post-war practice in Vienna, for example; his role as 'chosen mentor of Madison Avenue' (Edward Bernays, the leading 'adman' of the day was Freud's nephew) and the idea that 'Freud's definition of the analyst–patient relationship gave advertisers wooing their clients their model and their cue; the appeal of the 'terrible honesty', or pessimism, of psychoanalysis to a generation of American writers; Freud's anxiety that the popularization of psychoanalysis in America amounted to a vulgarization, a destruction, of his theories and therapy. If only for the insight it offers into a contemporary struggle between Europe and America over the legacy of psychoanalysis, *Terrible Honesty* (and, in particular, the chapter on 'Offstage Influences') is another contribution to a historical and cultural contextualization of psychoanalytic thinking. That work is also represented this year in José Brunner's *Freud and the Politics of Psychoanalysis*. Brunner offers a 'political reading of Freud's writings' which both scans the 'surface' of Freud's texts – 'politics provides the largest single repertoire of Freud's metaphors and analogies' – and excavates the political logic structuring Freud's thinking on the 'family and sexuality, his hypotheses on the development of the psychic and social structures, and the groundwork of his therapeutic practice'.

Noting the book's debt to Michel Foucault – 'I regard everying which has to do with the exercise of power as political' – Brunner is nevertheless concerned to produce a sympathetic account of the history and theory of psychoanalysis, starting with Freud's analysis of hysteria in 'Nervousness and Nationalism: Medical Politics and the Origins of Psychoanalysis'. This is a reading of Freud's studies in hysteria in the context of the 'bourgeois values, nationalist ideologies and racial prejudices which dominated medical and political thinking in the end of the nineteenth century', a reading which aims to 'assess the various ways in which Freud's utterances and silences on the relationship between hysteria, heredity and ethnicity departed from the prevailing medico-political discourse'. Such an approach may be familiar from the work of Sander Gilman (*Freud, Race, and Gender* 1993), referenced by Brunner as one of the few theorists to have attempted to think of Freud's Jewishness in relation to his scientific context. Brunner's aim, however, is to

> examine Freud's references to Jews and Judaism and differentiate
> from one another the four textual strategies which Freud adopted
> in his writings to express his attitude towards his ethnic identity.
> By no means, however, does my reading entail a neglect of Freud's
> Jewish consciousness; on the contrary, it means taking Freud's
> particular self-conception as a modern secular Jew more seriously
> than some of his more speculative commentators have done.

'Portrait of the Scientist as a Young Jew' tracks those four strategies in some detail through Freud's texts, only to discover a type of strategic universalism in

Freud's silence on 'ethnic and national matters': 'Freud's silence is *relevant* because it expressed his attempt to make his own and his patients' Jewishness *irrelevant* to his new science and the understanding of neuroses' – an irrelevance which would break the link between Jewishness and degeneracy which persists through the medical discourses of the nineteenth century.

Brunner's own strategic reading of Freud's 'silences' surfaces throughout the three remaining sections of the book: part II, 'A State of Mind: Metaphorical Politics in Freud's Metapsychology' starts with Freud's analogies between the work of censorship in dreams and in the political state; part III, 'Between Two Consenting Adults: Face-to-Face Politics in the Clinical Practice of Psychoanalysis' presents psychoanalysis as a 'dyadic face-to-face society' which, like all societies, is 'politically structured': 'Two persons never encounter each other only as analyst and analysand, but always also as members of their profession, nationality, social class and gender'; and part IV 'Empires of Passion: Oedipal Politics in Freud's Writings on Social Relations' includes a chapter on 'Brothers in Arms' and Freud's phylogenetic fantasies, in 'Totem and Taboo' and elsewhere. The breadth of Brunner's reading is obvious and the book is full of quotations which make you want to go and read yet another bit of Freud. The author is also keen to take on some of the more neglected dimensions of psychoanalytic experience. Thus chapter 11, 'A Touch of Class' returns, once again, to the treatment of hysteria, drawing on recent feminist studies of late nineteenth-century gynaecology to show up the difference of Freud's approach. Psychoanalytic therapy, Brunner suggests,

> originated in his [Freud's] attempt to transform patient–doctor relations from a public spectacle in which members of the lower class submit to commanding talk by a middle-class doctor, into private encounters where patients are of the same class and cultural background as the doctor. . . . Rather than illiterate, superstitious, poor peasants and factory workers, Freud's patients mostly were well-to-do women.

This begs the question of what happens to those women who fall outside the middle class, a question to which Brunner responds briefly with reference to Freud's own comments on the disaffected relation between psychoanalysis and the poor:

> Poor ourselves and socially powerless, and compelled to earn our livelihood from our medical activity, we are not even in a position to extend our efforts to people without means, as other doctors with other methods of treatment are after all able to do. Our therapy is too time-consuming and too laborious for that to be possible.

Too much time, too much work, it seems, for psychoanalysts to offer the talking cure, the cure through transference and love, to those who cannot afford to pay for it – and Brunner is properly critical. But, again, the turn to the history of what psychoanalysis does not talk about – or what it talks about only improperly – loses the opportunity to ask what happens to psychoanalysis as the result of such silence, such exclusions: what happens to psychoanalytic concepts themselves when they refuse to interpret racial fantasy or to find fantasy in the lower classes? As Brunner points out, but no more than that, Freud argued that ' " the poor" were less likely to fall ill, since they suffered less of bourgeois values'.

Given current critical interest in the medical and psychiatric discourses from which psychoanalysis emerges, Katrien Libbrecht's *Hysterical Psychosis: A Historical Survey*, offered as the 'first complete and authoritative historical study' of hysterical madness, seems well timed. Like Brunner, Libbrecht's point of departure is the turn-of-the-century recognition of hysteria: Charcot's work at the Salpêtrière and Freud's 'neurology'. Less familiar, perhaps, is the material collated in chapter 4, 'Congresses on Hysteria', which discusses events at three congresses held by French neurologists and alienists and one by Belgian neurologists and psychiatrists in 1894, 1907, 1921 and 1908. Part Two, 'The Interbellum: Hysteria in the Margin, Schizophrenia as a Refuge of Hysterical Madness' again treats the better-known material – 'The War Neuroses' – in the context of a history of psychiatry which is less familiar and which adds to the bibliographical source material. As its title suggests, 'The 1950s to the Present: The Marginal Psychotic Existence of Hysterical Madness, The Numerical Diaspora of Hysteria', the final section of the book considers the contemporary fate of hysteria in the wake of the anti-psychiatry movement, charting the re-emergence of hysteria in the category of 'hysterical psychosis' – a perspective which, among other things, offers Libbrecht a slightly different way into Lacan's elaboration of hysterical discourse.

Finally, published in the Makers of Modern Psychotherapy Series, Sheila Spensley's *Frances Tustin* is a critical introduction to Tustin's pioneering psychoanalysis of autism. Starting with two brief biographical chapters, Spensley places Tustin's clinical and theoretical treatment of approaches to autism in the context of both psychoanalysis (Bion, Meltzer) and of different approaches to childhood disturbance – including, tantalizingly, Kant's assertion in 1798 that all forms of derangement were inherited: 'There are no disturbed children!' This is, I think, a crucial introduction to one of the most suggestive, and brilliant, *oeuvres* within contemporary psychoanalytic thinking. Hopefully, it will make Tustin's work more widely available outside of psychoanalysis; certainly, the material has a contemporary critical purchase not only in the context of, say, Julia Kristeva's influential analyses of abjection and primary identification in *Tales of Love* (1987) and *Powers of Horror* (1982), but also, as Spensley's meticulous presentation makes clear, in light of a contemporary sense that something has gone wrong with 'our children'. At least three books published this year underline the relevance of Spensley's evocation of 'unnatural children' and Tustin's wondering at autism as a problem for our time. Oliver James's *Juvenile Violence in a Winner–Loser Culture*, David Jackson's *Destroying the Baby in Themselves: Why Did the Two Boys Kill James Bulger?* and Rosalind Miles's *The Children We Deserve* are all concerned with the problem of 'juvenile violence', of childhood and sexuality, of what children do to society as well as what society does to children – and all three draw on more or less explicit psychological-psychoanalytic models of child development. None, it should be said, make use of Tustin's work on the terrors, the 'black holes', of autism; to push the point, none exploit what Spensley describes as the 'extreme aloneness' of autism for its capacity to symbolize something about the dissociative, or disaffected, ways of being a child that are so much at issue for each of these authors. What would happen, for example, if Tustin's insights into the mental cataclysm of autism were brought to bear on the question of 'juvenile violence'? What might her account of an autistic use of objects as defences against a world felt to be unbearably hostile have to say about Oliver James's critique of a 'winner–loser' culture in which boys' violence is associated with increasing poverty, maternal depression and a widening gap between rich and poor? Or about what Jackson describes as the 'damaging struggle to be masculine in this culture', a struggle that, in his view, can end in the scene of murder?

Books Reviewed

Alexander, Franz, Samuel Eisenstein and Martin Grotjahn, eds. *Psychoanalytic Pioneers*. Transaction. pp. 616. pb £18.95. ISBN 1 56000 815 6.

Bollas, Christopher. *Cracking Up: The Work of Unconscious Experience*. Routledge. pp. 264. hb £40.00, pb £14.99. ISBN 0 415 12242 2, 0 415 12243 0.

Bollas, Christopher, and David Sundelson. *The New Informants: Betrayal of Confidentiality in Psychoanalysis and Psychotherapy*. Karnac Books. £21.99. ISBN 1 85575 116 X.

Brunner, José. *Freud and the Politics of Psychoanalysis*. Blackwell. pp. 238. hb £40.00. ISBN 0 631 16404 9.

Douglas, Ann. *Terrible Honesty: Mongrel Manhattan in the 1920s*. Picador. pp. 606. hb £20.00. ISBN 0 330 34683 0.

Elliott, Anthony, and Stephen Frosh, eds. *Psychoanalysis in Contexts*. Routledge. pp. 254. pb £12.99. ISBN 0 415 09704 5.

Hanly, Margaret Ann Fitzpatrick. *Essential Papers on Masochism*. New York University Press. pp. 532. ISBN 0 8147 3496 0.

Jackson, David. *Destroying the Baby in Themselves: Why Did the Two Boys Kill James Bulger?* Mushroom. pp. 46. pb £3.50. ISBN 0 907123 31 7.

James, Oliver. *Juvenile Violence in a Winner–Loser Culture: Socio-Economic and Familial Origins of Violence Against the Person*. Free Association Books. pp. 171. pb £15.95. ISBN 1 85343 302 0.

Libbrecht, Katrien. *Hysterical Psychosis: A Historical Survey*. Transaction. pp. 283. hb £25.95. ISBN 1 56000 181 X.

McDougall, Joyce. *The Many Faces of Eros: A Psychoanalytic Exploration of Human Sexuality*. Free Association Books. pp. 257. pb £15.95. ISBN 1 85343 326 8.

Miles, Rosalind. *The Children We Deserve*. HarperCollins. pp. 305. pb £6.99. ISBN 0 586 09231 5.

Ofshe, Richard, and Ethan Watters. *Making Monsters: False Memories, Psychotherapy, and Sexual Hysteria*. André Deutsch. pp. 340. pb £12.99. ISBN 0 233 98957 9.

Ragland, Ellie. *Essays on the Pleasures of Death: From Freud to Lacan*. Routledge. pp. 240. hb £37.50, pb £12.99. ISBN 0 415 90721 7, 0 415 90722 5.

Spensley, Sheila. *Frances Tustin*. Routledge. pp. 154. hb £30.00, pb £12.99. ISBN 0 415 09262 0, 0 415 09263 9.

4

Deconstruction

IAIN HAMILTON GRANT and KARIN LITTAU

'Philosophers', wrote Nietzsche, 'think they show respect for a thinker when they mummify him' – and not only philosophers, to judge from this year's leaps into the wake of deconstruction. It is not only that Derrida's own work is raided, like the tomb of a still living pharaoh, or that essays already widely available in English are recollected for a new book, appropriately entitled *On the Name*, to honour but also cash in on his name. Or that those contributions which genuinely admire his work, such as Royle's *After Derrida*, whilst leaving us with a fresh and inventive homage to Derrida, remains an essay in, on, about and around deconstruction rather than what it might have been, and what Royle might still produce, an invigorating shift beyond it. While yet others still are so enthralled by Derrida that their imitations of his clever ways are almost too much to bear, works in other words which remain so hermetically sealed or stuffy (Smith's *Derrida and Autobiography* sticks in the craw) as to suffocate its audience, as to satisfy solely its audience of one. Sometimes, however, things are very much done with deconstruction, and the conjunction of deconstruction with another field of enquiry produces new insights, as was the case with so many of last year's contributions, and a tendency best represented this year in Graham Ward's *Barth, Derrida and the Language of Theology*, which carefully unknits the 'ands' between theology and deconstruction, a carefulness that is sadly wanting in Bill Martin's 'synthesis' of Marxism and deconstruction, which might have done much more than merely touch on the parasitism of deconstruction. Equally, as is the case with many of the contributions in *Deconstruction and Phenomenology*, the conjunction – here between Derrida and Husserl – is often at the expense of the former, and as such represents a mummification also. For, whether in idolizing Derrida to the extent that his texts become seemingly sacred and untouchable, or an excuse for showing why he should be put on ice, it is perhaps time to translate theory across borders, texts, disciplines and cultures, the very topic of Hillis Miller's *Topographies*, so as to transform, even if it does deform, a body of work as it is recontextualized and assimilated in a new place. Let us take a look at Derrida's own publications for 1995 then, before moving on to what is a rather Frankensteinian collection of responses to deconstruction this year.

Of the three essays comprising Derrida's *On the Name*, two of them, 'Passions: An Oblique Offering' and '*Sauf le nom* (*Post-Scriptum*)', although rewritten prior to their recent publication in French (1993) as three separate booklets – the dubious occasion for the present volume – were originally published in English; the former in David Wood (ed.) *Derrida: A Critical Reader* (1992), and the latter in Harold Coward and Toby Foshay (eds) *Derrida & Negative Theology* (also 1992; see *YWCCT* 2 for review). Moreover, since the third of the essays, *'Khora'*, though appearing in English for the first time, first saw the light of day in 1987, cynics may find it taxing to decide whether Derrida's *prière d'insérer* (translated in *On the Name*) that accompanied the French editions, claiming that all three essays hang on the 'question of the name', is an attempt to justify their reappearance on thematic grounds or to comment on publishers' marketing strategies. That *'Khora'* appears here is, however, fortuitous, in that its core themes – philosophical versus literary discourse; the comparative virtues of close textual analysis as against abstract theorizing; how one can 'formalize', as Derrida quotes Jean-Pierre Vernant's question, prefacing *'Khora'* with a prescient summary of the logic of deconstruction; 'these see-saw operations, which flip any term into its opposite whilst at the same time keeping them both apart, from another point of view?' – recur throughout many of this year's publications. Firstly, however, it is difficult, in a text bearing this title, not to remark upon the absence of any direct reference to Derrida's erstwhile *Tel Quel* comrade Julia Kristeva, given the centrality of her discussion of the 'chora' in *Revolution of Poetic Language* (published 1974 in French and 1984 in English). Kristeva does figure indirectly, however, and may be an implied addressee, since this essay considers khora (marking the problem of prejudging the ontological status of khora, answering the question 'what *is* . . .', Derrida pointedly drops the article) from the points of view of textual analysis and the problem of deriving a politics or a politeia from, as it were, a written 'constitution'. This hypothesis is perhaps reinforced by a debate between Kristeva and Derrida regarding the interpretive strategies appropriate to and the political resources to be derived from treating Plato's *Timaeus*, that – Derrida gives us to infer by way of a footnote in this text echoing one in *Positions* – took place on the occasion of Derrida's 1970 lecture series entitled 'Theory of Philosophical Discourse: The Conditions of Inscription of the Text of Political Philosophy – The Example of Materialism'. The same reference recurs, under the rubric of the problem of 'ontologizing' (the) chora, in *Positions* (published 1972 in French and 1981 in English), which problematic, and Derrida's critical position with regard to it, Kristeva also remarks upon in a note in *Revolution*. It is to the extent that *'Khora'* readdresses the topics treated in that course – and in the debate which appears to have followed it – that it replays the 'putting to the test of the political' that Derrida argues it constitutes (perhaps an ironic rehearsal of the events recorded in *Positions*, where representatives of *Tel Quel*, including Kristeva, put Derrida's politics to an ideological test, failing which resulted in his expulsion from the community, just as Socrates claims he is, in the *Timaeus*, with regard to the 'political philosophers'). Derrida's reading of the *Timaeus* in this text draws attention to the pretexts and nested narrative contexts within which Plato's discussion of the khora occurs. The principal and initial context is provided by Socrates' summarizing the form of the ideal polity as it occurs in the *Republic*. Derrida's cue for the political reserve he demonstrates in *Positions* (and has more recently demonstrated in *Spectres of Marx* 1994 – for a review, see *YWCCT* 4) is taken from Plato's tale of Socrates' mournful recognition of the unbridgeable difference between an idea, a memory, a textual or a pictorial representation of the ideal city and the realization or *animation* of this idea. In consequence of this recognition, Socrates retreats and goes over a series of tales concerning the political origins of Athens told to him by Timaeus who, in turn, is retelling tales told to others and then, by those others, to him. Derrida's basic lesson is that, since the political cannot be reduced to, or animated from, a text, the difference between the inscription of political discourse and the institution of the polity inevitably involves this abyssal retreat to, and retreatment of, the question of origins and origination. From this, the idea, familiar from *Spectres of Marx*, of 'the revolution to come' through 'the retreat of politics' unsatisfyingly derives. The multiple narrative frames of the *Timaeus*, interrupted by the abyssally contaminated, 'hybrid or bastard' mytho-philosophical discourse on khora, indicate further, according to Derrida, that philosophical or 'ontologizing' theses *on* khora cannot be extracted from a text as narratively dense as Plato's most fictitious of fictions, since, by virtue of the metaphysics of the representation reiterated in that text, such theses would amount to simulacra, fictions abstracted from fictions, undercutting in advance the purity of philosophical discourse; nor, moreover, can the *Timaeus* serve as the support for a politics. Both discourses must instead 'retreat' to the hybridized and abyssal 'conditions of inscription' of philosophical or political discourse in the *Timaeus*: stories told, reported myths, unverifiable accounts, fictions of all kinds mesh with the more philosophical fictions of, for example, the *Republic*. Oddly then, this text, ten years out of date, serves to conjoin the problematic 'reserve' or 'retreat' informing the attempts to formulate a deconstructive politics which predominated in last year's works, with the hybridized discursive condition that it seems to be the mission of many of this year's works to redress, whether by asking if a deconstructive logic may admit of formalization – something Derrida claims in this text, after Vernant, is 'virtually impossible'; whether by subsuming literary discourses under philosophical mastery; or by contesting the interpretive adequacy of deconstructive against close, even intentional, readings of texts; or whether, finally, it is conceivable that old discourses can be discarded and, children like the Greeks, as the story goes, we may come to invent new ones.

Since khora is also a 'universal receptacle', receiving anything that happens to imprint upon it but having nothing, no identity, no property or propriety of its own to give, Derrida's essay offers another, albeit brief, reflection in a series on the economy of the gift, something that we might expect to be more fully explored in a text entitled *The Gift of Death*. Part of a continuing attempt to consider the gift 'apart from all anthropology', apart, that is, from its development under Mauss, Lévi-Strauss and Bataille, Derrida's take on the topic repeats Heidegger's criticisms of the limitations of humanism and returns the gift, so to speak, to the Heideggerian '*es gibt*', the 'there is' of Being, from which the former initially receives it. As in '*Khora*', Derrida addresses the problem of origination, albeit this time through an extended reading of Jan Patocka's *Heretical Essays on the History of Philosophy* (published 1975 in Czech and 1981 in French), the deferred origination of the Christian religion which, Patocka argues, will be co-extensive and co-eval with the 'birth of Europe', once it has come into its own and broken decisively with its Greek, philosophical prehistory. In offering such an intertwined history of philosophy and religion, Derrida argues, Patocka covers the same ground as Heidegger's history and *Destruktion* of onto-theology and yet, in that work, makes no overt mention of Heidegger. Derrida's mission here, then, is to reinsert Patocka's Heideggerian supplement into the problematic relationship between ontology and theology, a topic that in turn reinserts this text into Derrida's ongoing readings, beginning with 'Violence and Metaphysics', of Levinas, a context that echoes throughout this text. As in Derrida's early text on Levinas, *The Gift of Death* plays the latter's restricted sense of 'economy' – *oikos* and *nomos*, the law of the home – off against a general economy of sacrifice where no return can be expected, a theme played out in turn in Levinas's own critical reading of Kierkegaard's account of Abraham's preparedness, having received God's command, to sacrifice his beloved only son, Isaac. In brief, the problem is what to do when the 'absolutely other' appears unbidden at the threshold of your home and demands everything. In other words, this is a problem of how to respond to what Levinas calls the ethical priority of the 'there is [*il y a*]' of the other, a reformulation of the priority of Being in the *es gibt* – 'it gives'. Thus, just as for Heidegger, 'human being' is a degraded, merely 'ontic' stand-in that covers over Being or ontological difference, so Derrida here distinguishes two economies of the gift of death. In the former, the economy as the 'law of the home' (following Levinas), death appears as the condition under which I most fully and freely become myself, since my death cannot be shared by another; in the latter, death comes as a gift, something other than I am, and conditions the possibility of the former. Thus, reading Levinas through Heidegger through Patocka, provides Derrida's starting point for his analysis of the economy of the 'gift of death', 'a gift that is not a present, the gift of something that remains inaccessible, unpresentable', and being unpresentable and therefore unpresented, a gift to which there can be no countergift, no response. Challenging, then, both the 'absolute obligation' to the other that Levinas's ethical priority demands, and what Derrida criticizes, in 'Violence and Metaphysics', as the empiricism that, allowing the gift to appear 'face to face' with the other, as Levinas has it, makes the gift into a present, the present of the other, Derrida goes on to ask whether this gift can even be conceived; whether, in other words, if it cannot be sensible, it might yet be intelligible. Here, however, we run up against the Heideggerian problem, in so far as the ontological gift not only breaks the law of the home, but broaches the limits of conceptual thinking; we cannot *know*, therefore, of the gift. In the face of this exorbitant gift, then, there is no response, whether of ethical obligation or conceptualization, since the gift, the *es gibt*, not only does not appear, but, given that nothing appears, what *is* it that is being talked about? It is at this point that these Heideggerian questions are brought to bear upon one of the principal themes of Patocka's book, the chiasmic origins of Europe and Christianity. Rather, however, than asking 'what *is* religion', as Patocka does, Derrida's question retreats (from) its topic to ask: 'under what conditions can we speak of religion?' Here Derrida implicates Heidegger's *es gibt*, as he remarks in '*Khora*', in the apophatic discourses of negative theology, reiterating the continuing retreatment, after Heidegger, of ontology *with* theology and inscribing the economy of *différance* into the limits and conditions of theological discourse. Thus Heidegger is as implicated, however forceful his arguments against this may be, in theology as Levinas is, equally unwillingly, in ontology. While thus questioning the 'possibility of religion without religion', and especially, following Patocka's lead, in the context of Christianity, might seem to place *The Gift of Death* rather to the side of Derrida's concerns, it nevertheless draws attention to the extent that, heavily referenced in the present text, *Glas* (1986), for example, asks similar questions of Judaism, based on Hegel's theses on the topic. While, however, ethical, political, theological and philosophical themes and arguments intersect with the readings of Patocka, Heidegger, Levinas and Kierkegaard, they form a rather looser – certainly drier! – less developed weave than this reference might suggest.

In a timely follow-up to *The Gift of Death*, Graham Ward's *Barth, Derrida and the Language of Theology* takes up both this theological version of 'how to avoid speaking' and contends that Derrida's work is indeed 'situated within theological horizons'. While as raw assertion this may seem sweeping, Ward's text demonstrates sufficient attention to the theoretical and practical aspects of 'the economy of *différance*' at work to develop a strategy appropriate to this reframing. Adapting this strategy from Derrida's own in his encounters with Searle and, especially, with Gadamer, Ward argues that his 'negotiation' of the economy of *différance* and Karl Barth's theology of 'the Word in words' avoids the overbearing consensualist predeterminations of 'dialogue' and retains sufficient suspicion and oblique interrogation to avoid either the violence of appropriation or that of misrepresentation befalling either partner. Moreover, Ward's modest proposal is merely to demonstrate that Derrida offers a 'philosophical supplementation' to Barth's theology, one that takes care to 'avoid speaking', and to credit Derrida's critique of logocentrism, and the general postmodern crisis of representation, as generating theological investigation. Successive chapters therefore delineate Barth's theology alongside the philosophies of his contemporaries, Heidegger and Husserl, and demonstrate their shared indebtedness to the philosophies of language developed by Hamann, Herder and Humboldt, before considering the intricacies of Derrida's double-edged 'critique and supplementation' of Levinas's philosophical theology and, finally, negotiating, contaminating with reserve, Barth and Derrida in an investigation of postmodern theology and the 'metaphysics of liminality'. Irrespective of the immediate interest its specific thematics might arouse in Derrida's more textualist readers, Ward's book is exemplary in its attention to the distances, rather than simply the proximities, set to work throughout this complex text from the moment its title says 'and'.

Before we leave the question of Derrida and theology, however, *Diacritics* (25:iv) continues its deconstructive blitz with Jill Robbins's 'Circumcising Confession: Derrida, Autobiography, Judaism'. Beginning with Levinas's examination of Franz Rosenzweig's 'confession' that his passage to Judaism took a 'double detour' via the Christian faith from which, initially, he had hatefully regarded his eventual spiritual home, only now to have the tables turned, Robbins finds the same 'double movement', via the same stations, on his way to Judaism via the Christian saints. Finally, in 'Circumfession', Derrida too comes to Judaic philosophy by way of St Augustine. As a first clue to these thinkers as contributors to 'modern Jewish philosophy', these detours also translated in the expanded range of that philosophy, developing what Rosenzweig had already indicated as the task of recovering a 'lost dimension of Jewish philosophy'. Thus, in parallel with these three thinkers' circuitous detours to Judaism, Robbins notes the necessity that this recovery go by way of an additional detour via the Greeks, that 'Hebrew be translated into Greek', as she puts it, in order that Jewish philosophy might acquire its full ontological range. Robbins's fascinating essay does much to enhance the point, made by Ward, that Derrida's texts are written within a theological frame; in apparent revenge for detourning of Heidegger and Levinas against themselves in *The Gift of Death*, Robbins doubly binds Derrida's 'circumfession' within the economy of Judaic philosophy and its *différance*.

Derrida's *Points . . . Interviews, 1974–1994*, edited by Elisabeth Weber, is a hefty collection of conversations between Derrida and a hoard of different interviewers; of the twenty-three interviews (some of which are exchanges of letters), fourteen appear here for the first time in English. One interview is a new, specifically commissioned piece, and rehearses once more Derrida's indignation at the 'Wolin–Sheehan affair' which swept the pages of the *New York Review of Books* in 1993, after Wolin had both published and translated ('badly'), and moreover without Derrida's authorization, the latter's 'Heidegger, the Philosophers' Hell' essay. Dealing with a vast arena of themes – from in-depth commentaries on his own works, that of other philosophers, including the (in)famous essay on Heidegger just mentioned, to the teaching of philosophy, or its future at 'a Certain Collège International de Philosophy Still to Come', or responding to the question 'Is there a Philosophical Language', from letter exchanges with Verena Andermatt about sexual difference, an address to the question 'CHE cos'é la poesia?', explorations of the poetry of Trakl or Celan, to reflections on drugs, the media, AIDS, as well as translation, nationalism and politics – this volume contains both serious, witty and anecdotal insights into his work. As such it might not only appeal to the Derridaphile reading up on his other, often journalistic, pieces, but also to those who would wish to obtain a first introduction to his thinking, and read for the first time a Derrida who in the parameters of conversational prose is perhaps more lively, engaging and accessible than he is elsewhere in his work. If its editor, Weber, allowed herself to 'be guided' for this collection of interviews, as she puts it, 'above all by diversity, by the greatest diversity possible in the limits and the coherence of a single volume', Florian Rötzer, both editor and interviewer of *Conversations with French Philosophers*, takes a very different tack. This collection of interviews, first published in Germany in 1986, is not guided by Weber's 'diversity', but by Rötzer's attempt to introduce German readers to a whole range of philosophical voices from France. Rötzer's conversations with Derrida, Levinas, Lyotard, Baudrillard, but also Cornelius Costariadis, Gérard Raulet, Michel Serres and Paul Virilio, are therefore all geared towards what is specifically germane to the German critical scene, largely dominated by Habermas's cries for consensus, Gadamer's pleadings for dialogue, and Manfred Frank's decryings of what he takes to be French philosophy's celebration of 'irrationality'. That is, since fascism is associated with irrationality, the French love affair with Heidegger and Nietzsche is problematic for German thinkers, such as Rainer Rochlitz, for instance, whose foreword to this volume reminds his audience on the Black Forest side of the Rhine that French poststructuralism has a 'dark side that hardly comes out in conversation'. It is from this very specific background then, that Rötzer does not so much set himself to tease out this 'dark side', but elicit from his French interviewees some altogether more reassuring answers for his German readership. This does not mean, however, that this collection is only of limited interest to the Anglo-American world, rather it does give voice to certain fears also felt on this side of the Channel, or the other side of the

Atlantic; equally, however, the questions raised, and the answers given, show just how much these fears are driven by hysteria rather than informed by a close encounter with these thinkers' writings. While Rötzer's and Weber's volumes of interviews give a good, albeit partial introductory indication of what Derrida's work, for instance, is about, they do not save readers from the necessary task of reading the works themselves, or as Derrida makes clear in interviews in both volumes, 'to read the texts discussed and not just the article', or here the interview, 'that is devoted to it', and furthermore, 'to verify the information that is proposed to them and not take at its word what they are being told about a text or a fact', even if, we might add, it has Habermas's name (with its secondary readings of Derrida) stamped all over it.

Tom Rockmore's *Heidegger and Modern French Philosophy: Humanism, Antihumanism and Being* makes a contribution to an emerging sub-genre of what could be called 'popular philosophy', perhaps intended to rival the increasing appearance on the best-seller lists of works of 'popular science', from one particularly successful example of which – Stephen Hawking's *A Brief History of Time* – Rockmore quotes in the very first sentence of this work. Underscoring this populism with a constant barrage of disclaimers regarding minor points such as accuracy or even adequate familiarity with his topic, Rockmore aims this messy work at 'intelligent and good-willed men and women' who may lack a philosophical background, but who are none the less desperate to understand how Heidegger could have been a *Nazi*. Whereas popular science has a clear idea of its audience, this particular piece of popular philosophy seems addressed to one that is at best unlikely to exist. For academics from other fields wishing for a comprehensive guide to recent French philosophy, Vincent Descombes's *Modern French Philosophy* (1980) remains clearer, shorter and infinitely more adequate to its topic. The agenda behind Rockmore's book, however, has nothing to do with providing a guide either to Heidegger, or to modern French philosophy, but rather to add a voice to the familiar hysterical rant that 'fashionable French filth' is riddled with nazism, atoning for the night of the long knives with an apparent eternity of long wind. Where Rockmore does address contemporary French philosophy, then, it is predictably enough to show merely that Derrida, too, remains in ideologically unhealthy proximity to Heidegger, although, as per his treatment of Heidegger, the portrait of Derrida in this work is shielded by so many caveats as to become almost unintelligible, until, at last, a summarial account of 'Derrida's position' comes unexpectedly to the fore, a position assembled, Rockmore writes, from 'close exegeses of Heidegger's writings, criticisms of other theories in terms of the spirit of those writings, as he interprets it, and a number of characteristic doctrines that are invariably either borrowed from, consistent with, or extensions of, Heideggerian doctrines'. Evidence for this, and other claims in Rockmore's book (basing, as he does, a claim that French intellectual life is shrouded in Catholicism on two works from the seventeenth century) remains scant and under-researched, and, as such, provides a usefully condensed illustration of the many shortcomings of this book.

Roland A. Champagne's *Jacques Derrida* takes aim at a similarly broad range of targets, seeking to address the philosophical background alongside the literary, political and ethical engagements of the 'author' in question. Unfortunately, however, much of Champagne's contextualization remains too slight to be of use either as introductory material or as a contribution to ongoing debates. Hegel, for instance, typically figures as deconstruction's great enemy; but the Hegel we are offered is unrecognizably simplistic, or, in Champagne's intentionalist lexis, too 'single-minded' to provide even the remotest theoretical challenge. Nor is this an isolated example: elided differences, sloppy exegeses and erroneous ascriptions ('Kant's universal Spirit' springs to mind) abound, reducing the gamut of figures and themes this book touches on in its hundred or so pages – Husserl, Levinas, Freud, Lacan, de Man, feminism, the Heidegger affair, deconstruction and speech-act theory – to an indistinguishable mass of received ideas. It is, however, very much Derrida the author-and-person, rather than 'Derrida' the set of philosophical and theoretical problems, that figures as the guiding question of this work: encouragingly asserting his critical intentions from the outset, and noting the irritation and inevitable allegations of political irresponsibility attendant upon Derrida's 'expert avoidance of providing answers' to the 'provocative' and 'subversive' questions he poses, Champagne swiftly drops his critical commitment and rather clumsily avoids posing questions in order to allow his appreciation of Derrida the author to come to the fore. While theoretical problems are therefore smoothed over by reference to Derrida-as-poet (Champagne cites with approval Elizabeth Roudinescou's characterization of Derrida as a childish late-surrealist sniping at psychoanalysis from the wings, as his predecessors did), all political engagements, with, against or by deconstruction, such as Derrida's studied refusal to condemn Heidegger and de Man for their entanglements with nazism and anti-semitism, are immediately quashed by repeated but undeveloped reference to Derrida's 'problematic relation to his Jewish identity' and to his commitment to the presence of philosophy in France's academic curricula, while 'undecidability' becomes the watchword by which Derrida's ethics and politics are revealed as decidedly liberal.

Critical Encounters: Reference and Responsibility in Deconstructive Writing, edited by Cathy Caruth and Deborah Esch, is a collection of essays which explore different aspects of the relation between literature and reality, textuality and history, language and experience. The aim, as outlined in Caruth's introduction, is to redirect current critiques of deconstruction which assume that relevant understanding can only be derived from conscious, first-hand experience, and ask instead 'how we might learn to recognize and to respond to the realities of history, a politics, and an ethics not based on straightforward understanding'. One very direct response to these issues can be found in a specifically commissioned piece by Andrzej Warminski, entitled 'Ending Up/Taking Back (with Two Postscripts on Paul de Man's Historical Materialism)', which uses Marx not only to explain history and materiality in de Man, but in turn also illustrates just how much 'de Man is Marxian'. The crucial lesson to be learned from de Man, in Warminski's view, is that 'the materiality of language, materiality as such, is not ever something that we can know, and hence is never something that could be the object of consciousness'; thus we cannot 'step out of or beyond ideology' precisely because 'language *is* consciousness'. Cynthia Chase and Caruth also seek to negotiate de Man's engagement with history, the former by indicating how certain essays in *Resistance to Theory* 'locate "theory" in "history"', and thereby do the inverse as well'; and the latter by demonstrating how de Man's distinction between constative and performative language, 'far from denying access to history, is a way . . . of precisely keeping history from being swallowed up by the power of abstraction'. Two further essays, one by Esch on de Man, the other by Kevin Newmark on de Man and Nietzsche, continue this re-examination of history from the perspective of deconstruction, albeit with specific reference to the historical events that absorbed these thinkers' writings as anti-semitism *in toto*. E. S. Burt, perhaps the least explicit address to deconstruction in this volume, turns to literature in his 'Hallucinatory History: Hugo's *Révolution*' (reprinted from *MLN* 105.965–91) to reject the charge often brought against poetry's alleged 'retreat from the public arena of history and politics' by exploring 'where Hugo situates the historicity of poetry'. Another engagement with literature is Derek Attridge's 'Singularities, Responsibilities: Derrida, Deconstruction, and Literary Criticism', which is perhaps best read in conjunction with his introduction to *Acts of Literature* (1992). Rather than asking, as he did then, 'what is literature for Derrida?', this essay focuses on the assimilation of Derrida's work by literary critics to ask instead, 'what is literary deconstructive criticism?'

While the essays in the first part of *Critical Encounters* tend to interrogate history, literature and literary criticism from the perspective of deconstruction, the essays which make up the second part mostly translate, as they negotiate, the insights of deconstruction into the arena of political action and ethical responsibility. This widens the volume's frame of reference, but also rather stretches the thematics announced in the book's introduction. For instance, Judith Butler's 'Contingent Foundations. Feminism and the Question of "Postmodernism" ' (reviewed in *YWCCT* 3), concerned with the possibilities of agency once the subject is conceived as a discursive construct, or Fuss's 'Inside/Out' (reviewed in *YWCCT* 2), concerned with the material and political effects of gay and lesbian theories' rethinking of the conceptual grounds of sexual identity, are two contributions which – although in part related to Caruth's themes on text and reality, knowledge and action – clearly have a different agenda than merely to assess, as is announced in the prefatory note, 'the possible pasts and futures of what has come to be called deconstruction'. Harriet Davidson's '"I Say I Am There": Siting/Citing the Subject of Feminism and Deconstruction', on the other hand, echoes many of Butler's and Fuss's themes, but also brings the editors' express concerns back into line by responding directly to criticisms by feminists, Marxists and historians levelled against deconstruction's 'typical move from history to rhetoric'. Through a reading of Adrienne Rich's poetry, Davidson shows how the latter, contrary to claims by deconstructionists, 'shares a critique of the subject with deconstruction', and in turn, how Derrida, contrary to many a political thinker, and not unlike Rich, 'constructs a performative subject'. The final essays to round up this collection are Thomas Keenan's 'Deconstruction and the Impossibility of Justice', earlier versions of which have already been published twice, concerning rights and responsibilities, and about what it might 'mean to claim a right'; and Jill Robbins's reading of Derrida through Levinas which explores the ethics of responding to the other, and asks whether 'one can speak about an alterity that is rhetorical and textual' and if so, whether 'the alterity of the other and textual alterity [can] be even addressed in the same breath'.

Anselm Haverkamp's *Deconstruction is/in America: A New Sense of the Political* is also a collection of essays which, like Caruth's and Esch's, is based on a conference, and also boasts contributions by a number of leading proponents of deconstruction (with appearances once more by Attridge, Chase and Butler). It also includes a key address by Derrida himself, in which – picking up the thematics of his 1985 Wellek Library Lecture 'Deconstruction in America' (published in 1986 as *Mémoires for Paul de Man*) and the Hamlet theme from *Spectres of Marx* – he cobbles together Hamlet's phrase 'The time is out of joint' with the conference's brief 'Deconstruction is/in America' to follow through the dislocations, disjoinings and disarticulations at play not only in those two sentences and the 'disjunction at the heart of the is' which joins both phrases, but also the slash which puts out of joint the 'is' and the 'in' between deconstruction 'and' America. Gayatri Spivak and David Wills both follow suit: the former's 'At the *Planchette* of Deconstruction is/in America' is an autobiographical cum bibliographical record of her own person's/work's engagement with Derrida's, 'some-one who, like me was not quite European'; the latter's 'Jaded in America' is an exploration of the 'is/in' that disturbs any simplistic reading of the relation between deconstruction and America. In his introduction, Haverkamp too examines the 'is' and the 'in' between deconstruction and America, but from the perspective of 'what keeps [deconstruction] in America rather than elsewhere'. While Haverkamp seizes on the difference that America, as opposed to Europe, has made to deconstruction – for him 'pragmatism is the American name for this difference in the realm of philosophy' – Michel Beaujour seizes the opportunity to rather patronizingly remind his American audience of the difference that a French philosophical training can make. For him, the 'condition of philosophical innocence . . . and deprivation' of American students, as opposed to the philosophical acuity of their French counterparts, has led to a 'massive trivialization' of philosophical deconstruction in American literature departments. That literary criticism (and particularly the Yale School) has somehow distorted the philosophical thrust of Derrida's work has, of course, also been one of Rodolphe Gasché's long-standing concerns, and his essay in this volume returns to the relation of philosophy and literature to unknit once more – here, via a close reading of Derrida's Kafka essay 'Before the Law' – their 'irreducible difference'. J. Hillis Miller, on the other hand, defends deconstruction against the claims by critics like Jonathan Loesberg and others that as a philosopher Derrida has little to say to literary critics, exposing in this reclaiming of Derrida for philosophy an 'ideological storytelling' that justifies not only literary studies' turning away from deconstruction, but also its recent return 'to history', 'to the social', or 'to multiculturalism', 'cultural studies' and 'identity politics', without the scholarly prerequisite to engage with Derrida's work any longer. Miller's concerns, like Peggy Kamuf's in the following essay, are intimately tied up with the much stronger impact that deconstruction, and the political correctness debate it still fuels, has had in the United States rather than in the more sleepy United Kingdom. Another examination of the problematic place of deconstruction inside/outside the institution – here '*in*' the university – is thus offered by Kamuf, who compares the common goals of those who accuse deconstruction of having paved the way for political correctness in gender studies, Marxism or new historicism, and those who reject deconstruction on the grounds that, unlike the above critical movements, it is not political enough. One group (exemplified by Vann Woodward) is therefore happy to use deconstruction as an 'umbrella name for "multicultural innovations"'; the other group (exemplified by Clyde de L. Ryals) is unhappy to associate such a 'plurality of names' (feminism, Marxism, new historicism, etc.) with the generic name 'deconstructionist'. Since both Woodward and Ryals are, however, unhappy with deconstruction *per se*, Kamuf concludes that deconstruction has become 'the name of something that *has no place* in the university', by extension, it also names that which 'happens when instituted, referential boundaries shift'. As such, it is less pertinent 'to think about the place of deconstruction *in* the university', than to speak, as Kamuf in the end does, 'of the university in deconstruction'.

If for Kamuf deconstruction is a 'name in dispute', for Judith Butler in her essay 'Burning Acts: Injurious Speech' the dispute arises when we have to decide whether a word enacts what it names. When she asks whether 'the word and deed are one', and more specifically whether 'hateful remarks *are* injurious acts', she turns away from the themes of the conference towards a number of legal cases in the United States where she finds evidence of the courts' readiness on the one hand, in cases of pornographic representation, to accept the injurious quality of such acts (even if such representations could 'not be said to leave the page'), and on the other hand, their unwillingness to consider racist injuries on the same terms, demonstrating instead their readiness to dignify such injuries as 'protected speech' under the First Amendment. To condemn one injury but not the other exposes for Butler 'a heightened sexual conservatism [which] works in tandem with an increasing governmental sanction for racist violence'; it also, however, points up a certain problematic, as exemplified by Catherine MacKinnon's argument in *Only Words* (1993), for instance, which attributes to words on the page or a visual representation the 'performative power to bring about that which it depicts'. In Butler's view, MacKinnon renders the relation of representation to social reality in overly determinant terms. Butler therefore goes on to illustrate how pornographic images have a 'phantasmatic power' and remain 'compensatory fantasies', 'unrealizable' and 'uninhabitable positions'; arguing that whilst pornography does 'hold sway over the social reality of gender positions', it does not, however, 'constitute that reality', but fails to *deliver* what it *depicts*, or as she puts it, 'fails to wield the power to construct the social reality of what a woman is'. For MacKinnon this is a clear case where the offending text, precisely because it constructs a social reality, ought to be abolished; for Butler, it is neither a question of censorship – as if such an abolition would do away with gender inequalities – nor a question of merely locating a subject responsible for such inequalities – as if by pointing the finger to 'pornography as a subject who speaks and, in speaking, brings about what it names', one has found a subject who can now be held accountable at a 'prosecutable' level. Instead, a feminist reading ought to 'resist the literalization of this imaginary scene', ought to ask to what extent the relation between representation and the construction of reality is perhaps far 'more frail' than MacKinnon makes out. Although this essay does not address deconstruction – and its relation to feminism – directly, many of the issues raised by Butler feed into the wider debate on essentialism and deconstruction, and therefore also echo themes central to Barbara Johnson's book *The Wake of Deconstruction*, which was reviewed last year (*YWCCT* 4). In another, more explicit, address to feminism and deconstruction, Barbara Vinken, making a move not unlike Derrida's in his reading of Rousseau's *The Origin of Language*, reads Rousseau's '*Lettre à d'Alembert*' against the grain of its author's intention, to show how this 'text reveals that man is not a natural essence, but a figure, one that has to be produced by a rhetoric, which is qualified as feminine'. In a further move not unfamiliar from Butler's thesis on the performance of gender in *Gender Trouble* (1990), Vinken demonstrates how 'men are not men, but that they too play a role and that they imitate "men"'. In an effort, then, to bring de Beauvoir (women should become like men) and Irigaray (self-identical subjecthood must be deconstructed) together, or as she puts it, 'to plead for de Beauvoir's praxis in order to achieve Irigaray's aim', Vinken brings Butler onto the scene to give her argument a final twist: 'Through the female impersonation of the male role, the masculine turns out to be a mimickry.' Which is to say, 'By parodying masculinity intentionally or unintentionally, women decompose the illusion of male identity . . . disfigure the figure of referentiality, the congruence of biological sex and social role.'

It should be clear, particularly from the last two contributions discussed, that *Deconstruction is/in America* is a volume which contains a variety of responses to deconstruction. As we have already seen, some contributors have directly engaged with the conference's brief; what follows can be broadly divided into those responses which comment on other papers delivered at the conference, and those which very much pursue their own interests in the field of deconstruction. While Derek Attridge gives the briefest of responses, mostly to Derrida's key address, Perry Meisel both summarizes and comments, albeit fleetingly, on a number of other papers, namely Haverkamp's and Jonathan Culler's, before giving his own 'deconstructive reassessment of the political', or rather, before flying off into his own sexual/political reading of Woolf's *Orlando* to endorse Vinken's point as to the 'pure performative' of gender. Jonathan Culler also turns to literature in his 'Deconstruction and the Lyric' to give a very involved, if not hermetic, account of poetic performativity; while Elisabeth Weber's 'Writing Resistances' focuses on psychical censorship, taking her cue from Derrida's phrase in 'Freud and the Scene of Writing' that 'writing is unthinkable without repression', to turn this postulation into another hypothesis: 'writing as an aggression'. Cynthia Chase's 'Reading Epitaphs' also turns to the topic of writing from the initial, Wordworthian, perspective of 'the epitaph as a paradigm of writing'. She reads Wordsworth's 'Essay upon Epitaph', where '*literature* and *epitaph* define one another', in conjunction with de Man's essay on Benjamin's 'The Task of the Translator' where translation is that condition which guarantees the survival of writing and literature, and where the epitaph, just like the translation according to de Man, is 'secondary in relation to the original . . . to its writing', but also undoes the original by 'reveal[ing] an essential disarticulation which was already there in the original'. In 'Upping the Ante: Deconstruction as Parodic Practice' Samuel Weber also dwells on the borderlines between original and repetition, exploring both the relation of parody to iterability, and the possible differences between parody and parodic practice, to suggest – not unlike de Man does with reference to the relation between original and translation – that 'each "original" . . . becomes already in and of itself a potential *self-parody*', at the very moment at which 'parody is construed as the effect of an irreducible iterability'. Finally, two very different essays: one by Peter Eisenman on the unique relation of architecture to deconstruction, and architecture's unique challenge to deconstruction as a 'discourse where the sign and signified are more closely linked than in any other discourse'; the other by Avital Ronell on Nietzsche's *Gay Science*, a highly inventive piece, not so much about deconstruction, as Weber's or Eisenman's, but a kind of deconstruction *in situ*, experimenting with 'the *scientificity* of Nietzsche's use of "science"'.

Peter Baker's *Deconstruction and the Ethical Turn* and Bill Martin's *Humanism and its Aftermath: The Shared Fate of Deconstruction and Politics* are two studies which have in common a certain insistence, to use Baker's terms, on deconstruction's 'possible usefulness for negotiating the political terrain of the postmodern university, not to say the world'; or, in Martin's terms, on deconstruction's transformation of and by Marxism as a 'long-term project [which] must begin to come together with a more engaged sense of politics and transforming society'. Both projects therefore place a strong emphasis on what Baker calls 'the social and real world significance of Derrida's project' and what Martin, following Derrida's view of politics 'not simply as an opening to endless wordplay', names as a 'politics [that] has to be worked out . . . to be concretized'. Although both authors explore a similar set of themes – ethics, politics, justice, responsibility and alterity – and turn to some of the same theorists, Foucault and Habermas for instance (both also offering a stringent critique of Habermas), the different disciplinary contexts from which their work has emerged (Martin works in a philosophy department and has written on social theory, this book is a follow-up to his 1992 book *Matrix and Line: Derrida and the Possibilities of Postmodern Social Theory*; Baker works with literature and literary theory, his previous book is on the modern long poem) also means that they approach their topics very differently. In order to test what Martin refers to as 'the ethical moment in politics', and what Baker terms the ethical turn in deconstructive writing, Baker takes *Glas* as Derrida's 'most serious attempt to confront ethical issues', rather than merely as an example of one of Derrida's more playful, writerly texts, while Martin turns to the more sober *The Other Heading: Reflections on Today's Europe* (1992) where Derrida not only 'reconstitutes Kantian ethics', but 'raises', as he sees it, 'the possibility of an ethics and a politics oriented . . . to the impossible'. While Baker is content to stress that 'writing' can expose and 'does offer ways of performing (deconstructive) interpretive acts that are also transformative, and thus ethical', and sees theoretical texts not merely in abstract conceptual terms, Martin is much more concerned that 'theory becomes a material force'. This is to say, for Baker the 'activity of teaching, studying, analyzing, and discussing texts in a classroom is paradigmatic of the deconstructive mode in general', whereas for Martin, 'to get bogged down in etymological play', lacks in his view 'any political edge whatsoever'. Martin's attempt therefore to transform Marxism by attuning it to a deconstructive 'sense of alterity', and his concomitant endeavour to transform deconstruction by attuning it to a 'greater sense of historical concreteness', is a necessary step towards tackling the 'reality of marginalization in the world today' (which is both a result of imperialism, and a result of what is only too often marginalized or overlooked these days, the class system). The Marxism–deconstruction encounter, which Martin stages in *Humanism and its Aftermath*, and through which he seeks to articulate a 'deconstructive social theory', always hovers on the edges of theoretical writing and practical activism; his many examples from US politics, or of his own political activism outside the immediate context of the academy gives the term 'social theory' another flavour altogether: beneath the theoretical paving stones, the practical beach!

Another book to address the place or rather the institutionalization of deconstruction, and of theory more generally, in America, is Mark Edmundson's *Literature against Philosophy, Plato to Derrida: A Defence of Poetry*. What guides his argument from the very start is his belief that 'Literary criticism in the West begins with the wish that literature disappear.' He locates this 'disenfranchisement of literature' in the 'ancient quarrel between poetry and philosophy', a tradition born of Plato's hostility towards literature, on the grounds that it merely 'stirs up refractory emotions' amongst the populace, thus ruining the political life of the city, whereas philosophy asks vital questions as to 'eternal truth' and the just order of the polity. This tradition, according to Edmundson, with its concomitant striving 'to subsume [literature] in some higher form of thought', that is philosophy, is now perpetuated by those who would least want to be seen as Plato's heirs, namely contemporary theorists such as Bloom, de Man and Derrida. Equally, few theorists would now wish to acknowledge that they are descendants of a trend in this century principally initiated through Lionel Trilling's work on Arnold, and his adherence to the Arnoldian dictum that 'once authorative centres no longer hold' then 'it is up to criticism to provide grounds for humane social life'. Not only does literature merely matter here 'because of the guiding truths that one can draw from it', but literary criticism, elevated to a guardian of culture, withdraws into the academy, becomes the kind of highly professionalized pursuit which is in danger of losing the capacity to appreciate or 'to describe the difficult humanly enlarging pleasure that the work at hand offers'. Having aggravated the ancient quarrel between poetry and philosophy, or rather, having blown the apparent disenfranchisement of literature out of all proportion, Edmundson comes to poetry's defence (at, it should be remembered, Plato's grief-stricken behest), pointing to theory's limits and literature's power to outstrip, exceed and 'productively outdistance theoretical critiques'. Although Edmundson makes it very clear that his work is not anti-theoretical, that he does not wish to 'do away with theory' – after all he spends more time on what he calls 'some of the most impressive critiques [of 'major literary art'] theory can muster', than on poetry itself – the project leaves the distinct impression that his attack was less directed against those he names, against the big names like Bloom, Derrida or Greenblatt, who he clearly admires deeply, but against those he does not name, against the 'ideologues' who have questioned perhaps not so much literature but the canon. As one who clearly appreciates great poetry and major criticism when he sees it, it is less a question of conceding, for instance, as he does, that there may be good grounds for pointing up misogynist tendencies in Milton, or for that matter, for stressing that we must continue to read Milton even if 'we don't like the way he renders Eve', but of interrogating the ways in which some poets or theorists come to be included among the great, that is, enter the canon, and others do not. Thus, Edmundson's dispute was perhaps less to do with the quarrel between literature and philosophy, than with an unacknowledged war between literature and politics, which was precisely the platform from which Plato launched his famous exclusion order against the poets. In this sense Edmundson, like the poets Plato decries, distorts what he represents as the cause both of Plato's quarrel, and of his own.

If, under Edmundson's government, the poets are to be readmitted to the city, how will the philosophers guard against their contamination? Would it still be possible, were philosophers and poets to speak the same language, to tell them apart? The problem of where to situate Derrida with respect to this contamination of genres is still a major concern, judging by the essays collected in William R. McKenna and J. Claude Evans's *Derrida and Phenomenology*, for philosophers. These essays explore a terrain which, as Mano Daniels's concluding 'Bibliography of Derrida and Phenomenology' demonstrates, has already been so mined by the partisans of this attritious, albeit often inconspicuous, conflict as to make even the most cursory sweep a hazardous undertaking. Thus, while Rudolf Bernet's approach in 'Derrida and his Master's Voice' is to pay equal tribute to the philosophical voices of both Derrida and 'his master' Husserl, which would seem to guarantee a critical peace between their partisans, his light step inevitably trips further explosions. Even with the apparently uncontentious aim of providing a critical summary of Derrida's *Speech and Phenomena* (1973), Bernet's essay heightens the tension at each flashpoint this collection approaches. The first of these, which Natalie Alexander focuses on in 'The Hollow Deconstruction of Time', consists in raising the question of how to read Derrida, of what criteria to adopt when reading Derrida reading Husserl, a question whose answer Alexander prefaces, in good Husserlian manner, with the following 'essential distinction': *either* as philosophical argumentation, *or* as 'rhetorical (almost literary) narrative. If, she argues, one adopts the former approach to read Derrida's texts on Husserl, these texts fail to meet the required standard. If, however, the second approach is adopted, then these texts can be read as 'interpreting Husserl's texts as one interprets literature' at the expense, implicitly, of any philosophical status. Apparently granting Derrida that there exists no 'text in itself' (although not indicating whether the reasons for granting this point are 'philosophical' or 'rhetorical'), Alexander adopts the perspective that there nevertheless exist 'protocols of reading' by which the strength or weakness of particular misreadings may be judged, and concludes that, while Derrida's texts cannot fail when read in this manner, they can – and should – be judged weak in the light of the philosophical texts they set out to read. While Alexander finds it a simple task to dismiss the idea of a literary 'text in itself', she maintains something that Derrida solicits from Husserl: that there nevertheless exists a *philosophical* 'text in itself' to which overt criteria must be brought to bear if those texts are to maintain the authority that must be consistently negotiated in every mis/reading. Indeed, a certain rallying cry – 'to the texts themselves!' – highlights this phenomenology of the book, which Derrida, following Bachelard, christens 'bibliomenology': if, with the cry 'to the things themselves!', Husserlian phenomenology sought to pare appearances from the things they shroud, to strip phenomena to their noumenal bone, Derrida argues, this bone remains irreducibly graphic, the textual armature of the 'bibliomenon', the book-thing. This is not to say, however, that only phenomenologists practise it, or that deconstructors – even the arch-deconstructor himself – are immune from its influence, as can be seen from what Alan White calls the 'grammatolatry' of many of deconstruction's more scholastic or hermetic worshippers. With greater or less philosophical rigour or rhetorical strength, however, Alexander's schema of misreadings is implicitly applied, with its bibliomenological assumptions, by several other contributors, ranging from John Scanlon's outright and impatient dismissal, in 'Pure Presence: A Modest Proposal', of Derrida's 'preposterous' philosophical pretensions on the basis that the texts in question are 'sophisticated parodies' of Husserl rather than serious exegetical or philosophical analyses, to Alan White's defence of the philosophical integrity of deconstruction against the accusations of 'bullshit' Searle once quoted against Derrida, albeit from an unnamed source. Curiously, however, White's 'Of Grammatolatry: Deconstruction as Rigorous Phenomenology?' defends deconstruction by assimilating it to phenomenology, only thus enabling Derrida to be read in all his 'philosophical rigour'. White's thesis that 'the move from Husserlian phenomenology to Derridean deconstruction is made when the demand for philosophical rigour leads to the abandonment of the dream of a philosophical science' takes deconstruction as the necessary consequence of the adoption of a properly phenomenological rigour, carrying the latter's project beyond itself, a view shared by Thomas Seebohm in 'The Apodicticity of Absence', which demonstrates that Derrida's criticisms, in *Speech and Phenomena*, of the phenomenological 'principle of principles', the insistence on the veracity and instantaneity of 'originary intuition', are indeed phenomenologically well founded, but do not go far enough along the important new paths Derrida has opened for phenomenological research. Almost holding a mirror to this conclusion, Burt C. Hopkins's 'Husserl and Derrida on the Origin of Geometry' has it that the potential utility of Derrida's critiques of Husserl to phenomenology is hindered by his misreadings of the latter's texts, but further concludes that such misreadings may in some sense be strategic, raising the question of a Derridean methodology.

Thus Hopkins touches on the second of the philosophical flashpoints struck by Bernet's paper: the question of the generalizability or even the existence of a 'logic of deconstruction'. While in part lending itself to the further philosophical – which in this collection is equivalent to 'phenomenological' – rehabilitation of deconstruction, this question nevertheless strikes at the core of Derrida's consistent denials that deconstruction constitutes a 'method', a 'system' or even a 'critique', something that must itself be systematically negotiated throughout every strategic redeployment of deconstruction: how could such redeployment be possible in the absence of some minimal, logical consistency? Following a reprise of the theme of Derrida's misreadings, this is the thesis behind J. Claude Evans's contribution, 'Indication and Occasional Expression'. The beginnings of a response to this problem may be found in certain of Derrida's overtly methodological strictures concerning 'the operations of deconstruction' in *Of Grammatology* (1976), which must 'operate necessarily from the inside, borrowing all the strategic and economic resources of subversion from inside the old structure, borrowing them *structurally*'. With this methodological exclusion, as it were, of external resourcing, and the injunction to deploy such resources as provided within the field of deconstruction's 'structural' operations, an economic and critical logic of immanence appears to have been established as the operative core of deconstruction. As general and as delimiting as Kant's transcendental deductions, such strictures apply irrespective of the adaptations and transformations of deconstruction in accordance with the imperatives of the particular fields in which it operates – what White calls the 'law of undecidable contamination'. Dallas Willard, however, coupling an almost caricatural analytic sobriety with the ill-tempered bloodlusts of an inquisitor, manages to impoverish this important question by subjecting what he clumsily reconstructs as 'Derrida's position' to a test in 'standard logic', which once failed (as Derrida of course will – as indeed, would Kant, not to mention Hegel) will mean that position will be subject to criticism on the grounds of 'logical inconsistency' and, in consequence, be 'rationally indefensible'. While it is tempting to pose Scanlon's (serious or parodic?) question as to whether this is parody or to be taken seriously, Willard, by virtue of his particularly gruesome brand of what Heidegger called the 'violence of interpretation', at least invites accusations of hermeneutic inadequacy, a question explicitly addressed by Leonard Lawlor in 'The Relation as the Fundamental Issue in Derrida'. 'None' of Derrida's critics, he argues, 'adhere to one of the most basic hermeneutical rules: reconstruct the context.' To do justice to Derrida's readings of Husserl, Lawlor argues, Derrida's readers must not only reassemble every instance in Derrida's corpus in which Husserl figures, but must also reconstruct Derrida's 'entire thought', which extreme criterion, Lawlor concludes, imposes upon the reader the infinite task of reconstructing context, an ethical responsibility imposed under the rule of 'the form of the text itself'. Not only, once again, do we hear the echo of the bibliomenological injunction: 'to the text itself!', but we hear it in concert with the reinscription of the horizon of Derrida's 'entire thought'. The coincidence of these imperatives can only be made possible by an assumption of an intention recoverable through 'the being of the book', the transcendental condition of philosophical canonization, an assumption as clear from Bernet's question of what it is to read the 'master's voice' as it is from every address in this collection to the adequacy of readings of Derrida's readings of Husserl. These names do not, however, indicate the presence of an authorial intention, but rather of a bibliomenological intention, a legible propriety stored in the book. This is why bibliomenology is amongst the earliest of Derrida's critical targets, in his *Introduction to Husserl's 'Origin of Geometry'* (1989): 'when considering the . . . purity of intentional animation, Husserl always says that the linguistic or graphic body is a flesh, a proper body'. Thus, what is at stake in the delimitation of philosophical reading is not the determination of the authorial presence, but the 'book in its unity', the body of an 'entire thought'; and this is also why deconstruction distinguishes early on 'between the book and writing'.

While, then, many a reader not initiated into the lore of the 'collegium phenomenologicum' may feel that the question as to whether or not deconstruction is a late variant of Husserlian phenomenology is of merely scholarly interest and may therefore be dismissed as lightly as Bernet does the '*distortions*' of their master's voice by proponents of the (implicitly literary-theoretical) 'deconstructionist vogue', the questions around which this collection clusters, once any marginal question of Derrida's debt to phenomenology is 'bracketed off' or 'suspended', far from vanishing as mere points of scholarship, assume a broader significance for reading Derrida and practising deconstruction: whether deconstruction requires more logical consistency or politico-strategic impetus to survive beyond the sterile machinations of bibliomenological or grammatolatrous Derrideans.

M. C. Dillon's *Semiological Reductionism: A Critique of the Deconstructionist Movement in Postmodern Thought* again takes up the intertwining of deconstruction and phenomenology to argue, this time more from the perspective of Merleau-Ponty's than of Husserl's phenomenology, that deconstruction's principal philosophical strategy reiterates the problems of

reduction or 'bracketing' that occur in Husserl's work, but that in deconstruction and its postmodernist avatars in general, and in Derrida in particular,
the reduction in question is a reduction of reference, a 'bracketing off' of the
'other of language' from the field of possible signification. The strategy of
'semiological reduction', then, according to Dillon, consists in the constant
displacement of reference (to the signified) onto *différance* (in signifiers),
resulting in the abolition of referential purchase from deconstruction, making
the 'other of language' constantly invoked by Derrida – often in the context
of defending deconstruction against similar charges, as Dillon notes – a
transcendental idea devoid of content. In a series of closely argued chapters on
the 'Metaphysics of Presence', 'Time', 'Truth', 'The Unconscious' and 'Desire',
Merleau-Ponty's realist phenomenology of the flesh and the world is pitched
against both Husserl's idealism and Derrida's reductionism. While Derrida has
responded to charges of 'reducing everything to a question of language'
before, and while therefore it may seem to receptive Derrideans to be taking
aim at a straw target, the virtues of Dillon's book lie in the detail of its
argument and in its attempt to engage with Derrida on his own territory; and
while some of these arguments may be flawed (particularly the peculiar
inversions inflecting his discussion of the role of 'force' and 'quantity' in
Derrida's 'Différance' – here Dillon ought perhaps to have consulted some
basic physics, or even Manfred Frank's paper on Derrida, 'The Entropy of
Language'; but this opens up an entirely different problematic), they are laid
down clearly enough to engage a sustained and critical reading of what Dillon
carefully unravels as 'the operative strategy that reveals the coherence of
Derrida's thinking', generating more questions – both of Derrida and Dillon's
insistent interrogation of his 'thinking' – rather than, as all too often, closing
them down with empty assertion.

J. Hillis Miller's *Topographies* is a collection of his own essays, divided into
twelve chapters, all of which engage with different aspects of topography such
as mapping, places, place names, landscapes, border demarcations or territorial
appropriations; ten of the chapters have already been published, the earliest in
1981 and the most recent in 1996, and appear here in a revised form, while two
of them, one on Faulkner and one on Heidegger, are new. The twofold
question Miller poses in these essays, is: 'What is the function of landscape or
cityscape descriptions in novels and poems? What is the function of
typological terms in philosophical or critical thinking?' One cluster of essays
therefore engages closely with literary works, with a chapter each on Hardy,
Kleist, Dickens, Tennyson, Hopkins, Stevens; the other cluster of essays turns
to philosophical works, with chapters on Plato, Nietzsche, Derrida and
Heidegger. In tracing references to specific types of landscapes or certain place
names in novels, poems and philosophical works, Miller not only explores how
topographical terms follow a 'calculated arrangement' and can function
'poetically' or 'allegorically' (that is, 'naming one thing and meaning another'),
or indeed, 'have a function beyond that of mere setting, or metaphorical
adornment', but also how speech acts 'legislate meaning, including
topographical meaning', or rather, how a literary work might be said to be a
'speech act that inaugurates a new law' in the sense that a specific literary work
might use words to socially and historically performative effect. Since the
power literature has 'to make something happen in individual and social life
arises from some potency in language', it is literary theory's task to focus on

the 'performative powers of language' rather than, Miller has it, on 'non-linguistic, that is to say historical and aesthetic considerations'. As such, literary theory, and this is the gist of the book's final chapter, is a 'language about language'; what happens therefore, Miller asks, when a literary work, and crucially also, a work of criticism or a literary theory is 'translated', is transposed 'from one topological location to another'? Taking the Book of Ruth as an 'allegory of the travelling of theory', Miller illustrates not only that theoretical abstractions are always derived from local readings (in this instance his readings of the story of Ruth), but also that the transfer of such specific readings to another site or text, or the more general transfer of theory across borders, be they linguistic, cultural or disciplinary, both transforms and deforms a theory as it is recontextualized and assimilated in a new place. Theory's openness to translation, for Miller, clearly acts as a reminder that theory 'is a performative, not a cognitive, use of language', in other words, that 'A theory is a way of doing things with words, namely facilitating . . . acts of reading', it is also Miller's reminder, however, of theory continuing as a necessary linguistic and textual grounding. Furthermore, since theory is always based on a specific reading and as such holds 'good for this time, place and text', and is at the same time always open to be deployed and transferred elsewhere, it is only ever 'provisional', neither 'wholly amenable to conceptualization' nor wholly assimilable, but only ever remains a mere 'glimpse out of the corner of the eye of the way language works'. Which is to say that an original can never be wholly recovered, but remains 'lost'; and any translation of any original, be it the translation of a specific reading into a theoretical abstraction, or the translation of theory *per se*, is always a mistranslation. Which is why Miller can conclude that 'Translations of theory are therefore mistranslations of mistranslations, not mistranslations of some authoritative and perspicuous original.' This is undoubtedly Miller's answer to those who have, over the years, pointed their finger at the transfer of theory from a certain Paris philosophy department to a certain Yale school of literary criticism, and pointed out the misappropriations of French deconstruction by American boa-deconstructors, a misappropriation which now turns out (as) always already to have been mistranslations of mistranslations themselves.

While Miller, Dillon, McKenna and Evans debate the advantages and disadvantages of attention to philosophical detail, the six texts comprising Stanley Cavell's *Philosophical Passages: Wittgenstein, Emerson, Austin, Derrida* are marked by that nuanced sensitivity to reading that is often held up as deconstruction's chief literary-theoretical (rather than Natalie Alexander's 'literary-rhetorical': at what point does theory cease to be philosophical, and vice versa? – a question Cavell, a philosophical reader of literature and film, might well ask) virtue; also *initially* familiar from deconstruction's canon is the high-resolution textual focus: the minimalist *passage* of this collection's title. At the same time, however, Cavell never retreats from these passages to the structural security of abyssal metacommentary, but instead follows passages not simply between works, their themes or their tropic economies, but into the vitality of a 'thinking' freed from the metaphysical neurosis of the 'flight from the ordinary' – the common enemy of the analytic, continental and 'out-of-school' philosophers to whom Cavell patiently 'listens' in these texts. Cavell, like Rorty, is steeped in the Anglo-American analytic tradition, having been taught it from the sceptical stance of Austin; unlike Rorty, however (with whom he might be edifyingly contrasted), Cavell does not approach the Franco-German continental tradition from a recognizably analytic – or even post-analytic – perspective. Instead, his investigations of the philosophers with whom he crosses paths give voice to 'Man Thinking', a humane, Thoreauvian chorus at the heart of the Heideggerian mystery. Such unexpected philosophical conjunctions lead Cavell, turning to the continentals, as here, commenting on the Searle–Derrida debacle, to lament the aggression and ignorance that characterized that exchange, and to emphasize instead the proximity of Derrida's and Austin's concerns, concerns expressed, Cavell finds, in Derrida's sympathy for the nuances of Austin's text. Thus, rejecting the school-bound posturing of many philosophical commentators, such as those found in McKenna and Evans's collection, Cavell comes neither to praise nor to bury Derrida, but rather to resurrect Austin, the principal casualty of this recent affray. Since, he argues, this is the closest the two philosophical traditions have ever come, Cavell unceremoniously dismisses Searle's limiting and combative voice from its captaincy of the analytic tradition, and sets about re-reading Derrida reading Austin, clearing up what Cavell argues are Derrida's mistakes in that reading in order to sweep away the barriers between the schools and to continue thinking. If, however, Cavell finds a way to unite these projects rather than to use the one to criticize the other, he sometimes tends to sacrifice their specificity to an often unrecognizable unity. For example, the 'Man Thinking' that underwrites Cavell's readings, and the consequent presence of the 'human voice . . . in philosophy', clash noiselessly with Derrida's Heideggerian anti-humanism. Although Cavell offers caveats concerning his own ignorance of Derrida's work in general, and addresses the latter's exchanges with Searle due primarily to his own indebtedness to Professor Austin; and despite his stated philosophical affinity with scepticism, it is the questions that are never asked, and the inhuman dissonances that are never heard, that both frustrate and condition Cavell's 'thoughts out of school'.

If Cavell, confessing himself unfamiliar with Derrida's corpus, seeks traces of the human voice in philosophy, then in *Derrida and Autobiography*, Robert Smith – so self-consciously Derridean and so familiar with Derrida's corpus that he seeks to eradicate any difference between his own and his master's voices – is none the less similarly engaged in scouring philosophy for traces of autobiography. This, Smith claims, becomes necessary due to philosophy's determination to eradicate all traces of autobiography from its texts, the better to approximate the status of the science it 'wants' to become. Destining his project to success from the outset, Smith selects, under the curiously twinned rubrics of the indelible specificity of *his own* 'selection', on the one hand, and 'philosophy' (in general, Smith intends; in the event, however, Hegelian 'science', or a sentence reported from, and subsequently authored as, Hegel's lectures: at best, then, a second-hand science) on the other, only that 'philosophy' marking and informing Derrida's own reflections on that discipline's troubled origins. Aiming at a sustained discussion of Derrida's (writings on) autobiography, Smith begins an obsessive pilgrimage along the same 'autoroutes' his master travelled with Geoff Bennington in *Jacques Derrida* (see *YWCCT* 3). Furious that Bennington should have got into Derrida's auto before him, Smith tries after the event to expel the usurper on the grounds of the exorbitant claims to 'mastering the master' evident in the

latter's 'Derridabase'. The real problem in the constant inversions inherent in
the master–slave dialectic to which Smith obliquely refers is not, however, who
is on top, not who is master and who slave, but rather that there is always
someone else who wants to take the place of the master's slave, the better to
have the ear of the other and to be the scribe of his master's voice. This is the
autobiographical problem of philosophical mastery played out in Smith's text:
'how *dare* Bennington play Derrida's master!' Smith's assault on 'philosophy'
and its quest for autochthonous origins thus plays a dual role: on the one
hand, biographically, it reiterates Derrida's own dealings with Hegel's 'system'
(*Glas*, 'From a Restricted to a General Economy', 'The Pit and the Pyramid');
on the other – and this is where autobiography bites back at Smith's anxious
sententiousness – it perpetrates an internecine, clerical squabble over who has
the right to take Derrida as one's master. Like all priestly rows, this is a
struggle between slaves.

In the acknowledgements prefacing *After Derrida*, Nicholas Royle suggests
that Smith's work 'forms an indispensable supplement' to his own. Charitably,
this linkage may be due to their shared attempts at the 'ruination of
philosophy' as a genre and as an institutionalization of the discourse on
discourse, as Irigaray prefaces her assault on it. The question of institutions,
whether 'that strange' one 'called Literature', philosophy or psychoanalysis-
as-science, haunts Royle's text as it does Derrida's, and perhaps even drives this
text's will-to-experiment. Less charitably, it is the sort of link Royle could well
sever, since Smith's work merely instances that 'mummifying' purism Nietzsche
diagnosed as the means by which philosophers show respect. Mummification
has, meanwhile, spread well beyond the disciplinary confines of philosophy,
affecting even Royle's otherwise irreverent text, whose title, in this light, invites
diagnosis. Perhaps, however, such 'derridolatry' is only a foreign body in a text
that openly advocates generic iconoclasm in pursuit of 'the dream of
completely different kinds of psycho-literary-philosophical writing', that
shatters the order of discourse with unannounced deliria, that stages its theses
as dramatic dialogues (after Plato, then?) and that celebrates a communion of
foreign bodies in writing, working against their academic and disciplinary
hosts. Successive playful and wayward essay-chapters thus consider the
'mollusc' as figuring a body foreign to human history and, by extension, to the
new historicists' crowned anthropomorphism; Freud's *fort-da* with telepathy
and his 'fascination' with the Bacon–Shakespeare controversy emerge as
foreign bodies within the scientific corpus of psychoanalysis; while the import
and importation of foreign bodies to and from Derrida's texts forms the theme
of a dialogue culled from fragments of Beckett, whose work in its turn remains
at once familiar and foreign to Derrida, as he has recently professed, providing
Royle with a final foreign body. While Royle is playing up the exorbitant role of
the foreign body with respect to what it inhabits, *After Derrida* is at its most
irreverent and inventive; the other, reverent, side of the coin, however, comes
up whenever Derrida's text is at stake. Thus Royle's discussion of *Saving the
Text: Literature/Derrida/Philosophy* (1981) as an example of the reception of
deconstruction in America sets out straightforwardly to disabuse Hartman of
the validity of his 'misreadings and misrepresentations of Derrida's work',
despite the latter's insistence, as noted by Royle, that his text constitutes a
'counterstatement' taking a 'different turn' from Derrida's *Glas*: against Royle's
close readings, backed up by *Derrida's own words*, Hartman's 'different' turn

turns out merely to be a wrong turn. This economy of ir/reverence, ultimately funded, then, by returns on Derrida's texts, threatens to become unrecoverable only when Derrida is played for laughs, as a 'great comic writer' (Rorty) – *Glas* being recommended as a 'side-splitting' example. As Derrida writes in that text, however, 'you have to know how to *die* of laughter'; sides must *really* split and all reserves be fatally exhausted. Against this unrecoverable expenditure, there is, perhaps, a trace of anxiety, figured by the reserve and by what remains unthought in Derrida, that turns this economy into an economizing: what if Derrida were so funny, doubling us over with such turbulent and exhausting laughter that his textual reserves were all used up?

Is deconstruction dead, then? Answering this question – with a firm *yes and no* – is the first order of business in Paul Gordon's *The Critical Double: Figurative Meaning in Aesthetic Discourse*. The second order of business is to find the 'denominator', 'model' or 'formula' for analysing aesthetic discourse, which Gordon discovers in the 'double' or 'doubling' of discourse. Thirdly, and moving swiftly on from assertion to demonstration, the double is set to work in a variety of textual fields from which doubles may be recovered. Successive chapters locate and describe the actions of the double in texts as diverse as Kafka, Nietzsche, Freud, Henry James, Paul de Man and Protagoras the Sophist, the Bible and 'Romanticism' and 'comparative literature'. While Gordon's readings are stimulating in themselves, with some fascinating combinations of topics, they do not offer the formalization, or the 'effective conceptual grounds', that Gordon, doubled by Hillis Miller's preface, promises. In part, as Gordon's discussion of the adventures – metaphorically speaking – of logic and metaphor demonstrates, the lack of a general theory of the double, or a discourse that would be singularly proper to the double, is consequent upon the branching recursivity of the oxymoronic project of delineating a 'theory of metaphor'. While this is well handled, and while Gordon fields the suspended promise by means of Protagoras' rhetorical exercise book, distributed to his students just as Hillis Miller suggests *The Critical Double* should, the *Dissoi Logoi* – 'On every question there are two opposing statements – including this one' – there is too little discussion, rhetorical or logical, or sustained development of the thetic status of the double itself (or themselves) beyond the immediate context of Gordon's readings. While, then, there is plenty of analysis, and while it intricately negotiates the doubling and the dissonance of opposing claims; while the doubling of theoretical discourses on the status of metaphor admirably demonstrates Gordon's etymological link between 'double' and 'doubt'; the one point for which there is no double, no dissonant voice, and on which no doubt is cast whatever, concerns the status of the double itself.

Saving one of the best to last, *Titanic Light: Paul de Man's Post-Romanticism 1960–1969*, the second volume of Ortwin de Graef's extraordinary immersion in the world of Paul de Man begun in *Serenity in Crisis* (reviewed in *YWCCT* 3), charts de Man's critical progress from his 1960 essay 'Intentional Structure of the Romantic Image' up to the essays collected in *Blindness and Insight* (1st edition 1971). De Graef begins his odyssey from the problem de Man identified in his thesis as the 'post-Romantic predicament', which the latter derived from a comparative study of the Symbolist aesthetics of Mallarmé and Yeats. While Mallarmé's poetry remains interpretatively 'autonomous' or 'self-sufficient', interpreting Yeats demands,

according to de Man, historical or contextual augmentation, and it is here that
de Man locates the aporia that gives rise to the post-Romantic crisis. De
Graef's guiding question in this work is how to 'translate' de Man's concerns
with Symbolism into his later concerns with rhetorical analysis, on the one
hand, and with Romanticism, on the other. An initial guide to this winding
passage is sought in de Man's negotiations of the odyssey of consciousness
presented in the arch-Romantic *Phenomenology of Mind*, wherein Hegel
demonstrates the detours of consciousness on its way to coterminate with the
unfolding of history, combining thereby the elements split off from one
another in de Man's Symbolist aporia. The other companion on this journey,
however, is Rousseau, who comes to assume, as de Graef demonstrates
through detailed analyses of de Man's continuous engagement with him, the
burden of having finally buried the Hegelian dream, in so far as it is Rousseau
who paves the way for the general separability of internal from external worlds
in, as de Man puts it, his conversion to the 'ontological priority of
consciousness over sense-objects'. This effectively removes the possibility of
the conjunction of historico-political and poetic works of which Rousseau had
otherwise been so paradigmatic. Following Rousseau, then, the quest for
authentic being is radically exiled from external efficacy, so that even this
aporetic severance becomes lost to the nineteenth century. Moreover, as de
Graef ominously underscores, de Man's recognition of Rousseau's conversion
as an historical accident rather than a necessity of historical unfolding, of the
exile of consciousness from the field of history, has vast consequences for the
subsequent development of de Man's theorizing, motivating his move from
this post-Romantic predicament to the critical resurrection of the Hegelian
odyssey in the 'ideology of pure fiction' that functions in true Hegelian
fashion, both to relieve and to elevate contradictions in consciousness. The
renowned split in de Man's work between the epistemological and the
performative is the sublated echo of pre-conversion Rousseau, where
interiority and self-sufficiency were combined with external efficacy, although
since this crisis now appears solely at the level of criticism and rhetoric for
de Man, Rousseau's wrong turning is similarly and ineradicably troped.
As de Man puts it, troping de Graef's journey with him from Symbolism to
Romanticism to rhetorical criticism, 'Is criticism indeed engaged in scrutinizing
itself to the point of reflecting on its own origin? Is it asking whether it is
necessary for the act of criticism to take place?' De Graef's account has a
twofold virtue: firstly, it fleshes out the irremediable and labyrinthine
interiority of de Man's work by accompanying it, at each turn, with the works
of those in whose company he takes de Man to be travelling; secondly, its
detail and its clarity allow de Graef's text to challenge prevailing orthodoxies –
whether strictly critical or indeed political – that block access to this
challenging figure.

  In an apparent attempt to outproduce Derrida, volume 25 of *Diacritics*,
beginning with *Around Derrida* (25:ii), has hosted so much deconstruction that
one might plausibly wonder about the structural integrity of this venerable
institution. Marking its first quarter century, Jonathan Culler offers a brief
history of the journal and the changes in the 'theoretical scene' since its
inception and, following documentation of those who have held its editorial
reins, Derrida himself may seem to be commenting on this commemoration in
'Archive Fever' (9–63). Since, however, *Archive Fever* has, in 1996, been

published as a book, it will be reviewed in *YWCCT* 6. The remaining contributions, beginning with Gayatri Spivak's 'Ghostwriting' – a title Derek Attridge's contribution to *Deconstruction is/in America* shares – usefully stake out the terrains currently occupied by or with deconstruction. Spivak addresses herself (as she is wont to do) before addressing herself ghostwriting Derrida's *Spectres of Marx* to 'Marxist-feminists active in global economic resistance'. Using a passage from *The Gift of Death* on the place of woman in the economics of sacrifice to highlight the absence of woman in Derrida's offering to father Marx, 'Ghostwriting' offers an unusually Haraway-esque 'shorthand taxonomy of the coded discursive management of the new socialization of the reproductive body' in order to locate the other place of feminism within Marxism, and both in deconstruction. To effect this relocation, Spivak engages a twofold critique of Aijaz Ahmed's review essay '*Spectres of Marx* and Deconstructive Politics' (*New Left Review* 208.87–106) alongside a rereading of Derrida's text for what she calls its 'ontopology' of Marx. Regional at best, Derrida's text is therefore doubly haunted by other places and sexes, providing Spivak with a platform from which to extend this 'hauntopology' to a reading of 'the ghostwomen of Islam', represented by Assia Djebar's *Far from Medina*. Despite its resolute address to 'active Marxist-feminists', Spivak retreats too quickly from her topic, supplementing Derrida's 'ontopology' with an ultimately predictable 'ontropology'.

Unlikely though it sounds, the subaltern critic recurs in Herman Rapaport's 'Deconstruction's Other: Trinh T. Minh-Ha and Jacques Derrida'. Beginning with an 'antagonism' he locates between deconstruction on the one hand and cultural studies, identity politics and the return to agency on the other, Rapaport notes that, in many respects, this antagonism rehearses the one that is the object of the 'two Marxists' (not to mention, since Rapaport does not, an additional Maoist) to provoke Derrida into producing in *Positions*. Defining 'antagonism' after Ernesto Laclau and Chantal Mouffe in their *Hegemony and Socialist Strategy* (1985), Rapaport goes on to argue that antagonism occurs when there is a 'failure of difference'. Adding his voice to those who, like Gasché in *Inventions of Difference* (1994), lament the fate of deconstruction in America, it is precisely this, Rapaport argues, that pro-deconstruction cultural critics do when, like Trinh T. Minh-Ha, due care and attention is not given to 'what deconstruction is and is not'. Ernesto Laclau, in ' "The time is out of joint" ' takes issue with those critics who, like the anti-deconstruction practitioners of cultural studies Rapaport mentions, dismiss the very idea of a deconstructive politics for its want of any overt political agenda. Noting Derrida's attempt, in *Spectres of Marx*, to appropriate Marxism as one of the 'disadjustments' that made deconstruction both possible and necessary, along with his emphasis on the aporetic double articulation, in Marx's text, of the 'techno-ontological' agents of capital's social disadjustments that put 'time out of joint', alongside the consequent decentring of humanity as forming the 'condition of justice' in Marx's politics, Laclau makes good Derrida's failure to 'trace the genealogy of his intervention in the Marxist text'. Supplying this genealogy by way of the well-known break installed between 'scientific' and 'humanist' Marxism, Laclau's optimistic reading of *Spectres* in particular and deconstruction in general as 'an extension and radicalization' of this history, Laclau points to the necessity of a deconstructive politics as finally addressing the political from the horizon of its im/possible tasks.

While Rapaport would like to sever the study from the use of deconstruction (grammatolatrists in the one camp and grammatoloclasts in another), Elizabeth Grosz, in 'Ontology and Equivocation: Derrida's Politics of Sexual Experience', embraces deconstruction as a valuable means by which to question a feminism that has become too enamoured of 'clear-cut positions, answers, boundaries and divisions'. Feminism is by now, she argues, sufficiently well founded to make such critical analysis possible and necessary, however uncomfortable the loss of unequivocal political certainty may be. Grosz in turn, therefore, subjects Derrida's *'Geschlecht*: Sexual Difference and Ontological Difference' (*Research in Phenomenology* 13.65–83) to critical scrutiny on the basis of its asking the question of 'the ontological status of sexual difference', a question, Grosz argues, that has become one of the core issues in contemporary feminist debate. Derrida's equivocation, manifest in regard to this question and to politics in general, also highlights what Grosz argues is one of the strengths, rather than, as certain tropic critics of deconstruction would have it, the weaknesses of feminism: 'its openness to its own rewritings'. Finally, in a text obliquely concerned to redress the canonization of the Word of deconstruction as opposed to its heretical uses, Jane Gallop's '"Women" in Spurs and Nineties Feminism' re-reads Derrida's *Spurs* (published in English in 1979, but initially given in 1972 to a conference entitled *Nietzsche aujourd'hui*) in order to address, under the rubric of 'Derrida Today', the relation between deconstruction and feminism. Taking Derrida's essay as showing symptoms of the essentialist category of 'woman' dominant in feminist debate in the seventies, Gallop's text remains agonistically disposed to Grosz's assessment of this problem. In itself, however, the fact that Derrida's text has dated so much becomes another means by which to solicit the 'altared ego' that Derrida's more pious readers have made for him, since it highlights not only that texts take place within history (even if their topic is to dispute this), becoming archives of their topics, but also to alert us to symptoms of nineties feminist debate that may be manifest in Derrida's more recent texts.

As if this were not enough, *Diacritics* 25:iii continues to put matters Derridean to the fore. In 'Derrida Dry: Iterating Iterability Analytically', Gordon C. F. Bearn returns to 'Signature, Event, Context', the text that occasioned the fractious dispute between its author and Searle, in order to get to grips with what has never yet received adequate analytic attention: its *argument*. While formalizing that argument finally enables its consistency to be properly and clearly assessed, using the toolkit of analytic philosophy to do so does have its problems, as Bearn is careful to point out, in so far as it pre-empts its results in accordance with its primary schematization. In addition, having demonstrated that Derrida's arguments, since they admit of formalization, are satisfactorily rigorous and valid, the resultant 'truth' of the propositions concerning the context-dependent production of iterable meanings also reflects on the present context, making Bearn's 'serious attempt to be clear and precise somewhat ridiculous', reiterating, thereby, some of the themes of the Derrida–Searle deluge that it was this essay's mission to staunch.

Also in this volume, J. Hillis Miller's 'Ethics of Hypertext', while it does not address deconstruction *per se*, deserves mention, as does Peggy Kamuf's 'The Division of Literature', subject to the same caveats. In a consideration of the problems that literary studies must face up to in a post-literate visual – and increasingly cybernetic – culture, Miller looks at the theories of reading materialized in the form of the hypertext and the challenge they pose to the pre-digital, print-based theoretical orthodoxies that currently dominate the conceptual and institutional frame of literature. If Miller looks to the future, Kamuf complements his essay by staring down the past in so far as it examines the institutional history and context of the formation of literary canons. Concluding her discussion with a deconstruction of the 'self-presence of the institution', however, Kamuf rather predictably scorns the mere 'sociology of literary studies', from which arguably both the texts she examines here and Hillis Miller's speculations derive, for its naive claims to empirical certainty.

Finally away from *Diacritics*, Xiaoying Wang's 'Derrida, Husserl and the Structural Affinity between the "Text" and the "Market"' (*New Literary History* 26.261–82) uses Baudrillard's attempts in the early seventies to forge a 'critique of the political economy of the sign' to demonstrate that the text outside of which there is nothing is structurally affinous with the self-regulating or free market. Choosing to demonstrate his theses by stabbing away, with the weighty pointer of *logic, logic, logic*, at *Speech and Phenomena*, since Derrida's later, 'poetic' texts are, he claims, void of philosophical targets, Wang's urgent assault exhausts itself before Derrida's textual excess, grasping at what Baudrillard called the '*consommation* of signs'. Of a piece with Wang's tirade, although more polite, Russell Fraser's 'A Note on Deconstruction' (*Iowa Review* 25:i.67–77) is either *not* on deconstruction, since it includes Husserl and Frege amongst its luminaries, or it means to *serve notice* on deconstruction, to evict it from its still-high 'chart-position' (once number one, Fraser remarks; now, perhaps, just number two?). The question is, however, why should this matter if deconstructors are content, as Fraser suggests, to erase the world and play on the page? This stalwart defence of standards in poetic life implies that poetry is too serious a matter to be left to playboys of the textual world.

In a second half to a particularly dissonant 'critical double', to extend Paul Gordon's analysis, Barbara Leckie's 'The Force of Law and Literature: Critiques of Ideology in Jacques Derrida and Pierre Bourdieu' (*Mosaic* 28:iii.109–35) assesses the contributions made to a conception of critique appropriate to the law and literature project by the two theorists in their essays on the 'force of law'. Far from seeing in Derrida the merely textual gamester he is so often taken to be, Leckie argues that the force of 'Force of Law' bears upon the supposed self-sufficiency of the legal text in the performance of the law, alongside the performative force of the literary text, which demonstrates, she argues, Derrida's 'commitment to critique and politics'.

Jiewei Cheng's 'Derrida and Ideographic Poetics' (*British Journal of Aesthetics* 33:ii.34–144) engages Derrida's critique of phonocentrism via the oblique route of his unthemed assimilation of Chinese ideographic poetry. Drawing this enthusiasm from Pound and Fenellosa, Derrida inherits their already partial appropriation of Chinese poetics which he then amplifies when he addresses the poetries of Mallarmé and Ponge. Cheng therefore argues that while superficial similarities abound between the graphematic and the ideographic, Derrida's lack of attention to the poetics informing the latter seriously weakens the critique of phonocentrism. Although Cheng does not give sufficient attention to this latter critique to justify his own criticism in turn, the wayward genealogy of Western aesthetic importation of the ideograph, and the link thus established between Pound and Derrida, makes this an interesting contribution.

Finally, in 'Professah de Man – he dead' (*American Literary History* 7:ii.284–301), de Man's publisher, Lindsay Waters, returns to the *New York Review of Books* affair to ask why America should want, after his death, to expel de Man. It would never have been enough, Waters argues in this memoir, unfolding the series of prurient assaults that de Man's posthumous reputation has suffered, to have discovered the alien's wartime journalism, unless de Man had already been the object of considerable bile; after all, Lehman's 'hatchet-job', *Signs of the Times*, is more concerned with the discovery that de Man had been a bad tenant than with the problem of Europe-wide fascism in the 1940s. Waters, without idolatry, indicts America for its treatment of de Man, who, a modern-day rhetor, like Protagoras whose books were burnt, was also expelled from the city, since he was always a metic and a barbarian.

Books Reviewed

Baker, Peter. *Deconstruction and the Ethical Turn*. University Press of Florida. pp. 171. hb £34.95. ISBN 0 8130 1365 8.

Caruth, Cathy, and Deborah Esch, eds. *Critical Encounters: Reference and Responsibility in Deconstructive Writing*. Rutgers University Press. pp. 305. pb $50.00. ISBN 0 8135 2086 X.

Cavell, Stanley. *Philosophical Passages: Wittgenstein, Emerson, Austin, Derrida*. Blackwell. pp. 200. pb £10.99. ISBN 0 631 19271 9.

Champagne, Roland A. *Jacques Derrida*. Twayne. pp. 138. hb £17.50. ISBN 0 8057 4310 3.

De Graef, Ortwin. *Titanic Light: Paul de Man's Post-Romanticism 1960–1969*. University of Nebraska Press. pp. 289. hb £32.95. ISBN 0 8032 1695 5.

Derrida, Jacques. *On the Name*. Stanford University Press. pp. 150. pb £10.95. ISBN 0 8047 2555 1.

Derrida, Jacques. *Points . . . Interviews 1974–1994*. edited by Elisabeth Weber. Stanford University Press. pp. 499. pb £10.95. ISBN 0 8047 2488 1.

Derrida, Jacques. *The Gift of Death*. The University of Chicago Press. pp. 115. pb £8.75. ISBN 0 226 14306 6.

Dillon, M. C. *Semiological Reductionism: A Critique of the Deconstructionist Movement in Postmodern Thought*. State University of New York Press. pp. 241. pb £15.50. ISBN 0 7914 2376 X.

Edmundson, Mark. *Literature against Philosophy, Plato to Derrida: A Defence of Poetry*. Cambridge University Press. pp. 243. pb £13.95. ISBN 0 521 48532 0.

Gordon, Paul. *The Critical Double: Figurative Meaning in Aesthetic Discourse*. University of Alabama Press. pp. 176. hb £23.95. ISBN 0 8173 0710 9.

Haverkamp, Anselm, ed. *Deconstruction is/in America: A New Sense of the Political*. New York University Press. pp. 262. pb. $19.95. ISBN 0 8147 3519 3.

Martin, Bill. *Humanism and its Aftermath: The Shared Fate of Deconstruction and Politics*. Humanities Press. pp. 199. pb £9.95. ISBN 0 391 03894 X.

McKenna, William R., and J. Claude Evans, eds. *Derrida and Phenomenology*. Kluwer. pp. 214. hb £64.00. ISBN 0 7923 3730 1.

Miller, J. Hillis. *Topographies*. Stanford University Press. pp. 376. pb £10.95. ISBN 0 8047 2379 6.

Rockmore, Tom. *Heidegger and Modern French Philosophy: Humanism, Anti-humanism and Being*. Routledge. pp. 250. pb £12.95. ISBN 0 415 11181 1.

Rötzer, Florian. *Conversations with French Philosophers*. Humanities Press. pp. 109. pb £8.95. ISBN 0 391 03847 8.

Royle, Nicholas. *After Derrida*. Manchester University Press. pp. 178. pb £12.99. ISBN 0 7190 4379 4.

Smith, Robert. *Derrida and Autobiography*. Cambridge University Press. pp. 194. pb £10.95. ISBN 0 521 46581 8.

Ward, Graham. *Barth, Derrida and the Language of Theology*. Cambridge University Press. pp. 288. hb £35.00. ISBN 0 521 47290 3.

5

Feminism

JILL LeBIHAN with JANE GOLDMAN, ANGIE SANDHU
and DIANA WALLACE

This chapter has five sections: 1. Introduction; 2. General Feminist Theory;
3. Psychoanalysis and Feminism; 4. 'Race' and Gender; 5. Anthologies.

1. Introduction

The books reviewed this year suggest that feminist theory is continuing and consolidating trends undergone in previous years, with particular strengths in 'race'-related issues, and in the range of anthologies available for teaching. In addition, there are a number of texts that indicate a retrospective tendency in feminist theory: with the albeit grudging acceptance of feminism within the academy, academics are assessing the progress of the theory to date, and considering the future. Many of the latter retrospectives represent a significant materialist approach, which is perhaps to be welcomed in today's Britain. The texts this year also reflect the ongoing and fraught relationship between feminism and psychoanalysis, a relationship that is considered in several important texts reviewed here, and which seems to remain an area of both contention and rich discussion.

2. General Feminist Theory

Imelda Whelehan's *Modern Feminist Thought: From the Second Wave to 'Post-Feminism'* is a helpful account of what has become perennially familiar in feminist studies: 'the story so far'. Conscious of the dangers of habitual stock-taking which may occur at the expense of political action, Whelehan charts second-wave feminism as it has developed 'from the realms of grass roots political issues, and reached into more abstract areas of epistemology', a transition which 'mirrors the movement from activism to internal debate within feminism, which many feminists have lamented over the years' (238). Offering a critical résumé of the various strands of Anglo-American feminism from the 1960s to the fraught debates around 'Post-Feminism' in the 1990s, Whelehan finds hope for 'feminism's "lost" political edge' in the work of black and lesbian feminists (238). The most stimulating chapter (for those already only too familiar with 'the story so far') is 'Identity Crisis?: "Post-Feminism", the Media and "Feminist Superstars" ', in which Whelehan, exposing, for example, Naomi Wolf's 'reluctance to talk about collective activism, and indeed radical change', shows that this sort of liberal individualism merely repeats the sentiments of Betty Friedan in the early 1960s. It is unfortunate that Wolf's *The Beauty Myth* (1990) probably still has greater impact than Whelehan can expect for her own more intelligent analysis or for that of other feminists, such as Marilyn French, she also considers.

In *State and Civil Society: Explorations in Political Theory*, Neera Chandhoke provides a carefully written, well-researched and incisive analysis of political and philosophical theoretical history. The text provides excellent readings of Marx, Hegel and Gramsci. Chandhoke presents a carefully developed progressive argument, beginning with an analysis of the implications of readings that have focused upon state power, and then analysing the implications of prioritizing civil society. Chandhoke concludes by moving toward a vision of a politicized civil sphere that will facilitate the reorganization of existing state structures. Chandhoke uses contemporary Indian politics in order to argue for an 'organizational principle'; by which she means the practice of diverse, localized social movements coming together in a shared project of democratic concerns. Chandhoke points out that one of the main reasons such a project is needed arises because of the present fragmentation of the political agenda (that is, anti-caste movement, women's movement, environment movement, feminist movement). Chandhoke, in tackling the more difficult question of finding something around which diverse groups can organize, critiques postmodernism for replacing conceptions of class struggle. Chandhoke accepts that postmodernism is a useful tool for criticizing 'existing positions and terms' and for 'sensitizing us to neglected and repressed issues' (218), but laments its incapacity to assist in the creation of radical intelligible discourse. While I would agree that postmodernism can be used to evade the material reality of structural forms of domination, I would cite Gayatri Spivak's defence of postmodernism as an insurance against simplistic notions of oppression that is clearly necessary for any future restructuring of society. In this sense Chandhoke's criticism of postmodernism as an ineffective practical political tool, juxtaposed to her endorsement of it as an important check on existing structures, fails to position critiques of radical new structures as an equally important safeguard for any future society. Thus Chandhoke criticizes postmodernism for something that it is by definition incapable of achieving, namely a clearly defined programme that will guarantee human freedom. Nevertheless, the commitment of Chandhoke's text provides a welcome relief to the excesses of postmodernist speculations.

The couple-based nuclear family with working husband and non-employed wife is repeatedly held up to us as both 'norm' and ideal. As Nancy Bonvillain's *Women and Men: Cultural Constructs of Gender* argues, this is rationalized not only by religious and moral teaching but also by science itself, particularly sociobiologists who assert a biological basis for this gender model, offering it as a universal founded on the assumption that in hunter-gatherer societies 'men hunt and women stay at home' (Edward Wilson, quoted in Bonvillain, 1995, 173). Yet, as Bonvillain's wide-ranging survey shows, 'men are not the only people who hunt and women do not always stay at home' (173). Indeed, today only around one-third (33.5 per cent) of American families conform to this stereotypical 'norm'. Moreover, Bonvillain points out that not only has there been a long history of male bias in reporting the behaviour and beliefs of non-Western cultures but the effect of European colonization on the gender roles and constructs of indigenous peoples was almost always to alter them to fit a patriarchal/capitalist model, eroding women's autonomy by, for instance, only trading with men, therefore giving the men increased economic power and status. Bonvillain examines gender as a *cultural* (rather than 'biological') construction across a range of societies, looking at relations between their mode of production (foraging, horticulture, pastoralism, agriculture, industrialism) and their political organization (band, tribe, chiefdom, state, etc.), as well as the ideological constructs that support and justify the gender constructions which emerge from those relations. The picture that emerges is a complex one. While the potential for gender equality appears to be greatest in foraging band societies such as the !Kung of Botswana and Namibia or the Inuit/Inupiat of Arctic Canada and Alaska, for instance, where both men and women have access to resources, other factors, such as the Inuit/Inupiat reliance on hunting animals for meat can undermine women's status and legitimate male dominance (271). The more complex the hierarchical structure of a society (as in the agricultural societies of China or India, or the industrialized United States) the greater the gender inequality, while male dominance is given ideological support through philosophical and religious teachings that stress women's unworthiness. However, the extraordinary diversity of human life across the globe suggests that, despite the strength of ideological structures, people are able to adopt new ideological concepts and that therefore there is always the possibility of change.

Lise Vogel's *Woman Questions: Essays for a Materialist Feminism* is a revised and updated selection of her key essays written between the 1960s and the early 1990s. Vogel introduces each essay with information about the academic and social contexts that informed their production. The text is a clear and accessible one in which Vogel attempts to tackle the relationship between feminism and socialism through an analysis of key socialist feminist writers and canonical texts such as Engels's *Origin of the Family*. Vogel presents her text as constituting both a 'connection to and a critique of the socialist tradition' (xii). Her theoretical speculations are placed alongside auto-biographical information and she articulates her scepticism that theory is capable of producing real political change. The most challenging and successful aspect of the text lies in its refutation of readings that view the early days of feminism as lacking any insight into the dynamics of race, class and gender. Vogel also produces a good analysis of the domestic labour debate and, although she does not tackle it herself, points out that the issues of racial and national oppression are still inadequately confronted either theoretically or practically. However, this latter claim seems to ignore the growing body of work by feminists on precisely these issues. Vogel concludes her discussion by voicing her unease at recent feminist interest in diversity and difference, reminding readers that this can and has been equally effective as a means to omit analysis of structures of domination. The text is most useful as a historical corrective to feminist historical accounts that present 'women's' history as progressing towards an ever-improving analysis. Unfortunately, Vogel herself assumes that she can articulate a 'true history of women's history' (100–1), which undermines her own critical position.

The need to document feminist history, Gabriele Griffin suggests in her introduction to *Feminist Activism in the 1990s*, can lead to feminist activism being seen as a thing of the past, while those women who are actively engaged may feel isolated because they know little of work being done outside their specific area. The demise of *Spare Rib* and then, in 1996, of *Everywoman*, has undoubtedly contributed to such feelings of isolation at grassroots level in the United Kingdom. This accessible collection of essays is much-needed proof that, despite rumours to the contrary, 'feminist activism is alive and well in the 1990s' (1). The supposed 'fragmentation' of feminism in the 1980s and 1990s is often offered as evidence of its 'death' in contrast to the 'unity' of the 1970s women's liberation movement. Making the important point that this 'unity' is in itself a nostalgic myth, Griffin argues that the diversity of current activism is one of its strengths, allowing single issue/identity groups to develop a high level of expertise and impact. Moreover, many women are involved in more than one organization. The essays are loosely grouped around four key areas of activism – health, women's rights, Black and Asian women, young women, lesbians, and 'working for change' – and document the work of an impressively diverse range of organizations including the Bristol Crisis Service for Women; the National Abortion Campaign (NAC); Rights of Women (ROW); Justice for Women; Southall Black Sisters; the Bengali Women's Support Group; Lesbians Organising Together (LOT) and Lesbian Line in Dublin; and Women in Accountancy (WIA). There is much evidence here of success but the often problematic relationship between grassroots activism and academic theory is addressed in Alex Warwick and Rosemary Auchmuty's 'Women's Studies as Feminist Activism'. They defend Women's Studies as both 'a product and a producer of feminist knowledge' which 'actively works to change and to break down the structures of those institutions in which it is found, and gives students access to and support through the processes of change' (190). As they point out, one of the most visible measures of change is the increased use of inclusive language in institutional documentation. The problem of isolation is particularly acute in the case of the young women discussed by Debi Morgan in 'Invisible Women; Young Women and Feminism' which argues that feminism has failed young women who, although they may be doing activist work, do not see themselves as feminist or feel that feminism has anything to offer them. Finally, Ailbhe Smyth's 'Haystacks in my Mind or How to Stay SAFE (Sane, Angry and Feminist) in the 1990s' is an impassioned, informed, often witty meditation on the backlash that brilliantly succeeds in making those all-important connections between the personal and the political, the individual and the collective.

3. Psychoanalysis and Feminism

Feminist engagement with psychoanalytic theory has proved a rich resource for cultural analysis. The subjects of critical engagement range from the very personal family photograph to broad categories such as masculinity, and recent feminist psychoanalysis ranges from the highly modest to the most ambitious. In *Identification Papers*, Diana Fuss presents a detailed exploration of the concepts of identity and the process of identification, and in particular adds important discussion on how this process might work for the lesbian subject. In attempting to tackle the problem of theorizing and practising a 'politics of identification' (9), Fuss returns to the modernist concept of psychoanalysis as the first major discourse to attribute such significance to identification. Fuss begins by focusing on Freud's 1913 essay 'Totem and Taboo', in order to demonstrate the paternity of identification in Freudian analysis. She expands on this in the following chapter which, through a careful reading of Freud's 'The Psychogenesis of a case of Homosexuality in a Woman', succeeds in achieving the aim of the reading, which is to confront the shortfalls of pre-oedipality as an explanatory model for female homosexuality. Fuss's subsequent discussion of the film *The Silence of the Lambs* is an excellent reading, which clearly demonstrates how Freud's criminalization of socially 'different' groups, particularly homosexuals, remains a contemporary concern. Fuss expands on this with an incisive reading of Dorothy Strachey's *Olivia*, upon which she bases her wide-ranging discussion of the categories of 'adolescent' and 'homosexuals'. Fuss demonstrates that the shared history of these two categories links them as important subjects in discourses of psychoanalysis, criminal anthropology, ethnology and sociology. In her concluding chapter, Fuss makes two crucial claims. These are, firstly, that identification has a colonial history and, secondly, that this history poses serious challenges for contemporary uses of a politics of identification. Accordingly, Fuss discusses Frantz Fanon's work on colonization, providing biographical material about him and exploring the much debated relationship between the colonizer and the colonized. Overall the text is an accessible exploration of identity but seems limited in its potential scope because it is grounded in the work of Freud. It will certainly be of interest for readers who are interested in sexuality and identity/identification. However, Fuss's more hasty summaries about the roles of 'race' in her final chapter are problematic because, despite the fact that they are tagged on at the end, they are supposed to demonstrate how crucial the process of colonization is to examinations of identity and identification.

Annette Kuhn's *Family Secrets: Acts of Memory and Imagination* follows on from the work of Jo Spence and Carolyn Steedman. Kuhn provides a personalized examination of a working-class girlhood in 1950s London, through detailed analysis of family portraits, cinema, and stills from the public domain, such as photographs of the royal family and of the London blitz. In a process she calls 'memory work', Kuhn aims to retrieve the untold stories that linger behind the public face that is composed for the camera, and she argues that such personal revelations can be used to develop a new kind of cultural theory and to create an awareness of political reality. Throughout the text, she articulates the senses of dislocation or belonging she feels when stimulated by symbols of nationalism, by images of a disintegrating country, by stills that cover up an increasingly dysfunctional family. Her commentary on the growth of a working-class girl into an academic is convincingly related to an ongoing discussion about national identity, which concludes with an analysis of *The Last of England* and a mental image of a pile of books in a skip outside Senate House. However, despite Kuhn's wish to recover a memory of her father, he remains a somewhat shadowy figure in the text, the professional behind the camera who dwindled into ill-health and was eclipsed by a powerful matriarch. Although this text can be seen as a kind of phototherapy, Kuhn's relationships with her parents remain unsatisfactorily analysed. She retains a nostalgia for her elusive, distant father, and demonstrates blatant dislike for the mother that resented her daughter's education and refused to support her in her school career, kicking her out of her home and allowing her to take her A levels as a charity case. All Kuhn's resentment is directed towards the woman whose attempts are to create a daughter who will be 'a credit to her mother', and who had a penchant for kitting out her little girl in peculiar fancy dress costumes, and an oversized school-uniform (so it would last well into her grammar school career, becoming a shabby embarrassment). Her understanding is reserved for her sick father, dominated by his powerful wife, and she does not appear to resent him for his weakness. Her anger at her mother remains, and her melancholy at the loss of her father is unresolved.

Like Annette Kuhn, Mary Russo also makes use of limited auto-biographical material intertwined with public texts in *The Female Grotesque: Risk, Excess, Modernity*, which provides a successful and entertaining synthesis of the theories of Kristeva and Bakhtin, Freud and Zizek. Russo develops a convincing new gendered category through which to analyse a wide variety of texts. She makes an association between the grotto-esque and the woman's body, and makes use of this association of the woman's base and cavernous form in her assorted case studies. She stretches the term of the female grotesque across the uncanny, the abject, the freakish and the carnivalesque, and takes us from senile, pregnant hags (Bakhtin's grotesque image), to the cunning stunts of early aviatrices (Russo's own grandmother included). She analyses numerous cultural examples including Carter's *Nights at the Circus*, Cronenberg's *Dead Ringers*, Ottinger's *Freak Orlando*, and makes passing references to other texts and images, from Sherlock Holmes to Cindy Sherman. Russo reminds us that women activists have always historically been associated with the grotesque: feminism somehow makes women freakish and repellent, and this text reminds us that we would be wise to consider the continuum of the woman's body with the categories of the uncanny, deviant or abject. Russo's array of examples is dazzling, and her commentary witty and engaging. Most impressively, she takes some extraordinarily difficult theoretical discourse and makes it accessible through her use of cultural illustrations. If only all feminist cultural criticism were as entertaining and informative as this.

In a more ambitious, less personal work, *The Man Who Never Was: Freudian Tales*, Janet Sayers uses a series of case studies taken from her clinical work to illustrate the images of 'manhood' that continue to disturb our unconscious lives. The introduction suggests a psychoanalytic eclecticism on Sayers's part, with condensed, somewhat oversimplified explanations of the most familiar psychoanalytic theories, from Freud to Winnicott, from Klein to Chodorow, from Lacan to Kristeva. Interestingly, Jung gets no mention here, despite the organization of the book in terms of archetypal figures of masculinity: the pervert, the wimp, the Don Juan and so on. Sayers argues that contemporary psychoanalytic practice in Britain, with many of its roots in object-relations theory, places too much emphasis on the role of the mother. In a slightly alarming 'postfeminist' move, her study aims to return to the problem of patriarchy by looking at masculinity, which, she claims, is one of the more important aspects of Freud's work. *The Man Who Never Was* has the subtitle 'Freudian Tales', which is slightly misleading about the psychoanalytic practice being described: this is certainly not the fifty-minute hour on the couch five times a week. Indeed, in many of these fragments of case histories, Sayers visits the clients in their own homes and is lucky if she sees them more than once. The self-consciousness about narrativization implied by the title is also somewhat absent in this text. Sayers's writing has none of the rhetorical flourish of Adam Phillips, or even of Freud himself. She gives the bare material details of her clients' sad, often poverty-stricken or abuse-filled existences, but does not really elaborate on what she supposes is going on in their minds. This is left largely to the reader to deduce.

The purported aim of *The Man Who Never Was* is to discredit the shadowy figure of a mythical male that haunts and terrorizes men and women, in their attempts to live up to a realization of its ideal. Sayers suggests that if we can exorcize the 'imagined men' of our unconscious, we would all be much saner people. However, no matter how her clients choose do battle with this demonic male figure, like the frustratingly silent analyst in a classical session, Sayers does not elaborate on how they might make peace with masculinity and with themselves. For instance, in the case of 'Toni', who relates to men by trying to usurp the masculine position, Sayers pathologizes the 'tomboy' and argues that the transgressive potential of 'cross-dressing', although serving 'as a means of demonstrating gender's fictive character, acting out its categories only serves to reinforce them and the discrimination practised in their name' (115). There appears to be no way out of the perverse determinism offered by Sayers's assorted categories of masculinity, even when they are turned upside-down and played out by women. One cannot simply come to terms with certain types of masculinity just by recognizing that they are there and that they exert a powerful hold over our fantasies. The only way to change such constructions is to play with them, exploit them, use them creatively, and this is not something Sayers seems prepared to permit.

4. 'Race' and Gender

The relationship between race and gender is explored in a variety of different areas in the texts produced this year, from the infamous faces of Clarence Thomas and O. J. Simpson in the glare of the media spotlight, to the neglected issue of homeworking in Britain. *Race, Gender and Power in America: The Legacy of the Hill–Thomas Hearings*, edited by Anita Faye Hill and Emma Coleman Jordan, is a collection of essays drawn from colleagues of Anita Hill and addressing the issues raised by the 1991 Hill/Thomas hearings. The anthology explores in particular the contexts that provided Clarence Thomas with the African-American support that was crucial to his confirmation as a supreme court judge. African-American women in the text explore the lack of attention that has been paid to the history of black women and trace it through to the contemporary African-American political struggles for assimilation, civil rights and black power. Many of the contributors provide a much-needed corrective account of slavery, insisting that it be viewed as more than a racial issue. The hearings themselves are examined in detail and the text offers an excellent introduction to what are critical issues for cultural studies. The anthologies take the form of a debate but there is an overwhelming sense of relief that sexual politics is finally on the critical agenda. Particularly interesting is the inclusion of a lengthy essay by Orlando Patterson who was heavily criticized in Toni Morrison's 1993 anthology, which tackled many of the issues raised here. Unfortunately Orlando Patterson seems to remain convinced that black men are the true victims and that young black single mothers remain responsible for much of the current crisis in America. The anthology makes interesting reading for anyone interested in 'American' and 'African-American' studies.

In *Negotiating Difference: Race, Gender and the Politics of Positionality*, Michael Awkward attempts to produce a 'self-consciously black male enquiry' (5) and succeeds in doing so. The second chapter, 'A Black Man's Place in Black Feminist Criticism', is a particularly clear and accountable demonstration of why reading as a 'feminist' should be assessed in terms of the reading and not in terms of the sex/gender of the speaker. Awkward also details the particular relevance of feminism to many black men who, like himself, have been brought up by a black single mother. Moreover, Awkward correctly applies Alice Walker's conception of womanism to its wider reference point, pointing out that 'womanism . . . is useful because it is concerned with the psychic health of black people' (49). Awkward's incisive readings of current race- and gender-based debates are a welcome addition to the crucial debate taking place between African-American men and women about the intersections of race and gender which have followed the Clarence Thomas/Anita Hill hearings and the highly publicized trials of Mike Tyson and O. J. Simpson. However, Awkward's final chapter, devoted to the 'curious case of Michael Jackson', also raises several curious questions. First, in differentiating between 'passing' and 'transraciality' Awkward concludes that since passing necessitates the possession from birth of certain physical characteristics, whereas 'transraciality' requires radical revision of natural markings and therefore while both allow for a transgressive identity, transraciality offers more potential for 'uncovering the constructedness of racial designation'. This proposed difference reduces passing to 'a form' and lifts transraciality to a 'practice', and in the process, I would suggest, makes simplistic assumptions about both categories. Moreover, Awkward's subsequent celebration of Michael Jackson's transraciality manages to silence Jackson both as a person (as opposed to a useful interpretative strategy) and as the huge marketing army that promotes 'Jackson'. Unfortunately, Awkward's concluding discussion undermines what is otherwise an astute and careful text.

American Anatomies: Theorizing Race and Gender by Robyn Wiegman is a brilliant analysis of the categories of race and gender. Wiegman introduces her discussion by observing the limits of any theoretical claim to knowledge. Wiegman refers this both to her own work and to work by others, pointing out that for many anti-essentialism is sought as 'a newly found political guarantee' (6). For Wiegman the problem of registering and attending to multiplicity constitutes the central issue in contemporary culture, and for this, she argues, 'new approaches and different kinds of critical thinking about the relationships among power, identity and social subjectivity' (7) are required. In the text Wiegman explores how '"blacks" and "women" have become wedded in the cultural symbolic as our primary figure for the complicated relationship of race and gender' (8). What follows is a detailed analysis of the contexts that produced notions of sexual and racial difference and a very welcome attention to how black women fitted into this. Despite the vast range of her enquiry Wiegman provides a careful and illuminating reading of cultural history and politics in America. The text is also clearly organized and contains useful additional notes and references.

In *Manliness and Civilization: A Cultural History of Gender and Race in the United States 1880–1917*, Gail Bederman presents a detailed exploration of the cultural history that stimulated constructions of 'manliness' and 'masculinity' in turn-of-the-century America. Bederman's familiarity with historical and political mobilizations of discourses of gender and race makes this a particularly useful addition to current work in this area. Through a detailed examination of very different prominent figures such as Charlotte Perkins Gilman, Ida B. Wells and Theodore Roosevelt, Bederman clearly demonstrates how despite the inherent flexibility of dominant discourses their most effective power lies in their application by powerful white middle-class men. The text moves fluently between historical and literary material, concluding with an excellent discussion of the popular phenomenon of *Tarzan*, which, as Bederman demonstrates, encapsulated the connections that were being forcibly made by people like Theodore Roosevelt, between white male masculinity and 'civilization'. Bederman's focus on masculinity inevitably is also an incisive focus on 'femininity' and her examination of Charlotte Perkins Gilman is essential reading for anyone who is interested in the fraught racial history of feminism in America.

In *Homeworking Women: Gender, Racism and Class at Work*, Annie Phizacklea and Carol Wolkowitz present the results of their study of home-working in Coventry. The authors emphasize that this is not just a matter of representation: 'Privatisation in social welfare and housing policy increasingly defines the home as the axis of British social life' (14–15). The text is particularly good in challenging the dominant stereotype of Asian women choosing to work at home because of pressure from their husbands. The study shows that, compared to white women, Asian women are far less happy to work at home. The authors show that for British women, the problems involved with combining childcare with employment are reflected in the far higher level of interest in homeworking for women in Britain compared to surveys conducted in Germany, France and Italy. The authors also show how women are further isolated by the tendency of trade unions to view homeworking as a threat to on-site workers. The text provides an informative analysis of their findings and concludes with a number of questions and proposals on the subject of homeworkers, calling for both a minimum wage and increased networks of support.

In their 'Cross-cultural Perspectives on Women' series, Berg Publishers have continued to fill a much-needed gap concerning the lives of 'Third World' women. The series is particularly useful as it does not represent 'Third World' women as paternalistic subjects but demonstrates how their lives counteract such readings. *'Male' and 'Female' in Developing Southeast Asia*, edited by Wazir Jahan Karim, tackles key issues and assumptions that underpin many Western discussions of gender. Karim argues that discussions of the origins of patriarchy lack sufficient discussion of the ways in which systems might be equal or bilateral in form. Thus, Karim argues that in south-east Asia, power at the grassroots is as public and important as the power of men allied to the state. Karim also tackles Foucault's reading of 'power', in his *History of Sexuality*, arguing that Foucault merely replaces one Eurocentric grand narrative with another. Throughout the anthology the contributors stress the enormous significance of the informal sphere, and emphasize that calling it the 'periphery' is inaccurate in a south-east Asian context. The contributors all stress that Western themes of feminism cannot envisage a situation where male and female relations arc managed in a way as flexible and fluid as that found in south-east Asia. Accordingly, the essays in the text provide examples of the flexibility of gender, detailing 'unisexuality' in Indonesia, and the political strength of women in Malaysia. Other contributors stress the relevance of diminishing ecological reserves for gender relations. Mark Hobart provides a particularly good discussion of the erroneous assumptions that many Western scholars have applied to their discussions of 'kinship'. As Hobart argues, anthropological determinism has missed many of the complexities involved in kinship systems, an omission that reflects in large part the lack of critical time that has been given to both the ethics and the reliability of ethnographical methods. Overall the text offers a challenging and detailed survey of gender in south-east Asia and is produced in an organized and accessible form.

Deborah Fahy Bryceson's anthology *Women Wielding the Hoe: Lessons from Rural Africa for Feminist Theory and Development Practice* focuses on women as the backbone of agricultural production in Africa. The papers all analyse and report upon African women hoe cultivators and refer this to a critical assessment of prevailing Western theories about women as agricultural workers. The text is clearly organized. The five main sections deal with the reproductive and productive role of African women hoe cultivators and how this has been approached and developed by Western development agencies. The concluding section of the text is excellent as it draws together the contributors and presents an engaged summary of key areas of disagreement and accord between the commentators. The text has wide-ranging uses both for policy-makers, sociologists and anyone interested in broadening existing definitions of women and work.

The South Asian Petty Bourgeoisie in Britain: An Oxford Case Study, by Shaila Srinivasan, is an examination of south Asian entrepreneurship in Britain and its implications for the 'assimilation' of Asian small business owners into British society. Srinivasan provides detailed discussion based on her interviews of the underlying motives of Asian small businessmen but there are a number of problematic aspects to this discussion. Srinivasan places a good deal of emphasis upon the question of whether Asian small business does aid integration, and it is clear that this study is intended to document that it does. This leaves the issue of racism relatively unaddressed, as the overlying emphasis falls upon showing how Asian small businesses fit in to a relatively undiscussed 'British society'. Srinivasan presents such adages as 'working hard' as without doubt 'something that all South Asian migrants believe in. Similarly frugality, thrift and saving for the future, are essential characteristics of the South Asian population as a whole' (50). Such enormous over-generalizations are accompanied by a lack of analysis of the different gender positions within the 'Asian' small business community. In Srinivasan's reading, this is best described as 'collective commitment' (55) enabling otherwise impossibly long hours. However, Srinivasan's assertion that this allows 'each member' of the business family 'a certain space' ignores the fact that women and children often do provide longer hours. It also ignores the fact that Asian children are often working in the family business at a very young age. Srinivasan cites research carried out in Australia to support her contention that the assumption that family labour is exploitative is questionable: it ignores the facts that alternative employment prospects may be no better; it addresses the long-term needs of the family not the individual family member; and it should be viewed as a contribution. Lastly, children certainly are not cheap labour since education comes first. Srinivasan fails to differentiate between what are gendered options. Moreover, Srinivasan puts forward the argument that these children are sent to private school, thus putting family prosperity to the best possible use without considering how this fits in with an aspect of British society and not British society as a whole. The text is seriously undermined by the consistent lack of attention to what it is that constitutes 'family' or society, leaving the question of Asian integration at best unresolved.

5. Anthologies

Practising Feminist Criticism: An Introduction is designed as a companion piece to Maggie Humm's *A Reader's Guide to Contemporary Feminist Literary Criticism*, and both follow the series format initially set by Raman Selden's *A Reader's Guide to Contemporary Literary Theory* (1985) in providing basic introductions for student readers. Humm, however, explicitly avoids the kind of 'grand claims' she perceives in Selden and Widdowson's comment (in the third edition, 1993) that 'to theorise one's own practice – is to enfranchise oneself in the constituency of cultural politics', stating that her concern instead is with 'the question of what gender means when we read' (xv). While Humm's first volume outlined the theory, the emphasis in the second book is on practical explication through a series of readings of texts. The book covers eleven areas of feminist criticism: second wave feminism (which provides a brief historicized introduction through the work of Ellen Moers, Elaine Showalter and Kate Millett), myth criticism, Marxist/socialist criticism, French feminism, psycho-analytic criticism, poststructuralism, deconstruction, postmodernism, Black feminisms, lesbian criticism and Third World feminisms. The sheer range of theoretical approaches offers a testament not just to the diversity of feminist critical approaches but to the willingness of feminist critics to engage with 'mainstream' theory (poststructuralism, postmodernism, deconstruction and so on) and, by gendering it, to appropriate it for feminist uses. The chapters on Black, lesbian and Third World criticisms foreground the *political* content and commitment of feminist literary criticism at its best. Each critical approach is applied to two texts with some detailed analysis of a key passage. Within the remit of the book there is little room for sustained development of the critical analysis. However, Humm's readings are not only clear and succinct but sometimes open up texts in unexpected ways, as in her application of myth criticism to Ursula Le Guin's *The Left Hand of Darkness*, deconstruction to Elizabeth Robins's *The Convert* or postructuctualism to Iris Murdoch's *The Unicorn*. One minor quibble with this otherwise useful introduction is that initial publication dates for each of the literary texts are not given, and this lack of historical placing results in a curious homogenizing of what is an interesting range of carefully chosen texts.

Penny Florence and Dee Reynolds's collection, *Feminist Subjects, Multi-Media: Cultural Methodologies*, promises more than it delivers, but is nevertheless a stimulating multidisciplinary feminist enterprise. The contents do suggest a 'multidiscipline' approach: chapters by academics, freelance writers, a poet and artists, written in a range of styles, including theoretical, poetic and autobiographical, address a number of different ('high' and 'low') cultural activities such as fiction, painting, opera, photography, film, video. But this does not really constitute anything truly in the realm of the 'multi-media' invoked in the title, which might lead us to expect feminist investigations of more innovative technological experimentation. It comes in three parts: 'The Politics of Spectatorship' (five essays), which looks at the positioning of female spectators by aesthetic (film and painting mainly) and critical discourses; 'The Politics of Production/Performance' (three essays), which explores issues concerning the extents of women's power and involvement in the production of 'high' and 'low' media (examples from film, television, opera); and 'Repositioning Feminist Subjects' (four essays), which attempts to rewrite and reconceptualize feminist subjectivity. The framing of these contents is disappointing. Penny Florence's rather wordy introduction promises the collection will 'foreground consideration of how innovation by women in critical theory and methodology and in creativity participates in the dynamic of cultural change. In so doing, it should be no surprise that its own form is unconventional' (ix). But what follows, although interesting, does not need such portentous admonitions, appearing in fact rather tame in places.

Before turning to the contents, it is also worth considering some of the book's elisions, which are coyly brought to our attention in a somewhat defensive 'Afterword' by Anthea Callen. She explains the collection's origins in a 1992 conference on Feminist Methodologies which 'sought to facilitate the networking of ideas between all women active in the field, regardless of affiliation or status, and hence to assert the right to speech'. But such admirably pluralist ambitions were not realized, and Callen offers some uncomfortable reflections on this: 'Every effort was made to seek out contributions from black women, and it is a reflection, perhaps, of their differing agendas as much as of their small number in academe so far that none was forthcoming' (197). This clumsy attempt to speak on behalf of the absent betrays the narrow perspective of the collection's apparently broad 'cultural' pretensions. By citing only academe (in this worryingly glib dismissal), Callen not only seems to ignore the very possibilities of alternative cultural spheres the collection is supposedly embracing, but also signals the project's own limited sphere of interest and appeal. For all its gestures to the margins and to different cultural locations, this collection is predominantly academic, and seems to assume an academic audience.

That said, there are some very interesting and worthwhile individual contributions in the collection. In 'The "View from Elsewhere": Extracts from a Semi-Public Correspondence about the Politics of Spectatorship', Griselda Pollock impressively uses the epistolary form to explore issues of female spectatorship in a stimulating comparative analysis of Edouard Manet's painting, *The Bar at the Folies Bergère*, and Mary Cassatt's *Woman in Black at the Opera*. Penny Florence offers a 'video poem' on Manet's interference with Berthe Morisot's painting of her mother (he blacked out the figure), and Frances Presley offers some poems on women and surrealism inspired by the work of Leonora Carrington and Meret Oppenheim. Kate Chedgzoy draws on Kristeva's theory of the abject to examine 'grotesque bodies' in the paintings of Frida Kahlo. Annette Kuhn opens her own family photograph album to reflect on the issues of identity and mother–daughter relationships. In the second section of the collection there are feminist readings of the film *Thelma and Louise*, the opera *Carmen* (film and stage versions), and natural history television programs. In the third section Jean Grant movingly considers in word and image the personal and wider politics of her father's death in World War II; Lynne Pearce helpfully traces feminist subject positions and the politics of reading; and Sarah Radstone explores memory and subjectivity in a range of texts from the *Medea* to Toni Morrison's *Beloved*. The collection ends with the rigorous, theoretical formulations of Elizabeth Grosz in an excellent academic essay, 'Psychoanalysis and the Imaginary Body'. Not as ground-breaking or all-embracing as its editors would like to think, this book nevertheless has much to recommend it.

Helen Baehr and Ann Gray's *Turning It On: A Reader in Women and Media* is an excellent, highly useful collection aimed at media, communication and cultural studies courses. To avoid reduplicating the more readily available critical canon on film and film theory, the editors have tailored this reader well, offering a systematic and informative guide to the wide spectrum of perspectives on women and the media. It is divided into four sections of articles, essays and extracts, each with helpful introductions and lists of references and further reading. Section I, 'Representation: Image, Sign, Difference', looks at 'key shifts in feminist approaches to representation' from 'Images of Women' to questions of gender and postmodernist theories of fragmenting identities – from Noreene Z. Janus's 'Research on Sex Roles in the Mass Media' (1977) to Susan Bordo's thoughts on the media's most famous 'Material Girl', Madonna (1993). Section II, 'Genre: Textuality, Femininity, Feminism', looks at work on 'women's genres' such as soap opera and melodrama and includes Annette Kuhn on 'women's genres' and Kathleen K. Rowe on *Roseanne*. Section III, 'Audience: Texts, Subjects, Contexts', looks at women audiences and women's consumption of media output (magazines, television, videos and so on), with reference to women's domestic contexts, and explores feminist developments in methodology (including contributions from Tania Modleski on daytime television, Elizabeth Frazer on 'Teenage Girls Reading *Jackie*', and Evelyn Cauleta Reid on 'Television Viewing Habits of Young Black Women in London'). Section IV, 'Interventions: Industry, Organisation, Working Practices', looks at feminist practices and interventions in the media. This is a good collection, useful in many contexts.

Feminist Academics: Creative Agents for Change, edited by Louise Morley and Val Walsh, is a highly readable and fascinating collection of essays by feminist academics and teachers. The contributors discuss the effects of recent government educational legislation on women, the particular obstacles faced by black women academics, the insidious effects of the 'hidden curriculum' on teaching, and the continued masculinity of academic institutions. Tracey Potts and Janet Price's discussion of the difficulties posed by teaching in a classroom in a wheelchair is an excellent correction to the pervasive omission of the issue of 'disability' and is also an excellent critique of Diana Fuss's problematic classroom model in *Essentially Speaking*. This accessible and diverse text will be of interest to any woman working in education.

Feminist Cultural Theory: Process and Production, edited by Beverly Skeggs, is a welcome attempt to fill a gap in feminist cultural studies, that is, the 'serious lack of work which interrogates its own theoretical production'. It sets out to 'equip the reader with the requisite skills to interrogate the methodological underpinnings of any academic work [and] to evaluate theories in relation to their conditions of production' (2). The contributions of feminist cultural theorists invited to reflect on their methodologies in areas such as literary and film theory, sociology and history are divided into two parts: 'Texts and Responses', and 'Responses and Texts'. Part One includes Celia Lury on her work on gender and culture in *Cultural Rights* (1993); Alison Young on the reception and methodology of her work on the women of Greenham, *Femininity in Dissent* (1994); Pat Kirkham on issues arising from her book on the personal and professional partnership of designers Charles and Ray Eames; Kathleen Rowe on studying *Roseanne*; and contributions from Janet Thumm, Lynne Pearce and Jackie Stacey. Part Two includes Ellen Seiter on mothers, children and television viewing; Ann Gay on her research into women's use of domestic video cassette recorders; Beverley Skeggs interviewing Julia Hallam and Margaret Marshment on their research into the television version of Jeanette Winterson's *Oranges Are Not the Only Fruit* and viewers; and Skeggs on 'Theorising, Ethics and Representation in Feminist Ethnography'.

Books Reviewed

Awkward, Michael. *Negotiating Difference: Race, Gender, and the Politics of Positionality*. University of Chicago Press. pp. ix–225. £11.95. ISBN 0 226 03301 5.

Baehr, Helen, and Ann Gray. *Turning It On: A Reader in Women and Media*. Arnold. pp. 226. £12.99. ISBN 0 340 58016 X.

Bederman, Gail. *Manliness and Civilization: A Cultural History of Gender and Race in the United States 1880–1917*. University of Chicago Press. pp. 322. £15.25. ISBN 0 226 04139 5.

Bonvillain, Nancy. *Women and Men: Cultural Constructs of Gender*. Prentice Hall. pp. 291. £21.95. ISBN 0 13 103482 0.

Bryceson, Deborah Fahy, ed. *Women Wielding the Hoe: Lessons from Rural Africa for Feminist Theory and Development Practice*. Berg. pp. 288. £14.95. ISBN 1 85973 073 6.

Chandhoke, Neera. *State and Civil Society: Explorations in Political Theory*. Sage. £35.00. ISBN 0 8039 9246 7.

Florence, Penny, and Dee Reynolds, eds. *Feminist Subjects, Multi-Media: Cultural Methodologies*. Manchester University Press. pp. 218. £14.99. ISBN 0 7190 4180 5.

Fuss, Diana. *Identification Papers*. Routledge. pp. 179. £11.99 ISBN 0 415 90886 8.

Griffin, Gabriele, ed. *Feminist Activism in the 1990s*. Taylor and Francis. pp. 214. pb £13.95. hb £38.00. ISBN 0 7484 0290 X, 0 7484 0289 6.

Hill, Anita Faye, and Emma Coleman Jordan eds. *Race, Gender, and Power in America: The Legacy of the Hill–Thomas Hearings*. Oxford University Press. pp. vii–302. £25.00. ISBN 0 19 508774 7.

Humm, Maggie. *Practising Feminist Criticism: An Introduction*. Prentice Hall/Harvester Wheatsheaf. pp. 211. £10.95. ISBN 0 13 355371 X.

Karim, Wazir Jahan, ed. *'Male' and 'Female' in Developing Southeast Asia*. Berg. pp. vii–267. £14.95. ISBN 1 85973 027 2.

Kuhn, Annette. *Family Secrets: Acts of Memory and Imagination*. Verso. pp. 128. pb £9.95. hb £34.95. ISBN 0 86091 629 4, 0 86091 479 8.

Morley, Louise, and Val Walsh, eds. *Feminist Academics: Creative Agents for Change*. Taylor and Francis. pp. 203. £13.95. ISBN 0 7484 0300 0.

Phizacklea, Annie, and Carol Wolkowitz. *Homeworking Women: Gender, Racism and Class at Work*. Sage. pp. vi–152. £11.95. ISBN 0 8039 8874 5.

Russo, Mary. *The Female Grotesque: Risk, Excess, Modernity*. Routledge. pp. 233. pb £13.99, hb £35.00. ISBN 0 415 90165 0, 0 415 90164 2.

Sayers, Janet. *The Man Who Never Was: Freudian Tales*. Chatto and Windus. pp. 236. £15.99. ISBN 0 7011 6232 5.

Skeggs, Beverly, ed. *Feminist Cultural Theory: Process and Production*. Manchester University Press. pp. 235. pb £14.99, hb £40.00. ISBN 0 7190 4471 5, 0 7190 4470 7.

Srinivasan, Shaila. *The South Asian Petty Bourgeoisie in Britain: An Oxford Case Study*. Avebury. pp. v–237. £37.50. ISBN 1 8562 8972 9.

Vogel, Lise. *Woman Questions: Essays for a Materialist Feminism*. Pluto Press. pp. viii–162. £12.99. ISBN 0 7453 0676 4.

Whelehan, Imelda. *Modern Feminist Thought: From the Second Wave to 'Post-Feminism'*. Edinburgh University Press. pp. 270. £12.95. ISBN 0 7486 0621 1.

Wiegman, Robyn. *American Anatomies: Theorizing Race and Gender*. Duke University Press. pp. vii–268. £14.95. ISBN 0 8223 4591 2.

Yanagisako, Sylvia, and Delaney, Carol eds. *Naturalizing Power: Essays in Feminist Cultural Analysis*. Routledge. pp. vii–310. £13.99. ISBN 0 415 90884 1.

6

Colonial Discourse/Postcolonial Theory

PATRICK WILLIAMS and NAHEM YOUSAF

For some reason, publishers appeared not to want to have their 1995 offerings reviewed: from the mighty Routledge to little American university presses, almost every copy, or so it seemed at times, had to be fought – or wheedled – for. As a result, the Books Reviewed list is, unfortunately, thinner than ever before. Among the Routledge books that did arrive, *Imperialism and Its Contradictions*, by the veteran Marxist historian V. G. Kiernan, is not necessarily what everyone would immediately think of as postcolonial theory, but it represents the kind of historically grounded analysis of, and meditation upon, fundamental aspects of imperialism which postcolonial work ignores at its peril. This is the third edited volume of Kiernan's essays published by Routledge, but the first to focus on imperialism, which has arguably been his central concern throughout his long writing career, and consists of work produced over the last twenty years. Although entitled 'Imperialism' the collection is particularly concerned with the period of the colonial empires, from formation to dissolution. Most of the essays are wide ranging ('Imperialism and Revolution', 'Europe and the World: The Imperial Record'); others are more narrowly focused ('Antonio Gramsci and the Other Continents'); all, however, share a similar synthesizing aim. In several of the essays Kiernan examines the relation of capitalism to imperialism and produces a picture which in no way follows what has become something of an orthodoxy, namely that imperialism is simply the global spread of capitalism. He is also ready to address contentious questions, such as what imperialism could be said to have contributed to the development of particular countries or continents, and refuses to provide easy answers, or ones which might seem merely fashionable. He is at pains to remind readers that colonialist practices of territorial expropriation, economic exploitation and brutal repression were developed in Europe for use against other European nations, or segments of the national population, (referring, for example, to 'England's possession of all these colonial regions within the British Isles'). Most unfashionably, perhaps, Kiernan wants to retain a sense that 'In its own however distorted fashion, Europe often really was a civilising presence', or that 'The vicious Oriental potentate or the barbarous tribal chief was not always a figment of Western imagination: there were many ruling classes that their peoples were better off without.' Interestingly for someone whose work has been lavishly praised by Said, his opinions of Islam can seem remarkably

Orientalist (though they also need to be put in the context of his general low regard for religion). The final postimperial chapter, 'After Empire', exhibits a range of ideas which even Kiernan's editor is forced to call 'cranky', and it is tempting to see the volume as something like V. G. Kiernan and His Contradictions. Perhaps non-contradictory positions are too much to expect from someone engaged in the difficult process of – in the words of his editor – 'bringing theory face to face with history'.

Imaginary Maps continues Gayatri Spivak's practical and theoretical engagement with the work of Mahasweta Devi, presenting three of her translations of Devi's stories, the first two of which, 'The Hunt' and 'Douloti the Bountiful', she has already written about elsewhere. The stories are accompanied by an interview with Devi, a translator's preface and an afterword, in which Spivak addresses a range of textual, theoretical and political issues – and in many cases these also represent a continued engagement. Among the questions considered is the relation between postcolonialism and migrancy: 'a conflation of Eurocentric migrancy with postcoloniality lets drop the vicissitudes of decolonization and ignores the question: Who decolonizes?', as well as that between the subaltern and the organic intellectual : 'When the subaltern "speaks" in order to be heard and gets into the structure of responsible (responding and being responded to) resistance, he/she is, or is on the way to becoming, an organic intellectual', and the latter, of course, represents a brief further elaboration of points from her most famous article. A more recent emphasis is that on the need for an 'ethical singularity' – open, responsible, accountable – as the appropriate mode of contact with the subaltern, though at the same time there is an awareness that this constitutes 'an experience of the impossible, the sense that "something has not got across" '. Like this 'ethical singularity', another 'impossibility' that is sought for is the form of 'global justice through attention to specificity' – and such a linking of the specific and the global is something Spivak finds common to both Marx and Derrida. Finally, inevitably, there is the complexity of the postcolonial itself: 'Mahasweta's stories are *post* colonial. They must operate *with* the resources of a history shaped by colonization *against* the legacy of colonialism.' One such legacy, to which both Devi and Spivak repeatedly return, is the uneven, fragile or spurious nature of decolonization. Spivak's comments on the final story, 'Pterodactyl, Puran Sahay and Pirtha' – 'the scene is one of internal colonization in the name of decolonization' – indicate something of the complexity both for those inhabiting such a state and those attempting to analyse it.

Late Imperial Culture, edited by Roman de la Campa, E. Ann Kaplan and Michael Sprinker, is an interesting grouping of pieces which – especially editorially – express a current (and particularly US located) unease with postcolonialism. It could also be seen as part of a US located interest in the concept 'late imperial', following John McClure's *Late Imperial Romance* (reviewed in *YWCCT* 4). McClure uses the concept to refer to broadly contemporary American fiction, though with *Kim, Heart of Darkness* and *A Passage to India* as early examples. Sprinker in his introduction – and despite his altogether correct demand for accurate periodization – allows it even more elasticity, verging on vagueness: '"Late", then, can only mean "old", or "advanced".' (But what, for starters, are the differences and similarities between these? Old or advanced according to who? Old or advanced as equivalent, non-evaluative terms?) Surprisingly, neither book acknowledges a debt to Ernst Mandel's *Late Capitalism*, popularized in Jameson's famous article on postmodernism, nor to the earlier Frankfurt School discussions – indeed, neither advances any rationale for the term at all (though Sprinker's introduction at least provides a context). Both Sprinker and Aijaz Ahmad in the first of the contributions identify postcolonial work in general with the worst of its excesses – relentlessly discourse-centred, endlessly expandable and imprecise in its historical and geographical reference – thereby neglecting both the range of work produced (some of which is no doubt as bad as they suggest) and the extent of debate and (violent) disagreement among the practitioners. Sprinker and Ahmad criticize notorious *Empire Writes Back*-type positions, but then postcolonial critics have been queuing up to do that for some years now.

Aijaz Ahmad's piece, 'Postcolonialism: What's in a Name?', is both a timely reminder of an earlier debate around postcolonialism in political theory and a useful summary of that debate. Unfortunately, Ahmad seems to feel that neglect of that earlier work by current cultural analyses of postcolonialism constitutes instant disqualification. When he turns from his own area of expertise to the (improper) postcolonial, Ahmad's grasp is not particularly sure:

> But within the field of literature, we also have, alongside 'post-colonial criticism', the category of 'postcolonial writing'. This quite different, and in its own way equally common, usage, refers simply to literary compositions – plays, poems, fiction – of non-white minorities located in Britain and North America, while efforts are now under way also to designate the contemporary literatures of Asia and Africa as 'postcolonial' and thus to make them available for being read according to the protocols that metropolitan criticism has developed for treating what it calls 'minority literatures'.

This is quite simply wrong: wrong about the process (it is Asia and Africa which are already installed as postcolonial; non-white metropolitan populations are currently being vigorously fought over), and wrong about the critical apparatus ('minority literature' theories, especially as developed from Deleuze and Guattari, are almost never used in postcolonial theorizing). May Joseph's 'Performing the Postcolony: The Plays of Mustapha Matura' would, on the face of it, appear to be exactly the sort of work of which Aijaz Ahmad's critique is so dismissive: it is 'cultural'; it focuses on non-white minority groups in the metropolis; it is more interested in text and discourse than history or material circumstances; it revels in sentences such as 'The syncretism of these borders is simultaneously fractured by contradictions' – it is, nevertheless, a readable discussion of a neglected author and area.

Among the other contributions, two focus on nineteenth-century writers – Bram Stoker and Anna Leonowens – which creates further problems for the 'late' periodizing, while whatever the merits of Marianna Torgovnick's piece on body piercing it is difficult to see how it relates to imperialism, late or otherwise. Periodizing quibbles apart, Caren Kaplan's discussion of Anna Leonowens raises important issues in relation to feminism and imperialism, forms of domination and the politics of representation. The latter is taken up in a different way by Ella Shohat. In 'Casting, Coalitions and the Politics of Identity', Shohat emphasizes the complex locations, affiliations and identifications involved in cinema spectatorship: 'It is not only a question of what one is, or where one is coming from, but also of what one desires to be, where one wants to go, and with whom one wants to go there.' Politically, however, what matters most is the alliances which can be formed: 'intercommunal coalitions based on historically shaped affinities'.

The Decolonization of Imagination: Culture, Knowledge and Power, edited by Jan Nederveen Pieterse and Bikhu Parekh, assembles an interesting group of contributors, both expected (Pieterse, Spivak, Patrick Brantlinger, for example) and unexpected (the novelist Sol Yurick; the former United Nations departmental deputy director Marion O'Callaghan). The introduction by Parekh and Pieterse, 'Shifting Imaginaries: Decolonization, Internal Decolonization, Postcoloniality', is an ambitious overview, sometimes informative and occasionally irritating, as for example in the conceptual confusion (at least, I was confused) over image/imagination/imaginary [n., rather than adj.], or when it argues for a cultural pluralism which moves beyond 'the victimhood of North–South domination' – as if that relation of domination and exploitation could somehow be bracketed off – or when they identify 'play' as one of two keynotes of 'the postcolonial sensibility': 'because the postcolonial world is more fluid, less rigid than the space of confrontation and reconquest, boundaries, for those who have experience of crossing them, become a matter of play, rather than an obsession.' (Oh really?) If this brevity and selective quotation do not really do justice to Parekh and Pieterse, that is perhaps only returning the compliment – they, for example, dismiss Said in one brief unqualified sentence for purportedly 'uncritically recycl[ing] Noam Chomsky's ideas' in *Culture and Imperialism*. (What's wrong with Chomsky's ideas anyway? Shouldn't we be told?)

Marion O'Callaghan's 'Continuities in Imagination' ranges widely, both historically and geographically. Written without references, it is a very self-assured assessment of continuities across space and time in various processes and practices, especially in relation to capitalism (rather than in 'imagination', I would have thought, but at least it attempts to address the terms of the title, unlike everybody else). It is strongly dismissive of divisive identity politics, (especially, perhaps, racialized versions), and even more so of the economic or social circumstances to which capitalism gives rise and which make such (bad) political choices a necessity for some.

Bad political choices of a different kind abound in Bikhu Parekh's 'Liberalism and Colonialism', a careful, impressive dissection of the contradictions in the liberalism of Locke and Mill which allowed them simultaneously to champion liberty and support colonialism. It also establishes some links with modern liberalism, an aspect I would have liked to have seen further developed. Jan Berting's 'Patterns of Exclusion: Imaginaries of Class, Nation, Ethnicity and Gender in Europe' in some ways follows on from Parekh, highlighting contradictions and problems in the 'positive' model of the Enlightenment, but lacks the clarity and organization of the latter's piece. It does, however, bring the argument up to the present, which is what the book's final section addresses.

Given the current importance of work on globalization (and the fact that the introduction singles it out as an area which postcolonialism supposedly neglects), the section of the book which deals with it is disappointing, though Sol Yurick's piece, 'Metastate versus the Politics of Identity', was, like that of Marion O'Callaghan, punchy, assertive and unreferenced.

Anyone familiar with Anne McClintock's work, especially the increasingly anthologized and cited article 'The Angel of Progress', would expect her book *Imperial Leather: Race, Gender and Sexuality in the Colonial Contest*, to be intelligent, wide-ranging, insightful and theoretically astute, and they would not be disappointed. ('The Angel of Progress' is here too, though now divided to form the opening and closing pages of the book, it ironically works less well than it did as a unified piece.) As in the article, Anne McClintock takes a somewhat sceptical look at a number of approaches to, or positions within, postcolonial work, especially an overfondness for certain empty generalizations ('the post-colonial woman') or excessive theoretical enthusiasms ('The lyrical glamour cast by some post-colonial theorists over ambivalence and hybridity is not always historically warranted'). Ambivalence and hybridity inevitably connote Homi Bhabha, and while McClintock has some complimentary things to say about him, she also accuses him of a 'fetishism of form', in which the formal ambivalences of discourse are portrayed as more powerful anticolonial forces than the resistance of indigenous populations. However, far from dismissing the kind of psychoanalytically informed theory which Bhabha favours, McClintock argues for its fundamental importance, and rejects conventional oppositions between psychoanalytical and Marxist approaches: 'Perhaps one can go so far as to say that there should be no material history without psychoanalysis and no psychoanalysis without a material history.'

The book consists of a series of readings of texts from different forms and moments of colonialism, some obvious (*King Solomon's Mines, Kim, Heart of Darkness*), others less obvious (adverts for soap), and some quite surprising (the remarkable relationship between Arthur Munby and Hannah Cullwick). In the latter instance, McClintock skilfully draws out the ways in which the apparently private, intimate, even perverse dimensions of their relationship intersect with imperial concerns. The idea that the production of 'domesticity' was central to British imperial identity is also central to the book, with the domestic and the imperial constantly impacting on one another: 'as domestic space became racialized, colonial space became domesticated'. The final section of the book continues the southern African focus already introduced via the studies of Olive Schreiner and Rider Haggard, and brings it up to the present through discussions of black poetry, Elsa Joubert's controversial *Poppie Nongena*, and the relation of women to the nation state and the formation of national identity. This focus on the active participation of women reflects one of the book's central concerns: women's work, women's agency and the ways in which they are circumscribed, sidelined and ignored by men. Part of this involves the complex of discourses around idleness (especially the idleness of the working class, women and black people), and its paradoxical apogee in the staged idleness of middle-class housewives: 'Housewifery became a career in vanishing acts. A wife's vocation was not only to create a clean and productive family, but also to ensure the skilled erasure of every *sign* of her work.' The repeated attempt to deny the importance of female labour is an example of abjection – 'something rejected from which one does not part' –

which McClintock borrows from Kristeva and deploys as part of her development of 'a situated psychoanalysis'. Once again, as well as being a constitutive aspect of metropolitan domesticity, abjection emerges as a widespread colonial strategy. There are, inevitably, perhaps, aspects of the book which are less convincing. At the conceptual level, for example, it seems that McClintock rather exaggerates the possibility of deploying panoptical time ('the image of global history consumed – at a glance – in a single spectacle from a point of privileged invisibility') as a means of surveillance or control; also, the idea of commodity racism (McClintock's term) as a late nineteenth-century replacement for scientific racism seems oddly – given the author's approach – historically ungrounded, in view of scientific racism's persistence and power in the twentieth century. At the level of consistency, for example, a phrase attributed to Hannah Arendt turns up twenty pages later attributed to Rider Haggard; names change: Saartjie Baartman/Saadjie Baadman; Carl Linne/Carolus Linnaeus – all these, it has to be said, are minor points when set against the good things *Imperial Leather* has to offer.

Robert Young's *Colonial Desire: Hybridity in Theory, Culture and Race* manages to be very different from *White Mythologies* and yet interestingly similar. At a fairly obvious level both books are involved in tracing concepts: in *White Mythologies*, models of history, especially Marxist ones; in *Colonial Desire,* the concept of culture, and its relation to issues of race and sexuality. At the same time, the books have a very different feel: *White Mythologies* gave the impression of more passionate engagement, perhaps of scores to be settled; *Colonial Desire*, on the other hand – and despite its title – appears more relaxed, less desire-ridden, an altogether lighter work. A further area of similarity concerns some of the controversial aspects of the books, especially in connection with what might be called the (unspoken or only partially articulated) implications of Young's arguments. In *White Mythologies*, for instance, it is not clear whether, even if one accepts the contentions regarding the irreducible Hegelian content of Marxist thought, that should be taken as comprehensively invalidating Marxism, or whether it should simply make Marxists rather more circumspect in their claims. In *Colonial Desire*, Young demonstrates the way in which the concept of culture also has its dark side, in this case, a racist dimension: 'Culture has always marked cultural difference by producing the other; it has always been comparative, and racism has always been an integral part of it: the two are inextricably clustered together, feeding off and generating each other.' Clearly, historical amnesia or ignorance in such matters is unacceptable, and *Colonial Desire* performs an important function in attempting to rectify that state of affairs. What is less clear is how contaminated Young regards current intellectual work as a result. In *White Mythologies* he was scathing of Said's perceived desire for a position of relative autonomy for the intellectual; in *Colonial Desire*, he sees that, generalized or extended, as the characteristic flaw in postcolonialism: 'The fantasy of post-colonial cultural theory, however, is that those in the Western academy have at least managed to free themselves from the hybrid commerce of colonialism, as from every other aspect of the colonial legacy.' This is by now a very familiar accusation – see, for example, Arif Dirlik's article 'The Postcolonial Aura', reviewed in *YWCCT* 4 – (and one that always rather mystifies me, since I have never known anyone lay claim to such fantastic freedoms). Striving for some sort of critical or intellectual distance from certain institutions or operations of power ought not to be equated with dreams of total detachment, I would have thought. Young's position has already occasioned some forthright responses. Stuart Hall, for instance, has criticized 'the incredibly simplistic charge in Robert Young's *Colonial Desire* (1995) that the post-colonial critics are "complicit" with Victorian racial theory *because both sets of writers deploy the same term – hybridity – in their discourse!'* (see *YWCCT* 6 for the full review). Controversy apart, the book is a very interesting and very readable narrative (much more so than *White Mythologies*, both in terms of readability and terms of narrative organization). It makes important connections and (surprisingly – it is somehow not what I would expect in a Robert Young book), provides a powerful illustration of the scope of individual agency in deliberately structuring a discourse for political ends: the account of Henry Hotze, a Confederate agent based in London, his rise to membership of the Council of the British Anthropological Society, and the effects of the combination of racial ideas he represented and disseminated, is just one among numerous examples. Above all, perhaps, *Colonial Desire* is both a timely reminder that even those terms which are most valorized and appear most progressive may have historical connections which are at best problematic, and, hence, a plea for proper historical knowledge which it would be impossible to argue with: 'If we worry today that we have been unable to establish any true knowledge of other cultures, we also need to make sure that we have a knowledge of the history of our own.'

On the journal front, Salman Rushdie is currently a popular subject for postcolonial critics. Feroza Jussawalla in 'Of *The Satanic Verses*' Mohajirs and Migrants: Hybridity vs. Syncretism and Indigenous Aesthetics in Postcoloniality' (*Third Text* 32: autumn, 85–92) makes the point that the postcolonial usually signifies in relation to European colonization, rather than, as in the case of India, for example, Mogul colonization, arguing that this can lead to a fundamental misunderstanding and therefore misinterpretation of Rushdie's work: 'Rushdie is the European metropolitan intellectual who does not dislodge metropolitan definitions but instead reinscribes them into his roots and his history' which are post yet another colonization – Muslim colonization of India.' Jussawalla's point is that critics who use the term postcolonial to refer only to post-British colonization and post-European colonization tend to obfuscate previous forms of colonization like religious colonization. Whilst Anouar Majid's 'Can the Postcolonial Critic Speak? Orientalism and the Rushdie Affair' (*Cultural Critique* 32: winter, 5–42) does not specifically foreground the history of religious colonization, it nevertheless points to the ways the West has represented Islam and Islamists as in need of 'civilizing'. Majid, quite rightly, finds it problematic that negative representations and stereotypes of Islam have political and academic currency whilst level-headed debates are relegated and often left unheard. He argues that

the time has come to acknowledge that the Afroasian person (intellectual or not) is in deep trouble today, persecuted by the tyranny of a heartless capitalist regime which has cast its web across the globe, and which rewards only those who – dazzled by the ephemeral promise of the West – have unscrupulously abandoned the memory and wisdom of their ancestors. No amount of intellectual acrobatics can erase this painful and dangerous reality. We must reclaim our resources, *ourselves*, our Rushdies and others like him.

Majid's piece is thoughtful and carefully argued, so it comes as a surprise that he believes that the 'discourses of orientalism and racism will turn into the distant echoes of a culture that has condemned itself into regression. The West will then evoke pity, not horror.'

Vijay Mishra's 'Postcolonial Differend: Diasporic Narratives of Salman Rushdie' (*Ariel* 26:3.8–45) is a wide-ranging article that takes as its point of departure an examination of Britishness, inbetweenness, diaspora and hybridity. Mishra goes on to develop Jean-François Lyotard's conceptualization of the *differend* and concludes that in the Rushdie Affair 'compromise or justice is not possible because the grounds of the argument are incommensurate. There are no winners or losers in the Rushdie Affair, only the presencing of the differend through agnostic discourses and politics.' Revathi Krishnaswamy in her 'Mythologies of Migrancy: Postcolonialism, Postmodernism and the Politics of (Dis)location' (*Ariel* 26:1.125–46) complains that an uncritical focus on the similarities between postcolonialism and postmodernism has the effect of obfuscating the real historical and political differences between the two. She believes that the 'metaphorization of postcolonial migrancy is becoming so overblown, overdetermined, and amorphous as to repudiate any meaningful specificity of historical location or interpretation', and argues that politically charged words such as 'diaspora' and 'exile' 'are being emptied of their histories of pain and suffering and are being deployed promiscuously to designate a wide array of cross-cultural phenomena'. Her essay focuses on the work of Salman Rushdie and she argues that he is guilty of promoting such ideas. Krishnaswamy warns that the celebration of migrancy and migrant intellectuals is a myopic venture when it fails to differentiate between 'diverse modalities of postcolonial diaspora'.

Two essays that take Chinua Achebe's work as their focal point are Douglas Killam's 'The Interdisciplinarity of Pragmatics and Politeness Theory with Reference to Chinua Achebe's *No Longer at Ease*' (*Alternation* 2:2.5–14) and Neil Ten Kortenaar's 'Beyond Authenticity and Creolization: Reading Achebe Writing Culture' (*PMLA* 110.30–42). Killam's is essentially a position piece in which he suggests that the relationship between pragmatics and politeness theory could function as an 'apparatus for accounting for the dynamics of post-colonial texts whose intention is to redefine and reshape post-colonial societies'. Killam dismisses the approaches of Formalists, New Critics and Reception Theory schools as lacking 'something' (although precisely what that 'something' is he fails to make clear) and he suggests that critics follow the approach he outlines. His appropriation of politeness theory, developed from the work of Roger Sell, who in turn develops the work of anthropological linguists Penelope Brown and Stephen Levinson, is applied, rather simplistically, to *No Longer at Ease*. As interesting as Killam's essay is, it lacks detailed application and depth. This last failure is one that Kortenaar cannot be accused of. Kortenaar examines how the Igbo in Achebe's *Arrow of God* reinvent themselves in the light of the idea that culture has two faces: the first is 'a symbolic system that establishes values and horizons of common sense', whereas the second face is used, despite the variety of cultural meanings attached to symbols, to 'summon a community to collective action'. The second face is seen when 'as with authenticity and creolization, identity becomes a cultural resource'. He concludes that 'neither authenticity nor creolization has ontological validity, but both are valid as metaphors that permit collective self-fashioning'.

Alison Donnell worries that there has developed an acceptable 'model' postcolonial critical response. In 'She Ties Her Tongue: The Problems of Cultural Paralysis in Postcolonial Criticism' (*Ariel* 26:1.101–16) she questions the orthodoxies and prejudices that delimit the politics of postcolonialism. This is an important essay in which Donnell begins to think through some of the academic anxieties that result in 'a major political and intellectual impasse currently facing the discipline'. Donnell sounds a number of warning bells: she detects an apprehension on the part of cross-cultural readers who defer to those critics whose context mirrors that of the writer they read; she is, quite understandably, unimpressed by the strategic preface to engagement that names one's identity ('As a white European feminist . . .') but legitimates as it disclaims. In short, Donnell analyses the stresses placed on a critic's 'credentials' and goes on, via Jamaica Kincaid's deeply ironic *A Small Place*, to demonstrate how Kincaid's text parodies liberal angst through the tourists who visit Antigua, and points to ways in which the critical protocol Donnell has exposed may encumber the readers (and writers) of postcolonial texts (and contexts). Donnell never uses the term 'political correctness', and wisely so, but her discussion pursues the issues that the most interrogative critics of political correctness have begun to explore for postcolonial studies.

Peter Hulme's 'Including America' (*Ariel* 26:1.117–23) is an interesting short piece in which he urges the inclusion of America in postcolonial studies, arguing that its inclusion would enrich the field. Hulme questions the nature of temporal definitions and suggests that the ' "postcolonial" . . . is a descriptive, not evaluative, term' and the word should signify a '*process* of disengagement from the whole colonial syndrome'. In an extension of Hulme's idea, three articles which take Toni Morrison's fiction as their subject deploy, or state that they deploy, a postcolonial theoretical grid to explore issues of hybridity, otherness and agency. The first, Lynda Koolish's 'Fictive Strategies and Cinematic Representations in Toni Morrison's *Beloved*: Postcolonial Theory/ Postcolonial Text' (*African American Review* 29:3.421–38), asserts that 'by ethnicity, thematic concerns, and date of publication' *Beloved* 'qualifies' as a postcolonial text and demonstrates a postcolonial narrative strategy. It is something of an elliptical piece: interestingly so in that Koolish provides a cinematic reading of a never-filmed text, but irritatingly so in that the assertions of postcoloniality in her opening paragraph are never addressed. It is an interesting idea to read *Beloved* according to its visual images, but analogies to Hitchcock and Renais sit uncomfortably with the novel and do not illuminate its effects. The title's specific reference to postcolonial theory is misleading: *Beloved* is read as a neo-slave narrative, a subversive re-visioning of the genre, but there is no theorizing of its strategies and no postcolonial critics are referenced, even in the bibliography. It is an unsuccessful attempt at jumping on a speeding bandwagon.

'The Hypocrisy of Completeness: Toni Morrison and the Conception of the Other' (*Cultural Studies* 9:2.247–55) is much more successful and effective in the exploration of the affinity that exists between Morrison's work and 'a larger global community of postcolonial writers' involved in deconstructing Western grand narratives. This article is presented as the work of six authors – Cameron McCarthy, Stephen David, K. E. Supriya, Carrie Wilson-Brown, Alicia Rodriguez and Heriberto Godina – and cites connections between Morrison and writers of African, Caribbean, and Latin American backgrounds, ranging across continents and recognizing the ambivalence of the writer's position in whichever context. Finally, the six authors focus on the importance of language in representing subaltern subjects and subjectivities across a range of positions. The article is short and in many ways charts obvious territory but, after acknowledging the specificity of Morrison's American context, it recognizes the hybridity and oppositionality to Eurocentric forms and aesthetics that lies at the heart of her work and represents her as a writer with a postcolonial agenda. Nandini Bhattacharya's 'Postcolonial Agency in Teaching Toni Morrison' (*Cultural Studies* 9:2.226–46) is a self-conscious piece. Bhattacharya begins by locating herself, her context and her subject-matter in the manner of the self-revealing but often delimiting strategic prefaces of the kind that Alison Donnell criticizes in her article: 'As a diasporic, postcolonial female academic of middle-class Indian origin, I do not claim a history of racial oppression identical with that of African Americans.' However, the essay picks up momentum once one pushes through the jargon-laden prose to the examination of her role and agency as a teacher in an American university, teaching Morrison in an all-white classroom. The author questions whether Afrocentric and multicultural agendas may clash as pedagogic models. Using Spivak as something of a guide, and S. P. Mohanty and Chela Sandoval's observations on postcoloniality, Bhattacharya reflects openly on her experience of teaching *Song of Soloman*, its demands, her efforts to overcome resistance and her purposeful theorizing of a specific teaching context.

Saree Makdisi's '"Postcolonial" Literature in a Neocolonial World: Modern Arabic Culture and the End of Modernity' (*Boundary 2* 22:i.85–115) begins with a reading of Al-Tayyeb Saleh's *Season of Migration to the North* that focuses on its fusion of styles, European and Arabic, and its disruption of linear narrative forms. Makdisi here uses Saleh as a springboard from which to launch a discussion of Arabic culture torn between a classical heritage and a European appreciation of modernity, and, in turn, between an 'Arabic modernism' and a postcolonial identity. Makdisi provides an overview of twentieth-century Arab history and, whilst recognizing major differences across the Arab states, makes a case for a shared experience of imperialism and the persistence of neo-colonialism across the Arab world. Makdisi sees these circumstances echoed in 'a literature of crisis': in Saleh in Sudan, and Mahfouz in Egypt, for example, whose modernist novels historicize the sense of crises. These, and Palestinian and Lebanese writers, reject imaginary resolutions to crisis but may express hope in an Arab world via its common language. Identifying Arab 'modernism' and comparing it to European and American modernisms, Makdisi, following McClintock and Shohat, worries that 'postmodernism' is seen as a 'First World' term and 'postcolonial' as a replacement for 'Third World': 'After all just as we were all involved in colonialism together, we are now, it seems to me, either all "postcolonial" or we are not'. For Makdisi we are not, since 'postcolonial' implies the end of colonialism and concepts like 'Arabic modernism' posits one of a constellation of positions that seek to understand the complexity of the global situation.

Christopher L. Miller's 'Hallucinations of France and Africa in the Colonial Exhibition of 1931 and Ousmane Soce's *Mirages de Paris*' (*Paragraph* 18:i.39–63) is a detailed reading of Paris's 1931 International Colonial and Overseas Exhibition and Soce's 1937 novel about that exhibition. Miller examines the rhetoric of the exhibition and Soce's use of the term *metissage* within the confines of his definitional idea that 'the dominant ideology of colonial and postcolonial literary creation in the twentieth century has been the politics of identity, these texts [the exhibition and Soce's novel] seem to address questions of political and cultural identity within a hall of mirrors. They stage the encounter between Africans and French as a matter of *hallucination, mirage, anesthesia,* or *fantasm.*' Miller's study of the official literature of the exhibition prompts him to suggest that 'France *is* Africa' (in the context of the exhibition) which aligns with his notion that any consideration of francophone space must include France, since now many Africans live there: 'France, through a strange twist of fate, is now part of Africa.' He also examines the complexities and paradoxes in Soce's usage of *metissage* and suggests that 'recent investments in movement . . . hybridity, and extraneity . . . were already anticipated in the 1930s'.

Amani Konan's essay 'Paule Marshall: A Conradian Praisesong' in (*Critical Arts: A Journal for Cultural Studies* 9:i.21–9) examines Marshall's *Praisesong for the Widow*, and Conrad's *Heart of Darkness*. Konan argues that by employing Henry Louis Gates's idea of signifying we can read Marshall's text as an effort to revise Conrad's predominantly negative reading of Africans as Other. Furthermore, Konan suggests that we expand Gates's notion that black texts 'signify' on other black texts to 'texts signify on other texts'. This is obviously problematic but the real problem with Konan's essay is that he fails to say anything that is particularly new or different about *Heart of Darkness*, so he falls to examining the journey motif and the use of colours in Conrad's text in relation to *Praisesong for the Widow*, the examination of both these areas having already been undertaken by Benita Parry in her *Conrad and Imperialism: Ideological Boundaries and Visionary Frontiers* (1983). Jacqueline Jaffe's 'The Gentleman's War: The Ideology of Imperialism in Arthur Conan Doyle's *The Great Boer War*' (*Alternation* 2:ii.90–105) is a disappointing narrative replay of Doyle's war history which reiterates ideas of war as a mobilizing venture in its ability to unite classes whilst retaining class distinctions. Jaffe states that 'narratives of war' have not received a great deal of critical attention from colonial and postcolonial critics, something that she, unfortunately, is also guilty of. Susan Fraiman in 'Jane Austen and Edward Said: Gender, Culture, and Imperialism' (*Critical Inquiry* 21.805–21) notes how many critics and reviewers of Edward Said's work relish the focus on Jane Austen, and *Mansfield Park* in particular, as emblematic of the European canon's complicity with imperialism. Fraiman focuses on Austen to examine what she sees as 'a more general gender politics underlying Said's postcolonial project'. She argues cogently and convincingly that what Said misses in his reading of Austen is her ironic vision, a vision he attributes to Conrad but fails to discern in Austen, along with the significance of her status as a bourgeois English woman. Fraiman details Austen's ironic rendering of Sir Thomas Bertram and, at times, of Fanny the heroine, but allows that Austen typically uses slavery as a metaphor to symbolize wrongs at home and consequently, as Said argues, elides the slaves themselves, their history and their suffering. However, she notes that Said makes no mention of postcolonial feminist critics whose projects intersect with his own on Austen. Fraiman admires Said's *Culture and Imperialism* and seeks to complicate his reading of Austen, rather than rescue her from literary collusion with imperialist ideology.

Deepika Bahri's essay 'Once More with Feeling: What is Postcolonialism?' (*Ariel* 26:i.51–82) is a carefully written survey of the area of postcolonial studies that takes as its starting point an examination of the definitional problems associated with the term. She goes on to explore the ways the term has been appropriated by various critics for their agendas, but ultimately fails to come to any new or radically different conclusions. Instead, she opts to state that carefully theorized work is being carried out by the likes of McClintock, Shohat and Spivak, before listing her own concerns about the potentially problematic meanings the term has generated when inaccurately and poorly applied. In the same volume is 'Positioning the Subject: Locating Postcolonial Studies' (83–99) by Martina Michel in which she argues (once again with McClintock) that the label 'postcolonial' is dangerous as it allows for the homogenization of experience without addressing the problematic nature of power relations *within* the former colonies. Her project is one in which she offers the reversal of the postmodern fractured subject and celebrates a postcolonial subject formation which she argues is closely tied to the 'problem of defining space, the problem of positioning the subject'. She argues that we need to be wary of defining spaces as this necessarily requires that we attribute identities to those spaces: 'Postcolonial studies need to resist fixing postcolonial literatures to any particular terrain and, instead, to set out to analyze how these literatures acquire meaning in interaction with a variety of contested territories.' It should be clear from this that she advocates a position that is very similar to Henry A. Giroux's idea of 'border pedagogy'. She concludes with an example of how she might teach Kamala Markandaya's 1954 novel, *Nectar in a Sieve*.

E. San Juan, Jr in his 'On the Limits of "Postcolonial" Theory: Trespassing Letters from the "Third World"' (*Ariel* 26:iii.89–115) offers a Marxist reading of the exploitation of the 'Third World' and argues that the policies of the World Bank/International Monetary Fund do little but bolster Western capitalism and promote dependence. In the light of this, he believes that 'the literary conceits of undecidability and indeterminacy offer neither catharsis nor denouement, only mock-heroic distractions'. San Juan sees postcolonial discourse as lacking a space which gives natives agency: 'the revolutionary power of native agency absent in postcolonial discourse may be encountered in the current transvaluation of traditional beliefs and archaic practices'. Sangeeta Ray and Henry Schwarz in 'Postcolonial Discourse: The Raw and the Cooked' (*Ariel* 26:i.147–66) attack Arif Dirlik's 'The Postcolonial Aura: Third World Criticism in the Age of Global Capitalism' (*Critical Inquiry* 20:ii), arguing that he fails to live up to the premises of his title (which they see as suggesting 'an exciting engagement between Marxism . . . and the still largely undefined mass referred to here as "postcolonial discourse"') and falls to attacking the Indian critics Prakash, Spivak and Bhabha. Although they state that they do not want to rescue Prakash, from Dirlik's criticism, this is arguably what they end up doing. Their analyses of selected works by Spivak and Bhabha are quite interesting, but in the end *they* do not provide the kind of reading that they initially demanded from Dirlik. Aijaz Ahmad remains as controversial as ever in his 'The Politics of Literary Postcoloniality' (*Race & Class* 36:iii.1–20), which could be seen as a companion piece to his contribution to *Late Imperial Culture*. Here, he outlines in less detail the earlier deployment of the idea of postcolonialism in the field of political theory, and goes on to argue that its current reincarnation is highly problematic. He also repeats the notion that postcolonialism is unacceptably complicit with postmodernism, although in this essay he does not attempt to say what postmodernism might mean to him. He examines the work of Spivak and Bhabha and concludes that their ideas are more often than not unfocused and in need of some clarification and development *vis-à-vis* Marxism and the global expansion of capitalism.

Victor Li's 'Towards Articulation: Postcolonial Theory and Demotic Resistance' (*Ariel* 26:i.167–89) draws on the writings of the Guatemalan Rigoberta Menchu, Martinican Edouard Glissant and Nigerian Chinua Achebe. Li proposes that a stance of cultural apartheid is symptomatic of a problematic politics of identity, whilst the adoption of transculturation leads to an 'empowering politics of articulation'. M. Keith Booker's 'African Literature and the World System: Dystopian Fiction, Collective Experience, and the Postcolonial Condition' (*Research in African Literatures* 26:iv.58–75) engages with the utopian impulses and often dystopian realities of postcolonial writing. He reads Orwell's *1984* in order to explicate how global politics inform dystopian fictions, but also how 'the individualistic horror of collective experience' that characterizes *1984* and other Western texts is avoided by those African writers who envision the collective much more positively. He examines how the dystopias of Farah, Ngugi and Hama differ from Western models, and how writers like Ngugi are as likely to indict America's global capitalism as the policies of the former Soviet Union. In each case the failure of postcolonial African countries is linked to their seduction and betrayal by global capitalism. He pursues this idea via Ngugi and Soyinka's fictions and Fredric Jameson's theories of cultural production. Edith W. Clowes's article engages with some of the anomalies of postmodernist theorizing: its scepticism on the one hand and apparent inclusivity on the other, its elitist aesthetic and the popular expressive modes it often explores, before turning her attention to postmodernism's relationship to postcolonial and postcommunist cultures. In 'The Robinson Myth Reread in Postcolonial Postcommunist Modes' (*Critique* xxxvi:2.145–59) she reads Coetzee's *Foe* (1986) and a short story by Liudmila Petrushevskaia according to what she decides is the 'defining issue' in both cultures: the myth of economic individualism. Both narratives employ Defoe's *Robinson Crusoe* as the Urtext, but she detects other parallels in the situations of writers in South Africa and the Soviet Union whose commitment to telling 'the truth' results in their being labelled dissidents. It is refreshing to see the critically acclaimed *Foe* read alongside the short story 'The New Robinsons' (1989). *Foe* is the more deconstructionist text and in it postcolonial concerns combine with postmodernist claims more clearly than postcommunist and postmodernist ideas in Petrushevskaia's short story, but the comparison is lively and informed. Finally, Clowes wonders whether the non-communication between self and other that characterizes both texts may be an inevitable result of postmodernism's 'global reach'.

In 'Discontinuity and Postcolonial Discourse' (*Ariel* 26:iii.73–88) Sara Mills analyses a post-South African election picture which features a black man and a white woman sharing a shower on a beach. Mills uses Foucault's ideas of discourse structures and argues that 'certain discursive structures begin to decline or disappear only when they are challenged sufficiently by other discourses'. Her point is that Amnesty International may have unwittingly supplied a cover-picture that may be read in a number of contradictory and negative ways, and she outlines a series of possible interpretations in her essay. Karin Barber in 'African-Language Literature and Postcolonial Criticism' (*Research in African Literatures* 26:iv.3–29) makes a strong case for those literatures that are written in indigenous languages, rather than in English. She acknowledges that 'commonwealth criticism' allowed the inclusion of literatures written in English, as does its successor 'postcolonial criticism', but she also sees that the former advocated that writers had no choice but to write in English, whilst the latter 'eliminates virtually all hint of a choice: the discourses of empire were apparently all-encompassing and inescapable'. She argues that the key culprits in promoting this latter belief are Ashcroft et al. in their *The Empire Writes Back*. Barber provides a detailed reading of the Nigerian Yoruba writer Oladejo Okediji's *Agbalagba Akan* (1971) and *Atoto Arere* (1981), having read them in the original Yoruba. Olatubosun Ogunsanwo's 'Intertextuality and Post-Colonial Literature in Ben Okri's *The Famished Road*' (*Research in African Literatures* 26:i.40–1) opens with a statement by Ben Okri in which he values superstition and ritual, and criticizes 'the linear, scientific, imprisoned, tight, mean-spirited, and unsatisfactory description of reality and human beings'. Ogunsanwo does not engage with Okri's ideas head on, however; instead, he takes critical cover behind definitions of 'literary realism', 'postmodernism' and 'natural supernaturalism' until he begins his reading of *The Famished Road*. This is by far the better part of the essay: Ogunsanwo celebrates the novel as neo-traditional; a creative rewriting of a sociocultural past that combines folktales and legends with broad intertextual references to Nigerian literature and produces a 'cultural interdiscursivity'. Ogunsanwo has no problems with defining Okri as a postmodernist writer but his postcolonial status is rather taken for granted. Consequently, the 'interdiscursivity' so valued here does not quite draw in the terms of Ogunsanwo's own argument.

Kalpana Seshadri-Crooks in 'At the Margins of Postcolonial Studies' (*Ariel* 26:iii.47–71) reads Charles Taylor's article 'The Politics of Recognition' (1994) and Iain Chambers's book *Migrancy, Culture, Identity* (1994), and analyses their deployment of ideas of the 'margin', 'authenticity' and 'hierarchy' to suggest that the margin is the new centre. Although this is a thought-provoking piece, it is ultimately quite problematic. She argues that 'the exploration of postcoloniality from the point of view of the margin (as the excluded and the limit) can be thought of as the realm of postcolonial scholarship'. And, in her final analysis, postcolonial studies 'has no theory to speak of, concerned as it is with micro-cultural and micro-political practices and issues. Unlike other area studies, postcolonial studies has no identifiable object: it would be impossible to suggest that it pertains to one or another area of the world or that it is confined to a period, genre, or theme.' Seshandri-Crooks makes no effort to define what she means by 'micro-cultural and micro-political practices and issues' when it should be apparent, without wanting to make it a new orthodoxy, that postcoloniality, in one form or another, is now a lived condition for much of the world's population. Gwen Bergner's 'Who is that Masked Woman? or, The Role of Gender in Fanon's *Black Skin, White Masks*' (*PMLA* 110.75–88) is an essay which brings feminist and psychoanalytical film theory to a reading of Fanon's text in order to critique Fanon's elision of gender politics. She offers a brief reading of two chapters ('The Woman of Color and the White Man' and 'The Man of Color and the White Woman') and argues that, in Fanon's terms: 'Black women – even educated upper-class black women – cannot make the same claim to intellectual and social equality with white men that educated, professional black men can. Thus women's attempts to inhabit a whiteness that Fanon consistently defines in masculine terms becomes mimicry, a feminine masquerade both of race and gender.' Bergner does not say anything particularly new about Fanon *vis-à-vis* the black woman, but her use of feminist film theory, although underdeveloped, is quite interesting.

Books Reviewed

de la Campa, Roman, E. Ann Kaplan and Michael Sprinker, eds. *Late Imperial Culture*. Verso. pp. 226. hb £34.95, pb £12.95. ISBN 1 85984 950 4, 1 85984 050 7.

Devi, Mahasweta. *Imaginary Maps*. Translated and introduced by Gayatri Chakravorty Spivak. Routledge. pp. 213. hb £35.00, pb £12.99. ISBN 0 415 90462 5, 0 415 90463 3.

Kiernan, V. G. *Imperialism and Its Contradictions*. Edited and introduced by Harvey J. Kaye. Routledge. pp. 218. hb £37.50, pb £11.99. ISBN 0 415 90769 9, 0 415 90797 7.

McClintock, Anne. *Imperial Leather: Race, Gender and Sexuality in the Colonial Contest*. Routledge. pp. 449. hb £40.00, pb £13.99. ISBN 0 415 90889 2, 0 415 90890 6.

Pieterse, Jan Nederveen, and Bikhu Parekh, eds. *The Decolonization of Imagination: Culture, Knowledge and Power*. Zed Books. pp. 246. hb £39.95, pb £14.95. ISBN 1 85649 279 6, 1 85649 280 X.

Young, Robert J. C. *Colonial Desire: Hybridity in Theory, Culture and Race*. Routledge. pp. 236. hb £40.00, pb £11.99. ISBN 0 415 05373 0, 0 415 05374 9.

7

Historicism

SCOTT WILSON

The publication of Edward Anthony's *Thy Rod and Staff*, a history of flagellation, illustrates an odd quirk of recent times. It seems that the more the infliction of physical violence, particularly authoritarian, officially sanctioned violence, has become taboo in the West, the more respectable has become its reproduction in fantasy either as a form of popular entertainment or object of academic study. The term 'corporal punishment' (or CP) is as likely to conjure up, or promise (often ribald) images of pleasure as the anticipation of painful correction. Corporal punishment as a model of juridical sanction has become virtually outlawed in the West, even in the armed forces. While rum no doubt remains aplenty in the Royal Navy, and sodomy a tacit tradition that is struggling towards official acceptance, there has been no lash for sturdy matelots since the 1950s. The civilizing arm of the law has, in some Scandinavian and EU countries, even penetrated into the hitherto sacred space of domestic privacy, and the parental spanking of children, or 'the Solomonic method of child raising', has also been criminalized. At the same time, in the same countries as well as elsewhere, the style and paraphernalia of S/M practices, once the acme of the perverse, has become a constant reference point of a transgressive aesthetic for the chic and the fashionable. I think it would be fair to say that S/M is situated not only in the avant-garde of haute couture, but also at the cutting edge of dissident sexual practices, at the limit of consensus on sexual mores, at least where 'minors' are not involved. As such, S/M is also located at the centre of debates about political freedom, rights and the politics of identity. S/M marks the limit of acceptability, and the law's point of entry into the private intimacy of consensual acts: for example in the recent 'Spanner case', in Britain, where fifteen men were sentenced at the Old Bailey for willingly and privately engaging in S/M acts with each other for sexual pleasure.

While the Spanner case verdict seems to have been an effect of, at the very least, rank homophobia and absolute incomprehension, it also highlights the inability of conventional legal, or moral, discourse to distinguish fantasy from reality. The switch from reality to fantasy in the field of physical violence is surely a good thing and ought to be encouraged. There is a world of difference between fantasy and reality; logically they ought to be mutually exclusive, since the one necessarily precludes the other. Only in psychosis is the world of fantasy taken for reality. Fantasy can, of course, be 'acted out' in consensual games that involve physical contact, but it is still fantasy, still a pretence that depends upon the acknowledgement of a violent reality that it is not. There is no reason why S/M, for example, should be seen as any less acceptable or more violent than Rugby Union; its relation to actual violence is no closer than an international between England and France at Twickenham is to war. Which is to say that a Rugby international is of course to a large degree a *fantasy* re-enactment of war between rival nations; and, moreover, the enjoyment of the competitive (not to say erotic) edge between the teams and among the spectators depends upon the *frisson* produced by the asymptotic proximity between fantasy and an absent reality, a *frisson* that requires that fantasy and reality never converge.

It is a distinction that Anthony's book does also not adequately make, since it tends to fetishize violence and the infliction of pain *per se*, rather than discuss different practices in which the meaning and significance of violence is incommensurate. The book is divided into two parts; the first concerns the gradual disappearance of corporal punishment as a mode of disciplinary or penal correction, while the second, entitled 'The Flagellant Experience', discusses the adoption of corporal punishment as a mode of physical pleasure. While the book is more interested in pleasure than punishment, it accepts that the two are intimately related. The book (which contains, according to the *Literary Review*, 'all you ever wanted to know about spanking') is nevertheless courageous because unlike previous treatments of the topic, most notably Ian Gibson's *The English Vice* (1978), it does not already presuppose perversion or 'vice', nor does it condemn the practice under a specious mask of academic or scientific objectivity. It is instead a vigorous defence and celebration of the history of flagellation. There are two main problems with it, it seems to me, that are linked to the way that Anthony tends to conflate pleasure and punishment. The first concerns its clumsy denunciations of the retrospective censorship of the representation of CP in popular children's literature and reproductions of classic comics like the Billy Bunter books, the *Beano* and so on, by so-called PC publishers and librarians. These complaints, which are certainly justified in so far as one respects an archive, do not sit well with Anthony's 'PC' attempt to characterize the practitioners of CP as an oppressed minority.

For Anthony spanking has been misrepresented as a 'disgusting vice', but worse in many ways, it has also been caricatured as 'a Male Vice, [and] a Right Wing Vice, a Tory Vice – even a Fascist Vice' (19); spanking types being generally characterized as 'red-faced ex-colonels, city brokers and the aristocracy' (19). Given this, Anthony highlights some rum characters to defend. I doubt that there would be many willing to stand up for the right of Lieutenant-Colonel Brooks, the owner of a cruiser moored on the Thames, to 'spank the bare bottoms of the young ladies who crewed for him' (18), or for Harvey Proctor, then Conservative MP for Billericay, to be spanked by sixteen-year-old boys, or for Frank Bough, BBC sportscaster, to have his balls scourged with cacti by a dominatrix (one of a menu of tortures offered in a London basement apartment Bough was alleged to have patronized), but since none of these practices involved coercion and all were apparently consensual, it is probably correct that someone should defend them.

Anthony is keen to 'normalize' the practice of flagellation and his book runs through the most common fantasy scenarios – 'Lord and master', 'Lady with the lash' and so on. Knowledgeable about the rules and rituals, he provides a connoisseur's account of the various weapons of choice, their historical

development and literary treatment: from the humble palm to the slipper,
hairbrush, paddle, strap, cane and birch rod, as well as the various whips, crops
and martinets. The book also includes tips about how to get your own partner
started in the domestic home:

> 'But how do you put it into his mind?'
> 'As a joke to start with. Find fault with him on some account.
> Suppose that he's unpunctual. Then you can say, "Next time you
> are late I shall have to whip you". Watch how he reacts. If he
> seems to relish the idea, if he says, "Oh, you wouldn't do that
> would you?" you'll know he's nibbling. "Oh, yes I will," you'll say,
> "and it won't be a laughing matter, I can promise you." . . .Then
> one day you will produce a whip, or a birch – there's a lot to be
> said for a birch. It stings rather than bruises; you show it to him
> and say: "Do you see this? This is for the next time you are late.
> One stroke for every minute". As likely as not he'll be late on
> purpose'. (*A Spy in the Family*, cit. Anthony, 126)

All this is very amusing, but the most controversial part of the book concerns
corporal punishment as a mode of punishment, both parental and judicial.
While, as Anthony notes, there is almost universal condemnation of spanking
children among S/M 'communities and schools of thought', Anthony is
sceptical about the universal taboo on physical correction. While he says he
would not advocate corporal punishment, he does take a quasi-Foucaultian
view about the non-progressive movement from the judicial infliction of pain to
disciplinary power. Anthony laments the shift from 'naughtiness' to
'hyperactivity' or 'behavioural difficulties', the move from 'the stinging and
cathartic rite of passage in the head's study' to 'humiliating parental
involvement, psychiatric studies and, ultimately, the inevitable banishment to
"special" classes, "special" schools or "behaviour units" ' (61–2).

Anthony also makes a distinction between the so-called 'cathartic' effect of
localized forms of physical punishment and the widespread, dangerous
'sadomasochism' of society itself: 'whether we like it or not, or even realise it,
we are constantly bathed in other people's misery, loss, pain, humiliation and
destruction' (304), from images at home and abroad. Anthony cites, among
other examples, the globally syndicated photograph of a drowning man, 'the
face of a boy in fear of death and about to die', the reproduction of which
was, at best, 'cruelly irresponsible; at worst something a good deal closer to
"sadism" than nearly all of the activities detailed in this book' (300). Further,
Anthony considers that the prurient pursuit, into every aspect of private life,
of cruelty and abuse to be the very mirror of, and handmaiden to, the media's
theatre of cruelty. Public enjoyment is constantly stimulated by the continual
exposure of scandal, the exhibition of shame for huge commercial profit.

It is a view put in a more lurid form by Alphonso Lingis in the collection
Sade and the Narrative of Transgression edited by David B. Allison, Mark S.
Roberts and Allen S. Weiss. For Lingis, in his essay 'The Friends of the Society
of Crime', the anaemic yet no less dangerous contemporary equivalents of
Sade's 'Friends' are to be found 'in key positions in mass media, industry, and
the Intelligence Division of governments' (117). Something like the Sadean
dystopia is already upon us: 'We live in an infantile world where the demand

for equipment and gratifications can be satisfied and any possibility of sexual mutations brought about on ourselves or on others, or racial extinction, can be realized immediately. Our present has swallowed up the future as merely one of an infinite array of possibilities open now' (118). If that were not enough, contemporary society is being driven to self-destruction by the same eroticized death-drive that (de)animates Sade's: 'we acquiesce to the release of the germ of the race into the electronic and radioactive excrement. We lasciviously acquiesce to being disemboweled' (120). According to Lingis, we are fucking ourselves up the arse with a really big dick; things are that bad.

Sometimes it seems, given the continual use to which they are put as an index of all of the wrongs of society and the inherent cruelty of so-called human nature, that if Sade had not taken the endless pains to write his works, someone else would have to. If it were necessary, clearly Lingis would be the man to do it. His work is characterized by the same Sadean combination of satire, fiction and philosophy peppered with highly selective ethnographical detail. His characteristic method is to contrast the hopelessly alienated, shallow, mediatized world of the West with the wholesome, ritualistic vitality of some tribe recently visited by ethnographers. In this essay, the Sambia of Papua New Guinea are offered for the West's admiration and envy. Interestingly, Lingis has chosen to highlight what, in the West, has become easily the most taboo sexual practice. He is particularly interested in the tribe's ritual exchanges of bodily fluids where 'men give the milk of their penis to boys that they grow into men. When these boys are filled with the milk of men to the point that the milk flows into their penises, they will give it orally to young girls, until the milk fills them and their breasts swell . . .' and so on (103). The Sambia of Papua New Guinea apparently exemplify a happy organic community based around the common pursuit of child abuse; no wonder this tribe is so frequently cited in American academic and journalistic articles concerned with the problems raised by cultural difference.

Other essays in the collection include Georges Bataille's 'The Use-Value of D. A. F. Sade', in which Bataille resists the gullible co-option and celebration of Sade by his former colleagues in the Surrealist movement. Instead of aestheticizing Sade, Bataille wants the world to acknowledge and engage with the unruly affects and disruptive energy that shaped the texts, an energy which they continue to produce. As an investigation into 'heterogeneity' and 'non-productive expenditure', the essay is an early exploration of what would become his concern in his major theoretical work, *The Accursed Share*. Also included is Pierre Klossowski's 'Sade, or the Philosopher-Villain'. As author of *Sade mon prochain*, Klossowski is one of the most important commentators on Sade this century, and, along with Sade, he is the object of Jean-François Lyotard's critical scrutiny in 'Libidinal Economy in Sade and Klossowski'. Also in the collection, Philippe Roger gives an account of what he sees as the 'minimalist' politics of Sade, and Jane Gallop looks at some versions of the maternal in 'Sade, Mothers and Other Women'; other essays include Marcel Hénaff's 'The Encyclopedia of Excess', Dalia Judovitz's '"Sex" or, the Misfortunes of Literature', Allen S. Weiss's 'Structures of Exchange, Acts of Transgression', Nancy K. Miller's 'Gender and Narrative Possibilities', Lawrence Schehr's 'Sade's Literary Space', and Chantal Thomas's 'Fantasizing Juliette', in which the author luxuriates in the liberating fantasy of female criminality.

Most of the authors in *Sade and the Narrative of Transgression* are either French or American and Britain awaits its first major study of the notorious writer. Perhaps now that most of Sade's major work has, for the first time, been available in high street bookshops in Britain, this will happen. That Sade has not thus far been appreciated by the British might seem surprising given that flagellation has so often been seen as 'the English vice'. Yet as Edward Anthony attempts to show, flagellation among consenting adults aims at generating pleasure not pain and humiliation. Sade's books are interested neither in moral correction (in any conventional way, at least), nor in pleasure (not even pain-as-pleasure), they are, as Timo Airaksinen attempts to prove, purely interested in pain.

Timo Airaksinen's *The Philosophy of the Marquis de Sade* is a book that attempts to understand and test the philosophical rigour of Sade's ideas, the justification or *raison d'être* of his violence. Given that most of the renowned critics of Sade have been either French or specialists in French literature and continental philosophy, Airaksinen's book is remarkable as a philosophical work that situates itself in the Anglo-American 'mainstream' of philosophy and the history of ideas, yet still manages to take Sade seriously as a thinker. Airaksinen pitches Sade's version of nature, or rather his two versions of nature, and his favoured idea of the social contract, in with Hobbes, Locke and Rousseau. The result is illuminating not only because of the light it sheds on Sade's ironic philosophical ambitions, but also on the fantastic darkness it discloses in the very nature of these versions of nature upon which the social contract is based. At the same time, Airaksinen is aware that there is nothing natural about Sade's system, nor is there anything of it that is dedicated to lust, pleasure or the enjoyment of the good in any 'natural' or utilitarian way based on the needs and satisfactions of the body. On the contrary, Sade's evil is moral in that it is aware of the difference between right and wrong and chooses wrong as a matter of principle, in the full knowledge that such a choice will necessarily bring about harm or injury to oneself as part of a commitment to universalize such harm. Sade's desire and method is pitched well beyond the pleasure principle and pervades every aspect of his texts, not just in their content but their narrative style, making them, for Airaksinsen, so difficult and unpleasant to read: a deliberate act of aggression towards their reader.

One disappointment about Airaksinen's book is the lack of an engagement with French and European commentators on Sade, though some are briefly footnoted and cited in the bibliography. Given Airaksinen's insights about Sade's Kantian morality, it is a pity that there is no mention of Jacques Lacan for whom it is not just Sade that is Kantian, but Kant that is Sadean. Kant's theory of consciousness, Lacan contends,

> when he writes of practical reason, is sustained only by giving a specification of the moral law which, looked at more closely, is simply desire in its pure state, that very desire that culminates in the sacrifice, strictly speaking, of everything that is the object of love in one's human tenderness – I would say, not only in the rejection of the pathological object, but also in its sacrifice and murder. That is why I wrote *Kant avec Sade*.
>
> (*Four Fundamental Concepts*, tr. Alan Sheridan,
> Penguin, 1979, 275–6)

Airaksinen's book broadly illustrates Lacan's point, though it comes from a completely different theoretical direction. While Aireksinen emphasizes that Sade is not interested in pain-as-pleasure (that is, pain subordinated to a pleasure principle), but purely 'pain and disgust' (179), a concept such as *jouissance* might add another nuance to the pain/pleasure opposition that Airaksinen remains within. Nevertheless, Airaksinen's analysis is acute when he rigorously develops the distinction between the (Kantian) *morality* that informs the Sadean problematic and the essentially Epicurean or utilitarian politics that determine debates about pornography and censorship. For Airaksinen, Sade is not a pornographer because his books are not dedicated to pleasure of any kind: 'they do not describe pleasure in its Epicurean hedonist or psychological sense', nor are they pleasurable to read. The mutually defining relationship between censorship and pornography, however, is precisely concerned with the deployment of pleasures and the distribution of the good; pornography must necessarily be recognized as some kind of 'good', as a desirable object, in order for the censor to require its restriction or prohibition. As has been shown elsewhere, it is a matter of historical fact that the category of 'pornography' is an invention of the desire to censor, the particular objects of censorship being indicative of a matter of sensitivity, in one way or another, to the censoring subject. As Airaksinen argues, 'the fact that the censor is a pornographer does not follow only for the reason that he enjoys the material consciously or unconsciously. . . . On the contrary, it is difficult to see why one could not fight successfully against perverse pleasure as a psychological fact' (179). Ultimately, for Airaksinen, censorship is not a question of morality, but always one of politics and power:

> The method of censorship entails an important point: if *x* is defined as evil, and an agent does not reject *x*, he has created an ambiguous situation by refusing to reject something which is undesirable and as such already rejected. Evil facts logically entail their objectionable nature; one cannot claim that there is an open choice in this matter. . . . Since definition is control, and control is definition, ethics is primarily power in this sense. (179)

To push the argument further, following Airaksinen, though the censorship of materials representing sex and violence is purely a question of power and interests, the way that the management of pornography prosecutes those interests is quite complex. Censorship is generally presented as necessary for the good of society; censorship attempts to maintain the social good while restricting goods. The trouble with this is that no one has ever been entirely clear what the social good is, whether it is good*ness*, or virtue, whether it is happiness, pleasure, enjoyment or satisfaction, nor is anyone sure about the best way of getting it. The one thing most people are sure about, however, is that, whatever it is, the good has been unfairly distributed. The genius of censorship is that it conjures up an ideal image the good, of that very good that is missing, *in the shape of the pornography it censors*. It is in pornography that the good is seen to be enjoyed; pornography establishes the good as a retroactive effect of its being fucked, raped, abused and murdered. The absence of the social good, then, the good that no one can quite define, that cannot be located except in so far as it is unfairly distributed, can be explained and justified by censorship. Censorship justifies the withdrawal of the good from the grasp of 'the people' because it needs to be protected from the exploitation and enjoyment of the pornographers, the pornographers who have taken over from the filthy aristocrats, the Sadean libertines or the obscene nineteenth-century capitalists who enjoyed it before.

It is censorship that, in its eternal vigilance, maintains the connection between fantasy and reality, affirming fantasy *as* reality, to produce a pornographic reality. The depressing thing about pornography is that, as a product of censorship, it really *does* construct the fantasy-scene that determines ideas about the (absence of the) good. Put symbolically out of reach, on the top shelves, pornography discloses, even as it withholds, the scene and properties, the objects, that transfix the political, desiring economy of those Western democracies that are dedicated, in the name of the people, to the commercial production and exploitation of the pursuit of happiness, the pursuit of the good.

Tony James, in *Dream, Creativity, and Madness in Nineteenth-Century France*, explores the nineteenth-century understanding of dreams before Freud. Although it is not a work of theory, it might be of interest to psychoanalysts, historicists or Foucaultians interested in the relationship between the madness and the work of literature. While James does not mention Foucault, his concerns are similar since his book is concerned with a paradox, an opposition between Rationalist and Romantic conceptions of dreams and madness. For the Enlightenment rationalist Voltaire, for example, dreams are a kind of madness; they are identical with or analogous to madness. For the philosopher Condillac, however, dreaming can be a creative or problem-solving process, and dreams are seen as the well-spring of literary inspiration (2). This latter view is of course very familiar to the English Romantics, Coleridge and Blake in particular. James looks at medical as well as philosophical accounts of dreaming and their relationship to creativity, and looks at the relationship between dreaming, somnambulism and hallucination. His main concern is with French literature, however, and James discusses some major representatives of the French nineteenth-century canon: Balzac, Baudelaire, Gautier, Nerval, Hugo and Rimbaud, among others.

The collected writings and correspondence of a twentieth-century French writer not usually included in the canon is published in English translation, annotated by Georges Bataille and Michel Leiris, and edited by Jeanine Herman. The work of Colette Laure Lucienne Peignot has been collected as *Laure: The Collected Writings*, and published by City Lights in a particularly hideous cover featuring a pair of stockinged legs sticking in the air. Readers looking for the *risqué* memoirs of some inverted or perverted Sally Bowles will be disappointed, however, since the book contains, in difficult, fragmented prose and poetry, Laure's intense explorations of heterogeneous existence and apprehensions of the sacred in secular experiences of anguish and ecstasy. Laure has presumably been deemed worthy of such a pornographic cover because she is best known as the lover of Georges Bataille, and is allegedly the model of the fictional character 'Dirty' in Bataille's novel *The Blue of Noon*, written in 1935. Since that character existed in an early draft written before Bataille met Laure, this is unlikely. What does seem to be the case, however, is that biographers and Bataillophiles have attempted to locate her, like Dirty, Simone and Madame Edwarda, as one of Bataille's 'characters'. Certainly

Bataille was traumatized by her death, at the age of thirty-five, at his house in 1938 and *La Coupable*, the first section of Bataille's *La Somme atheologique*, begun in 1939, is haunted by her memory.

Another important part of Bataille's *oeuvre* is translated into English this year, the complete Critical Dictionary from the journal *Documents*. It is collected in Georges Bataille (ed.), *Encyclopaedia Acephalica* and Robert Lebel and Isabelle Waldberg (eds) *Encyclopaedia Da Costa* assembled and introduced by Alastair Brotchie, with short biographies by Dominique Lecoq, translated by Iain White. Along with Bataille's contributions to the Dictionary, there are entries from Michel Leiris, Marcel Griaule, Carl Einstein and Robert Desnos, among others. The Dictionary is idiosyncratic, deliberately non-comprehensive and comprised of terms such as 'Aesthete', 'Architecture', 'Dust', 'Formless', 'Museum', 'Mouth' and so on that plot the peculiar interests, obsessions and loathings of the compilers. It also includes Bataille's famous ruminations on the 'Eye', which, as he notes, has traditionally been commended for its poetic virtues, having been the metaphorical reference point for countless lyrical comparisons and allegories concerned with truth, beauty, insight, spirituality, philosophical speculation, conscience, interiority and so on, and yet is also, in some cultures, 'a cannibal delicacy'.

The second half of the volume, comprising the *Encyclopaedia Da Costa*, is an anonymous late surrealist and pataphysical revue, believed to be an assemblage of contributions written in the 1950s by Jacques Brunius, Marcel Duchamp, Andre Breton, Jean Ferry, Robert Lebel and Isabelle Waldberg.

One entry in the Critical Dictionary is entitled 'Materialism' and refers to a conception of 'matter' heterogeneous to its reduction by scientific and dialectical materialism. 'Despite wanting to eliminate all spiritual entities', claims Bataille, materialists have ended up describing an order of things whose hierarchical relations mark it out as specifically idealist. 'They have situated dead matter at the summit of a conventional hierarchy of diverse types of facts, without realising that in this way they have submitted to an obsession with an *ideal* form of matter, with a form which approaches closer than any other to that which matter *should* be' (58). But there are other notions of matter, as Bataille notes both here and elsewhere. As specifically base, matter was associated with 'darkness', or a monstrous formlessness that was deforming of all modes of rational comprehension and systematic knowledge. This is a 'matter' located beyond the idealizations of materialism, but locatable as neither presence nor absence, good nor evil, yet apprehended or experienced, in moments of horror or revulsion, as an utterly alien, exuberant force that tears subjects apart, rendering them continuous with irrepressible expenditures of energy.

Ivo Kamps's edited volume, *Materialist Shakespeare: A History*, also seems to have little to do with scientific or dialectical materialism, being concerned with no other matter than the maximization of student consumption of Shakespeare in the mass academic market. As such, the collection indicates that these days materialism has more in common with Madonna than Marx. Unfortunately, though it is a repackaging of great hits from the 1980s, Madonna's 'Material Girl' is not included. There are, however, very familiar numbers from Paul Delany, Louis Adrian Montrose, Walter Cohen, Alan Sinfield, Stephen Greenblatt, Michael Bristol, James R. Andreas, Robert Weiman, Graham Holderness, Lynda E. Boose, John Drakakis, and some newish tunes from Katharine Eisaman Maus and Clare McEachern that are rounded off by an afterword by Fredric Jameson, in the role of Marxist *eminence gris*, who has the job of saying how good the essays are and how much they deserved to be hits. Complementing *Materialist Shakespeare* is a collection also edited by Kamps, and Deborah E. Barker, entitled *Shakespeare and Gender: A History*. In this collection the role of feminist doyenne is played by Lisa Jardine. She compares the collection to 'the kind of record to be found in the front of an Elizabethan family Bible – key names in the genealogy of critical descent' (325). These names are: Catherine Belsey, Carol Cook, Gayle Greene, Coppélia Kahn, Leah Marcus, Carol Thomas Neely, Gabrielle Bernard Jackson, Lisa Jardine, Jacqueline Rose, Ann Thompson, Marianne Novy, Joseph Pequigney, Phyllis Rackin, Valerie Traub, William C. Carroll and William Van Watson. The latter two Williams are not as familiar to me as the other august names in this feminist genealogy – indeed William Van Watson's essay is not about women at all but about gay homoeroticism in Franco Zeffirelli's Shakespeare films. It is, though, a good essay, and I think I prefer this collection to the *Materialist* one, which, with the exception of Drakakis's essay, is pretty dour. It is disappointing that Kamps found no room for an essay by Terence Hawkes, one of the premier materialist Shakespeareans of the last twenty or thirty years, who would certainly have lightened up the new historicist stodge with a bit of lively wit. But of course Hawkes does not provide handy student-friendly readings of the plays; he does not disclose the material truth about seventeenth-century Shakespeare; he reads instead the twentieth-century ideological uses to which Shakespeare is put. While Kamps mentions this political tendency in some branches of Shakespeare studies, the one representative piece, by Holderness, is significantly about a popular cinematic version, Branagh's *Henry V*, readymade, in video format, for the classroom. The point of both *Materialist Shakespeare* and *Shakespeare and Gender* is spelled out in the section of the introduction that is reproduced in both volumes: 'In keeping with the familiar seminar format that combines a Shakespearean text with one or more pieces of criticism canonical essays are grouped around several plays' (*Feminist Shakespeare* 3, *Materialist Shakespeare* 13). The point of these books is not to attempt to break the hegemonic grip that Shakespeare holds in the Anglo-American academy, not to dissolve the slavish adherence to the author and his work that fits in so snugly with capitalist individualism, property and propriety, it is not to displace the focus of study on to economic or material or even unconscious processes that escape the late twentieth century's comfortable grasp of Elizabethan and Jacobean culture, it is not to make a contribution to a Marxist or Marxist-informed account of revolutionary struggles in the seventeenth century, or to reconfigure the boundaries of literature and open up early modern studies into hitherto neglected areas of women's writing. But even assuming the book contained such essays, it would make no difference because the point of the book has nothing at all to do with its content. The book has been produced for two reasons: first, the reproduction of these already reproduced essays is another attempt to exploit cheaply the mass American academic market. For this reason, it is the sort of book that academic presses are most keen to publish, almost to the exclusion of any other kind of book. But if academic presses would rather reprint, yet again, a famous Greenblatt essay from the 1980s, than commission a new one, the implications for research generally are dire. Second, the books lay down a critical orthodoxy that is inscribed in a predetermined pedagogy. A neat triangle is established in which text and tutor authorize themselves in relation to a safely packaged and historically distanced Bard. This authority is then purchased by the student who takes away Shakespeare as the marker of a certain cultural capital exchangeable in the market determining entry into future corporate careers. In academic terms, the depressing thing about these books is not so much the complacency of their self-affirmed radicalism, nor is it the self-congratulatory nature of their introduction to new readers (essays are not only 'exemplary' in every case, but often 'marvellous' and 'wonderful' as well – 13, 15), the worrying thing is that they mark a limit to academic work beyond which even the editor Kamps cannot see. There is no space left for questioning: 'it is difficult to divine where materialist criticism of Shakespeare will go from here' Kamps asks (13), and then repeats, 'so what is still to be done?' (16), but fails to come up with anything. If these essays are unable to stimulate their editor into any fresh thought, what are they going to do to students?

A slightly different approach to Shakespeare is offered by Naomi Conn Liebler in her *Shakespeare's Festive Tragedy: The Ritual Foundations of Genre*. The title obviously recalls C. L. Barber's seminal *Shakespeare's Festive Comedy*, which in itself is a testament to Liebler's ambition and critical scope, but this is a return to Barber that returns with a difference. Precisely because of Barber's influence, Liebler's title might, at first sight, seem oxymoronic. Festival has been pre-eminently associated with comedy, carnival, pantomime, romance and so on. But it is of course a mistake to subordinate the historical significance of festival to generic literary categories. Festival, as a sacred ritual, traditionally involved sacrifice, death and the playing out of a symbolic exchange with the gods, or with God, a relationship out of which tragedy emerges as a theatrical form. Liebler's book is important, then, since it reintroduces, to critical thinking, both the festive element of tragedy and the tragic, sacrificial, element of festival. At the same time, Liebler respects the conventional generic boundaries in her attempt to negotiate her ideas about festive tragedy in relation to them. Comedy 'recognizes, negotiates, and celebrates the social operations that reaffirm and revitalize social institutions, while [tragedy] discloses the consequence of misrecognizing or debasing those operations by diverting or disjoining them from the structures through which a society normally derives its meaning' (8). Liebler examines the generic differences with recourse to anthropologically informed criticism, and some incisive readings of Shakespeare's plays. The notion of festive tragedy in the Shakespearean canon would immediately conjure up *Julius Caesar* and *Hamlet*; these are indeed addressed, but Liebler also reads *Richard II*, *Romeo and Juliet*, *Coriolanus*, *King Lear* and *Macbeth*. One disappointment for this reader is that the book contains no reference to Georges Bataille, for whom the tragic side of festival was always apparent. Flicking through the pages of the Critical Dictionary, for example, an unlikely place emerges as one of the descendants of the tragic festival that is 'linked to religion in so far as the temples of bygone eras served two purposes: used both for prayer and for killing. The result (and this judgement is confirmed by [its] chaotic aspect [in the] present-day) was certainly a disturbing convergence of the mysteries of myth and the ominous grandeur typical of those places in which blood flows.' This place, where the preparations for the festive meal were made, is known as the Slaughterhouse ('Slaughterhouse', Bataille et al., 72–3). While pertinent to the conditions of Elizabethan and Jacobean theatre, this kind of description, though written in the 1930s, seems remote from the industrialized abbatoirs of the late twentieth century. Yet at the time of writing, the reputation of contemporary slaughterhouses for producing horror, disgust, abjection and guilt, not to mention their association with filth and disease, seems undiminished. Indeed, British slaughterhouses, having failed properly to implement the regulations imposed after the outbreak of BSE, have been imputed with the responsibility for condemning untold numbers of consumers of British meat products to madness and an early death. The British still do not know, as their brains gradually become spongey, if they are about to be turned into a nation of Hamlets, Ophelias and Lears. Perhaps there is a history to write here, or rather a genealogy, of heterogeneous spaces, heterotopias of tragedy and the festival.

In *Textual Practice* Stephen Orgel makes a more conventional but no less interesting contribution to a perennial theme of festive critical concern in his essay 'Insolent Women and Manlike Apparel' (9.i.5–26). Here, Orgel stresses the ubiquity, in Elizabethan and early Jacobean society, of cross-dressing – from the negative identification of masculinity with socially offensive female behaviour to courtly male appropriations of femininity. It is illustrated with contemporary paintings that include a miniature of a very camp-looking, ringletted Lord Mountjoy. This image is accompanied by an anecdote concerning the same Mountjoy, conquering hero of the so-called 'Wild Irish', that finds him returning in triumph from Ireland festooned with feathers, coquettishly concealing his blushing modesty behind a large feathery fan. Orgel points out that Elizabethans identified certain types of beauty with femininity and youth, of either gender, and argues for the erotic interchangeability of boys and maids. Cross-dressing was 'thoroughly naturalized in Renaissance England', 'the only people who found it reprehensible were those for whom theatre itself was reprehensible' (23).

There are, of course, some critics who see this sort of 'naturalization' as repressive or as a strategy for containment. Fitting into this category would appear to be Jonathan Crewe, in his 'In the Field of Dreams: Transvestism in *Twelfth Night* and *The Crying Game*' (*Representations* 50.100–21). Here the resolution of *Twelfth Night* is compared with the sexual and racial politics of Neil Jordan's *The Crying Game*. The romantic entanglements between a British West Indian, an Irish ex-IRA man and a transvestite is criticized as an example of the 'absorptiveness' of the English civil imaginary.

Outside Shakespeare, there is a highly theoretical work on Spenser published this year: Louise Schleiner's *Cultural Semiotics, Spenser, and the Captive Woman*. This work situates itself as a continuation or application of Fredric Jameson's method in *The Political Unconscious* (1981). Schleiner is particularly interested in Jameson's use of the Greimasian square that provides the internal structure of an 'ideologeme' which, for Schleiner, is 'a set of interrelated oppositional possibilities whereby people of competing socio-economic classes and class factions "talk" to each other' (13). The ideologeme that Schleiner focuses on in Spenser is 'the captive woman' which is used as shorthand for an intertextual assemblage of a variety of captive or repulsed or independent or tolerated women that are organized by Schleiner in a square that functions 'as carrier of socio-political legitimation and hegemony' (16).

While there are lots of diagrams, I was never quite sure what, beyond a certain patriarchal obsession with woman as figure and metaphor, the specific nature of the political hegemony this assemblage was supposed to legitimate.

The most 'monumental' historicist work on the Renaissance published this year, at least according to the publicity emblazoned on its cover, is Jonathan Sawday's *The Body Emblazoned: Art and Dissection in Renaissance Culture*. It is a handsome and, unusually for Routledge, distinctively produced, well-illustrated study of Renaissance anatomy. Taking 'anatomy' and 'the body' as its governing metaphors, Sawday's text traces these terms' metonymic associations and transformations in the science of dissection and early modern 'literature', the term 'anatomy' being common to both. Always a rather vague metaphor, 'the body', becomes a convenient signifier for the purposes of gathering up and unifying unruly elements. It functions as a means of categorizing and establishing limits to the human figure, to cultural products, discourse and so on, as discrete yet dissectable units. Often entertainingly written, Sawday's rather gamey style suggests that he enjoyed researching the topic. An unfortunate effect of all the praise heaped on the book, however, is that it cannot fail to disappoint to some degree. There is very little here that is surprising, except the realization of how familiar the metaphorical movements of the body are in the early modern period. Anyone even vaguely familiar with Elizabethan poetry knows that the body is figured as a battlefield, an arena over which various forces, physical as well as spiritual, are ranged, just as they would recognize its characterization as a prison, not to say dungeon, of the soul. Similarly, countless undergraduate essays have no doubt been written on John Donne and the erotic body as an object of protocolonialist desire: the female body as 'my America, my newfoundland', a desire attributed by Sawday also to anatomists who sought out in the depths of a corpse's mortified flesh 'an (as yet) undiscovered country, a location which demanded from its explorers skills which seemed analogous to those displayed by the heroic voyagers across the terrestrial globe' (23). Whether or not it was an effect of cutting up corpses, an understanding of the body in the mid to late seventeenth century shifts from a feudal realm or the unknown terrain of an imperial power, a realm to be conquered, to a lump of dead matter. Or rather, as every student of the Enlightenment knows, the body becomes material organized as a machine. The sovereignty of the body, its conception as a 'realm', as a seat of royalty or sovereign alterity, gives way to its conception as machinic reality, in the modern sense. It is a revolutionary metaphorical shift, and Sawday notes the profound effects such a shift has on the body politic.

Sawday's work with metaphors of the body provides rich material for the sort of investigation Lana Cable undertakes in *Carnal Rhetoric: Milton's Iconoclasm and the Poetics of Desire*, which focuses on metaphor as an agent of political transformation. The type of transformation effected by the affective metaphors of 'carnal rhetoric' hovers between transgression and dialectic. There appears to be a certain sublation involved in the movement from one term to another, from the negated thesis to the new revolutionary synthesis, but this movement does not, according to Cable, following Milton, result from the work of rational discourse. Cable's analysis recalls the Blakean argument about Milton being of the Devil's party without knowing it when she suggests that 'Milton writes a prose whose affective impetus splits away from its rational progression . . . the richly sensuous metaphoric arguments in these tracts actually feed on and derive their energy from the images of those he attacks' (6). Cable's first example is in many ways her most arresting, it is the case of Milton's 'vomitting God'. In *Of Reformation*, Milton compares moderate Episcopal ministers to cooling stewpots whose rising lukewarm scum 'gives a vomit to God himself'. The idea of God doubled up in an Episcopal kitchen vomitting over his representatives is an intriguing one, but Cable stresses its affectivity, as opposed to its satirical, or indeed theological, meaning. As Cable writes, 'we accomplish little by asserting that what Milton *really* means is that the Almighty prefers ministers of strong religious conviction' (9). Such a reading turns away from the affectivity of the metaphor and the complicity such an apparently iconoclastic image has with idolatrous representations of the deity. It is this complicity that, in sophisticated readings of Milton's metaphors, Cable examines. Much of the violence of iconoclasm is drawn from the affects of attraction and repulsion produced by the icons themselves. In so far as iconoclasm is a transgressive as opposed to rational process, it depends upon the continual production of carnal icons. It is, for Cable, the transgressive paradox that animates literature in so far as metaphor lies as its defining figure: it is the 'iconoclastic activity of metaphor that marks the creative impetus behind all literary art – an impetus by force of which iconic high places are thrown down precisely to *liberate* imaginative desire in a propulsive thrust toward the unknown (3); it is in metaphor 'where linguistic affect and the iconoclastic impulse coalesce'. Specifically, it is Milton's 'instinct for forceful expression of conviction [that] leads him indiscriminately to accept forcefulness as a test of validity: if it *feels strong*, it *must* be True' (74). So what was God reading, then, at the moment of creation? What powerful feeling, what unfathomable force of horror and revulsion, caused God to vomit forth the world? Perhaps it was *Paradise Lost*.

Beyond Milton, in the seventeenth century, there is a very interesting collection of interdisciplinary essays focusing on the relatively neglected Restoration period. Gerald MacLean's *Culture and Society in the Stuart Restoration* collects literary historical and cultural critical essays by John Patrick Montaño on Lord Mayor's Day Shows in the 1670s; Andrew R. Walkling on the politics of the Restoration Masque; Nancy Klein Maguire on John Crowne's *Henry VI*; James Grantham Turner on Pepys and the private parts of monarchy; Blair Worden on Milton, *Samson Agonistes* and the Restoration; Stephen N. Zwicker on Milton, Dryden and the politics of literary controversy; Robert Iliffe, on Issac Newton and idolatry that sees Newton turning himself, after the *Principia Mathematica*, into a *fin-de-siècle* 'priest of Nature'; Elaine Hobby on Hannah Wolley; N. H. Keeble on Royalist women's *mémoires*; Moira Ferguson on Quaker women; Steven C. A. Pincus on English popular sentiment during the third Dutch war; Bridget Hill on Catharine Macaulay and the radical response to the 'Glorious Revolution'. While there is much fascinating and scholarly work on view here the essays are very self-contained; they do not address shared issues or open up contiguous areas of debate.

Just as interdisciplinary, but more focused, is Jonathan Lamb's *The Rhetoric of Suffering: Reading the Book of Job in the Eighteenth Century*. This is an excellent, well-written, researched and originally assembled text that is happy to 'eschew questions of chronology or discursive coherence'. Instead, it wanders through the eighteenth century following the circulation of stories about Job and his manifold sufferings. Lamb traces the dissemination of what Louise Schleiner would probably call an 'ideologeme', that is a set of narrative coordinates, a story, that the eighteenth century used to think, negotiate and complain about the disjunction between human suffering and contemporary systems of secular and divine justice. Job, Lamb argues, provided a locus of excess – an excess of suffering that enabled an excess of complaint about suffering: Job brings 'excess out in the open, and makes articulate the agitated and complaining voice of the first person singular' (5). Lamb attempts to identify the energy and power of the complaint, the energy of which fights or confronts law or authority with its own excess. In so doing he offers considerations of Richardson, Fielding, Hawkesworth and the South Pacific, Goldsmith and Godwin, Hume and Bolingbroke, Blackstone, Bentham, Burke and Longinus, and Blackmore and Wright of Derby.

If Lamb ignores, or rather skips over, disciplinary boundaries between literature, history, law, religion and so on, Michael Naas looks back to a time when apparently there were no boundaries because there was only one mythic discourse. Naas looks back to the Ancients, to a time when areas now supposed to be disciplines were largely indistinct, or gathered up into an art of rhetoric, or 'persuasion', that articulated the relationship between mortals and gods. Naas's *Turning: From Persuasion to Philosophy* reads well alongside both Cable's and Lamb's books since they all turn on the difference between the meaning and the affectivity of metaphor. *Turning* is another contribution to the literary-philosophical or deconstructive debate concerned with the 'origin' of the split between philosophy and rhetoric, a split that seems to boil down to the difference between persuading someone of something or telling them the truth. Naas looks at the 'history' of persuasion in Ancient Greek myth as the 'third term' between, or anterior to, reasoned argument and the threat of physical violence – 'persuasion' in a sense familiar, in popular culture, to the Mafia. As neither reasoned argument nor physical violence, 'persuasion' for the Greeks was not, apparently, perceived as a belated supplement to or intermediary between debate and violence, but as the necessary 'prelude' 'to reasoned law and civil debate' (3). Without persuasion, it was believed, the lawless would overrun the lawful; without persuasion, there would be no political space, no reliable rule of law, no stable community. Yet this priority was of course to shift. The book argues that 'by the time of Plato, but perhaps already in Aeschylus, a fundamental transformation had taken place in the Greek understanding of persuasion'. It was no longer thought of in terms of a turning that precedes law or philosophy, but had rather 'become a tool or practice in the service of law and philosophy' (5). By the time of Plato the essential ambivalence of persuasion had been mastered and ordered by philosophy so that good persuasion could be distinguished and separated off from the bad – the good persuasion of the Furies that led to the salvation of Orestes was rigorously distinguished from the bad persuasion of the Athenian jury that led to the execution of Socrates. Needless to say, the book is philosophically well-argued and persuasively written.

Another book that addresses the issue of rhetoric, reason and narrative persuasion, though from a different millenium, is Mária Minich Brewer's *Claude Simon: Narrativities without Narrative*. It is a welcome monograph on Simon, a relatively unread writer in the Anglo-American world who, nevertheless, won the Nobel Prize for literature in 1985. Brewer's readings 'pursue the intersections between the narrative elements of literature and of material, symbolic culture, history and technology'. She is particularly interested in the example Simon provides of a narrativity without narrative, a style that resists the totalizations of narrative. Brewer is sceptical of Lyotard's famously affirmed general incredulity about (grand) narratives, considering that

> postmodern theory was perhaps too hasty in announcing the end of the master narratives of emancipation in the name of nationalism, identity, and territory. It may also have assumed too readily that just because they are plural, decentred, and diverse, all truly 'postmodern' micronarratives of the avant-garde would be free of the legacies and problems of master narratives. Narratives, like cultures, never simply disappear unless they are extinguished . . . such dispersive narrativity is always susceptible of being mobilized into new totalizing narrative orders.   (xxxiv)

This is an intelligent and sympathetic book that situates Simon in the context of post-war French literature and the critical, philosophical and theoretical movements that have flourished alongside it, and provides a fine introduction to the novels.

Fred Ankersmit and Hans Kellner's *A New Philosophy of History* provides a philosophical rather than literary or deconstructive return to the example of the pre-Socratics. This collection of essays self-consciously undertakes to develop a rhetoric of persuasion rather than philosophical certainty. The editors argue that the contributors share a vison that history can be recast as a rhetorical discourse, that representing the past takes place through the creation of powerful, persuasive images which can be understood as metaphors about reality (2). The essays include Nancy F. Partner's 'Historicity in an age of Reality-Fictions', Richard T. Vann's 'Turning Linguistic: History and Theory 1960–75', Arthur C. Danto's 'The Decline and Fall of the Analytical Philosophy of History', Linda Orr's 'Subjectivity and History – Staell, Michelet, and Tocqueville', Philippe Carrard on the *Annales* School, Ann Rigney on 'Relevance, Revision and the Fear of Long Books', Allan Megill on 'Grand Narrative and the Discipline of History', Robert F. Berkhofer on 'Viewpoints in Historical Practice', Stephen Bann on 'History as Competence and Performance', and Frank Ankersmit on 'Statements, Texts and Pictures'. Kellner's introduction speculates interestingly about different histories, noting that 'histories of nature, of the bodily functions, of almost anything that can be named, are beginning to appear, regularly amazing us with the ingenuity of their authors in resituating object after object from the realm of the ostensibly natural to the realm of the historical' (18). But a certain unease is also evident: 'the notion of a congeries of incompatible historical worlds is potentially as troubling as the idea of the universe as a chaotic fun-house where different physical rules prevail in different places' (18). Whether Kellner is himself troubled by this notion, there is very little evidence of a 'congeries of incompatible worlds' in his book. The collection provides thoroughly academic, institutionalized accounts of Western, high cultural topics. It is another offering that provides much more of the same packaged in the name of difference and the new that is unlikely to persuade many.

Another big collection that, in its subtitle, claims to cover history from the point of view of cultural studies is Jessica Munns and Gita Rajan's *A Cultural Studies Reader: History, Theory, Practice*. It is a very big book (694 pages) in a market where big books are becoming more common as publishing houses attempt to colonize the cultural studies coursebook market in the new age of mass higher education. So there is virtually nothing here that historicist specialists will not already have in their possession or have seen before. To a certain extent, the collection sketches in a 'history' of cultural studies in Britain and America from Matthew Arnold in Britain, and Frederick Jackson Turner in United States, to Stuart Hall and J. Hillis Miller who are interviewed at the end of the book and offer their reflections on the history of cultural studies. In between, the areas covered are: 'The Impact of European Theory' which reprints cultural studies favourites from critical theory, structuralism and poststructualism including Walter Benjamin's 'The Work of Art in the Age of Mechanical Reproduction', Antonio Gramsci's 'Intellectuals', 'A Writing Lesson' from Claude Lévi-Strauss, and familiar selections from Jacques Derrida, 'The Violence of the Letter', Jacques Lacan, 'The Mirror Stage', and the first chapter from Michel Foucault's *History of Sexuality*; 'Cultural Studies in Britain' has familiar pieces from Richard Hoggart, Raymond Williams, E. P. Thompson, Germaine Greer and Stuart Hall; 'Cultural Studies in America' has extracts from Henry Nash Smith, Marshall McLuhan, Clifford Geertz, James Clifford and Mary Ellman; 'Media Studies' includes work by Richard Ohmann, Jean Seaton, Laura Mulvey, Janice Radway, Simon Frith and Lawrence Grossberg; 'Race Studies' is represented by Paula Gunn Allen, Gloria Anzaldua, Cornell West, Paul Gilroy, Seamus Deane, Abdul R. JanMohammed and Gayatri Spivak; 'Gender Studies' includes extracts by Sherry B. Ortner, Penelope Brown and Ludmilla Jordanova, and under this section is also work on gay and lesbian studies by Jonathan Dollimore, Simon Watney, Eve Sedgwick and Ann du Cille.

It would probably be too much to expect a cultural studies reader to contain an essay that questions the relevance of the very concept of culture, so for that the reader should consult Bill Readings, 'The University without Culture?' (*New Literary History* 26.465–92). This essay develops Readings's argument that 'culture' has been replaced, as the governing idea of the university, by the empty notion of 'excellence'. This issue of *New Literary History* also contains a reply to Readings by Gerald Graff (*NLH* 26.493–97).

Still fighting the culture wars from the Marxist corner is E. San Juan, Jr, whose *Hegemony and Strategies of Transgression* is published this year. The veteran Marxist and Filipino anticolonialist campaigner provides, in this book, a wide-ranging critique of American cultural imperialism, and reviews developments in Marxist, post-Marxist and poststructuralist criticism of the past twenty years or so. While San Juan, Jr offers an informed critique of postmodern theories, he is much more interested in 'evoking the world of Marxist anticolonialist writers, Fanon, C. L. R. James, Che Guevara' (2). These he compares favourably to current, so-called radical academics in the United States who 'only advance transnational capital's ascendancy for now and throughout the next century' (2). While he urges his academic colleagues to engage in the 'multitudinous reality' (1), it is not easy to see how his own book provides an example of such an engagement with its literary critical readings of Hemingway, Baldwin and McDiarmid.

San Juan, Jr is impatient with the 'culture wars' and considers his 'brief' to be to provide 'a critical analysis and transvaluation of the discourse of multiculturalism and its mirror image, "the common culture." We need to go beyond celebrating fluid identities, hybridity, borderline or liminal bodies, uncanny deconstructive ventriloquisms setting "postcolonial" gurus [such as Homi Bhabha and Gayatri Spivak] as a new breed and so on' (257). For San Juan, Jr, multiculturalism is a demagogical device used 'to legitimize existing class divisions'. While he acknowledges the creativity of different folk traditions, these need to be brought into line in 'a broad socialist agenda, for equalizing wealth and recovering the sources of meaning and self-worth from the commodifying reach of a tendentious, patriotic "common culture" that has now almost colonized the planet' (257). While it remains his project to search for those parts of the planet that the culture of capital has not colonized, E. San Juan, Jr not only risks bringing that culture with him, but also finding that the only opportunity for spending his retirement years in an unalienated environment of unmediated communication is among the penguins on South Georgia.

Books Reviewed

Airaksinen, Timo. *The Philosophy of the Marquis de Sade*. Routledge. pp. 200. hb £37.50, pb £12.99. ISBN 0 415 11228 1, 0 415 11229 X.

Allison, David B., Mark S. Roberts and Allen S. Weiss, eds. *Sade and the Narrative of Transgression*. Cambridge University Press. pp. 275. hb £35.00. ISBN 0 521 44415 2.

Ankersmit, Fred, and Hans Kellner, eds. *A New Philosophy of History*. Reaktion Books. pp. 289. hb £29.95, pb £12.95. ISBN 0 948462 78 7, 0 948462 77 9.

Anthony, Edward. *Thy Rod and Staff*. Abacus. pp. 323. pb £8.99. ISBN 0 349 10709 2.

Barker, Deborah E., and Ivo Kamps. *Shakespeare and Gender: A History*. Verso. pp. 323. hb £39.95, pb £14.95. ISBN 0 86091 458 5, 0 86091 669 3.

Bataille, Georges. *Encyclopaedia Acephalica*. edited and introduced by Robert Lebel and Isabelle Waldberg and *Encyclopaedia Da Costa* assembled and introduced by Alastair Brotchie, biographies by Dominique Lecoq, translated by Iain White. Atlas Press. pp. 173. pb £12.99. ISBN 0 947757 87 2.

Brewer, Mária Minich. *Claude Simon: Narrativities without Narrative*. University of Nebraska Press. pp. 183. hb $38.50. ISBN 0 8032 1261 5.

Cable, Lana. *Carnal Rhetoric: Milton's Iconoclasm and the Poetics of Desire*. Duke University Press. pp. 231. hb £42.95, pb £16.95. ISBN 0 8223 1560 2, 0 8223 1573 4.

Herman, Jeanine, ed. *Laure: The Collected Writings*. City Lights. pp. 156. pb £11.95. ISBN 0 87286 293 3.

James, Tony. *Dream, Creativity, and Madness in Nineteenth-Century France*. Clarendon Press. pp. 304. hb £37.50. ISBN 0 19 815188 8.

San Juan, Jr, E. *Hegemony and Strategies of Transgression*. State University of New York Press. pp. 286. hb $36.00. ISBN 0 7914 2527 4.

Kamps, Ivo. *Materialist Shakespeare: A History*. Verso. pp. 342. hb £39.95, pb £14.94. ISBN 0 86091 463 1, 0 86091 674 X.

Lamb, Jonathan. *The Rhetoric of Suffering: Reading the Book of Job in the Eighteenth Century*. Clarendon Press. pp. 329. hb £40.00. ISBN 0 19 818264 3.

Liebler, Naomi Conn. *Shakespeare's Festive Tragedy: The Ritual Foundations of Genre*. Routledge. pp. 266. hb £45.00, pb £14.99. ISBN 0 415 08657 4, 0 415 13183 9.

MacLean, Gerald, ed. *Culture and Society in the Stuart Restoration*. Cambridge University Press. pp. 292. hb £37.50, pb £13.95. ISBN 0 521 41605 1, 0 521 47566 X.

Munns, Jessica, and Gita Rajan, eds. *A Cultural Studies Reader: History, Theory, Practice*. Longman. pp. 694. pb £19.99. ISBN 0 582 21411 4.

Naas, Michael. *Turning: From Persuasion to Philosophy*. Humanities Press. pp. 298. hb £39.95. ISBN 0 391 03821 4.

Sawday, Jonathan. *The Body Emblazoned: Art and Dissection in Renaissance Culture*. Routledge. pp. 327. hb £35.00. ISBN 0 415 04444 8.

Schleiner, Louise. *Cultural Semiotics, Spenser, and the Captive Woman*. Lehigh University Press. pp. 277. hb £32.50. ISBN 0 934223 36 X.

8

Queer Theories/Cultures

TAMSIN SPARGO

This chapter has three sections: 1. Monographs/Studies; 2. Readers/Anthologies/Collections; 3. Journals.

1. Monographs/Studies

One of the most compelling studies of 1995 was David M. Halperin's *Saint Foucault: Towards a Gay Hagiography*. In addition to offering one of the most lucid and persuasive accounts of Foucauldian theory, prompted by the 'phobic construction of Foucault' which has caricatured the theorist's work and life, Halperin's study traces the ways in which Foucauldian strategies of resistance have been enacted in queer politics and practices. Although he presents a positive case for the possibilities of the positionality of 'queer', '"Queer", in any case, does not designate a class of already objectified pathologies or perversions; rather, it describes a horizon of possibility whose precise extent and heterogeneous scope cannot in principle be delimited in advance' (62), he makes no claim that it is of greater political value than 'gay' or 'lesbian', suggesting rather that endless debates over terminology have wasted time, generated ill feeling and 'inhibited careful evaluation of the *strategic* functioning of those terms' (63). Instead he makes a convincing case for the possibilities of queer identity as positionality and resistance to the norm, rather than as positivity, and supports this by a thorough and strategically useful exploration of Foucault's theoretical and political interventions.

Elizabeth Grosz's *Space, Time, and Perversion* is described in the introduction as

> a celebration of the (re)finding and (re)situating of the body in the mysterious – and perhaps ultimately abyssal – space between feminism and philosophy, cultural analysis, or critical thought . . . an enjoyment of the unsettling effects that rethinking bodies implies for those knowledges that have devoted so much conscious and unconscious effort to sweeping away all traces of the specificity, the corporeality, of their own processes of production and self-representation. (2)

Although I am usually deterred by the conjunction of the words 'celebration' and 'body', Grosz's 'provisional forays into epistemic domains where the neutrality, transparency, and universality of the body are founding (if implicit) assumptions' (3), essays written separately over a number of years, are more enjoyable than celebratory. The volume is presented in three sections, 'Bodies and Knowledges', 'Space, Time, and Bodies' and 'Perverse Desire', with essays ranging in subject matter from feminism and the crisis of reason to architecture and queer subjectivity, engaging throughout with the work of Derrida, Foucault, Butler, Deleuze, Lingis and de Lauretis.

A number of other studies this year explored the position of lesbian subjects and the subject of lesbians in culture and the academy. Claudia Card's *Lesbian Choices* begins with a 'reminiscence' of 'how I learned to speak with my own voice as a lesbian feminist philosopher with a certain set of histories' (1), setting the tone for a highly personal study which explores ethical and political questions about lesbian identity and outlines a model of lesbianism as determined by 'choice', developed from the philosophical work of de Beauvoir and elaborated through a combination of genealogical study and exploration of issues such as violence, consensual lesbian sadomasochism, incest and the military ban on gays in the United States. Tamsin Wilton's *Lesbian Studies: Setting an Agenda* makes a claim, and outlines an agenda, for a specific arena dedicated to lesbian studies. The study explores issues including models of sexual identity, lesbians and feminists, lesbian literary studies, history, sociology, lesbian culture, and lesbians and the state, and presents a tentative syllabus for lesbian studies which would include five major endeavours: affirmation; theoretical critiques of sexuality; feminism and lesbianism: theory and practice; lesbian cultural studies; and the social sciences: lesbian subject, lesbian object.

Paula C. Rust explores the challenges to dualistic models of sexuality in *Bisexuality and the Challenge to Lesbian Politics: Sex, Loyalty, and Revolution*, a sociological study of recent debates on bisexuality in a range of different contexts. Rust's work is based on a questionnaire survey of lesbian and bisexual women and a study of the lesbian and gay press, with an appendix offering statistical and graphical interpretations of responses, as well as Rust's own analysis of the debates and of sexual politics. Bernice L. Hausman's *Changing Sex: Transsexualism, Technology, and the Idea of Gender* examines medical discourses, popularizations of medical theories and transsexual autobiographies in order to explore transsexualism and the broader operation of gender in culture. In so doing she asserts the need to move beyond the antitechnological position adopted by a number of influential feminist theorists of transgender identity and to examine the ways in which medical technologies can be read not only as effects of gender ideologies but as changing the body's capacity to signify sex, so affecting the potential relation of the body to those ideologies.

Moving from the technologically and discursively constructed transsexual body to the plastic body, *Barbie's Queer Accessories* by Erica Rand is an enjoyable, and thought-provoking, analysis of a key figure of pleasure and abjection in contemporary cultural politics, Mattel's Barbie doll. Rand's study covers her construction and marketing, from the improbably shaped, straight white blonde of 1959 to the multiethnic Barbies and earring Magic Ken of the 1970s and 1980s, as well as the 'naked, dyked out, transgendered, and trashed versions favored by many juvenile owners and adult collectors'. In Rand's analysis Barbie becomes a tool for discussing the difficulties as well as the subversive potential of cultural appropriation in terms of the dynamics of intention, reception and resistance which make consumers queer accessories, often both acting as unlikely allies in Mattel's construction of a straight world for Barbie and as accessories in the crime of helping her to escape.

The interrelationship between straight and queer cultures is examined more broadly in David Van Leer's *The Queening of America: Gay Culture in a Straight Society*, a collection of essays which collectively 'argue that in our century, gay and straight cultures are already informed and shaped by elements of each other, and that the creation after Stonewall of a "gay sensibility" is better understood as a foregrounding of sexuality in a sensibility that had long since been presented to (and assimilated by) the mainstream' (2). The essays explore the crossing of gay motifs into straight culture in the decades before Stonewall, the packaging of Joe Orton, the work of Eve Kosofsky Sedgwick, postmodern rhetoric of representation, and the possibility of working beyond the gay/straight dichotomy through attending to minority convergence.

Ken Plummer's *Telling Sexual Stories: Power, Change and Social Worlds* examines the rites and sociohistorical conditions of a sexual story-telling culture, focusing on three main types – rape stories, coming-out stories and recovery stories – and suggesting that attention to the production of such narratives from a sociological perspective might ask different questions to those posed within cultural studies. Plummer's study culminates in an optimistic delineation of a politics of 'intimate citizenship' which moves beyond emancipation and one of whose axes is in gender/sexual/erotic politics, which itself depends on the kind of stories invented about the roles of intimacy within it. Although, as the author acknowledges, this is not a 'sexy' book, its articulation of cultural theory and sociological method is unusually attentive to the possibilities for intervention of both traditions and constitutes a welcome departure from interdisciplinary bickering and misrepresentation.

A number of texts were published by writers better known for their work as journalists. *Homosexuality: A History* is an accessible historical survey written by Colin Spencer, best known for his food columns in the *Guardian*. Spencer acknowledges the limited scope of his study, which includes little on lesbian history and is primarily focused on Western cultures, but his work is informed by the work of a number of critical and cultural theorists. Paul Burston's *What Are You Looking At? Queer Sex, Style and Cinema* is a collection of short essays, articles and interviews by the gay editor of *Time Out*, divided into sections on sex, stars, men, cinema and symptoms, which stands as a useful (and entertaining) record of the concerns and style of one of the most successful popular gay cultural critics. Terry Sanderson's *Mediawatch: The Treatment of Male and Female Homosexuality in the British Media* is a development from the author's 'Mediawatch' column in *Gay Times* which has monitored press coverage of lesbian and gay issues for the past twelve years.

A new edition of Emmanuel Cooper's *Fully Exposed: The Male Nude in Photography*, which combines photographic essay and art criticism, includes a new chapter on the subject in the 1990s, exploring, among other topics, the impact of AIDS on the representation of the male body. 1995 also saw a new edition of B. R. Burg's *Sodomy and the Pirate Tradition: English Sea Rovers in the Seventeenth-Century Caribbean*, which investigates the social and sexual world of buccaneers and asserts that in contrast to regimented and regulated all-male institutions such as prisons, the society of piracy accepted homo-sexuality as the norm. This new edition includes an author's introduction analysing responses to the book since its first publication in 1983 and assessing changes in historical perspectives on all-male societies.

The slimmest volume of 1995 was Chris Woods's *State of the Queer Nation: A Critique of Gay and Lesbian Politics in 1990s Britain*, published in Cassell's 'Listen Up!' series. Woods asserts that 'The once dominant hegemony of gay radicalism is collapsing, elbowed aside by the re-emergence of gay assimil-ationalist politics and the increased power of a new commercialism' (1) and presents a persuasive, if stylistically polemical, analysis of the political and cultural developments which have led to the current state of the queer nation in Britain, from the fraught relations between different groups such as Stonewall, OutRage! (of which Woods was a founder) and TORCHE, and the development of an AIDS 'industry' dominated by white, middle-class, HIV-negative 'professionals', to the rise of the pink pound and commodification. Woods's reading of the development of queer as identity and politics, in Britain, is as 'a manifestation of the insecurities of those who having grown comfortable with the politics of opposition, balk at the prospect of an end to hostilities and thus invent a political identity which has no goal but the generation of contradiction and hostility itself' (29), an alternative to the '"mundanity" of gay, with its utopian ideology' (31) taken up by an elitist minority while the majority 'are making the transition from homosexual to a neutered form of gay' (32). One of the most interesting aspects of Woods's analysis of the phenomenon of queer is his suggestion that it is bound up with the maintenance of a cult of perfection which alienates those whose style does not fit, and of the production of 'communities' which 'are fast becoming mere warped reflections of a wider society we still claim to fight' (60). Although the form of the essay allows a rhetorical tone which seems, at times, to be glib or scathing, in contrast with some other critiques of the individualism, commodification and hedonism of some aspects of queer culture, which appear to be grounded in nostalgia for a remembered radicalism and frequently caricature rather than seek to understand cultural developments that are at odds with earlier versions or visions of community, identity or sexual politics, Woods's study is both uncompromising and attentive. His analysis may be condensed and his conclusions contestable, but this is a timely critique of the state of queer, gay and lesbian cultures beyond the primary terrain of academic theory.

2. Readers/Anthologies/Collections

Performativity and Performance, edited by Andrew Parker and Eve Kosofsky Sedgwick, is a collection of essays from the English Institute which follows the traces of these two key terms in recent theoretical work within a broad range of cultural, historical and discursive contexts. The contributions are: Timothy Gould, 'The Unhappy Performative'; Joseph Roach, 'Culture and Performance in the Circum-Atlantic World'; Sandra L. Richards, 'Writing the Absent Potential: Drama, Performance, and the Canon of African-American Literature'; Cathy Caruth, 'Traumatic Awakenings'; Andrew Ford, '*Katharsis*: The Ancient Problem'; Stephen Orgel, 'The Play of Conscience'; Elin Diamond,

'The Shudder of Catharsis in Twentieth-Century Performance'; Cindy Patton, 'Performativity and Spatial Distinction: The End of AIDS Epidemiology'; Judith Butler, 'Burning Acts – Injurious Speech'. The performative is also explored in *Cruising the Performative: Interventions into the Representation of Ethnicity, Nationality, and Sexuality*, edited by Sue-Ellen Case, Philip Brett and Susan Leigh Foster. This collection presents work which originated in the 'Unnatural Acts' conference in Riverside and comprises: Ellen Brinks, 'Who's Been in My Closet? Mimetic Identification and the Psychosis of Class Transvestism in *Single White Female*'; Cynthia J. Fuchs, 'Michael Jackson's Penis'; Ellis Hanson, 'The Telephone and its Queerness'; Ricardo L. Ortiz, 'John Rechy and the Grammar of Ostentation'; Richard Rambuss, 'Homodevotion'; Katrin Sieg, 'Deviance and Dissidence: Sexual Subjects of the Cold War'; Parama Roy, 'As the Master Saw Her'; Marta E. Savigliano, 'Tango and the Postmodern Uses of Passion'; Jennifer DeVere Brody, 'Hyphen-Nations'; Brian Currid, '"We Are Family": House Music and Queer Peformativity'; Michael Davidson, 'Compulsory Homosociality: Charles Olson, Jack Spicer, and the Gender of Poetics'; Jane C. Desmond, 'Performing "Nature": Shamu at Sea World'; Michael E. McClellan, '"If We Could Talk with the Animals": Elephants and Musical Performance during the French Revolution'.

Sexy Bodies: The Strange Carnalities of Feminism, edited by Elizabeth Grosz and Elspeth Probyn, investigates the production of sexual bodies and sexual practices from a position which seeks to 'ask rather than presume what sex, sexuality or sexiness are' (x). The shared approach is succinctly formulated by the editors as characterized by an emphasis on 'sex' and 'queer' as verbs rather than as nouns or adjectives: 'Conjugated, they could be fully conceived as activities and processes, rather than as objects or impulses, as movements rather than identities, as lines more than locations, as motions of making rather than as forms of expression' (x). The collection comprises: Elspeth Probyn, 'Queer Belongings: The Politics of Departure'; Dianne Chisholm, 'The "Cunning Lingua" of Desire: Bodies-Language and Perverse Performativity'; Mary Fallon, 'Sextec: Excerpt from *Working Hot*'; Barbara Creed, 'Lesbian Bodies: Tribades, Tomboys and Tarts'; Lisa Moore, 'Teledildonics: Virtual Lesbians in the Fiction of Jeanette Winterson'; Nicole Brossard, 'Green Night of Labyrinth Park: La Nuit Verte du Parc Labyrinthe'; Anna Gibbs, 'Acts of Creation: The Brainchildren of Certain Psychoanalytic Fictions'; Melissa Jane Hardie, '"I Embrace the Difference": Elizabeth Taylor and the Closet'; Sue Golding, 'Pariah Bodies'; Sue Best, 'Sexualising Space'; Sabina Sawhney, 'The Jewels in the Crotch: The Imperial Erotics in *The Raj Quartet*'; Chantal Nadeau, 'Girls on a Wired Screen: Cabvani's Cinema and Lesbian S/M'; Angela Y. Davis, 'I Used To Be Your Sweet Mama: Ideology, Sexuality and Domesticity in the Blues of Gertrude "Ma" Rainey and Bessie Smith'; Catherine Waldby, 'Destruction: Boundary Erotics and Refigurations of the Heterosexual Male Body'; Elizabeth Grosz, 'Animal Sex: Libido as Desire and Death'.

Solitary Pleasures: The Historical, Literary, and Artistic Discourses of Autoeroticism, edited by Paula Bennett and Vernon A. Rosario, II, is described on the cover as 'the first book to take masturbation seriously, as seriously as did those who subjected people to unusual physical and mental torture to curtail the "vicious pleasures of solitude"'. It includes essays by historians, art historians, literary and cultural critics. The contributions are: Paula Bennett and Vernon A. Rosario, II, 'Introduction: The Politics of Solitary Pleasures'; Laura Weigert, 'Autonomy as Deviance: Sixteenth-Century Images of Witches and Prostitutes'; Kelly Dennis, 'Playing with Herself: Feminine Sexuality and Aesthetic Indifference'; Roy Porter, 'Forbidden Pleasures: Enlightenment Literature of Sexual Advice'; Vernon A. Rosario, II, 'Phantastical Pollutions: The Public Threat of Private Vice in France'; Eve Kosofsky Sedgwick, 'Jane Austen and the Masturbating Girl'; Thomas W. Laqueur, 'The Social Evil, the Solitary Vice, and Pouring Tea'; Christopher Looby, '"The Roots of the Orchis, the Iuli of Chestnuts": The Odor of Male Solitude'; Paula Bennett, '"Pomegranate-Flowers": The Phantasmatic Productions of Late-Nineteenth-Century Anglo-American Women Poets'; Lawrence R. Schehr, 'Fragments of a Poetics: Bonnetain and Roth'; Roger Celestin, 'Can Robinson Crusoe Find True Happiness (Alone)? Beyond the Genitals and History on the Island of Hope'; Earl Jackson, Jr, 'Coming in Handy: The J/O Spectacle and the Gay Male Spectator in Almodóvar'.

Out in Culture: Gay, Lesbian, and Queer Essays on Popular Culture, edited by Corey K. Creekmur and Alexander Doty, charts lesbian, gay and queer engagement in and with popular and mass culture in a collection of essays that 'develop antihomophobic and antiheterocentrist critical approaches to some of the major forms of contemporary mass culture: film, television, popular music, and fashion' (1). It includes two 'dossiers', on popular music and on Hitchcock, the latter chosen in preference to a gay-identified Hollywood director because his films have become 'test cases' for new positions in film theory and criticism. The volume comprises: Corey K. Creekmur and Alexander Doty, 'Introduction'; Robin Wood, 'Responsibilities of a Gay Film Critic'; Edith Becker, Michelle Citron, Julia Lesage and B. Ruby Rich, 'Lesbians and Film'; Chris Straayer, 'The Hypothetical Lesbian Heroine in Narrative Feature Film'; Al LaValley, 'The Great Escape'; Alexander Doty, 'There's Something Queer Here'; Patricia White, 'Supporting Character: The Queer Career of Agnes Moorhead'; Valerie Traub, 'The Ambiguities of "Lesbian" Viewing Pleasure: The (Dis)articulations of *Black Widow*'; B. Ruby Rich, 'From Repressive Tolerance to Erotic Liberation: *Mädchen in Uniform*'; Corey K. Creekmur, 'Acting Like a Man: Masculine Performance in *My Darling Clementine*'. The dossier on Hitchcock comprises: John Hepworth (with 'Letter to the Editor' by Robin Wood and 'Response' by John Hepworth), 'Hitchcock's Homophobia'; Robin Wood, 'The Murderous Gays: Hitchcock's Homophobia'; Sabrina Barton, '"Crisscross": Paranoia and Projection in *Strangers on a Train*'; Rhona J. Berenstein, '"I'm not the sort of person men marry": Monsters, Queers, and Hitchcock's *Rebecca*'; Lucretia Knapp, 'The Queer Voice in *Marnie*'; Michael Moon, 'Flaming Closets'; Thomas Waugh, 'Men's Pornography: Gay vs. Straight'; Heather Findlay, 'Freud's "Fetishism" and the Lesbian Dildo Debates'; Nayland Blake, 'Tom of Finland: An Appreciation'; Jan Zita Grover, 'Visible Lesions: Images of the PWA'; Bruce La Bruce, 'Pee Wee Herman: The Homosexual Subtext'; Essex Hemphill, '*In Living Color*: Toms, Coons, Mammies, Faggots, and Bucks'. The dossier on popular music comprises: Richard Dyer, 'In Defense of Disco'; Arlene Stein, 'Crossover Dreams: Lesbianism and Popular Music since the 1970s'; Michael Musto, 'Immaculate Connection'; Anthony Thomas, 'The House the Kids Built: The Gay Black Imprint on American Dance Music'; Mark Thompson, 'Children of Paradise: A Brief History of Queens'; Jeffrey

Hilbert, 'The Politics of Drag'; Marlon Riggs, 'Black Macho Revisited: Reflections of a Snap! Queen'; Arlene Stein, 'All Dressed Up but No Place to Go? Style Wars and the New Lesbianism'; Danae Clark, 'Commodity Lesbianism'. The volume also includes a bibliography of work on gay, lesbian and queer popular culture.

Popular culture is also the focus of *A Queer Romance: Lesbians, Gay Men and Popular Culture*, edited by Paul Burston and Colin Richardson. The volume explores debates about the gaze, a new theory of queer viewing, lesbian vampires, mainstream cinema, home shopping catalogues, Monika Treut, homocore fanzines, pornography and 'out' television. The contents are Part I, 'A Queer Framework', including Caroline Evans and Lorraine Gamman, 'The Gaze Revisited, or Reviewing Queer Viewing'; Z. Isiling Nataf, 'Black Lesbian Spectatorship and Pleasure in Popular Cinema'; Steven Drukman, 'The Gay Gaze, or Why I Want my MTV'; Part II, 'Queer Genes?', including Tanya Krzywinska, 'La Belle Dame Sans Merci?'; Paul Burston, 'Just a Gigolo? Narcissism, Nellyism, and the "New Man" Theme'; Cherry Smyth, 'The Transgressive Sexual Subject'; Part III, 'Masquerade', including Gregory Woods, 'We're Here, We're Queer and We're Not Going Shopping'; Part IV, 'The View from the Other Side', including Colin Richardson, 'Monika Treut: An Outlaw at Home'; Bruce LaBruce, 'The Wild, Wild World of Fanzines: Notes from a Reluctant Pornographer'; Part V, 'The Mirror Image', including Anna Marie Smith, '"By Women, for Women and about Women" Rules OK? The Impossibility of Visual Soliloquy'; Colin Richardson, 'TVOD: The Never-Bending Story'.

Negotiating Lesbian and Gay Subjects, edited by Monica Dorenkamp and Richard Henke, is motivated by a desire to turn from questions of identity to a concern with a politics of location. The contributions are: Monica Dorenkamp and Richard Henke, 'Introduction'; Samuel R. Delany, 'Aversion/Perversion/ Diversion'; Sylvia Molloy, 'Too Wilde for Comfort: Desire and Ideology in Fin-de-Siècle Latin America'; Simon Watney, 'AIDS and the Politics of Queer Diaspora'; Marcia Ian, 'How Do You Wear Your Body? Bodybuilding and the Sublimity of Drag'; Richard Meyer, 'Warhol's Clones'; Richard Fung, 'The Trouble with "Asians"'; Eve Kosofsky Sedgwick, 'Inside Henry James: Toward a Lexicon for *The Art of the Novel*'; Joseph A. Boone, 'Rubbing Aladdin's Lamp'; Julia Creet, 'Anxieties of Identity: Coming Out and Coming Undone'.

Constructing Masculinity, edited by Maurice Berger, Brian Wallis and Simon Watson, examines the standards by which masculinity is defined through analysis of representations in the media and the arts, and consideration of masculinity in relation to science and the law. The collection is presented in five sections – Section 1: 'What is Masculinity?', including Eve Kosofsky Sedgwick, '"Gosh, Boy George, You Must Be Awfully Secure in Your Masculinity!"'; Judith Butler, 'Melancholy Gender/Refused Identification'; Carole S. Vance, 'Social Construction Theory and Sexuality'; Wayne Koestenbaum, 'The Aryan Boy who Pissed on my Father's Head'; Homi K. Bhabha, 'Are You a Man or a Mouse?'; Section 2: 'Masculinity and Representation', including Abigail Solomon-Godeau, 'Male Trouble'; Paul Smith, 'Eastwood Bound'; bell hooks, 'Doing it for Daddy'; Michael Taussig, 'Schopenhauer's Beard'; Leo Bersani, 'Loving Men'; Section 3: 'How Science Defines Men', including Anne Fausto-Sterling, 'How to Build a Man'; Philomena Mariani, 'Law-and-Order Science'; Simon Watney, 'Gene Wars'; Andrew Ross, 'The Great White Dude';

Sander L. Gilman, 'Damaged Men: Thoughts on Kafka's Body'; Section 4: 'Masculinity and the Rule of Law', including Derrick Bell, 'The Race-Charged Relationship of Black Men and Black Women'; Richard Delgado and Jean Stefancic, 'Minority Men, Misery, and the Marketplace of Ideas'; Kendall Thomas, '"Masculinity", "the Rule of Law", and Other Legal Fictions'; Patricia J. Williams, 'Meditations on Masculinity'; Marjorie Heins, 'Masculinity, Sexism, and Censorship Law'; Section 5: 'Male Subjectivity and Responsibility', including George Yúdice, 'What's a Straight White Man to Do?'; Barbara Ehrenreich, 'The Decline of Patriarchy'; Richard Fung, 'Burdens of Representation, Burdens of Responsibility'; Michelle Wallace, 'Masculinity in Black Popular Culture: Could it be that Political Correctness is the Problem?', Stanley Aronowitz, 'My Masculinity'.

A Simple Matter of Justice? Theorizing Lesbian and Gay Politics, edited by Angelia R. Wilson, explores the relationship between lesbian and gay politics and the idea, and systems, of legal and social justice in Britain, America and Europe. The collection comprises David Smith, 'The Anatomy of a Campaign'; Anya Palmer, 'Lesbian and Gay Rights Campaigning: A Report from the Coalface'; Paisley Currah, 'Searching for Immutability: Homosexuality, Race and Rights Discourse'; Jean Carabine, 'Invisible Sexualities: Sexuality, Politics and Influencing Policy-Making'; David T. Evans, '(Homo)sexual Citizenship: A Queer Kind of Justice'; Angelia R. Wilson, 'Their Justice: Heterosexism in A Theory of Justice'; Didi Herman, 'A Jurisprudence of One's Own? Ruthann Robson's Lesbian Legal Theory'; Shane Phelan, 'The Space of Justice: Lesbians and Democratic Politics'. Battles and debates about legislation are also a primary focus of Sex Wars: Sexual Dissent and Political Culture, a collection of essays, written over the past ten years, by Lisa Duggan and Nan D. Hunter. The 'sex wars' of the title were/are, in Duggan's words, 'a series of bitter political and cultural battles over issues of sexuality' which 'convulsed' the United States from 1980 to 1990, over issues including the regulation of pornography, the scope of legal protections for gay people, the funding of allegedly 'obscene' art, reproductive freedom for women, and sexual abuse of children in daycare centres. The essays, which are presented in three sections on 'Sexual Dissent and Representation', 'Sexual Dissent and the Law' and 'Sexual Dissent, Activism and the Academy', are mostly developed from collective projects in which the authors participated, including work with FACT, the Feminist Anti-Censorship Taskforce.

Conceiving Sexuality: Approaches to Sex Research in a Postmodern World, edited by Richard G. Parker and John H. Gagnon, presents an overview of cross-cultural research on sexuality. The volume comprises an introduction, John H. Gagnon and Richard G. Parker, 'Conceiving Sexuality'; Part One, 'Histories of Desire': Karin Lützen, 'La mise en discours and Silences in Research on the History of Sexuality'; Jeffrey Weeks, 'History, Desire, and Identities'; Mattias Duyves, 'Framing Preferences, Framing Differences: Inventing Amsterdam as a Gay Capital'; Part Two, 'Gender, Sexuality, and Identity': Gilbert Herdt and Andrew Boxer, 'Bisexuality: Toward a Comparative theory of Identities and Culture'; Michael L. Tan, 'From Bakla to Gay: Shifting Gender Identities and Sexual Behaviors in the Philippines'; Dennis Altman, 'Political Sexualities: Meaning and Identities in the Time of AIDS'; Part Three, 'Gender Power': Lori L. Heise, 'Violence, Sexuality, and Women's Lives'; Roger N. Lancaster, '"That We Should All Turn Queer?":

Homosexual Stigma in the Making of Manhood and the Breaking of a Revolution in Nicaragua'; Barbara de Zalduondo and Jean Maxius Bernard, 'Meanings and Consequences of Sexual-Economic Exchange: Gender, Poverty and Sexual Risk Behavior in Urban Haiti'; Part Four, 'Social and Sexual Networks': Edward O. Laumann and John H. Gagnon, 'A Sociological Perspective on Sexual Action'; Anthony P. M. Coxon, 'Networks and Sex: The Use of Social Networks as Method and Substance in Researching Gay Men's Response to HIV/AIDS'; I. O. Orubuloye, 'Patterns of Sexual Behaviour of High Risk Populations and the Implications for STDs and HIV/AIDS Transmission in Nigeria'; Part Five, 'The Social Construction of Sexual Risk': Carl Kendell, 'The Construction of Risk in AIDS Control Programs: Theoretical Bases and Popular Responses'; Geeta Rao Gupta and Ellen Weiss, 'Women's Lives and Sex: Implications for AIDS Prevention'; and an afterword by Shirley Lindenbaum, 'Culture, Structure, and Change'.

Perhaps the most ambitious interdisciplinary project in the field of queer studies is *Sex, Cells, and Same-Sex Desire: The Biology of Sexual Preference*, edited by John P. De Cecco and David Allen Parker, which reports, reviews and analyses recent biological research on sexual preference. While the most rapid expansion of gay, lesbian and queer studies has been in the humanities and social sciences, biological studies of sexual preference have received little attention except where they appear to endorse or sustain negative popular assumptions. The aim of this collection is to make biological research accessible to those unfamiliar with its terms and techniques, but also to review such work both in relation to the transhistorical and universalizing logic of sexuality which has grounded biological studies since the nineteenth century and in relation to the challenges posed to that logic by recent work in queer studies. The collection is divided into sections, each prefaced with an explanation of key concepts and terms. The contents are: Section I, 'Introduction': John P. De Cecco and David Allen Parker, 'The Biology of Homosexuality: Sexual Orientation or Sexual Preference?'; Section II, 'Historical and Conceptual Background': Rainer Herrn, 'On the History of Biological Theories of Homosexuality'; Günter Haumann, 'Homosexuality, Biology, and Ideology'; Nelly Oudshoorn, 'Female or Male: The Classification of Homosexuality and Gender'; Section III, 'Is Sexual Preference Determined by Heredity?': James D. Haynes, 'A Critique of the Possibility of Genetic Inheritance of Homosexual Orientation'; Terry R. McGuire, 'Is Homosexuality Genetic? A Critical Review and Some Suggestions'; Mildred Dickemann, 'Wilson's Panchreston: The Inclusive Fitness Hypothesis of Sociobiology Re-Examined'; Debra Salais and Robert B. Fischer, 'Sexual Preference and Altruism'; James D. Weinrich, 'Biological Research on Sexual Orientation: A Critique of the Critics'; Section IV, 'Is Sexual Preference Determined by Hormones?': Anne Fausto-Sterling, 'Animal Models for the Development of Human Sexuality: A Critical Evaluation'; Louis J. G. Gooren, 'Biomedical Concepts of Homosexuality: Folk Belief in a White Coat'; Amy Banks and Nanette K. Gartrell, 'Hormones and Sexual Orientation: A Questionable Link'; Gunter Schmidt and Ulrich Clement, 'Does Peace Prevent Homosexuality?'; Section V, 'Is Sexual Preference Determined By the Brain?': D. F. Swaab, L. J. G. Gooren and M. A. Hofman, 'Brain Research, Gender, and Sexual Orientation'; William Byne, 'Science and Belief: Psychobiological Research on Sexual Orientation'; Ruth G. Doell, 'Sexuality in the Brain';

Section VI, 'Mislabelling, Social Stigma, Science, and Medicine': Paul H. Van
Wyk and Chrisann S. Geist, 'Biology of Bisexuality: Critique and Obser-
vations'; John A. Hamill, 'Dexterity and Sexuality: Is There a Relationship?';
Daniel C. Tsang, 'Policing "Perversions": Depo-Provera and John Money's
New Sexual Order'; and a conclusion by David Allen Parker and John P. De
Cecco, 'Sexual Expression: A Global Perspective'.

   Lesbian Erotics, edited by Karla Jay, addresses the questions 'What exactly
qualifies as lesbian sex?', 'What is the relationship, if any, between lesbian
erotica and heterosexual pornography?', and examines the cultural production
of sexually charged images of lesbians in film, law, literature and popular
culture. The volume comprises an editor's introduction, 'On Slippery Ground:
An Introduction' and three parts. Part I, 'Reading/Writing/Teaching the
Lesbian Body', includes Marny Hall, 'Not Tonight, Dear, I'm Deconstructing
a Headache: Confessions of a Lesbian Sex Therapist'; Ruthann Robson,
'Pedagogy, Jurisprudence, and Finger-Fucking: Lesbian Sex in a Law School
Classroom'; Anna Livia, 'Tongues or Fingers'; Elizabeth Meese and Sandy
Huss, 'Give Joan Chen my Number Anytime'; Donna Allegra, 'Between the
Sheets: My Sex Life in Literature'. Part II, 'Qu(e)eries into People, Theories,
and Deeds', includes S. Elaine Craghead, 'Camille Paglia and the Problematics
of Sexuality and Subversion'; Colleen Lamos, 'Taking on the Phallus'; Ann
Cvetkovich, 'Recasting Receptivity: Femme Sexualities'; Jennifer Travis, 'Clits
in Court: *Salome*, Sodomy, and the Lesbian "Sadist"'; Anna Marie Smith,
'The Regulation of Lesbian Sexuality through Erasure: The Case of Jennifer
Saunders'. Part III, 'Lesbian Erotics in Film and Literature', includes Karin
Quimby, '*She Must Be Seeing Things* Differently: The Limits of Butch/
Femme'; Ronie Burns, '*Dracula's Daughter*: Cinema, Hypnosis, and the Erotics
of Lesbianism'; Sharon P. Holland, 'Abrotica: The Lesbian Erotic and the
Erotic Abject in Anaïs Nin's *House of Incest*'; Jane Garrity, 'Encoding
Bi-Location: Sylvia Townsend Warner and the Erotics of Dissimulation'.

   The practices of lesbian and queer film-making, from directing to
spectatorship, are the focus of *Immortal, Invisible: Lesbians and the Moving
Image*, edited by Tamsin Wilton. The collection comprises Tamsin Wilton,
'Introduction: On Invisibility and Mortality'; Cindy Patton, 'What is a Nice
Lesbian Like You Doing in a Film Like This?'; Julia Knight, 'The Meaning of
Treut?'; Hilary Hinds, '*Oranges are not the Only Fruit*: Reaching Audiences
Other Lesbian Texts Cannot Reach'; Louise Allen, '*Salmonberries*: Consuming
kd lang'; Susan Ardill and Sue O'Sullivan, 'Sex in the Summer of '88'; Jackie
Stacey, '"If You Don't Play, You Can't Win": *Desert Hearts* and the Lesbian
Romance Film'; Penny Florence, 'Portrait of a Production'; Lizzie Thynne,
'The Space Between: Daughters and Lovers in *Anne Trister*'; Tamsin Wilton,
'On not Being Lady Macbeth: Some (Troubled) Thoughts on Lesbian
Spectatorship'; Paula Graham, 'Girl's Camp? The Politics of Parody'; Jocelyn
Robson and Beverley Zalcock, 'Looking at *Pumping Iron II: The Women*'; Ros
Jennings, 'Desire and Design – Ripley Undressed'; 'Visible Mortals: Andrea
Weiss and Greta Schiller' interviewed by Nazreen Memon.

   Professions of Desire, edited by George E. Haggerty and Bonnie
Zimmerman, addresses issues concerning lesbian and gay studies in the
undergraduate classroom. The collection is divided into four sections. Part 1,
'Teaching Positions', includes George E. Haggerty, '"Promoting Homosexuality" in the Classroom'; Joseph Litvak, 'Pedagogy and Sexuality'; Joseph

Chadwick, 'Toward an Antihomophobic Pedagogy'; Sue-Ellen Case, 'The Student and the Strap: Authority and Seduction in the Class(room)'. Part 2, 'Canons and Closets', includes Lillian Federman, 'What is Lesbian Literature? Forming a Historical Canon'; Stephen Orgel, 'Teaching the Postmodern Renaissance'; Karla Jay, 'Lesbian Modernism: (Trans)Forming the ©Anon'; Cheryl Clarke, 'Race, Homosocial Desire, and "Mammon" in *Autobiography of an Ex-Coloured Man*'; Paula Bennett, 'Lesbian Poetry in the United States, 1890–1990: A Brief Overview'. Part 3, 'Sameness and Differences', includes David Róman, 'Teaching Differences: Theory and Practice in a Lesbian and Gay Studies Seminar'; Yvonne Yarbro-Bejarano, 'Expanding the Categories of Race and Sexuality in Lesbian and Gay Studies'; Earl Jackson, Jr, 'Explicit Instruction: Teaching Gay Male Sexuality in Literature Classes'; Marilyn R. Farwell, 'The Lesbian Narrative: "The Pursuit of the Inedible by the Unspeakable"'; Gregory W. Bredbeck, 'Anal/yzing the Classroom: On the Impossibility of a Queer Pedagogy'. Part 4, 'Transgressing Subjects', includes Jeffrey Nunokawa, 'The Disappearance of the Homosexual in *The Picture of Dorian Gray*'; Eve Kosofsky Sedgwick, 'Tales of the Avunculate: Queer Tutelage in *The Importance of Being Earnest*'; Phillip Brian Harper, 'Private Affairs: Race, Sex, Property, and Persons'; Michael Moon, 'Memorial Rags'.

Defiant Desire: Gay and Lesbian Lives in South Africa, edited by Mark Gevisser and Edwin Cameron, combines testimony from those involved in the history of lesbian and gay activism in South Africa with analysis, focusing on the intersection of issues of sexuality and race. The collection comprises six sections. Section One, 'Overviews', includes Mark Gevisser and Edwin Cameron, 'Defiant Desire'; Mark Gevisser, 'A Different Fight for Freedom: A History of South African Lesbian and Gay Organisation from the 1950s to the 1990s'. Section Two, 'Where We Stand: Moffies and the Laager', includes Edwin Cameron, '"Unapprehended Felons": Gays and Lesbians and the Law in South Africa'; Glen Retief, 'Keeping Sodom out of the Laager: State Repression of Homosexuality in Apartheid South Africa'. Section Three, 'Making Space: Queer Societies', includes Dhianaraj Chetty, 'A Drag at Madame Costello's: Cape Moffie Life and the Popular Press in the 1950s and 1960s'; 'Lesbian Gangster: The Gertie Williams Story' (excerpted from *Golden City Post and Drum* by Dhianaraj Chetty); Peter Galli and Luis Rafael, 'Johannesburg's "Health Clubs": Places of Erotic Langour or Prison-Houses of Desire?'; Jack Lewis and François Loots, '"Moffies en Manvroue": Gay and Lesbian Life Histories in Contemporary Cape Town'; Hugh McLean and Linda Ngcobo, 'Abangibhamayo bathi ngimnandi (Those Who Fuck Me Say I'm Tasty): Gay Sexuality in Reef Townships'; 'Five Women: Black Lesbian Life on the Reef' (as told to Tanya Chan Sam); Vera Vimbela with Mike Oliver, 'Climbing on her Shoulders: An Interview with Umtata's "First Lesbian"'; Neil Miller, 'Going Underground: A Visit to Gay Welkom'; Julia Beffon, 'Wearing the Pants: Butch/Femme roleplaying in Lesbian Relationships'. Section Four, 'Making Noise: Queer Cultural Forms', includes Matthew Krouse, 'The Arista Sisters, September 1984: A Personal Account of Army Drag'; Gerrit Olivier, 'From Ada to Zelda: Notes on Gays and Language in South Africa'; Gerry Davidson and Ron Nerio, 'Exit: Gay Publishing in South Africa'; Shaun de Waal, 'A Thousand Forms of Love: Representations of Homosexuality in South African Literature'. Section Five, 'Making Waves: Lesbian and Gay Activism', includes Simon Nkoli, 'Wardrobes: Coming Out

as a Black Gay Activist in South Africa'; Ivan Toms, 'Ivan Toms is a Fairy?:
The South African Defence Force, the End Conscription Campaign, and Me';
Hein Kleinbooi, 'Identity Crossfire: On Being a Black Gay Student Activist';
Derrick Fine and Julia Nicol, 'The Lavender Lobby: Working for Lesbian and
Gay Rights within the Liberation Movement'; Mark Gevisser and Graeme
Reid, 'Pride or Protest?: Drag Queens, Comrades, and the Lesbian and Gay
Pride March'; Rachel Holmes, '"White Rapists Made Coloureds (and
Homosexuals)": The Winnie Mandela Trial and the Politics of Race and
Sexuality'; Mary Armour and Sheila Lapinsky, '"Lesbians in Love and
Compromising Situations": Lesbian Feminist Organising in the Western Cape';
John V. Pegge, 'Living with Loss in the Best Way We Know How: AIDS and
Gay Men in Cape Town'; Digby Ricci, 'Of Gay Rights and the Pitfalls of the
"PC": A Polemic'. Section Six, 'Testaments', includes Koos Prinsloo, 'Promise
You'll Tell No-One: A Memoir'; Zackie Achmat, 'My Childhood as an Adult
Molester: A Salt River Moffie'; Neville John, '"Pretended Families": On Being
a Gay Parent'; Anne Mayne, 'In Memory of Rocky: An Obituary'.

The cover notes of *Mapping Desire: Geographies of Sexualities*, edited by
David Bell and Gill Valentine, make a tantalizing, and presumably tongue-
in-cheek, claim: 'discover the truth about sex in the city (and the country)'. As
the image of a gilded navel (presumably not Freud's) on the cover might
suggest this discovery may be only an alluring prospect, but *Mapping Desire*,
while it may not present the truth, takes lesbian/gay/queer analysis into a new
territory which is well worth exploring. The volume analyses geographies of
sexualities, the spaces of sex and the sexes of space, across Europe, America,
Africa, Australasia, the Pacific and the imaginary, deploying a range of
theoretical and empirical approaches. It is divided into four sections. Section
One, 'Cartographies/Identities', comprises Julia Cream, 'Re-Solving Riddles:
The Sexed Body'; Clare Hemmings, 'Locating Bisexual Identities: Discourses
of Bisexuality and Contemporary Feminist Theory'; Glen Elder, 'Of Moffies,
Kaffirs and Perverts: Male Homosexuality and the Discourse of Moral Order
in the Apartheid State'; Alison Murray, 'Femme on the Streets, Butch in the
Sheets (A Play on Whores)'; Linda McDowell, 'Body Work: Heterosexual
Gender Performances in City Workplaces'. Section Two, 'Sexualised Spaces':
Global/Local, comprises Lynda Johnston and Gill Valentine, 'Wherever I Lay
My Girlfriend, That's My Home: The Performance and Surveillance of
Lesbian Identities in Domestic Environments'; Sally Munt, 'The Lesbian
Flâneur'; Gregory Woods, 'Fantasy Islands: Popular Topographies of
Marooned Masculinity'; Lawrence Knopp, 'Sexuality and Urban Space: A
Framework for Analysis'. Section Three, 'Sexualised Places: Local/Global',
comprises Tamar Rothenberg, '"And She Told Two Friends": Lesbians
Creating Urban Social Space'; Jon Binnie, 'Trading Places: Consumption,
Sexuality and the Production of Queer Space'; Jerry Lee Kramer, 'Bachelor
Farmers and Spinsters: Gay and Lesbian Identities and Communities in Rural
North Dakota'; Angie Hart, '(Re)Constructing a Spanish Red-Light District:
Prostitution, Space and Power'. Section Four, 'Sites of Resistance', comprises
David Woodhead, '"Surveillant Gays": HIV, Space and the Constitution of
Identities'; Michael Brown, 'Sex, Scale and the "New Urban Politics":
HIV-Prevention Strategies from Yaletown, Vancouver'; Tracey Skelton,
'"Boom, Bye, Bye": Jamaican Ragga and Gay Resistance'; Tim Davis, 'The
Diversity of Queer Politics and the Redefinition of Sexual Identity and

Community in Urban Spaces'; David Bell, 'Perverse Dynamics, Sexual Citizenship and the Transformation of Intimacy'.

3. Journals

As is now customary, many special issues of a number of journals were dedicated to this topic. *Genders 21: Forming and Reforming Identity*, edited by Carol Siegel and Ann Kibbey, included a number of relevant essays including Mrinalini Sinha, 'Nationalism and Respectable Sexuality in India', Jonathan C. Lang, 'Some Perversions of Pastoral: Or Tourism in Gide's *L'Immoraliste*', Albert Rouzie, 'The Dangers of (D)alliance: Power, Homosexual Desire, and Homophobia in Marlowe's *Edward II*', Kate Cummings, 'Nasty Broads and Tender Bitches: The Televising of AIDS Mothers We Love (to Hate)', and Carol Siegel, 'Compulsory Heterophobia: The Aesthetics of Seriousness and the Production of Homophobia'. *Index on Censorship* 24:i, edited by Ursula Owen, was entitled 'Gay's the Word in Moscow', and included personal accounts, fiction and analysis of gay experience in the Soviet Union, with contributions by Alberto Manguel, Andrew Graham-Yooll, Zufar Gareev, Alexander Shatalov, Gennady Trifanov, Yevgeny Kharitonov, Sofia Parnok, Yaroslav Mogulin, Ryurik Ivnev, Elizabeth Wilson, Emma Donaghue, Lionel Blue, Scott Long, Masok, Paul Bailey, Radu Afrim and Edmund White.

An issue of *Radical History Review* entitled 'The Queer Issue: New Visions of America's Lesbian and Gay Past' comprised feature articles: Martha M. Umphrey, 'The Trouble with Harry Thaw'; Donna Penn, 'Queer: Theorizing Politics and History'; Henry Abelove, 'The Queering of Lesbian/Gay History'; Elizabeth Lapovsky Kennedy, 'Telling tales: Oral History and the Construction of Pre-Stonewall Lesbian History'; John D'Emilio, 'Homophobia and the Trajectory of Postwar American Radicalism: The Case of Bayard Rustin'; Terence Kissack, 'Freaking Fag Revolutionaries: New York's Gay Liberation Front, 1969–1971'; David Harley Serlin, 'Christine Jorgensen and the Cold War Closet'; John Howard, 'The Library, the Park, and the Pervert: Public Space and Homosexual Encounter in Post-World War II Atlanta'; a section on public history: Lisa Duggan, '"Becoming Visible: The Legacy of Stonewall," New York Public Library, June 18–September 24, 1994'; Kevin Murphy, 'Walking the Queer City'; and a section on teaching radical history: Van Gosse and Priscilla Murolo, 'Introductory Comments'; Geeta Patel, 'Crosscultural Sexuality'; Dagmar Herzog, 'Topics in the History of Sexuality: 19th- and 20th-Century Europe'; Nikhil Pal Singh, 'Sex and Sexuality in the US since 1800'; George Chauncey, 'The Social History of American Sexual Subcultures'.

The 'Gay Lives?' volume of *Critical Quarterly* (37:iii), with criticism edited by David Trotter, is described as motivated by 'the outing of outing as a political practice . . . which raises any number of questions about the relation between inner and outer, private and public, inclination and consequence' and by 'the proliferation of queer theory within English studies (1). The articles are Suzanne Rait, 'Charlotte Mew and May Sinclair: A Love-Song'; Peter Swaab, 'Hopkins and the Pushed Peach'; Philip Horne, 'Henry James: The Master and the "Queer Affair" of "The Pupil"' (discussed in detail below); Kasia Boddy, 'Conversation with Dennis Cooper'.

Individual articles reflected the diversity of work in this field. Bradd Epps's 'Proper Conduct: Reinaldo Arenas, Fidel Castro, and the Politics of Homosexuality' (*Journal of the History of Sexuality* 6:ii.231–83) contributes to the growing body of work which attends to the historical and cultural specificity of particular constructions of homosexuality and homosexual identities and practices through a careful reading of the construction in Cuba of 'a homosexuality of performance and appearance, in which positionality is the dominant, or most visible, mark' (233). Epps combines social history, psychoanalytic theory and poetics in an impressive essay which is as attentive to the implications of the theoretical models deployed as to the specificity of its historical and cultural focus and which subtly builds a compelling reading of desire and of writing.

In the same volume, Shannon Bell's '"Pictures Don't Lie. Pictures Tell it All"' challenges Canadian obscenity legislation in the wake of the 'child' pornography scare and Butler Decision of 1992 by interrogating the relationship between philosophy and pornography and suggesting the possibility of 'pornosophy: a strategy of conscious porn resistance through representation (thoughts, words, and images) of lesbian, sadomasochistic, and youth sexualities' (285). A more traditional approach is taken in Patricia Duncker's "Bonne Excitation, Orgasme Assuré': The Representation of Lesbianism in Contemporary French Pornography' which presents a familiar reading of the representation of a contained and confined form of lesbianism within mainstream pornography (*Journal of Gender Studies* 4:i.5–15).

Jonathan Dollimore's 'Sex and Death' (*Textual Practice* 9:i.27–53) explores the inseparability of homosexuality and death in homophobic representations of AIDS, and, more disturbingly, in apparently positive representations of homosexual culture, in which 'homoerotic desire is construed as death-driven, death-desiring, and death-dealing' (27). In response to texts by Oscar Moore, John Rechy, James Baldwin and Michael Rumaker, among others, Dollimore rejects the temptation to read the association of desire and death in gay writing as the result of internalized homophobia, locating it instead as an example of the established dynamic of Western culture, a dynamic which is 'crucial in the formation of the western subject, and in its (our) gendering, and its (our) fantasy life' (36). This, by now conventional, reading is developed through an examination of work by Leo Bersani, Bataille, Foucault and Barthes, into a subtle examination of the tensions between the desire for unity and the drive to undifferentiation.

Lynda Hart's 'Blood, Piss, and Tears: The Queer Real' (*Textual Practice* 9:i.55–66) explores the 'uncommon concern and unselfconscious new naiveté about representation' (57) elicited by S/M performances by queer artists such as Ron Athey and Anna Munster which have repeatedly provoked demands to know whether the 'scenes' enacted are 'real'. Arguing that S/M sexuality is permeated with theatrical rhetoric, that it is about *doing* whereas 'straight' sex is about *having*, Hart explores the challenges posed by S/M to the distinction between the 'real' and the 'performed'. She develops a reading of lesbian S/M which recalls aspects of Dollimore's analysis, 'Accepting that we are always already in representation, even when we are enacting our most private experience, the lesbian sado-masochist is aroused by the dialectic of appearance/disappearance and the pleasurable suffering that constitutes the persistent failure to master its implacable necessity' (60), and connects this with the dialectic of forgetting and remembering one's self in performance. Hart's argument that S/M sexuality 'pushes hard against the referent that feminism needs to make its truth claims' is balanced by an acknowledgement that it too 'longs for a referent, something that provides an anchor, or ground, beyond representation' (62). Lesbian S/M, in particular, is seen as searching, like Artaud, for a scene which is not haunted by the father, a desire which Hart suggests would be shared by most feminists. Hart's analysis ends not with an attempt to find common ground(ing) for S/M and feminism but with a brief, theoretical and lyrical, reading of performance and temporality. In this reading the transformative potential, as well as the eroticism, of S/M is located not in any ultimate appeal to the 'truth' of the experience, but in its striving to hold, 'while forever failing to capture, lovers mingled in that tense more impossible than the future anterior – the present, where they are suspended together (64).

Questions about the subversive potential of queer and S/M practices are also the spur to Bruce R. Smith's 'Rape, Rap, Rupture, Rapture: R-rated Futures on the Global Market' (*Textual Practice* 9:iii.421–44). In an attempt to identify the reasons why '(homo)sex and violence come together in just the way they do now' (424), Smith examines philological, physiological, legal, sociopolitical and psychological reasons within early-modern and contemporary cultures. He explores, among other things, the ambiguities of early-modern English meanings of 'rape' and 'ravish', and asserts that in the period forced sexual intercourse was only a species within the genus of violent aggression. Smith identifies forms of rape in *Edward II*, *Troilus and Cressida*, *Coriolanus* and *Sejanus* which can be read as enacting a violent punishment in kind on the bodies of men who 'have in some way entered publicly into homoerotic transactions' (424), suggesting that the psychological pleasure in conflating homoerotic desire of the spectator who identifies with the object and pleasure may subvert, rather than simply internalize or strengthen, the forces which would control or police.

In 'The New Queer Narrative: Intervention and Critique' (*Textual Practice* 9:iii.477–502) Gregory W. Bredbeck examines the work of writers, including Bruce Boone, Robert Glück, Kathy Acker, Dennis Cooper, Michael Amnasan, Dodie Belamy, Sarah Schulman, Bo Huston, Gary Indiana, Kevin Killian, 'Dumb Bitch Deserves to Die', Dorothy Allison, David Wojnarowitz and Vaginal Creme Davis, who have all been associated with the generic label of new queer narrative, in order to question the simplistic model of chronological development which identifies a development from lesbian and gay identity politics to the postmodern diaspora of the late 1990s, a model which is frequently deployed to differentiate between gay and queer. In opposition to this chronological distinction, Bredbeck argues that what really distinguishes between gay and queer is different, yet possibly complementary, attitudes to power and social change, evident in gay and queer narratives. Gay narrative is read as participating in *activist* critique, a form of social reflection and intervention which can be compared to the model of critique in traditional Marxist social theory; queer narrative, Bredbeck suggests, enacts a programme of *pure* critique, deeply inflected by poststructuralist literary theory and postmodern social theory. So far, so predictable. Bredbeck initially seems to be describing an all too familiar distinction which seems to offer little more than the chronological narrative he rejects, but moves in a more interesting direction, albeit only a little way, when he suggests that both modes of critique, and their associated social movements, 'participate in the lineage of liberation theory, but they continue the tradition with a *difference* achieved through prohibition' (495) and that 'the general segregation that now renders these two modes distinct can be viewed as an enabling strategy, a means of preserving the multiple strands inherent in liberation theory while still allowing the repudiations that necessarily attend the assertion of identity' (497).

Questions of performance differently concern Philip Brian Harper in 'Walk-On Parts and Speaking Subjects: Screen Representations of Black Gay Men' (*Callaloo* 18:ii.390–94) and Sue-Ellen Case in 'Performing Lesbian in the Space of Technology: Part I' (*Theatre Journal* 47.1–18). Harper's brief article suggests that recent acknowledgements that the figure of the black gay man has become a key figure for crises which threaten the foundations of institutionalized culture in the United States should not be allowed to mask the fact that representations of the black gay man have often served to buttress, sometimes by challenging, normative conceptions of race, gender identity and sexuality. The argument is supported by readings of such representations from *Portrait of Jason*, *Beverly Hills Cop* and *Tongues United*. Case suggests that in recent queer theory the body and the order of the visible have been subsumed by writing and the order of print and connects this with the withdrawal of feminist critical theory from the activist agendas of the 1970s. Her critique of the work of Butler, Sedgwick and Hart is accompanied by a call for a recognition of the impact of new technologies which disrupt the linear prescription of print, and Case argues for the performing of lesbian within 'the regime of the visible', constituted as 'a screening device that somehow retains the body, the flesh, and "lives" in tandem with technology' (18). 'Visibility' is explored as a 'struggle term' in Rosemary Hennessy's 'Queer Visibility in Commodity Culture' (*Cultural Critique* 29.31–76), which argues that 'for those of us caught up in the circuits of late capitalist consumption, the visibility of sexual identity is often a matter of commodification, a process that invariably depends on the lives and labor of invisible others' (31). In a wide-ranging essay Hennessy examines examples of what she terms 'the postmodern fetishizing of identity' in the work of Butler, Fuss and de Lauretis; argues against the limited view of social relations which underpins some queer politics; and suggests that we 'need a way of understanding visibility that acknowledges both the local situations in which sexuality is made intelligible as well as the ties that bind knowledge and power to commodity production, consumption, and exchange' (71).

Donald Morton's 'Queerity and Ludic Sado-Masochism: Compulsory Consumption and the Emerging Post-al Queer' (*Transformation: Marxist Boundary Work in Theory, Economics, Politics and Culture* 1.189–215) opens with an assertion that the recent films *Exit from Eden* (on S/M) and *Ed Wood* (on transvestism) should be read not as markers of a 'progressive' or increasingly tolerant attitude to other sexualities but as 'symptoms of the new ideological training needed to produce the different forms of subjectivity required by contemporary capitalism' (189), and argues that what Morton terms 'post-al' theory has performed the work needed by late capitalism by 'changing the concept of radicality . . . so that the "radical" has lost its decided oppositionality' (190). Morton develops his, often rehearsed, argument that 'Queer Theory has become a principal ideological arm of late capitalism' (192) through analysis of key texts which he reads as contributing to the elevation of desire and the near exclusion of need, including work by Anne McClintock, Gayle Rubin and John D'Emilio. Morton's earlier criticisms of queer theory are addressed in Elspeth Probyn's 'The Outside of Queer Cultural Studies' (*University of Toronto Quarterly* 64:iv.536–46), a brief intervention in recent debates about the direction of academic political interventions which seeks to 'position Queer Cultural Studies within and through the optic of [a Foucauldian concept of] governmentality in order to figure the constitution of the terrain in which as an intellectual project it would intervene' (537). The problem of celebrity in cultural studies is explored in Richard Burt's 'Getting Off the Subject: Iconoclasm, Queer Sexuality, and the Celebrity Intellectual' (*Performing Arts Journal* 50/51.137–50), which asserts that 'celebrity constitutes the sacred of cultural criticism' (149) and examines the ways in which a range of feminist and queer cultural critics, notably Judith Butler, Terry Castle and Camille Paglia, have participated in, and been constructed by, 'antagonistic contestation over what counts as properly (progressive) queer criticism' (142).

Practical concerns about the positions of queer theory and of lesbian and gay academics are also addressed in 'The Discipline Problem: Queer Theory Meets Lesbian and Gay History' in which Lisa Duggan argues that in the United States history departments remain largely hostile environments for new work in lesbian and gay studies, failing to hire historians of sexuality; examines the strained relations between lesbian and gay history; and queer theory which have reinforced the isolation of those working in history and calls for a more productive intellectual and political exchange between the two (*GLQ: A Journal of Lesbian and Gay Studies* 2:iii.179–91). Primarily historical articles and analyses included Sarah Waters's '"The Most Famous Fairy in History": Antinous and Homosexual Fantasy', which explores the multiple resonances of Antinous as the key homosexual icon of the late nineteenth century (*Journal of the History of Sexuality* 6:ii.194–230). Others were Kathleen Brown, '"Changed . . . into the Fashion of Man": The Politics of Sexual Difference in a Seventeenth-Century Anglo-American Settlement' (*Journal of the History of Sexuality* 6:ii.171–93); Karen V. Hansen, '"No *Kisses* Is Like Youres": An Erotic Friendship between Two African-American Women during the Mid-Nineteenth Century' (*Gender & History* 7:ii.153–82); Patricia Crawford and Sara Mendelson, 'Sexual Identities in Early Modern England: The Marriage of Two Women in 1680' (*Gender & History* 7:iii.362–77).

Primarily literary critical articles included Edward Hughes' 'The Mapping of Homosexuality in Proust's *Recherche*', which examines the ramifications of the political and cultural recognition triggered in by the narrator's anagnorisis in the area of homosexuality, notably the strains of European colonialism and questions of ethnic and national identity (*Paragraph* 18:ii.148–62), and Eric Savoy's '"In the Cage" and the Queer Effects of Gay History', which explores *queerness* in the writings of Henry James which is taken to signify 'the uncanny, the circuitous, the displaced that more often than not are locatable in prescribed sexualities and their discursive marking' (284) and connects this with the scandals that shaped gay history in the 1890s (*Novel: A Forum on Fiction* 28:ii.284–307). In 'Henry James: The Master and the "Queer Affair" of "The Pupil"' Philip Horne raises some issues of critical purpose and procedure suggested by recent work on James from gender studies and queer theory positions, with particular reference to Eve Kosofsky Sedgwick's writing. Horne questions the restricted list of shadings of sexual possibility deployed by much queer theory, the abuse of speculation and develops his critique through a reading of 'The Pupil' and its critical history (*Critical Quarterly* 37:iii.75–92).

Finally, Eric Savoy's 'The Signifying Rabbit' (*Narrative* 3:ii.188–209) gloriously recuperates Bugs Bunny as 'a queer cultural icon, a parodic diva, whose campy excesses and canny games are profoundly though tacitly indebted to the African-American rhetorical tradition of Signifyin(g), especially in their potential to short-circuit the self-congratulation of an impercipient adversary' (188). He locates Bugs Bunny's 'decidedly liminal position in the regulatory mechanisms of gender and his ambiguous relations to sexuality' (191) within a long tradition of the representational association of the rabbit with deviant or perverse sexuality, featuring, for example, Brer Rabbit, and addresses the possibility of establishing meaningful connections between the narrative conventions of Signifyin(g)-as-Trickstering and the multiple performative modes that constitute camp, or queer Signifyin(g). Savoy's essay explores the relationship between the Bunny and Henry Louis Gates's Signifying Monkey, through analysis of cartoons and of theoretical and political strategies, arguing that animation 'is a powerful space in which to discern the constructedness of gendered taxonomies because of the rapid juxtaposition it permits' (207), and asking, along the way, one of the best questions of 1995: 'Does Bugs Bunny have a penis, or is he a *signifying manqué*?' (197). And that's all folks!

Books Reviewed

Bell, David, and Gill Valentine, eds. *Mapping Desire: Geographies of Sexualities*. Routledge. pp.370. hb £47.50, pb £15.99. ISBN 0 415 11163 3, 0 415 11164 1.

Bennett, Paula, and Vernon A. Rosario, II, eds. *Solitary Pleasures: The Historical, Literary and Artistic Discourses of Autoeroticism*. Routledge. pp. 286. hb £40.00, pb £12.99. ISBN 0 415 91173 7, 0 415 91174 5.

Berger, Maurice, Brian Wallis and Simon Watson, eds. *Constructing Masculinity*. Routledge. pp. 342. hb £45.00, pb £14.99. ISBN 0 415 91052 8, 0 415 91053 6.

Burg, B. R. *Sodomy and the Pirate Tradition: English Sea Rovers in the Seventeenth-Century Caribbean*. New York University Press. pp. 215. hb £30.00, pb £12.00. ISBN 0 8147 1235 5, 0 8147 1236 3.

Burston, Paul. *What Are You Looking At? Queer Sex, Style and Cinema*. Cassell. pp. 179. £12.99. ISBN 0 304 34300 5.

Burston, Paul, and Colin Richardson, eds. *A Queer Romance: Lesbians, Gay Men and Popular Culture*. Routledge. pp. 258. hb £40.00, pb £12.99. ISBN 0 415 09617 0, 0 415 09618 9.

Card, Claudia. *Lesbian Choices*. Columbia University Press. pp. 310. hb £22.95, pb £12.00. ISBN 0 231 08008 5, 0 231 08009 3.

Case, Sue-Ellen, Philip Brett and Susan Leigh Foster, eds. *Cruising the Performative: Interventions into the Representation of Ethnicity, Nationality and Sexuality*. Indiana University Press. pp. 259. pb £12.95. ISBN 0 253 32901 9, 0 253 20976 5.

Cooper, Emmanuel. *Fully Exposed: The Male Nude in Photography*. Routledge. pp. 296. hb £45.00, pb £14.99. ISBN 0 415 03279 2, 0 415 03280 6.

Creekmur, Corey K., and Alexander Doty, eds. *Out in Culture: Gay, Lesbian and Queer Essays on Popular Culture.* Cassell. pp. 535. £15.99. ISBN 0 304 33488 X.

De Cecco, John P., and David Allen Parker, eds. *Sex, Cells, and Same-Sex Desire: The Biology of Sexual Preference.* Harrington Park Press. pp. 470. hb $49.95. ISBN 1 56024 700 2.

Dorenkamp, Monika, and Richard Henke, eds. *Negotiating Lesbian and Gay Subjects.* Routledge. pp. 199. hb £40.00, pb £12.99. ISBN 0 415 90832 9, 0 415 90833 7.

Duggan, Lisa, and Nan D. Hunter. *Sex Wars: Sexual Dissent and Political Culture.* Routledge. pp. 310. hb £37.50, pb £11.99. ISBN 0 415 91036, 0 415 91037 4.

Gevisser, Mark, and Edwin Cameron, eds. *Defiant Desire: Gay and Lesbian Lives in South Africa.* Routledge. pp. 376. hb £40.00, pb £14.99. ISBN 0 415 91060 9, 0 415 91061 7.

Grosz, Elizabeth. *Space, Time, and Perversion.* Routledge. pp. 273. hb £40.00, pb £11.99. ISBN 0 415 91136 2, 0 415 91137 0.

Grosz, Elizabeth, and Elspeth Probyn, eds. *Sexy Bodies: The Strange Carnalities of Feminism.* Routledge. pp. 303. hb £40.00, pb £11.99. ISBN 0 415 09802 5, 0 415 09803 3.

Haggerty, George E., and Bonnie Zimmerman, eds. *Professions of Desire.* Modern Language Association of America. pp. 246. hb $37.50, pb $19.75. ISBN 0 87352 562 0, 0 87352 563 9.

Halperin, David M. *Saint Foucault: Towards a Gay Hagiography.* Oxford University Press. pp. 246. £14.99. ISBN 0 19 509371 2.

Hausman, Berenice L. *Changing Sex: Transsexualism, Technology and the Idea of Gender.* Duke University Press. pp. 245. hb £47.50, pb £16.95. ISBN 0 8223 1680 3, 0 8223 1692 7.

Jay, Karla, ed. *Lesbian Erotics.* New York University Press. pp. 283. hb £40.00, pb £14.50. ISBN 0 8147 4221 1, 0 8147 4225 4.

Parker, Andrew, and Eve Kosofsky Sedgwick, eds. *Performativity and Performance.* Routledge. pp. 239. hb £40.40, pb £11.99. ISBN 0 415 91054 4, 0 415 91055 2.

Parker, Richard G., and John H. Gagnon, eds. *Conceiving Sexuality: Approaches to Sex Research in a Postmodern World.* Routledge. pp. 307. hb £40.00, pb £13.99. ISBN 0 415 90927 9, 0 415 90928 7.

Plummer, Ken. *Telling Sexual Stories: Power, Change and Social Worlds.* Routledge. pp. 244. hb £40.40, pb £12.99. ISBN 0 415 10295 2, 0 415 10296 0.

Rand, Erica. *Barbie's Queer Accessories.* Duke University Press. pp. 213. hb £43.50, pb $14.95. ISBN 0 8223 1604 8, 0 8223 1620 X.

Rust, Paula C. *Bisexuality and the Challenge to Lesbian Politics: Sex, Loyalty, and Revolution.* New York University Press. pp. 367. hb £36.00, pb £14.50. ISBN 0 8147 7444 X, 0 8147 7445 8.

Sanderson, Terry. *Mediawatch: The Treatment of Male and Female Homosexuality in the British Media.* Cassell. pp. 246. £13.99. ISBN 0 304 33186 4.

Spencer, Colin. *Homosexuality: A History.* Fourth Estate. pp. 448. hb £20.20, pb £8.99. ISBN 1 85702 143 6, 1 85702 447 8.

Van Leer, David. *The Queening of America: Gay Culture in a Straight Society.* Routledge. pp. 222. hb £40.00, pb £12.99. ISBN 0 415 90335 1, 0 415 90336 X.

Wilson, Angelia R. *A Simple Matter of Justice? Theorizing Lesbian and Gay Politics*. Cassell. pp. 223. £15.99. ISBN 0 304 32957 6.

Wilton, Tamsin, ed. *Immortal, Invisible: Lesbians and the Moving Image*. Routledge. pp. 235. hb £40.00, pb £12.99. ISBN 0 415 10724 5, 0 415 10725 3.

Wilton, Tamsin. *Lesbian Studies: Setting an Agenda*. Routledge. pp. 234. hb £40.40, pb £12.99. ISBN 0 415 08655 8, 0 415 08656 6.

Woods, Chris. *State of the Queer Nation: A Critique of Gay and Lesbian Politics in 1990s Britain*. Cassell. pp. 60. £4.99. ISBN 0 304 33339 5.

9

Discourse Analysis

SHAFQAT NASIR

Despite various attempts over the last 15–20 years to define the range and scope of discourse analysis the term still covers a number of distinctive disciplinary approaches within both modern and postmodern paradigms. Some of this work seems more closely related to sociological conversation analysis whilst other work, which does not necessarily use the term 'discourse analysis', does in fact analyse discourses through text and image. There is therefore no one clear focus on a particular aspect of discourse analysis in this chapter. Rather the chapter deals with a constellation of studies in the fields of semiotics, language, discourse, social constructionism and postmodernism. Also, since the context of this chapter is firmly that of critical and cultural studies, more emphasis will be given here to books and articles which fit into its theoretical terrain. Some books which may be of interest to those studying discourse, but which are more conventionally sociological or psychological in orientation, are covered more briefly.

This chapter is divided into three sections: 1. Introductory and General Textbooks; 2. Discourse, Race and Nation; 3. Gender and Discourse.

1. Introductory and General Textbooks

Vivien Burr's *An Introduction to Social Constructionism* is published this year and provides an excellent introductory text to its field. In addition, it deserves detailed attention here since it also places discourse analysis amongst a whole set of further debates about essentialism, postmodern theory, language and subjectivity. As such, the text also forms a useful introduction to, and framework for, the rest of this chapter.

An Introduction to Social Constructionism is structured through a series of pertinent and often asked questions, divided into ten logically sequenced chapters: 'Where Do You Get your Personality From?'; 'Does Language Affect the Way We Think?'; 'What is a Discourse?'; 'What Does it Mean to Have Power?'; 'Is There a Real World Outside of Discourse?'; 'Can Individuals Change Society?'; 'What is Social Constructionism?'; 'What Does it Mean to Be a Person? I. The Person as Discourse User'; 'What Does it Mean to Be a Person? II. The Self as Constructed through Language'; 'What Does it Mean to Be a Person? III. Subject Positions in Discourse'; and What Do Discourse

Analysts Do?' – which applies the concepts, arguments and questions covered in the book to the practice of discourse analysis itself.

The book covers a vast range of issues both comprehensively and elegantly, with substantial points clearly signposted, and no effort is spared in terms of crafting the connections which hold the whole project together. Those who are well versed in discourse analysis may find this a little tortured and repetitious – though I think most will find it presents a useful, well-thought-through critical framework. This clarity is enhanced by the glossary of terms provided by Burr at the end of the book.

The audience Burr speaks to primarily are those with a background in psychology, yet the discussion is wide enough to draw in anybody interested in popular psychology, or in everyday discourses of personality. Burr notes that her aim is to be readable yet critical – which is something that is certainly achieved. Terms are carefully and clearly explained, often with the use of metaphors, illustrations and reference to further reading. Her approach throughout is refreshingly reflective and unpretentious, she positions herself as an advocate, but also gives comprehensive expositions of theories in a non-reductive way. In this way, Burr is not making an argument as much as taking her reader on a journey, emphasizing that what is produced by such an exercise is: 'Like any snapshot . . . a likeness that is recognisable without passing itself off as the only true image' (viii).

Thus Burr begins not by trying to forge a definition of social constructionism but rather a list of things 'you would absolutely have to believe in order to be a social constructionist'. This leads into a discussion of the problems of essentialism and realism which form the main ingredients of everyday logic about personhood. Dissecting and problematizing these terms, Burr argues that knowledge must be seen as something which is in the process of ongoing production, through language, within changing historical and cultural contexts.

The first chapter replaces a traditional psychological account of personality with a social constructionist one, exposing how the former is organized by logics of individualism with its essentialized components of stability, coherence and binary metaphysics. Within this context the nature–nurture debate is shown to be a discursively produced and socially constructed dichotomy. Following on from this, chapter 2 addresses the ways in which language structures consciousness and therefore perception and experience. In order to bring the reader to an understanding of the ways in which language constitutes people as subjects, the text begins with an outline of an analysis of Saussure's structuralist theory of language, as a system of signs which construe reality. This is followed by an analysis of the problems with seeing meaning as fixed (if arbitrary) that led to the succession of Saussure's work by a poststructural approach underpinned by a critique of humanism, identifying language 'as an approach which, as Burr points out, is a site of struggle, conflict and potential personal and social change' (40).

Having established the theoretical foundation, Burr then goes on to discuss what discourse is or might be, by way of a series of expositions of discourse theory, discourse analysis and relations between discourse, identity and person-hood, social practices and agency, social structure and reality.

Chapter 3 takes this exposition further by introducing the reader to Foucault's work on power and knowledge, being careful in the subsequent chapters to connect this to the reader's understanding of ideology, agency and false consciousness so that the charge of idealism and conservatism often levelled at postmodernism is dismantled before a much more complex discussion of personhood and agency explored in chapters 7–9.

Chapter 7's treatment of 'the person as discourse user' covers the performative view of language, interpretive repertoires and the person as moral actor. As with all of the chapters, Burr avoids closing the debate by outlining a number of theoretical positions. However, with each step she constructs the unanswered questions – in this case unintended consequences of accounts – which then open the next chapter, 'The Self as Constructed in Language'. The basis of this chapter is Harre's work on the grammatical self, the language of selfhood and the related critique of the notion of cause and effect as merely providing a narrative account of events. The final chapter in this set, 'Subject Positions in Discourse', is particularly well illustrated, using various pieces of text to show how subject positions are constructed and negotiated within interpersonal contexts. Together, these chapters, with the various theoretical contributions and Burr's critical questioning, avoid any kind of reductionism. Each theorist has something to offer – but clearly no one can offer either an all-encompassing theory or the truth.

The substantive points and theoretical questions that have been raised throughout the book are then applied to texts in the final chapter – 'What Do Discourse Analysts Do?' – not only in relation to theory underpinning practice, but also to the subjectivity of the researcher, where the researcher is positioned culturally, socially and in relation to their research subjects. An open but critical stance is adopted in relation to the practice of research: like others (Erica Burman and Ian Parker, *Discourse Analytic Research*, 1993), Burr feels it is counterproductive to talk of set guidelines, the pursuit being characterized more by critical enquiry than 'scientific method'. Towards the end of this chapter a full range of problems are raised, including the possibility that reflexive accounts may create merely the illusion of democratization.

Whilst Burr argues for an awareness of the political uses and effects of discourse analytic research, Lemke takes it as a promising tool of radical research in a postmodern world. *Textual Politics: Discourse and Social Dynamics* is part of the 'Critical Perspectives on Literacy and Education Series', which the series editor introduces as an 'attempt to resituate functional linguistics and social semiotics within a political framework' (4). Both the series editor and the author seem to share a concern that trendy and/or fashionable postmodernism *should* be used for leftist political ends. However, it is possible to argue that the authors themselves are not sufficiently critical or reflective about how they position themselves within this framework (perhaps because they read 'radicalism' as today's brand of Marxism) – the metanarrative is not completely abandoned.

Textual Politics consists of seven chapters and a retrospective postscript. Chapter 1 introduces the reader to the theoretical framework to be used and sets out the organization of the book as a whole. Meaning, ideology, language, discourse and semiotics form the reference points through which Lemke constructs both himself as subject and his theoretical project. There is a constant note of suspicion and concern that approaching politics in this way – unless you really know what your politics are – might lead to a naive and uninformed (by Marxism) understanding of the role of language in maintaining power relationships.

Having set out the parameters and reference points for his project in this way, Lemke takes the next step – in chapter 2 'Discourse and Social Theory' towards outlining the theoretical contributions and positions that have informed his understanding of discourse. This includes Bakhtin's work on heteroglossia, Halliday and Bernstein on register and code, Foucault's discursive formations, and Bourdieu's theory of discourse and habitus. This exercise is useful in that it equips the reader with some of the theoretical background needed to travel with Lemke. However, each argument is introduced for very specific purposes in terms of the author's argument, which makes it quite difficult to engage with them as theories in their own right.

This difficulty is overcome to some extent in following chapters, which take a more in-depth look at particular theorists and their contributions. Thus in chapter 3 'Discourses in Conflict', heteroglossic relations and intertextuality are discussed. Heteroglossia promotes the study of presentation, orientation and organization in text semantics, and is used here to 'read' two texts: the discourse of the moral majority and the discourse of gay rights. Each of these provides rich material for analysis. Next, in chapter 4, Lemke turns his attention to Foucault in a discussion of 'technical discourse and technocratic ideology' – the power/knowledge discourse dynamic.

This is an interesting and engaging book for people who want to use discourse analysis in 'radical' political projects. However, for someone primarily interested in discourse analysis and its underlying principles, the examples of texts may be of more use than Lemke's theoretical framework.

Another book in the field which draws extensively on different theoretical traditions in order to advance a particular line of enquiry is *The Social Semiotics of Mass Communication* by Klaus Bruhn Jensen. Jensen is particularly interested in developing Peircean theory in order to advance a pragmatic approach to mass communication also referred to as an integrative social semiotic theory of mass communication.

The Social Semiotics of Mass Communication consists of eleven chapters divided into three parts: 'Sources of Social Semiotics'; 'Community Theory: First Order Semiotics'; and 'Theory of Science: Second Order Semiotics'. Jensen argues that recovering pragmatism could inform a new theory of mass communication which utilizes Peircean concepts of abduction, ontology and semiotics. He also argues that there are problems with the current expansion of postmodern approaches to communication. One of these problems is that it has, as he sees it, developed from dyadic semiology rather than triadic semiotics. Furthermore, he suggests that postmodern approaches may obscure the politics of communication, ending this chapter with the statement that: 'The key issue may not be how to ensure the right to engage in dialogue but how to develop procedures for ending dialogue and transferring it into other social action (180). This is, perhaps, a point of convergence with Lemke.

Lemke is also not the only person this year to be inspired by Bernstein. *Discourse and Reproduction*, edited by P. Atkinson, B. Davies and S. Delamont, is a set of essays in 'honour' of Basil Bernstein, which the editors stress is about the continuing importance of his work as a basis for current and future work rather than a book about Bernstein himself, or indeed merely a refinement and/or expansion of his theoretical contributions. There are essays on ethnopoetics, cultural semantics in occupations in relation to gender, official knowledge and morality. Several of the essays focus on education as a site of the reproduction of discourses using current texts such as the National Curriculum as their focus.

Language: The Basics, written by R. Trask, is an invitation to the study of language. It is addressed to a more general 'reader' rather than targeting a specific group, using questions to encourage thinking about the role and importance of language in our lives. Indeed, the author argues that 'nothing is more important than language' (xiii).

Emphasis is placed early on in this book on cognitive and physiological aspects of language. The first chapter, 'The Uniqueness of Human Language', includes many anatomical drawings using the language and discourse of science and anthropology as its authority. The emphasis then shifts to a more linguistic study, with chapter 2 examining the rules of grammar, carefully noting that rules vary from context to context. In chapter 3, language and meaning are explored through a discussion of semantics, structure and context. This emphasis on context continues in chapters 4 and 5, which address variation and change in language.

Having explored some 'social' aspects of language, the author returns to questions of neurology and genetics in the production of language, while the final substantive chapter, 'Attitudes to Language', is concerned with linguistic pluralism and the relationships between language and identity.

Whilst it may serve as a kind of social science introduction to language, there is little new in this book. Indeed, it mainly brings together a range of issues in language in a rather conventional and predictable way. Analysis stays at a fairly superficial level, the organization betrays a rather narrow focus and, whilst the newcomer may find the book of interest, it is neither comprehensive nor inspiring to anyone who has any knowledge of the subject matter with which it deals.

Montgomery's second edition of *An Introduction to Language and Society* is better. It positions itself clearly as a book for students of sociolinguistics within a set of 'Studies in Culture and Communication'. The book is divided into four parts. The first covers 'The Development of Language' and the second 'Linguistic Diversity and the Speech Community'. Whereas this entire area was covered in a couple of separate chapters in Trask's book, here a set of chapters cover a whole range of issues in a well-organized sequence. First regional variations are discussed in relation to social structure with reference to 'accent and dialect'. This then leads into a chapter entitled 'Language and Ethnic Identity', with further chapters on subcultures, situation (register), social class and gender.

2. Discourse, Race and Nation

Though not directly about discourse analysis, A. L. Stoler's *Race and the Education of Desire: Foucault's* History of Sexuality *and the Colonial Order of Things* is an important book for those using Foucault's work on discursive formations. The book is a well-grounded and thorough analysis of Foucault's 1976 lectures on 'Racisms of the State' – and a critique of Foucault's limits in dealing with the sexual politics of race. Stoler's project in this book is clearly to examine 'the tensions between what [Foucault] wrote and what he said' (viii). As such the book makes fascinating reading, illuminating the 'networks of scaffolding' Foucault described as carrying him from one position to another, and then with respect, and in a tradition of critical enquiry and conceptual development encouraged by Foucault, Stoler turns the deconstructive mirror towards the subject/author. Stoler expresses this as 'at once a recuperation and departure from themes addressed in his earlier work' (ix).

The questions that emerge from her analysis are of central importance. Of those she asks directly, perhaps the most urgent might be characterized as 'What explains the incessant search for racism's originary moment? What truth-claims about modernity and the post-colonial condition are lodged in the wide spectrum of stories constructed about the imperial history of race?'. She also argues that 'We need to think through not only why colonial history appears as manichean but also why so much historiography has invested (and continues to invest) in that myth as well' (199). In addition to this enquiry, Stoler also engages with recent debates in what might be called 'subaltern studies' about 'strategic essentialism' which she argues may represent:

> the *contre-histoire* in racial discourse, the form in which subjugated knowledges make their space. That may be its political virtue. But as a political strategy for rewriting histories that reflect both the fixity and the fluidity of racial categories, that attend to how people reworked and contested the boundaries of taxonomic colonial states, it is, if not untenable, at least problematic. (199)

In all, this book offers a highly sophisticated approach to the way that discourse theory might inform 'radical' politics, and studies around the concept of race. As Stoler herself asserts, 'Periodising racisms is so problematic because racisms are not, and never have been, about race alone' (204).

Another book that does not actually emphasize discourse but makes a very important contribution to thinking about race (in particular, in relation to Stoler's work on the way in which discourses of race relate to others in the discursive field at any given time) is *Colonial Masculinity: The 'Manly Englishman' and the 'Effeminate Bengali' in the Late Nineteenth Century* by Mrinalini Sinha.

Whilst the book is perhaps more orientated to specifically literature-based discourse analysis, there is much of wider interest offered, particularly in relation to interdependent constructions of colonial masculinity during the time of the British Raj. Fascinating historical narratives are woven together in an exceptionally well-grounded and perceptive analysis. One of the aspects of masculinity examined in this way, for example, is the construction of Bengali men as feeble – racially – such as is illustrated by a quote from Lord Macaulay: 'During many ages he has been trampled upon by men of bolder and more hardy breeds' (15). This colonial construction of masculinity is exposed and deconstructed as highly instrumental in justifying India's loss of independence to Britain.

Chapter 1 of Sinha's book focuses on the Ilbert Bill in which she shows various moves made discursively to reconfigure hierarchies and the way in which 'The politics of colonial masculinity in the Ilbert bill controversy links the "New Woman" in Britain no less than the "Effeminate babu" in India to the changing imperatives of late nineteenth century imperial social formation' (63). Further chapters give an equally well-researched analysis of documents such as the Age of Consent Bill which passed into legislation in 1891. The book as a whole shows how it is both possible and necessary to go beyond reductive categorizations in relation to race, class and gender, and it promotes a recognition of various relationships between colonialism and feminism. Imperial social formations are clearly discursive ones. Sinha's book is both fascinating and important – subtly but carefully making space for non-reductive historical analyses through the study of official documents.

On the other side of the Imperialist coin, *Banal Nationalism* by Michael Billig explores the effects of the way in which nationalism is produced and sustained in everyday forms in the West, specifically focusing on the United Kingdom and the United States. Billig challenges orthodox theories of nationalism which tend to focus on its more extreme manifestations: nationalist war campaigns, the rhetoric of political parties and racial violence. In the introduction he argues that nationalism (in various forms and types) is not something that only emerges at particular crisis points in the West. It is seen constantly, for example in the case of Bosnia, as a sign of intolerance, of ethnic absolutism often with undemocratic outcomes. Further, it is something, he argues, that is so deeply discursively ingrained, both in discourses of nationalism and discourses of the 'other', that it can be described as being installed in our consciousness.

Billig goes on from this to argue that when nationalism is invoked to mobilize citizens it becomes more important than life itself, worth the ultimate sacrifice. Clearly then, as Billig argues, 'there is something misleading about the accepted use of the word "nationalism". It always seems to locate nationalism on the periphery. The property of others not us' (5).

In demonstrating these points Billig focuses on the political rhetoric surrounding the Falklands and the Gulf War. In one useful example, he draws attention to George Bush's claim during the Gulf War that 'Saddam Hussein systematically raped, pillaged and plundered a tiny nation no threat to its own' (1). This is, indeed, a rich example; where for instance, is the former president positioning America in this scenario? Analyses like those of Noam Chomsky and Jean Baudrillard examine the ways in which the construction of an 'us' and 'them' dichotomy works, and also the irony of statements like that shown above when it is not clear, given the odds and obvious imbalance of power between the United States and Iraq, that what happened was a 'war' at all (see particularly Baudrillard's work *The Gulf War Did Not Take Place*, first published in 1991 by Editions Galillee and reprinted in 1995 by Power Publications).

The way in which nation and race are collapsed lexically is also shown in Margaret Thatcher's statement at the time about the people settled on the Falkland islands as 'British in stock and tradition'. As Billig points out, the 'gaps in political language are rarely innocent . . . banal not benign' (6).

In chapter 2, 'Nations and Languages', language, which is often assumed to be the communicative glue of nationalism and the central pillar of ethnic identity 'projecting and naturalising theories of nation' is examined. It is suggested that language has no such natural existence, but rather that it is fully engineered and subject to 'hyperstandardisation' – a disciplinary discursive structure standing as a symbol of uniformity and order.

In chapters 3 and 4 what Billig calls the 'complex dialectic of remembering and forgetting' and the rise of the modern nation state are analysed. Chapter 4,

'National Identity in the World of Nations', uses political speeches to show how the United States regularly positions itself as the world, the voice of universality and of impartiality, thus demonizing and positioning outside of the world of nations those countries that become its enemies. As with much of the discourse around humanitarianism, like the pigs in *Animal Farm*, some of us (Europeans) are more human than others – or at least have a clearer, hegemonic, if Eurocentric, conception of what universal humanity looks like.

The last five chapters of the book look at the way news, sport and even the weather also 'flag the homeland daily'. This serves cumulatively to bring out important questions of the effects of postmodernity on national identity. Whilst much of the discussion in these chapters is repetitive, the project as a whole is coherent, though not as textually grounded as some will need in order to be convinced of Billig's argument.

Like Billig, David Sibley believes that too much emphasis is given to stark expressions of spacial boundaries in relation to questions of nation, nationalism and identities. Whilst others look at places like South Africa (see Gerhard Schutte's *What Racists Believe: Race Relations in South Africa and the United States*, Sage, 1995) or Nazi Germany, his project is to turn the tables on this Orientalist gaze to 'anthropologise the West' (ix). In his book *Geographies of Exclusion: Society and Difference in the West* he states that his intention 'is to foreground the more opaque instances of exclusion, opaque that is, from a mainstream or majority perspective, the ones which do not make the news or are taken for granted as part of the routine of daily life' (ix).

In order to effect this stated project, Sibley draws on a wide range of theoretical frameworks and disciplines – an approach which, in the end, proves to have both strengths and weaknesses. The strength is that the issue of exclusion in anthropology is opened out, to enable it to be examined from a number of perspectives. The weakness is that this opening out affects the coherence of the project as a whole. Whilst the problems of a totalizing discourse of Marxism are outlined, the framework offered is in transit. This may of course be intentional (Sibley does not claim that his account achieves any real synthesis) in the sense that it does avoid closure. However, despite some very interesting pieces, Sibley seems less aware of metanarratives as a whole – the project in many ways is still modern, and not as post-disciplinary as he suggests.

The book consists of eleven chapters, which are divided into two parts: 'Geographies of Exclusion' and 'The Exclusion of Geographies'. The first substantial chapter (after the introduction) is entitled 'Feelings about Difference'. Here Sibley refers to object relations theory, Klienian psychoanalysis and Kristeva's account of abjection, in order to discuss the phenomena of simultaneous attraction and repulsion, and processes of introjection and projection. Chapters 2–5 are less theoretical and more practical, with more analyses of images and geographies. One of the examples of spaces of exclusion is nation, and like Billig, Sibley discusses the Gulf War in this context.

Part 2 focuses on the exclusion of knowledge, in particular the eclipsing of the work of black academics, such as W. E. B. Dubois, within the project and history of spacial geography. Overall, this is an interesting and highly readable book, giving the reader several reference points from which to look at the construction of geographical boundaries, border-crossing, and physical and intellectual acts of inclusion/exclusion.

In *Race, Myth and the News* C. P. Campbell also provides a textual analysis of the construction of the racialized other this year. This time the analysis has particular focus on the media, specifically on national, local and newspaper coverage of events. Campbell's project here is a study of the ways in which newsroom practices perpetuate racial myths, using a textual analysis. Applied to a medium which is commonly regarded as the most accurate representation of reality, a textual analysis which shows how authority is conferred, a critical analysis of the subject position and discursive field of the journalist, particularly in relation to how myths are reconstructed lexically and through the structure of narratives, is of crucial importance.

Campbell also picks up on what he calls 'enlightened' racism. This, it turns out, is the form of racism which is used by people who acknowledge and believe themselves to be beyond the social taboo around overt racism in society. Through a whole range of textual analyses, however, 'enlightened' racism is shown to be in no way benign. Campbell argues, as a result of his research, that its cover of awareness serves to deflect criticism – a clear argument for the use of discourse analysis – and meaning and effect here are far from transparent.

In addition to 'enlightened' racism, aversive, everyday, assimilationist as well as some examples of overt racism are outlined and illustrated with a set of well chosen pieces of text in the form of the written word, talk and image. The way in which these support each other is also highlighted. The effect, for instance, of brief stories which consist of little more than soundbites, often with rapid-fire video overlaid, gives the illusion of presenting a picture of the truth. The people involved give their 'eyewitness testimony' and the video footage gives what audiences see as transparent access – 'seeing' what is 'actually' happening.

Separate chapters examine national and local news, and this is compared with newspaper coverage (which has the capacity to structure a much more meaningful argument) and also contrasted with research findings on fictional television. Campbell suggests that a more accurate picture is ironically given by fictionalized narratives and accounts, such as those in Spike Lee films, and discussions in Oprah Winfrey-type talk shows. Certainly they foreground the issues related to any one subject, and allow much greater room for exploration, whilst resisting the closure involved in summarized truths.

In many ways the discussion of negative stereotypes, the narrow confines of positive images (sport/singing) and the analysis of different types of racism (or manifestations) repeat earlier work. What this book does provide, however, are plentiful texts to work on, from a wide range of perspectives, contrasting formulaic reporting with negotiated, preferred and oppositional readings. It is also important to note here the 'sameness' which results from the striking similarities of readings from a journalistic perspective. The only reservation I have about this otherwise useful text is that it seems as though Campbell is looking for, and indeed assuming, a truth in relation to the material examined. This, itself, needs to be examined in terms of its discursive constructions.

This book would work well in conjunction with Norman Fairclough's *Media Discourse*, which is methodologically more thorough and more grounded in critical discourse analysis. Whilst being theoretically sophisticated, the book is also highly readable and informative, in relation to both theoretical influences (linguistic and poststructural) and 'guidelines' (as far as one can have them in discourse analysis) for practice. Chapter 1 for instance, 'Media and Language: Setting an Agenda', outlines a kind of formula for critical discourse analysis, emphasizing the interrelatedness of three interdependent fields: Representation, Identity and Relationships.

Chapters 2 and 3 set Fairclough's discussion firstly within the context of 'approaches to media discourse' and then in relation to the sociocultural political and economic context. Having established this theoretical foundation, chapters 4–7 develop his own theory of 'Critical Analysis of Media Discourse' involving detailed discussion of 'Intertextuality and the News', 'Representations in Documentary and News' and 'Identity and Social Relations in Media Texts'. The latter discussion focuses on several case-studies of media texts, including *Medicine Now*, *High Resolution*, *The Oprah Winfrey Show* and the *Today* programme.

Chapter 8 similarly concentrates on case-studies – this time *Crimewatch UK* and *999*. Adding to the kind of analysis given by Campbell, Fairclough explores the format of such programmes. The format gives a generic analysis constructed through video footage and several voices in the voice-over. The voices become discursive intertextuality, creating an unstable boundary between the official (public) and the life-world (private), as well as between information and entertainment. Fairclough argues that this has the effect of building a communicative bridge between those two 'worlds', thus serving to rebuild trust in the police and participating in the act of surveillance.

In chapter 9 'Political Discourse in the Media', Fairclough regroups the threads of his argument addressed so far and strengthens the theoretical and critical basis, still applying analysis to media texts, but bringing in considerations of Bourdieu's work on the field of politics and the order of mediatized political discourse. The book ends with a chapter entitled 'Critical Media Literacy', arguing that 'If culture is becoming more salient, by the same token so too are language and discourse. It follows that it is becoming essential for effective citizenship that people should be critically aware of culture, discourse and language, including the discourse and language of the media' (201). Perhaps a little tokenistically, or uncommittedly, Fairclough ends with a short paragraph, subtitled 'What can be done about this text?'

3. Gender and Discourse

Several books address specifically feminist discourse analysis this year. The argument for such an approach is outlined by the editors of *Feminism and Discourse*, Sue Wilkinson and Celia Kitzinger. The book is described as a showcase of feminist work in the field of discourse analysis, mainly within the discipline of psychology. The editors argue that within psychology as a whole, and discourse analysis in particular, feminist work has been marginalized. The issues of 'invisibility' and 'voice' are foregrounded, alongside the claim that this is unfair, as the editors claim that feminists have always been concerned about language and its effects (or at least since before the 'fashionable' orientation towards discourse began within critical psychology).

Discourse analysis is recognized here as having both benefits and limits in relation to feminist activism. On the one hand language is clearly a key site for 'feminist resistance', in terms of the construction of subjectivity for instance. However, it is argued that the emphasis on difference denies a single identity around which to organize (this is seen by the authors as a major problem). They also argue that in emphasizing micro-power, macro-power is, at least to some extent, eclipsed. Perhaps this concern arises from the fact that the book is positioned within psychology and a particular form of discourse analysis. After all, Foucauldian discursive formations encourage a dismantling of a macro/micro binary.

The book consists of nine substantive chapters divided into two parts. Part 1 focuses on empirical work on menstruation, sexual harassment, masculinity and anorexia nervosa, while part 2 offers several theoretical advances. Here women's heterosexual desire, identity and politics in everyday talk, and romantic discourse are covered. The last three chapters are more clearly theoretical: investment, pragmatism, extravagance, relativism and reflexivity in relation to feminist work are explored.

The editors qualify the work as feminist by reference to content, focus, approach and aim (in relation to political outcomes), as does Sara Mills, the author of *Feminist Stylistics*. This book is also divided into two parts, the first being general theoretical issues, and the second, analysis. Each part contains three chapters. Like Wilkinson and Kitzinger, Mills regards her work as drawing attention to the way in which gender is represented, with a view to changing it. She writes, for example, that 'feminist stylistics is concerned not only to describe sexism in text, but also to analyze the way that point of view, agency, metaphor, or transitivity are unexpectedly closely related to matters of gender' (1). Also, like Wilkinson and Kitzinger, Mills believes that feminism was 'there' first: 'work undertaken by men into masculinity . . . draws productively on feminist studies . . . research by gay and lesbian theorists has also drawn on feminist theory' (17). And again a similar set of concerns are expressed around discourse analysis and stylistics needing to move 'away from analysis of the language of the text, as if that language were simply there, to an analysis of socioeconomic factors which have allowed that language to appear' (17).

These points, in conjunction with the statement that 'feminism sets itself in opposition to the kind of academic work which aims to mystify the uninitiated and keep out all but a select few' (4), position the book as more advanced, more inclusive and more accessible than other non-feminist books in the field. This seems more of (or works as) a marketing ploy, though that is not to question the feminist intentions.

Part 1 comprises 'Feminist Models of Text'; 'The Gendered Sentence'; and 'Gender and Reading', all of which draw on a wide range of mainly feminist works. While no new material is produced, these chapters are none the less a good introduction to things like 'ecriture feminine' and the multiple positions that women occupy as within discourses. Part 2 is more substantial, covering three levels of analysis: 'The Word'; 'Phrase/Sentence'; and finally 'Discourse'. There is some insightful analysis in chapters 4–6 on linguistic determinism, the semantic derogation of women, presuppositions, inferences, transitivity choices, and fragmentation and focalizing.

Throughout the book the pieces of text and images used are shown in their original form and cover a vast range of mediums: Page 3 of the *Sun*, singles columns, advertisements (hair removal creams to cars), fictional and non-fictional books, job advertisements, institutional guidelines and cartoons. Thus, the book contains a rich source of examples through which Mills successfully draws attention to the way in which gender is represented in culture and women positioned in relation to that. This is perhaps stronger than its theoretical contribution.

Talking Difference: On Gender and Language by Mary Crawford is part of the Sage series 'Gender and Psychology: Feminist and Critical Perspectives'. This book is more questioning of assumptions that are based on essentialist logics, thus the question of gender rather than feminist accounts of gender is the focus. Crawford looks at both academic and popular work on gender and language. In the end the critique offered leaves an opening for the study of gender and language that is needed in order to introduce reflexivity and to question various levels of essentialism and reductionism in feminist work on language.

While one of the problems with *Feminism and Discourse* and *Feminist Stylistics* is the conception of feminism as almost a self-evident truth, with very little reflexivity in relation to discourses of feminism, which both employ, *Messages Men Hear: Constructing Masculinities* by I. M. Harris has similar problems, but on a larger scale. It may sound from its title as though the book is based on social constructionism, perhaps that of Luckman and Berger, but it is certainly not that associated with current critical theory. In an attempt to answer the question 'Why do men behave the way they do?' Harris develops a qualitative/quantitative hybrid methodology. Based on ten years of research with a 'diverse' sample of 500 men, the book is divided into three parts: 'Learning to Be a Man', 'Acting Like a Man' and the now obligatory, but peripheral, 'Differences between Men'.

Part 1 discusses cultural norms, and it is no surprise to learn that Harris is heavily into men's groups himself when the somewhat naive statement that 'with constant love and nourishment boys have the capacity to grow into cuddly teddy bears. With hatred, abuse and abandonment they can become fierce grizzlies' (9) is made. Harris also seems to have what I would consider a suspect view of 'difference' when he says 'Although this list has been generated in the United States, it has universal application' (9). This, it is argued, is a result of a 'hegemonic message heard throughout the world' – clearly this is a very different approach from the intellectually rigorous critical treatment of masculinities given by Sinha.

In part 2 various 'types' of male subject positions are broken down into categories. So, standard bearers are divided into scholar, nature lover and good samaritans, whilst lovers are categorized as breadwinners, nurturers and playboys. The construction of each category is fairly well grounded in the pieces of text/talk used, but this makes Harris's analysis open to the charge of being too narrow and offering a closed reading.

The final chapter talks of the importance of message therapy, arguing that men's groups can help men cope better with 'gender role strain'. Overall this is a book for those starting work on masculinities (undergraduates), and perhaps also for counsellors. There are some interesting points raised and it does offer examples of texts that can be used for further analysis.

Moving out of the confines of separate studies of race and gender, but onto issues which concern each of these, as well as discourse analysis in general, two books published this year are of interest. Theoretically rigorous and able to negotiate a maze of debates which bridge the gap between academic work and issues in linguistics which concern and effect all of us is *Verbal Hygiene* by Deborah Cameron. This book consists of six chapters which address in detail, through a variety of case studies, the sociopolitical practice of language regulation. Of particular interest to the author is the purpose served by such acts of engineering, for those with investments in the notion of good and bad language.

Chapter 1, 'On Verbal Hygiene', constructs a sophisticated argument around the instability of the binary opposition in theory of descriptive and prescriptive positions. Cameron shows how both of these operate within the same system of norms and therefore can never be mutually exclusive, since they work within a societal consensus of authority and identity. She also here locates the need for verbal hygiene within the fear of a breakdown of communication and fragmentation in society.

The first case-study, which comprises chapter 2, is of restrictive practices in the printed word. Here Cameron analyses the strict adherence to guidelines, hyperstandardization and uniformity which is often assumed as being a defence of democracy via the argument for plain language – the notion of language being transparent (the more transparent the better). Again the case of journalistic reporting of the Gulf War and the use of terms like 'collateral damage' are deconstructed, thus demonstrating that plain language, far from being neutral, can instead be seen as part of the politics of discourse, in a world where the notion of instant access to transparent accounts and images actually obscures the role of language in positioning ourselves in relation to 'others'.

Similar concerns are raised in chapter 3 where the focus is on 'the great grammar crusade' which has in recent political discourse connected moral panic firmly to national culture in the United Kingdom via the National Curriculum. Again formulaic writing and hyperstandardization are shown to be entirely engineered, not natural or necessarily logical.

Chapters 4 and 5 take two very different examples of language regulation. Chapter 4 is a brave and timely comment on 'political correctness' in an age in which the power to define is recognized as the same power that reproduces inequalities at odds with the idealized notion of democracy. Cameron does not come down on any one side of this debate. Instead, what she offers is simultaneously a deconstruction of the argument that political correctness merely tampers with natural language (thus trivializing meaning) and a demonstration of the impossibility of the assumption of there being a fixed value neutral term for those wishing to promote politically correct language – not least through the phenomena of discursive drift in which language as it is socially negotiated involves transfers of meaning.

'The New Pygmalion' (chapter 5) looks at the way in which assertiveness, and the personal advice genre related to it, involve verbal hygiene for women in the late twentieth century. Here language and power are again assumed to have a straightforward connection which underpins both the logic of 'talking like a man' and empowerment. Cameron does not use this investigation into its workings to dismiss this logic but rather to understand the role of what she calls 'empowering fictions'. This position, in relation to the various arguments, is restated in the final chapter, where Cameron argues that this knowledge will be more effectively used to work with fears about language and cultural communication rather than against them.

Again addressing the issue of the regulation of language in the context of cultural social movements is *Hate Speech*, edited by R. K. Whillock and D. Slayden. This book is a well-researched and intellectually stimulating approach to how hatred of the 'other' in society is constructed, produced and expressed in political rhetoric, media representation and popular culture. Language and voice come together here in a study of hatred in public and private, without polarizing the two.

At first the narrative of hatred resulting in a lack of understanding and clash of values with its simplistic cause and effect formula is critiqued, as is the crisis model of hate which positions it at the fringe of society or extrasocietal. It is argued (similarly to Billig, Campbell and Sibley) that hate is integral to each culture, and whilst it may in the context of 'democracy' be marginalized as distasteful, it nevertheless mutates and manifests itself in subtle and hidden forms, as van Dijk shows in his chapter, 'Elite Discourse and the Reproduction of Racism'.

The construction of identity, the acquisition of power and the need to blame which underpin the use of hate as a stratagem for achieving political and social goals is addressed by Whillock in chapter 2. Examples are used from a US election campaign of the way in which hate speech inflames the emotions of the outgroup which has been separated due to the denial of hate as unproductive and illiberal in society, but also the emotions of those who cast the group out for offending liberal democracy (i.e. those who hate then become legitimate targets of hate themselves). Denigrating this outgroup positions those who seek to silence no less than those seeking to use the voice of hate.

This paradox is also explored in chapter 7, 'Hating for Life: Rhetorical Extremism and Abortion Clinic violence' by Janette Muir.

In chapter 3 Marguerite Moritz looks at the way gay and lesbian communities in the United States have marketed hate speech to the media, asking 'Do you really want to buy into this hate?' Having challenged the logic and conclusions of attacks on gay men and lesbians, the group used experts and a 'you decide' tactic to produce the debate not as something which the media passively reflected, but one which it must actively buy into first, thus engaging the press in a discourse of responsibility and ownership.

Other chapters cover work hate narratives in the management of change, again, like Cameron, exploring the functions these serve: symbolism and representation of hate in visual discourse; the politics of US iconography in relation to federally funded art; and the value-laden notion of free speech. There is also an excellent chapter on narrative accounts of convicted rapists (something which could add to and enhance Harris's work). Whilst consisting of several divergent chapters, the book works very well as a whole project. Each chapter is connected to the others via the general introduction and the editor's preface to each essay. In this way a vast range of issues are considered in depth in a non-reductive project which always resists closure. These chapters, which each involve the close application of theory to practice, are followed by an afterword on 'Hate or Power?' by David Theo Goldeberg. The book is intellectually, theoretically and methodologically coherent, it is a book that will interest and inform academics, activists, politicians and Joe Bloggs; an important contribution to discourse analysis which connects it in a non-simplistic way to politics – be they described as radical or populist.

Books Reviewed

Atkinson, P., B. Davies, and S. Delamont. *Discourse and Reproduction: Essays in Honor of Basil Bernstein.* Hampton Press. pp. 297. pb £21.50. ISBN 1 881303 05 5.

Baudrillard, J. *The Gulf War Did Not Take Place.* Power Publishers. pp. 87. £8.99. ISBN 0 909952 23 X.

Billig, M. *Banal Nationalism.* Sage. pp. 200. pb £13.95. ISBN 0 8039 7525 2.

Burman, E., and I. Parker, eds. *Discourse Analytic Research: Repertoires and Readings of Text in Action.* Routledge. 1993. pp. 192. £13.99. ISBN 0 415 09720 7.

Burr, V. *An Introduction to Social Constructionism.* Routledge. pp. 198. pb £11.95. ISBN 0 415 10405 X.

Cameron, D. *Verbal Hygiene.* Routledge. pp. 264. pb £13.99. ISBN 0 415 10355 X.

Campbell, C. P. *Race, Myth and the News.* Sage. pp. 173. pb £17.50. ISBN 0 8039 5872 2.

Crawford, M. *Talking Difference: On Gender and Language.* Sage. pp. 224. £13.99. ISBN 0 8039 8828 1.

Fairclough, N. *Media Discourse.* Edward Arnold. pp. 214. pb £12.99. ISBN 0 340 58889 6.

Harris, I. M. *Messages Men Hear: Constructing Masculinities.* Taylor & Francis. pp. 214. pb £12.95. ISBN 0 7484 0230 6.

Jensen, K. B. *The Social Semiotics of Mass Communication.* Sage. pp. 228. pb £14.95. ISBN 0 8039 7810 3.

Lemke, J. L. *Textual Politics: Discourse and Social Dynamics.* Sage. pp. 196. pb £12.95. ISBN 0 7484 0216 0.

Mills, S. *Feminist Stylistics.* Routledge. pp. 230. pb £13.95. ISBN 0 415 05028 6.

Montgomery, M. *An Introduction to Language and Society.* Routledge. pp. 272. pb £10.99. ISBN 0 415 07238 7.

Sibley, D. *Geographies of Exclusion: Society and Difference in the West.* Routledge. pp. 206. pb £13.99. ISBN 0 415 11925 1.

Sinha, M. *Colonial Masculinity: The 'Manly Englishman' and the 'Effeminate Bengali' in the Late Nineteenth Century.* Manchester University Press. pp. 191. pb £14.99. ISBN 0 7190 4653 X.

Stoler, A. L. *Race and the Education of Desire: Foucault's* History of Sexuality *and the Colonial Order of Things.* Duke. pp. 238. pb £18.45. ISBN 0 8223 1690 0.

Trask, R. L. *Language: The Basics.* Routledge. pp. 197. pb £8.99. ISBN 0 415 12541 3.

Whillock, R. K., and D. Slayden, eds. *Hate Speech.* Sage. pp. 294. pb £18.99. ISBN 0 8039 7209 1.

Wilkinson, S., and C. Kitzinger. *Feminism and Discourse.* Sage. pp. 193. pb £13.95. ISBN 0 8039 7802 2.

10

Postmodernism

MICHAEL RYAN

Postmodernism – always hard to pin down, always glad not to be pinned down – remains, as a word, a lesson in postmodernism: it means what you want it to mean depending on your perspective, your physical or geographical location, your bodily, intellectual and political interests, your defining differences, and, to use a more postmodern term, your line of flight. As someone raised on poststructuralism (Foucault, Deleuze, Guattari, Derrida, the late Kristeva, Barthes, Irigaray, etc.) it took me a while to figure out that what my Marxist friends were trashing in the early to mid-eighties when they denounced something I had never heard of – postmodernism – was, in part at least, the very poststructuralism I had always found so politically inspiring. And it did not take me long, knowing poststructuralism as I do, which is to say, knowing it to be one of the most interesting radical projects of the past half century, to figure out that what those political compatriots (Jameson and Eagleton, especially) were doing constituted one of the more irresponsible intellectual and rhetorical manoeuvres executed on the academic left in the past half century. (By irresponsible here I mean not responsible to the prevailing standards of intellectual honesty and scholarly accuracy in academia.)

Why should Marxists be so dead set on getting everyone to believe that the most interesting radical political and social theories since Marxism are nothing more than a symptom of capitalist decadence? The question, I think, answers itself. But what is it about these new radical discourses that so upsets Marxists and obliges them to engage in such a disreputable and dishonest sleight of hand? The answer might be found in the nineteenth century, when Marxists succeeded in expelling anarchists from the First International. Like the poststructuralists (especially Deleuze and Guattari), the anarchists were committed to non-statist, non-authoritarian solutions to social problems, and they believed political organizations had to be prefigurative; they could not be non-democratic and hope to create a democratic society. What the post-structuralists, like the anarchists before them, suggest is that other options are available, other avenues open. The Party/State game is not the only one in town, the dialectic not the only dance one can learn. But to identify post-structuralism with anarchism would be to engage in a kind of conceptual analogizing (equating one thing absolutely and totally with another because of partial, historically differentiated overlaps) that poststructuralism finds to be at the heart of a rather bad kind of identity-making that has been one of the worst features of the accumulated bad thinking that gets called Western philosophy, and which includes the dialectic so dear to Marxists.

Such identity-making is in fact what the Marxist critics of poststructuralism (what they call postmodernism) do when they (and here I am thinking of Jameson in his book on postmodernism and of Eagleton in his recent *The Illusions of Postmodernism*) identify a very diverse cluster of left radical thinkers – from Derrida to Lyotard – with 'the last stage of capitalism'. The very profound indifference to truth embedded in this claim leaves one gasping. It also leaves one secure in the perception that the academic publishing system has attained a point where someone who has accumulated a sufficient amount of status (and book marketability) can say just about anything, no matter how uninformed or partisan or tendentious or dishonest, and get away with it. Here is how the sleight of hand works: take some radical critics of capitalism and of Western culture – Deleuze, Derrida, Lyotard, etc. – and say that what characterizes all of their works is something called 'postmodernism'. They share this common chemical element, no matter how diverse and heterogeneous their various, multiple, highly differentiated endeavours. In the end, they are all one thing. Then describe the latest stage of capitalism (which is not all that different from recent stages and is hardly a latest stage at all) as also being something called 'postmodernism'. Presto! You have it. Deleuze, Derrida and company are the latest stage of capitalism! Now wasn't that clever? And easy? Perhaps a little too easy?

Eagleton's *The Illusions of Postmodernism* demonstrates that the difference between Marxists and poststructuralists can be summed up in two words: politics and epistemology. The poststructuralists favour on the whole non-statist, small-scale or molecular forms of political engagement that confront power in all its forms, from the sex gender system to the sociology of criminalization to the imposition of work under capitalism. Marxists like Eagleton hold to the twin ideals of the party and of the state, and to the single goal of the liberation of the proletariat. All well and good, but there is much more to be done – from exorcizing power to liberating violated identities – and Marxists like Eagleton, apparently, do not like being told that. Understandably. They have had a monopoly on political virtue for too long, and although the lease, according to poststructuralism at least, has run out, they will not relinquish it without a fight. Or at least some good name-calling and mud slinging. Not to mention slander and calumny.

Second, epistemology. Marxists believe in a certain arcane model of authoritative scientific knowledge (defined as different from the imaginary doxa of the proles) and in a procedure for establishing true knowledge that has been discredited by poststructuralism. The dialectical method locates logic in history and reason in society. Contradictions converge into resolved identities. But in order for this to occur, discrete parts and material surfaces must be sublated (annulled and preserved in more conceptual form), turned from vagrant particulars into securely tucked in and buttoned down universal truths. This is fine, but the holders of the truths were, for some reason, always heterosexual males of a certain masculine temper, good patriarchs who held their families together with a firm hand and believed in the virtues of the nation and of the race. Examples of the universal truths the dialectic produced were always tainted in some way by a lot of rottenness whose sheer materiality had to be ignored or sublated into the ideal ether that is the only place where such universals can exist as such without being betrayed by empirical examples. And the derided or expelled particulars were always disliked ethnic or regional minorities, despised gender groups, or dissident voices who wanted no part of such totalities or had second thoughts about accepting the invitation to the party. What Marxists call postmodernism is essentially the breaking away of those groups from the Marxist round-up, the straying off of energies and particularities that want no part of yet another reform socialist, male-led, patrocentric state that exchanges socialist managers for capitalist managers and leaves power in all its forms intact. Their accidental contingency in relation to the absolute necessity of the core universal truths of the dialectic have taken on new significance in the light of postmodernism.

Until Terry Eagleton wrote *The Illusions of Postmodernism*, his engaging argument with poststructuralism, Marxists had been content to name-call instead of argue over these issues. Eagleton, while nevertheless clinging to the fundamental slander (left radical poststructuralists = one thing, that one thing = postmodernism, capitalism has entered a new stage also called post-modernism, ergo left radical poststructuralist writers = the latest stage of capitalism), displays his usual wit and intelligence in contending with all of the bogeypeople of poststructuralism/postmodernism – from the insight that we actually live in history and that we actually have bodies, to the insight that we actually use words when we communicate with each other and that words actually wield power and that we might want to attend to how they do that. His response to all of these 'illusions' is convincing, true, absolute, universal, total and, as intended, beyond all possible response.

Eagleton is joined this year in the Marxist (we've nothing better to do than rebut poststructuralism) camp by David Simpson (*The Academic Postmodern and the Rule of Literature*). While Eagleton tries to convince an imaginary undergraduate that he never even had the dirty thoughts of postmodernism in his head in the first place, Simpson tries to argue that postmodernism has no effect on the real world anyway. Fine and good, if you can locate the so-called real world. If it is the one 'out there' that is largely defined by the business community, then we are all in trouble. And maybe the postmodernists are right about needing to transform it from top to bottom, on 'multiple fronts', as they say, instead of simply angling for a re-elected Labour Party that will reduce the working day, as Eagleton, in one of his more apocalyptic utopian moments, promises.

Fortunately, these are not the only voices speaking out or up. The year has witnessed some wonderful work that either derives its method from postmodernism (understood now as a congeries of French theories from Deleuze and Guattari to Lyotard, and not as a cultural phase or an economic stage) or meditates upon the link between those theories and the contemporary world. Vincent B. Leitch's *Postmodernsim: Local Effects, Global Flows* is an extremely informed, very rich set of engagements with a range of postmodern issues and art forms, from teaching to poetry. Caren Kaplan's *Questions of Travel: Postmodern Discourses of Displacement* is a complex, extremely intelligent meditation on what it means to be in exile or in between in a national or ethnic sense. Kaplan theorizes a mediation between the imperatives of world politics and postmodern theory. The volume of postmodern studies edited by Jane Dowson and Steven Earnshaw entitled *Postmodern Subjects/ Postmodern Texts* brings together a particularly wide array of writers and topics, from Larry McMurty's westerns to the theory of the state. Michael Dillon's *Politics of Security: Towards a Political Philosophy of Continental Thought* adds another secure plank to the bridge between political theory and continental philosophy, a bridge that is already well established by the work of thinkers like Thomas Dumm, William Connoley and Michael Shapiro. Richard Beardsworth's *Derrida and the Political*, while, like Dillon, spending perhaps too much time on Heidegger and not enough on contemporary political philosophy, is nevertheless the definitive work on Derrida's politics in print. Barbara Maria Stafford, in *Good Looking: Essays on the Virtue of Images*, offers a vision of a world in which visual images would be released from their site of denigration and become the basis for new ways of teaching and knowing. And finally, William Simon's *Postmodern Sexualities* suggests how a postmodern notion of contingency allows sexual 'nature' to be redefined and reconstructed. Well done all. Worth checking out also: the recent work of Elisabeth Grosz and Rey Chow.

Books Reviewed

Beardsworth, Richard. *Derrida and the Political*. Routledge. pp. 174. £12.99. ISBN 0 415 10967 1.

Dillon, Michael. *Politics of Security: Towards a Political Philosophy of Continental Thought*. Routledge. pp. 252. £45.00. ISBN 0 415 12960 5.

Dowson, Jane and Steven Earnshaw, eds. *Postmodern Subjects/Postmodern Texts*. Rodopi. pp. 251. $13.95. ISBN 09 5183 875 1.

Eagleton, Terry. *The Illusions of Postmodernism*. Blackwell. pp. 147. £9.99. ISBN 0 631 20323 0.

Kaplan, Caren. *Questions of Travel: Postmodern Discourses of Displacement*. Duke University Press. pp. 238. £15.95. ISBN 0 8223 1821 0.

Leitch, Vincent B. *Postmodernism: Local Effects, Global Flows*. State University of New York Press. pp. 195. £15.50. ISBN 0 7914 3010 3.

Simon, William. *Postmodern Sexualities*. Routledge. pp. 179. £12.99. ISBN 0 415 10627 3.

Simpson, David. *The Academic Postmodern and the Rule of Literature: A Report on Half-Knowledge*. The University of Chicago Press. pp. 199. $34.00. ISBN 0 226 75949 0.

Stafford, Barbara Maria. *Good Looking: Essays on the Virtue of Images*. Massachusetts Institute of Technology University Press. pp. 259. £20.61. ISBN 0 262 19369 8.

Part II

Culture and Communications

11

Cultural Studies: General

JOHN STOREY

Cultural studies has always been an unfolding discourse, responding to changing historical and political conditions and always marked by debate, disagreement and intervention. Ioan Davies' *Cultural Studies and Beyond* offers a fascinating account of this unfolding, tracking its historical development and geographic proliferation, following its emergence in the cultural struggles of the British new left in the late 1950s and early 1960s.

The growth and geographic expansion of cultural studies is also evidenced by three volumes published by the Clarendon Press, *French Cultural Studies*, edited by Jill Forbes and Michael Kelly, *German Cultural Studies*, edited by Rob Burns, and *Spanish Cultural Studies*, edited by Helen Graham and Jo Labanyi. Each volume provides an excellent introduction to cultural studies in the respective three countries.

To call cultural studies an unfolding discourse does not mean that it is a completely open postdisciplinary field. One cannot simply rename as cultural studies what one already does in order to impress publishers or to salvage a declining area of academic work. Cultural studies does mean something. Although there can be little doubt that it has been experiencing great success recently, and that success is something to be welcomed, there are those who suspect that it might not be all that it seems. Lawrence Grossberg, in *We Gotta Get Out of This Place: Popular Conservatism and Postmodern Culture*, for example, makes the point that 'Many of those now describing their work as cultural studies were attacking cultural studies only a few years ago although they have not changed their project in the interim. Many of those who now appropriate the term want to read only very selectively in the tradition.'

Cultural Studies, by Fred Inglis, may be a case in point. There was a time when Inglis ('Culture and Cant', *Universities Quarterly* 29) attacked cultural studies for its 'jargon-laden absurdities' and its 'self-confident ignorance'. Nowadays he is part of the fold, writing, according to the 'blurb' of *Cultural Studies*, 'a much-needed critical introduction to an exciting new field of inquiry'. What I find most interesting about Inglis's book is the bibliography. It makes very interesting reading in terms of who is absent and who is present. The 'exciting new field of inquiry' does not include, for example, Martin Barker, Roland Barthes, Tony Bennett, Rosalind Coward, John Fiske, Paul Gilroy, Dick Hebdige, Richard Johnson, Angela McRobbie or Meaghan Morris. Even when key figures are present, the material selected to represent them is often very strange. For example, although there are four references to work by Stuart Hall, missing are foundational essays, such as 'Encoding and Decoding', 'Notes on Deconstructing "The Popular"' and 'The Rediscovery of "Ideology": Return of the Repressed in Media Studies'. There are also four references to work by Raymond Williams. But again, key texts are missing. For example, there is no mention of *Culture and Society*, *Keywords* or *Marxism and Literature*. So who are the major players in this 'exciting new field of inquiry'? Well, according to the bibliography, Fred Inglis (five books) and F. R. Leavis (eight books). Perhaps Grossberg is not as paranoid as some might say.

A Cultural Studies Reader: History, Theory, Practice, edited by Jessica Munns and Gita Rajan, may represent a continuation of the process identified by Grossberg. It is not so much a case of who is in and who is outside cultural studies that marks this book for inclusion so much as its concerted, not to say contorted, attempt to twist and shape cultural studies to fit academic consumption in the United States. This is particularly clear in the editors' attempt to define cultural studies. Sometimes cultural studies means little more than the 'study of culture' and at other times it refers to the academic recycling of 'cultural critique'. Defined in this way, it includes – without contradiction – the ideas of both Matthew Arnold and Karl Marx. Moreover, in this spirit the editors regret the fact that they were unable to include work by Allan Bloom. It might be reassuring to some to know that 'cultural studies is not so much a new and terrifying subject, as it is a re-examination, a re-negotiation, and a re-interpretation of major Enlightenment and humanist ideals'.

There are times when the focus tightens and a recognizable image comes into view. One example is the editors' account of what they call the 'development of a cultural studies consciousness' in late 1950s Britain. But even here the focus falters. Richard Hoggart's contribution is reduced to nothing more than 'nostalgia'. E. P. Thompson's foundational contribution, *The Making of the English Working Class*, we are asked to believe, consists of little more than an 'interpretation of the "worker" in British society'.

On a more positive note, the reader seeks to present 'a body of knowledge to students as one view of the origins of cultural studies'. The book is organized into eight sections (each with an introduction and further reading): 'The Nineteenth Century', 'The Impact of European Theory', 'Cultural Studies in Britain (edited by Roger Bromley)', 'Cultural Studies in America', 'Media Studies', 'Race Studies', 'Gender Studies' and 'Voice-Overs: Definitions and Debates'.

Acknowledging Consumption: A Review of New Studies, edited by Daniel Miller, opens with a long and fascinating account by Miller of the place of consumption in our contemporary global–local postmodern world. The book closes with an authoritative overview by David Morley of theories of consumption in media studies. In between there are essays on new thinking about consumption in historical studies, geography, political economy, psychology, sociology, anthropology and consumer behaviour. The collection makes a substantial contribution to contemporary understandings of consumption. It is undoubtedly destined to become a set text on programmes where these matters are discussed.

Cultural consumption is also the subject of the collection of essays edited by Ann Bermingham and John Brewer, *The Consumption of Culture 1600–1800*. Although modern and postmodern consumption is now established as a field of critical inquiry, attention to early modern consumption is still in its preliminary stages. Bermingham and Brewer's volume makes a major contribution to the further development of this work. Arguing against the claim, found in some versions of postmodern theory, that consumer society is a product of late capitalism, the twenty-six essays collected here implicitly and explicitly (especially in Bermingham's excellent introduction) argue the case for locating the birth of consumer society in the sixteenth, and certainly no later than the eighteenth, century. The coming to dominance of capitalism witnessed not only an expansion of production but also the rapid growth of consumption.

Bermingham argues that the neglect of consumption in our understanding of these historical changes is the result of the hegemony of:

> a vision of modernity which has turned largely on an economic analysis of the social organization of production, and on an ideology of modernism which has taken upon itself the task of defending 'culture' against the very forms of mass consumption that we now seek to examine. In short, modernism's master narrative of culture has obscured the early history of consumption and its relationship to social and cultural forms, substituting in its place a history of culture focused on artistic production, individualism, originality, genius, aestheticism, and avant-gardism. This would help to explain why critics of postmodernism like Fredric Jameson, nostalgic for a more 'authentic' culture, see consumer society as part of the superficial, schizophrenic, 'logic' of late capitalism. Indeed, it is only by operating outside the limits of modernism that we can see a 'consumer society' that is nearly four hundred years old. This vantage point reveals cultural and social formations which by the later eighteenth century had come to represent all that a nascent modernism both needed – and needed to suppress – in order to constitute itself.

The book seeks both to contribute to our knowledge of early modern consumption and 'to interrogate its relation to particular modernist conceptions of culture as they came to be formulated in the seventeenth and eighteenth centuries and naturalized in the twentieth'.

Bermingham does not argue that consumer society is a monolithic entity, unchanging since its inception in the sixteenth century. Rather she insists that we must reject the notion that it is simply a phase of late capitalism and we should see it instead as 'intrinsic to all phases of capitalism, even the earliest'. Moreover, she thinks that 'perhaps the thing that distinguishes the modern period from any that preceded it, is the fact that consumption has been the primary means through which individuals have participated in culture and transformed it'.

The Consumption of Culture 1600–1800 should be essential reading for anyone seriously interested in the historical development of consumption.

Understanding Media Cultures: Social Theory and Mass Communication by Nick Stevenson presents a critical overview of a range of theoretical approaches to popular media culture. Discussion of individual theorists ranges from the early work of Marshall McLuhan to the more recent work of Jean

Baudrillard. Cultural studies, feminism and Marxism are also covered. The book provides a useful introduction to different ways of thinking about the place of popular media in contemporary culture.

Television, Ethnicity and Cultural Change, by Marie Gillespie, offers an account of 'the role of television in the formation and transformation of identity among young Punjabi Londoners'. In a fascinating study, based on ethnographic research carried out between 1988 and 1991, she explores the relationship between media consumption and the cultures of migrant and diasporic communities, demonstrating how the young (mainly in the 14–18 year age group) Punjabi Londoners are 'shaped by but at the same time reshaping the images and meanings circulated in the media and in the market' – what she calls 're-creative consumption'. Gillespie does not wish 'to celebrate consumer creativity any more than consumer culture itself', but she does insist, following Michel de Certeau, that 'consumption, despite its overdetermination by the market and the unequal distribution of access to economic and cultural capital, is not a passive process but an expressive and productive activity'. Therefore, she contends that it is never enough to study the images and narratives of television; we must also examine how these are used by viewers.

Given the growing reputation within cultural studies of the work of Michel de Certeau, it is surprising to think that Jeremy Ahearne's excellent *Michel de Certeau: Interpretation and its Other* is the first full-length study of his contribution to cultural theory. Similarly, it also surprising to find that de Certeau is not the subject of one of the one hundred entries in the otherwise very useful *The A-Z Guide to Modern Literary and Cultural Theorists*, edited by Stuart Sim.

John Frow's *Cultural Studies and Cultural Value* 'is a book about the organization of cultural value in the advanced capitalist world'. In a stimulating and wide-ranging argument, Frow contends that as a result of changes in audience structure, the integration of the cultural into the economic, the changing role of intellectuals in the circulation and consumption of culture, 'there is no longer a stable hierarchy of value (even an inverted one) running from "high" to "low" culture'. The book is essential reading for anyone concerned with questions of cultural value in the postmodern world.

Theorizing Culture: An Interdisciplinary Critique After Postmodernism, edited by Barbara Adam and Stuart Allan, brings together seventeen short essays on 'culture' after postmodernism. From a range of disciplinary locations, and in the knowledge that in each location 'culture' may signify something quite different, even unrecognizable as culture from another location, the various essays attempt to interrogate and rethink 'culture' as it is theorized and lived as form, text, practice and identity in our postmodern world.

In a thoughtful and thought-provoking 'Introduction' to *Critical Theory: A Reader*, Douglas Tallack claims that 'Critical Theory is on the way to becoming established – so much so that its radical credentials are being challenged by a revived (*sic*) Cultural Studies. . . . It sounds almost heretical to say so, but there is [now] the basis for a canon.' Tallack's version of the canon consists of thirty-two essays and extracts, including work by Roland Barthes, Jacques Derrida, Julia Kristeva, Michel Foucault, Herbert Marcuse, Kate Millet, Jacques Lacan, Gilles Deleuze and Felix Guattari, Helene Cixous,

Gayatri Chakravorty Spivak, Walter Benjamin, Theodor Adorno, Louis Althusser, Raymond Williams, Fredric Jameson, Ernesto Laclau and Chantal Mouffe, Jurgen Habermas, Jean-Francois Lyotard and Luce Irigaray. What unites this body of work, it is claimed, is a commitment to 'a set of [four] theoretical discourses': (i) 'ground-breaking methodological advances'; (ii) 'deconstructive self-reflexivity'; (iii) 'immanent critique'; and (iv) 'the substitution of power for truth as the primary focus of analysis'.

A book that may well challenge the radical credentials of critical theory is *Cultural Politics: Class, Gender, Race and the Postmodern World*, by Glenn Jordan and Chris Weedon. They describe their book as 'a political and theoretical intervention in the broad field of Cultural Studies'. It is an ambitious attempt, ranging over more than 600 pages, to map the relationship between power and culture and 'to contribute to critical cultural enquiry and liberating political practice'. As they explain:

> Power is our central concern and we see *Cultural Politics* as an attempt to use theory in the interests of change, as a contribution to an emancipatory cultural politics. We hope that many different groups of reader – from students and teachers to arts and cultural workers – will find it accessible and above all useful.

This is cultural studies as social intervention – a perspective which dominated the field in the 1970s and seems increasingly less dominant in the 1990s. For some, to reverse this trend requires a return to questions of political economy. This is certainly the position of Nicholas Garnham, 'Political Economy and Cultural Studies: Reconciliation or Divorce?' (*Critical Studies in Mass Communication* 12. 62–71). Garnham's is the opening essay in a debate on the state of cultural studies. The other contributors are Lawrence Grossberg, 'Cultural Studies vs. Political Economy: Is Anybody Else Bored with this Debate?' (72–81), James W. Carey, 'Abolishing the Old Spirit World' (82–8), Graham Murdock, 'Across the Great Divide: Cultural Analysis and the Condition of Democracy' (89–94) and Nicholas Garnham, 'Reply to Grossberg and Carey' (95–100). In an often bad-tempered debate (Oscar H. Gandy's introduction [60–1] informs us that one would-be participant, Angela McRobbie, 'was so outraged and insulted by Garnham's initial draft that she simply could not respond') about the place of political economy in cultural studies, Garnham's concluding words to the debate are worth remembering, 'let the conversation continue across as wide a civic and civil discourse as possible'. As I said at the beginning of this short essay, cultural studies is an unfolding discourse.

Books Reviewed

Adam, Barbara, and Stuart Allan, eds. *Theorizing Culture: An Interdisciplinary Critique after Postmodernism*. UCL Press. pp. 256. hb £35.00, pb £12.95. ISBN 1 857 2832 95, 1 857 2832 87.
Ahearne, Jeremy. *Michel de Certeau: Interpretation and its Other*. Polity Press. pp. 227. hb £45.00, pb £12.95. ISBN 0 7456 1347 0.
Bermingham, Ann, and John Brewer, eds. *The Consumption of Culture*

1600–1800: Image, Object, Text. Routledge. pp. 672. hb £95.00. ISBN 0 415 12135 3.

Burns, Rob, ed. *German Cultural Studies: An Introduction*. Clarendon Press. pp. 384. hb £35.00, pb £13.99. ISBN 0 19 871502 1, 0 19 871503 X.

Davies, Ioan. *Cultural Studies and Beyond: Fragments of Empire*. Routledge. pp. 224. hb £40.00, pb £12.99. ISBN 0 415 03837 5.

Forbes, Jill, and Michael Kelly, eds. *French Cultural Studies: An Introduction*. Clarendon Press. pp. 336. hb £35.00, pb £12.99. ISBN 0 19 851500 5, 0 19 871501 3.

Frow, John. *Cultural Studies and Cultural Value*, Clarendon Press. pp. 190. hb £25.00, pb £10.99. ISBN 0 19 871128 X, 0 19 871127 1.

Gillespie, Marie. *Television, Ethnicity and Cultural Change*. Routledge. pp. 256. hb £35.00, pb £12.99. ISBN 0 415 09675 8.

Graham, Helen, and Jo Labanyi, eds. *Spanish Cultural Studies: An Introduction*. Clarendon Press. pp. 464. hb £35.00, pb £14.99. ISBN 0 19 815195 0, 0 19 815195 3.

Grossberg, Lawrence. 1992. *We Gotta Get Out of This Place: Popular Conservatism and Postmodern Culture*. Routledge. pp. 436. ISBN 0 415 90330 0.

Inglis, Fred. *Cultural Studies*. 1993. Blackwell. pp. 280. hb £40.00, pb £12.99. ISBN 0 631 18454 6, 0 631 18453 8.

Jordan, Glenn, and Chris Weedon. *Cultural Politics: Class, Gender, Race and the Postmodern World*. Blackwell. pp. 624. hb £35.00, pb £12.99. ISBN 0 631 16227 5, 0 631 16228 3.

Miller, Daniel. *Acknowledging Consumption: A Review of New Studies*. Routledge. pp. 304. hb £50.00, pb £15.99. ISBN 0 415 10688 5, 0 415 10689 3.

Munns, Jessica, and Gita Rajan, eds. *A Cultural Studies Reader: History, Theory, Practice*. Longman. pp. 694. hb £48.00, pb £18.99. ISBN 0 582 21411 4.

Sim, Stuart, ed. *The A-Z Guide to Modern Literary and Cultural Theorists*. Harvester Wheatsheaf. pp. 432. pb £12.95. ISBN 0 13 355553 4.

Stevenson, Nick. *Understanding Media Cultures: Social Theory and Mass Communication*. Sage. pp. 238. hb £37.50, pb £12.95. ISBN 0 8039 8931 8, 0 8039 8930 X.

Tallack, Douglas, ed. *Critical Theory: A Reader*. Harvester Wheatsheaf. pp. 501. pb £14.50. ISBN 0 7450 1533 6.

12

Popular Culture

HILLEGONDA RIETVELD

Dominic Strinati, Lecturer in the Sociology Department at Leicester University, suggests in *An Introduction to Theories of Popular Culture*, that 'popular culture cannot be defined except in relation to particular theories' (xviii). He therefore limits a general definition of popular culture to 'a set of generally available artefacts' (xvii) or 'a specific set of artefacts' (xviii). The main focus of this book pivots around discussions of approaches to the analysis, interpretation and evaluation of popular culture. This particular overview of perspectives has proven to be useful to course leaders and students in media, cultural and popular music studies. Topics follow each other in a semi-chronological order. 'Mass Culture' is the first stop and charts the development of the notion of popular culture as commodification and industrialization set in, whereby Strinati defines mass culture as 'popular culture which is produced by mass production industrial techniques and is marketed for a profit to a mass public of consumers' (10). The British pre-war debates of high versus low culture (elite versus mass) and, more importantly, folk versus mass culture are addressed, as well as post-war British fears of Americanization. Next is 'The Frankfurt School and the Culture Industry', where the ideas of mass culture theory are discussed from a German–American perspective, as it developed during the two decades after World War II. The Frankfurt School has been included because of the continuing influence of Adorno's ideas on the British study of popular culture and because of the importance of Benjamin's critique in this. Adorno's approach is criticized mainly for being ahistorical and for lacking an empirical basis. 'Structuralism, Semiology and Popular Culture' follows neatly, in a historical sense, as a chapter which deals with approaches which became prominent first in France during the 1950s. In this chapter, Strinati differentiates between the trajectories of semiology, 'the scientific study of signs', and structuralism, which 'is said to make general claims about the universal, causal character of structures' (88). Semiology is explained by taking Saussure's linguistic theory as a basis with some additions from Barthes's critical methods. Structuralism is focused on through the work of the anthropologist Lévi-Strauss, whose 'version of structuralism is concerned with uncovering the common structural principles underlying all the specific and historically variable manifestations of culture and myth' (96). An example of a structuralist analysis of contemporary popular culture is provided by a discussion of Eco's study of the James Bond novels, while Barthes's writing on popular culture provides examples of how semiology can be applied combined with a 'crude' notion of ideology. This brings us to 'Marxism, Political Economy and Ideology', a chapter which, with the exception of the already discussed Frankfurt School, addresses a history of thinking about popular culture based on ideas developed within a Marxist tradition. Starting with the concept of ideology, this chapter then moves on to the notion of political economy. Althusser's structuralist Marxism takes the discussion on ideology further, after which Gramsci's approach to popular culture and his notion of hegemony is put to the test. Here Strinati gives us a glimpse of his political colours by stating that: 'It may well be the case that the theory offered by Gramsci will prove the best way forward for the study of popular culture, especially if it is combined with the stress of the political economy approach on the importance of economic constrains' (171–2). It seems that Strinati wants to avoid economic determinism without being accused of 'culturalism'. What he does not avoid is reiterating the white, male and heterosexual points of view which, despite internal struggles, dominate social sciences and the humanities to this day. In all of the chapters discussed so far, the politics of identity are not explicitly addressed. The chapter on 'Feminism and Popular Culture', however, deals with some of these issues. Although Strinati pointed out in his introduction that he wanted to avoid a discussion of internal debates on the study of popular culture, these are central to this chapter. He first addresses the issue of 'symbolic annihilation of women' (180) and then moves on to the work of feminist critique concerning the analysis of advertising. After this he usefully summarizes internal debates consisting of feminist critiques of various approaches to the study of (popular) culture. Some of these approaches were already discussed in previous chapters (mass culture, ideology, semiology) and some are new to the narrative of the book (content analysis, psychoanalysis, audiences). Yet, I wonder why some of the feminist critiques could not have been integrated into the appropriate chapters, rather than ghettoizing them in a special chapter on feminism. As a result, feminism is structured as an 'other' to cultural and social theory. One could argue that this is a historical fact, but if Strinati set out not to give a history or an overview of internal debates, but rather to provide a good overview of approaches to the analysis of popular culture, then, structurally speaking, this chapter is an odd one. As he puts it himself: 'In this chapter I have not tried to present an exhaustive discussion of the feminist *analysis* of popular culture' (215; my emphasis). Ignoring issues of sexuality and the post-colonial debate, this book moves on to its final chapter, which reviews 'Postmodernism and Popular Culture'. After first pointing out some characteristics of this concept, such as the end and breakdown of the world as we used to conceptualize it, he then discusses 'some examples of popular culture in order to see if the existence of postmodernism can be detected' (228). It may be that a reader who is new to these debates could get confused here between theoretical analysis on the one hand and artefact on the other. The concrete examples show the mixing and merging of aesthetic styles, but do not convince that there is anything especially characteristic about that, since through history many styles and genres have developed out of hybrids. Only an approach which accepts hybridization, rather than 'progress', as a valid explanation for cultural changes and developments could, perhaps, be called postmodern. This chapter continues with a discussion of some of the 'social and historical conditions under which postmodernism emerges' (235). The shift to consumerism and to a media-led British society as well as the erosion of a stable sense of identity are given brief attention, followed by a critique of these ideas and characteristics. The chapter finishes with a critical assessment of popular cinema; the examined examples disappoint in postmodern potential, which could be because Strinati applies a non-postmodernist approach. In the 'Conclusions' section, discourse analysis and poststructuralism are mentioned, as well as the dialogical approach and cultural populism. Although each of these approaches would make for interesting chapters in themselves, Strinati uses them in order to end his tale. This means that although this is a useful and readable book, when teaching an overview of theoretical approaches it is limited to mainly sociological debates within a dated version of British Cultural Studies. Although useful as an educational device, one will need to use complementary reading material to teach those ideas which gave rise to the specific study of popular culture in the last ten years. To give Strinati credit, however, perhaps one of the problems in producing an ambitious overview like this is that the methods of analysis change just as rapidly as its ephemeral subject.

So, onto a book which took time to develop, but which was written in a relatively short time, providing a fast yet dense read of contemporary ideas in a not so bulky format. Enter *Unpopular Cultures,* written by Steve Redhead, founding joint director of the Manchester Institute for Popular Culture, and Reader in Law and Popular Culture based at the Manchester Metropolitan University. This text sets out Redhead's ideas on how to develop popular cultural studies as an academic discipline. This can be achieved, Redhead suggests, by focusing on the theorization of the margins rather than the centre of popular culture, where its limits and limitations are made apparent through its clashes with the law and with notions of 'common sense': 'It is the "regulation" of popular culture which marks out the terrain of study, where popular and unpopular clash' (105). Part I traces a history of jurisprudence, the sociology of law and of deviance on the one hand and of cultural studies on the other. He contends that 'deviance' theory has been an important theoretical interest (especially with a focus on youth and popular culture) within the development of cultural studies during the 1960s and 1970s, an interest which, Redhead claims, was lost 'in the "literary" and "postmodern" turns within cultural studies' (39). Redhead places his ideas within the spectrum of cultural theory as follows: 'if the commodification of everyday life was the focus of earlier critical theory, influenced by the Frankfurt School, the aim in this book is to take into account the aestheticisation and sexualisation of everyday life' (4). Part II develops the central thesis of the book and discusses 'the disappearance of law into popular culture' (6). In other words, the authority of the law in the regulation of 'the boundaries of certain social discourses and practices' is fragmenting in a 'media-saturated, self-referential, culture'; for example, in the occurrence of media-led moral panics (7). Redhead provides a critique on contemporary media-based culture which has been influenced by the work of Jean Baudrillard, while his interest in the 'margins' of popular culture draws on ideas developed by Gayatri Spivak, Michel Foucault and Jacques Derrida. In his own words, Redhead prefers: 'the notion of a low (as opposed to high) modernism . . . to some of the more outrageous – and ultimately, in my view, futile – connotations of postmodernism' (11). By discussing the regulation of cultural production such as copyright and licensing laws, as well as occasions of censorship, Redhead first establishes a notion of the law of art, providing plenty of case-studies in the process. After this he provides 'a postmodern law review' (84), whereby the subject of law, especially that in relation to popular culture, is problematized. Law seems to have become an object in itself, without a referent, thereby revelling in its pure form, its aesthetics, resulting in an 'art of law'. We find ourselves in an era of 'post-law', which in its turn produces a desire for law, which Redhead calls an 'erotics of law'. Taking on the rhythm of a roller coaster, Redhead demonstrates, by pointing out narratives from the 'margins' of contemporary 'global' culture (using genres such as slipstream, post-punk, post-youth, queer and gangsta), that the authority of official law seems to have disappeared. Redhead explains in the last chapter how some of the above ideas have been put into practice by the Unit for Law and Popular Culture, which joined the Centre for Urban and Cultural Analysis under the umbrella of the Manchester Institute for Popular Culture (MIPC) at the then Manchester Polytechnic. Like the Birmingham Centre for Contemporary Cultural Studies two decades earlier, it has favoured ethnographic methodological approaches and has produced working papers ('Working Papers in Popular Cultural Studies') in order to present up-to-date research and theoretical work. The MIPC encouraged participant observation by researchers, most of whom were actively involved in their fields of study. In the process, it acquired a huge archive of small press and other documentation on (un)popular cultures. The MIPC also produced a book series in 'Popular Cultural Studies', which charts its research activities and interests, such as rave culture, dance music, representations of the Gulf War, gay men's lives and lots of football. This book, then, sets out Redhead's ideas of 'the story of the birth and subsequent history of "law and popular culture" ' (100), a project which evolves with its subject matter.

During his time as a researcher for the Unit for Law and Popular Culture, Richard Haynes used football fanzines for his unique discourse analysis of contemporary football fandom. In addition to an impressive collection of British football-related small press at the MIPC, the result is *The Football Imagination: The Rise of Football Fanzine Culture*. Small press publications by British football fans started to occur in the 1980s and give a good indication of the discursive field of football fandom. Being a fan himself, Haynes has an intimate knowledge of this type of writing. His book:

> critically document(s) the rise of fanzines as an integral part of
> the new affective sensibility within football – from its subcultural
> roots in punk to its bricolage of football nostalgia and satirical
> humour – analysing textual content and tracing the ontology of
> the 'alternative football fan network'.   (147)

Using a methodology which can partly be traced back to the study of women's magazines, he shows how identities, which are tied in with concepts of masculinity and community, are redefined continually. Not only have fanzines provided a voice in defence against the (mis)treatment of fans as 'hooligans' by various authorities, but also against 'the erosion of a varied and vibrant football culture by sustaining interest in all professional and semi-professional clubs in the UK' (152). This book is an excellent example of how a study in popular culture from the 'inside' can significantly deepen the reader's knowledge of a specific subject, whilst remaining critical of the meanings that are produced within its various discourses.

In *The Language of Youth Subcultures: Social Identity in Action*, Sue Widdicombe and Robin Wooffitt, both lecturers in social psychology, acknowledge that there is a need in social research to let people talk for themselves about their sense of identity. In order 'to take heed of (subculture) members' own accounts' they want 'to consider the nature of the medium through which those accounts are produced' (28).

The first one-third of this book provides an overview and critique of debates on subcultural theory, conversation analysis in sociology and discourse analysis in social psychology. In their discussion of the work of the Birmingham Centre for Contemporary Cultural Studies, the authors point out that subcultures had become vehicles for the centre's theoretical and political projections, thereby showing a 'mild contempt for the actual members', silencing them 'before they have even been allowed to speak' (23). As an alternative, Widdicombe and Wooffitt feel that more empirical research is necessary. They first provide examples of how identities are constructed in conversations, such as interviews, before embarking on an analysis of empirical examples which focus on the content of conversations that 'resonate with issues addressed in social psychological and sociological studies' (5), in particular, youth subcultures and social identity. Although the thesis of this book is important to social research in popular culture today, it is a pity that the examples are rather dated. For instance, interviews are analysed with members of 'subcultures' which were more relevant twenty years ago (punk), and a type of formal style is employed which is equivalent to someone trying to explain a joke to the extent that it is not a joke anymore. Ironically, in the attempt to be as precise a possible, a phonetic representation of colloquial language is provided which gives the impression that the interviewees suffer from speech impairments; this is in contrast to the speech of the interviewers, which is transcribed in a correct English spelling. This format places the social researcher in a 'normal', 'objective' and unproblematic position, while their subject of study is structured as an 'abnormal' and fetishized object. Nevertheless, Widdicombe and Wooffitt do achieve some useful, though minimal, conclusions. By listening to 'the discursive actions produced by young people themselves'(227) one learns that 'being seen to conform to the critical features of a subcultural group is taken to be a sign of inauthenticity. . . . The ascription or denial of conformity is therefore a live interactional concern for members' (226).

In other words, one has to be careful not to put people into sociocultural categories without carefully listening to their opinions about that.

Club Cultures: Music, Media and Subcultural Capital is an example of thorough empirical research combined with academic objectification. It was researched and written partly as a Ph.D. project by Sarah Thornton, now a Lecturer in Media Studies at the University of Sussex. Like the previous title, this book is a result of a social science inquiry into the notion of 'subcultures'. Yet, it is very different in its choice of methodologies and of subject matter – the latter is the contemporary young dance audiences that attend nightclubs. This book is useful as an educational aid, since it provides fresh examples to explain key notions in British cultural studies such as 'moral panics', 'cultural capital', 'authenticity' and 'youth'. In doing so, it uses club culture as a vehicle for theoretical projections which have a history in debates in media and cultural studies. Despite the wealth of insightful information collected, certain

gaps in ethnographic knowledge are glossed over by a self-assured use of
'traditional' cultural theory. Thornton makes her position clear by stating that:
'Despite having once been an avid clubber, I was an outsider to the cultures in
which I conducted research' (2). Thornton gives several reasons for this. In the
first place, as a social observer she was working and not playing, like the staff
at these establishments and unlike the punters she studied. Secondly, as an
American she felt like a stranger in British clubs. However, in my opinion, this
sense of alienation could have lifted if she had actively taken part in British
club culture. Finally, at the age of twenty-three at the start of her research, she
claims she was older than most of the social group she observed. It is funny to
think that her age group was in some way an alienating factor in the study of
club cultures; it is a mistake to collapse club cultures and youth cultures onto
each other, unless the concept of 'youth' is stretched to well beyond the
youthful age of twenty-three. Therefore, the most important obstacle to
Thornton's involvement in the club scenes she describes is her choice of
methodology, which favours a 'detached' type of empirical observation over
participant observation. This seems to lead to a foregrounding in her study of
media representations of youth in dance environments. Thornton concludes
that 'subcultures are best defined as social groups that have been labelled as
such. . . . Communications media create subcultures in the process of naming
them and draw boundaries around them in the act of describing them' (162).
This study seems to indicate that the people who populate those 'social groups'
are, if not passive, certainly malleable. This argument echoes some of the
pessimism formulated by mass culture theorists and the Frankfurt School.
Thornton contends that the media are crucial in the shaping of distinctions in
'subcultural capital' (a variation on Bourdieu's concept of 'cultural capital')
and adds on her position towards popular culture that:

> This approach interrogates the 'popular' not just in terms of its
> etymological root, 'of the people', nor in the sense of being 'pre-
> valent' or 'common', but specifically in the sense of being
> 'approved', 'preferred' and 'well-liked'. In other words, issues of
> taste are essential to the conception of *popular* culture.
>
> (164; author's italics)

A different view on popular culture and communication media is offered in
Out in Culture: Gay, Lesbian and Queer Essays on Popular Culture, an anthology
edited by Corey K. Creekmur and Alexander Doty, both American Professors
(Lecturers to the British) in English. Here we can find a critical approach from
the 'inside' out onto the world of mass media. This collection of critical essays
on film, television, fashion and popular culture provides a wealth of theoretical
projections and insightful narratives which offer a refreshing alternative to
theorizations produced by the gaze of social observers who presume a status of
'neutrality'. After pointing out 'the metaphor of *the closet* – a private (or
'sub'cultural) space one comes out of to inhabit public space honestly and with
one's identity intact' (2; author's italics), the editors state that:

> the inevitability of the symbolic and social 'limits', 'margins',
> 'borders', and boundaries maintaining these oppositions [of
> 'inside' and 'outside'] has been continually challenged by the

unconventional participation of gays and lesbians in mainstream culture. For the writers in this anthology, a central issue is how to be 'out in culture': how to occupy a place in mass culture, yet maintain a perspective on it that does not accept its homophobic and heterocentrist definitions, images, and terms of analysis. (2)

Creekmur and Doty explain that 'this queerly "different" experience of mass culture was most evident, if coded, in the ironic, scandalous sensibility known as camp' (2). 'These days', they observe:

> there really is no critical or political 'bottomline' on the uses of camp . . . sometimes it re-inscribes queerness on the margins of popular culture, sometimes it questions the notion of a mainstream culture or preferred (read straight, white middleclass male) cultural readings, while at other times it places queerness at the heart of the popular. (4)

This anthology charts a history of increased visibility of lesbian and gay people in popular culture, both as mass culture (mass produced for a 'mass audience') and as a type of folk culture ('of the people'). Not only academic essays, but also texts from the 'alternative' gay and lesbian press have been compiled producing a wide 'range of modes as well as topics in queer cultural commentary' (7). Some of the thirty papers are seminal classics, such as Richard Dyer's often reprinted piece on disco and Anthony Thomas's important article on the gay African-American origins of house music. Topics include early to later pieces of explicit gay and lesbian film criticism; a special dossier on Hitchcock's films (which are employed as 'test cases'); gay avant-garde and pornography (for example, a piece on cult cartoonist Tom of Finland); lesbian dildo-debates; visual representations of AIDS in the mass media; a special dossier on popular music (disco, house, 'women's music' and a piece on Madonna's queer fans); and a section on 'style', from drag to 'commodity lesbianism'. In aid of the interested reader and researcher, this book also includes 'a general bibliography of gay, lesbian and queer work on mass culture. While this bibliography is not exhaustive, it . . . turned out to be very long indeed' (9). This anthology shows a diversity of points of view. It is a useful collection to anyone interested in the study of popular culture, on the one hand because of its engaging content and important commentary, and on the other because it is witness to popular culture as it is lived – where audiences actively negotiate and produce meanings within and outside the constraints of the mass media.

In *Family Plots: The De-Oedipalization of Popular Culture*, Dana Heller (Associate Professor of American Literature, Gender Studies and Literary Theory at Old Dominion University) contributes to the discussion of how a notion of the family is constructed in narratives of mass-mediated popular culture. It is pointed out that our concept of the family is on the one hand derived from a narrative form which Heller calls (with Sigmund Freud) the 'family romance' or (with Alfred Hitchcock) the 'family plot'; on the other hand, these types of narratives are a result of a cultural (re)mapping in a postmodern society. Heller uses contemporary critical theory in order to analyse (post)family romances which:

demonstrate . . . the ongoing debate over the possibility of self-formation in the wake of cultural/familial dissolution . . . they allow us to foreground some of the various fault lines of the family, lines along which desires and identifications . . . become mobile and transgressive, moving toward an affirmative practice of familial description. (xiv)

She shows that the metaphor of the Oedipus complex (a central concept in psychoanalysis in relation to the acquisition of a gendered sense of identity) is crumbling, as is the concept of the nuclear family.

The critique of the Oedipus complex does not stand in isolation; in a different way, it is also indicated by, for example, Joanna Ryan's short polemic 'Feminism, Sexuality and Psychoanalysis' in the Autumn issue of *New Formations* (devoted to the discussion of psychoanalysis in a cultural context), which argues that psychoanalysis fails to provide a satisfactory explanation for the formation of sexual orientations.

Heller reviews a variety of popular narratives, from the modernist 'normal' family, via monster families like *Bewitched* (a sitcom which Heller mentions in one breath with *The Addams Family*) to queer narratives (or how to recognize these) and the lesbian detective story. The last discussion of the book centres on the (cyborg) family grouping in the Hollywood film. *Terminator 2* Heller interprets (during a home video viewing experience) as a right-wing backlash for nuclear family values. She also remarks, on the popular fascination with cyborgs, that 'Insofar as cyborgs offer appropriate emblems of fragmented identities, they may also serve as fitting tropes for fragmented families, a kind of genealogical systems breakdown' (193).

Heller's book updates some of the feminist psychoanalytical debates in narrative theory which centre around issues of gender identity and sexuality. The use of contemporary examples makes her dense theorizations relevant to the narrative study of popular culture in the context of gender and sexuality.

A pragmatic view on how North American middle class children deal with mass-produced popular culture can be found in *Kid Culture: Children & Adults & Popular Culture* by Kathleen McDonnell. Children are constructed in this book as active readers of mass-mediated popular texts. In a liberal–humanist vein, McDonnell argues that popular culture may perhaps have a deteriorating effect on children, but it also creates a global environment which liberates children. In this way, it seems like ALL children are part of the same global 'subculture', namely, 'KidCulture', as though they were of one homogeneous social category, regardless of location, ethnic background, class or sexuality. There is one concession to this idea of global culture: central in the book is a discussion of the way in which (middle-class heterosexual North American) children differentiate themselves on the basis of gender in their creations of narratives. Together with film narratives, television programmes feature high as popular cultural media. Keeping in mind the limitations of the social parameters within which the observations have been made, this book is relevant as a contribution to the debates on the moral panic over children in the context of mediated sexism and violence.

Sandra Weber and Claudia Mitchell, Lecturers (Associate Professors) in Education, Curriculum Theory and (in the case of Weber) Popular Culture in Montreal, are also concerned with identity constructions in mass-mediated popular culture, this time of the professional educator, the teacher. *'That's Funny, You Don't Look Like a Teacher': Interrogating Images and Identity in Popular Culture* traces how knowledge about the concept of the teacher is constructed in various contexts, not only at schools, but also outside, such as in films, on television and in books. The text supplies readings of a great variety of cinematic narratives, such as *Kindergarden Cop* and *Blackboard Jungle*, or of North American television series, such as *My Little Pony*. Dress codes are discussed, as are images of teachers in drawings by children and student teachers. Stereotypes and other representations ('images') of teachers are put into a historical context and discussed in terms of gender politics and class dynamics. Although this book is of obvious interest to anyone involved in education, it can also be used as source material for research into interaction between representation and lived experience.

In *Spanish Cultural Studies: An Introduction*, edited by Helen Graham (Lecturer in the Department of History at Royal Holloway) and Jo Labanyi (Reader in Modern Spanish and Latin American Literature at Birkbeck College), the debates in cultural studies and on the use of mass media are given a Spanish dimension, whilst using the English language. The editors explain that Spanish cultural studies is relatively new, partly because the earlier theoretical writings about Spanish culture seem to be rather elitist and concerned with notions such as national identity. In the late nineteenth century, the Krausists from the Institucion Libre de Ensenaza explored ideas parallel to the British 'culture and civilization' tradition, whereby education was seen to be beneficial in the 'civilization' of the masses. Some of the Spanish debates on culture as everyday life started in the 1930s, but no tradition of thought developed out of this, due to an influential cultural thinker, Ortega y Gasset, who on the one hand argued that modernist 'high' culture was too dehumanizing to be promoted to 'the masses' and on the other hand had no interest in (rural) popular culture. In addition, the 'Nationalist victory in the civil war, restor[ed] power to the traditional elite. . . . What Francoism discouraged was not popular and mass culture, but the exercise of independent critical thought necessary to the development of any form of cultural analysis' (3).

Cultural debates, it seems, were influenced by Gramsci's notion of the 'national popular' but, according to Helen Graham and Jo Labanyi, on the whole this body of work was rather naive. 'The postmodern stress on heterogeneity – allied with the Gramscian notion of hegemony – has been especially fertile in Latin American cultural theory' (4). Yet in Spain this is a relatively new concept, perhaps due to the success of Francoist totalitarian ideas. Now, with the 'globalization' of mass culture, these issues are being discussed. Thereby, the editors:

> take 'culture' to mean both lived practices and artefacts or performances, understood as symbolic systems. The notion of 'performance' effectively ties the various categories together, inasmuch as they are all forms of signification produced for an audience. . . . One must, however, remember that lived practices have material effects on human beings that are more deadly than those of any art object. . . . Nevertheless, all cultural forms . . . have an underlying narrative: culture can be defined as the stories

people tell each other to explain what and where they are. This brings us to the second point we want to stress: that culture is a site of power that is always negotiated and contested (5)

The editors distinguish three categories of culture: 'high' culture, mass culture and popular culture. The latter is viewed as a Romantic notion, referring to an oral folk culture which is pre-literate, and which serves to create a sense of national tradition in the modern state. Mass culture is seen as the culture of 'the masses' or the urban proletariat, and is a product of modernity. However, in the postmodern era, the editors explain, the terms 'popular culture' and 'mass culture' seem to have become synonymous. At the same time, we are reminded that 'The persistence in Spain into the modern period of strong rural cultural traditions means that Anglo-Saxon – and even French – theoretical models have to be applied with caution' (8). So the term 'cultura popular' is reserved for Spanish popular traditions, while mass cultural media are used to promote a national identity by bringing 'high' cultural forms to the rural areas. These contemporary concepts of culture, which developed in conjunction with modernity, are discussed in this collection (including postmodernism) from 1898 to 1992. It offers a wide scope of material on a variety of subjects, which are grouped in a historical overview. 'Elites in Crisis 1898–1931' includes two essays on popular culture: Jose Alvarez Junco discusses 'Rural and Urban Popular Cultures' and Serge Salaun tackles 'The Cuplé: Modernity and Mass Culture'. The next part, 'The Failure of Democratic Modernization 1931–1939', carries two articles which are of interest to readers and researchers in popular culture: Alicia Alted's 'The Republican and Nationalist Wartime Cultural Apparatus' and Jo Labanyi's 'Propaganda Art: Culture By the People or for the People?' Part III, 'Authoritarian Modernization 1940–1975' includes several pieces relevant to this review section: 'The Ideology of Sport' by John London, 'Censorship or the Fear of Mass Culture' again by Jo Labanyi, 'Popular Culture in the "Years of Hunger"' by Helen Graham and 'The Politics of Popular Music: On the Dynamics of the New Song' by Catherine Boyle. The last part, 'Democracy and Europeanization: Continuity and Change 1975–1992', is packed with essays which discuss notions of popular culture, such as 'The Politics of Language: Spain's Minority Languages' by Clare Mar-Molinero, 'Redefining Public Interest: Television in Spain Today' by Barry Jordan and 'The Film Industry: Under Pressure from the State and Television' by Augusto M. Torres, as well as 'Artistic Patronage and Enterprise Culture' and 'Designer Culture in the 1980s: the Price of Success' both by Emma Dent Coad. Apart from popular culture, this collection of papers addresses issues like government politics (republicans, democracy, Francoism, anarchism, nationalism, pluralism), gender politics, sexual politics, education and religion.

The academic journal *New Formations* published a collection of their papers (covering the period 1987 to 1991) in book form this year – *Cultural Remix: Theories of Politics and the Popular*, edited by Erica Carter, James Donald and Judith Squires. Although this team 'welcome legitimacy for interdisciplinary and popular cultural studies', 'there is a troubling political ambiguity in the cultural studies commitment to interdisciplinarity, coupled with its anti-hierarchical reflex – its drive to shift the academic focus from high culture to popular forms' (vii). The editors argue that democratization in education may seem like a good thing, but there may be a danger that students are seduced by commodified courses which are clearly populist and which, instead of a solid critical underpinning, offer a hedonist pluralism where everything goes: 'There is a point, in other words – as is underlined by Ien Ang, Charlotte Brunsdon and others in this volume – when critical criteria must be formulated, and judgements made' (viii).

However, how does one consolidate, as a teacher, the political project of cultural studies ('pedagogy in the service of democratic transformation' [viii]) with the institutional expectation that one invests time and money in the acquisition of knowledge that hopefully provides the student with a career? In addition, how can a New Left politics be maintained in the face of an even newer New Right? For example, the collapse of the East European communist block and the rise of an authoritarian woman in British politics, Margaret Thatcher, have meant some blows to Marxist and feminist critical approaches: 'It is to these key questions of popular politics adequate to this *fin-de-siècle* moment that *New Formations* has addressed itself since the late 1980s' (vix, author's italics). The editors point out that the focus is therefore not specifically on everyday culture or on alternative methods of reading, but rather on the production, through critical discourse, of a way of making sense of the cultural objects it refers to. Many of the pieces in this collection have been written by familiar 'names' in the field of cultural studies, such as Homi K. Bhabha, Jaqueline Rose, Stuart Hall, Dick Hebdidge, Ien Ang and Susan Willis (co-author of *Inside the Mouse: Work and Play at Disney World*, a 1995 publication on popular culture). Subjects range from deeply abstract to concrete readings of the politics of everyday life. For example, Willis discusses the cultural politics of Afro hairstyles, while Hebdidge embroiders on Bourdieu's theme of a sociology of taste and the use of cars in his street. The last paper in the book may provide an answer to the question of how the New Right can have such a stronghold on British cultural politics; Anne Marie Smith concludes her piece on British legislation of homosexuality with conceptualizing 'Thatcherism as a floating signifier' (326), which can be found in different guises at different locations, including our own self-policing. This is a useful book, which provides examples of how to apply a politicized cultural theory to questions in the study of popular culture.

Chris Jenks, Head of the Department of Sociology at Goldsmiths' College, is the editor of *Visual Culture*, a timely collection of scholarly texts which explores the centrality of vision as perceptive sensibility in Western culture. Illustrating a varied sociology of visual modernist cultural production, this book offers, in addition to some dense theoretical discussions, a review of popular cultural topics such as cinema, pop art, television, Nazi aesthetics, advertising and photography. Contributors David Morley and Dick Hebdidge are well established within the tradition of British Cultural Studies, while many of the others in the thirteen headed all-male writers team of this collection have distinguished themselves in the field of sociology, media studies, art history and critical theory. In 'Television: Not So Much a Visual Medium, More a Visible Object', David Morley gives a literature review which indicates that television has historically developed as an aural rather than visual medium and that, as a part of our contemporary domestic furniture, the television fulfils several roles including that of a fetish object which in more ways than one has become an extension of our sense of self. Both James Donald's 'The

City, The Cinema: Modern Spaces' and Malcolm Barnard's 'Advertising: The Rhetorical Imperative' are relevant to this review section. Another interesting paper is Justin Lorenzen's 'Reich Dreams: Ritual Horror and Armoured Bodies' on Nazi propaganda and its project of the aestheticization of everyday life, which points out that a Nazi way of using imagery is still a source of fascination in contemporary society and can be found, for example, in cyborg science fiction movies. Although he does not mention Susan Sontag's much earlier essay 'Fascinating Fascism', or Walter Benjamin's notion of Nazi 'aestheticization of everyday life', the argument in this essay reads like an update of these ideas. Using quotes from work by Felix Guattari, Jean Baudrillard and George Bataille, Lorenzen argues that the imagery, as well as certain attitudes which he identifies with both fascism and Nazism (two terms he uses, perhaps confusingly, in an interchangeable manner), are still with us today:

> In one sense Nazism's secret was transcendence and self- destruction made into one. Yet these impulses, far from being defeated, survive in the social space finding expression in a diverse range of popular cultural forms. . . . The problem is not simply how we respond to the fascist imagery, but also how and where it emerges next. . . . As someone quite famous once said, 'the next time the Nazi's come they won't be wearing brown shirts'. (168)

With one eye on Anne Marie Smith's previous conclusion and another on the work of Steve Redhead, it is tempting to add that perhaps nazism is a type of 'floating signifier', providing an erotic and aesthetic pleasure in an excessive and destructive striving for law and order.

Andreas Huyssen, 'born in the Third Reich, but too late to have conscious remembrances' (4) and for many years a Professor at Columbia University, has collected his papers from the last seven years in *Twilight Memories: Marking Time in a Culture of Amnesia*. Huyssen contends that all representation is based on memory, while memory itself is based in representation: 'The past is not simply there in memory, but it must be articulated to become memory' (3). A project which started in the debates of postmodernism in the 1980s led Huyssen to explore memory in contemporary culture, not only in the media (for example, in an essay on Baudrillard's inspiration by McLuhan) and German avant-garde art but also and especially in 'the surprising popularity of the museum and the resurgence of the monument and the memorial as major modes of aesthetic, historical, and spatial expression' (5).

Huyssen observes that contemporary representations of the past have ceased to be a linear narrative. This is in contrast to a high modernist conceptualization of history, which was designed to forge nation states and to show that the present was better and the future would be best. On the one hand, this shift is tied in with the fact that we are now able to travel around the globe, physically or virtually: 'we have accumulated so many non-synchronicities in our present that a very hybrid structure of temporality seems to be emerging' (8). Yet, on the other hand: 'The jumble of the non-synchronous, the recognition of temporal difference in the real world . . . clashes dramatically with the draining of time in the world of information and data banks' (9).

So, Huyssen suggests that what we can witness in the boom of remembrances is a struggle of 'mortal bodies that want to hold on to their temporality (9) 'against high-tech amnesia' (5). Huyssen's meticulous methods of critical writing are rooted in a German tradition of cultural philosophy, while his keen observation of Western society gone haywire in its memory banks seems to be steeped in an identification with German culture whilst living in New York. This book can provide some theoretical underpinning to the study of museums, memorials and representations of 'traditions'.

An overview of live issues and theory in cultural politics can be found in an epic volume (624 pages) entitled *Cultural Politics: Class, Gender, Race and the Postmodern World*, edited by Glenn Jordan, Lecturer in Cultural and Media Studies at the University of Glamorgan, and Chris Weedon, Lecturer in Critical Theory, Cultural Studies and Women's Studies at the University of Wales. It provides a historical perspective on cultural politics and policy, mainly in the area of the arts, literature and intellectual life in Britain and it contextualizes this with case-studies from abroad, such as class politics and the German Democratic Republic or feminist politics and African-American literary criticism. A large part of the book is devoted to the cultural politics of race in art, addressing primitivism and postcolonialism, using Australian Aboriginal writing as a non-British case-study. It is a book one can dip in and out of, since each section discusses specific case-studies. It questions whose voice is allowed to be heard and remembered, and what tactics of empowerment can be employed by those who have been marginalized or oppressed. Popular culture does not seem to feature much in its narrative; rather, it seeks empowerment in Western middle-class 'high' cultural activities, such as a writing group for Asian women in the United Kingdom. Jordan and Weedon describe their project as follows:

> We look precisely at those areas that constitute the dominant 'high' culture: Literature, Art and History. Many social groups do not find themselves or their interests reflected in these traditions. Working-class people, women and people of Colour find themselves marginalised or excluded. We focus on examples of how these groups have attempted to reclaim and transform the dominant in their own interests.

One could argue that no case can be made for a reclaiming of 'high' culture, since historically it belongs with dominant social groupings. Yet, what these writers chart is the great variety of existing projects which enable people to gain a voice in the transformation of dominant formats in our culture (and its projections). Out of this a cultural production develops, which in some cases is a type of popular culture in the senses of folk culture and unpopular culture, rather than mass culture. Examples of these can be found Redhead's *Unpopular Cultures* or in Creekmur and Doty's *Out in Culture* (discussed above), and in many other types of contemporary fiction.

Music seems to be more accessible to a wide range of people than other media. A book which centres on the pleasures of a particular North American popular music genre is *Country Music Culture: From Hard Times to Heaven* by Curtis W. Ellison, Dean of the School of Interdisciplinary Studies at Miami University in Ohio. Ellison's realist narrative shows that:

Commercial country music was invented during a period of intense modernization in the twentieth-century American South. It evolved rapidly from rustic radio programs of the mid-20s through the marketing of recording artists to an extensive national network of performers and fans unparalleled in other forms of popular music.   (xvi)

An informative study, full of ethnographic and historical detail with a focus on commercial country music and the persisting devotion of its fans, it places this musical genre in a wider cultural framework:

for nearly seventy years, even with its complexity, this entertainment has maintained a distinctly personal tone and a sustained focus on domestic social life. This persistence has achieved an impressive irony in American society: while the marketing of commercial country music and its trappings fully embrace modernity, the resulting popular culture community functions as an imaginative means for transcending the negative effects of modernity.   (xvii)

Ellison argues that the devotion to country music should be understood in the context of the 'hard times' of social change; it provides an antidote to the resultant traumas in the form of celebrations of several versions of love (romantic, family, spiritual). In this way, so the argument goes, economic and broader social issues are individualized to the extent that country music itself is said to give a sense of hope of escape. Indeed, it may be said to offer a pleasure akin to (pastoral) romance fiction, with the added dimension that country music fans can share their emotions in large groups, thereby creating a sense of community and of identity. In this way, country music offers a type of cultural function which could be compared with religion. As Ellison puts it: 'this music can lead us from hard times to heaven' (270).

Ecstasy can also be bought as a chemical and, since it is illegal in countries like Great Britain, one has to hope that it does not contain some lethal concoction. Ecstasy has been at the centre of various British moral panics since the late 1980s. Although several studies on the cultural context of the use of this drug are available abroad (The Netherlands, for example), no British publisher seems to have dared to support a study on this topic. In this political climate, Nicholas Saunders made the brave step of self publishing *Ecstasy and the Dance Culture*. Uncensored by institutional (academic or government) interests, this book is quirky (for instance, what is *the* dance culture?). It is part of an ongoing updating process, which started with an earlier version called *E is for Ecstasy*, and has a parallel website on the internet. These books could be seen as cult classics; they are now part and parcel of the imagination and mythology of ecstasy users. *Ecstasy and the Dance Culture* covers a history of the drug ecstasy and reviews physiological, psychological, social, legal and cultural contexts of its use. Saunders relies on specialist contributors for additional information, such as its various user groups, including, amongst others, contemporary British dance (club) cultures (which, like country music culture, seem to function as secular versions of religion), and related dance drugs. It also provides a large, but by no means exhaustive, bibliography (including brief descriptions of contents), mainly in the areas of toxicology, law and social commentary. Thereby, it is one example of a rich resource for further study in this area of (un)popular culture.

Books Reviewed

Carter, Erica, James Donald, and Judith Squires eds. *Cultural Remix: Theories of Politics and the Popular*. Lawrence & Wishart. pp. 332. pb £14.99. ISBN 0 85315 794 4.

Creekmur, Corey K., and Alexander Doty, eds. *Out in Culture: Gay, Lesbian and Queer Essays on Popular Culture*. Cassell (and Duke University Press). pp. 535. pb £16.99. ISBN 0 304 33488 X.

Ellison, Curtis W. *Country Music Culture: From Hard Times to Heaven*. University Press of Mississippi. pp. 314. £14.95. ISBN 0 87805 722 6.

Graham, Helen, and Jo Labanyi, eds. *Spanish Cultural Studies: An Introduction*. Oxford University Press. pp. 455. hb £37.50. ISBN 0 19 815195 0.

Haynes, Richard. *The Football Imagination: The Rise of Football Fanzine Culture*. Popular Cultural Studies No. 8. Arena. pp. 169. pb £12.95. ISBN 1 85742 213 9.

Heller, Dana. *Family Plots: The De-Oedipalization of Popular Culture*. University of Pennsylvania Press. pp. 237. pb £13.95. ISBN 0 8122 1544 3.

Huyssen, Andreas. *Twilight Memories: Marking Time in a Culture of Amnesia*. Routledge. pp. 292. hb £37.50. ISBN 0 415 90934 1.

Jenks, Chris, ed. *Visual Culture*. Routledge. pp. 269. pb £13.99. ISBN 0 415 10623 0.

Jordan, Glenn, and Chris Weedon, eds. *Cultural Politics: Class, Gender, Race and the Postmodern World*. Blackwell. pp. 624. pb £13.99. ISBN 0 631 16228 3.

McDonnell, Kathleen. *Kid Culture: Children & Adults & Popular Culture*. Second Story Press. pp. 179. pb £11.99. ISBN 0 929005 64 3.

Redhead, Steve. *Unpopular Cultures: The Birth of Law and Popular Culture*. Manchester University Press. pp. 136. pb £10.99. ISBN 0 7190 3652 6.

Saunders, Nicholas. *Ecstasy and the Dance Culture*. Self publication. pb £9.95. ISBN 0 9501628 9 2.

Strinati, Dominic. *An Introduction to Theories of Popular Culture*. Routledge. pp. 301. pb £11.99. ISBN 0 415 12470 0.

Thornton, Sarah. *Club Cultures: Music, Media and Subcultural Capital*. Polity Press. pp. 191. pb £11.95. ISBN 0 7456 1443 4.

Weber, Sandra, and Claudia Mitchell. *'That's Funny, You Don't Look Like a Teacher': Interrogating Images and Identity in Popular Culture*. The Falmer Press. pp. 156. pb £13.95. ISBN 0 750 70413 6.

Widdicombe, Sue, and Robin Wooffitt. *The Language of Youth Subcultures: Social Identity in Action*. Harvester Wheatsheaf. pp. 250. pb £13.95. ISBN 0 7450 1419 4.

13

Australian Popular Culture and Media Studies

TARA BRABAZON

The phrase 'imagined communities' has almost reached the level of cliché in cultural theory. Within Australian popular culture and media studies, the expression is inflected by a resonance beyond Anderson's theorizing. The debates emerging from 1995 articulate a troubled imagining, a fraying and dissociating social subjectivity. While there are increasing forays into cultural history, with accompanying attempts to reconcile race relations, the study of contemporary popular cultural practices and media sites has been tentative in direction and reticent in ideological stance.

The debates explored in this review are presented in five sections: 1. Framing Popular Cultural Studies; 2. Representing the Nation; 3. Difference and Diversity; 4. Popular Cultural Practices; 5. Media Studies: From Poaching to Policy.

1. Framing Popular Cultural Studies

The time has ended when a cultural critic could state with certainty that popular culture is resistive and high culture is hegemonic. The texts published during 1995 display the breadth and complexity through which the terrain of popular culture is being framed. One book in particular serves to demonstrate the maturity of contemporary cultural theory within Australia: Peter Goodall's *High Culture, Popular Culture*.

Goodall investigates the contextual questions that encircle the spheres of high and popular culture. While working over familiar territory, attending to Matthew Arnold and the Birmingham Centre, the textual and research material is inflected for use by Australian scholars and students. Continually, Goodall pulls abstract debates back to 'the history of Australia, which, like all postcolonial societies, has struggled with questions of its identity, but which has interpreted them to a peculiar extent in terms of a conflict between elitist and populist definitions of its culture'. The analysis remains sharp and innovative because Goodall links cultural analysis to the construction of Australian nationalism. He also shows the distinctiveness and overlap between populist and elitist renderings of the White Australia Policy.

The investigation of past cultural formations remains a key directive of the text. Goodall is wary of cultural studies because of its fetishization of contemporary sites. Similarly, he decries the lack of treatment granted to the canon. He argues, quite effectively, that theorists within contemporary cultural studies must stop shadow-boxing Leavisites. He also warns that 'uncritical populism . . . has threatened to become the house style of Australian Cultural Studies'. He works against the reification of popular culture as a counter-aesthetic and questions why simplistic presentations of resistance and struggle have been a characteristic problem of Australian theorists. With remarkable contextual reflexivity and analytical fluency, Goodall has shown how texts function within social processes. His most evocative research is found in chapter 4, where the analysis of elitism and populism feeds into identity politics. The mutual exclusivity of Australianness and high culture is inscribed on the bodies of both the bushman in the 'outback' and Noeline Donaher from *Sylvania Waters*. Goodall reconciles both populism and elitism in the image of the (ex)Prime Minister, Paul Keating.

Although vitriolic at times, *High Culture, Popular Culture* offers a reading of Australian culture and critical theories that must be considered. His attack on contemporary cultural studies is timely, recognizing it as 'a well-marked and small pond inhabited by a few large fish'. The book is appropriate for upper level undergraduates, serving to assist their reading of the seminal moments in critical theory. Yet the currency of the text also extends to scholars wanting to understand the form and direction of cultural studies in a small antipodean pond.

Two big fish in this pond are Meaghan Morris and Stephen Muecke. During 1995, they founded the *UTS Review*. Like Goodall, they are concerned with the state of Humanities in Australia. Morris and Muecke, in their 'Editorial' (*UTS Review* 1.1–4), argue that cultural studies is not as resilient as suggested within publishers' catalogues. With fewer places to submit articles, Australian cultural studies is being squeezed into a shrinking niche market. They realize that 'the economic and technological changes are . . . forcing publishers to insist that cultural studies be produced for an international market – by which they mean, in practice "US readers" '. The *UTS Review* has been published to provide a place for critical theorizing of Australian culture. Yet, as Morris and Muecke suggest, the formation of this new journal has been necessary because of the dwindling Australian spaces for intellectual inquiry.

The journal's articles display an awareness of the changing state of cultural theory. Ruth Barcan's article, 'A Symphony of Farts' (*UTS Review* 1.83–92), explores the slippages between consumption practices and notions of resistance. The piece questions how to be politically active while working in cultural studies. Barcan states that 'it seems to me that much cultural studies work on popular culture (including my own) still works within a paradigm structured around the twin poles of containment and subversion'. By demanding a reconsideration of social change and struggle in contemporary theory, the politics of everyday life can be shaken from simplistic readings of power relationships.

Some contributions to the journal assert the political imperatives within contemporary theory. Tani Barlow, editor of the journal *Positions*, argues in 'Triple Double Bind' (*UTS Review* 1.57–83) that 'Right now . . . I think that cultural studies consists of nothing less in practical terms than a method for renegotiating relations between Britain and its former colonies and settler societies'. The article considers the difficulties in using a cultural studies framework beyond the United Kingdom. She suggests that any affirmation of difference within cultural studies be mediated through an anglophone filter. Significantly though, she traces the decline of the journal as a forum for intellectual work. The increasing publication of readers, or edited collection of essays, is seen by Barlow to be transforming journals into databases.

Cultural studies is not the only theoretical methodology seen to be losing its resilience. Helen Borland, in the article 'Contested Territories and Evolving Academic Cultures' (*Australian Journal of Communication* 22.14–30), recounts the history of the Australian Communication Association (ACA). The ACA has grown beyond New South Wales and Queensland through to the other Australian states and New Zealand. Yet in the economic rationalist environment, the lack of academic recognition of communication studies leaves both the scholars working in the area and the ACA itself vulnerable. Borland warns of the dangerous overlap between English and communication studies, where declining academic spheres piggyback the success of newer terrains.

The debates encircling both communication studies and cultural studies show that the exploration of popular culture and the media is moving through a transitional phrase. The embodiment of this trend, and the most significant book to be published in the area during 1995, is John Frow's *Cultural Studies and Cultural Value*. This text has been greeted with enormous critical interest, as befits a theoretician of Frow's calibre. The major humanities journals interrogated the text carefully.

Cultural Studies and Cultural Value investigates the way in which cultural value is understood and discussed within advanced capitalist society. Frow shows that the division between high and low culture is no longer stable and cannot be allocated to class-based behaviours. In this theoretical, social and economic context, Frow is considering 'on what basis I can and do continue to make and to apply judgments of value within this disrupted and uncertain universe of value'. Frow's analysis is strongest when considering the positioning of the cultural critic. At times, though, the text falls into a restatement of Pierre Bourdieu's *Distinction*. The criticisms of John Fiske and Iain Chambers underestimate the role that these writers have played in the establishment of cultural studies as a student-friendly discourse. Frow states: 'I am deeply suspicious of this claim that 'the people' can speak *through* the position of the analyst, or, conversely, that the class position of a middle-class intellectual can be put to one side when one writes "as a fan" '. Such a reading oversimplifies the critical positioning of Fiske. Frow suggests that Chambers 'appropriates this streetwise epistemology for his own academic discourse'. A point not considered by Frow is the audience for Chambers's work. Instead he maintains Bourdieu's thesis that the principal aim of cultural practice is to ensure distinction. No cultural critic would deny Frow's premise that 'judgments of value are always choices made within a particular regime [of value]'. The only resolution reached in his discussion is that the cultural intellectual cannot deny the possession of knowledge.

It is not surprising that John Hartley, Frow's one-time colleague at Murdoch University in Western Australia, utilizes the text as a springboard for a vigorous critique. Hartley chose to explore *Cultural Studies and Cultural Value* in the article 'Capitalised Language' (*UTS Review* 1.215–28). He discusses the book 'as a material object sitting there on the desk, and as an object circulating in the sphere of readerships'. Displaying Hartleyesque humour and a sharp turn of phrase, he interrogates the space in which Frow is writing. He is most critical of Frow's tendency to forget Welsh national identity and the process of internal colonization. Hartley argues that 'the difference between "English" and "British" may not seem very great to a lad from Wagga Wagga, but for Frow to accuse [Raymond] Williams of racism in this context is quite shocking, even if he isn't interested in Williams' lived identity'. Pivotally, Hartley questions Frow's reading of the knowledge class and the desire not to speak on behalf of others. There are options outside Routledge-derived populism and Oxford University Press-based abstraction. Hartley's response to Frow's dilemma is clear: 'but what are you going to *do* about that, John?'.

Cultural Studies and Cultural Value is also the springboard for the first polemical interchange within *Social Semiotics*. Malcolm MacLean grounded his critique in New Class Theory. In 'But What Sort of Value?' (*Social Semiotics* 5.281–97), MacLean formulates a detailed investigation of the knowledge class's relationship to use value and ownership of the means of production. MacLean faults Frow on his theorization of the relationship between the intelligentsia and the bourgeoisie. This article remains significant, however, because of its careful rereading of Appadurai's regimes of value and their place in intellectual work.

The reply to MacLean's polemic is written by Tony Schirato. In 'Not What, but Whose Value?' (*Social Semiotics* 5.299–308), Schirato re-establishes the significance of Frow's text, suggesting that it is important because it generates resonant connections between the economic sphere, cultural institutions and cultural practices. He argues that Frow 'keep[s] alive the question of the significance of the role of the economic sphere in always strongly informing, but not necessarily overdetermining, the cultural/ideological sphere'. Both Schirato and Frow (re)affirm the political role of cultural studies and the interdependence of economic and cultural spheres. Yet they are responding to theoretical phantoms. Fiske and Chambers never suggest that culture is an autonomous field of study, yet they must necessarily perform the role of playful populists if Frow's critique is to be granted weight and relevance.

Frow does serve to prioritize questions of value within the study of culture. His careful readings of Bourdieu, de Certeau, Laclau and Mouffe render the text important for theorists of culture. A major disappointment remains his dismissal of the teacherly component of the cultural studies project.

A strong example of how the project of cultural studies may be furthered through accessible, engaged theory is Richard Waterhouse's *Private Pleasures, Public Leisure: A History of Australian Popular Culture since 1788*. The text has a clear aim: to move theory from English regimes of value to diversified cultural models. The text is ideal for undergraduates, exploring how the parameters of culture are demarcated through time and space. The study is, as Waterhouse suggests, 'the first comprehensive and overall history of Australian popular culture'. By reworking values and institution within the context of Australian popular culture, the book investigates the ambiguous and complex status of Englishness in colonial life. Obvious absences exist in the text: Aboriginal popular cultural practices are not presented. However, the scope of the research through the post-contact years displays the class-based behaviours of the pre-Federation population. From cock fighting to the formation of the Melbourne Club, the narrative is convincing and thorough. *Private Pleasures,*

Public Leisure embodies the careful cultural theorizing that is lost through Frow's overview of 'the big names'. While Waterhouse does not mention Bourdieu, he is able to investigate the process through which popular culture is produced:

> By the end of the nineteenth century . . . an identifiable urban popular culture had emerged in Australia. Because it embraced gambling, drinking, professionalism and an acceptance of recreation as an enjoyable rather than an educational experience, it was essentially a culture that was shaped by and reflected the values of the working class. (85)

Waterhouse carries his thesis from the modernist challenge of 1914–54 to the Superleague challenge in the mid-1990s. Yet his engagement with multi-culturalism makes the text profound and important, particularly considering the historical scale of his project. He argues that critics like the historian Geoffrey Blainey, who oppose multiculturalism as damaging to 'the majority of Australians', have poorly theorized the Australian past. Waterhouse reminds these scholars that 'cultural diversity rather than unity for the most part has characterised Australia's history'. His words are verified by the detailed and capable scholarship of the preceding 249 pages.

The framing of popular cultural studies remains a challenging task because the sphere is dynamic and reflexive. Yet good scholarship that is also accessible to students is an intellectual goal. The vitriol and rigour of the Frow debate demonstrates that the capacity to *write the popular* remains the aim of many. The breadth and care of Waterhouse's research shows that it is an attainable target.

2. Representing the Nation

The iconography of Australian nationalism is fragmenting: split between a hyperconfident excessiveness and a tentative, questioning and at times destructive relativism. As the republican debate continues, the essence of Australianness has dominated debates waged by popular cultural critics. From popular music to the film industry, the representations of the nation have been increasingly disturbed.

Ross Poole embodies much of this transitional imagining in his essay 'Nationalism: The Last Rites?' (*Arena Journal* 4.51–68). He assembles a theory that accommodates the violent forms of nationalism in Australia. While recognizing its populist and egalitarian form, Poole shows the way in which nationalism is both a consciousness and self-consciousness. The aim of the piece is to display how conceptions of culture and identity are changing. The nation is, to Poole, a dying mode of societal organization.

Within the same edition of the *Arena Journal*, Paul James suggests that the nation state will survive through late modernity. In 'Reconstituting the Nation-State' (*Arena Journal* 4.69–89), James shows that cultural formations are being reconstituted rather than dissolved. Importantly, he argues that Australia's history must be separated from the narratives of other nations. The lateness of federation (1901) and the convict past 'could not easily be resolved with the ideologies of modernism'. Rather than exploring consciousness, James investigates the affectivities and subjectivities experienced within the nation state. He argues that the shift in spatial and temporal structures will change the mechanism through which history is understood, but continuities will remain through the transitional phase to the postmodern republic.

A popular culturalist inflection on this nation building/destruction is offered in the David Headon, Joy Hooton and Donald Horne edited collection, *The Abundant Culture: Meaning and Significance in Everyday Australia*. This collection of essays is structured into three sections: 'Representing Australia', 'Having a Good Time' and 'Rethinking'. The text is well written, succinct and accessible. In their introduction (xiii–xvi), the editors state that 'not one essay here shows the slightest interest in the academic debate about the pure theory of "Cultural Studies" presently preoccupying too many cultural commentators here and overseas'. They argue that an emphasis on meaning and significance is pivotal to interpretations of Australian history and culture. By moving beyond oppositional communities, the editors have formulated a collection that questions 'how to articulate this new Australia of such abundance and diversity'. The most successful essay in the collection is David Carter's 'Future Pasts' (3–15). He investigates how histories formulate narratives of national sense making, being critical of a linear, singular and Anglo-Saxon reading of Australia's past. By focusing on the period between 1938 and 1988, Carter discovers 'multilayered histories . . . a sense of historical density'. Significantly, he spatializes the analysis, exploring the distinctiveness of country life when compared with Sydney or Melbourne. The rhetorics of contemporary Australian nationalism and the emphasis upon unity in diversity are aimed at forming many 'future pasts' for Australia. Carter remains unconvinced of Australia's status as either an Asian or a Pacific nation, but remains hopeful of the multiple identities possible within a republican Australia.

Theorizing this republican future is continued by Peter Cochrane's contribution to the collection, 'The New Heroes – Inventing a Heritage' (16–25). His study of symbolism in national culture and the contestation of Anglocentrism interrogates the place of UK iconography and ideas in popular memory and public culture. Similarly, Ken Taylor's 'Things We Want to Keep' (26–33) frames heritage as a process of both remembering and forgetting. He suggests that contemporary Australians have 'a history and national culture that promotes a sense of identity'. Both these chapters are quite optimistic in their republican vistas, yet other essays delve into more problematic representations of the nation.

Joy Hooton dips once more into the fully inked well of 'Laurie and Noeline and *Sylvania Waters*' (61–70). The strength of her analysis is the unravelling of the constructedness of the programme, falling between soap opera and documentary. She forms an innovative feminist reading of this overworked text, realizing that Noeline is framed as another Dame Edna, 'presented externally, from the male position: she is the classic phallic mother'. As a reading of misogyny in contemporary national representations, Hooton's research has mobilized convincing evidence from *Sylvania Waters*.

Richard Harris has investigated a new representative field: Australian comedy ('The Funny Country', 91–8). By questioning how a national culture is formed, he argues that 'the sharp eye of comedy was helping us to use both who and what we were'. The intense contextualization of Australian humour is based on a collective awareness of story telling forms and practices. He reviews the revival of stand-up comedy in Melbourne in the early 1970s, the growing presence of female comics and the arrival of *The Comedy Company* in 1988. This television programme was the highest rating comedy series in the history of Australian television. Other programmes followed: *The D Generation, Fast Forward* and *The Big Gig*. Harris argues that the specificity of Australian humour will counter the 'insidious influence' of US and UK sitcoms. As with many essays in *The Abundant Culture*, Australianness becomes a goal for which to strive, an affirmative identity to construct.

Filmic representations are also a part of *The Abundant Culture*'s Australia. David Headon reviews 'Strictly Stomper – The New Australian Films' (71–9). Constructing a brief history of the film industry, through the Australian Film Commission years and the 10BA tax rebate scheme, he shows how *Romper Stomper* and *Strictly Ballroom* were formulated and financed. For Headon, the decision is clear: 'either respond to the challenges implicit in contemporary, multicultural Australia, or risk sliding into obscurity and irrelevance'. These two odd films, one detailing the story of an inner-city Melbourne skinhead group and the other a couple of radical ballroom dancers, are seen by Headon to be necessary for the long-term survival of the industry.

Besides filmic representations of the nation, aural texts are also considered with *The Abundant Culture*. Specifically, Philip Hayward explores contemporary Oz rock in his essay 'It's SONY Rock and Roll' (86–90). He situates music into the cultural practices of drinking, screeching and proto-mosh dancing. Hayward activates a study of sex and femininity within Oz rock, rewriting the cliché that 'if music is the food of love then Australian rock is a Four "n" Twenty pie and the kind of love involved takes place in the back seat of the car'. At times the commentary is brutal in its language, matching the muscled power chords of his subject.

Other critics outside *The Abundant Culture* have investigated the Oz rock genre. Michael George Smith's study ('Ozrock: The State of Play', *Overland* 139.32–7) explores how the live scene feeds into recorded music, radio and television. Crucially, though, he recognizes the importance of free weekly music papers in sustaining and changing the music industry. Because of the numerous cultural sites for contemporary music, it is not surprising that Smith affirms that 'there is no single identifiable Australian popular music culture'. The education of the audience in musical/cultural literacies has formulated a knowing and demanding aural, visual and corporeal readership.

Perhaps the most corporeal of dancing forms is located in the mosh pit. Dominic Pettman's 'It'll All Come Out in the Mosh' (*Southern Review* 28.213–25) activates the interconnected relationship between death metal, or thrash, and moshing. Most significantly, Pettman traces the parallel treatment of UK ravers and Australian moshers. The difference between the two cultural phenomena is that the ravers' dancing spaces were policed, while thrash fans had their music banned by the Australian Censorship Board and seized by Customs. Pettman accounts for the formation of the thrash subculture through Sydney-based fanzines like *In Your Face* and significant music stores in Melbourne. Yet his analysis of moshing as 'completing the deconstructive legacy of punk' remains most convincing. He probes the carnivalesque aspects of the practice, matching it with the panic sex of the contemporary era.

Two of the most innovative articles that question representations of

Australianness return to film. Tony Safford, Vice President of Acquisitions at Miramax Films, relates 'Two or Three Things I Know about Australian Cinema' (*Media Information Australia* 76.27–9). He discusses the complex meaning of the phrase 'different, but similar' when situating Australian films in the American market. The importance of a similar language and cultural system is argued by Safford to be vital to the commercial success of films from peripheral origins. The line between familiarity and uniqueness is difficult to judge and limits the options for the industry. Martha Ansara offered a rejoinder to Safford in her article 'Telling Our Own Stories' (*Public History Review* 4.41–50). By moving outside nationalist sentimentality, she affirms that 'we should tell our own stories. . . . But I want to take a closer look at the "we" who are creating the story-telling process.' She asks the industry to be reflexive in the writing of Australian cinematic history, recognizing contemporary changes and the mistakes of the past.

The most mythologized component of the Australian past is the 1950s. With Robert Menzies in the Prime Ministership, Australia was embedded in its own 'Age of Affluence'. Nicolas Brown scrutinizes the representations of this period in *Governing Prosperity*, focusing particularly on the conceptualizations of the self and society in the midst of what he terms 'a milk bar economy'. Carefully, he unravels the way in which phantoms of the 1950s are summoned in the present, 'to establish discontinuities rather than to affirm familiarity and continuity'. Brown shows how, through hailing the 1950s, the societal ruptures of the 1960s can be discredited. He shows how the economy of the milk bar, which incorporated excessive personal consumption, inflation and economic inefficiency, changes understandings of citizenship.

Jane Connors also interrogated national representations circulating during the 1950s, highlighting the 1954 Australian tour of Queen Elizabeth and the Duke of Edinburgh ('Betty Windsor and the Egg of Dukemburg', *Journal of Australian Studies – Special Edition* 47.67–80). This incisive study explores the gendering of those who followed the British Royal Family. From the 1940s, news of the royalty was becoming confined to women's magazines. This connection between the Royal Family and women's issues is unravelled by Connors, suggesting that popular monarchism is a far more complex ideological movement. As she states, 'the best-known advocates for the retention of the monarchy are male, they shy away from any discussion of the Royal Family as such, preferring to concentrate on the constitutional position of the Crown'. Connors shows that seven million Australians, of a total population of nine million, were present at events held to honour the Queen and Duke of Edinburgh during the 1954 tour. She carefully unwinds a distinctly gendered reading of Australian popular monarchism.

Susan Sheridan, too, critiques a clear gendering of national representations. Her *Along the Faultlines* investigates the interrelationship of race, sex and nation within women's popular fiction and journalism. Particular stress is placed on romantic fiction, as 'that genre has been so denigrated and dismissed as having no significant bearing on cultural life'. The text effectively untangles conceptualizations of literariness and popularness. By researching well-known writers, such as Miles Franklin, Mary Gilmore and Katharine Prichard, and the less recognized, such as Capel Boake, the rationale for national success can be articulated. The multiple intersections of difference, constructed from a myriad of social subjectivities, have generated faultlines where ambiguities and conflicts emerge. The clash between dominant renderings of feminism and nationalism means that 'women can only be admitted to the ranks of Australian literature despite their gender; they cannot be writers, Australians, and women all at once'. The book remains valuable for its exploration of sexual politics in romance fiction, feminist journalism, and the placement of race and nation in women's writing. In looking to a postcolonial feminism, Sheridan validates work in the crevices of social struggle.

Representations of Australia, through women's journalism during the period of nation building or by skinheads roaming through Melbourne streets in *Romper Stomper*, work on the faultlines that Sheridan has isolated. The debates of 1995 show a tendency to explore gaps, divisions and inequalities, rather than wallpaper over societal divisions. The next component of this review probes the theorizing of this diversity and difference within popular cultural studies.

3. Difference and Diversity

The most significant research in contemporary Australian popular culture and media studies displays a consciousness of difference and diversity. The need to theorize speaking positions and the marginalizing strategies of the media signal a movement away from easy linkages between popular culture and power. Postcolonial thought has enabled this study, but an investigation of multiculturalism outside the confines of policy has formulated an awareness of difference as a lived practice, not as a transcendent framework of imagined communities and perpetual alienation.

The most notable contribution to these debates is the collection edited by Penny van Toorn and David English, *Speaking Positions: Aboriginality, Gender and Ethnicity in Australian Cultural Studies*. In their introduction (1–13), the editors ask how speaking positions inflect the cultural practices of the media. The scrutiny of living space adds a complexity to their understandings of identity politics. By moving beyond the UK cultural studies lexicon of class, gender and ethnicity, the editors argue that Australian scholars can address integrated concerns with history, land and language. No longer is Aboriginality a marginal or minority concern. Instead van Toorn and English show that by looking for positioned speakers, representations may be politicized and subjectivity historicized.

The book's other papers interrogate these positions, critiquing rigid restatements of the essentialism versus social constructionism dichotomy. In 'Reclaiming Tru-ger-nan-ner' (31–42), Ian Anderson investigates the death and life of the 'last' female Tasmanian Aboriginal. Dying in 1876, her body was exhumed and the skeleton displayed in the Royal Society of Tasmania Museum from 1904 to 1947. Anderson terms her remains 'a totem for triumphant colonialism'. He is able to demonstrate how the construction of knowledge about Aboriginal people mobilizes essentialized notions of race that blocked full citizenship until 1967.

Barbara Milech continues Anderson's study, deploying Spivak's inquiry into whether the subaltern can speak. By assessing the effectiveness of the trope of colonization in feminist theorizing, Milech invokes 'Metaphoric Strategies' (107–29). She asks if radically disenfranchised groups 'can . . . be spoken for by liberationist theorists and critics'. She carefully unravels the contradiction of an empowered scholar speaking for disempowered communities who, by definition, exist outside discursive structures. Stephen Muecke is more direct than Milech. In 'Towards an Aboriginal Philosophy of Place' (167–79), he states: 'don't just write or think, learn how to behave yourself. Don't write a philosophy *about* Aboriginal concepts, make a philosophy *become* Aboriginal, and make an Aboriginality become philosophical'. The motif of speaking positions remains both an intellectual and political directive for Muecke, with *becoming* rather than writing being a greater imperative.

Shifting away from concerns with Aboriginality, Catherine Driscoll investigates the sexuality of adolescent women's magazines. In 'Who Needs a Boyfriend?' (188–98), she explores the liminal state of young women, who are not fully formed subjects or women. The sexuality exhibited in these magazines is deeply contradictory, featuring 'hunks' while remaining focused on what Driscoll terms 'the social definition of the feminine'. By close analysis of the major Australian magazines, *Dolly, Girlfriend, Looks, Sassy, Seventeen* and *19*, she presents 'an eroticisation of commodities and a commodification of erotics'. This dynamic interchange normalizes the adolescent girl's body, while concurrently idealizing a sexualized projection. The 'unresolved ambivalences' of the image renders these texts, and Driscoll's analysis, a highly charged and significant site for continued study.

These papers, in their original form, were derived from the 1993 Australian Cultural Studies Conference. Interestingly, this research distended bodily representation from articulated speaking positions. This agenda is explored in Anne Cranny-Francis's *The Body in the Text*. She investigates how the narratives of everyday life are embodied practices. Her theoretical framework is situated between 'the representation' and 'the real'. This matrix evokes an articulation of the strategies through which the body is defined and how meanings flood the spaces and places of the body. Challenging the mind–body relationship by working with Deleuze and Guattari's rhizomatic discourses, Cranny-Francis maps topographies of meaning on the corporeal. The theoretical framework of the book is well chosen, providing exemplary reviews of Michel Foucault and bell hooks. Her examples, too, are strong. Moving from the 1955 Australian film *Jedda* to Madonna, from D'Arcy Niland's *The Shiralee* to the character of Baines in Jane Campion's *The Piano*, Cranny-Francis studies the popular positioning of the body within Western society. Strongly affirmed in the book is the need to understand identity in a way that is multiple and shifting, rather than fixed and stereotyped. She proves that the mind–body split is both gender- and class-bound, with bodily inscription being a highly discursive practice.

This concentration on theoretical framing devices is continued by Ken Gelder and Jane Jacobs. Their 'Uncanny Australia' (*UTS Review* 1.150–69) researches the formation of postcolonial racism. Their reading of space, place and culture demonstrates how dominant representations of Aboriginal people, as both disempowered through health care and housing, and overcompensated in terms of welfare, are not contradictory. As they realize, 'In an uncanny Australia, one place is always already another place because the issue of possession is never complete, never entirely settled'. In this context, reconciliation will only be partially successful.

The role of newspapers in constructing this ideology of Aboriginality is the focus of David Trigger's article, 'Everyone's agreed, the *West* is all you need' (*Media Information Australia* 75.102–22). Poaching its title from an advertising campaign for Western Australia's only daily newspaper, he displays how systematic bias and institutional racism continue 'the portrayal of Aboriginal or ethnic labels in criminal contexts'. Trigger demonstrates how the common-sensical ideologies circulating through Perth-based radio and newspapers impact on the understanding of Aboriginal issues in the state.

The key concern expressed by Trigger is that very few news reports present the perspective of Aboriginal people. John Welchman's *Modernity Relocated: Towards a Cultural Studies of Visual Modernity* rectifies some of these concerns. Much of the text explores modernism and the transgressive nature of the avant-garde. Particular attention is granted to the impact of contemporary critical theory and cultural studies on the future of visual modernity. Working through borders and frameworks, he presents a carefully theorized analysis of Western cultural politics and Aboriginal representations. By reading First World cultural practices against the visuality emerging from the Western Desert, the Dot paintings 'offer the possibility for a re-territorialization of visual practice'. The attention to margins and transgressions grants his analysis of Papunya art a resonance outside binarized frameworks of black–white, modernist–postmodernist and past–present.

The cultural value placed on popular renderings of Aboriginal texts is also the investigative site for Melinda Hinkson. Her 'Making Meaning of the Yuendumu Doors' (*Arena Journal* 5.5–15) explores the history of Aboriginal cultural sites. In 1983, senior Warlpiri men were commissioned to paint school doors with Dreaming designs. In the subsequent years, art dealers have offered the painters large sums of money for the sale of the doors. Hinkson wishes 'to explore the meaning that objects such as the doors hold in the contemporary period, and . . . to briefly consider some aspects of intercultural exchange'. She proves how White critics, concerned with the preservation of the artefacts, are ignoring the Warlpiri ideology of cultural formation, which emphasizes the process of production, rather than the completed, saleable object. Hinkson applies Appadurai's regimes of value with great effectiveness. She realizes that ' "we" want the Warlpiri to put cultural maintenance in the form of objects such as the doors before economic gain, because if they no longer do, then what hope is there for the rest of us?' By problematizing the singularity of cultural heritage, definition of cultural value moves beyond a rigid colonial framework.

While the colonial relationship has activated a critique of the dominant ideologies circulating through popular culture and media studies, wider theories of cultural diversity have also generated productive cultural sites. Shirley Fitzgerald and Garry Wotherspoon have edited a collection of essays entitled *Minorities: Cultural Diversity in Sydney*. This collection includes a piece by Yu Lan Poon, entitled 'The Two-Way Mirror: Contemporary Issues as Seen Through the Eyes of the Chinese Language Press, 1901–1911' (50–65). The chapter looks at the gap between perceptions about 'Asians' prevailing in the dominant ideologies when compared with the self-perceptions circulating in the Chinese press in Sydney during the foundations of the Australian nation. Yu shows how the 'ethnic press' socializes minorities into their setting. Concurrently though, the rupture between values, particularly around the issues of women's suffrage and equal wages, presents a distinct rendering of the events surrounding the formation of the Australian nation.

Ashley Carruthers updates Yu's analysis in the article 'Suburbanasia' (*Media International Australia* 77.86–90). This article effectively frames contemporary debates within critical theory, focusing on the trend towards critical multiculturalism. As Carruthers suggests, there is 'a schism almost, in contemporary critical multicultural approaches to the Australian media. The source of this divergence is, put simply, a disagreement about just how multicultural the established media really are.' The question remains, is multiculturalism a mainstream or a minority discourse? This piece is significant, as it charts the reception of multiculturalism and historicizes the 'multicentric media'. Similarly, Terry Flew, in 'Pay TV and Broadcasting Diversity in Australia' (*Media International Australia* 77.130–8), positions cultural diversity into contemporary Australian media policy. He explores the impact of pay television on catering for the shifting allegiances and identities of 'the public'.

A more critical stance on the role and place of multiculturalism in Australian society is displayed by Lorella Di Pietro's 'A User's Guide to Multicultural Success – The Australian Version' (*Social Semiotics* 5.239–64). This article investigates the ethics and practices of nation-building in Australia. The contradictory role of fluid, globalized capital against the fixity of citizenship in the nation state renders the federal framework of multi-culturalism inappropriate within contemporary social spheres. Di Pietro demonstrates that the discourses of difference do not reconcile the employ-ment conditions of migrants as an adaptable labour force. She argues that ethnicity is used 'to reaffirm the authenticity of Anglo-Australian, middle class identities as opposed to the impostor status supposedly embodied by migrants'. A case is strongly assembled that shows how multiculturalism has allowed the continual importation of immigrants without challenging Anglo-Celtic cultural norms.

Popular literature has reinforced the conservative agenda of multi-culturalism. Ruth Brown researches this history 'From Nino Culotta to Simon During' (*Australian Studies* 9.35–44). The novel *They're a Weird Mob* is a major success story of Australian publishing. Brown understands though, how it may 'be read as 1950s Liberal party propaganda in its representation of a homogenised society in which immigrants assimilate, everyone is so well off that complaint would be churlish, and the bush ethos in its new suburban habitat is cured of its rebellious streak'. Brown retheorizes the politics of the suburb, suggesting that it may be a place where class, race and gender inequalities are confronted, and new models of community assembled.

The role of multiculturalism in the maintenance of dominant ideologies is also recognized by David Pearson. His 'Multi-Culturalisms and Modernisms' (*Sites* 30.9–30) commences a comparative investigation of Australian, Canadian and New Zealand immigration practices. However, he verifies Di Pietro's argument that 'Multiculturalism . . . is a hegemonic tool of control wielded by major power holders in society'. With ethnicity reduced to cultural practices and symbolic modes of life, structural inequalities are perpetuated.

Many distinct understandings of multiculturalism circulate through these debates. John Docker adds some structure to this heated and committed controversy in 'Rethinking Postcolonialism and Multiculturalism in the *Fin de Siècle*' (*Cultural Studies* 9.409–26), suggesting that the term is used quite distinctly as both a governmental policy and a pro-pluralism statement.

Instead of viewing multiculturalism as a tool of Anglo-Celtic hegemony, Docker explains that 'throughout white Australian history there has been a continuing tension between multiculturality and an insistence on a singular British identity'. The convoluted relationship between ethnicity and race has, for Docker, rendered a critical discourse that re-establishes a modernist model of identity.

Like Docker, Andrew Theophanous discovers the many applications and meanings of multiculturalism. His text, *Understanding Multiculturalism and Australian Identity*, provides a well written and researched history. As a parliamentarian elected into office in February 1980, he was present during a period of major shifts in the configuration of Australian identity and citizenship. This text remains significant to theorists of Australian media and popular culture as he explores how the presence of the Special Broadcasting Service (SBS) contributes to changing understandings of multiculturalism. Integral to the SBS charter is the shift from the easy rhetoric of plurality to confronting serious concerns with social justice. The text provides strong analytical work on multiculturalism, citizenship and Australian identity. The writer's political involvement in the formation of multicultural policies grants the book a candour and depth of research.

Many of the ideologies circulating between postcolonialism, multiculturalism and identity are discussed within Martin Hirst's jaunt into 'The Coming Republic' (*Australian Journal of Communication* 22.13–39). This article probes the extent to which the mass media, as the site of the contemporary public sphere, instigates democratic struggle and change. The effectiveness of the media presentation of various interests and contested speaking positions raises questions about the public–media sphere. Hirst reads through Jurgen Habermas's notion of the public sphere, as positioned between civil society and the nation state, and acknowledges that the theorist does not assess the media's role as public representative. By enacting a reading of the Australian media in a global context, and evaluating the republican issue, Hirst suggests that newspapers and the media 'constitute an important public sphere tied to the nation-state, and one that distorts the true nature of class society in favour of a generalized, *idealised*, and reconstituted national public'. By not feeding into individualist notions of citizenship, Hirst shows how the media summon a phantom of participatory decision-making.

A gentle, lilting reminder of the pre-war diversities walking through Australian streets is Patrick O'Farrell's article, 'St Patrick's Day in Australia' (*Journal of the Royal Australian Historical Society* 81.1–16). He conveys the history of the day in Ireland and how the celebration remained 'in the penal colony [the] only one social expression of Irishness [that] was tolerated'. He highlights for contemporary analysts of critical multiculturalism that articulations of difference were present from the foundations of colonial society.

The constitution of the public–media sphere in contemporary Australia is currently a volatile debate within popular culture and media studies. The sharply contested interpretations of multiculturalism and postcolonialism prove that politically hollow presentations of minority voices and spaces are no longer functional components of critical theory. The next component of this review explores how popular cultural practices can serve to patch the punctures in the Australian body politic.

4. Popular Cultural Practices

Identities are affirmed and performed through popular cultural texts and behaviours. Increasingly, Australian media and popular culture studies have granted attention to the formation of national subjectivities. The analyses from 1995 focus on a myriad of identity-building tendencies: sport, fashion, shopping, eating and suburban life. As theorists approach the Sydney 2000 Olympics, a reflexive detailing of everyday life and nation-building experiences will increase in frequency and rigour.

The ecstatic response to Sydney's winning bid for the Olympics has been tempered by recent critical investigations. Paul Gillen, in 'The Olympic Games and Global Society' (*Arena Journal* 4.5–15), explores how the invocation of Sydney 2000 has entered public debates about the future of the city and the nation. Arguing that 'every Olympic festival is an advertisement for the politics and culture of the host city and nation', he displays how the Games have been utilized in political discussions ranging from republicanism to visual pollution. Yet he also suggests that the jubilation of successful contemporary Olympic bids be tempered by concerns of social costs and losses, as much as profits and gains.

One of the major concerns framing debates about the Olympics is the role and place of Aboriginal people within the symbolism and politics of the Games. Aboriginal sport remains a deeply under-researched area, which makes Vicky Paraschak's essay in Headon, Hooton and Horne's edited collection, *The Abundant Culture*, so significant. In 'A Sporting Chance?' (187–97), she analyses sport as an oppositional cultural practice. Paraschak discusses how sport 'provides a site for challenging as well as reproducing dominant societal values, along with their formative underlying power relations'. By working through the representations and meanings of national Aboriginal sports carnivals, she explores the transformational role of popular cultural practices in race relations.

Paraschak displays how sport can change attitudes and counter prejudice. Richard Cashman's chapter from *The Abundant Culture* also displays the politically activating role of sport in society. His piece on 'Packer Cricket' (80–5) shows how World Series cricket 'was a catalyst of broader media, economic and cultural change'. Cashman researches the way in which the Englishness of cricket was attacked by Packer, bringing a new audience to the game, including migrants, women and the working class. The 'chauvinistically Australian' temperament of the game, that was advertised using the sing-a-long chant 'come on Aussie, come on, come on', remade it for television. No longer was it a transplanted colonial practice. Instead, Packer's cricket placed Australia at the centre of the sporting world – if only in the minds of its Australian viewers.

Although the new audience for Packer cricket included women, the status of female cricketers has continued to be low in Australia. Angela Burroughs, Leonie Seebohm and Liz Ashburn confront this politically complex issue in their article '"A Leso Story": A Case of Australian Women's Cricket and its Media Experience' (*Sporting Traditions* 12.27–46). The article focuses on the media reports of Denise Annetts, who believed that she was excluded from the Australian women's cricket team because of her heterosexual, married status. The story first appeared in a local Sydney newspaper, the *North Shore Times*, during January 1994. By the time the issue had been exhausted, at least 140 articles and letters had appeared in newspapers and magazines: all television networks covered the story. Burroughs, Seebohm and Ashburn investigate these media sites against the low status and credibility allocated to women's cricket. They argue that 'maintaining socially constructed sex specific sports, labelling opposite sex participation in those sports as deviant and accepting the notion that homosexuality is deviant, ensure that a sexist and heterosexist sports structure is preserved'. The writers do not concern themselves with the allegation that women are excluded from cricket teams for their hetero-sexuality: instead, they show how 'the media's preoccupation within women's cricket served only to titillate the public, trivialise the game itself and denigrate women's sport in general'. The writers argue that the sexism and homophobia resonating in representations of women's cricket are worse than the invisibility of the sport the rest of the time.

Television is not only pivotal in forming the high profile of men's cricket: it is also becoming crucial to the continued success of Australian rules football and rugby league. Chris Masters's 'Barbarians at the Game' (*Media International Australia* 77.15–19) investigates how television sponsorship is changing sports marketing. The arrival of Superleague, the Murdoch-led challenger to the Australian Rugby League, and the increasing movement of Australian rules football away from its Melbourne base are formulating a new sporting marketplace. As Masters states, 'The turnstile no longer generates the big footy dollar – major revenue comes through sponsorship and television advertising, and so too does major power'. He also argues that the crowds are a nuisance for football managers, as the Melbourne-based supporters of Australian rules are blocking club closures and mergers, thereby preventing the televisual expansion of the game. The 'unleashed testosterone' both on the field and in the boardroom is changing the dynamic between sport and the fan.

Masculinity and nationalism are intertwined ideologies. Both inscribe meaning onto the panels of a motor vehicle. Richard Strauss, in 'Up for Rego? Masculinity and the Kingswood' (*Public History Review* 4.104–119), explores the 'ships of the suburbs'. This humorous, well-written article researches 'Kingswood culture' and the lifestyle practices that scrape the panel work of Australia's most popular car. He researches the television situation comedy scripted in honour of the vehicle, *Kingswood Country*, and the actions of the programme's protagonist Ted Bullpit. As the mobile symbol of Australia's post-war reconstruction, Strauss demonstrates how 'the Kingswood way of life appeared within the context of a national culture which was predominantly suburban, consumerist and heavily in favour of the automobile.' Significantly, he also shows how this symbol of Australian manufacturing has lost lustre through the changes in the economy.

A more visual, less vehicular, commentary on suburbia is articulated by Ian Craven. His 'Cinema, Postcolonialism and Australian Suburbia' (*Australian Studies* 9.45–69) explores the discursive devaluation of suburbia in Australian film and television programmes. Little work has been conducted that explores the representation of suburbia in cinematic texts. He argues that the familiarity of suburbia makes this space difficult to inscribe with otherness or the mysterious. This premise is used by Craven to explain the distinctive iconography of television and film:

Clearly the banality of the suburbs which synchronises with TV as a medium and an aesthetic, is less easily negotiated within cinema, partly because that medium has been socially-constructed as so disposed towards 'fatal' experience and the fascinations of the exotic, because cinema's relationship to this audience is so premised upon the possibilities of a displacement.

For Craven, televisual renderings of suburbia have radically altered the definition of Australian identity, far beyond the jurisdiction of cinematic imaginings.

Suburban life is also the focus of Mark Peel's evocative and timely cultural history of the Adelaide suburb Elizabeth, entitled *Good Times, Hard Times*. Elizabeth was Australia's first new town that was not a colonialist rendering of London, Coventry or Newcastle. It was a town built for and by migrants derived from the industrial regions of Britain. As Australia's first planned city, it provides a metaphor for the social and economic reconstructions of the post-war period. Peel's study is judicious in its judgements and carefully researched. As a one-time 'local boy', his analysis of the town planning, employment prospects and immigration experiences is affective as much as analytical. As 'a city for industry', community life was negotiated between the demands of migrant services and the job requirements of General Motors-Holden. Yet its role in the immigration history of Australia remains significant. As Peel articulates, 'Journalists and commentators looking for the local colour of English migrant picturesque, or the hunt for pommy wingers and shopfloor militants . . . have always mimicked the Elizabeth voice and the Elizabeth identity'. The changes to Elizabeth, from a home for new arrivals to 'a place for the poor', grant importance to this research for theorists grappling with the role of suburban life in understanding popular culture.

Two elements of suburban ideologies and cultural practices are the focus of research in *Arena Magazine*: eating and shopping. Jane Dixon, in 'Kitchen Cultures' (19.35–8), explores how the globalization of food has been matched with hopes for a national cuisine. Stating that 'food policy is cultural policy', Dixon seeks to understand the impact of immigration and class on cooking and eating practices. Memories of home sauté the meanings of food, while the desire for healthier, diet-friendly food has made eating an enterprise fraught with tension. Similarly, Kim Humpheries investigates the stress-filled changes to shopping in 'Talking Shop' (*Arena Magazine* 19.30–4). She shows how the supermarket has conquered food retailing in Australia, transforming the nation into 'the most highly concentrated grocery market in the Western world'. She carefully removes the layers of meaning from shopping spaces, arguing that we 'make them social, take from them what we want, but they are never . . . ours'. This short article is a clever invocation of spaces between public debates about retail ownership and consumption practices. Rob White also works in this space, showing how 'The Forbidden City' (*Arena Magazine* 15.34–7) blocks the social and physical movement of young people. He shows how concerns with amusement parlours and shopping centres 'pertain both to the increasing polarization of wealth and poverty in society and to the overall distribution of community resources, including public space'. These three short articles demonstrate a close reading of cultural geographies, applying social semiotic theory with a feminist directive.

Continuing this study of material culture, consumption practices and memory is Jean Duruz's investigation of fashion, 'Dressing up Daydreams' (*UTS Review* 1.130–49). By exploring the positioning of fashion in terms of waste and desire, the piece uses interviews to show how clothing can be a personal burden, rather than a pleasure. Focusing on the 1950s and 1960s, Duruz enacts an emotionally engaged rendering of Australian femininity. She remains concerned with 'tensions of competing identities – shaped both within and outside consumerist discourses and practices – and active searches for pleasure and for comfort in spite of femininity's contradictions'. Her research problematizes the cultural populist tendencies of much recent feminist reclamations of desire and consumption.

Margaret Maynard also explores the role of fashion in constructing Australian femininity within the Headon, Hooton and Horne edited collection, *The Abundant Culture*. Her chapter, 'The Mirrored Ceiling' (220–5), interrogates the problematic connection between style and womanhood. The disciplines of dress, diet and deportment summon specific difficulties for women renegotiating power relationships. As Maynard states, 'the ceilings they encounter are not simply made of glass. They are actually made of mirrors.' The bodily surface is moulded and tamed so that gestures and appearance convene the spectre of the feminine.

Beach holidays smooth over rigid controls of fashion and femininity. George Seddon's *Swan Song: Reflections on Perth and Western Australia 1956–1995*, explores the cultural geography of one of the most isolated capital cities in the world. While many essays in this collection are formed at the nexus of literature and geography, his chapter on 'The Rottnest Experience' (130–7) investigates the small holiday island to the west of Perth. He shows how 'Rottnest has played a significant part in sustaining Western Australians' self-image as a society that is friendly, gregarious, simple, unpretentious, physically oriented, pleasure loving and egalitarian'. He discusses the history of the island formerly as a site for Aboriginal prisoners and now as a place for contemporary tourists. He shows how the behaviours on the island are seen to be outside the law, as holidaymakers are released from the restraints of the mainland. The essay remains a fluent and accessible reading of holidaying spaces.

From sport to fashion, and shopping to holidays, popular cultural studies has moved beyond the simple divisions of production and consumption, authenticity or complicity. The complex struggles between genders, classes and races have left a residue on theories of pleasure and an awareness of the social costs involved in having a good time. The final component of this review focuses on Australian media studies, exploring how research is inflected by these ruptures in the contemporary social and theoretical field.

5. Media Studies: From Poaching to Policy

Contemporary Australian media studies is split between northern and southern theorists. The Brisbane-based Centre for Cultural Policy links critical work with governmental and media structures. Sydney, Melbourne and Perth theorists continue textual and contextual investigations untethered from politically volatile 'pragmatic concerns'. The articles and books emerging during 1995 show this divide, varying from the entertaining and engaging work by de Certeau and Gramscian-inspired critics to the Foucauldian-framed, dry analyses of media policy theorists.

An example of the former category is the John Tulloch and Henry Jenkins's text, *Science Fiction Audiences: Watching Doctor Who and Star Trek*. While the chapters by Jenkins focus on American-based fans, Tulloch researches Australian audiences of the BBC programme, *Doctor Who*. Both writers explore fandom as a reading formation, moving beyond Jenkins's earlier work, *Textual Poachers*. The writers still maintain the premise of the early book, however, arguing that fan activities are defined more through relations of consumption than production. They state that 'scholars move into a space already heavily colonized by other discursive constructs, mapped by popular journalism and preconceived by the reading public'. John Tulloch researches the interpretative community of Australian *Doctor Who* fans. His best work explores how these programmes are inserted 'within specific national broadcasting contexts'. The interplay of text, analysis and fandom makes the book theoretically rewarding reading, particularly in its consideration of 'foreign' content within a national broadcasting framework.

A distinct rendering of reading formations occurs within Susan Hopkins's article 'Generation Pulp' (*Youth Studies Australia* 14.14–18). She investigates the relationship between Generation X-ers and the media discourse. As she states, 'in the 1990s, understanding youth necessitates consideration of postmodern popular culture as a formative experience'. While Tulloch explores the place of an English timelord within Australian media schedules, Hopkins focuses on Tarantino's *Pulp Fiction* as the embodiment of X-er media literacy. The piece questions how new economic and cultural forms construct a consciousness. For Hopkins, 'the problem is how to invent and reinvent an identity out of a chaotic mix of consumer goods, advertising appeals and media cliches'. This piece is relevant, well written and innovative: it is an ideal teaching aid to introduce contemporary youth culture.

Another significant teaching text is Barry Lowe's *Media Mythologies*. He initiates a thoughtful history of media studies in Australia. Not being a journalistic, sociological or literary text, the book is framed as a general, first year undergraduate introduction to media studies. He reviews the Frankfurt School and structuralism, while choosing relevant examples for an audience of Australian students. The representations of the Queen in the context of the republican debate are well handled, as is the analysis of the (mis)informed construction of Asia and the Pacific in the Australian media. He also assesses 'The Murdoch Syndrome', showing the impact of the media baron's 65 per cent share of nationally circulated newspapers. With discussions of ethnic and Aboriginal stereotyping, Lowe prepares students for further courses in race, gender and media studies.

An under-researched area of the Australian media is radio. Two books have emerged in 1995 that alleviate some of this absence. Colin Jones has published *Something in the Air: A History of Radio in Australia*. This large-format book is well illustrated and cuts through the nostalgic ideologies that seep into histories of the medium. Jones focuses on the immediacy of radio, arguing that it is 'a parochial medium, and does best when it emphasises this'. He theorizes the failure of American serials among an Australian audience, while also showing how radio changes understandings of space, speed and news. The movement from a ham's hobby to a well-financed industry grants the book's narrative both accessibility and rigour.

A small, but politically significant, moment in Australia's radio history is researched within the Liz Fell and Caroline Wenzel edited collection, *The Coming Out Show: Twenty Years of Feminist ABC Radio*. The chapters recount the formation of the *Coming Out Ready or Not Show*, which first went live to air on International Women's Day in 1975. This programme was aired for one hour each week; it remains significant because women had editorial control. The contemporary show, which is now titled *Women Out Loud*, is what Liz Fell describes as 'a unique public space for a plethora of previously unheard female voices and feminist perspectives'. The battle between the Australian Broadcasting Corporation management, who critiqued the programme for its production standards and intellectual rigour, and the Australian Women's Broadcasting Cooperative is well displayed in this text. Other chapters focus on the internal changes to feminism and the programme during the twenty-year run: from the articulation between race and gender to the role of pleasure in feminist thought and feminism in the workplace. The text also features a listing of the *Coming Out Show* tape archives from March 1975 to 25 December 1994. Any review of media politics must include reference to both this significant programme and the book derived from its twentieth anniversary.

A more scholarly, and bland, investigation of the Australian media is the edited collection assembled by Jennifer Craik, Julie James Bailey and Albert Moran, *Public Voices, Private Interests: Australia's Media Policy*. The book has five parts: 'The Context of Australia's Media', 'Key Media Policy Issues', 'The Public Broadcasting Sector', 'Indigenous Broadcasting Initiatives' and 'Australian Media in Asia'. As the editors explain in their introduction (xvi–xxv), the book is framed between 'the role of the media in disseminating information in the public sphere, and patterns of ownership and regulatory strategies in favour of private interests'. There are strong chapters in this collection: Anne Davies's review of 'Broadcasting under Labor' (3–14) investigates how deregulation led to a greater concentration of media ownership in Australia. The changing media models of the Labor years are well catalogued, moving from concerns with the public interest to market-based doctrines. Toby Miller's 'Striving for Difference: Commercial Radio Policy' (86–100) shows how radio has become the 'most ethnocentric medium'. Other chapters peruse the 1992 Broadcasting Services ('Privatising the Public Interest' by Jo Hawke, 33–52) and community radio ('Multiplying Minorities' by Albert Moran, 147–64). The book attempts a theorizing of media/ citizenship and the contemporary public domain. Much of the research is significant and important. However, the plodding narratives and predictable theoretical tropes render this text a mediocre example of policy-inflected media studies.

More vibrant is Murray Goot's review of 'Pluralism in the Polls: Australian Attitudes to Media Ownership, 1948–95' (*Media International Australia* 77.5–14). He reviews post-war public opinion polls of the media ownership issue. This study places the contemporary arguments about concentrated media ownership into a longer term. He argues that 'like the nation's real estate . . . there does seem to be something about the media that people want to think of as "their own"'. Goot realizes that parliamentary debates lead public opinion: surveys do not take place unless the issue has been raised in Canberra.

The place of Rupert Murdoch in the media ownership debate remains pivotal. Ian Weber's 'The Moral Market' (*Media International Australia* 77.45–53) researches Murdoch's News Corporation as a global media infrastructure. As a 'media baron', Murdoch embodies a dynamic capitalism that is reaching into Asia through Star TV. As Weber suggests, 'Murdoch's discourses of media, choice and modernity are constructed around the meaning of technology to win the consent of the audiences for his vision of a new communications environment'. This study of Star TV is continued by Will Atkins in 'Friendly and Useful: Rupert Murdoch and the Politics of Television in Southeast Asia, 1993–95' (*Media International Australia* 77.54–64). He shows how Murdoch reshapes commercial and political strategies in Asia. The shift from citizens to consumers is argued by Atkins to be significant in understanding the Chinese broadcasting market.

While News Corporation is starting to gain knowledge of, and success in, the Asia market, other televisual programmes have completely misunderstood their audience. Stuart Cunningham and Elizabeth Jacka analyse 'The Wash-Up on *Paradise Beach*' (*Cinema Papers* 103.22–3). This serial was launched in Australia and the United States simultaneously between May 1993 and June 1994. For Cunningham and Jacka, the failure of *Paradise Beach* in the American market demonstrates that sharing the English language is not enough to guarantee success overseas. Not being a prime-time serial or a daytime soap opera, '*Paradise Beach*' was an easy, if probably misplaced, target'.

An even easier target for local commentators is the Sydney Gay and Lesbian Mardi Gras. In 1994, the Australian Broadcasting Corporation screened an hour-long presentation of the event. The resulting furore generated numerous commentaries from cultural critics. The strongest is Samantha Searle's 'Our ABC?' (*Media International Australia* 78.12–19). The competing rhetorics of a national broadcaster and cultural pluralism are seen by Searle to be the basis for the outraged response. The gulf between the 'normal audience' for the ABC and the desire to embody the diversity of the population was clearly crossed in this broadcast. As she argues, the ABC 'constructs the audience as straight, and . . . constructs that audience's potential to be offended as "reasonable", rather than as a site for educative work'. The impact of public standards on another community's rights is also the topic of Rebecca Huntley's article 'Queer Cuts: Censorship and Community Standards' (*Media International Australia* 78.5–12). This research displays how the Office of Film and Literature Classification works against the presence of queer cinema. The banning of gay and lesbian documentaries and the Australian censorship histories of the films *Salo, Tras El Cristal* and *Pixote* provide a reminder to media theorists that the ideologies encircling phrases like public opinion and good taste need to be monitored and critiqued. Huntley's piece demonstrates that film culture, even on the festival circuit, is enmeshed in national imaginings of normality and transgression.

Australian popular culture and media studies are changing. While some critics are working in policy spaces, others seek out social faultlines and sites of difference. Simplistic renderings of nationalist ideologies are avoided in the search for evocative sites of meaning-making. Multiculturalism is an ideology to be critically assessed, not celebrated. These debates, while being at times too detailed and avoiding more overarching theses, are taking media theorists and cultural studies scholars to a more complex, and rewarding, critical plane.

Books Reviewed

Brown, Nicholas. *Governing Prosperity*. Cambridge University Press. pp. 300. pb A$29.95, hb A$90.00. ISBN 0 521 47732 8, 0 521 47160 5.

Craik, Jennifer, Julie Bailey, and Albert Moran, eds. *Public Voices, Private Interests: Australia's Media Policy*. Allen & Unwin. pp. 296. pb A$29.95. ISBN 1 86373 628 X.

Cranny-Francis, Anne. *The Body in the Text*. Melbourne University Press. pp. 148. pb A$14.95. ISBN 0 522 84575 4.

Fell, Liz, and Caroline Wenzel, eds. *The Coming Out Show: Twenty Years of Feminist ABC Radio*. Australian Broadcasting Corporation. pp. 205. pb A$17.95. ISBN 0 7333 0433 8.

Fitzgerald, Shirley, and Garry Wotherspoon, eds. *Minorities: Cultural Diversity in Sydney*. New South Wales Press. pp. 220. pb A$19.95. ISBN 0 7305 8926 9.

Frow, John, *Cultural Studies and Cultural Value*. Clarendon Press. pp. 190. pb A$26.95. ISBN 0 19 871128 X.

Goodall, Peter. *High Culture, Popular Culture*. Allen & Unwin. pp. 208. pb A$24.95. ISBN 1 86373 833 9.

Headon, David, Joy Hooton, and Donald Horne, eds. *The Abundant Culture: Meaning and Significance in Everyday Australia*. Allen & Unwin. pp. 264. pb A$24.95. ISBN 1 86373 644 1.

Jones, Colin. *Something in the Air: A History of Radio in Australia*. Kangaroo Press. pp. 150. pb A$29.95. ISBN 0 86417 700 3.

Lowe, Barry. *Media Mythologies*. University of New South Wales Press. pp. 165. pb A$27.95. ISBN 0 86840 006 8.

Peel, Mark. *Good Times, Hard Times: The Past and the Future in Elizabeth*. Melbourne University Press. pp. 328. pb A$24.95. ISBN 0 522 84628 9.

Seddon, George. *Swan Song: Reflections on Perth and Western Australia 1956–1995*. Centre for Studies in Australian Literature. pp. 250. pb A$24.95. ISBN 0 86422 428 1.

Sheridan, Susan. *Along the Faultlines*. Allen & Unwin. pp. 304. pb A$24.95. ISBN 1 86373 867 3.

Theophanous, Andrew. *Understanding Multiculturalism and Australian Identity*. Elikia Books. pp. 470. pb A$16.95. ISBN 1 875335 04 8.

Tulloch, John, and Henry Jenkins. *Science Fiction Audiences: Watching Doctor Who and Star Trek*. Routledge. pp. 288. pb £12.99, hb £40.00. ISBN 0 415 06141 5, 0 415 06140 7.

van Toorn, Penny, and David English. *Speaking Positions: Aboriginality, Gender and Ethnicity in Australian Cultural Studies*. Victoria University of Technology. pp. 240. pb A$24.95. ISBN 1 86272 461 X.

Waterhouse, Richard. *Private Pleasures, Public Leisure – A History of Australian Popular Culture since 1788*. Longman. pp. 260. A$29.95. ISBN 0 582 86968 4.

Welchman, John. *Modernity Relocated: Towards a Cultural Studies of Visual Modernity*. Allen & Unwin. pp. 330. A$29.95. ISBN 1 86373 582 8.

14

Popular Music

DAVID BUCKLEY

This chapter has four sections: 1. Introduction; 2. Biography, Autobiography and Critical Surveys of Artists; 3. Anthologies, Collections and Encyclopedias; 4. History and Analysis.

1. Introduction

The more popular music studies develops within the academy as a valid and vibrant discipline, the more it is evident that an analytical pluralism is appropriate for its future direction. One of the central tasks facing popular music studies is the need to develop a genuinely pluralistic approach – a good-natured tolerance of different traditions and analytical approaches – which is sufficiently weighty to explain contesting phenomena and which also connects with those who want to read about pop music in a meaningful way. Jon Savage in his introduction to *The Faber Book of Pop*, co-edited with Hanif Kureishi, reminds us that 'pop hits the head, the heart, the soul and the feet' and yet it is the case that some academic writing still carries with it a curiously disengaged air. Whereas the best pop journalism is still gritty and emotional, the average academic account of pop lacks a sense of advocacy or prophecy, thus rendering levelled, flat and insipid the brilliance and contradictory collision of music and people which drives popular culture. More than fifteen years after the formation of the International Association for the Study of Popular Music, and almost fifty years since the first sociological analyses of youth culture and music, there are still precious few meaningful links between academia and journalism. This is a great shame, particularly since many academics who started life as journalists and who are in a better position to foster such links seem disinclined to do so.

Furthermore, within academia there is also the beginnings of a crisis of confidence in terms of the critical language. Many musicologists with an interest in popular music now find more comfortable bedfellows in sociologists or communication studies theorists rather than music theorists still embroiled with the Western European canon. For some critics, certain academic analyses of the institutional rationale which provides the economic *raison d'être* for popular music come perilously close to reaching an accommodation with big business itself. Just as pop journalists were historically accused of simply providing copy based on a blandly rewritten press release from a given band or artist, so academics such as Keith Negus have been criticized for their neutral assessment of how capital and big business cordially cooperate with small-scale entrepreneurship. Marcus Breen puts the case forcefully in his article 'The End of the World as we Know it: Popular Music's Cultural Mobility' (*Cultural Studies*, 9:3):

> Perhaps . . . we have been too eager to be culturalists – promoters of our musical obsessions – rather than analysts and critics. Scholars are readily acceding to the cultural–industrial cooptive pressures. Our research and writing can look increasingly like promotional material for the sector in which we work. In this respect I have to express deep disappointment with Keith Negus's recent book, *Producing Pop*, which occasionally read like an industry endorsement pamphlet. (492)

This sort of critique, which attempts to reassert some sort of oppositionality after the alleged noncommittal and levelled stance of some postmodernist-influenced writing, does suggest a certain crisis of confidence in how popular music studies should progress. For in berating Negus as some sort of quisling engaged in 'bland administrative research' (a reading which this author does not find convincing), Breen points to the larger problem of how close academic writers can comfortably get to their sites of inquiry. What I think we are witnessing, therefore, is both a semantic problem for academics (how do I write about music in a way which conveys my passion for my object of inquiry and still remain theoretically 'credible'?) and the diffusion of academic energies in a way which somehow implicates researchers as co-authors of, or co-respondents for, the structures they wish to critique. As more academics become increasingly involved in local initiatives, national projects, and taste-affirming/formulating projects and events which elide the boundaries between observer and participator, this phenomenon will become increasingly important to the way popular music studies develops in the future.

2. Biography, Autobiography and Critical Surveys of Artists

The overwhelming majority of pop biographies are trade books, and most of these deal with rock musicians (hardly ever with producers, engineers or executives). A good number are concerned with the three seminal figures of the early years of the rock period: Elvis Presley, Bob Dylan and the Beatles. A real breakthrough in terms of applying a theoretical protocol to biographical material has come with Henry W. Sullivan's unpromisingly titled *The Beatles with Lacan: Rock'n'Roll as Requiem for the Modern Age*. Sullivan provides an excellent analysis of the Beatles' career – perhaps, along with Ian MacDonald's *Revolution in the Head* (Fourth Estate, 1994), the best so far available. But in using the work of Lacan Sullivan offers a psychoanalytical framework to discuss personality and creativity. He also provides a provocative analysis of the roots of rock'n'roll, arguing that the paternal guard of the time, born in the first two decades of the twentieth century, were traumatized on a subconscious level by the mistakes of their parents and, in losing respect for them, turned a blind eye to, and as a result tacitly supported, the flaunting of moral codes by their own sons and daughters in the 1950s and 1960s 'without having been placed under any real obligation to do so'. It is out of this that the Beatles' individual biographies are discussed. Furthermore, Sullivan argues that what gives the Beatles and their music their real distinction is their location, temporally, on the cusp between the modern and postmodern world views. The albums 'between *Rubber Soul* in 1965 and *Abbey Road* in 1969 constitute . . . the first popular post-Modern Classic'. This is an innovative though never obtuse piece of writing, and stands as the first real attempt to theorize the Beatles' life and work.

Two other major studies of the Beatles fall a good way short of Sullivan's innovative analyses, both for similar reasons. During the mid-1960s the Beatles drew strength from both the counter-culture and from the Establishment. Their music had a pan-sexual and cross-generational appeal. Furthermore, their melodies won, and have continued to win, the respect of lovers of classical music and high cultural musical critics. This respect was further strengthened when, in the mid-1960s, the band began using orchestral arrangements and conceptualizing their music so as to invite parallels between it and symphonic works. All this has led to certain critics working within the established musical canon who seek to win acceptance for the Beatles, not on their own terms – as a pop phenomenon – but on the grounds that they brought pop closer to classical music, thus making it loftier, more complex and therefore more credible. Allan Kozinn's book *The Beatles*, in Phaidon's 'Twentieth Century Composers' series, argues this line throughout, without much success. Kozinn's writing is polite and readable, without ever really being incisive. The main weakness in his analysis of the Beatles' music is a rather fundamental one: he appears totally unaware of recent musicological work on pop in general, and on the Beatles in particular, written by those who deal with the music on its own terms as something distinctive and unanalysable as art music (for example, Middleton, Tagg, Wicke, McClary, Moore, Shepherd and Brackett). This leads him to express something akin to incredulity that the Beatles managed such sophistication without even a jot of formal musical training. The Beatles' lyrics are deemed 'unusually articulate' (thus in one descriptive phrase patronizing the Beatles and rendering as dross the vast majority of pop lyrics, since presumably they fail to read as exquisite poetry). Some of their music is 'great art', and, of course, 'the world has seen nothing like them since'. Kozinn's book is not without its merits, containing as it does some enlightening informational nuggets along the way (I was particularly interested to read that 'Get Back' was originally entitled 'No Pakistanis', a parody of the 'Britain for the British' Powellite stance of 1968). But overall, I found Kozinn's approach rather middle-brow and outmoded. The idea that the closer pop gets to classical music in terms of complexity the more lasting it ultimately will be also seems to be the reasoning behind *A Day in the Life: The Music and Artistry of the Beatles* by Mark Hertsgaard. Hertsgaard's view is that the personal biographies of the four individual members, the way in which the music was packaged and the sensationalism of the counter-cultural experience was mere froth, an unfortunate adjunct to the truth of the Beatles' power and a distraction from any analysis of the music: 'A principal aim of this book is to encourage readers to listen to the Beatles' music for themselves – separate from the myth – and to develop their own views accordingly' (xi). To achieve this aim Hertsgaard ploughs an already very worn furrow. The book is a readable, sporadically interesting, but ultimately run-of-the mill and humourless chronological analysis of the Beatles' records, with absolutely no new theoretical approach. Indeed, in endeavouring to reveal the music behind the myth, Hertsgaard is, of course, following the hackneyed biographical line based on the assumption that the myth is somehow a less valid object of inquiry than any notional 'truth' which it allegedly obfuscates. He also makes the same sort of appeals to high culture as Kozinn in order to validate his subject of inquiry, despite invalidating his own phony bases of comparison with rather bland statements: 'Comparing Mozart and the Beatles is . . . like comparing apples and oranges. But the Beatles may well be regarded as the twentieth-century counterpart of Mozart. Like him, they created music that was not only the most popular of its time but also of the highest quality artistically.' The Beatles as classical composers manqué is the overriding theme of both Kozinn and Hertsgaard. Perhaps the next book on the Beatles should be an examination of why this is so.

A most welcome (re)addition to the welter of comment surrounding the Fab Four is Michael Braun's seminal *Love Me Do!: The Beatles' Progress*. Originally published in 1964, this long-out-of-print book is a contemporary account of life on the road with the band at the height of Beatlemania. As a piece of ethnography/sociology it is undeniably important: although this is no academic treatise, Braun gives a real taste of the social mores within which the Beatles were embedded. The band show themselves as incurably laddish, punning their way from interview to interview in something of a haze of coke and whisky. Braun punctured the then prevalent view of the Beatles as friendly mop-topped funsters, recording discussions centring on topics such as female masturbation at their concerts and their deep hatred of Cliff Richard's music. Back in 1964 such talk was bordering on the blasphemous. But it is the rearticulation of US popular culture, the Beatles' deep knowledge of which Americanisms were in and which were out, and Lennon's avowed declaration not to sound like an American singer, despite his love for Presley et al., which provides some telling first-hand testimony as to why 1960s UK popular music, and much since that decade, has remained such a powerful force. The United States codified rhythm and blues, blues, country and rock'n'roll (the *software* of pop), and the United Kingdom stylized it, jumbled it up, mixed it with sources from outside of music and provided the casing (both conceptual and sartorial – the *hardware* of pop). It is this general theme which Braun's thirty-year-old piece of reportage exemplifies so well, capturing as it does the very birth of UK pop as a global force.

The rise of rock'n'roll a decade before Beatlemania is inextricably linked with that of Elvis Presley, the topic of two new studies. Robert Matthew-Walker's *Heartbreak Hotel: The Life and Music of Elvis Presley* is yet another traditional analysis of the Presley *oeuvre*, and of note mainly only for its useful 'Documentary' section detailing his main recordings and films. But *True Disbelievers: The Elvis Contagion* by R. Serge Denisoff and George Plasketes is a worthwhile addendum to the huge weight of comment on the man. The book focuses on the Elvis cults and followers – the Gatheringites and Elfans (Elvis fans) who believe in the second coming of the King. The authors draw interesting comparisons between this phenomenon and other quasi-religious cults such as the Millerites, who believed the world would end in 1843. A second grouping of Elvis followers are also identified, the 'true disbelievers' of the book's title, a group 'who reject the religious rationale and reasoning regarding Elvis's life arguing that the worship and adulation is nothing more than idolatry of a false god', but who still, however, have 'explored alternate sets of belief regarding Elvis's life and death and adopted them with the same passion and enthusiasm as the true believers of the Elvis religious sect' (273). This wing of Elvis devotees have posited a wide range of theories regarding Presley's demise in August 1977, and the authors assess each hypothesis in turn. The possibilities range from natural causes (heart attack, cancer, brain tumour) and accidental death (suffocation in the bathroom rug after a fall), to suicide, murder and, finally, the case that Presley is still alive, having faked his own demise and arranged for a terminally ill Elvis impersonator to die in his place. There are two main theories for why this may be so: the first centres on Presley's wish to retire from the public domain after over twenty years of the success which had corrupted him. The second claims that Presley, who served as a government agent for the Drug Enforcement Agency, is hiding out under the Federal Government's witness protection scheme after receiving numerous death threats. After assessing the evidence, the authors still fail to completely rule out the latter theory that Elvis is in the underground, 'figuratively, not literally'.

Sue Wise's reading of Elvis Presley, 'Sexing Elvis', reprinted in Simon Frith and Andrew Goodwin's *On Record: Rock, Pop and the Written Word* (Routledge, 1990), is the starting point for John Gill's analysis of Presley in *Queer Noises: Male and Female Homosexuality in Twentieth-Century Music*. In 'Sexing Elvis' Wise wrote how she came to terms with her lesbianism through a close identification with the feminine side of the King, and the softer, less macho element in his music and his iconography. Gill argues that similar readings of our pop icons would destroy the myth perpetrated by male heterosexual rock writers that pop, machismo and rebellion go hand in hand, maintaining that 'we should marvel at the achievement of one lesbian and apply such readings to the rest of rock history. If a lone dyke can bring this monstrous fiction crashing to earth, who knows what an army of lovers might do.' This quote neatly exemplifies the bitchy tone of the narrative, which eventually begins to pall and detracts from the undoubted quality of intellect on display. *Queer Noises* is a polemic against the heterosexual enemy written 'as a refutation of the heterosexual propaganda – spookily echoed in the editorial policies of some of the gay media – that queers don't make or listen to music'. *Queer Noises* is not so much a sustained piece of analysis as eighteen rather disparate mini-sketches of a whole variety of gay or bisexual musicians. Gill writes aggressively and unsympathetically about those closet queers who have, for personal reasons, found it necessary to hide their own sexuality. That said, there is a welter of interesting material here: I particularly liked the critique of classical music in the chapter on Benjamin Britten, as well as the essays on John Cage, Bessie Smith, Sun Ra and Patti Smith. Gill also analyses the 'myth of Queer David', arguing that Bowie, although straight (and maybe even a homophobe), created the space for 'real' gays to come out. But ultimately the tone of the book is often spiteful, as the author's homosexual purism replaces the old chestnut of rock authenticity with a sort of hardline and ungenerous gay authenticity.

Equally bitchy is Boy George's 'autobiography', *Take It Like a Man*, co-written with Spencer Bright. As a testimony to ego-gratification and style fascism George's memoirs make for illuminating reading, particularly his account of his pre-stardom years in the New Romantic maelstrom of early eighties London club culture, and his report of the sexual prejudices of BBC TV and Radio One (one reporter apparently told his record company 'we don't interview transvestites').

Punk remains one of the most written about moments in pop history, and Marcus Gray's *The Last Gang in Town: The Story of The Clash* is a weighty addition to the punk debate. At over 500 pages the book is too long: Gray seems unable to spare the reader even the most mundane of facts concerning the band's career, with – seemingly – every equipment change, every gig and every recording earnestly described in minute detail. Gray overcompensates for his failure to win the cooperation of the band members themselves by quoting excessively from second-hand sources, with mixed results. He also follows the standard biographical line in attempting to reveal the hidden and hitherto ineffable 'truths' behind the media 'myth'. There are some sharper sections, and Gray is undoubtedly extremely knowledgeable about the band, but the analysis comes nowhere near the sort of cultural contextualization to be found in Jon Savage's *England's Dreaming: The Sex Pistols and Punk Rock* (Faber, 1991).

Also around 500 pages in length, but significantly less prosaic, is Bill Flanagan's *U2 At the End of the World*. Flanagan's main advantage over Gray is the simple fact that he had access to the band members. The narrative runs from the recording of the epochal *Achtung Baby* in Berlin in late 1990 through to the conclusion of the *Zooropa* tour three years later. The action never flags: I particularly appreciated Flanagan's candid accounts of studio tensions and the way in which the band dynamic changed throughout the period of investigation. Whereas many long-lived bands who start out writing together 'regress' to a point where each member begins working separately (the Beatles being the most glaring example of this), Flanagan describes how, by 1993, the band had regained a more organic approach to writing and recording with their *Zooropa* album. As an insider account of perhaps the biggest rock band of the last decade, Flanagan's reportage is most welcome, revealing as it does some interesting details of U2's financial dealings, the importance of corporate image, the development of stage personae by Bono and U2's love–hate relationship with Americana.

Finally, *Touching from a Distance: Ian Curtis and Joy Division* by Deborah Curtis (his wife) details the life and tragic early death at the age of 23 of one of pop's most enduring icons. In the foreword Jon Savage writes:

> When you're young, death isn't part of your world. When Ian Curtis committed suicide in May 1980, it was the first time that many of us had had to encounter death: the result was a shock so profound that it has become an unresolved trauma, a rupture in Manchester's social history that has persisted through the city's worldwide promotion as Madchester, and through the continuing success of New Order, the group formed by Joy Division's remaining trio. (xii)

As an *exposé* of the male-dominated rock world, this first-hand evidence gives a voice to the way in which wives and girlfriends of stars are often patronized, marginalized and emotionally abused. Many research projects into music-making, such as Sara Cohen's *Rock Culture in Liverpool: Popular Music in the Making* (Cambridge University Press, 1991), make similar claims about the marginality of women, and stories such as Deborah Curtis's are important in that they are useful validators of academic research. The picture of Curtis which emerges as the narrative progresses is that of a talented and creative man who was haunted and obsessed by his own personal demons. Deborah Curtis details how her husband became transfixed by the dark power of Nazism, how he became fixated with death and human suffering, and how he became something of a paranoid misogynist, mistreating his wife through a regime of emotional cruelty. Interestingly, Deborah Curtis also talks about how her husband's maniacal stage presence was a distressing parody of his off-stage epileptic seizures. This is a moving book which never pulls its punches.

3. Anthologies, Collections and Encyclopedias

The Faber Book of Pop, edited by Hanif Kureishi and Jon Savage, is a treasure trove of short extracts from 1942 to the present day. In his introductory essay, 'The Simple Things You See Are All Complicated', Savage reiterates the central theme of his 1993 article co-authored with Simon Frith, 'Pearls and Swine: Against Cultural Populism' (*New Left Review* 198:107–16). Savage bemoans baby-boomer nostalgia in the media, arguing that far from losing its politics and radical edge, pop, in embodying the future, is 'one of the few places in modern communications which transcends cynicism and populism to offer hope, joy and love'. For Savage, pop music has cultural resonance because:

> it stands, by default, at the intersection between two quite separate perceptions – the public world of news, current affairs and media chat, and the private world of life as lived. In this pops perennial concentration on love is only the most obvious sign of its intention to make the private public. Hence also its flagrant concerns with sex and gender. (xxxii)

It is these issues of sex and gender which provide the overriding schemata for the collection. Savage and Kureishi's selections seek to reveal the roots of pop in the conflicted terrain of youth culture, and in particular gay subculture. Although this is a much-needed corrective to the disappointing machismo of Clinton Heylin's earlier collection, *The Penguin Book of Rock'n'Roll Writing* (Viking, 1992), at times it is hard not to conclude that the proselytizing is a little overplayed. Kureishi and Savage split up their material into ten main sections, each with an introduction which expertly contextualizes the cultural topography (however, like so much of Savage's writing, the tone is avowedly earnest, engaged, but rather humourless throughout). Section 1, dealing with the period 1942–56, is especially interesting, particularly the reprint of a 1955 article by Bernard McElwaine which describes the scenes of mass hysteria at an early Johnny Ray concert. Section 2, which deals with the rock'n'roll explosion, contains a priceless left-wing put-down of phony Americana by Richard Hoggart extracted from the classic *The Uses of Literacy* (Chatto & Windus, 1957). The rest of the anthology contains numerous other gems from the likes

of Tom Wolfe, Nick Cohn, Angela Carter, Charles Shaar Murray, Lester Bangs,
Simon Reynolds, Kodo Eshwun and David Toop. *The Faber Book of Pop* is by
far and away the best anthology of journalistic writing yet published, and is
essential reading.

However, *The Faber Book of Pop* contains very little on the role of women
in the music business. In the wake of the Riot Grrl, a loose confederation of
noisy feminist guitar bands which started in 1991 in the United States and
which was imported into the United Kingdom a year later, Virago have
published two edited anthologies which deal with women as musicians in their
own right. Amy Raphael's *Never Mind the Bollocks: Women Rewrite Rock*
contains a dozen interviews with contemporary female musicians such as
Courtney Love, Sonya Aurora Madan, Björk and Kirstin Hersh. In the short
introduction Raphael points out how women have been marginalized into
cartoon-like caricatures in a male-dominated music business. She writes: 'The
fact is that gender will remain an issue as long as the industry is dominated by
men, and female musicians remain an exception to the rule'. Karen O'Brien's
collection of interviews, *Hymn to Her: Women Musicians Talk*, follows an
almost identical format, this time with a much shorter introduction prefiguring
fifteen interviews. O'Brien's selection is more eclectic than Raphael's, and
includes interviews with Moe Tucker from the Velvet Underground, singer-
songwriter Kirsty MacColl and doyenne of the avant-garde Yoko Ono.
Interesting, but hardly essential.

The work of Fred and Judy Vermorel in the 1980s, particularly their book
Starlust: The Secret Fantasies of Fans (Comedia, 1985), started a trend towards
the 'pop confessional'. *Starlust* collected dozens of testimonies which revealed
in a brutally frank manner the psychology of the devoted pop fan. And the
1990s have witnessed any number of attempts to fetishize fanatism, whether it
be with regard to pop music and its icons or, more likely, in the United
Kingdom at least, with regard to football. *The Smiths: All Men Have Secrets*,
edited by Tom Gallagher, Michael Campbell and Murdo Miles, is a collection
of confessionals about arguably the signature UK band of the 1980s, The
Smiths. Never a real force in purely commercial terms, the group did have a
fanatical following of arty bedsit suburbanites. But with no proper introduction to contextualize the band's achievements and the most arbitrary of
chapter headings, *All Men Have Secrets* is poorly organized and unalluring.
And the reprinted letters themselves vary from the unremarkable to the
downright embarrassing. Here's one representative extract:

> The night after I'd first heard this song is one I'll cherish forever. I
> actually had a dream that Morrissey, wearing a brown woolly
> jumper, embraced me in his arms then took me flying. It was
> dusk, and as we floated serenely over my home town of Maltby he
> would whisper points of interest in my ear.   (107)

For this sort of ethnographic material to be of any real use, it has to be placed
in a much wider discursive framework and must breathe life into the main text
rather than stand isolated as these letters do here, uncontextualized and
ultimately pointless.

Music, Culture and Experience, edited by Reginald Byron, is a collection of
selected papers by the ethnomusicologist John Blacking, who died in 1990.

Blacking's *How Musical is Man?* (Seattle: University of Washington Press, 1973) argued that the structure of music commented on the way humans organize themselves socially. This link between music and 'the social' was a theme developed in the 1980s and 1990s in the work of musicologists such as John Shepherd. For anyone coming to the work of Blacking for the first time, this collection is the perfect place to start, with the introductory essay 'The Ethnomusicology of John Blacking', by Reginald Byron, of particular use. According to Byron, Blacking's greatest contribution was in arguing for a formulation which is now read as axiomatic, that: 'music conveys everything but itself. If musical structures per se are non-referential, then their meanings cannot be found in "scientific" musical analysis, but only in the constructions that people put upon them within particular social and cultural milieus' (26). Much of Blacking's writing sought to break down the artificial categorizations which bedevil the music scholar. In probably the most useful essay for the non-musicologist, 'Expressing Human Experience Through Music', he argues that:

> Our understanding of people as music-makers can be retarded by attempts to classify music according to its sound or the culture of its creators. Terms such as 'art', 'folk' or 'popular' can be misleading: although they may suggest the kind of experience the music is intended to convey, they are too often used to refer to the technical complexity it displays. (31)

This essay goes on to explore the whole concept of what music is and what it is not. For Blacking, 'music is humanly organized sound', dependent for its success 'on the kind and quality of human experiences involved in its creation and performance'.

This year also sees the publication of a revised edition of *The Faber Companion to Twentieth-Century Popular Music*, by Phil Hardy and Dave Laing. Always the most readable of the welter of popular music encyclopedias on the market, this edition was updated to include newer acts such as Boyz II Men, Garth Brooks, Nirvana and Soul II Soul, although it was obviously collated too late to reflect the newer 'trip-hop' and Britpop' bands from the United Kingdom. Each entry comprises basic biographical details, followed by a short introductory paragraph summarizing the artist's influence, before a critical chronological survey. A short 'Glossary of Styles and Genres', concentrating on those forms of music which 'might be unfamiliar to the general reader', is included too. There is now also a useful index of song and album titles.

alt.culture: An A–Z of the 90s – Underground and Online by Steven Daly and Nathaniel Wice is, despite its rather self-conscious trendiness, a very useful guide to US popular culture in the Internet age. It contains profiles of individuals from film, music, art, sport, fashion, philosophy and literature, definitions of musical styles and interesting discussions of such phenomena as body piercing, phone sex and toad licking. The material is clearly presented and cross-referenced, with information on various relevant web sites and numerous black-and-white photographs.

Finally, the tenth edition of *British Hit Singles*, compiled as ever by Paul Gambaccini, Tim Rice and Jonathan Rice: published every two years, this volume contains the 1993/1994 chart update. In their introduction, 'Back To Life', the authors give a brief survey of the changed terrain. The single's format, far from dying out as predicted in the first years of the decade, merely transposed itself from vinyl to CD, and by the end of 1994 sales were as buoyant as they had been for nearly a decade, with two million-selling singles in that year alone. Dance emerged as the genre with the quickest turnover of hits: 'In no two-year period has there been as high a number of entries in the top 75 as in 1993–94' (5). This trend would continue, of course, throughout the decade, causing much industry promotional panic as a top 3 single's chart life could be as short as three weeks in the top 75. *British Hit Singles* follows the tried and trusted format, with the chart performances of each entrant into the UK charts from 1952 listed in Part 1, each charted song listed in Part 2, and a facts and feats section to round off an always entertaining read.

4. History and Analysis

As popular music studies has developed into a recognized academic discipline, so the need to draw together for the undergraduate the various competing analytical traditions which make up this 'hydra-headed monster' has become all the more pressing. Brian Longhurst's sociological critique of the intellectual terrain, *Popular Music and Society*, is the best attempt so far. Livelier than Roy Shuker's *Understanding Popular Music* (Routledge, 1994), Longhurst gets the pitch just right for those coming to the serious study of popular music for the first time. He writes clearly and the text is liberally punctuated with long extracts from apposite secondary sources. Part 1, 'Production', discusses the pop music industry and the social production of music. Part 2, 'Text', gives a brief history of pop and its genres, defines black music and briefly engages with musicology. This is the weakest section in the book, as Longhurst fails to discuss much important work by musicologists in adequate detail, but by part 3, which deals with how pop is consumed, with audiences and subcultures, his touch is once again assured. In short, this is a very clear sociological account (although Longhurst's propensity to tabulate seemingly everything does become weari-some), much weaker on textual analysis but ultimately the best introduction yet to come on the market. Peter J. Martin's *Sounds and Society: Themes in the Sociology of Music* is unlikely to have the same immediate pedagogical impact in that it primarily addresses fellow researchers in the relatively small field of the sociology of musical practice. That said, perseverance does pay off: Martin's cogent and fluid style is a treat. In his introduction, Martin defines the sociological perspective in general terms (sociology as 'guided by the perception that the words, thoughts and deeds of individual human beings are profoundly influenced by the nature of the social circumstances in which they occur'), before fitting music into the sociological framework as an 'autonomous sphere of social activity'. Martin goes on to argue that the sociology of music must be inclusive and must 'encompass all the sounds that people describe as music and all the things they say and write about such sounds'. Martin's analysis is particularly valuable in that it summarizes existing work in the field so expertly. I found his critique of the work of musicologist John Shepherd, and his roots in the work of Marshall McLuhan in the 1960s, particularly helpful in this respect.

David Brackett's enthusiastic *Interpreting Popular Music* also comes recommended. In the main body of the work Brackett's musicological readings of Billie Holiday, Bing Crosby, Hank Williams, James Brown and Elvis Costello are astute, but the real benefit of the book is its excellent introduction, in which the author discusses the notion of authorship, for the pop music text is a conflation of the 'singing voice, body, image, and biographical details'. Brackett argues for a sort of strategic or pragmatic musicology, one free from totalizing dogma:

> One of the arguments throughout is that there is not necessarily one way of interpreting popular music, but that different types of popular music use different types of rhetoric, call for different sorts of interpretation, refer to different arguments about words and voices, about musical complexity and familiarity, and draw upon different senses of history and tradition.   (31)

Brackett obviously feels that traditional musicology, in its conservatism and its bias towards examinations of 'masterworks', has entered into the pop debate late, well after the first sociological encounters with music and culture, but that musicologists 'have had difficulty establishing why one kind of music and not another is used in a particular way, and *how* one kind of music produces one effect while a different kind of music produces another'. Brackett's engaged musicology, cognizant of the social and political content of music, is an attempt to answer some of the questions straight sociology has failed to answer effectively.

Richard Middleton's 'Authorship, Gender and the Construction of Meaning in the Eurythmics' Hit Recordings' (*Cultural Studies* 9:iii.465–85) puts forward a more problematized and sophisticated notion of authorship through an application of Mikhail Bakhtin's dialogical theory of creativity to music and its creation. Middleton argues that 'Modes of singing help to delineate styles but they also move across them, responding to them, perhaps changing meanings as they go' (471). He identifies a high proportion of such stylistic boundary-breaking, particularly in the early work of the Eurythmics, and contends that the gender map is crucial in terms of understanding their music fully. Middleton's review of their later work is, however, less convincing, in that no theory is put forward as to why the playfulness and daring went out of their music so quickly. This is perhaps because he fails to consider, or is perhaps unaware of, the mid-1980s drive towards 'rock authenticity' which the band were caught up in. Middleton's work is provocative here as always, but lacks the weight of lived experience, the experience of someone who actively consumed the music at the time and who was aware of the sort of critical agenda set by both practitioners and writers which impacted on musical styles themselves.

The journal *Popular Music* also contains three very useful musicological analyses which even the non-music theorist will find of interest. In 'The Stax Sound: a Musicological Analysis' (*Popular Music* 14:iii.285–320), Rob Bowman argues that, apart from Robert Walser's recent book-length study of heavy metal, *Running with the Devil* (Wesleyan University Press, 1993):

> there has been no academic musicological work . . . that has attempted to ferret out the component parts of a given genre through an analysis of a sizeable body of repertoire. There is an

acute need for such work if popular music scholars are going to begin to understand in concrete terms what is meant by such terms as rock, soul, funk, Merseybeat and so on.   (285)

Bowman's article, derived from work in progress for a book on Stax records, analyses the Stax sound with commendable authority by breaking down the components of that sound into its constituent analysable parts. Hence there are sections on instrumentation, repertoire, musical structure (including discussions of key signatures, chord structures, harmony, tempo, vocals and timbre) and the available recording equipment and technology. Bowman concludes that 'all aspects of composition and performance practice in this music were geared towards an overall aesthetic ideal on each recording' and 'that there were two basic aesthetic ideals operative at Stax: one for dance/groove tunes . . . and one for "love" songs . . . aiming for emotional catharsis' (318). Doug Miller, in his article 'The Moan with the Tone: African Retentions in Rhythm and Blues Saxophone Style in Afro-American Popular Music' (*Popular Music* 14:ii.155–74), looks at the 'honkers' and 'screamers' of the forties and fifties. After a general discussion of the role of the saxophone within American popular music, Miller gets to grips with the actual sounds themselves and discusses pitch, timbre and tone colour, looking at performance technique itself, the phrasing and building of a solo within a live context. Lastly, the analysis focuses on the huge popularity of the music with the white audiences of the day before concluding: 'We are left with an important residual question concerning the extent to which the dominant white culture – notably the social, economic and political context of the black urban working class and the hostile environment of white racism – may have had their own impact on the psyche of the black musician and his audience' (170). Finally, Jon Fitzgerald's short article, 'Motown Crossover Hits 1963–1966 and the Creative Process' (*Popular Music* 14:i.1–11), rightly draws attention to the lack of scholarly interest, even by those writers who have written eloquently about black music, in the most commercially successful black music phenomenon of its day. Fitzgerald states that 'Motown's chart success appears all the more remarkable when one considers the limited previous achievements of black performers and songwriters in terms of crossover sales' (1). Fitzgerald concludes that, although melody and lyrics were important to the overall effect of Holland–Dozier–Holland's vast repertoire, 'it is fair to say that the concentration of session players and writers on details of "the groove" made these Motown songs very different from other pop songs of the day, and allowed for an elusive balance of repetition and variety which was undoubtedly a contributing factor to their crossover success' (8).

Although not so straight a piece of musicological analysis, Benjamin Noys's article 'Into the "Jungle" ' (*Popular Music* 14:iii.321–32) is extremely useful in sorting out the complicated terrain of contemporary dance music. According to Noys, 'Jungle is Techno hip-hop, taking the rolling break-beats of hip-hop and speeding them up to 150 beats per minute (b.p.m). The result is a distinctive clattering sound of drum and bass which cannot be mistaken for other forms of House and Techno' (321). Whereas punk has been traditionally theorized by the likes of Jon Savage as a suburban musical form which migrated to urban centres, Noys writes that jungle 'constantly transgresses the urban/suburban binarism both ideologically and materially and as such both confirms and denies it' (325). Noys argues against much subcultural readings of the relationship between music and culture in that he maintains that 'Jungle as a musical form shapes its subcultural expression', and calls for the reopening of debate concerning how past subcultures have been historically framed based on a re-examination of the function of music 'in integrating the subcultural style':

> The preoccupation with the political effects of subcultures or the concentration on style and consumption have both tended to obscure questions around musical evolution and competition. Instead it is possible that a concentration on musical forms may lead to new ways in answering questions about the politics, style and practices of consumption of subcultures. (330)

The impact and development of techno music in Australia is the subject of Ross Harley's article 'Acts of Volition: Volition Records, Independent Marketing and the Promotion of Techno-Pop' (*Perfect Beat*, 2:3.21–48). Harley usefully contrasts techno music 'which privileges the use of "synthetic" instruments, "robotic" rhythms, vastly varying tempos and "futuristic" sounds in order to create a highly percussive and danceable soundtrack' with the more melodic song-based 'dance-pop' which 'tends to mask the synthetic origin of sounds'. Harley defines techno as an oppositional music designed to 'grate against the system of commercial music. . . . A kind of *musique concrète* you can dance to', and maintains an '"underground" status despite its appearance in the mainstream charts'. The rest of the article is concerned with tracing the success of Sydney's Volition records and their increasingly global reach. Harley's conclusion echoes the work of Keith Negus in *Producing Pop* (Edward Arnold, 1992), particularly his theory of 'webs' of 'major' and 'minor' companies locked in interdependence rather than conflict. Harley concludes:

> The success of Volition records also demonstrates the extent to which major record companies rely on smaller independent labels to supply them with products and audiences they may not understand. Instead of competing with the smaller labels as they may have done in the past (by signing similar acts to the company directly), major record companies are happy to capitalize on techno-pop by way of distribution alone. Unable to beat independent labels at their own game, majors now join them instead. (45)

Ocean of Sound: After Talk, Ambient Sound and Imaginary Worlds is another valuable contribution. David Toop, with endless enthusiasm and commitment, writes about the sort of music which deals primarily with timbres and textures, the ethnic styles of music which only very occasionally impinge on the mainstream, and the formless, ambient, oceanic musics which create a sense of otherness, loss or *jouissance* for the listener. Toop traces the development of ambient music ('music that aspires to the tradition of perfume') from its introduction into European culture through Javanese Gamelan music, through futurism and sound collagists, the minimalism of

Satie, Cage and later Eno, the experimentalism of Sun Ray and Lee Perry, into the nineties and 'ambient house', and its relationship with the curator club culture. A trip by the author into an Amazon rainforest makes for a startling finale. But sometimes Toop drifts off into the obscure; too many allusions and illusions spice the narrative with a self-conscious arcaneness, and the book could certainly have profited from some photographic illustrative material. A double CD, also called *Ocean Of Sound* (Virgin, 1996), containing much of the music analysed in the book is available and provides an almost essential adjunct to the main text.

In *Plunderphonics, 'Pataphysics and Pop Mechanics: An Introduction to Musique Actuelle*, Andrew Jones looks at the work of the likes of Fred Frith, Chris Cutler, John Zorn and The Residents, those musicians who work largely outside of the mainstream and whose music is 'fuelled by the art of bricolage'. *Musique actuelle* is defined as 'music about music, a metamusic that sounds like your parents' copy of *The Readers' Digest Collection of Music of the World* put through a Ronco Veg-o-matic'. This is an interesting read in parts, but Jones lacks Toop's gift for contextualization and quick-wittedness. And this book, more than Toop's, would have benefited from an accompanying CD, so obscure is some of the material under discussion to all but the aficionado. However, Joseph Lanza's *Elevator Music: A Surreal History of Muzak, Easy-Listening and other Moodsong* is a historical *tour de force* and beautifully written at that. Lanza is at pains to point out the ubiquity of mood music (he calls it 'the music world's Esperanto') in our lives, that music which 'shifts music from *figure* to *ground*, to encourage peripheral hearing' to 'provide an illusion of distended time'. Lanza tells the story of the development of mood music from its roots in the folklore of antiquity, through the utility music and sound experiments of the futurist movement, the development of 'wired music' and the Muzak Corporation, and the use of mood music on radio, to discussions of the work of Mantovani and the The Mystic Moods Orchestra, elevator music and the development of New Age music. Fascinating reading.

Despite the occasional appearance of genuine works of quality such as Lanza's, there are surprisingly few serious or academic histories of popular music, and the best introductions to popular music and culture, such as Iain Chamber's *Urban Rhythms* (Macmillan, 1985), are now long out-of-date. Whilst not an academic history as such, *The Rise and Fall of Popular Music* by Donald Clarke, over 600 pages in length, does contain much useful information, tracing as it does the origins of popular song back into the nineteenth century and beyond. The main advantage of Clarke's approach is also its principal weakness: his non-academic tack means that he is not afraid to assess and evaluate rather than simply take a neutral stance. But this leads him into real difficulties when the discussion turns to contemporary popular music. What ultimately emerges is a sort of menopausal blues of a history in which the tone becomes more patronizing and high-mannered: 'Many people hate rap. Considered purely as music, it is the ultimate reduction of pop to absurdity. Charles Shaar Murray claims that rap was the most exciting thing to happen to pop in the 1980s, but that's not saying much' (550).

As a corrective to Clarke's wrong-headed portrayal of black American rap and hip-hop culture as inane and offensive, readers should be directed to *The New Beats: Exploring the Music Culture and Attitudes of Hip-Hop* by S. H. Fernando Jr, a new account of contemporary black styles which traces the roots of hip-hop and rap to the nineteenth-century African-American oral tradition, and provides authoritative readings of the major players in an uplifting way and with a sense of history.

As popular music studies further widens its scope, the work of historians, now a tiny minority within the overall academic interest in popular music, will hopefully become more prominent. Social and cultural historian John Blaxendale has an essay, '" . . . Into Another Kind of Life in which Anything Might Happen . . ." Popular Music and Late Modernity, 1910–1930', in *Popular Music* (14.ii.137–54). Blaxendale shows how the Victorian musical system 'in which songs were produced as commodities, and their exchange value realized by charging people to hear them performed professionally' was, under the impact of new technologies and 'massification' in the first three decades of the century, superseded by a new system, essentially still in operation today, 'in which commodification through mass reproduction and social dance partly displaced live performance'.

A much-needed curative to those histories of popular music which have tended to marginalize the role of women is Lucy O'Brien's excellent *She Bop: The Definitive History of Women in Rock, Pop and Soul*. This is a flowing, well-researched and passionate journalistic account. In her introduction O'Brien makes the point that 'Women need to become active as consumers, to discriminate, to argue, to read, to listen and therefore alter preconceptions of what popular music should be' (6). The first six chapters describes the travails and contributions of a succession of female singers and performers, from the blues and jazz period to the present day. O'Brien argues that blueswomen such as Billie Holiday and disco singers such as Donna Summer, far from following in a male-dominated world, formed and led public appreciation of these musical genres. The critical assessments are almost always spot-on. Of Ella Fitzgerald she writes: 'Her pioneering scat predates the vocal gymnastics of later eras, in which stars like Whitney Houston and Mariah Carey race around the octaves yet somehow render their material meaningless' (27). What a non-academic writer like O'Brien lacks in theoretical knowledge is more than made up for by her overall feel, as a consumer of popular music and as someone who is obviously passionate about her endeavours, for the material she is writing about. The second half of the book looks afresh at issues such as iconography and MTV, androgyny, disco, rap and world music. Highly recommended.

Simon Reynold's *Blissed Out: The Raptures of Rock* (Serpent's Tail, 1990), a collection of his eighties journalistic writings, is as committed an aesthetic defence of popular music as one could wish for. Reynolds, like perhaps no other pop writer, is able to write partial, dynamic analyses which are also wedded to a flexible and eclectic theoretical approach. His new book, *The Sex Revolts: Gender, Rebellion and Rock'n'Roll*, co-authored with his wife Joy Press, is, however, a mild disappointment. The main problem is that the book is far too discursive. The short, sharp shock in the form of a review or journalistic set-piece is Reynolds' *métier*; he fails to fully make the transition to more weighty sustained cultural analysis. *The Sex Revolts* is simply a succession of rather disconnected sketches tacked together. There is no unity of argument or flow to the book. There is admittedly a huge territory to cover, and Reynolds and Press try everything from the Stranglers' misogyny to Tori Amos's confessionals. Another problem is that of political correctness, as the authors signal in the introduction: 'If you choose to venture along the path of critical awareness, though, and start to dissect rock's psychosexual underpinnings, you quickly arrive in an interesting interzone of double allegiances – torn between the conflicting criteria of rock fandom and feminism, aesthetics and ethics' (xiii).

Despite its failings, this is still an important book and should certainly be consulted; the analysis is often brilliantly thought-provoking and engaged. Has anyone better captured the spirit of rave culture than this?: 'Rave culture is "about" nothing: it's a celebration of celebration. Where fascism is a killing machine, rave is an orgasmatron: a system for generating euphoria and excitement out of nothing, and for no good reason' (106).

The institutional monitoring and attempted control of the rave culture of the late 1980s reconfigured not only youth culture but also youth cultural theory. As a direct response to the impingement of law on popular culture, Steve Redhead's writings have sought to confront head-on issues of law, postmodernism and subculture. His latest book, *Unpopular Cultures: The Birth of Law and Order*, attempts to bring law as a discipline into the mainstream of popular cultural analysis. The most novel aspect of the work is Redhead's neologism for a new area of study, 'popular cultural studies', committed to an analysis of the '"regulation" of popular culture . . . where popular and unpopular clash. . . . Popular cultural studies parodies and pastiches previous contemporary cultural studies just as pop parodies and pastiches its own socio-musical history.' Martin Cloonan's article, '"I Fought the Law" – Popular Music and British Obscenity Law' (*Popular Music* 14:iii.349–63), also takes institutionalized methods of control and censorship as its central theme. Cloonan looks at two main areas: 'first, attempts to prosecute records because of their covers and second, because of their content', arguing that the Obscene Publications Act of 1959, which was not envisaged for use against pop, but nevertheless has been, should be replaced by a more Draconian law in the future. Cloonan concludes: 'It is interesting to note that all attempts to prosecute covers and records have come since the Conservatives came to power in 1979.'

Deena Weinstein, like Steve Redhead, also sees the development of a highly ironic stance within youth culture as an important part of its make-up in the 1990s. In her article 'Alternative Youth: The Ironies of Recapturing Youth Culture' (*Young* 3:i.61–71), Weinstein argues for the emergence of 'ironic youth'. After the countercultural 1960s the idea of an oppositional youth culture collapsed, movements such as punk and metal being merely subcultural fragments as the concept of youth as a signifier became detached from its temporal locus as the embodiment of an adolescent world-view. She writes:

> Youth, in the sense of young people in a specific biological and
> social predicament, became marginal to 'youth' as a cultural code
> of beliefs, values, sentiments, and practices. Youth did not have its
> own 'youth', but instead the 'youth' that was given to them by the
> media. Young people did not have a culture that was theirs. Rock,
> like youthful looks, was no longer the province of the young.   (63)

Weinstein goes on to show how the early 1980s American college bands, the 'alternative' rockers such as Sonic Youth, the Replacements, Husker Du and

REM, cleverly 'nurtured a counter-cultural pop–rock music that was potentially acceptable in its sonic values to a more mass audience but defied the regnant values of capitalist greed and the "youthfulness" projected by the commercial leisure culture' (65).

Entrapped in the simulacra of Disney World, the shopping mall and MTV, the new 'hipoisie' of the 1980s, those fans of 'alternative' rock, 'became figures of self-irony – knowing and declaring themselves to be lies/truth, heart/ garbage. Hence the "endless self-conscious shrug".' The apogee of this indifference came with the self-loathing of grunge, the 'Baby Bust' generation who created a '(simulation of a) counter-culture' with media events such as the mid-nineties Lollapalooza festival. Weinstein's critique makes for depressing reading but rightly highlights the almost mythic status the sixties as an era has over the popular culture of today.

Finally, a celebration of a loose confederation of bands and attitudes which, unlike so much of the Anglo-American pop of the 1960s, still seem fresh and untarnished by endless recycling: *Krautrocksampler: One Head's Guide to the Great Kosmische Musik – 1968 Onwards* is really only a glorified fanzine by pop singer Julian Cope. But it is written with such dash and with such a love for the music that it should be essential reading. Cope discusses those bands integral to the Krautrock scene, including Kraftwerk, Can, Cluster, La Dusseldorf, Ash Ra Temple and Neu!, and shows that this new wave of German experimenters, often with a classical or avant-garde musical training, were interested in those musical parameters – dynamics, space, atonality and daring – which the British progrock scene forsook in search of virtuosity:

> the new rock'n'roll in W. Germany was not rock'n'roll at all. It was a meltdown music-form which defied all categories but that which the W. German musicians called it – Kosmische music. The term has been credited to Edgar Froese, future leader of Tangerine Dream, but in 1969 all the young idealistic W. German musicians talked about Kosmische music with a great reverence, a great idealism, as though they knew it was their way to the stars. (12)

Three major mainstream styles originated out of Krautrock. The late-1970s/ early-1980s British synth-pop of the likes of OMD, Ultravox, Depeche Mode and the Human League was particularly indebted to the work of Kraftwerk (and it was in 1982 that Kraftwerk had their only UK Number 1 single with their 1978 track 'The Model'). What in the late 1980s became known as techo also had its origins in a marriage of Kraftwerk's music with dance styles such as disco and hi-energy. And ambient music, later to be codified in the work of Brian Eno, was part of Krautrock's armoury of musical styles too. A more detailed analysis of Krautrock's legacy would be a fascinating topic for future research.

Books Reviewed

Brackett, David. *Interpreting Popular Music*. Cambridge University Press. pp. 260. hb £35.00. ISBN 0 521 47337 3.
Braun, Michael. *Love Me Do! The Beatles' Progress*. Foreword by Mark

Lewisohn. Reprint of 1964 original. Penguin. pp. 140. pb £5.99. ISBN 0 14 002278 3.

Byron, Reginald, ed. *Music, Culture and Experience: Selected Papers of John Blacking*. Foreword by Bruno Nettl. University of Chicago Press. pp. 268. pb $17.95, £14.25. ISBN 0 226 08830 8.

Clarke, Donald. *The Rise and Fall of Popular Music*. Viking. pp. 620. hb £22.50. ISBN 0 670 83244 8.

Cope, Julian. *Krautrocksampler: One Head's Guide to the Great Kosmische Musik – 1968 Onwards*. Head Heritage. pp. 139. pb £7.99. ISBN 0 9526719 1 3.

Curtis, Deborah. *Touching from a Distance: Ian Curtis and Joy Division*. Faber & Faber. pp. 212. pb £9.99. ISBN 0 571 17445 0.

Daly, Steven, and Nathaniel Wice. *alt.culture: An A–Z of the 90s – Underground and Online*. Fourth Estate. pp. 300. pb £12.99. ISBN 1 85702 378 1.

Denisoff, R. Serge and George Plasketes. *True Disbelievers: The Elvis Contagion*. Transaction. pp. 307. pb $29.95. ISBN 1 56000 186 0.

Fernando, S. H. Jr. *The New Beats: Exploring the Music Culture and Attitudes of Hip-Hop*. Payback Press. pp. 330. pb £9.99. ISBN 0 86241 524 1.

Flanagan, Bill. *U2 at the End of the World*. Bantam. pp. 480. hb £16.99. ISBN 0 385 31154 0.

Gallagher, Tom, Michael Campbell, and Murdo Miles. *The Smiths: All Men Have Secrets.* Virgin. pp. 256. pb £6.99. ISBN 0 86369 874 3.

Gambacini, Paul, Tim Rice, and Jonathan Rice. *British Hit Singles*, 10th edn. Guinness. pp. 456. pb £11.99. ISBN 0 85112 633 2.

George, Boy, with Spencer Bright. *Take It Like a Man: The Autobiography of Boy George*. Sidgwick & Jackson. pp. 490. hb £15.99. ISBN 0 283 99217 4.

Gill, John. *Queer Noises: Male and Female Homosexuality in Twentieth-Century Music*. Cassell. pp. 184. hb £45.00, pb £14.99. ISBN 0 304 34304 8, 0 304 34302 1.

Gray, Marcus. *The Last Gang in Town: The Story of The Clash*. Fourth Estate. pp. 512. pb £12.99. ISBN 1 85702 146 0.

Hardy, Phil, and Dave Laing. *The Faber Companion to Twentieth Century Popular Music*. Revised and updated edition. Faber & Faber. pp. 1211. pb £20.00. ISBN 0 571 17148 6.

Hertsgaard, Mark. *A Day in the Life: The Music and Artistry of the Beatles*. Macmillan. pp. 434. hb £16.99. ISBN 0 333 62824 1.

Jones, Andrew. *Plunderphonics, 'Pataphysics and Pop Mechanics: An Introduction to* Musique Actuelle. SAF. pp. 256. pb £12. 95. ISBN 0 946719 15 2.

Kozinn, Allan. *The Beatles*. 20th Century Composers series. Phaidon. pp. 240. pb £14.99. ISBN 0 7148 3203 0.

Kureishi, Hanif, and Jon Savage. *The Faber Book of Pop*. Faber & Faber. pp. 862. hb £16.99. ISBN 0 571 16992 9.

Lanza, Joseph. *Elevator Music: A Surreal History of Muzak, Easy-Listening and other Moodsong*. Quartet. pp. 280. pb £10.00. ISBN 0 7043 0226 8.

Longhurst, Brian. *Popular Music and Society*. Polity. pp. 277. hb £45.00, pb £12.95. ISBN 0 7456 1437 X, 0 7456 1464 7.

Martin, Peter J. *Sounds and Society: Themes in the Sociology of Music*. Manchester University Press. pp. 298. hb £40.00. ISBN 0 7190 3223 7.

Matthew-Walker, Robert. *Heartbreak Hotel: The Life and Music of Elvis Presley*. Castle Communication. pp. 250. hb £15.99. ISBN 1 86074 055 3.

O'Brien, Karen. *Hymn to Her: Women Musicians Talk*. Virago. pp. 241. pb £9.99. ISBN 1 85381 805 4.

O'Brien, Lucy. *She Bop: The Definitive History of Women in Rock, Pop and Soul*. Penguin. pp. 464. pb £12.50. ISBN 0 14 023232 X.

Raphael, Amy. *Never Mind the Bollocks: Women Rewrite Rock*. Virago. pp. 233. pb £9.99. ISBN 1 85381 887 9.

Redhead, Steve. *Unpopular Cultures: The Birth of Law and Order*. Manchester University Press. pp. 136. pb £10.99. ISBN 0 7190 3652 6.

Reynolds, Simon, and Joy Press. *The Sex Revolts: Gender, Rebellion and Rock'n'Roll*. Serpent's Tail. pp. 406. pb £14.99. ISBN 1 85242 254 8.

Sullivan, Henry W. *The Beatles with Lacan: Rock'n'Roll as Requiem for the Modern Age*. Peter Lang. pp. 217. DM48.00. ISBN 0 8204 2183 9.

Toop, David. *Ocean of Sound: After Talk, Ambient Sounds and Imaginary Worlds*. Serpent's Tail. pp. 306. pb £10.99. ISBN 1 85242 382 X.

15

Virtual Cultures

IAN SAUNDERS

This chapter has four sections: 1. Hypertext; 2. The Politics of the Virtual; 3. The Space of Cyberspace; 4. From *CTheory* to Cyberpunk.

1. Hypertext

Michael Joyce is the pre-eminent creative writer in hypertext. His hypertext fiction *afternoon: a story* was one of the first, and is certainly the most cited, in the medium, and the writing environment he co-developed (Storyspace) has become the standard for creative writing programs in hypertext. One would expect, then, his book-length meditation on the nature of hypertext, *Of Two Minds: Hypertext, Pedagogy and Poetics*, itself to set a new benchmark in the area, but it is more diffuse – and engaging – than that. *Of Two Minds* is a diverse collection of pieces, some previously published, written for a range of different contexts. It is not an easy book in which to navigate, and indeed one begins to see why Storyspace seemed a natural (forking) path for him: that is just the way he thinks. As he disarmingly remarks in the Introduction, 'the essays collected here talk sometimes confusingly, although, I hope, also pleasurably and permeably, about teaching and writing . . . [they] are made up in the way that a bed is, a day-to-day process of billowing, shaking, refitting' (3). The result is (deliberately) uneven. Joyce ranges from a formal account of hypertext in 'Hypertext and Hypermedia' to a series of anecdotal accounts of the writing and teaching process. It is in the latter that the real interest of the book lies, although they are not all equally successful. 'What the Fish Lady Saw', for example, offers a quasi-sociological report on the electronic communications of two classes, one in creative writing, the other in composition, but it remains unclear what the results of the survey are, or just what it is that Joyce is trying to say about them. 'The Geography of the World: The Textfile as Landscape', by contrast, is as lucid as it is poetic in its suggestive argument that the key to understanding both environment and computer-file is the structure and process of memory (and, of course, Simon Schama's *Landscape and Memory* [HarperCollins, 1995], springs to mind in that connection). It is not an argument that reaches conclusion, though; it is not clear what we are to make of the apparent link, or whether and in what ways it might change the way we think about either environment *or* computer-file. What difference does this argument make? For Joyce, though, that is not the point. His conclusion is borrowed from the 'great and dreaming geographer of the world', Gaston Bachelard: 'Dreaming of the secret power of substances, we dream our secret being. . . . The dream interior is warm, never burning . . .' (171). Perhaps I am more critic than creative, but suggestive as this essay is, I could not help thinking that it, and the book as a whole, would have been stronger for a little less indirection.

In a way, though, that indirection is in part the result of the fact that hypertext criticism as a genre is itself barely formed. We do not yet know the standard steps in the way we know the standard (and non-standard) modes of literary criticism. Christiane Paul's 'Reading/Writing Hyperfictions: The Psychodrama of Interactivity' (*Leonardo* 28:4.265–72) can be cited here as an interesting, if limited, attempt to practice such criticism. In it she tries to tease the way causality, logic, time and closure work in J. Yellowlees Douglas's 'I Have Said Nothing' (*Eastgate Quarterly* 1.2). For the most part, however, this does not get beyond the now expected observation that all these things work a bit differently freed of the constraint of single linear narrative form. I should add that *Leonardo*, the MIT Press-published journal that takes as its theme the intersection of art and technology, is a rich source of work on digital art – especially in the issue devoted to the annual New York Digital Arts Salon (issue 5 in 1995), but as its focus is with the visual arts I will not review it here.

Does hypertext imply an ethics? J. Hillis Miller thinks so, and in 'The Ethics of Hypertext' (*Diacritics* 25.27–39) argues that since 'hypertext demands that we choose at every turn' we are obliged to 'take responsibility for our choices' and it is in this that 'the ethics of hypertext' lies (38). This article is an early offering from a work in progress on literature and the new technologies which will, I am sure, generate a great deal of interest upon publication. That said, the argument here seems unsteady in two different ways. On the one hand, Miller defines this ethical implication as the result of the difference between hypertext and linear text. In the case of latter, he contends, 'a fixed text imposed on its readers a single unified meaning generated by a single linear reading from the first word to the end' such that 'the meaning was there, waiting to be generated in me in an act of essentially passive reception' (38). Hypertext, by contrast, is about readerly choices. On the other hand, though, Miller concludes that such choice '*brings into the open* the way the generation of meaning in the act of reading is a speech act, not a passive cognitive reception' (38; my emphasis). If that is so, the 'ethics' Miller identifies pertains to all reading: if hypertext does anything different, it is that it makes that general condition clear, but there is no reason for the reading of a 'linear' text to be just as ethical as the reading of any other text. Furthermore, it is not obvious to me why the fact of having to make choices is necessarily an ethical matter. In fact, choice in the reading of hypertext (since generally one will not know in advance what the choice will reveal or entail) is usually more a matter of whim or curiosity. Moreover, it seems odd to say we must 'take responsibility for our choices'. After all, if the screen one arrives at turns out to be uninteresting, one can usually move back, or start over at some different place. It does not seem promising ground to nurture the kind of ethics in which Miller is interested.

2. The Politics of the Virtual

If a dominant theme emerges in the year's work on virtual cultures, it is the need for political critique of both the reality and rhetoric of computer life. This issue is taken up (in very different ways) by Dale Spender's *Nattering on the Net*, Julian Stallabrass's 'Empowering Technology', James Brook and Iain Boal's collection *Resisting the Virtual Life*, and Dinty Moore's engagingly titled *The Emperor's Virtual Clothes*. The subtitle of Dale Spender's *Nattering on the Net: Women, Power and Cyberspace*, promises an engaged, politicized reading of the cultural possibilities and problems of internet culture, but in fact only the last section of the book takes up these issues in any detail. For the most part, Spender's book is an anecdotal rehearsal of the history of the transition from manuscript to print culture, and a revisiting of the kind of gender critique of language practice set out in her earlier volume, *Man Made Language* (Routledge, 1980). In both respects the present book is useful in its way (although less repetition and more cautious argument would have been welcome) but rather different from the project the title sets up. By the time the last section appears one has traversed so much potted history, quirky anecdote, bland paraphrase and untested assertion that patience begins to ebb, which is a pity, because Spender's most important material is in it. We all know, of course, that the internet has tended to be male dominated, and that – at least according to some users – sexual harassment on it is commonplace: Spender brings a wealth of detail, claim and counter-claim that makes that knowledge, anecdotal though it may be, urgent. The chapter is not without contradiction, though – the central one being that, on the one hand, there is something about computer technology that both models and amplifies the worst aspects of masculinist aggression and, on the other, that there is something about computer technology which makes it uniquely suited to the communicative practices of women, and so will empower them to be freed of just such male domination. The fact that neither claim is given much defence does not undermine one of Spender's fundamental points – that it is not good enough to note gender bias on the net, one ought to be doing something about it: 'priority must be given to dealing with the endemic sexual harassment in cyberspace. . . . Sexual harassment is becoming the modus operandi of the new world; the medium of communication for the generation of wealth and the support of power. It is the means by which some males are conquering and claiming the new territory as their own' (210).

Less happy, though, is the rhetoric of 'new territories' itself. Spender's liberation politics is simplicity itself: overthrow gender bias and the new communications technology will deliver an open, anarchistic realm of self-creation. 'If connected to cyberspace, then every user has the potential to be author, to put information on the net which can be transmitted to the world. There will be no teacher, editor, publisher or bookseller to vet or validate what goes public' (86). The difficulty with this is twofold. First, an exponential increase in the amount of information available to be read is not the same as an exponential increase in our ability to read information. If every user were an author, most would go unread. Second, the system is far from even-handed. To be sure, Spender notes that 'we should never lose sight of the fact that, even as we talk of the democratisation of authorship, we are speaking of First World societies and highly privileged communities' (86), but the point is that if we are talking of 'First World societies and highly privileged communities' we are *not* talking about democratization. No doubt wealthy white girls should be given the same chances as their wealthy white brothers (and Spender's account of the success of electronic teaching at Melbourne's affluent Methodist Ladies' College shows how it can be done), but the outcome looks more like increased class privilege than anything else. Spender's rhetoric of the 'new territory' might well remind us that the imperialist logic of the phrase was to suggest tabula rasa, and to deny the interests of anyone who did not happen to have a hand on the bright new flagstaff. Now, unlike countless other 'new territories', cyberspace does not have an indigenous population, but the fact that the contours of its distribution and control precisely match those of the political world which created and maintains it renders glib talk of the inevitable democratization that will follow in its wake frankly implausible.

'Empowering Technology: The Exploration of Cyberspace' (*New Left Review* 211:May/June, 3–32) is a cogent, compelling critique of just such unreflective utopianism. Julian Stallabrass reads cyberspace as a cultural and political phenomenon, and as such it is less what cyberspace can do than the way we talk about it that matters. Cyberspace is nothing if not future-looking, but Stallabrass points out that there is much that is conservative in the dreams that underpin it, too. As he remarks, 'a number of old bourgeois dreams are encompassed in the promise of this technology: to survey the world from one's living room, to grasp the totality of all data within a single frame, and to recapture a unified knowledge and experience' (4). At the heart of the idea of cyberspace there is, on his reading, a strange contraction between excited future-talk and the very old values that talk endorses. Of the utopian future-talk Stallabrass is flatly dismissive, describing the 'unholy alliance' of:

> postmodern disintegration theorists with wise-eyed New Agers, producing a ludicrous image of the world immersed in a great, shifting sea of data, each person jacking in and finding exactly what they want, in their own personalized order and format. People will live intensely in this digital utopia, forgetting their grosser material needs in an affective, intellectual search for companionship and knowledge. In this ostensibly democratic forum, a chairman of some Western conglomerate and an impoverished peasant in Central Africa will both use a device, much the size of a Walkman, to communicate by satellite with a panoply of open information systems. (10)

As Stallabrass observes, 'as soon as this utopian vision of global information-sharing is baldly stated, its stupidity becomes obvious' (10). The technology is not the real issue: what will drive its use is the political and economic reality from which it feeds. 'There is no interest in selling electronic commodities at the price the world's poor can afford, nor is there likely to be. The idea that high-band global networking will become truly universal in a world where only a fifth of the population currently have telephones is laughable' (11). Indeed it is, but – as the observation about the 'old bourgeois dreams', above, makes clear – the underlying logic is in reality little to do with democratization or utopia. Rather, cyberspace and the system of communication it maintains is at once a new market for capital and an apparent guarantor of its inevitability. Indeed, in cyberspace the very possibility of political critique is eroded: critique assumes the possibility of unearthing a covert agenda obscured by the saccharine promotional rhetoric of capital, but from the outset cyberspace has a kind of guileless transparency. Speaking of William Gibson's fictional creation in *Neuromancer* (Victor Gollancz, 1984), Stallabrass writes that 'cyberspace is a visual environment in which, while deception is occasionally a feature, things generally look much like they are: large databases look large, corporations look powerful, military complexes look remote and dangerous, electronic countermeasures look threatening' (5). In the end, 'the invention of cyberspace is . . . the attempt to create a world where to perceive is the same as to understand, where "objects" are entirely adequate to their concepts, and are even, through their dematerialization, identical with them' (31). If Stallabrass is right, then the key to the power of the rhetoric of cyberspace is its promise of personal self-definition freed of the necessity to think reflectively on the political context which enables the very process of that self-definition; indeed, freed of politics altogether. Of course capital has always been quick to debunk politics as 'just' politics, and it should be no surprise that it does so in the electronic world, too. The virtue of Stallabrass's essay is the way he uncovers the logic of the process, deftly relating it as discursive formation to its fictional and philosophical antecedents, and to the *Boy's Own* world of the first Net.

Resisting the Virtual Life: The Culture and Politics of Information, edited by James Brook and Iain Boal, is a collection of twenty-one essays which aim to address 'the impact of the convergence of video, computer, and networked communication technologies on work, education, health, entertainment, art, and literature' (xiv). The result is, not surprisingly, rather diverse, although there is more than a whiff of sixties San Francisco drifting through its pages. Iain Boal's 'A Flow of Monsters: Luddism and Virtual Technologies', for example, argues that no technology is inevitable, and that it is possible to unplug the system before it overwhelms us – claims which in themselves seem plausible enough. The case he makes, though, is less than compelling.

> It is a lie that direct action against the instruments of production has always been hopeless. . . . The Elizabethan gig-mills were successfully suppressed for generations by legislation that followed agitation from below. The Japanese for a time gave up the gun. Captain Swing and the agricultural Luddites who smashed the threshing machines in the 1830s got themselves and their children a reprieve for half a century. (11)

On this kind of history, the only question is when, not if – and, perhaps, how 'good' the protest was. His essay begins with an account of a staged television smashing on the Berkeley campus, and it is difficult not to think that the electronic Luddism he advocates is rather like this: a quasi institutionalized rite of passage for the next generation of the bourgeois elite, a rite that in reality is powerless to unsettle (and perhaps does not really want to unsettle) the system of commodity production and control to which it is, in name alone, a protest.

Rather more successful is Boal's interview with George Lakoff, 'Body, Brain, and Communication'. Lakoff's work on metaphor is well known, and here he offers a critique of what he calls, following Michael Reddy, the conduit metaphor, or the belief that language 'is a container for ideas, and you send ideas in words over a conduit, a channel of communication to someone else who then extracts the ideas from the words' (116). The implication of the conduit metaphor is that communication is in principle independent of people, and it is this belief, Lakoff thinks, that underpins the confident assumption that computers themselves can communicate. Reject the conduit metaphor, though, and much of our 'common-sense' thinking about computer culture begins to look unpersuasive. Lakoff offers a number of reasons to suggest why we ought to drop that model, the most fundamental of which is also the most simple: reason is embodied, and the concepts with which we reason are embodied. We cannot extract a 'pure' content from our embodied thought. 'How we function in the world, how we perceive things, how our brains are organized', the 'schematic spatial relations' (121) with which we organize thought, the metaphors with which we model the world and our understanding of it: all of this is of our world and our embodied place within it, and no mathematical logic (and thus, no computer generated algorithm) could replicate it. To talk of computer communication as if it could supersede human communication is, according to Lakoff, to simply misunderstand the nature of communication itself.

While on the subject of metaphor, I ought to digress from *Resisting the Virtual Life* to mention Raymond Gozzi's 'Virtual Reality as Metaphor' (*Etc.: A Review of General Semantics* 52:4). This is one of a series of brief, quirky pieces by Gozzi on metaphor that have appeared over a couple of years. Here he argues that the power of the idea of virtual reality (VR) (and he is especially thinking of the helmet-wearing kind) stems from its status as a metaphor of miniaturization. According to his argument all experience is a kind of 'virtual', in that we construct a version of the world from the sensory data we collect. We do not, however, control that experience, but take it as it comes – a situation Gozzi finds in extreme form in the routinely exaggerated accounts of the real that the news media offers us. Those exaggerations, and the emphasis on violence and conflict typical of the news, threaten to totally overwhelm any sense of reader control, and it is in response to that threat that the metaphor of VR works its appeal: here is a miniature version of the real, but it is one we control. As he puts it, 'The news creates for us a virtual reality every day [which] leaves us thinking the world is a more dangerous place than it really is. . . . At least with "virtual reality" technology, we know we have a headset and we've chosen to have this experience' (459). It is a neat argument in its way, and not dissimilar to others mentioned in these pages, but I cannot leave it without pointing to the elementary collision between the view that *all* our experience is of a virtual reality, and the claim that news 'leaves us thinking the world is a more dangerous place than it really is'. If indeed – Descartes-like – we are locked in the virtual sensorium, the phrase 'than it really is' has no bite. Gozzi cannot have it both ways (and should know better than to resurrect the rather tired claim that what we know is in some way fatally compromised by the fact that all knowledge is mediated).

Daniel Harris reconfigures the ground Gozzi covers in an arresting way in his contribution to *Resisting the Virtual Life*, 'The Aesthetic of the Computer'. Harris is interested in the epiphenomena of computing the screen savers, the desktop palettes, and the variable typefaces and colours operating systems such as Windows and Macintosh offer. Rather than putting them aside as not worthy of serious attention, Harris asks how they function, and concludes that the primary point of the gimmickry is to maintain precisely that metaphor of control. As he notes, in reality, and in stark contrast to the narrative of empowerment and liberation which accompanies the introduction of new technology, the 'average' officeworker has little or no control over the system in which he or she has a role, and usually even less understanding of the actual mechanics of the information technology that defines that role. It is here, Harris argues, in response to the contradiction between the ideological representation of the new technology and its degrading reality, that the ephemera of computing come into their own:

> The Pac Man aesthetic of the computer turns us, first into child-ren, and then back again into adults – or at least into children who imitate adults by playing a game of dress-up in which we live out an occupational fantasy that our responsibilities, as seasoned technicians, the foot soldiers of the information age, are far less menial than in fact they are. By providing a multiplicity of choices for nearly every decorative feature offered, from the color of the monitor to the size of the design, manufacturers encourage us to manipulate the images on the screen and thus to achieve an illusory sense of being crack-shot telecommunications engineers. The malleability of the aesthetic of the computer transforms unskilled members of the work force into software virtuosos, artistic collaborators who, in the act of constructing these complex desktop diorama, remake themselves in the image of their superiors. (199–200)

Not all contributions to *Resisting the Virtual Life* do 'resist' the virtual life. Richard Sclove, for example, is optimistic about the possibility of 'making technology democratic' through more widespread public participation in the design process, while Laura Miller, in 'Women and Children First: Gender and the Settling of the Electronic Frontier', takes up the theme of gender bias and harassment on the Internet, and argues that in her experience (and contrary to the prevailing wisdom rehearsed by Dale Spender, above) it is not a problem, and that the idea of 'virtual rape' is unpersuasive. Rape is about real bodies, and so on-line ('where I have no body and neither does anyone else', 54) rape is impossible. In fact, Miller contends, 'the idea that women merit special protections in an environment as incorporeal as the Net is intimately bound up with the idea that women's minds are weak, fragile, and unsuited to the rough and tumble of public discourse' (57). By her account, talk of sexual harass-ment on the Internet paradoxically maintains the very ideology it seeks to reject. In this context I should also mention Andrew Calcutt's 'Computer Porn Panic: Fear and Control in Cyberspace' (*Futures* 27:7.749–62), a contribution to an issue devoted to the exploration of cyberspace (subtitled *Cyberspace: To Boldly Go*). Calcutt argues that the oft-repeated notion of an epidemic of computer-mediated pornography sweeping through schools is a nonsense without empirical support. In his view, it is a 'moral panic': 'it is false, but it is also true to our times' (754). The plague fantasy, he contends, is generated by the fear of social and environmental degradation, and the experience of personal vulnerability in an economically and morally dysfunctional com-munity: 'The panic over computer pornography is virulent because the notion of the epidemic of software slime purports to provide an explanation for the widespread sense of violation. In fact it explains nothing, but has a resonance in that it *describes* the prevailing social mood of nervousness, disquiet and vulnerability' (755). The outcome of such panic, he thinks, is the nurturing of a 'dependency culture' in which we 'are encouraged to rely on the embrace of those in authority to save us from each other and from the beast within ourselves' (760). Ziauddin Sardar's contribution to the same issue of *Futures*, 'alt.civilizations.faq: Cyberspace as the Darker Side of the West', adopts an equally distrustful view of the nature of cyberspace, although in his case from a postcolonial perspective. Noting the colonial colour of the familiar rhetoric of the 'new frontier', Sardar argues that cyberspace – like the Orient before it – has become the other of the West, onto which the West projects its colonial prejudices, its fears and its desires. In this case, though, the other has become a form of control: 'the romantic, liberating notion of information technologies draws our attention away from its more real potential: to enslave us in its totality' (789). Sardar's critique is a useful and continually interesting one but, as was the case in Calcutt's paper, there seems too ready an inclination to blame an unnamed 'them' at work behind the spread of computer culture. Just who, for example, is using the 'instrument' here: 'Cyberspace, with its techno-utopian ideology, is an instrument for distracting the Western society from its increasing spiritual poverty, utter meaninglessness and grinding misery and inhumanity of everyday lives' (793). Can things be quite this conspiratorial?

Of the other contributions to the cyberspace issue of *Futures*, let me mention Nigel Clark's 'Being Consoled? Virtual Nature and Ecological Consciousness' (735–47), which takes a striking line on the possible interaction between cyberspace technology and ecological consciousness. Noting that the stark visual logic of early computer environments was giving way to a more 'natural' one, and despite the seeming irony of his title, Clark celebrates the potential for such alternative 'natures' in which 'life forms' can grow, interact and evolve. We turn, he thinks, to such cyberspace worlds not to substitute them for the real world, but to improve upon it: 'cybernetic simulation will prompt not so much the preservation of an extant biophysicality as its conspicuous enhancement' (745). There is more than a bit of gee-whiz description of some of the available software, but Clark manages to balance that with an argument that the escape into the virtual may well enable us to see the real for what it is. After all, he argues, the chief difficulty of the ecological case is that it too often relies on a naive view of an unmediated apprehension of the natural world, and of a model of nature more mystical than mundane. 'One of the foremost challenges for the ecology movement,' he writes, 'is to develop representational practices which draw attention to ecological issues without further inflating the model of "nature".' To do so requires a degree of self-reflexivity about the nature of representation which, he concludes, 'suggests the need for an ecological praxis which focuses more on the processes of constructing nature than on the interaction with a nature constructed as "given"' (745). So, as the experience of cyberspace nature is plainly the experience of a constructed nature, we ought to be able to draw from that experience lessons (although to be sure Clark does not say what they might be) about how we can better read the constructedness of natural 'nature'.

Dinty Moore's *The Emperor's Virtual Clothes: The Naked Truth about Internet Culture* deserves mention for its title alone. To my disappointment, that is just about the only reason to justify its inclusion here: rather than an exploration of the politics and implications of 'Internet culture', Moore offers

a low-key, outdated and anecdotal account of his experience as a newcomer to
a corner of the Internet that could well be called Cyberspace Middle America.
It is a pretty depressing place. Here is his description of the occasional
real-space get-together of the inhabitants of one virtual community he visits:

> When I arrive, Tony's house is packed with folks, around thirty of
> them, and his wife looks understandably nervous – more than a
> few unattended children are tearing up and down the stairs,
> looking for loose glassware. The adults are all white, seemingly
> middle-class, of varying ages, and few are obvious computer
> nerds. Judging from the volleyball action in the backyard, not
> many of them will be headed to the Olympics any time soon, but
> they are certainly nice enough to a visiting writer, and boy can
> they cook. (83)

3. The Space of Cyberspace

A key component of the imagining of cyberspace is that of space itself, and a
number of texts, perhaps emerging from the reinvestment in notions of space in
the wake of work like that of Edward Soja's *Postmodern Geographies* (Verso,
1989), take up the question of just what kind of space cyberspace might be.
William J. Mitchell's project in *City of Bits: Space, Place and the Infobahn* is to
'reimagine architecture and urbanism' in the context of 'the digital
telecommunications revolution, the ongoing miniaturisation of electronics, the
commodification of bits, and the growing domination of software over
materialized form' (5). It is an elegant book, complete with World Wide Web
virtual double (http://www-mitpress.mit.edu/City_of_Bits/) and associated
electronic discussion pages, but there is little that could be called a 'reimagining'
of space. Rather, *City of Bits* asserts (again and again) that traditionally
architectural design is very much directed by the distribution of the real human
bodies who will come to inhabit and use the completed structure – not perhaps
a claim that needs a great deal of defence – and that in the space of the future
electronic city this will no longer be the case:

> For designers and planners, the task of the twenty-first century
> will be to build the bitsphere – a worldwide, electronically medi-
> ated environment in which networks are everywhere, and most of
> the artifacts that function within it (at every scale, from nano to
> global) have intelligence and telecommunications capabilities. It
> will overlay and eventually succeed the agricultural and industrial
> landscapes that humankind has inhabited for so long. (167)

For the 'bitsphere' to 'overlay' the agricultural and industrial landscape is one
thing, to 'succeed' it is, however, a very different matter, and it is difficult to
know how to make sense of a claim like this. A crucial issue is just what form the
'overlay' will take, and how the agricultural and industrial landscapes will
accommodate it (and, if we assume we will still need to eat, and the keyboards
will still need to be built, it is hard to suppose either of those will dematerialize).

Mitchell's leap from one realm to the other sets aside that issue, substituting instead pages of gee-whiz description of what the new technology feels like:

> Anaheim Convention Center. I line up with the computer graphics geeks and off-duty demo-dollies to check out the Sega R360. Doug Trumbull's Luxor ride milks all of its thrills out of sliding motions along just two axes, but this one does 360-degree rotations. And I strap on a head-mounted display instead of watching a projection screen. The illusion of flying like Superman is complete. Killer vestibulars!   (37)

Or again, and sounding depressingly like one of the progress-is-good-for-you spiels at Disney's Epcot Center or the mighty Bill Gates himself: 'Pizza. Interactive television will replace the telephone. You enter a virtual parlor and see a menu of available toppings. As you choose, a displayed pizza is modified accordingly and the price is tallied. When you are satisfied, the nearest pizzeria is notified and the order speeds to your door' (91). This is not 'reimagining', but hype, and of a rather old-fashioned kind where delight in a workerless wizardry sweeps aside analysis for something simple and familiar – familiar as the reassuring promises capital made (and routinely broke) before it found itself in cyberspace.

More plausible, if equally programmatic, is Marcos Novak's electronically disseminated 'Transmitting Architecture: The Transphysical City' (*CTheory* 29 November 1995: see next section for web address). Novak argues that the possibility of virtual communities highlights the essential conservatism of architectural thinking. As a conceptual discipline architecture is at home with Euclidean space or a Galilean universe, but beyond that it falters. 'The efforts of Lobachevsky and Reimann, the descriptions of electromagnetic fields by Maxwell, and the world view that was slowly assembled via relativity, quantum mechanics, and that led to today's theories of hyperspace and stochastic universes, created a condition that architecture, burdened by its materiality, could no longer follow.' Of course, for utilitarian architecture that materiality is the point. Novak's case is not, however, that we could in any meaningful way abandon the one realm for the other, but that architecture is a system of imagining as well as a material practice, and it is that imaginative dimension that is extended by the possibility of virtual space in a way that forces it beyond the paradigms of Enlightenment mathematical thought. That system of imagining ought to feed back into the way we understand the interface between the real and the virtual; or, as Novak usefully puts it, the way we understand the 'transphysical' city. Novak eschews simplistic binary oppositions, and the notion of the 'transphysical' is a case in point: 'As distant as this may appear from the city as we know it, the transphysical city will not be the postphysical city. As the prefix *trans-* implies, it will be at once a transmutation and transgression of the known, but it will also stand alongside and be interwoven into that very matrix.'

In *Virtual Geography: Living with Global Media Events* (1994, it reached me too late for inclusion in the previous year's review), McKenzie Wark undertakes to trace what he calls the 'media vectors' of four 'weird' events: the Gulf War, the fall of the Berlin Wall, the Tiananmen Square massacre and the 1987 Wall Street stock market crash. The underlying premise of the text is straightforward enough: we live in a familiar, local terrain, yet at the same time we vicariously inhabit a global one: 'the terrain created by the television, the telephone, the telecommunications networks crisscrossing the globe' (vii). This 'crisscrossing' is what Wark means by media 'vectors', the information flows which create, he contends, a virtual geography. Wark himself does not attempt to sum up his theory or method in any kind of extended way, and indeed concludes that, because each of the chapters 'grew organically out of the constellations thrown up by the particular events', his own work 'does not lend itself' to any summary (228). I have to say I found it difficult to find anything of note to summarize, too. In particular, it is not clear what makes this expanded comprehension of the real local and global that television and other media enable a 'virtual' geography, nor is it clear just why the concept of the 'vector' is thought to be invested with such explanatory power. We know, for example, that one's own state media appropriates the output of other state media in a self-serving fashion, just as such foreign media appropriate our own. For Wark, though, this is an astonishing revelation:

> in the crisis atmosphere of the event, the international news vector is not a form of *communication*. No mutually accepted 'messages' passed through this channel from one community to another. There was no commonality between encoding and decoding practices at either end. Rather, the vector allows each side to exploit images that come from the other in a narrative framework which constructs the attributes of the other entirely at 'our' media sites. The fact that the image is an authentic product of 'their' media merely legitimates a construction of the other that is entirely 'our' doing. (36)

This is hardly surprising (although the use of the word 'entirely' seems simplistic, and in effect destroys the need for the appropriated product to be originally 'their' own doing; one might equally wonder about the word 'authentic' in Wark's account), but one could hardly hang much on it. Wark does, claiming that what this shows is that 'the guarantee of "our" identity comes not from "our" intrinsic qualities, nor from our difference from the other, but *from the vector itself*. The vector makes this other possible, and makes an "us" possible' (36). However, the vector or information path in this example does not guarantee anything. Of course, to represent an other one needs a mode of representation, and that mode of representation will determine the parameters of any such representation. But the vector that Wark describes, at least as I understand it, seems little more than a generic form of the electronic transfer of information from one place to another: it is necessary to set up instantaneous global communication, but it does not, in that bland formulation, indicate anything more than that an instance of just such information transfer has taken place.

4. From *CTheory* to Cyberpunk

One of the reasons for the relatively slight list of published work on cyberspace and virtual culture is that a great deal of the writing about the virtual occurs in cyberspace itself; as such it is often ephemeral, and teasingly difficult to locate in a way that paper and board is not. The most prominent site is *CTheory: Theory, Technology and Culture*, the cyberspace journal edited by Arthur and Marilouise Kroker. Rather than list www addresses for each of the pieces mentioned here, I will note the address of the *CTheory* catalogue, in which all *CTheory* publications can be located. It is http://www.ctheory.com/ctheory_dated.html. *CTheory* is itself powered by an ambivalent relationship with the technology that is its *raison d'être*: there seems to be genuine celebration of the possibilities of electronic communication (and academic Internet publication in particular), yet many of the pieces so published take a darkly pessimistic view of the likely outcome of the advent of cyberspace. So, for example, Arthur and Marilouise Kroker write 'it is no coincidence that the "shipping out" of Windows95 and the fall of Srebrinica take place on the same weekend' ('Windows on What?', 24 August 1995):

> These are deeply entwined events. What takes place in Redmond and Srebenica is the final settlement of human flesh in the last days of the 20th century: the bitter division of the world into virtual flesh and surplus flesh. Windows95 opens out onto the dominant ideology and privileged life position of digital flesh. It installs the new codes of the master occupants of virtual worlds: frenzied devotion to cyber-business, life in a multi-media virtual contest, digital tunnel vision, and most of all, embedded deep in the cerebral cortex of the virtual elite an I-chip: I, that is, for complete indifference. Technological acceleration is accompanied by a big shutting-down of ethical perception.

Geert Lovink ('Organized Innocence and War in the New Europe: On Electronic Solitude and Independent Media', 11 October 1995) argues in a similar vein. Part of the reason for the ineffectual internal resistance to the build-up of war conditions in the former Yugoslavia was the mistaken belief that the world of electronically mediated civilization was poised ready to embrace the newly independent nation. As Lovink puts it, drawing on the work of David Rieff (*Slaughterhouse: Bosnia and the Failure of the West* [Vintage, 1995]), 'the citizens of former Yugoslavia could not believe that the "CNN effect" would not occur in their case. They waited in vain for a live broadcast of the arrival of a rapid intervention force, come to set them free.' That failure to intervene in turn was underwritten by the indifference of which Kroker and Kroker speak or, in Lovink's words, 'organised innocence' – the devotion to banal routine for which the extraordinary, be it technological failure or (as in this case) emotionally distant social failure, is read as a threat, to be avoided if at all possible. Lovink concludes ambitiously if somewhat mysteriously that, in the light of this, the political task of independent media is to 'ridicule' the split between virtual and surplus flesh, 'and in an ironic, existential manner, to give shape to the universal technological desire, cyberspace'. Perhaps future work will make clear just what this might mean. Certainly, the interview with Lovink published earlier in the year ('Slaves of the Cyber-Market: An Interview with Geert Lovink', 28 June 1995) does not help much. To the question 'Can a future without computers be imagined?' Lovink responds:

> It's possible to be on-line without a computer – with the
> imagination, with drugs. Being on-line is not a hardware question.
> Finally it all boils down to exciting the senses. What does a
> four-color, 600-dpi picture do? It excites the senses. What is the
> computer? It simply has a range of technical ways of jiving up the
> senses. The virtual senses, that is!

This is, to say the very least, unpersuasive, and would in effect destroy both the
'on-line' and the 'virtual' as categories with conceptual content. If that is what
on-line means, it is hard to see just what the phrase adds to our pre-electronic
vocabularies.

Paul Virilio, in 'Speed and Information: Cyberspace Alarm!' (*CTheory* 27
August 1995), echoes a number of the sentiments expressed by Stallabrass in
the *New Left Review* article discussed above. The article is a longer version of
one that appeared at the same time in *Le Monde Diplomatique*, itself translated
three months later as 'Red Alert in Cyberspace!' in *Radical Philosophy* (no. 74,
November/December 1995). Of the prospect of a 'virtual democracy' Virilio
writes 'we have to acknowledge that the new communication technologies will
only further democracy if, and only if, we oppose from the beginning the caricature of global society being hatched for us by big multinational corporations
throwing themselves at a breakneck pace on the information superhighways'.
The 'alarm' of the title is the alarm that in the wake of the globalization of
telecommunications 'one should expect a generalised kind of accident, a
never-seen-before accident', to which phenomena like the 1987 stock market
collapse is the merest pre-figuration. Of course, the trouble with talking about
'never-seen-before' events is that one is inevitably stumbling about in the dark,
but Virilio does point in an interesting way to two features of the cyberspace
world: the loss of personal orientation and the globalization of time.
Cyberspace, he suggests, is a 'new form of perspective' in which we no longer
simply speak and hear at a distance, but also touch at a distance. That
contact-at-a-distance comes at a price – the loss of personal orientation:

> A duplication of sensible reality, into reality and virtuality, is in
> the making. A stereo-reality of sorts threatens. A total loss of the
> bearings of the individual looms large. To exist, is to exist *in situ*,
> here and now, *hic et nunc*. That is precisely what is being threat-
> ened by cyberspace and instantaneous, globalized information
> flows.

That is to say, social locatedness is critical to personal identity, but it is precisely
that which Internet culture may threaten. Moreover, Virilio argues, if the
specificity of locatedness is so eroded at the level of the individual, it is equally
eroded in terms of specific community. In a realm of instantaneous
communication, 'local time' is impossible, but it is precisely the nature of local
time that allows history itself to be local, specific to the community it describes.
'If history is so rich, it is because it is local, it was thanks to the existence of
spatially bounded times which overrode something that up to now occurred
only in astronomy: universal time.' That historical wealth will be displaced by
universal time and universal history; and in universal history, Virilio contends,

there will be reduced possibilities of individual identity and, by implication, autonomous identity.

By contrast, Jean Baudrillard ('Radical Thought', 19 April 1995) celebrates the virtual, if in a somewhat idiosyncratic way. 'Radical Thought' is a counter to the common-sense disbelief with which Baudrillard's model of universal simulation is sometimes greeted; far from retracting, Baudrillard goes further, and proclaims that nothing is real, or only the virtual is. By his account the virtual, the world of thought, never connects with an empirical reality and any truth that might anchor it: 'thought is not so much prized for its inevitable convergences with truth as it is for the insuperable divergences that separate the two'. One could and perhaps should take issue, but arguably that would be to mistake the kind of game to which this piece belongs. As he remarks in conclusion, 'the absolute rule of thought is to return the world as we received it, unintelligible. And if it is possible, to return it a little bit more unintelligible.' Take it or leave it.

Positive in a different way to Baudrillard, Siegfried Zielinski ('Seven Items on the Net', 31 May 1995) argues that the language of the net is an 'affirmation of life': 'As a principle, the language is positive, animated, apologetic, smart. It bristles with energy. It is an electronic fountain of youth.' In a curious mirror image of Baudrillard's celebration of the positive orbit that recalls no body around which it travels, for Zielinski it is just that positive energy that to date has limited the possibility of art on the Internet. Art, Zielinski observes, requires a sense of the negative other, of what has been lost or destroyed, but it is just such nostalgia that the affirmative language of cyberspace cannot accommodate.

Douglas Kellner does take issue with the Baudrillardian model of depthless simulation, in the last chapter of his engaging and wide ranging *Media Culture: Cultural Studies, Identity and Politics between the Modern and the Postmodern*. If I do not say as much about Kellner's text as it deserves, it is because the section that attends to questions concerning the virtual is a very small part – indeed, something of an aftersight – of a text which is primarily about the audio visual media of television and cinema. As such it is a fine book, and one which offers a sharp, politically alert critique of the values that circulate in contemporary media texts. In the last section Kellner develops a comparison between Gibson's cyberpunk world and Baudrillard's theoretical work to highlight what he sees as the limitations and even delusions of the latter. The key to cyberpunk, of course, is the marriage of street and technology, the interaction of a model of fleshless consciousness with an all too fleshy urban life. Baudrillard, according to Kellner, misses the significance of the 'street', of the material world of poverty, class difference and exploitation. Rather, his 'cool' America is 'a play of pure signs, devoid of meaning, purpose, or value' (317). 'Speeding through America, with his car stereo blasting and a trusty bottle of whiskey as a companion' results in the evacuation of meaning and presents 'the spectacle of pure speed, pure travelling, pure signs floating by in an empty indifference, absent of meaning' (317). And yet, as Kellner neatly observes, all is not as it appears in Baudrillard's virtual United States. Far from being just signs, it turns out that everything for Baudrillard signifies something, 'everything is a sign of something else' (317):

Break-dancers signify to him, as they spiral around on the
ground, an attempt to dig a hole for themselves, radiating 'the
ironic, indolent pose of the dead' (19); California jogging is
'like . . . so many other things . . . a sign of voluntary servitude'
(38); the 'smiling eyes' of squirrels at Irvine betray 'a cold,
ferocious beast fearfully stalking us' (48); television sets left on in
empty rooms in the Porterville hotel reveal TV 'for what it really
is: a video of another world, ultimately addressed to no one at all,
delivering its messages indifferently, indifferent to its own
messages.'

As Kellner makes clear, there is a curious irony in all of this, as an argument
against the content of signs is pursued in terms of a reading of the content of
cultural signs. And, he continues, there is a disturbing outcome, namely that
Baudrillard's game blinds him to the real material conditions of what he is
observing (although it has to be said that Kellner's case seems to be a little
motivated by national loyalty, too): 'the French tourist reduces everything to
signs and fails to see their material underpinnings and effects, the social
structure in which signs are embedded, or the history that produces sign and
structure' (318). According to Kellner, cyberpunk, albeit in a provisional,
exploratory way, offers an alternative which makes Baudrillard's 'radical'
thought look both partial and reactionary. It is a contrast that enlivens Kellner's
prose in a rather unexpected way; for example, when he writes that 'Baudrillard,
the old fart, makes fun of intellectuals on their word processors . . . not
knowing that they are plugging into cyberspace, accessing incredible amounts
of data at unforeseen speed, engaging in new types of communication through
bulletin-boards, e-mail, computer data-bases and on-line discussion, and
writing at new speeds with new intensities' (321). I take the point of Kellner's
critique, but, if anything, his description here of 'new speeds and new
intensities' (whatever that might mean) prompts me to think the 'old fart' might
have had a point, after all: it looks like vacant jogging to me.

For Kellner the virtue of Gibson's work is the way it problematizes the
intersection of the real and hyper-real, and in particular the way in which it
confronts the nature of techno-capitalism: information rich, socially and
ecologically ruinous. For Joseph Tabbi, on the other hand, the imagined worlds
of cyberpunk are understood in terms of the 'technological sublime' they
evoke. As is the case with Kellner's *Media Culture*, Tabbi's *Postmodern Sublime:
Technology and American Writing from Mailer to Cyberpunk* is only marginally
concerned with the virtual, but is worth mentioning here for the way it situates
the rhetoric of the virtual within an ongoing cultural response to the
technologies of communication (and, by implication, raises the question of
just what can count as 'virtual': television images? Radio broadcasts? For that
matter, why not the print text itself?). Tabbi takes as a key example the
description of the computer virus (the 'Kuang') *Neuromancer*'s Case needs to
use in cyberspace. As the 'Flatline' (the computer-preserved memory of a
now-dead hacker) puts it,

This ain't bore and inject. It's more like we interface with the ice
so slow, the ice doesn't feel it. The face of the Kuang logics kinda
sleazes up to the target and mutates, so it gets to be exactly like the

ice fabric. Then we lock on and the main programs cut in, start talking circles 'round the logics in the ice. We go Siamese twin on 'em before they even get restless. (*Postmodern Sublime* 217–18)

For Tabbi, it is an interesting moment first in the way Gibson is able to assume a strong familiarity with the language and rhetoric of the virtual. As he writes,

> Gibson's least turn of phrase heralds an unprecedented familiarity not with technology itself but with its image. . . . The merest mention of a 'Sense/Net', an 'Ono-Sendai', or a cyberpunk cowboy who 'flatlines on his EEG' . . . call up a ready-made aesthetic and reinforce a popular intuition of technological abstraction that earlier novelists had to *create* in their audience. (218)

The virtual, that is to say, has a rhetorical life that exceeds its 'real' life, an observation that may well recall the Stallabrass *New Left Review* piece discussed above. For Tabbi, though, the critical thing here is the way in which the penetration of the corporate library in the passage 'may be read as an allegory of the compositional process that has preoccupied all of those postmodern writers that have sought to redefine realism in an age of expanding information':

> The technique spelled out by the Flatline is worthy of a classical rhetorician: one hides behind the mask of a powerful opponent, all the while diverting that opponent's language to other purposes. . . . Gibson's strategy in this extraordinary passage is, in other words, possibly the most direct example yet of what I have been calling (with my own overlays onto Jameson, Lyotard, Leo Marx and Weiskel) the technological sublime: the Kuang enacts a conceptual integration without a loss of personal identity, leaving the representing mind . . . separate from the complex of forces being represented. (219)

Plausible as Tabbi's reading is, it is about – as he notes – a rhetorical strategy, a way of solving a material paradox (the desire to maintain personal independence and integrity in a technologically controlled world) through the vehicle of an imagined narrative resolution. However, as the allusion to Jameson in the preceding paragraph might remind us, consoling as an imagined narrative resolution can be, in the end it is in effect complicit with the ideological structure that is the material cause of the contradiction that it putatively solves.

As I have already mentioned, although discussion of the virtual is more coda than anything else in *Postmodern Sublime*, Tabbi's conceptualization of it challenges the categorical distinctness of the virtual itself. Before reaching cyberpunk his study attends to a range of US postmodern fiction, from Pynchon's *Gravity's Rainbow* (Jonathan Cape, 1973) to DeLillo's *White Noise* (Viking Penguin, 1984) and *Mao II* (Jonathan Cape, 1991), and he is able to recast the familiar account of postmodernism which thinks of our experiential world as linguistically mediated and, perhaps, linguistically contained, as an anticipation of the virtual. In *Gravity's Rainbow*, for example, the linguistic world seems to break free from the empirical one in a way that inspires belief and fear: belief in the ability to go beyond the natural, fear of the loss of freedom that the complete connectivity of a completely informational world might herald. Recalling Father Rapier's argument in Pynchon's text that 'once the technical means of control have reached a certain size, a certain degree of being connected, the chances for freedom are over for good' (as cited in *Postmodern Sublime* 75), Tabbi notes the way it has been 'elaborated with a remarkable literalness by cyberpunk writers such as William Gibson and Kathy Acker . . . because Rapier's vision of an unlimited yet complete connectivity speaks to the virtual world these younger writers inhabit' (75). In a similar vein, one could argue that the way in which Jack Gladney becomes the sum of his data after the toxic event in *White Noise* rehearses the trajectory into the virtual, as does Bill Gray's transformation from corporeal novelist to an obsessively maintained library of print and visual traces in *Mao II*. Of course, as Tabbi observes, even here the escape to proto cyberspace is never completed: 'DeLillo never loses sight of the embodied reality beneath the information grid' (207). From my perspective, though, what is most curious, and exciting, here is the way in which the exploration of a rhetorical and conceptual terrain seems to anticipate the outcome of a revolution in communications technology. Virtual culture is still of the future, and yet the rhetorical means through which it will be understood have circulated well before 'that last historical act of writing', the moment in the early seventies when 'Intel engineers laid out some dozen square meters of blueprint paper . . . in order to design the hardware architecture of their first integrated microprocessor' (Friedrich Kittler, 'There is No Software', *CTheory*, 18 October 1995).

Books Reviewed

Brook, James, and Iain Boal, eds. *Resisting the Virtual Life: The Culture and Politics of Information*. City Lights. pp. xvi + 278. pb US$15.95. ISBN 0 87286 299 2.

Joyce, Michael. *Of Two Minds: Hypertext, Pedagogy and Poetics*. University of Michigan Press. pp. viii + 277. hb £22.95, pb £12.50. ISBN 0 472 09578 1, 0 472 06578 5.

Kellner, Douglas. *Media Culture: Cultural Studies, Identity and Politics between the Modern and the Postmodern*. Routledge. pp. x + 357. hb £45.00, pb £13.99. ISBN 0 415 10569 2, 0 415 10570 6.

Mitchell, William J. *City of Bits: Space, Place and the Infobahn*. MIT Press. pp. vi + 225. hb £15.95, pb £8.50. ISBN 0 262 13309 1, 0 262 63176 8.

Moore, Dinty. *The Emperor's Virtual Clothes: The Naked Truth about Internet Culture*. Algonquin Books. pp. xviii + 219. pb US$17.95. ISBN 1 56512 096 5.

Spender, Dale. *Nattering on the Net: Women, Power and Cyberspace*. Spinifex. pp. xxvi + 278. pb £11.95. ISBN 1 87559 09 4.

Tabbi, Joseph. *Postmodern Sublime: Technology and American Writing from Mailer to Cyberpunk*. Cornell University Press. pp. xii + 243. hb £27.00, pb £11.95. ISBN 0 8014 3074 7, 0 8014 8383 2.

Wark, McKenzie. *Virtual Geography: Living with Global Media Events*. Indiana University Press, 1994. pp. xviii + 253. hb £27.50, pb £12.99. ISBN 0 253 36349 7, 0 253 20894 7.

16

Film Theory

SUSAN PURDIE

This chapter will concentrate on a group of books which explicitly attack 'film theory'. Although these attacks are made from differing positions, they share a view of this theory as a single, undifferentiated position that is dourly obsessed with demonstrating film's pernicious control of its audience's minds. As well as indicating the inadequacy of that account (not least through discussion of some particularly diverse and subtly interrogative theoretical writing published this year) I also want to consider what may be at stake in the emphatic reiteration of such demonstrably inaccurate arguments.

Approaches to Popular Film is a book of separately authored chapters written to the overall plan of its editors, Jane Hollows and Mark Jancovich. The usefulness of the chapters, at least in the context of studying film, varies considerably. As a whole the book raises some interesting questions about the development of film theory and of current critical attention to cinema, but they are not always the ones it sets out to address. The cover blurb concludes that this 'is an ideal textbook for students coming to film theory for the first time', but such students could be badly confused if they read the book as such an introduction, not only because some important current areas are almost or entirely unmentioned, but also because in those chapters where 'film theory' is attacked, the account of it is seriously misleading.

The chapters on 'Genre Theory and Criticism' by Peter Hutchings and on 'Star Studies' by Paul McDonald do work very well as introductions to their respective fields. Both Hutchings and McDonald know the past and present of their areas thoroughly and present them succinctly and clearly. Similarly, Henry Jenkins's chapter on 'Historical Poetics' offers a positive and stimulating argument for an historicized account of aesthetic norms and their relationship to 'shifting conditions of production, distribution and exhibition in contemporary Hollywood' (116). (This is a refreshing surprise, since he focuses on work by David Bordwell and Kristin Thompson, both strongly associated with the largely negative Cognitivist position discussed below.) Helen Stoddart covers a great deal of ground, as coherently as possible in the given space, in her chapter on 'Auteurism and Film Authorship'. However, she is grappling with the problem of recounting the 'death', as well as the creation of the film 'author', and of situating the complex political implications of the latter within the rather blunt schema of the book's remaining sections.

The Introduction, jointly written by the editors, includes chapter summaries which suggest that a single argument is pursued throughout the book. In fact, the four chapters described above neither pursue nor support the central argument of the other four chapters, that current film theory is insufficiently aware of the sociopolitical and economic issues involved in the mechanisms of production. Film theory is also taken to be elitist, on the grounds that it treats popular film as wholly bad for the populace and treats popular audiences as passive dupes. This error is attributed to its reliance on the mistaken (i.e. 'wrong', not 'mis-taken') ideas of psychoanalysis. The solution is to turn to the approaches 'associated with the Centre for Contemporary Cultural Studies at the University of Birmingham' which has 'a quite different conception of the popular to that available in earlier approaches' (10). This attack is made plausible by taking film theory in 1995 to be identical with apparatus theory at a point around the mid-seventies. Twenty years of development and debate within the arena are ignored. Beyond merely challenging the passivity of audiences, discussion has progressed (amongst many other things) to investigating the complexities of audience experiences, recognized as simultaneously restricting *and* empowering, through the pleasures that they offer (as I shall illustrate below). This would be evident if spectatorship had been identified as a currently central 'approach' and allotted a chapter (Hutchings mentions it, usefully but briefly).

Hollows's own chapter, 'Mass Culture Theory and Political Economy', concludes:

> theorists who see texts as ideological tend to share the belief that popular films support capitalism ideologically simply because they are a product of a capitalist economy. But . . . Although films are not produced outside a capitalist mode of production, they may challenge the system that their profits help to maintain. . . . Indeed, it is quite common for heroes and heroines in Hollywood films to be placed in opposition to exploitative economic interests, as films such as *Terminator 2*, *Total Recall*, *The Big Knife* and *Broadcast News* illustrate. (33–4)

This is an extremely simplified view of what are 'dominant classes' and of texts as supporting or challenging their interests, which is not current in film theory. It is puzzling that Hollows does not debate any more recent positions than those of Adorno, Horkheimer and Dwight MacDonald.

Hollows's chapter and its conclusion also point to one major and crucial lack in the book: it never explicitly discusses its own definition or designation of 'popular film'. If it had, it might have considered how interestingly differently the term operates in relation to cinematic film than to, say, literature; and especially how inappropriate it is as a defining term in relation to current production practices. This lost opportunity is especially disappointing given that *Approaches to Popular Film* seems to be the first book in a Manchester University Press series – 'Inside Popular Film' (general editors Mark Jancovich and Eric Schaefer) – which the blurb promises will 'present these areas as altogether more complex than is commonly suggested by established film theories'.

What is given includes a rather plodding discussion of the term 'popular' itself – i.e. of the distinction between 'of the people' and 'well-liked' – in the Introduction (which is rather odd since you would have to look a long time to find a 'people's folk tradition' of film). There is also Hollows's account of the mid-century pejorization of 'mass culture', which indeed included 'movies' in its condemnations and, in Helen Stoddart's brave chapter, an account of the attribution of art status to a limited class of 'authored' films. The book does therefore set out the politically important history of the evaluative binary 'avant-garde/popular' film (Bordieu is mentioned a lot); and following this path, Jancovich is surely correct in asserting, in his chapter on 'Screen Theory', that early work on cinematic textuality, whose 'ambitions . . . were global rather than local' (124), often reproduces this position's contempt for mass audiences and the films they watch.

However, in the nineties the term 'avant-garde' has a quaint ring unless it is used historically. Screen text production has proliferated and diversified within and without mass distribution, and into sliding gradations of budget and audience attraction between the poles (Jarman, Terence Davies, Mike Leigh, Merchant–Ivory . . .). At one extreme we find not 'avant-garde film' but the '4D' work of, for example, Bill Viola and Mona Hatoun, usually produced and exhibited under the aegis of 'visual art' rather than 'film'. If the other extreme is, perhaps, the Hollywood 'blockbuster', this is recognizable as one, distinctive, production strategy. The term 'popular film' therefore has very little use now, except in discussion of historical developments. It may designate one characteristic of a film's achieved or intended audience (though budget and box-office figures are more helpfully precise) but it simply does not designate a distinct category of film today and it probably never did.

(One area where 'popular' may still be a useful critical term is in discussion of non-Western film. Probably the most damaging unacknowledged omission in a book with this title is the absence of any reference to Third and Fourth World production and reception, except for Henry Jenkins's brief allusion to black US film.)

I suspect that the book's unproblematized acceptance of the term is linked to a project that underlies its deceptively anachronistic presentation of the film theory which was mainly developed in the pages of *Screen*. Thus, if the chronological sequence begun in the first two chapters were followed through, Jancovich's chapter on this thinking should be number three. It is, however, placed after the chapters discussing current work, and Jancovich slides to the present rather than past tense as he concludes his objections to 'screen theory'. The impression is clearly created that Laura Mulvey's 1975 'Visual Pleasure and Narrative Cinema' constitutes the present position, undeveloped and undebated, of 'film theory'. This is reinforced by the following chapter, Lisa Taylor's tellingly titled 'From Psychoanalytic Feminism to Popular Feminism', which begins with another account of Mulvey's essay (with no reference to its several earlier discussions) and another critique of its assumed passive, undifferentiated audience. This is opposed by ethnographic research, described with little account of recent work (someone has put Jackie Stacey's *Stargazing* [Routledge, 1994] into the list of further reading on feminism, but it is not mentioned in the chapter); and also by the argument that films do sometimes represent women as active and can therefore empower female audiences. Again there is a failure to examine the current state of 'approaches to film'. Taylor may be amongst those who distrust feminism's expansion into issues problematizing all distinctions of gender and sexuality, but a book offering an introduction to present thinking needs some focused discussion of these areas.

Andy Willis concludes the book with a chapter offering an interesting and succinct history of cultural studies; but this suddenly concludes, after (another) discussion of Bourdieu, with the argument that: 'the simple distinction between popular film and avant-garde film found in much writing on film becomes untenable [because t]he meaning and political significance of texts . . . are defined through their appropriation or rejection by different groups' (189). The implication is that only within the demarcated area of 'cultural studies' has this argument ever been mobilized.

Thus, in its beginning and its end, *Approaches to Popular Film* implies that a set of important considerations belongs only to cultural studies and that something completely separate, film theory, exists which has never paid attention to any of the issues these considerations raise.

It follows that film must be rescued from such theorists. It also follows, of course, that if film is to be carried off to the land where popular culture is the defining subject of attention, 'popular film' must exist. Film is quite clearly a valid part of cultural studies' area of attention, but it is difficult to see any good reasons why this claim needs to be made with such a jealous clamour, or why an 'enemy' camp of monolithically ignorant film theorists needs to be constructed.

Bad reasons suggest themselves in the economic pressures on academic work in the nineties to claim fields and so students, courses and correlated textbooks, in order to secure the income, and even the continued professional existence, that these alone can bring. (The pressure of time under which this book was produced is suggested by three out of eight illustrations' being credited as 'credit to come'.)

The appropriation in particular of film, for whatever reasons, does suggest several strengths in the site. One is that film is popular (I mean in the sense of 'well-liked') with students, who in my experience identify it as especially and empoweringly available, pleasurable and relevant. (Several book titles which include the word 'cinema', although film is not a central part of their subject, also testify to film's current pulling power.) This can be related to the intrinsic interest and importance of film's study, in interrogating so many traditional boundaries of textual/economic production, of textual/social segregations and of academic disciplinary divisions. Demonstrably, film theory over the last twenty years has been characterized by debates that recognize the complexity of cinema's allure and also its ambiguity given the power relations at play in its social and economic contexts. Arguably, willingness to participate in those debates, from whatever finally held position, is presently 'film theory's' only single identifying characteristic.

The actual strength of current film theory is a comforting reflection which is also raised by the attacks made from the Cognitivist position, though their tone is generally far from comfortable. Individual exponents may claim differences amongst themselves and even adopt different theoretical titles, but they are commonly grounded in the assumption linking Cognitive Science and Analytic Philosophy: that mental experience is best explained as a sum of separable, voluntary and rational mental acts. There is nothing careless here. Stretching back to the late seventies, produced by academics of high standing and published by eminent publishers, the work has persisted in offering an intense and repeated version of the crude 'film theory' that Hollows and Jancovich present (although the politics of their project is very different).

Bewildering in their refusal to engage with the actual variations within theory's developing debate and fascinating in its inability to examine its own premises, Cognitivists (their usual but not invariable label) stalk across the site of film, declaring rightful possession. Tempting as it is to dismiss them, I think it is worth trying to work out what is actually at stake.

Two books appeared in 1995 that pursue this line of thought: *Theorizing the Moving Image* (copyright date 1996), a collection of essays by Noël Carroll, and *Image and Mind: Film, Philosophy and Cognitive Science*, by Gregory Curry. Also *Philosophy and Film*, edited by Cynthia A. Freeland and Thomas E. Wartenberg, offers 'essays [which] approach film in many different ways and with a wide range of philosophic commitments' (5), including that exemplified by a contribution from Carroll and others with a similar stance.

A clear and remarkably good-tempered account of cognitivism's attack on what it persists in calling 'dominant film theory', and of responses to this, is given by Judith Mayne in *Theories of Spectatorship* (Routledge, 1993). One detailed response to Carroll's first anti-theory polemic, *Mystifying Movies: Fads and Fallacies in Contemporary Film* (1988), is Warren Buckland's extended review in *Screen* (30:4). Carroll's book, a mixture of new and reprinted essays, includes his response to Buckland which, apparently, *Screen* refused to print (321). The cognitivist arguments put forward in these books are thus not new and they have been challenged elsewhere. Here I only intend to discuss them sufficiently to establish that their persistent repetition, despite their evident refutability, does ask for explanation.

Carroll and Curry might point to differences which do exist between their positions (each refers briefly, but complimentarily, to the other), which I shall try to make clear, but it is in what unites them that the puzzle arises.

First of all they attack 'dominant' film theory, fundamentally because of its basis in psychoanalysis. They ignore the evolving debates about the interpretation of psychoanalytic theory and the value of its application to film, which have in fact characterized critical writing for the last quarter of a century; or worse, because it so culpably begs the question, they make occasional references to them in footnotes (for example, Carroll, 272 n. 4). Their common ground of complaint, that psychoanalysis is not scientific, is again unoriginal and also unargued. Here there is some difference: while Curry simply dismisses psychoanalysis as being as 'wildly, deeply and unrescuably false as Aristotle's physics is' (xiv), Carroll constantly suggests that psycho-analysis is not scientific and that this is a problem for film theorists who refer to it (for example, 272-3 n. 5) but explicitly insists that his rejection of its use in understanding moving images stems from its explaining only 'breakdowns in rationality or in normal cognitive processing that are not otherwise explicable in terms of nonrational [i.e. physiological] defects' (333). Both turn instead to rationalist positions. Thus for Carroll 'my theories not only challenge psycho-analytic alternatives, but preclude them. For they show that the responses in question are not in the appropriate domain of psychoanalysis' (333).

Carroll's route to sidestep, rather than confront, psychoanalysis is bizarre in that if psychoanalysis can be accepted as explaining clinical neurosis via reference to extreme malfunctions of the kind of unconscious processes Freud postulated, it must be accepted that those processes exist and are therefore always in play. Curry's position then is more logically consistent, treating the mind as 'a hierarchically organized structure with levels of more or less intelligent decision making going on in it' (xv). However, he thereby precludes himself from giving an answer such as Carroll has provided to the obvious objection that people often behave with self-damaging irrationality (I assume he would appeal to physical malfunction in the brain).

The nub of their problem, I think, lies in this insistence both want to make upon the fundamental rationality of the human mind, and on all mental experience (*pace* Carroll's exception of clinical patients) as exhaustively explained by rational redescription.

To cut to the chase, within a broadly psychoanalytic perspective a coherent explanation can be given for the anxiety its theorization of the mind may produce, whereas it is difficult to see how cognitive theories can account for what they take to be an extremely irrational attachment to such perspectives. To suggest that cognitivists experience anxiety in the face of theories postulating the universal influence of unconscious process, is not simply the appeal to Freudian 'resistance' ('if you say I'm wrong that proves I'm right') that they would, I take it, allege. It offers a coherent explanation for their consistent, and frequently demonstrated, misrepresentation of critical film theory: that is, not only their picking out positions which have been debated and modified for a long time, but also repeatedly claiming that positions are held which are evidently absurd. In particular, critical film theorists are claimed to believe that film 'causes the viewer to have the false belief that the fictional characters and events represented are real' (Curry 22). Curry's support for this is the following footnote, which I quote in its entirety (this is the only support he gives for the statement I have just quoted):

> 'In cinema it is perfectly possible to believe that a man can fly' (John Ellis, *Visible Fictions* 40); 'One knows that one is watching a film, but one believes, even so, that it is an imaginary [*sic*] reality' (Maureen Turim, *Flashbacks in Film* 17); Conditions of screening and narrative convention give the spectator an illusion of looking in on a private world' (Laura Mulvey, 'Visual Pleasure and Narrative Cinema' 806); 'The camera becomes the mechanism for producing the illusion of Renaissance space' (ibid. 816). This view is by now more or less standard; see, for example, Robert B. Ray, *A Certain Tendency of the Hollywood Cinema* 38.   (22)

Similarly, the alleged position that 'film is a language' is attacked by demonstrating the impossibility of impossible positions which have never been taken, or else by evasion (see, for example, Carroll's discussion of 'some rather straight-forward objections' to 'the film/language analogy' [403] or Curry's refusal to define the semiotic approach to film which he dismisses [116–17]). It is all too tempting to try to meet these cognitivists on their own ground, painstakingly picking up each point of misrepresentation, demonstrating that their own rationalism is unsound, adducing alternative theories of the validation of theories, appealing to a basic, missing, expectation that to engage in debate involves some attempt to understand one's opponents' actual position and finally to point out the power claim involved in their intellectual claim to superior rationality. Buckland's *Screen* review tries all of these and, as Carroll's reply demonstrates, they can all be evaded by employing exactly the strategies which are criticized.

I think a better strategy of response is to take up the implied challenge to articulate what it is about film that we find illuminated by elements of psycho-analytic and/or semiotic theory, what we actually take such theories to be, how far we take them to be analogies for or descriptions of the effects of film (or something else) and, in all these instances, *why*. In other words, the refutation of cognitivism's excluding claim to the site of film probably lies less in trying to pin down their misrepresentations and evasions and more in demonstrating the greater explanatory power of other approaches. This might involve examining what we take to be valid and valuable as 'explanation', which could be a tedious or pompous project. However, I think it is useful to ponder over the question sometimes, for the following reason. The multifaceted nature of film as a medium and cinema as a practice, which produces its stimulating hospitality to academically hybrid discussion, also involves its considerable ambiguity within any category to which it can be allocated. Because of this, it is a site where any explanation is going to be especially implicated with the belief systems of the person who is offering it. I suspect it is a clash of belief systems that is centrally at stake in the opposition between cognitivists and the various positions they lump together as dominant theory. In particular, I think conflicting anxieties about rationality and control – control of others, control by others and control of one's self – are in play.

Awareness of 'the need to subject the basic assumptions of a discipline to critical study' is claimed as the distinguishing characteristic of 'philosophers studying film' (2) in Freeland and Wartenberg's introduction to their compila-tion of such essays. Their approach to the site is much more eclectic than those discussed so far. They argue that 'the field of philosophy' is emerging as 'an important sub-discipline, of interest to both serious students of film and philosophy' (10) and also that 'the contributions of philosophers will encourage consideration of broader alternatives to those currently dominant in cinema studies' (2), but they do not engage in appropriating or hostile polemic and nor do most of their contributors. Noël Carroll's 'Ontology of the Moving Image' (of which 'Defining the Moving Image' in his own book is more or less a point-by-point rewriting – or vice versa) pursues quite calmly its dryly stipulative 'four necessary conditions for the phenomena that we are calling moving images' (81). Karen Hanson bases her assumption that 'film theory' developed to establish film as 'art', and that therefore it constituted itself as 'scientific', upon (respectively) a quotation from Noël Carroll and then from Dudley Andrews's *Major Theories of Film* (1976), thus reproducing the kind of confusion about current theory I have already discussed. However, she goes on to an interesting discussion of problems in the concept of scientific enquiry in general which actually critiques the stance of cognitivists rather than of current 'theorists'. Only George M. Wilson, inveighing against the assumed 'theorist' belief in the passively indoctrinated audience, thunders that: 'the plausibility that has been attributed to the claim I have mentioned is almost wholly a function of the grand obscurity with which it is normally formulated combined with a wholesale failure to think through even the limited implications of a minimally adequate account of cinematic point of view' (50). His argument is that, on the contrary, 'the audience enjoys an epistemic position superior to that of the fictional agents' and therefore it cannot be true that 'classical film essentially restricts the epistemic situation of the viewer in a radical and deplorable fashion' (51).

In fact, many if not most of these essays are engaged within the issues and debates to which apparatus theory (amongst other things) gave rise, in the way that I have suggested characterizes current 'film theorists' who do not define themselves as philosophers. Notably, Naomi Scheman's chapter, 'Missing Mothers/Desiring Daughters', debates with (rather than merely 'against') Freud-based views of the female's gender identity as 'com[ing] into existence only in relation to her father's desire for her; that is, she needs to acknowledge him as her one true parent' (93). Asserting that other factors are in play, and especially that 'The mother/daughter connection is the most important of those elsewheres' (96), Scheman argues that Hollywood melodrama, through its faulty or else wholly 'missing' mothers, operates to enforce the sole value of the father/husband as validator. Most of the essays in this volume are highly intelligent and carefully positioned, although I am not sure that they represent a distinctively 'philosophical approach' in the way the Introduction claims.

Freeland and Wartenberg list the 'widely divergent schools of thought' represented here as 'analytical, "Continental", Marxist, feminist, pragmatist, post-modern, anti-post-modern, classical' (4). It would be useful, especially to students, if they had discussed which of their contributors can be placed in which of these categories, because if you are not already familiar with the terms it would be difficult to work out which essay exemplifies which stance. Instead, the Introduction seems anxious to demonstrate that these essays on film do conform to traditional philosophical concerns such as 'aesthetics' or 'conceptions of virtue, vice, or political and social interaction' (7). The editors' tolerant inclusiveness is welcome, but a more robust Introduction, indicating the points of difference between contributors' 'basic assumptions', would have made the volume as a whole more valuable to many readers.

The contents of *Screen* itself in 1995 (volume 36) are a good place to begin demonstrating the variety of positions and debate I have been attributing to current theory. In the Spring issue (no. 1) three of the main articles are concerned with broadcast television, while dealing with issues such as gender, representation and its (re-)contextualization that connect directly with cinema. Julia Hallam and Margaret Marshmont, in 'Framing Experience: Case Studies in the Reception of *Oranges are Not the Only Fruit*' (1–15), examine the responses of a small group of women whom they invited to view the television adaptation of Winterson's novel, identifying this as 'a text . . . whose preferred reading was counter to dominant ideological constructions of marriage and heterosexuality' (3). In 'From the Dark Ages to the Golden Age: Women's Memories and Television Re-runs' (16–33), Lynn Spigel considers her University of Southern California students' responses to images of women in rerun situation comedies, with some anxiety about 'the role television plays in creating images of women's pasts and the idea of women's progress now' (17). Janet Thumin analyses post-war television's simultaneous address to women's economic power as housekeepers and suppression of the labour they performed in '"A Live Commercial for Icing Sugar": Researching the Historical Audience: Gender and Broadcast Television in the 1950s' (48–55). Three films dealing with past male childhoods (Davies's *The Long Day Closes*, Tornatore's *Cinema Paradiso* and Gyllenhaal's *Waterland*) form the site of Susannah Radstone's investigation of 'Cinema/Memory/History' (34–47). Her concern is both with the general relationship that may obtain if 'Memory emerges as the fruit of a fertile encounter between History and Theory' (38) and the more specific gender issue that in these films 'Though undoubtedly "in question", phallic masculinity remains in place and History shores itself against the incoming tide of memory' (45).

In this number of *Screen,* issues of gender and popular genre also appear in Lizzie Francke's review (75–8) of Carol J. Clover's *Men, Women and Chainsaws: Gender in the Modern Horror Film* (British Film Institute, 1992) and Barbara Creed's *The Monstrous-Feminine: Film, Feminism and Psychoanalysis* (Routledge, 1993). Franke concludes that both suggest good reasons why 'in the kinky and mucky arena of horror cinema there is much for those interested in gender to delve into rather than walk out on' (78). Kay Richardson extends the focus on popular television in her review (79–82) of Sonia Livingstone and Peter Lunt's *Talk on Television: Audience Participation and Public Debate* (Routledge, 1994).

Additionally, John Fletcher writes a longish review article (65–74) of Kaja Silverman's *Male Subjectivity at the Margins* (Routledge, 1992), starting from the observation that 'The psychoanalytic and Foucauldian perspectives might be said to occupy the blindspot of each other', the former 'characteristically impervious to the historicity of the categories it relies on' and the latter 'render[ing] invisible and unthought the complex histories of identity and desire' (65). Fletcher describes Silverman's exploration of marginalized sexualities as in fact able to say '"no" to power', via a re-examination of 'the interface between Althusser and Lacan which had been so crucial for the anglephone circulation of radical theory in the 1970's', praising it as 'a heartening recovery of scope after the postmodern rejection of grand narratives and structural theory' (66). Whilst noting the difficulties Silverman's wide sweep of theoretical reference could produce for a reader, he concludes that Silverman's book 'renews and refreshes one's attention to the necessary incommensurability of the psychic and the social at a time when the pressure to reduce or abandon one in the interests of the other have never been so great' (74).

Fletcher notes that '*Screen* played an important vanguard role' (66) in disseminating the perspectives from which Silverman starts: in both her book and its review we clearly have, then, the kind of theory that readers are warned about by the Cultural Studies and Cognitivist books I began by discussing. Here, though, is an unavoidable example (for anyone who really wants to know) of its continuing dynamic and (summed up in Fletcher's careful and crucial use of the epithet 'necessary') of the subtlety and importance of the issues it addresses.

The Summer issue of *Screen* 1995 is a 'video issue'. The only attention specifically to film comes in Barry Taylor's review of Joan Copjec's (ed.) *Shades of Noir: a Reader* (Verso, 1993) and Frank Krutnik's *In a Lonely Street: Film Noir, Genre, Masculinity* (Routledge, 1991). The titles of other books reviewed, and of the major articles, nevertheless indicate the permeability of questions and approaches across screenic sites (and of course other forms of textuality): José Muñoz writes on 'The Autoethnographic Performance: Reading Richard Fung's Queer Hybridity' (83–99); Dimitris Eleftheriotis on 'Video Poetics: Technology, Aesthetics and Politics' (100–12); Sean Cubitt writes 'On Interpretation: Bill Viola's *The Passing* (113–30); and Janine Marchessault on 'Reflections on the Dispossessed: Video and the "Challenge for Change" Experiment' (issues around the alleged empowerment of 'ordinary people' through access to camcorders) (131–46). The remaining reviews are by Lisa Cartwright, of Hamid Naficy's *The Making of Exile Cultures: Iranian Television in Los Angeles* (University of Minnesota Press, 1993) (159–67) and by Christine Gerhaghty of Julie D'Acci's *Defining Women: Television and the Case of Cagney and Lacey* (University of North Carolina Press, 1994).

The focus of the major articles in the Autumn issue is 'masculinities'. In 'Masquerade or Drag?: Bette Davis and the Ambiguities of Gender' (179–92), Martin Shingler considers the 'several instances where Bette Davis exploited the ironies and ambiguities of gender' (181) and maintains that 'by employing both concepts we can leave room for ambivalence in our reading of [her] performance of femininity' (192). 'Masquerade' is again a term Jeffrey A. Brown puts to use in analysing the attractive ambiguity of a Hollywood star's screen sexuality, in '"Putting on the Ritz": Masculinity and the Young Gary Cooper' (193–213). In 'Gender, Ethnicity and Cultural Crisis in *Falling Down* and *Groundhog Day*' (214–32), Jude Davies considers 'the implications of the figuring of an American cultural crisis in terms of a crisis in white masculinity' (232). Dimitris Eleftheriotis's essay 'Questioning Totalities: Constructions of Masculinity in the Popular Greek Cinema of the 1960s' (233–41), not only examines this particular site but also constructs a critique 'of "The construction of masculinity" as a discursive category within Film Studies' in terms of its 'focus on its non-historical, universalistic nature' (241). Murray Healy, on the other hand, mounts a defence in 'Were We Being Served? Homosexual Representation in Popular British Comedy' (243–56). Starting from his own pleasure as a young gay male in what are in obvious ways stereotypically effeminized portrayals, he argues that 'to be sure, these representations were not confrontational or challenging. But neither were they oppressive, outright demonizations; they were sensitive negotiations' (256).

The 'reports and debates' section of this issue returns attention to the female, being occupied by three essays on Jane Campion's *The Piano*. Stella Bruzzi and Sue Gillett find the film's subversion of cinematic and sexual norms offering an affirmation of female subjectivity ('Tempestuous Petticoats: Costume and Desire in *The Piano*' [257–66]; 'Lips and Fingers: Jane Campion's *The Piano*' [277–87]). In 'The Return of the Repressed? Whiteness, Femininity and Colonialism in *The Piano*' (267–76), however, Lynda Dyson finds in the film a 're-present[ation of] the story of colonisation in New Zealand as a narrative of colonisation. In doing so, the film addresses the concerns of the dominant white majority there, providing a textual palliative for post-colonial anxieties generated by the contemporary struggles over the nation's past' (267).

Reviews in this issue do not focus on its main theme. Sue Street (288–91) writes on Sue Harper's *Picturing the Past: the Rise and Fall of the British Costume Film* (British Film Institute, 1994); Susan Haywards (292–6) on Richard Abel's *The Cine Goes to Town: French Cinema 1896–1914* (University of California Press, 1993) and Colin Crisp's *The Classic French Cinema 1930–1960* (Indiana University Press, 1993); Leslie Felperin (297–300) reviews Ellen Seiter's *Sold Separately: Parents and Children in Consumer Culture* (Rutgers University Press, 1993); and Philip Simpson (301–4) reviews Kevin Jackson's (ed.) *The Humphrey Jennings Reader* (Carcanet Press, 1993).

The last 1995 issue of *Screen* has no overall theme. Ravi S. Vasudevan's 'Addressing the Spectator of a "Third World" National Cinema: The Bombay

"Social" Film of the 1940s and 1950s' (305–24) brings a basically psychoanalytic model to examples of close textual analysis to disclose a 'disaggretive
address' in Hindu films of this period. This he sees as 'perform[ing] a symbolic
remapping of identity and suppress[ing] other more complicated traditions of
gender, of Hinduism and other forms of popular culture' (324). Vasudevan
also uses contextual material to locate these films' production and activity
within a historically significant moment.

Vasudevan thus brings diverse approaches together to illuminate film-as-
text, film as (complex) ideological influence and film as instance of cultural
industrialization, on a site whose exoticism (seen from the West) not merely
extends the scope of Western popular culture studies, but also extends its
understanding.

This is dense writing which would be well beyond the expected capacity of
the first year undergraduate student at whom Hollows and Jancovich's book
seems aimed. It is, however, work that such books should be leading them
towards, not warning them off.

In 'Women Reading Chinese Films: Between Orientalism and Silence'
(325–40), Stephanie Donald notes the difficulty of writing 'from outside' in her
suggestive study of films which, as she argues, negotiate models of identity in
an ideologically destabilized post-Mao China, amongst competing constructions of the (inter)national, of gender and of traditionally hostile ethnicities.
However, it might be useful to consider further the complex implications of
translating models of identity, both ideological and psychoanalytic, between
the West and China.

John Fletcher uses the psychoanalytic model of 'fantasy', as elaborated by
Laplanche and Pontalis, to investigate 'Primal Scenes and the Female Gothic:
Rebecca and *Gaslight*' (341–70), suggesting that this account of fantasy
'challenges the functionalist tendency of much 1970's apparatus theory'
because 'if the primal fantasies map the terrain of a phallocentric Oedipal
order, they do so without necessarily determining the position and investment
of the subject along pre-given gender lines' (343). With close textual analysis
he convincingly argues that in his two examples 'the filmwork . . . sets up a
scene and a narrative involving various figures and positions within which the
spectator, the film's fantasising subject, is invited to find "herself" through the
film's work of enunciation, of cinematic identification and disidentification'.

Jeffrey Sconce's '"trashing the Academy": Taste, Excess, and an Emerging
Politics of Cinematic Style' (371–93) offers an exhilarating defence of 'para-
cinema' and its followers, defining this as 'a most elastic textual category . . .
[including] "badfilm", splatterpunk, "mondo" films, sword and sandal epics,
Elvis flicks, government hygiene films, Japanese monster movies, beach-parties
musicals, and just about every other historical manifestation of exploitation
cinema from juvenile delinquency documentaries to soft-core pornography'
(372). Sconce deals with this (undoubtedly a manifestation of popular culture)
without self-distancing patronage but equally from an undisguised politically
theorized position. His claim is that:

> Perhaps paracinema has the potential, at long last, to answer
> Brecht's famous call for an anti-illusionistic aesthetic, by
> presenting a cinema so histrionic, anachronistic and excessive that
> it compels even the most casual viewer to engage it ironically,

producing a relatively detached textual space in which to consider,
if only superficially, the cultural, historical and aesthetic politics
that shape cinematic representation. (393)

Finally, Ramona Fotiade considers the significance of surrealism within
Avant-Garde theories and practices of the 1920s and 1930s, in 'The Tamed
Eye: Surrealism and Film Theory' (394–407).

Most of the reviews in this issue deal with music in film. Robynn Stilwell
discusses Theodor Adorno and Hans Eisler's *Composing for the Films*
(1947; reprinted by The Athlone Press, 1994); Royal S. Brown's *Overtones and
Undertones: Reading Film Music* (University of California Press, 1994);
George Burt's *The Art of Film Music* (Northeastern University Press, 1994);
and Michel Chion's *Audio-Vision: Sound on Screen*, translated by Claudia
Gorbman (Columbia University Press, 1994). Will Straw reviews Andrew
Goodwin's *Dancing in the Distraction Factory: Music, Television and Popular
Culture* (University of Minnesota Press, 1992), and Erica Carter discusses
Gender and German Cinema: Feminist Interventions (Berg, 1993, 2 vols).

The pages of *Screen*, which must, if anything does, represent film theory's
domain, surely refute the hostile constructions currently offered. Far from the
perversely blinkered thinking attributed to it, there is not only an enormous
range of approaches and topics but also an awareness of political issues in the
lived world within which most writers firmly implicate themselves.

The difficulties that may be encountered in reading work (such as some
Screen articles) in which, in order to get somewhere new, the writer has not
space to give a full account of older arguments that are cited can (as I have
suggested) be met by reading other kinds of work specifically designed as
introductions to relevant areas. (Call me old-fashioned, but I always thought
that this is what 'studying a subject' involved.) A really useful example of such
secondary work is *Psychoanalytic Criticism: A Reader*, edited by Sue Vice. As
well as carefully selected extracts that progress through applications to
textuality of (more than 'in') Freud, Lacan, Kristeva and Irigaray, Vice
provides a substantial general introduction charting the different ways in which
textual criticism and psychoanalysis have been brought together and also
lucidly informative introductions to the particular theoretical positions whose
use is exemplified in each section. Amongst other things, this book
demonstrates that 'introductory' writing is most successfully produced by
those with a thorough and intelligent grasp of their subject.

Some prior knowledge of Freud's work and the debates it has engendered
would probably make for a more confident reading of Vicky Lebeau's *Lost
Angels: Psychoanalysis and Cinema*. This is an interesting example of books
which are taking the psychoanalytic debate forward and articulating their own
'oscillation, or . . . uncertainty, about the status of psychoanalysis as an object
of or a means to a critique' (16). Lebeau identifies 'a coincidence between the
mass and feminine in Freud's texts as the effect of a form of preoccupied or
fixated fantasy life' (16). With some similarities to Naomi Sheman's argument
(above), Lebeau sees patriarchy insisting that the daughter look only to her
father for confirmation of her subjectivity, here seen to coerce her into a
repeated demand for love, which is then condemned as perverse. For Lebeau,
though, the problem lies in the daughter's exclusion from the fraternal (rather
than maternal) bond, from the band of brothers whose comradeship in

opposition to, and final murder of, the primal father enables escape from the Oedipal triangle into a social sphere of subject experience.

I find some problems, perhaps rather in the writing of this book than in the argument itself. Persuasive parallels are indeed explored between Freud's pronouncements and 'the different critiques of the mass and feminine spectator in feminist and critical theories of film' (16). Also, though, examples are given of films allegedly soliciting a female teenage audience into the same pattern of enthralled but punished desire (these are two moments in John Hughes's *Ferris Bueller's Day Off*, taken as the starting points, respectively, for chapters 2 and 3). So the question does arise here of where the mistake is being made. For example, to the extent that films do have such an effect, it would be accurate to critique this and to demonstrate, though not to blame, their audiences' enthralment; but to what extent is Freud's formulation taken to influence film critics' interpretations, or film-makers' plots of exploitation; or else how far are all these to be seen as symptoms of a common cause, a pattern of unrecognized unfairness, produced within (say) the bourgeois nuclear family. In the latter case Freud's culpability lies in his lack of discernment but not in initiating this pattern. How far, then, is it specifically 'the gesture within Freud's theory which moves to preoccupy femininity with the father and so to dispossess the woman of a certain access to fantasy . . . which locks us – women – and the feminized others *into* an interminable oscillation between perversity and narcissism'? (154; original emphasis).

I suspect that Lebeau may well have responses to these questions; but these might have appeared more clearly if she had given more concentrated attention to film texts and the cinematic experience.

On the subject of female spectatorship and specifically the question 'what are women in their millions doing in the cinema, where most of our time is spent watching images of men rather than of women'? (73), I doubt if anything better will be written for some time than Christine Gledhill's essay 'Women Reading Men' in *Me Jane: Masculinity, Movies and Women*, edited by Pat Kirkham and Janet Thumin. Gledhill argues that women have not been sufficiently recognized as 'makers of meaning out of male images' (73), and yet if, in cinema, '"woman" is image – a fantasy – is this not true of "man" too?' (74). With particular attention to melodrama, she points to the '*dual* function of the human body in popular fictions', which both commands 'recognition by its reference to social, cultural and psychic attributes' and functions 'metaphorically, symbolically, mythically' (74). Therefore 'the concept of representation has . . . proved inadequate . . . because it precipitately refers the work and its reception to a reality constituted and theoretically known outside the work'. Alternatively, 'Attention to the aesthetic requirements of melo-drama . . . suggests a gap between imaginative and representational functions, which should delay the immediate translation of one in terms of the other' (75). Gledhill works through (with some compression of a complex view into an allotted space) to the question of the ways in which female fantasy both 'bind[s] us to atavistic social and psychic structures' and 'contribute[s] to resistance and the imagining of something different' (85), focusing on effects producing gender identity either in 'difference, separation, fixity' or in 'rapprochement'. She finally arrives 'back at making ideological readings of these conflicts between male and female figures, but readings which attempt to work with the aesthetic dynamic and pleasure offered by film, rather than

demanding they be accountable to analytic paradigms of the social formation
or the patriarchal psyche' (91).

The pleasure offered by texts whose effects can nevertheless simultaneously
be recognized as patriarchal (and which is not disavowed when it is
problematized) is often importantly acknowledged by this book's contributors:
examples are Kirkham's own 'Loving Men: Frank Borzage, Charles Farrell
and the Reconstruction of Masculinity in 1920s Hollywood Cinema' (94–109);
Susannah Radstone's 'Too Straight a Drive to the Tollbooth: Masculinity,
Mortality and Al Pacino' (148–65); and Gillian Swanson's 'Burt's Neck:
Masculine Corporeality and Estrangement' (203–22). This book is the
promised companion to *You Tarzan: Masculinity, Movies and Men* (Lawrence
& Wishart, 1993): the editors have thus put together two volumes of essays
about cinematic masculinity, one by male and one by female writer/spectators.
Thanks to their very careful procedures, the whole is even greater than the sum
of its parts, partly because contributors have worked with awareness of each
other's work and also because the thorough Introduction to the second volume
is able, besides considering relationships between its own chapters, to compare
these with the men's approaches. Interesting differences emerge. One is the
'delicate, fragile, provisional' nature of masculinity 'marked time and again' in
the films chosen by women (11), something not unacknowledged by the men
but given 'striking[ly] . . . more detailed attention, probing and speculation'
(13) here. Another is that while 'In *You Tarzan* discussion frequently focused
on action and spectacular display of the male body, and the epic, war, horror
and science fiction genres were each the subject of at least one essay; in *Me
Jane* the recurring genres are thrillers, westerns and melodramas' (12).

Kirkham and Thumin suggest the women may be 'more readily prepared to
examine elements of that construction [i.e. masculinity] which pose, in
themselves, no threat to the (always already) disempowered female subject'
(13). If any grumble occurs in relation to such a useful book, it might be that
there is not very much attention to the continuing reality of our disempower-
ment, which is legitimated by many cinematic images of masculinity, even
though they mobilize other effects and meanings. I am not suggesting that any
of the contributors is unaware of this, but that the illuminating investigation
of our pleasures, even while marked as paradoxical, can sometimes become a
bit too comfortable. The choice and treatment of masculinities here suggests
that when women are attracted to men it is very much in virtue of their
contradictory flaws and weaknesses (as the editors note, amongst the
socio-economic spheres represented in chosen texts, very many contributors
'have shown less concern with aristocrats or successful capitalists, big or small,
than with more ordinary and flawed men' [21]). Recognizing this forgiving
fondness is clearly empowering to both sides in the context of understanding
interpersonal male–female relationships, actual and cinematic. I think it does
still remain important explicitly to keep an eye on the inequities of social,
political and economic relationships. One criticism of film theory over the last
twenty years, which does seem to hold up, is that the understandings we have
been evolving have not yet done very much to reduce the exploitations they
help to explain.

This said, there is a great variety of attitude, methodology and cinematic
text in this volume. Besides the essays already noted, Gill Branston's
' . . . Viewer, I Listened to Him . . . Voices, Masculinity, *In the Line of Fire*'

(37–50) considers relationships between voice, body and gender, especially in Clint Eastwood's maintained, though ageing, 'masculinity'. In 'Relations between Men: Bernardo Bertolucci's *The Spider's Stratagem*' (51–61) Lesley Caldwell sees the film as an exploration of 'The family and its place, the relations between fathers and sons, and the power of the *idea* of the father' (52) in the context of Italy's construction of a national character. Christine Geraghty, in 'Albert Finney: A Working Class Hero' (62–93), considers how Finney was established as a star by a film, Karel Reisz's *Saturday Night and Sunday Morning,* that presented a new type of working class and compromising British hero. In 'Petro Almodovar's *Tie Me Up! Tie Me Down!*: The Mechanics of Masculinity' (113–27), Rikki Morgan offers a cautious defence of the film's ironization, rather than promotion, of misogyny. Grizelda Pollock traces a 'disruption of Oedipal narrativity' which nevertheless entails 'that the condition for this dramatisation is still the dehumanisation of Africa' (144) in 'Empire, Identity and Place: Masculinities in *Greystoke: The Legend of Tarzan*' (128–47). Charlene Regester examines and celebrates 'Oscar Micheaux's Multifaceted Portrayals of the African–American Male: The *Good*, The *Bad* and The *Ugly*' (166–83). In 'Melodrama and Men in Post-Classical Romantic Comedy' (184–93), Kathleen Rowe identifies a trend which threatens not only to appropriate the site of melodrama 'to tell the story of *men's* lives and *male* suffering' (as opposed to their traditional focus on women) but, more dangerously, to make this telling a tale of women as oppressors. Focusing especially on Robert de Niro, Helen Stoddart considers ways in which male body marking (scars and tattoos) functions to construct a masculine body whose contradictions are significant to male rather than female onlookers in '"I Don't Know Whether To Look at Him Or Read Him": *Cape Fear* and Male Scarification' (194–202). Sarah Street, in '"Mad About the Boy": Masculinity and Career in *Sunset Boulevard*' (223–33), suggests that readings of the film which construct Joe as purely the victim of Norma Desmond suppress the 'overwhelming male anxiety about age, mortality and career' (224) which is figured in his role as gigolo/male prostitute. Janet Thumin, in '"Maybe He's Tough But He Sure Ain't No Carpenter": Masculinity and In/competence in *Unforgiven*' (234–48), considers 'competence' as a signal of masculinity, complexly foregrounded in this film's depiction of older men handing down the strengths and skills of the 'real' West; and also that, despite its recognition of a feminist agenda, this resolutely remains 'men's talk'. In 'From Proletarian Hero to Godfather: Jean Gabin and "Paradigmatic" French Masculinity' (249–62), Ginette Vincendeau contends that this actor created and epitomized a model of masculinity, 'that of the rebellious and occasionally tragic "proletarian hero", who in his middle age becomes a strong patriarchal figure' (249), which is central to the domestic, if not international, popularity of male stars in French film. Margaret O'Brien is unusual amongst contributors in focusing on a director in 'Changing Places? Men and Women in Oliver Stone's Vietnam' (263–72). She argues that all three of his films concerned with that war display a progressively deepening anxiety about the survival of American masculinity. Finally, Lola Young's '"Nothing Is As It Seems": Re-Viewing *The Crying Game*' (273–85) considers the suppression of difference, difficulty and also of Northern Irish politics produced in this film; to which she attributes the surprisingly positive reception accorded to its portrayal of a black man who passes as a woman. She demonstrates the complicity with, rather than critique of, this in press reviews.

Adding to its other virtues, this book has a film index and a very full, reliable general index.

In her own book, *Fear of the Dark: 'Race', Gender and Sexuality in the Cinema* Lola Young's exploration of 'film-making and the resulting critical work [as] a crucial political activity' (192) is explored at greater length, within a focus on black characters represented in UK cinema. Methodologically, this book is an exemplary instance of an ability to work with psychoanalytic theory, to be selectively critical of it from an authoritatively inhabited politicized position, and yet to insist upon and to demonstrate the necessary expansion of explanation it generates. Young not only argues but demonstrates that questions of 'negative or positive representation' are insufficient without address to issues of relationship between viewer and text, especially of 'who may look at whom?'. Also, with no diminution of its intrinsic importance, the production and reception of racialized images (positive and negative) is located as imbricated within other 'discriminations' of distincted sexuality, gender and class. Thus amongst many other things this book is a reminder to its white readers that our concerns about colonialism's racial abjection need to be pursued as genuinely, and not by charitable adoption, our own.

Books Reviewed

Carroll, Noël. *Theorizing the Moving Image*. Cambridge Studies in Film Series, Cambridge University Press, 1996. pp. 419. hb £50.00, pb £16.95. ISBN 0 521 46049 2, 0 521 46607 5.

Curry, Gregory. *Image and Mind: Film, Philosophy and Cognitive Science*. Cambridge University Press. pp. 296. hb £35.00. ISBN 0 521 45356 9.

Freeland, Cynthia A., and Thomas E. Wartenberg, eds. *Philosophy and Film*. Routledge. pp. 249. pb £12.99. ISBN 0 415 90921 X.

Hollows, Jane, and Mark Jancovich. *Approaches to Popular Film*. Inside Popular Film Series. Manchester University Press. pp. 196. hb £40.00, pb £10.99. ISBN 0 7190 4392 1, 0 7190 4393 X.

Lebeau, Vicky. *Lost Angels: Psychoanalysis and Cinema*. Routledge. pp. 165. pb £12.99. ISBN 0 415 10721 0.

Kirkham, Pat, and Janet Thumin. *Me Jane: Masculinity, Movies and Women*. Lawrence & Wishart. pp. 291. pb £14.99. ISBN 0 85315 802 9.

Vice, Sue, ed. *Psychoanalytic Criticism: A Reader*. Polity Press. pp. 217. hb £45.00, pb £12.95. ISBN 0 7456 1049 8, 0 7456 1050 1.

Young, Lola. *Fear of the Dark: 'Race', Gender and Sexuality in the Cinema*. Gender, Racism, Ethnicity Series. Routledge. pp. 203. pb £13.99. ISBN 0 415 09710 X.

17

Science, Technology and Culture

ANNE BALSAMO

This chapter includes three sections: 1. The Philosophy of Technoscience Studies; 2. Posthuman Corporeality; 3. Cyberculture and New Information Technologies.

1. The Philosophy of Technoscience Studies

The matrix of interests identified by the conjunction of the terms 'science', 'technology' and 'culture' covers a broad spectrum of scholarly work. Andrew Feenberg and Alastair Hannay's edited volume, *Technology and the Politics of Knowledge*, offers an exceptional introduction to the equally broad range of philosophical issues implied by new developments in scientific and technological practice. Not only does the volume include several essays that review and clarify the major debates among foundational figures in the philosophy of technology (notably Habermas, Marcuse and Heidegger), it also includes essays that point to those new areas of social life that demand a similar philosophical review and explication. On this point, Don Ihde's chapter on 'Image Technologies and Traditional Culture' and Helen Longino's on 'Reproductive Technologies and their Scientific Context' attest to the fact that philosophical discussions of the nature of technology must also take into account the actual application of technology as these techniques, devices and forms of knowledge literally construct the human condition. These essays mark a philosophical shift from a consideration of technology in terms of 'techne', 'tools', or even a 'world-view', where the human being was understood to be an entity whose ontological status was not influenced or determined by the technological – as a 'species' for Habermas, as a 'tool-user' for Marcuse – to a consideration of the 'technological' as constitutive of the very nature of human being. Thus we read in Ihde's chapter how new technologies of representation influence phenomenological dimensions of technologically mediated perception; people literally see (and consequently live) differently in such a mediated world. According to Longino, new reproductive technologies contribute to the continuing alienation of human beings from the bodily experience of reproduction. She describes how the development and deployment of procreative technologies transforms reproduction into a technological event. One of the consequences of this transformation is that socially and politically constructed beliefs become institutional realities. Beliefs in the possibility of a scientific mastery of nature, in the facticity of biological determinism, and in the notion of woman as reproductive vessel become increasingly concretized through the institutional arrangements that structure the use of new reproductive technologies.

There are different implications to be drawn from this notion that technology is constitutive of the human condition. Following one line of reasoning, Richard E. Sclove considers technology as a social structure. In this view, technology influences the organization of human life as it is simultaneously constructed by human beings. Sclove's book, *Democracy and Technology*, is an attempt to elucidate a conceptual framework for the development of a democratic politics of technology. Although he begins with a review of the ways in which technologies have an impact on human life, he is careful to remind readers that all social structures are fundamentally ambiguous in that they always create opportunities as well as constraints. Following this line of reasoning, he suggests that it is more useful to think about the ways in which technologies 'influence' rather than 'determine' social existence. His choice of terms here is not merely rhetorical; the book is filled with concrete examples whereby technologies were themselves shaped to fit the social values and interests of the communities within which they were introduced. To see technologies as having a purely determining influence on social experience would be to deny the possibility of human or community intervention, thus denying also the possibility of a politics of technology. Sclove's notion of the politics of technology is not a banal rehearsal of the claim that technologies are used for political ends. Rather, he argues that a politics of technology entails the understanding that technologies have multiple effects. He uses the term 'polypotent' to describe the situation whereby technologies have not only focal functions, but also many other functions, some of which are realized, others that remain latent. The formation of a democratic politics of technology rests on the possibility that communities can exercise control and governance over the use, design and deployment of technologies. He devotes several chapters of his book to the explication of the role technology can play in the development of strong democracy, in terms of how it can be assessed, how it can be managed and finally how it can augment democratic self-governance. By the end he outlines several key steps that are required for the realization of a democratic politics of technology. These are: (1) lay citizens need to be involved in the determination of technology use and policy; (2) questions about the latent effects of technology need to be raised in the early phases of technology development and application; (3) technologies need to be seen in combination with one another, as systems of interrelated social structures that often reinforce and necessitate the use of other technologies; (4) communities need to focus on all technological developments, especially the simpler innovations that can accumulate effects over time; and (5) communities need to explicitly address the relationship between a given technology and democratic decision-making and self-governance, asking questions about how the technology aids or impedes the democratic project. In short, Sclove offers readers a set of analytical tools to use to guide our efforts to reclaim social control of our technological future.

Yet another way to explore the implications of the philosophical shift in thinking about the human being as constituted by technology rather than standing in (some external) relationship to it is to think 'the human' and 'the technological' together. This is the basic conceptual move grounding the work of 'cyborg studies' – a body of work by scholars who explicitly draw on cultural theory in their study of the intersections among science, technology and everyday life. A long-awaited book that begins to map the broad terrain of cyborg studies is *The Cyborg Handbook*, edited by Chris Hables Gray. The book includes essays by key figures such as Donna Haraway and Kate Hayles, as well as historical papers and interviews that trace the genesis of cyborg theory, particularly in the thinking of Manfred Clynes, the man who coined the word 'cyborg' in 1960 in the context of speculating on the adaptability of the human being for space travel. Of particular interest are two sections: one includes work on cyborg theory in the context of medicine and the other introduces the work of scholars in the nascent field of 'cyborg anthropology'.

The essays collected in the section on 'The Proliferation of Cyborgs in Medicine' collectively demonstrate that medicine, as one form of contemporary technoscientific practice, is bringing us ever closer to the realization of cyborg identity – both as organic bodies are refashioned with inorganic replacement parts and as new medical sciences such as genetics and reproductive engineering break new ground in the manipulation of human life. These essays suggest that we are already engaged in the ethically fraught project of engineering cyborg embodiment. From this perspective, the cyborg is not a science fictional or even metaphoric future vision of the human being; rather, the cyborg already exists among us through our use of organ transplants, artificial body replacement parts and gene therapy.

Cyborg anthropologists also study the cultural dimensions of science and technology. Their work addresses such issues as the analysis of the ideological impact of scientific knowledge as well as the ethnographic investigation of the laboratory practices of scientists and engineers. Even more interesting is the suggestion, offered by Gary Lee Downey, Joseph Dumit and Sarah Williams (authors of the essay 'Cyborg Anthropology' in *The Cyborg Handbook*), that the 'cyborg' may be a more adequate figuration of the subject/object of contemporary culture than the traditional figure of the organic 'human' being. Thus they argue that the notion of the 'cybernetic organism' – the cyborg – is a more robust framework for understanding the situation of human subjects in a postmodern, technologically saturated age. Mapping the figure of the cyborg onto the figure of the postmodern body politic, editors Gray and Mentor assert that 'cyborgs offer a new map, a new way to conceive of power and identity', because they offer a way to conceptualize the construction of multiple subjects and the perspective of strategic (multiple and partial) subjectivities. The promise of cyborgs is tied to the way in which they are 'not just potential sites for enacting . . . new subjectivities; they are also internships and embodied practices in the modes of operation and power of material bodies politic of the 20th and 21st century' (459).

2. Posthuman Corporeality

Although the 'cyborg' has become a potent figure in recent cultural studies to name the condition of the human subject in late capitalism, other terms are used as the springboard for related, but slightly different projects. Addressing similar issues as the ones discussed in *The Cyborg Handbook*, Judith Halberstam and Ira Livingston's edited volume, *Posthuman Bodies*, includes several essays that extend the range of topics from those that focus on the relationship between the human and the technological, to include studies of the 'posthuman condition'. A foundational assumption for these critics is that the identity of the body has been reconfigured in postmodernity through the work of various 'posts': poststructuralism, postcolonialism, postindustrialism and, most broadly, posthumanism. Like the cyborg, the posthuman body is the site of multiple subjectivities: 'posthumans have been "multiply colonized, interpenetrated and constructed" – as well as paradoxically empowered' (10). Reading the narratives of posthuman identity is a shared methodological practice among the writers collected in this volume. The texts they read range from newspaper accounts of the trial of a person diagnosed with multiple personalities (Sandy Stone, 'Identity in Oshkosh') to advertisements for electronic appliances (Alexandra Chasin, 'Class and its Close Relations: Identities among Women, Servants, and Machine') to films (Paula Rabinowitz, 'Soft Fictions and Intimate Documents: Can Feminism be Posthuman?'). A notable contribution offered by this collection is a collection of essays in a section titled 'Queering'. These essays provide interesting statements about the queer 'nature' of posthuman identity. As the editors write:

> The posthuman body is not driven, in the last instance, by a teleological desire for domination, death or stasis; or to become coherent and unitary; or even to explode into more disjointed multiplicities. Driven instead by the double impossibility and prerequisite to become other and to become itself, the posthuman body intrigues rather than desires; it is intrigued and intriguing just as it is queer: not as an identity but because it queers. Queering makes a postmodern politics out of the modernist aesthetics of 'defamiliarization'. (14)

For example, in her essay in the 'Queering' section called 'The Seductive Power of Science in the Making of Deviant Subjectivity', Jennifer Terry investigates the paradox of queering when she asks why lesbians and gay men volunteer to be studied by those who belong to a profession that has historically, and to this day continues to pathologize, homosexuality. In her efforts to assemble a response, Terry reviews the history of the scientific study of homosexuality. As she reminds us, homosexuals have been (historically) constructed as deviant subjects by science and medicine. In the process of confronting a scientifically marked 'deviant' nature, homosexuals experience the construction of 'deviant subjectivity'. But as her historical review illuminates, the construction of deviant (homosexual) subjectivity is not singular, predictable or unified. It is instead a multiply constituted queer subjectivity that is contradictorily lived in relation to systems of power such as those represented by the institutions of medicine and science. In Terry's analysis of the construction of deviant subjectivities we read how 'being Queer in America is a posthuman agenda.' In this sense, 'being Queer' represents an epistemological position endemic to the posthuman condition – where the body and the self are always defined in reference to a network of signifying relationships, in the process both the body and the self are denaturalized and deformed, even as they are simultaneously disciplined and staged.

The focus on the 'body' – posthuman, cyborg or otherwise – has become an increasingly popular subject of scholarly attention during recent years for several reasons. In ways similar to Terry's review of the history of the scientific study of the homosexual body, other scholars have turned their attention to the role that the body plays in the historical development of other scientific enterprises. Jonathan Sawday, for example, examines the role of the body in the 'culture of dissection' that flourished during Renaissance culture. His book, *The Body Emblazoned: Dissection and the Human Body in Renaissance Culture*, is an extended study of the ideological treatment of the body during the early stages of the scientific enlightenment. He traces the treatment of the body as it is embedded within a cultural matrix that includes not only various literary and artistic works of the Renaissance period – works that are frequently studied by literary historians and critics – including the poems of Donne and the dramas of Shakespeare, but also the work of early physicians and scientists such as Robert Boyle and William Harvey. His point is to suggest that the birth of modern science and the emergence of an anatomical understanding of the body were equally influenced and expressed by the poetry and literature of the period. The determining factor for the birth of anatomical science was not the separation of the discourse of poetry from the discourse of reason. Rather, this separation, and consequential devaluing of the discourse of poetry as a 'rational' discourse, is a consequence of the early attempts to institutionalize a particular type of knowledge about the body. As he writes: 'the study of anatomy was in the forefront of the new philosophical regime. . . . The exploration of the body was paradigmatic of the possibilities of science itself' (231). In Sawday's book, we read how the 'body' functioned, historically, as a site for the working through of various cultural tensions – about the status of knowledge, of truth, of identity and of authority.

In more recent historical periods, we find that the body still functions as the site for the working through of cultural tensions. A new journal called *Body and Society* dedicated its first issue to the topic of the body in contemporary cyberculture. Subsequently, Mike Featherstone and Roger Burrows, editors for the journal issue, reprinted it in book form under the title *Cyberpsace, Cyberbodies, Cyberpunk: Cultures of Technological Embodiment*. This volume offers a comprehensive overview of the main topics of technological embodiment, including a discussion of the role of the body in the science of cybernetics, in virtual reality applications and in cyberspace. Featherstone and Burrows's Introduction offers an encapsulated overview of the key aspects of a 'cyberculture' as a new technocultural formation. They tease out the nuances of the use of the term 'cyborg' to name the identity of the human being in this new cultural moment. Moreover, they offer a taxonomy of concepts of cyberspace by describing the subtle differences between a 'Barlovian cyberspace' (named after John Barlow, a founding member of the Electronic Freedom Foundation) and those of Gibsonian cyberspace (named for science fiction author William Gibson). One of the key differences between this book and *The Cyborg Handbook* is the recurring attention given to cyberpunk science fiction in various essays in the Featherstone/Burrows volume, and the prominent role this literature plays in providing a narrative structure for the analysis of contemporary cyberculture. In this sense, the Featherstone/Burrows volume comes closer to providing a coherent analysis of the complex social structure of cyberculture by showing how it is multiply constituted by new sciences, new fictions and new forms of embodiment. The social theory that emerges from these essays, considered collectively, is a significant revision of traditional social theoretical frameworks. In other words, this volume suggests that the meaning of social life is as much a construction of our sciences, our fictions, our simulations and our bodies as it is a consequence of the interaction between social practices and disembodied institutions.

3. Cyberculture and New Information Technologies

Cyberculture is the name for an emergent cultural logic produced through our collective engagement with cybernetic technologies. These technologies, including new information technologies, electronic communication devices and new technologies of representation, are changing the topography of human culture. Not only are our bodies reconfigured in relationship to these technologies; so too are our social practices and forms of cultural expression. Not since Marshall McLuhan published *Understanding Media* has there been so much attention directed on the impact of new media on the shape of human life. Simon Penny's edited book, *Critical Issues in Electronic Media*, presents several essays that consider the impact that these new technologies have on artistic practice. As Penny writes in his Introduction: 'Pre-electronic cultural ideas like "plagiarism" and "fakes", and the value systems attached to them, conflict with media designed specifically for precise rapid copying: videotape, photocopying, and par excellence, computer media' (3). Here Penny identifies only one of the 'critical issues' provoked by the wide-scale availability and use of electronic technologies. As digital media offer new possibilities for the production and reproduction of artistic practice, so too do they demand something in return. As Penny argues, not only must we develop new frameworks for understanding the production and consumption of digital art, we must also build 'new aesthetic models, new ethical models, new institutions . . . and new conventions of consumption' (3). This, according to Penny, requires the development of an interdisciplinary framework of analysis that can take account of the many facets of a particular cybercultural formation.

    The first essay in the Penny book, 'Suck on This, Planet of Noise!' by McKenzie Wark, explicitly considers the impact of electronic art on the development of cultural criticism. Wark argues that 'electronic art is an experimental laboratory, not so much for new technologies as for new social relations of communication' (9). He takes issue with those critics who see in the new technologies a simple and unmodulated continuation of the sins of older technologies: cultural homogenization, alienation and cultural exploitation, for example. He cajoles readers to think historically, about both the history of criticism and the history of cultural change. To begin this project, he speculates about the 'third nature' of our historical moment:

> The passage from modernity to postmodernity seems to me to involve the passage from one form of abstraction to another – from the *second nature* of abstract social spaces created by sea and rail transport to the abstract communicational spaces created by the telegraph, telephone, television, and telecommunications. These are the techniques of telesthesia, of perception at a

distance. . . . The decline of modernity is in many respects a loss
of faith in second nature. (12)

'Third nature' is Wark's term for the (vectoral) power relations constituted and
circulated within electronic communication networks, where the belief in the
possibility of redemption is now not a matter of colonizing geographic territory
(as it was a part of second nature), but rather is a matter of additional
computational power and speed. 'With an extra ten megabytes I can finally
RAM down the doors of data heaven!' (12). Our second nature of cities and
roads has been etched over by a third nature of data flows and information
exchange. As Wark writes: 'Both postmodernism in theory and cyberspace in
literature are explorations of the landscape of third nature' (17).

Several other essays in the book implicitly explore the 'third nature' that
Wark theorizes. In an essay entitled 'Consumer Culture and the Technological
Imperative: The Artist in Dataspace', Simon Penny points out how the
material production of 'digital art' implicates electronic artists in the politics
of consumer culture by virtue of the technologies they use in the production
of their art. In this sense they are equally subject to the ideological impact of
such technologies. According to Penny, this makes the production of 'critical'
electronic art difficult, if not outright impossible, for several reasons. Not only
does the 'technological imperative' force artists to keep current in the use and
consumption of new technologies; when they do so they inadvertently
participate in a system that devalues the practice of art: 'The technology,
moreover, may have the insidious ability to reify a value system that precludes
art practice' (50). Electronic art fosters the development of conventions such as
collage, 'sampling' and other forms of 'appropriative creative practice' which
challenges, but does not overturn or invalidate, the power of current legal
systems of intellectual property and copyright. It is clear from Penny's article,
as well as others in the book, that electronic artists will be among the most
active and invested participants in the struggle to define the cultural landscape
of our 'Third Nature'.

As an extension of Wark's reading of the implications of the historical
transformation of a second nature into a third nature, other scholars have
focused their attention on what happens when these two natures collide. John
Pickles's edited book, *Ground Truth: The Social Implications of Geographic
Information Systems*, includes several articles that explore the practices of
geographic world-making aided now by developments in new information
technologies and surveillance devices. At the centre of this cultural formation
is the reinvigorated importance of the visual image and the logic of spatial
geographic mapping. The chapters collected in this book suggest that new
information technologies – the data flows and information vectors of our
'third nature' – are rewriting the contours of that second nature by literally
restructuring global, regional and local geographies. In this sense, our second
nature is being actively rewritten as our third nature evolves. Many of the
articles in this book take as their starting point a concern for the relation
between science and democratic society, where the use of geographic
information systems (GIS) is understood to involve a set of scientific and
technological practices that have profound social and cultural implications.
Although Pickles suggests that 'the chapters include detailed case studies of
the societal and disciplinary roles being played by technologies of surveillance'

(xi), there are actually few examples of concrete uses or misuses of GIS practices. Noteworthy is the discussion of the role of spatial GIS data in the historical implementation of apartheid in South Africa in Trevor M. Harris, Daniel Weiner, Timothy A. Warner and Richard Levin's chapter, 'Pursuing Social Goals through Participatory Geographic Information Systems: Redressing South Africa's Historical Political Ecology'. None the less, the book offers a thoroughly accessible and important introduction to the political implications of the development and deployment of such 'mapping systems'. Not only are the various aspects of GIS well theorized throughout the various articles, but the book offers a significant contribution to a developing theory of technological representation. For example, in their chapter, 'Earth Shattering: Global Imagery and GIS', Susan M. Roberts and Richard H. Shein examine advertisements that feature representations of world symbols: the surface of the earth as seen from space, iconic depictions of GIS information and globes of various sorts. Roberts and Shein argue that the use of such images in the representational space of advertisements functions to reinforce a visual regime of power and objectivism: they literally teach us how to have a 'world-view' that ascribes to the viewer/reader exaggerated notions of power and objectivity. Advertisements also normalize the representational practices of GIS by making such 'scenes' part of the iconography of everyday life. This, according to Roberts and Shein, is one of the ways that geographic imaging technologies are implicated in the reproduction of a dominant ideological project of control, manipulation and objectification of not only the world, but also everything in it.

Addressing similar concerns from a different, yet related, critical framework is the work collected in the book *Spaces of Identity: Global Media, Electronic Landscapes and Cultural Boundaries*, co-authored by David Morley and Kevin Robins. The authors' prime concern is the 'question of identity under the conditions of postmodern geography – specifically with the complex and contradictory nature of cultural identities and with the role of communication technologies in the reconfiguration of contemporary (and often diasporic) identities' (1). While the broad focus of the book is on European identities and communication politics, their more specific theoretical problem concerns the paradox between globalism and localism – between the 'deterritorialization of audiovisual production' and the development of transnational delivery systems, and the growing emphasis on local production and distribution systems. In contrast to Pickles's book *Ground Truth*, the technology in question here is not geographic information systems, but global imaging technologies. The shift is from thinking about technologies of representation – GIS in the above example – to a discussion of technologies of distribution and circulation – such as satellite television, cable television and cinema. Although Morley and Robins discuss the role that technology plays in the construction of national identities and an attitude of nationalism, they do not focus exclusively on the determinant effects of specific communication technologies. The book goes beyond a simple preoccupation with the export of images from Western (mainly US) nations to explore the multiple effects of a wide-scale global restructuring of identities and nations. In the service of reassessing the theoretical implications of charges of cultural media imperialism, Morley and Robins review the process whereby cultures construct notions of home, of self, of community, of time and, most centrally, of history. Taking issue with certain variants of postmodern theory that offer claims about the technological reconfiguration of identity tied to the development of global media, Morley and Robins assert that the impact of technological developments are differently and unevenly experienced in different national situations. The claim that postmodernity is a period marked by an increase in global connectedness is, according to the authors, a claim about the reach of American cultural imperialism; in this sense, 'global connectedness' is less a characteristic of an evolutionary, historical condition and more a consequence of the continued development of a particular world power bloc. This leads them to suggest, at the end, that one of the most significant consequences of US media imperialism is the erasure of national histories and specific national narratives of identity and community.

Books Reviewed

Featherstone, Mike, and Roger Burrows, eds. *Cyberspace, Cyberbodies, Cyberpunk: Cultures of Technological Embodiment*. Sage. pp. 280. $26.95. ISBN 0 7619 5085 0.

Feenberg, Andrew, and Alastair Hannay, eds. *Technology and the Politics of Knowledge*. Indiana University Press. pp. 288. $15.95. ISBN 0 253 20940 4.

Gray, Chris Hables, ed. with the assistance of Heidi J. Figueroa-Sarriera, and Steven Mentor. *The Cyborg Handbook*. Routledge. pp. 540. $22.95. ISBN 0 415 90849 3.

Halberstam, Judith, and Ira Livingston, eds. *Posthuman Bodies*. Indiana University Press. pp. 275. $17.95. ISBN 0 253 20970 6.

Morley, David, and Kevin Robins. *Spaces of Identity: Global Media, Electronic Landscapes and Cultural Boundaries*. Routledge. pp. 257. $18.95. ISBN 0 415 09597 2

Penny, Simon, ed. *Critical Issues in Electronic Media*. State University of New York Press. pp. 298. $19.95. ISBN 0 7914 2318 2.

Pickles, John, ed. *Ground Truth: The Social Implications of Geographic Information Systems*. The Guilford Press. pp. 248. $19.95. ISBN 0 89862 295 6.

Sawday, Jonathan. *The Body Emblazoned: Dissection and the Human Body in Renaissance Culture*. Routledge. pp. 327. $19.95. ISBN 0 415 04444 8.

Sclove, Richard E. *Democracy and Technology*. Guildford. pp. 336. $18.95. ISBN 0 89862 861 X.

18

Cultural Policy

ROBIN TROTTER

Although the texts on cultural policy reviewed here inherently integrate theory, history and practice, each tends to prioritize one of these perspectives over the other two. This, then, provides a basic framework for the review. However, intersecting these broad categorizations is a set of common concerns – national identity, civilizing mission, consensus and national unity, and relations between state and culture. Many of the concerns raised relate to common experiences, nevertheless the accounts of cultural policy initiatives in America, Britain and France reviewed demonstrate that historically constituted assumptions also frame national debates and give a national colour to these common concerns. At the same time these studies also reveal some nationally specific concerns and cultural policy initiatives.

This chapter has three sections: 1. Theory; 2. History; 3. Practice.

1. Theory

Cultural policy has developed as an empirical area of research and practice with its origins in a diverse range of theoretical traditions such as cultural studies and arts management. Sociology, economics and managerialist theories have been opening up the terrain even further to new interpretations; and even within cultural studies different perspectives are being proposed such as Tony Bennett's Foucauldian approach (see: T. Bennett, 'Putting Policy into Cultural Studies', in L.Grossberg, C. Nelson, and P. Treichler, eds, *Cultural Studies*, Routledge, London and New York [1992], and T. Bennett, 'Useful Culture', *Cultural Studies* 6:iii [1992]). It is this latter approach which Jim McGuigan takes issue with in '"A Slow Reach Again for Control": Raymond Williams and the Vicissitudes of Cultural Policy' (*European Journal of Cultural Policy* 2:i. 105–15). Bennett's argument is that neo-Gramscian cultural studies, in focusing over-much on the imposition of top-down power, is unable to deal adequately with dispersions of power, particularly as these are expressed through governmental instrumentalities and institutional organizations. McGuigan's response is to return to Raymond Williams to register his contributions to the critical analysis of cultural policy (as an activist in cultural policy areas such as the Arts Council, adult education and ongoing criticism in media and communications areas), to identify Williams's key theoretical arguments relevant to cultural policy (in particular his writings on democratic communications and technological determinism), and to flag the research possibilities of comparing and contrasting cultural materialism with Foucauldian analysis. In conclusion, McGuigan suggests that Bennett's work tends toward an ideology of 'managerialism' and in so doing reduces *praxis* to *techne* which, in turn, divests cultural studies of its 'critical edge'.

Against this theoretical debate it is interesting that the publication in 1995 of several histories of cultural policy are largely framed around Gramscian theory with the works of Bourdieu, Foucault, Poulantzas and so on playing a more subordinate role.

2. History

Two historical perspectives on cultural policy that probe the precursors of current cultural policies and contemporary debates, but from different national perspectives, are Robert Hewison's *Culture and Consensus: England, Art and Politics Since 1940*, and David L. Looseley's *The Politics of Fun: Cultural Policy and Debate in Contemporary France*. Both Hewison and Looseley look back to the 1930s and 1940s as critical years in which the ideological, political and ideational foundations were laid for nationalist cultural policies in, respectively, Britain and France. Issues central to both writers – but given different priorities – are those of consensus, nationalism and national identity, democratization, creativity, and the role of the state in relation to arts and culture. For both Hewison and Looseley the leading cultural policy institution in the state – the Arts Council in Britain and the Ministry of Culture in France – is a focus point.

Hewison's account of Britain 'in triumph and disarray' is somewhat less given to polemicism than his previous works and, as a consequence, somewhat less passionate. Drawing on the concept of consensus, which he defines as a theoretical parallel to Gramsci's notion of hegemony and, in historical terms as the 'broad national political agreement that has kept Britain's social and economic institutions functioning throughout the shifts of power between Labour and Conservative governments since the war', Hewison charts a 'decline of consensus' from the late 1970s. This culminated in the monarchical crisis of 1992 (the Queen's 'annus horribilis'). Also critical to Hewison's charting of the shifting fortunes of cultural consensus is the contribution, or lack of contribution, that Britain's intelligentsia has made to the construction and challenging of consensus. This allows him to draw into the discussion an account of Britain's Left.

Underlying Hewison's concern with culture and cultural policy is his belief that 'culture . . . is the shaping, moral medium for all society's activities, including the economic', and flowing from this a 'nation's culture is not a purely private matter nor a marginal public responsibility, but vital to national existence' (xiv). But the connective links between cultural activity, cultural policy and identity are tenuous despite the centrality given to the theme of a 'crisis of identity' (ranging from the national to the personal), and an assertion that this is a problem that artists are 'uniquely qualified' to address.

For the origins of the current situation Hewison returns to wartime Britain and the conservative traditions and values that proved hegemonic in defining 'Deep England'. These, he argues, were 'constructed as much out of folk memories, poetry and cultural association as actuality'. Nevertheless, they projected a new national identity – one built on shared war experiences and a common heritage.

The post-war period brought pressure for change: for removal of the old class system, for state control and educational reforms. These were confirmed with the rise of the welfare state with its origins in the Beveridge Report of 1942.

CEMA (the Arts Council's predecessor) was established in 1940 but even then contradictions were inherent in the problematic aims of preserving high artistic standards and of providing widespread opportunity for arts. These aims became the source of ongoing confusion between the interests of professionals and amateurs, between artists and audiences, and in defining standards that established as priorities professional organizations and metropolitan values. In 1945 CEMA became the Arts Council. The new agency inherited CEMA's 'cultural conservatism' and commitment to an 'arm's length' principle. But, as Raymond Williams later noted of the Arts Council, it achieved 'consensus by co-option', a process based on the British state's ability to delegate certain official functions to a

> whole complex of semi-official or nominally independent bodies because it has been able to rely on an unusually compact and organic ruling class. Thus it can give Lord X or Lady Y both public money and apparent freedom of decision in some confidence . . . that they will act as if they were indeed state officials.
> (R. Williams in R. Gable, ed., *Resources of Hope: Culture, Democracy, Socialism*, Verso, 1989, quoted p. 33)

By the early 1950s the Arts Council had undergone a shift from its original mission (preserving the highest standards, ensuring widespread provision of opportunities for artists, and enabling cultural activities of 'the people') to administering a safe metropolitan cultural consensus, consolidating its own power and strengthening its relationship with the establishment. It was, declared W. E. Williams, the Council's first secretary-general, 'an instrument of State patronage' (80).

Decade by decade, and with a broad but conventional brush, Hewison maps the ways in which consensus was maintained. Although the monarchy and its role as a consensual 'branding device' is a sub-theme running through the study, Hewison ranges widely to develop this argument. He covers the development of a cultural studies movement, challenges for reform in higher education, the 'counterculture', the women's movement, ongoing literary/ cultural debates, and debates about cultural regeneration. More critically, he identifies a number of shifting interpretations of consensus ranging from a new left-culturalism or liberal-culturalism which articulated a more popular approach to the arts and a dilution of elitism during the early 1960s, to the Labour Party's endorsement of a new concept of culture in the first-ever government paper on cultural funding, *A Policy for the Arts* (1964). This document announced: 'Diffusion of culture is now so much a part of life that there is no point at which it stops. Advertisements, buildings, books, motor-cars, radio and television, magazines, records, all can carry a cultural aspect and affect our lives for good or ill as a species of "amenity"' (122).

Despite these shifts, at a political level and within the Arts Council, consensus on welfare state ideology continued. This, however, began to fragment by the end of the decade.

Until the 1970s the relationship Hewison establishes between art and politics is again somewhat tenuous; however, with the election of Margaret Thatcher and the implementation of Thatcher-economics (Hewison's *bête noire*) the connections are more clearly enunciated. Crises of capitalism and social democracy led to breakdown of the 'contract consensus' by which both parties had governed. Thatcher's position was clear: 'I am not a consensus politician, or a pragmatic politician. I'm a conviction politician' (208). Despite this stance, Thatcher required a degree of consent to govern and maintain power, hence the strategy of an 'enterprise culture' based on law and order, the traditional family, and patriotism (see also J. Corner, and S. Harvey, eds, *Heritage and Enterprise*, Routledge, London [1991]). As Thatcher recalled in 1988: 'Economics are the method. The object is to change the soul.' This, according to Hewison meant that: 'The British soul was to be remade, by creating a new myth of economic individualism to replace the old ideas of community and collectivism' (212).

This political revolution was paralleled by a revolution in the arts: with new communications technologies, globalization of capitalism, and the shift from production of things to production of images and ideas. Commodification of information became a factor in the breakdown of barriers between high and popular culture, as did the postmodernist invasion of literature and introduction of new technologies, new creative forms and postmodern theory. Thatcher's enterprise culture was a fusion of these two revolutions. Under Thatcher cultural policy direction involved withdrawal of funds to individuals, division of responsibility for government funding of performing and creative arts between the Arts Council and the Ministry for the Arts, Heritage and Tourism, and devolution of Arts Council clients (and funding) to regional arts associations. By 1985 the arts were enmeshed in Thatcher's 'culture of wealth creation' and the arts had undergone a transformation to become the 'cultural industries'.

Hewison's concentration on consensus (and the ideological context) as the overriding issue in the history of British cultural policy designates the British Arts Council as an agent for forging cultural consensus and subordinates other issues, in particular that of democratization. Although the activities of the Arts Council and bureaucratic moves within the Council are well covered, there is little in-depth analysis of the Council or its real impact on British culture other than at a superficial level. This partly reflects Hewison's underlying theme that the Council is, in the main, an organization that has failed to develop innovative strategies to take up cultural initiatives; instead it has consistently taken a reactive role.

Looseley's more complex analysis of the history of cultural policy in France is facilitated by an integrated analysis that brings together institutional history and discourse analysis along with political and economic themes. His examination of the four dominant 'missions' of French cultural policy – conservation, creation, diffusion and democratization, and formation – and the shifting priorities given to each of these, provides an exploratory framework for analysing the relationship between culture, society and the state. Although the Lang–Mitterrand era (1981–95) is seminal to this study, the period's historical precursors are critical foundations which subsequent policy-makers built upon, reformulated or reacted against. Looseley examines the different strategic programmes by which the state's primary cultural body, the Ministry of Culture (created in 1959 under André Malraux) set about interpreting and implementing its responsibilities. Against a historical background of the Sun King, revolution and the Napoleonic state's administrative system established to oversee the nation's heritage, and the immediate precursors of the Popular Front, the Vichy and the liberation, Looseley argues (taking up an argument of cultural historian Pascal Ory) that a continuity in cultural policy runs from the Popular Front through to the present. However, in this broader pattern Looseley also identifies ideological shifts in response to political, cultural, social, technological and commercial developments as well as the personalization of cultural agendas by key figures, in particular Jack Lang, France's colourful Minister of Culture in the years 1981–86 and 1988–93, and President Mitterrand with his programme of *grands projets:* 'the grandiloquent cultural temples with which he recently transformed the face of Paris' (3).

Frontist cultural policy was a product of Communist theory and the French Communist Party's repudiation of national high culture as bourgeois and corruptive of authentic proletarian cultural practices. It also projected a wider notion of culture inclusive of youth, sport, popular education and leisure. Looseley argues that the democratizing accomplishments of the Front failed, however, to put cultural proposals into effect, proved incapable of overruling traditionalism and academicism, and displayed an overriding concern with disseminating an accepted 'national' culture at the expense of exploring new creative territories. Moreover, despite aspirations of reforming the state education system as a vehicle for achieving the objectives of a cultural policy, neither the Frontist government nor subsequent governments have successfully brought education into the remit of culture.

Whilst Britain in the 1960s was considering a new model of culture the new French Minister for Culture, André Malraux, was setting a democratizing agenda, albeit one with a 'nationalist edge' based on a traditional model of the *beaux arts* or the best of artistic achievement. Malraux's Fourth Plan (1962–65) established a commission devoted to creation (*action culturelle*) with three areas of responsibility: promotion of national heritage, encouragement of contemporary creation, and democratization. His strategy included expanding regional facilities and setting up of a nationwide network of 'houses of culture'. He has, however, been criticized for disseminating a Parisian high culture that contracted earlier concepts of culture as a broad field of activities. On the other hand, Malraux's measures for heritage did broaden definitions of national heritage and encourage its popularization.

In 1981 the socialists came to power under François Mitterrand. Jack Lang was appointed his Minister of Culture. Early in his ministry Lang defined his aim of achieving an integrated culture that would remotivate and dynamize French art and economy as well as provide the national community with a 'new morality', a new value system and a new lifestyle. There should be no hierarchy in ministerial terms or between major and minor arts. No one class or city should be privileged. These objectives represented a synthesis of various socialist party attempts to shape cultural policy through democratization, pluralism, creativity and difference, with the concept of an integrated global culture.

In summary, Looseley argues that in respect to high culture, the socialist government, on one hand cast itself in an 'old Left, old fashioned, high cultural image' that followed on Malraux's 'heritage–democratisation–creation trilogy', yet on the other, achieved a respectable budget increase, created a fund for national contemporary arts, revived the tradition of state commissions and attempted to restore a community function in theatres and centres of cultural action (EACs). In respect to popular culture, the socialist government moved to put more emphasis on creativity, pluralism and difference through its notion of *developpement culturel* in which a new department (Direction du developpement culturel) became the instrument of new policies. These new policies focused on decentralization, the recognition of new practices and publics and the cultural industries, and expressed a faith in local democracy and cultural specificity. To further these objectives, a programme of political and administrative 'colonization' of the regions by Paris was implemented with the decentralization laws of 1982 and 1983, the revival of the contracts policy of Michael Guy (Giscard d'Estaing's first Secretary of State for Culture), and the redressing of inequities of access to high culture for minorities and underprivileged groups whilst recognizing the cultures of such groups. These moves represented development of a regionalist policy at the same time as they advanced European integration.

Lang's support for the cultural industries was not only motivated by economic concerns. It was another strategy for tackling cultural inequalities in terms of creative forms instead of audiences and for dynamizing French society by encouraging creation across a range of new cultural forms that were so diverse that the policy became labelled as *le tout-culturelle*. However, achievements in respect to new publics and practices remained limited by funding constraints, various forms of resistance, and the Ministry's reluctance to cede power (and funds) to local government. Consequently, 'pursuit of a new cultural democracy was a policy more symbolic than voluntarist' (120). A compensatory move was promotion of a festive concept of culture to release energies and break down barriers between individual and collective, professionalism and amateurism, and culture and economy – hence the first Fetê de la musique in 1982 which involved a variety of festivities spread across France that came to represent Lang's trademark as leader of an 'image-conscious, media-wise fun culture' (122).

Mitterrand's trademark, on the other hand, was his commitment to the presidential *grands projets,* three of which, ironically, had been Giscard d'Estaing's initiatives. The programme would give Paris, and France, a number of sites which would contribute to the state's architectural heritage, enhance its international prestige and help restore its reputation as the cultural capital of the world. The programme would also provide jobs, keep traditional crafts and skills alive, and act as a showcase for French construction and design. Importantly, the programme would restore national self-confidence. Moreover, the projects would become

> beacons of socialist cultural policy as a whole, monuments to the boost given to creation. They illustrated the Ministry's belief in reinterpreting the heritage by commissioning new works like the Pyramid [in front of the Louvre] or by converting historic buildings to new purposes as with the Orsay station [converted to

a museum]. And in particular, they enshrined the traditional
conception of democratisation [particularly the Opera Bastille
conceived as an antithesis of the elitist Opera de Paris and La
Villette where science and art would be united and science and
technology demystified]. (141)

But here also, contradictions, and controversies, mark the intent and
effectiveness of Mitterrand's programme. He was accused of monarchism (*fait
du prince*) while the rhetoric of participation, communitarianism and democratization appeared at odds with the 'centralised, personalised and statuesque'
conception of the programme (151). The *grand projets* were, in effect, part of a
raft of other consensual projects: the prioritizing of national heritage, a crusade
to unify France and implementation of Lang's 'culture of fun'. And, in all this
Lang became, through his flamboyant public image and energetic capacity for
work and politicizing, 'a consensual figure bestriding the gulf between Left
and Right' (161). But, as Looseley suggests, the 'spell' was broken by the loss
of a majority by the Socialist Party in the 1986 election, and a series of
critiques that marked the emergence of a debate on cultural policy and state
intervention.

Looseley's suggestion that 'much of the sound and fury of the Mitterrand
years was in fact about an alleged ministerial drift from the humanist to the
anthropological sense' (4) demonstrates an argument common to Hewison's
claim that differing views of culture (culture as Matthew Arnold's 'best which
has been thought and said in the world' and culture as the common expression
of a people) became the 'fundamental issue' in post-war critical debate and
subsequent conflicts. This is only one of several points of complementarity
and difference between these two historical accounts.

The traditions of cultural policy hold that nations differentially construct
the relationship between state and culture, with Britain's 'arm's length'
principle being contrasted with the more direct state involvement in arts and
heritage that has prevailed in France. These are, however, simplistic readings of
relationships that have been, and continue to be, dynamic and complex.

An example of nationalized attitudes to arts is noted by Hewison when, in
1992, John Major established a new department of National Heritage to act as
a catalyst for generating new forms of funding. Hewison suggests this is, in
fact, a *de facto* Ministry of Culture:

> In almost any other country, this new department would have
> been called a Ministry of Culture, but the British have shown
> themselves uncomfortable with the idea of Culture, whereas they
> have become extremely comfortable with the word 'heritage'.
> 'Culture' still suggests at best the preoccupation of a snobbish
> intellectual elite, at worst a Stalinist state imposition promoting
> official artists backed by an overweening bureaucracy. (300–1)

In contrast, Looseley acknowledges in his introduction that France has always
distinguished itself from other nations by the state's direct intervention in
culture and by the investment of state powers in a Minister of Culture, yet, in
conclusion he asks how far the state should go in constructing national taste
and shaping national culture:

Is its task simply to go with the flow, to act as 'the nation's impresàrio' by providing improved access to whatever kind of entertainment today's 'customers' demand? Interventionism or *clientelism*. And finally, this dilemma points to what is possibly the most intractable problem of all for future policy . . . the contradiction between a state policy still dedicated to promoting a shared national culture . . . and one espousing a communications revolution which is steadily isolating individuals within their private domestic space, unpicking the very fabric of community life. (244)

Whilst France has been depicted as a model of state intervention in cultural affairs, and Britain as a model of an 'arm's length' relationship between state and the arts, the United States' might be more aptly described as a 'hands-off' approach. This would, however, ignore the role of state-funded agencies such as the National Endowment for the Arts and the National Endowment for the Humanities. It would also ignore an important period in American art history when the arts were drawn directly into the state's agenda of ideological and social reconstruction under the auspices of Roosevelt's New Deal.

Jonathan Harris's study of this period, *Federal Art and National Culture: The Politics of Identity in New Deal America*, is part art history, part sociological study and part cultural studies theory and technique. The analytical framework is a synthesis of critical Marxism and what Harris calls the 'social structuralisms' associated with Foucault and Bourdieu. But again, the dominant influence is Gramscian, in particular his notion of the 'national-popular' and how this was implemented in the discursive practices of the New Deal wherein an idea and ideal of 'citizenship' (and 'the people') became the central 'articulatory principle' (9). Poulantzas's notion of the state as an ensemble of institutions, powers and interests is also an informing reference for demonstrating how the Federal Art Project, from 1935 to 1943, through its practices and discourses, offered a 'different set of social, aesthetic and ideological priorities' that appeared to be 'antimodernist' and 'anticapitalist'. Harris's objective is to redress this elision of a decade of art and artists, and the historical neglect of a decade of state intervention into cultural production.

Adopting a methodology of discourse analysis of New Deal rhetoric allows Harris to avoid a tight chronological structure and to facilitate a thematic approach that engages with issues of modernism, national identity and populism through the ideas and practices of New Deal administrators. This is also a problem for the study in that the reader has little recourse, other than in the extensive and useful footnotes, to alternative readings of the period, or to the experiences of cultural practitioners or 'the people'.

This analysis of a project that was essentially 'small beer' within the wider agenda of the New Deal administration also provides insight into the ideology and effectiveness of Roosevelt's programme. Harris's argument is that although the New Deal administration presented itself as capable of resolving contemporary crises on the economic and political fronts by offering policies that promised a social utopia, its achievements were, at best, limited reforms, and, at worst, the preservation and deeper entrenchment of monopoly capitalism. As Barton J. Bernstein claims, the New Deal failed to raise the impoverished, it failed to redistribute income, it failed to extend quality and generally countenanced racial discrimination and segregation. It failed generally to make business more responsible to the social welfare or to threaten big business's pre-eminent power. In this sense, the New Deal, despite the shifts in tone and spirit from the earlier decade, was profoundly conservative, and continuous with the 1920s.

('The New Deal', in Barton J. Bernstein, ed., *Towards a New Past: Dissenting Essays in American History* [1968], quoted p. 180, n. 56)

The period also represents a break from the view of culture as elitist, separatist and alienated from society, and from the reality of an 'unstable and shifting' context for artists and the arts that the late 1920s and early 1930s brought. *Federal Art and National Culture* has a revisionary function to bring to light the challenge to a 'triumphantalist modernist philippic', and to aesthetic modernist ideas and practices. Its purpose is also to establish the American historical context of the shift in the meaning of culture (from an aesthetic and specialized activity to being representative of a whole way of life) and to show how this was mobilized by the New Deal administration for its political agenda of reconstructing American society and for repositioning the artist as citizen and as a productive worker in society.

In the first hundred days of his presidency (1932) Roosevelt supervised the creation of numerous federal agencies and legislative acts aimed at, first, relieving an economically demoralized population by introducing relief measures, employment agencies, distress relief boards, mortgage relief, public works agencies and the Civilian Conservation Corps, and, second, restoring American capitalism through Keynesian deficit-financing. These strategies have been variously described as a 'co-operative and progressive federalism', a compromise between *laissez-faire* capitalism and authoritarian statism, or a 'confined, confused, contradictory pragmatism which only reproduced monopoly capitalism'. The central agencies and organizations established by the New Deal administration to effect the programmes of artistic production, work creation and assimilation of arts into society included: the Civil Works Administration (established 1933), the Public Works of Arts Project (PWAP, 1933–4), the Section of Painting and Sculpture financed by the Treasury (1934–3), the Works Progress Administration (WPA, 1935–9), the Federal Arts Project (FAP, 1935–43) and the Treasury Relief Art Project (1935–43). Harris examines the roles of each of these subgovernment bodies and their effectiveness in ideological terms and practical outcomes.

The role of the state in administration of arts/culture was to be a central issue of New Dealism. It was, for example, the FAP's expansion of employment that became a central issue in conflicting representations of New Dealism. On one hand, this project was seen as an attempt to limit reform of capitalism in crises; on the other, it was represented as an attempt to introduce a 'transitional programme' designed to transform the United States into a socialist society. External opposition to New Dealism focused also on social, political and cultural issues; Congressional opposition to direct involvement in cultural production that by 1939 led to changes in the nature and extent of funding for New Deal projects. By the late 1930s New Dealism projects were being challenged as 'un-American activities', its work-creation schemes were attacked as wasteful and subversive; the programme products were criticized as 'bad art'; and the artists employed on federal projects accused of being at best, parasites, or at worst, communist agents. Increasingly state intervention was represented as totalitarian and 'socialist and realistic art' as the product of totalitarian regimes. Consequently, in the US context popular frontism was represented in negative terms in stark contrast to the French context. Increasingly vocal support was articulated for the superiority of private patronage of art, and for validation of European-derived modernist art theories and practices. Moves were made to 'relegitimise production of art in economic and social relations between private individuals and capitalist corporations and to reposition artists as dependent on market and individual buyers instead of part of a wage labour system' (153–4). Harris argues that tensions outside the Roosevelt Administration were also reflected internally with differences emerging between federal and local policy and implementation, and between liberal administrators wanting to save capitalism and those supporting socialist alternatives.

By the late 1930s and early 1940s state interventions had been modulated by Congressional pressures, the demands of rearmament and security measures. But, as Harris argues, this was not necessarily anathema to FAP thinking as Holger Cahill (National Director of the FAP) had, as early as 1937, advocated a shift to surveillance and regulation when he asserted 'The function of the state must be, paradoxically, both visible and invisible. . . . It must be visible because of the role of the state in constituting "the people" as citizens through diverse cultural activities. It must be invisible because there must never be any sense of "superimposed" or "arty" subject matter in these events' (114).

The New Deal ostensibly concluded with the end of Roosevelt's first presidential term (1933–1937), and this study of the FAP as a microcosm of New Dealism demonstrates the fragility of its ideology both within and external to the administration, the limitations to its agenda, and the politico-economic constraints that weakened support for New Deal programmes. At the same time, external factors (cultural and political events in Europe and the imminence of war) and domestic developments (dissolution of the Roosevelt coalition, rearmament and reassertion of a military-industrial corporate coalition and emergence of an anticommunist, security-driven ethos, a press increasingly hostile to the FAP, and an FAP that was internally centralized and ill-equipped to defend itself), provided both catalyst and fuel for conservative forces to regroup and re-engage with New Dealers. By 1944 the WPA had been given over to war services and its statewide projects closed. Support from artists' groups split, with many giving their support to the war effort. In 1940, arts critic Beyton Boswell claimed that there had been 'a return to aesthetics' and it was time for 'the fog of gloom that shrouded American painting during the terrible thirties' to be lifted (quoted 154). Despite the failure of the New Deal attempt to assert cultural democracy and the social function of art, Harris concludes that 'the state's use of cultural forms in aiding the construction of both internal (national) and external (international) hegemony did not end with the Federal Art Project or the War Services Program. Instead, the state's economic, political and ideological investments in culture have grown, increased in complexity, and become a permanent feature of late twentieth century societies' (157).

The legacy of the New Deal has been challenged yet again in 1995 when the Republicans carried a vote in the US House of Representatives to 'zero out' by October 1997 all funding for the National Endowment for the Arts (NEA), which had been founded in 1964, and to phase out the agency. In the Senate this decision was watered down to a 40 per cent budget cut for the NEA in 1996. Robert Hughes, in a *Time* cover story, 'Pulling the Fuse on Culture' (7 August 1995, vol. 146, no. 6) attacked the Republican leadership, Newt Gingrich and his fellow 'ideologues . . . including their insatiable Fundamentalist Christian right wing', the Reverend Donald Wildmon and his 'religious hit squad', the American Family Association, for their all-out assault on federal funding. The assault, Hughes argues, is 'unenlightened, uneconomic and undemocratic'. He denies the conservative economic argument. Their motive, he claims, is, in fact, 'cultural defoliation' – an attempt to destroy 'liberal habitat'. In terminating the NEA (as well as the National Endowment for the Humanities [NEH] and the Corporation for Public Broadcasting [CPB], which are also under attack) the conservatives will destroy the 'fabric of America's public culture', place America in the same category as Haiti, Zaïre, Rwanda and Iraq (the 'bogey boys' in an American hagiography), isolate it from 'more civilized' parts of the world, and eliminate 'our best guarantee that our cultural heritage will be available to all Americans, regardless of how much money they make or where they live'.

This is the latest development in the 'culture wars' that have engulfed the United States since the late 1980s, and which are the concern of Kevin Mulcahy and Margaret Jane Wyszormirski as editors of a collection of essays: *America's Commitment to Culture: Government and the Arts*. The 'culture wars' are also the concern of Jennifer A. Peter and Louis M. Crosier who have collated, in *The Cultural Battlefield: Art Censorship and Public Funding*, a series of accounts from activists on the frontline of the war zone.

The first of these anthologies, *America's Commitment to Culture*, comprises a collection of sociologically informed studies that, concentrating on the NEA, explore the history, controversies, organisational structures and state–agency relationships surrounding government support for culture and the arts in the United States.

Again a major concern is with consensus (or 'accord') between the state, the NEA and the NEH, and the public; however, the focus is on the NEA, the historico-political contexts in which it has operated, its internal structures and organizational practices, and its relationships with the government (in particular through the reauthorization process), the arts community (particularly through its panels) and the public. Wyszormirski and Mulcahy in 'The Organisation of Public Support for the Arts' (121–43), contend that American attitudes to arts have historically been 'ambiguous and contrary' and that 'neither the public nor its elected representatives have developed a clear public philosophy about the value and place of art either in their personal lives or in society at large. Therefore no consensus has evolved regarding the legitimate relationship between government and the arts in the United States' (121). The United States was backward in introducing a public art agency such as the Arts Council in the United Kingdom or providing state support such as in France or West Germany, and even with establishment of the Endowments in 1964, cultural programmes were fragmented through a range of agencies and congressional committees. That the government has eschewed the idea of establishing an official culture is, in part, a legacy of US history and, in part, a reaction to the New Deal era.

In this context, Wyszormirski sets the historical framework in 'From Accord to Discord: Arts Policy During and After the Culture Wars' (1–46). From its inception in 1964 to the early 1980s, the policy problem was defined as a 'distribution problem': how to provide cultural equity and maintain the nation's artistic resources. For fifteen years an activist and expanding state enabled the NEA to achieve policy objectives, but in the 1980s Reagan's attack on the welfare state (alongside international economic changes) provided a less supportive environment for the arts policy. When a series of public controversies broke out, the vulnerability of the NEA was revealed in the ensuring battle and 'the clamour from the right was joined by outrage from the left in a battle over community standards versus professional standards, of obscenity and blasphemy versus artistic freedom', with conservatives and religious groups on one side and the NEA and its artistic constituency on the other (4).

A factor in shift from accord to discord, argues Wyszormirski in 'The Politics of Arts Policy: Subgovernment to Issue Network' (47–76), has been developments in the concept of the role of arts policy. From a simple distributive policy implemented by a subgovernment agency, this matured into a tripartite system that involved the NEA, the arts community and its authorizing and appropriations subcommittees in Congress. However, in the 1980s a regulatory element was introduced around issues of tax revisions, copyright, record labelling, artists' rights and community standards. This brought into the equation new players and new policies. As a result 'since 1989 federal arts policy has changed from a subgovernment with politics typical of distributive policy to an issue network concerned with policies that encompass not only distributive, but redistributive and regulatory aspects as well'. The 1990s has seen this scenario exacerbated by regulatory conflicts that have reduced the arts policy context to a 'loose, volatile and conflictual issue network . . . characterised by debate over both indirect administration . . . and indirect decision-making' (70–1).

David B. Pankratz and Carla Hanzal, in an analysis of the structure and leadership of the NEA, in 'Leadership and the NEA: The Roles of the Chairperson and the National Council of the Arts', conclude that leaders 'can make a difference' and that successful organizations occur when there is a match between individual skills of leaders and organization tasks that is reinforced by historical conditions. However, in the case of the NEA few operational directives were established at the outset in order to allow flexibility. This has allowed different interpretations of legislation, so that 'what emerges is a set of recurring, perennial dilemmas over the respective roles and responsibilities of the Chairperson and the National Council'. Nor are the roles and relationships of the panels, arts community or the public defined or established in any way.

Mulcahy develops this argument by focusing on the reauthorization process in 'The NEA and the Reauthorisation Process: Congress and Arts Policy Issues' (169–88). Lack of legislative guidelines on purpose and policies, or guidance on programmes, standards or methods of decision-making has resulted in the NEA acting as a *de facto* policy-maker, with Congress perennially concerned about the nature of distribution of public funds, and whose values are being furthered by such grants. Consequently, the most persistent concern of reauthorization committees is the advisory panels – the third tier of the NEA structure from 1967. Mulcahy describes this panel system as 'the administrative bedrock on which the NEA has rested' and claims it has increasingly been expected to incorporate the political task of preventing the process being subverted to a 'cultural pork barrel' and an opportunity for 'artistic logrolling', and that this has taken priority over its distribution task of ensuring equity. Here the debate revolves around whether grants should be awarded for artistic excellence alone, as defined by the professional arts world, or whether grants should develop social and political values of 'cultural democratization'. This is a question that can also be interpreted in terms of choice between a metropolitan emphasis on established cultural institutions and organized arts groups, and a community emphasis predominantly on the sphere of grass-roots cultural groups and their congressional representatives. The underlying problem, suggests Mulcahy, is the lack of a national cultural policy. This vacuum has opened the door on political controversy and called into question the notion of public support for the arts. The NEA has failed to recognize its responsibilities to the US public, with its discipline-based panels being seen as interpreting public culture in terms of the interests of private culture to such an extent that the NEA 'came to look like a closed circle of cultural cognoscente practicing "cronyism" in the distribution of the "cultural porkbarrel"' (211). Mulcahy advocates reorganization of NEA goals and administrative procedures. First, he suggests a recognition of the public interest involved in public cultural policy; second, a shift from administration by 'art discipline' to administration by 'cultural objective' (such as institutional support, arts development, arts education, support for artists); and finally, a restructuring of the peer review process from discipline based to inter-disciplinary based and inclusive of representatives of the public at large. Ideally, then: 'Arts policy as a public policy will be most successful as it addresses both, the general cultural interests of the American public as well as particular needs of the various art disciplines' (220).

In *The Cultural Battlefield* Peter and Crosier have published a selection of accounts of the 'culture wars' that are personal, immediate, emotive and confrontational. They represent different perspectives (black and white), different positions (artists and administrators), yet articulate concerns that are not adequately addressed elsewhere. Here the issues are different – but interrelated: the special role of the artist, censorship, defence of the First Amendment, and protection of individual and artistic rights. And the contributors are also representative of a different community: the arts community in general, and more specifically, arts practitioners, gallery directors, activists, cultural administrators, consultants and advocates. Several of the accounts bring home the effects of conflict at an individual level such as Jock Sturges's description of the McCarthy-like invasion and destruction of his studio, his life and his work during two years of investigation by the FBI for suspected violation of pornography statutes ('Chronicles of an Invasion: A Personalised Account', 19–38); or Susan Wyatt's 'Setting the Record Straight: Diary of a Controversy', 77–105), which chronicles the 1989 withdrawal of an NEA grant for an exhibition dealing with AIDS, and argues that this was less a case of controversy over content than an example of a reactive response and mismanagement by the NEA in the context of the Mapplethorpe and Serrano furore.

Wyatt's work supports the argument of several other contributors that a repercussion of the culture wars is 'cultural self-censorship' both within the NEA as well as in cultural production in general ('Cultural Arson', by visual artist Jock Reynolds, 53–61; 'Confessions of a Literary Arts Administrator', by Liam Rector, director of Bennington Writing Seminars, 63–75; 'The P Question: A Satirical Examination of Self-Censorship', by Joyce J. Scott, 107–10).

As Jill Bond argues ('Rebuilding the Public Consensus behind Free Expression', 3–5), the artist's voice is 'crucial' to society: 'it informs how we think about our own lives and provides a bridge to understanding others' (3). But contemporary intolerance and an 'angry climate' has invoked efforts to silence artists by censoring their critical comments or advocacy roles: 'Every act of censorship represents a lost opportunity to engage the public in a dialogue about the issues involved and about the larger principles represented by the First Amendment' (4). Art's capacity to 'touch the raw nerve in society' and to expose social, moral and ethical issues draws censorial attention; similarly, systematic attacks on the NEA are, likewise, depicted as attacks on the First Amendment ('The Raw Nerve in Politics', Thomas Birch, 12).

The contradictory position of racism within the cultural debate is raised by Kimberly Camp ('A Brand of Censorship', 111–19). Camp notes that the arts community attempted to co-opt the support of African-American artists in the culture wars and in defence of the First Amendment, but points out that Eurocentric values inimical to those of people of colour form the 'backbone of American tradition', that the values and moral standards of African-American artists are more often aligned with conservatives, and that struggles over the Thirteenth and Fourteenth Amendment rights (ability to participate in democratic society without oppression and racism) are more important to the African-American constituency. In conclusion, Camp forecasts that until solutions to racism are found, 'other battles for equity will lose energy and be defeated for lack of sincerity' (119).

Ironically, apprehension of the imposition of a totalitarian culture is a legacy of the myth of the New Deal that has had a direct influence on the structure of the NEA and on its responses to criticism. In seeking to appease right-wing fundamentalists, the NEA has become complicit in imposing orthodox religio-cultural values on national culture.

3. Practice

Growing recognition of the need for governments to formulate specific cultural policy rather than the tradition of *ad hoc* and/or fragmented and compartmentalized policies is evidenced in developments of national policies and programmes, a recent example being the Australian government's cultural statement, *A Creative Nation* (1994), which called for a charter of cultural rights, and the UNESCO publication, *Our Creative Diversity: Report of the World Commission on Culture and Development* (1995), which included a chapter entitled 'Rethinking Cultural Policies'. Here, the key issues are those of cultural development, pluralism, broadening the scope of 'culture', national identity, new technologies, tensions between commercial and public interests in culture, government responsibility for culture, and cultural development and management. And the 'key challenge' is identified as a need 'to move from principles to practice'. The report also identifies a need to redirect cultural policies. In the 1980s Western European and North American urban cultural policies were designed with economic objectives, but what is now required, argues the report, is an approach 'more integrated with the cultural fabric of the city'. National cultural policies have, on the other hand, been directed more to nation-building, but based on limited concepts of the nation, of culture and of cultural activity. Participatory and pluralistic policies with more holistic concepts of culture are required. An exception cited is Sweden where a governmental cultural committee has proposed a broadening of cultural policy by recognizing that participation in cultural life be linked to areas generally considered outside the domain of arts, such as education. As the preamble to the chapter suggests: 'Our biggest problem in cultural policy is not, I would suggest, lack of resources, lack of will, lack of commitment or even lack of policy co-ordination to date. It is, rather, a misconstrual or only partial formulation and recognition of the policy object itself: culture' (Colin Mercer, from a paper given at the conference 'Enhancing Cultural Value', organized by the Centre for International Research on Communication and Information Technologies, Melbourne, December 1993).

The practical implications of cultural policy and cultural management were the topic of the 1994 Symposium on Cultural Policy and Management held at the University of Warwick, the proceedings of which were published in 1995 (*Cultural Policy and Management in the United Kingdom*). In the opening address ('Cultural Policy in the UK: An Historical Perspective') Oliver Bennett outlined the history of government intervention in culture in Britain from which he identified five rationales for government support of culture: *laissez-faire* doctrine, national prestige, economic importance of the arts, civilizing mission, correcting market forces, and post-war reconstruction and the welfare state. Four of these grounds, he argued, are no longer valid and, as a consequence, the previous consensus has now collapsed. It has been acknowledged that cultural achievement cannot compensate for loss of political and economic influence; numerous economic impact studies of the 1980s have discredited the economic argument; the idea of art, in particular European high art, has been challenged; given a more eclectic view of culture and dismissal of high forms of art over more popular forms, the argument that public subsidy is no more than a means to correct the market is no longer valid; and with the rolling back of the welfare state and social services the provision of cultural services has become unjustifiable. In conclusion, Bennett suggests two alternatives remain: to construct a 'new vision' that will win back intellectual and political support, or rely on the market as adjudicator: 'back to the old ideas of laissez-faire, but forwards to a new era of post policy, finally liberated from the last traces of dependency culture' (26).

The following discussions and papers addressed a variety of issues around the problems identified by Bennett, issues which in contemporary cultural practices are also being raised in a global context. Decreasing state funding has been a catalyst for exploring sponsorship models, but, as has been recognized elsewhere, sponsorship is proving less successful than hoped. Sponsorship cannot replace the loss of government funds, it introduces constraints on artistic development and content, and it requires arts organizations to develop new techniques and management practices. At the same time some potential strategies can open up through sponsorship. These include: partnership arrangements involving 'private and public sharing of responsibilities in culture'; and encouraging better management of arts and professionalization of arts organizations. Moreover, the skills and management techniques developed through sponsorship relations can be applied elsewhere: 'Once you learn how to research, negotiate, pitch, make a proposal, tie up a negotiation and sell, you can apply those skills elsewhere' (Ugo Bacchella, 'Business Sponsorship', 35–40, and response from Andrew McIllroy, 41–4).

Debates about sponsorship and arts funding link into a wider question about the relationship between arts, culture and the economy. This is a question with increasing validity given the growth in economic importance of the culture industries, cultural tourism, the electronic media and telecommunications developments. In this context, Peter Bendixen ('The Arts and Economic Development', 101–04) argued against a purely economistic approach and proposed that:

- To argue for arts funding on the basis of expected economic effects tends to neglect other important links;
- Effects of arts activities on the economic sector are not one-way impacts. Actions in social systems set processes going that spread through the network of links within the system with often unknown and far away impacts;
- Figures and statistics created according to schemes, which appear to reflect a neutral logic but which actually conceal an ideology, should be regarded with great caution;
- To find a working balance between preserving the arts and heritage and keeping them accessible for the public is not easy, but is feasible. 'Money speaks, and this expresses convincingly how the balance might easily be upset'.   (104)

Other issues explored by delegates covered cultural diversity (Mary Ann DeVlieg and Colin Prescod), the relationship between arts and the media (Adrian Litvinoff), and differences between British and European contexts for cultural policy. Some of the differences noted included the conflicting definitions of culture that, in turn, coloured different social and political evaluations of culture. Britain was seen to be characterized by its more marked class structure, a strongly centralized media, and marginalization of the artist in respect to cultural policy concerns with its concomitant effect on cultural policy. Britain's strong metropolitan and international ethos was also noted, as was a predisposition to ignoring regional issues.

Development and expansion of communications technologies, the implications for economic and industrial policy, and reconstruction of national political structures such as the European union are raising fresh concerns for cultural policy. In this context Philip Schlesinger and Gillian Doyle set out to examine the contradictions associated with the European Union's aspirations to create a new economic space for media whilst also constructing a cultural and political one ('Contradictions of Economy and Culture: The European Union and the Information Society', *European Journal of Cultural Policy* 2:ii.25–42). 'The current state of European Union policy debate', they argue, 'exemplifies with increasing sharpness the contradictory pull between industrial policy and cultural policy. We are being offered two quite distinct images: one of a society of consumers founded in notions of economic choice, the other – increasingly marginalised now at least in respect of media and communication policy – of a society of complexity rooted in persistent cultural difference' (26). They express doubts as to whether the European Union will be able, or willing, to balance the increased concentration, vertical integration (and power) of media conglomerates with resultant pressure for deregulation of markets and elimination of national controls, regulatory constraints, and political and cultural barriers (language, norms and values) against the imperatives of cultural and national pluralism and social interest.

The prevalence of analyses that concentrate on the relationship between economic and cultural policy-related concerns relates not only to new forms and fields of culture, but to culture in general, as is well illustrated in Trine Bille Hansen's study of Danish cultural policy ('Cultural Economics and Cultural Policy: A Discussion in the Danish context', *European Journal of Cultural Policy* 2:i.87–103). Drawing on cultural economics theory, Hansen's objective is to 'link the theoretical and empirical results and observations' from this area of study with 'practical cultural policy' in order to test the validity of 'welfare economic demand analyses' for the allocation of public subsidies to the arts (187). From the rationales for public subsidies identified in cultural economics literature (economic impact or stabilization function, production of public goods and values [allocation function]), and access (distribution function), Hansen analyses the effectiveness of different demand-oriented analyses (economic impact analyses, willingness-to-pay studies and measurement of cultural amenities usage), and concludes that, although these methodologies need further refining and tailoring to the particular conditions that characterize the area of arts and culture, they do have value for cultural policy.

Whilst some of the differing priorities articulated by the writers reviewed might be seen as products of alternative disciplinary and political perspectives, historical shifts in contexts also have a contributory function. Globalization, new technologies and exploration and implementation of social policies devoted to pluralism and diversity are all changing the expectations of cultural policies and research priorities of the field.

Books Reviewed

Bennett, Oliver, ed. *Cultural Policy and Management in the United Kingdom.* Proceedings of an international symposium, published by the Centre for the Study of Cultural Policy, School of Theatre Studies, University of Warwick, Coventry CV4 7AL. ISBN 0 9526831 0 5.

Harris, Jonathan. *Federal Art and National Culture: The Politics of Identity in New Deal America.* Cambridge University Press. pp. 236. £45.00. ISBN 0 521 44268 0.

Hewison, Robert. *Culture and Consensus: England, Art and Politics since 1940.* Methuen. pp. 366. £20.00. ISBN 0 413 69060 1.

Looseley, David L. *The Politics of Fun: Cultural Policy and Debate in Contemporary France.* Berg. pp. 279. £34.95. ISBN 1 85973 0132.

Mulcahy, Kevin, and Margaret Jane Wyszormirski, eds. *America's Commitment to Culture: Government and the Arts.* Westview Press. pp. 235. $59.50. ISBN 0 8133 0692 2.

Peter, Jennifer A., and Louis M. Crosier, eds. *The Cultural Battlefield: Art Censorship and Public Funding*. Avocus. pp. 179. $19.95. ISBN 0 9627671 7 4.

World Commission on Culture and Development. *Our Creative Diversity. Report of the World Commission on Culture and Development*. World Commission on Culture and Development, France. £22.00. ISBN 0 11984415 X.

19

Law and Culture

JONATHAN MORROW and NINA PUREN

This chapter has five sections: 1. Introduction: Theory and the Law; 2. Decentred Law; 3. Literature and the Possibility of Justice; 4. Limits of the Law: Theory in the Law School; 5. Conclusion.

1. Introduction: Theory and the Law

There is a sense in which law is one of the most volatile and productive thresholds for the project of critical theory and cultural studies, and by the mid-1990s this has become increasingly obvious. The already marked impact of critical theory on academic activity in Western law schools represents a major *coup* for the stakeholders – those legal academics working within new domains in the law school, and those practitioners of 'theory' who are increasingly preoccupied with the mode of knowledge that is the law. The volatility and magnitude of the *coup* is all the more remarkable since it has taken place against a background of increasing conservatism in the broader political economy. Moreover, this academic activity has had practical effect: it is already possible to point to real gains which have been made, against real resistance, on behalf of legal subjects who, for example, had previously been denied the protection and benefit of the law, or who had too long suffered the effects of deleterious legal intervention.

The nature of the collision between critical theory and the law can be identified in the collocation of concepts that surround law: first, when law is considered as a rational, positivist master narrative of the enlightenment; and second, when it is considered as a discourse. The concept of law as an enlightenment narrative is organized around a series of carefully policed coordinates: first, that it is a positivist apparatus that can apprehend 'the truth' of an event; second, that preconstituted, autonomous subjects come 'before' it to be judged; and third, that events in the world have a stable existence which can then be unproblematically reiterated in the courtroom. Connected to these points is the notion of law as a disembodied tool of abstract rationality, and thus preserved from the predations of cultural contingency and modalities of difference.

The most striking feature of critical theory's engagement with this model is its rewriting of the master narrative as a *discourse*. Far from being a simple change in nomenclature, this reconception radically alters the terms of the field. From this perspective, the following consequences can be unfurled: first, that law as discourse does not 'discover the true', but rather attaches particular *effects* of truth to certain statements and not others; second, that it produces normative subject positions and subjectivities; third, that the legal reiteration of an event is always structured by the genres and bodies of its *locus classicus,* the courtroom; and fourth, that just as the law's violence is discursive, legal doctrine can, in turn, be deployed as a tool for deliberate and consciously strategic interventions in a political sphere at the level of language. Law on this model is one discourse among many, with no discernible author, and cannot claim transcendent or even unique status. Derrida has posed the question as to whether the law is 'a thing, a person, a discourse, a voice, a document, or simply a nothing that incessantly defers access to itself, thus forbidding *itself* in order thereby to become something or someone?' (see 'Before the Law', in Derek Attridge, ed., *Acts of Literature* [New York: Routledge, 1992]).

To figure law in this fashion is also to alter its role in general cultural transformation. If law is no longer a master narrative, then to pose it as a privileged site of reform may be to reiterate its own notion of itself as central. As Rebecca Huntley et al. have noted:

> Often forgotten . . . is the reality that law, as a vehicle for social conciliation, is considerably limited. Law students are apt to immerse themselves so deeply in the discourse of law that they lose the capacity to view society outside that rubric. In reality, the law is not necessarily the most constructive tool for solving problems, whether public or private.
> ('Talking with the Teachers', *Polemic* 6:58)

Similarly, in *Law's Desire: Sexuality and the Limits of* Justice Carl Stychin observes:

> The role of law in inscribing, constituting and regulating [identity] proves important. At the same time, it also must be recognised that law is not an 'all-powerful' discourse. Too often legal scholars place law in isolation at the centre of struggles for (or against) social change. On the other hand, scholars in other disciplines are sometimes dismissive of the role of legal discourse. Neither position is viable. (9)

This attitude, steadily gaining ground as critical legal theory becomes more institutionalized, is one that reveals an important tension in the move to pose law as a discourse: first, law is cast as just one of many discourses, with its privileged enlightenment status (and pre-enlightenment status) correspondingly diminished (competing most prominently with discourses of, for example, medicine, public administration, sociology and economics); while second, there is a need to identify law as an important, even crucial, site of critique, since the effects that law produces, even as one discourse among many, are so powerful and ubiquitous.

In this contemporary context, law is no longer quite so capable of conceiving of itself as being nothing more than a pragmatics, or as being capable of theoretical articulation only through idiosyncratic, self-serving jurisprudences based on legal process and 'fundamental rights'. A point has been reached, at a political level, where the law can no longer pretend, either to itself or to the wider community, that it is a prior term, an institution that is ahistorical and unified. The law curriculum in the Western law school may still be dominated by positivism – and may continue to be so for the foreseeable future – but there can be little question that, as a result of multifarious political struggles within the corridors of humanities departments, theory has written itself on the body of the law.

2. Decentred Law

The volatile interaction between law and cultural studies/critical theory, however, is not taking place only within the enclaves of the law school and legal profession to which theory has been imported. There are, as well, instances where 'pure' or 'high' critical theory in one form or another has been invited, or forced, to countenance claims made by legal discourse. And it is arguable that interactions of this latter variety are currently providing the most interesting examples of work in this interdisciplinary area.

Indeed, if law is beginning to claim the attention of theory, it is significant that these claims have most often been recognized by people working outside a 'legal' environment. It has been noted frequently, for example, that philosophers inside, but also outside, Europe are once again becoming involved in public debate not only about issues of ethical and political theory, but also about more concrete issues in business and law (see, for example, Nussbaum's remarks in *Poetic Justice: The Literary Imagination and Public Life*). One may speculate that this trend is, in large part, a residual and perhaps unpredictable effect of the fact that legal education in most Western countries has, at least until recently, strictly separated practice and theory, typically relegating the latter to a status which is inferior or negligible. This has been the unhappy fate even of those theories which are produced by lawyers for legal consumption (liberal/positivist jurisprudences). It is a highly political pedagogic move which has had the effect that traditionally trained lawyers are, as such, ill-equipped to appreciate the scale and complexity of the theoretical and philosophical importance of law. By default it has been left to theorists, remote from the law school, to establish much-needed connections with the law. Another important indirect effect of legal pedagogy has been the establishment of a relationship between law and theory that is characterized by mutual hostility. There is now outside the legal academy a widespread perception of a juridical stupidity, a tunnel-vision that, as Bruce A. Arrigo has put it in *Radical Philosophy of Law: Contemporary Challenges to Mainstream Legal Theory and Practice* (edited by David S. Caudill and Steven Jay Gold): 'is constituted through law's claim to truth manifested in its lofty vision of itself – even more striking than exercising power in concrete effects (judgments) is its ability to disqualify other nonlegal experiences or knowledge, or to relegate them to second-class status' (90). At any rate, we are faced with the paradoxical situation in which the most important legal thought seems to be finding expression outside the law school. The discursive nature of the law is far more powerful and complex than lawyers have allowed themselves to realize. In particular, law is increasingly being selected from the field as being a crucial linguistic agent to the extent that it constructs and problematizes the relationship between language, desire, transgression and violence.

In large part the terms of this problematic derive from Marxist work conducted in earlier decades, and it is worthwhile briefly rehearsing this work here. Marx had posited law as 'only the official recognition of fact' (*The Poverty of Philosophy*), and refused to see political life regulated by law. Within this model, law is merely a disguise for the ugly face of property relations. Instrumental Marxists typically set law aside as a mere epiphenomenon and fetish of capitalism which would, at least on the Leninist view, vanish as the capitalist state is dismantled. Law emanates from pre-socialist historical and economic conditions, and is not part of the economic substructure. Marxists deny the inevitability of law, placing trust in the informal, customary prescriptions and prohibitions that hold a culture together. To this extent, even bearing in mind Aleksandr Zinoviev's proleptic statement that a society of terror is 'a civilization without law', law has not been seen as a contested site for Marxism. Indeed, if Marxism is the originary 'critical theory', Marxist indifference to the law can be seen within a great deal of critical theory writing. Foucault's concern with power, inasmuch as it is invested in non-juridical sites, may owe more to Marxism than is commonly thought.

However, Marxism has occasionally attempted to present law as a crucial agent to the extent that it can be redefined as the minion of ruling-class interests. Evegeny Pashukanis, for example, claimed that notions of the abstract legal subject with universal rights could be traced directly to commodity exchange taking place in the competitive capitalist marketplace. (This is explored in Dragan Milovanovic's 'Postmodern Law and Subjectivity: Lacan and the Linguistic Turn', in Caudill and Gold's *Radical Philosophy of Law*.)

Gramsci suggested that law, legal institutions and legal discourse are part of the process by which dominant elites and classes strive to maintain power and hegemony in a society and are resisted. It has been acknowledged that the law poses difficulties for instrumentalist Marxism because law is, at least ostensibly, autonomous, functioning independently of the will of particular groups or individuals. Judicial personnel are independent of political parties and, in the West at least, a strict separation of powers is maintained between the judiciary and the legislature and executive.

Post-Marxist theorists have attempted to show that law, as a discursive formation, nevertheless reflects and articulates the form of capitalism itself and that law operates more powerfully as an ideological, discursive apparatus than as a coercive apparatus (Althusser). Raymond A. Belliotti, in 'The Legacy of Marxist Jurisprudence' (*Radical Philosophy of Law*), shows not only how Marxism impacted upon American legal realism in the 1920s and, later, upon critical legal studies (CLS), but how it has informed contemporary feminist struggles: MacKinnon's arguments, for example, that law inadvertently contributes to the hegemonic process that reinforces gender hierarchy, owe much to Marxist accounts of law – as Wendy Brown, in her essay 'The Mirror of Pornography' (in *States of Injury: Power and Freedom in Late Modernity*), also reminds us. Belliotti also traces Marx's influence on critical race theory.

Some recent Marxist work which sets law firmly on centre stage includes David Ingram's 'Legitimation Crisis in Contract Law' in *Radical Philosophy of Law*. Ingram shows how contractualist assumptions have permeated liberal democratic theory from its very inception, and have continued to thrive in the political and legal institutions of the welfare state. In Ingram's view contractualism becomes a vital term in political critique because it operates as a barometer of the social antagonism permeating capitalist society, for the reason that it presupposes the separation of public reason and private interest. This is a view which is shared by, among others, Patricia Williams in her book *The Rooster's Egg*.

Reconceptualized in this way as an apparatus and as an ideological discourse, legal practice has introduced theoretical and political concerns which cannot be ignored by those who wish to advance forms of neo-Marxism. It also remains clear that it is a Marxist paradigm which continues to suggest that critical theory should not merely appraise and criticize, but should either dismiss or, more recently, subvert and decentre, the project of law.

Non-juridical models of power, discipline and governance advanced by Michel Foucault rival Marx's work in their ability to direct attention away from the politics of substantive law. Such poststructuralist interventions into law which have been made are frequently overlooked when theoretical projects are officially mapped out. In *Unpopular Cultures*, for example, Steve Redhead remarks that writings on the history and politics of poststructuralism have tended to ignore more recent forays into legal theory (of Foucauldian and feminist varieties), noting that the bulk of poststructuralist theory is inspired by semiotic analyses and expounded on the pages of literary theory and cultural studies journals such as *Textual Practice* and *Cultural Studies*.

However, Foucault's work has not always had this effect. In some of his later essays, Foucault had called for a new economy of power relations, and suggested (for example) that legality should be investigated by examining the field of illegality. Despite the sparseness of Foucault's own work on legal institutions, it is becoming increasingly apparent that law is crucial to poststructural enterprises; indeed, few disciplines are more eligible for a Foucauldian analysis than the law itself. This is now being reflected in a renewed interest in the legal implications of Foucault's idea of 'participatory democracy'. This interest is represented this year in Ian Ward's *Law and Literature* (see below for review). In *The State and the Rule of Law* (original publication 1979, first English translation 1995) one of Foucault's collaborators, Blandine Kriegel, has subjected the law – and specifically the state under the rule of law – to a searching examination using Foucauldian and poststructuralist vocabulary. Kriegel takes up the idea of pre-nineteenth-century, pre-biopolitical sovereignty, only touched upon by Foucault in *Discipline and Punish,* and calls for a political or 'juridico-institutional' method of history, as distinct from a Marxist/Romantic emphasis upon economics and society. Kriegel attempts to rehabilitate the idea of the state under the rule of law, arguing that sovereignty is an obstacle which must be overthrown in any gravitation towards totalitarianism. Thus does an investigation of the field of illegality reveal the need for legality. Kriegel endorses the link between morality and law which was forged by Spinoza and Kant, and later (unsuccessfully) defended against Fichte and German romanticism by Hegel. It may be that, in the course of her sustained argument, Kriegel fetishizes (or reifies, to use the CLS term) certain categories such as 'the rights of the individual' and 'the common law', but her work is of considerable importance if only to the extent that it posits law and legal history as a basis from which to mount a critique of power and its relation to ethics. In particular, she calls for a deeper understanding of the familiar micropolitical and social sphere which is defined by law, the recognizably Foucauldian level of 'fact' and 'event'. She complains that: 'our own political science is so taken with revolutions and grand movements in politics that it neglects the legal niceties of day-to-day governance and rarely conceives of power in terms of law' (58). Kriegel rethinks the law not by exposing its partiality, but by suggesting its presence as a political institution whose genealogy reveals a resistance towards certain forms of domination and absolutism.

In what is perhaps a more conventional use of Foucault's work, Ros Mills in her paper 'The Confession as a Practice of Freedom: Feminism, Foucault and "Elsewhere" Truths' (*Law/Text/Culture* 2.101–27), redirects Foucauldian concerns back towards the law and, like Kriegel, to the micropolitics of the courtroom. She examines Foucault's discussion of the confession and the way in which the confession is implicated in the exercise of truth as an exercise of knowledge/power. In the context of the trials of women who kill, she argues that the confession is pivotal, not only to the outcomes of the trials, but to the way in which women's subjectivity is constructed. Mills notes that in Foucault's work on the confession, there is an emphasis upon historical moments of domination at the expense of resistance. Mills performs a close reading of the trial in the Supreme Court of Queensland, Australia of Tracey Wigginton, who was one of four women charged with the seemingly random murder of forty-seven-year-old Edward Baldock. In a confession to the police, Wigginton took full responsibility for the killing. Mills reads this confession: 'to see if – at the extremes or limits of discourse . . . at the extremes or limits of "woman as victim versus woman as predator", of woman as the unconscious bearer but not the articulator of truth – there is a place within liberal/legal "language" for an ethical female self' (112). Mills concludes that, contrary to what might be expected from her use of Foucauldian vocabulary, Wigginton's confession and her subsequent guilty plea disrupt medico-legal discourse and situate her, if only precariously, inside/outside the dualisms of domination and resistance, and place her, if only momentarily, in the position of 'an ethical female self in connection with other women' (116). By this argument the juridism of the courtroom is shown to be yet another site for productive power and resistance.

Indeed, it is arguably feminism which is, more than any other praxis, responsible for presenting law as the crucial object of critique for critical theory. Carol Smart in *Law, Crime and Sexuality: Essays in Feminism* articulates many of the strands of postmodern legal feminism. It was not until Smart's writing appeared that Foucault's theory concerning power–truth–knowledge was fully applied in the area of jurisprudence. *Law, Crime and Sexuality* brings together the various trajectories of Smart's work over the last ten years, in the areas of feminism, criminology, jurisprudence and critical theory. For Smart, the law – a heterogeneous ensemble of discourses and bodies – is one of Western culture's most powerful technologies for the production and reproduction of gender (191). This position marks the latest transformation in feminist theorizations about law, which has travelled from a narration of the law as a sexist institution (187–9), to a consideration of law as a masculine institution (189–90). Smart explores the limitations and possibilities of each of these articulations, and then outlines her own. Following Judith Butler in *Gender Trouble* (1990), Smart conceives of the law not as an apparatus that acts upon preconstituted women and men, and then treats them inequitably (that is, law as a sexist institution); rather, she identifies the law as an apparatus that demarcates and reiterates sexually and racially different bodies in the first instance. (See also Kendall Thomas, in *Constructing Masculinity* 1995, who discusses this issue in relation to masculinity.)

From this position, Smart variously tracks the production of 'the prostitute', 'the rape survivor', 'the bad mother', 'the criminal woman' and 'the sexual woman', noting that these legal apparitions have material effects upon women who come before the law. (See also Helen Koureskas, 'In a Different Voice: The Prostitute's Voice', *Australian Feminist Law Journal* 5.99–110.) Smart's examination of the discursive constitution of the female body in no way signals an abnegation of the reality of violence (a common charge laid with poststructuralist and postmodern theorists: see particularly Friedrichs and Schwartz, 'The Value of Postmodern Theory to Critical Criminology: Violence against Women and Corporate Violence' in *Legality and Illegality: Semiotics, Postmodernism and Law*, edited by Richard W. Janikowski and Dragan Milovanovic). Rather, it is a recognition of the fact, first, that violence between sexually and racially specific subjects is made possible by the discourses that constitute them. Secondly, it is a recognition of the fact that the exigencies of the courtroom mean that for the law, the only meaningful existence that violence possesses after the event is discursive. Thus, an examination of the subject positions offered to women in legal discourse is imperative (221). Smart, however, goes on to reaffirm her commitment to the discipline of sociology, with the warning that by focusing on the Woman of law, theorists must remember the women who come before it (231). In making this distinction, which can appear a reinstitution of the 'real' versus the 'discursive' opposition, it must be remembered that Smart has already demonstrated that every woman is already saturated with the various discourses of 'Woman', so that the binary is a spurious one (101–23). Most importantly, for Smart, unlike other theorists, the analysis of Woman/women is not mutually exclusive, but rather mutually implicated and necessary.

Smart maintains a profound ambivalence about the possible relationships that feminism can forge with law, consistently articulating the danger that feminism can become complicit in the overlegalization of everyday life, if it continues to privilege legislative solutions to the ethical dilemmas of patriarchy. In this way, then, she remains wary of the project of feminist jurisprudence(s), despite its transformative intent, because by definition it 'retains law as the central focus of feminist strategy' (184). She also outlines the epistemological problems involved in departing from (the fiction of) a 'unitary' set of principles, that is, 'feminist', that would lay the foundation for law, a move which of course risks exchanging one set of totalizing procedures for another (184). While convinced that traditional jurisprudence must be subjected to a vigilant feminist critique, for Smart the response should be perhaps 'resistance, rather than calling for more law' (184).

Throughout this text, Smart maintains her commitment to the recognition of difference, even if this makes the production of an homogenous feminist strategy unworkable. In many ways, it could be said that it follows from Smart's commitment to the poststructuralist and postmodern feminist position that any engagement with law is both necessary and impossible.

One fascinating example of a necessary engagement with the law, played out within the law's logic but on feminist terms, can be found in Therese

McCarthy's '"Battered Woman Syndrome": Some Reflections on the Invisibility of the Battering Man in Legal Discourse, Drawing on *R v Raby*' in the
Australian Feminist Law Journal 4.141–52. In this article, McCarthy considers
the limits of the 'battered woman syndrome' (BWS) defence in Australian
criminal law, and traces a possible solution to the difficulties that it presents.
BWS was developed to redress the legal situation in which women who kill
abusive partners are unable to plead self-defence, because of the structure of
that law. However, as McCarthy explores in reference to *Raby*, the defendant in
that instance was only able to use BWS for 'the partial defence of provocation,
not the defence of self-defence, which could have led to a full acquittal' (144).
Further, BWS 'pathologises and medicalises' the actions of the woman, with
an explicitly normalizing effect. The construction of a 'syndrome' means that
in a legal context, the heterogeneous responses that women may have within a
violent intimate relationship must be subjected to the law's understanding of
what that syndrome involves. To successfully signify as such a subject, the
woman's reactions *must* converge with those reactions that the law recognizes
as 'authentically' BWS, or else the woman may find herself outside of the
purview of the defence.

Most importantly, BWS erases the actions of the battering man. The lethal
force used by the defendant in *Raby* was in the context of an eleven-week
marriage in which Keith Raby subjected her to: 'constant sexual assaults,
humiliation, and degradation in the form of him defecating, urinating and
vomiting on her. She was constantly threatened with the possibility of
mutilation and death, as Keith Raby's *modus operandi* was to place lethal
weapons throughout the home for ready accessibility to threaten and injure
Margaret Raby' (141). McCarthy notes the 'invisibility of any kind of
condemnation of the acts perpetrated by Keith Raby in the judge's sentencing
remarks, and in the subsequent media coverage' (142).

McCarthy explores the different legislative issues around codifying, and thus
making visible, the different forms of abuse which provide the context for
women who use 'lethal force' (146). She also includes suggestions for judge's
directions to the jury which do not construct the violent man as a villain, but
rather underline the systematic and pervasive nature of violence against
women in our culture (149).

In this way, then, McCarthy hopes to institutionally highlight men's
violence, and contextualize self-defence in this kind of case. It is a reform
suggestion that is designed to help those women who come before the law; it is
not presented as a solution to the problem of male violence generally in our
culture. McCarthy concludes with Smart's double warning about using the law
in this fashion: that while reform can potentially extend the hegemonic influence of law, phallocentric practices can not, however, go unchallenged (151).

Beverly Horsburgh in 'Lifting the Veil of Secrecy: Domestic Violence in the
Jewish Community' (*Harvard Women's Law Journal* 18:spring) also attempts to
make male violence legible in the context of Orthodox Jewish culture.
Horsburgh points to the extremity of the problem facing Orthodox women –
up to 20 per cent of whom face violence in the home (175, n. 5) – and goes on
to discuss the explicitly patriarchal aspects of Orthodox culture which create
conditions of marked gender inequality. Horsburgh focuses particularly upon
Jewish divorce law, which can only be brought by the husband, thus leaving
many women trapped as *agunah* (neither married nor unmarried) for years.

Horsburgh insists that the Jewish community acknowledge the public status of Jewish women, and not perpetuate their concealment and isolation in violent homes. She ends her article with two prayers to be included in the synagogue's public worship: the first articulates a genealogy of battered and defamed women through the Torah, and the second establishes the contemporary battered woman in solidarity with them.

Margaret Thornton's 'The Gender of Judgements: An Introduction' (in *Public and Private: Feminist Legal Debates* edited by Margaret Thornton) explores this point further, in relation to the gendered nature of epistemology in the courtroom. Her point of departure is the very contemporary question of whether women judges would make a substantive difference to the way that law is enacted. From there, she considers what male judges do when they call on 'common-sense' and 'experience' in a range of diverse and troubling cases. On examination, these purportedly neutral concepts are seen to have a phallocentric basis. For example, Justice Bollen of the South Australian Supreme Court in *Johns* used the concept of 'human experience' to demonstrate that women fabricate claims of sexual assault. He further claimed that it was 'acceptable' for a husband to use 'a measure of rougher than usual handling' to 'persuade' his wife to intercourse (271). This was a case involving anal rape and rape with a bottle. As in *Raby*, the violent man in *Johns* had his actions rewritten or erased. Thornton's article provides striking evidence of the political and *embodied* context of any institutional renarration of an event.

Wendy Brown in *States of Injury: Power and Freedom in Late Modernity* offers a brilliant analysis of the contemporary political scene in America, with similar emphasis on the production of subjectivity. Through a series of connected essays, she explores the way in which particular modes of oppositional politics ironically end up reinscribing the formations of power which they seek to transform. She attends very closely to the materialization of the subject through regimes of unfreedom, and the consequent resistances within that subject to a radically democratic politics. In the context of feminist theorization about the law, she offers a highly original reading of Catherine MacKinnon in the essay 'The Mirror of Pornography'. Her preoccupation is the very important question as to why MacKinnon's form of radical feminism has had such extraordinary political purchase in America, as opposed to the more complex poststructuralist feminisms, which have no comparable hold over the mainstream political scene. After outlining the limitations of MacKinnon's translation of a Marxist analysis for 'feminist' purposes, Brown argues that, ironically, MacKinnon has succeeded in ontologizing the gendered terms of pornography. She 'encodes, the pornographic age as the truth rather than the hyperbole of gender production: [she] fails to read the $10 billion a year porn industry as a "state of emergency" . . . of a male dominant heterosexual regime' (88). Further, she argues that MacKinnon's theory of gender transpires within a pornographic genre itself, in terms of its modes of substitution and its chains of prohibition and transgression (91). In this way, Brown concludes, she offers mainstream politics an easily recognizable model of ontologized gender and sexual pleasure. Brown's work underlines the risks involved in any engagement with discourses of the state.

The work of Drucilla Cornell in *Imaginary Domains* converges with and extends Brown's position on MacKinnon in this context. Cornell, like Smart, is wary of reiterating the law's authority as the central site of reform and transformation; however, as she points out, the law's saturation of everyday life, its role precisely as producer of subjectivity, means that it cannot be ignored. In *Imaginary Domains* Cornell develops, through Lacanian psychoanalysis and Rawlsian jurisprudence, the idea of 'minimum conditions of individuation', an idea based heavily on 'bodily integrity' and put forward as a means of developing an adequate conception of a legal theory of equality and as a means of moving away from a system of 'negative freedoms'. Using this framework, she proceeds to analyse the law of abortion, pornography and sexual harassment, proposing new definitions of seemingly familiar legal categories.

So in the context of pornography, for example, Cornell supports the concept of a civil statute which would protect 'the minimum conditions of individuation' of workers in the industry, conditions which include freedom from degradation by way of protection of their 'imaginary domain'. However, Cornell does not support legal interventions in the style of Dworkin/ MacKinnon, in so far as they reify the subject positions articulated in heterosexual pornography as 'the true'. For Cornell, the sexed subject positions offered in the straight pornographic scene do not exhaust the imaginary domains of all individuals. Like Brown, Cornell argues that MacKinnon's conflation of the scene of pornography with the nature of sexual difference is itself a pornographic move – it takes porn literally. Instead, Cornell reads straight male porn through a Lacanian lens as a parable of castration anxiety. Rather than imposing legal restrictions, she recommends the production and proliferation of other sexual imaginaries.

In this way, Cornell distinguishes between a political and a legal response to pornography, advocating in particular that women outside the sex industry support those women acting inside to unionize and gain control over the production of films and images. She supports legal zoning of porn, on the basis that the inappropriate visibility of the images in some spaces may restrict the imaginaries of women. Accordingly, Cornell is only interested in the regulation of graphic images, not the written word. She is concerned with the 'passing glance' and its direct effect on women in their daily lives; Cornell's reasoning here seems to be the potential for the immediate impact contained in the image. We would have liked her to develop this point further, since it is such an important one.

Ngaire Naffine in *Gender, Crime and Feminism* has produced a fascinating collection of articles in the field of feminism and criminology this year. (See also *Gender and Crime: An Introduction* by Sandra Walklate.) In an illuminating introduction, 'Feminism and Modern Criminology', Naffine tracks the various positions that feminism has taken up in relation to criminology; and most interestingly in this context, these positions can be seen to echo the history of feminist encounters with the law. Feminist empiricism, for example, worked uncritically with the methods and assumptions of the criminological apparatus, and saw its role as adding information about women to a system that was to be left effectively unchallenged. This approach assumed the positivist principles that underlie traditional readings of law, in terms of the notion of a gender-neutral methodology apprehending an already constituted world, which the criminologist could take as his (*sic*) unproblematic object. Feminist engagements with criminology have since put these propositions into question in a variety of ways, including interrogating the subject position of the criminologist, and examining the conditions of the categories that criminology as discourse uses to 'know' the world. Naffine has provided a number of key articles from the various moments of this engagement, giving the reader a good overview of the critical scene.

The idea of law – and criminology – as discourse has propelled legal debates into what might be termed postmodernist theory, where law has not typically been the subject of scrutiny. So much so that Steve Redhead in *Unpopular Cultures: The Birth of Law and Popular Culture* observes that some writers in the United Kingdom, including Stephen Pfohl and Norman Denzin, have moved directly from being practitioners of criminology into high priests of postmodern theory (40). In the United States, the critical legal studies critique of legal rights and legal subjecthood ('rights discourse'), often performed in the name of postmodernism, has led to a retaliation by some feminists and critical race theorists against that postmodernism, a retaliation which has ramifications for 'theory', particularly as it relates to transatlantic debates surrounding textuality and political action.

It is interesting to note that much writing in the area of postmodern legal theory adopts a millenarian tone which is open to highly conservative interpretations. Gary Minda, for example, in *Postmodern Legal Movements: Law and Jurisprudence at Century's End* frequently makes such disturbing observations as this:

> By the end of the 1980s, the jurisprudential 'stew' had simmered to a boiling point. . . . The Generation X of future lawyers, judges, and legal academics is coming of age during an extremely contra-dictory and confusing era in legal education. It is experiencing the breakdown in the theories of law that had defined traditional jurisprudence. The breakdown is a manifestation of the skepti-cism and criticism of the current intellectual and social condition. This generation, Generation X, belongs to a particular epoch, namely, that of postmodernism. (68)

Minda sees jurisprudential studies not as undergoing a transformation, but rather as 'in decline', afflicted by 'a general disenchanted condition that has affected contemporary legal scholarship – *postmodernism*' (79). A crisis in representation which Minda identifies in legal thought becomes an impasse. It is perhaps not surprising that those for whom most is at stake in law's transformation are often highly critical of any 'postmodernist' conception of law in its endgame.

Critiques of postmodernism, however, are often as misguided as post-modernism's defence. Friedrichs and Schwartz in 'The Value of Postmodern Theory to Critical Criminology: Violence against Women and Corporate Violence' (*Legality and Illegality: Semiotics, Postmodernism and Law*) provide an exemplum of the backlash against postmodernist theory from the field of law. For the authors, the postmodern 'rejection' (147) of categories like 'state' and 'working class' means the destabilization of critical criminology's founding agenda. That postmodernism does not so much 'reject' categories, as subject their functioning (that is, their exclusions and effects) to a critical analysis appears lost on the authors.

Their critique goes on to establish a series of binaries, in which postmodernism is opposed variously to any form of effective political action.

For example: 'The problem remains as to whether the discourse now being recommended advances our understanding of the suffering of real people, or whether it becomes increasingly irrelevant to us' (152), and 'Those who do not agree with postmodernism tend to find the core experience outside the realm of language, and to find that "word games" tend to trivialise or diminish their view of the essential nature of violence' (152). These formulations oppose postmodern theory to the domain of the real and suffering body, and admonish the postmodern concept of textuality for its incapacity to deal with violence. In this way, critical criminology is able to claim an unmediated access to this suffering body, and to establish violence as a self-evident and transparent event in the world.

The functioning of a rape trial, however, which by definition is inevitably immured within the postmodern problematic of signification, would suggest that Friedrichs and Schwartz are mistaken in this regard. The event, the 'truth', of which the trial is concerned to find has already occurred, and within the legal system can only have a meaningful existence as a narrative, whether that be medical, psychiatric or legal. Rae Kaspiew in 'Rape Lore' (*Melbourne University Law Review* 20:2.350–82) examines the legal stories that circulate in trials that make sexual violence against a woman's body anything but transparent. Kaspiew specifically examines the destiny of the raped woman's narrative of the event, from the police statement (which Kaspiew calls the 'documentary starting point' of the case, 357), to the cross-examination. The woman's story suffers infinite transformations as it is translated from legal genre to legal genre, with the telling and retelling subject to the exigencies of legal method: that is, principles of relevance, rules defining procedures and general principles of jurisprudence (357–8). And of course, as Kaspiew remarks, the narrative that is catapulted into this metamorphosis is already one that has succeeded in signifying as a rape worth prosecuting; many kinds of sexual assault must be expelled from this domain of signification so that these rapes can even begin to circulate, in particular the sexual assault of those women, such as prostitutes, deemed to be worthy of less protection than more 'respectable' women.

Kaspiew explores the profound phallocentrism of the law's response to rape, in the context of Victorian's criminal justice system, which has actually undergone quite substantial feminist reform (see 'Rape: Reform of Law and Procedure', Victorian Law Reform Commission report no. 43, [1991]). The discursive existence of the event of rape is extremely unstable: the actions of the woman in the real, and the narrative of her actions during her cross-examination by the defence, are separated by the 'perceptual chasms' that Kaspiew identifies. In the six cases that she examines, the already highly edited and constrained police statement – which constitutes the survivor's only real chance to tell her story – was subject to a series of aggressive rewritings at different stages in the court process. In this way, rape and internal damage were turned into 'tender loving care' by the defence barrister in *Ellis* (357), and a man who had assaulted two women other than the rape survivor was described as having a non-violent history by the judge presiding over another case, that of *Stanbrook* (363).

The actions of women in a sexually violent culture are perpetually rewritten in this fashion, by the hegemonic discourse of law, so that the actions of a woman in a rape encounter are never separate from the potential for this unjust and damaging revision. Contrary to the claims of Friedrichs and Schwartz, her actions do not exist in a context in which their meaning can be made transparent: the moment in which those actions are re-enacted, discursively, is the moment in which the body of the woman is subject to, and inseparable from, the body of the law. Kaspiew thereby recoups a postmodern account of law, and problematizes suggestions that an appreciation of narrative indeterminacy is politically enervating. (See also Lisa A. Binder, '"With More than Admiration He Admired": Images of Beauty and Defilement in Judicial Narratives of Rape', *Harvard Women's Law Journal* 18:spring, 265–301.)

Alinor Sterling in 'Undressing the Victim: The Intersection of Evidentiary and Semiotic Meanings of Women's Clothing in Rape Trials' (*Yale Journal of Law and Feminism* 7:i.87–132) provides an explicitly semiotic analysis of the rewriting of rape in the courtroom. By focusing on the function of women's clothing in a series of rape trials, she shows the way in which the necessary *recontextualization* of the garments in a conservative courtroom context works to create the image of the provocative woman: that is, the clothing worn in a context outside of the courtroom is bound to be less demure than that worn inside it, thus creating a negative differentiation in the minds of the court. Clothing is used in this context in an explicitly metonymic fashion: a short skirt can be made into a sign of consent to full intercourse in the narrative of the defence (115–20).

If these discursive and semiotic rewritings seem to be the destiny of every narrative told within the courtroom, what will be the fate of those that are told by speakers whose first language is not English? *Language in Evidence: Issues Confronting Aboriginal and Multicultural Australia*, edited by Diana Eades, is a collection of essays that superbly charts language as a field of violence – both in terms of the relation between the dominant language and those marginal to it, and in terms of the specific register differences within the courtroom scene. Of particular concern to this collection is the status of the Aboriginal person in the courtroom. Aboriginal people are consistently denied access to interpreters at each stage in the court system, from the giving of the police statement to the cross-examination. Despite the 1966 International Covenant on Civil and Political Rights, and the 1966 International Covenant on the Elimination of All Forms of Racial Discrimination, there are no statutory guidelines in Australia which enshrine the right of every person to have an interpreter (11). Judicial discretion thus determines the participants' access to this facility, and the authors of this collection note that access is consistently refused. As Cooke notes (73), this refusal was often at the request of legal counsel, whose strategy to 'upset, unsettle, confuse or otherwise intimidate such witnesses through an aggressive barrage of questions' was often thwarted by interpreters, 'if only through impeding the pace of ques- tioning, or through relaying the questions in a more civil (and therefore less threatening) tone of voice. Also, the word-traps that can be set by counsel are commonly, often inevitably, defused in the translation.'

The standard expectation of the interpreter's role is that they are to provide a '"word for word" or "literal" translation without altering the meaning of the communication between lawyer and witness or judicial officer and witness' (19). Of course, this configuration does not begin to approach the cultural, linguistic and conceptual difficulties involved in courtroom translation. For example, there have been several inadequate attempts to produce the oath in Aboriginal languages in a way that makes it meaningful for the participants (47–4), and the author notes that, in another cultural context, 'a Zulu equivalent to guilty has yet to be "fully developed" ' (49).

As well as the extreme conceptual difficulties involved in interpreting the text of a trial for an Aboriginal participant, one must also consider the profound discursive differences between English and Aboriginal languages. For example, as Cooke documents extensively, the adversarial question–answer structure of the cross-examination, in which counsel asks questions and cuts short the response of the witness, tends to be considered highly offensive and inflammatory in any Aboriginal social context, and effectively ensures that the witness remains tense. Also, the respect accorded to the aged in Aboriginal communities is often realized, first, in a reluctance on the part of young witnesses to challenge those who command respect out of age and status – such as barristers – and secondly, in the offence given to an elderly witness when their testimony is questioned.

Thus, despite the fact that the participants in the courtroom are speaking what is ostensibly the same language, justice for witnesses in this situation is consistently compromised. The courtroom does not provide a transparent window onto the event that has occurred prior to it. Instead, the legal-discursive apparatus actively produces the event in a very specific way. Language, narrative and discourse, then, are entirely implicated in structures of violence.

Narrative coherence and incoherence recur as preoccupations in work which is now being undertaken in the newly emerging field of psychoanalysis and the law. Steve Redhead, in *Unpopular Cultures*, speaks for a growing number of writers when he argues that poststructuralist writings on law have moved on to an important and fruitful terrain when trying to theorize 'desire' and particularly the complex and fraught field of legal desire or 'the desire of the law' (82). He goes on to say that: 'without a theory of legal desire, theorising of subjects-in-law remains in a pre-structuralist or structuralist quagmire. A notion of the "sliding signifier" always already underneath the signified is helpful here. The idea of the body-in-the-law . . . could be re-posed in this context, as well as, to mistranslate Pierre Legendre, "the love of the law" ' (83).

Slavoj Zizek, in 'Ideology Between Fiction and Fantasy' (*Cardozo Law Review* 6.1511–32) uses psychoanalysis to develop a theory of legal desire that would describe the disjunctions that, in the modern world, lie between 'the Public Law' and its 'ritualistic obverse' (1530). This disjunction has important political consequences for Zizek, who sees the interruption between law and ritualistic phantasm as opening up the way for totalitarianism. Dragan Milovanovic in 'Postmodern Law and Subjectivity: Lacan and the Linguistic Turn' (in *Radical Philosophy of Law*) also indicates how the law is exemplary of the Lacanian conception of desire and the symbolic order, because in law, narrative coherence is a function of subjects embodying desire within legal categories and within acceptable semantic and syntagmatic structures: 'To be in the law is to insert oneself in these discursive subject-positions and to confine oneself to the dominant discourse of the courts. Accordingly, some voices are heard in court; many, however, are not. . . . Women . . . are denied a full voice. They are, according to Lacan, relegated to pas-toute' (43). It is precisely this denial, understood in Lacanian terms, which prompts Drucilla Cornell in *Imaginary Domains* to mount her powerful idea of the legal right to the 'minimum conditions of individuation' upon a Lacanian 'imaginary domain' which can be explained in terms of the mirror stage. And if women are denied a full voice in the law, then on a Lacanian analysis the law is also unable to provide coherent support for masculinity. Kendall Thomas also returns, in *Constructing Masculinity*, to Lacan's observation that although the father must be the author of the law, yet he cannot vouch for it any more than anyone else can, because he, too, must submit to the bar, which makes him, in so far as he is the real father, a castrated father.

However, it appears that psychoanalytic legal theory can offer some promise. Writing in the same volume as Milovanovic, David Caudill provides an account of critical-legal theorist Peter Gabel's reflections on collective desire, which Caudill argues 'provide a richer analogy between the critical-legal and the social-psychoanalytical projects' ('Re-Returning to Freud: Critical Legal Studies as Cultural Psychoanalysis', in *Radical Philosophy of Law*). Caudill sees in Gabel's work the possibility of a transformation of legal and social structures by renouncing reality, 'not in the mode of repression, which hampers the possibilities of the present under the impact of an unlived and untold past, but in the mode of a liberation which, comprehending the past and demanding a new future, condemns the present' (53). Although the work is not fully developed, it is becoming apparent that psychoanalytic jurisprudence and the writing of legal desire are having a marked effect in the areas of feminist and queer legal theory – perhaps precisely because of its apparent promise of liberation.

For Delgado and others writing within critical race theory, narrative has a radical function. It is not used to provide the privileged with access to difference, as some strands of law and literature movement would claim (see Martha Nussbaum, *Poetic Justice: The Literary Imagination and Public Life*); on the contrary, it is used to critique the conditions of economic and racial privilege itself. This position has been challenged by some writers as ignoring the potentially damaging effects of an unrestrained proliferation of legal narratives; however, Delgado maintains that narrative in this context will function to 'test and challenge reality, to construct a counter reality, to hearten and support each other, and to probe, mock, displace, jar or reconstruct the dominant tale or narrative'. Delgado uses this model to great effect in *The Roderigo Chronicles: Conversations about Race and America*, in which he constructs a narrative encounter between himself and a young law student, a man of indeterminate age and ethnicity (xviii). Delgado creates an interesting rhetorical effect by setting the militance of the law student against the more circumspect and cautious figure of the professor. These fictional constructions provide the occasion for an analysis of racism in the United States in many dimensions: the interpersonal, the political, the institutional. Their staged discussions range from the failures of affirmative action legislation to the ontological role of democracy in maintaining racist oppression. While their relationship is basically unsatisfying from a 'literary' point of view, the conceit of 'a conversation' allows enormous freedom for Delgado to think through legal and ethical strategies to transform a racist culture.

Delgado's edited collection *Critical Race Theory: The Cutting Edge* offers a comprehensive overview of work done in the area, which Delgado notes follows several main themes: 'the call for context, critique of liberalism, insistence that racism is ordinary and not exceptional, and the notion that traditional civil rights law has been more valuable to whites than to blacks' (xv). The essays collected here are an excellent illustration of the extremely complicated ways in which law is taken up by critical theorists: it is posed as deeply implicated in structures of racist violence ('Documents of Barbarism: The Contemporary Legacy of European Racism and Colonialism in the Narrative Traditions of Federal Indian Law', Robert A. Williams, Jr), and thus for some, engagement with it for radical ends is seen as impossible. Girardeau A. Spann, for example, in 'Pure Politics', details the US Supreme Court's negative response to claims made by minorities, and recommends minority activism in the political process instead, where the values in place are overt rather than covert. Delgado, on the other hand, in an early essay which is collected here, 'Words that Wound: A Tort Action for Racial Insults', still poses law as a site of useful engagement, while acknowledging the limitations of trying to fight racism with legislation. This collection demonstrates that in the struggle against institutionalized oppression, every point on the field must be occupied, and that a heterogeneous approach complicates and strengthens the form of the attack.

Patricia Williams's *The Rooster's Egg* also extols the utility of a hetero-geneous approach and the radical possibilities of narrative – or, indeed 'narrative jurisprudence'. Although not highly theoretical, Williams (once again) draws the discourses of law, race, sex and class into a sustained critique of US identity politics. In the midst of, and perhaps in defiance of, criticism of autobiographical legal scholarship (see Anne M. Coughlin's 'Regulating the Self' in *Virginia Law Review* 81:5.1229–340), Williams seamlessly incorporates personal narrative into her objective analysis, and makes striking connections between race and the often neglected discourse of class. Although suspicious of law's claim to be a central agent of progressive social change, Williams is aware of the alarming fact that law, for all its multiple and distressing faults, is already under siege from a theory which is as 'bad' as critical race theory is 'good': that is, the 'law and economics' school of (most famously) Richard Posner and its endorsement of the marketplace as the arbiter of social value. Where Williams is able to admit that the seminal US Supreme Court decision in *Brown v Board of Education* shaped the possibilities of her life, she must also complain that, 'legal discussions involving housing, employment, and schooling have shifted from the domain of civil rights to that of the market and thus have become "ungovernable", mere consumption preference' (18). Williams goes on:

> those who by one set of criteria are living in states of cultural, economic, or physical subjugation may be redescribed as ineffi-cient wealth maximizers, mere depoliticized shoppers who are irrational and undeserving by either choice or resistance. A model of constitutional jurisprudence based on this contractarian vision therefore fails to anticipate the situation in which an aggregate of private transactions in a society begins to conflict with express social guarantees: those express protections or ideals are robbed of their force as law and become 'external', implicit interference.
>
> (103)

The emerging field of queer legal theory has also derived from a feminist and postmodernist recognition of the importance of narrative, subjectivity and performativity. Michael Dobber is able to point to future work that would be able to link more complexly the detailed and instantiated work of the law and the construction of sexual identity. In 'Hegemon: Tracing Power Through Bodies of Law' (*Law/Text/Culture* 2.61–99) he writes, for example:

> There must be more to a new oppositional jurisprudence than the cry for 'common-cause signifiers', like 'queer'. . . . What we need is a model of power, and hence a jurisprudence or theory of 'legal power', that is capable of mapping the processes by which identity and experience and voice are produced. . . . Hence a politics/micropolitics of generation – of bodies, of subjects. (91–2)

Wayne Morgan in his article 'Queer Law: Identity, Culture, Diversity, Law' (*Australasian Gay and Lesbian Law Journal* 5.1–41) provides an excellent ground for just such a project. (See also Sarah Zetlein, 'Lesbian Bodies Before the Law: Chicks in White Satin', *Australian Feminist Law Journal* 5.49–64.) Morgan maps the political trajectories of 'gay liberation' and 'queer' in terms of their very different relations to the law and, in particular, critiques the commitment of gay liberationists to unproblematic, liberal conceptions of 'the law', 'justice', 'the state' and 'gay' or 'lesbian' identity. Reform on this model involves an affirmation of the homo–hetero binary, and the struggle to demonstrate that gays and lesbians can be 'as good as' heterosexual citizens – 'good parents', 'good teachers', 'good soldiers' for example (29). As Morgan explains, this strategy does not interrogate the construction of these categories, which are predicated, institutionally, on the exclusion of gays and lesbians for their coherence. Working for assimilation into the purview of these categories serves only to 'reinforce, legitimate and recreate the dominant culture' (29). Following Smart, Morgan contends that the liberationist project confirms the hegemony of law by posing it as a defining centre of culture, with the power to designate certain stories, identities and knowledges as 'the true' (37). A queer approach to law seeks not to augment this situation, but rather to decentre it. Morgan documents the continuing homophobia of supposedly 'reformed' legislatures, noting that, for example, 'In 1989, convictions for consensual male/male sex in the United Kingdom were four times greater than in 1966 (the year before decriminalisation)' (19). The homosexual community thus cannot entrust the outcomes of activism to legislation: 'the homophobia of law . . . is just as apparent in law's "gay friendly" voice (decriminalisation and anti-discrimination discourse) as it ever was in the former "gay unfriendly" voice of law in the past. Queer strategy thus does not revolve around reforms, but around transgressive readings of the corpus of legal knowledge: its texts and other forms of discourse' (37).

To this end, Morgan borrows the concept of 'vengeful counter-surveillance' from queer historiographer J. Terry, who adopts the role of 'deviant' in her readings of hegemonic texts. This position enables the theorist to expose the partiality of dominant discourses about homosexuality, and to chart its institutional pathologization. The deviant reader is able to track the law's production – not just repression – of homosexual subjectivities.

However, this 'vengeful counter-surveillance' is not a practice limited only to the critique of the legal system:

> we must remember that law is only one of the discourses along with others which construct views about homosex. The power to control is located within and among many discourses and is countered by directly challenging the truth claims of those discourses. Achieving legal reforms does not, of itself, do anything to contest this power. 'Vengeful counter-surveillance', on the other hand, is a technique which can be used by gay and lesbian theorists to directly dispute the law's claim to 'know' our lives'.   (41)

(See also Amy D. Ronner, '*Bottoms v Bottoms*: The Lesbian Mother and the Judicial Perpetuation of Damaging Stereotypes', *Yale Journal of Law and Feminism* 7.307.)

Carl Stychin, in *Law's Desire: Sexuality and the Limits of Justice*, also takes up the theme of law's relative importance for the constitution, consolidation and regulation of sexuality, and in particular the hetero–homo division, relying heavily upon the work of Judith Butler. Stychin sees the importance of law as great. In an argument that is reminiscent of those put by abortion activists in the United States, Stychin details the way in which US government funding decisions have proved to be at least as important as legal rights when it comes to the public articulation and presentation of gay and lesbian identities – his example is the recent controversy over the policies of the United States' National Endowment for the Arts, policies which, he argues, had the effect of a denial to gays and lesbians of the right to political expression and equal protection of the law.

Most interestingly, Stychin argues that law is not simply prohibitive regarding sexuality. He does not adopt the term 'vengeful counter-surveillance', but nevertheless emphazises: 'Legal "prohibitions" can inadvertently create discursive spaces for the articulation of the identity of the excluded "other" in a field of legal and political contest (7). Stychin discusses, in this context, the struggle in late 1980s Britain over section 28 of the Local Government Act and, more generally, laws prohibiting the publication of gay male pornography. Stychin continually links these legal contexts – and others – back to the production of identity, and to the gay identity in particular, the 'paradigmatic postmodern entity' (111), and he stresses the law's unconscious importance in revealing the failure of the universal conception of the subject.

But it is telling that Stychin, optimistically, sees resistance borne of law as potentially 'liberating' (55), facilitated by an exercise of 'liberatory imagination' (73); there is, in Stychin's vocabulary, not only an eroticized resistance (*pace* Butler) but also potential redemption to be enjoyed as an unintended by-product of homophobic legal surveillance. Law is cast as the unwitting agent of postmodernism, and against Stychin's stated intention, the law tends to become, once again, reified as an enlightenment, even quasi-theological presence.

One of the most radical recent perspectives on the relationship between theory and law is offered by Steve Redhead in his collection of essays, *Unpopular Cultures: The Birth of Law and Popular Culture*. Hoping for a broad view by standing back from the whole 'law and theory' phenomenon, Redhead seeks to show how the law is prolific in the production of cultural artefacts, and identifies the need for cultural theory to accommodate this production; that is, for cultural theory to colonize the law. He states: 'There is an urgent need, in my view, to narrate the (hi)story – or indeed, more accurately, (hi)stories – of a specific regime of power/knowledge which I have labelled as "law and popular culture"; in other words, to tell tales of its formation, scope and influence' (2). Redhead argues that the academic disciplines of jurisprudence, the sociology of law and the sociology of deviance have themselves helped to create and sustain, as well as criticize, a global popular culture industry. In this context he anticipates and encourages the formation of an aesthetics or erotics of law. For Redhead, law is crucial to cultural studies precisely because law is disintegrating; that is, the legal modernism of the law school is, in Redhead's view, currently fragmenting in such a way that law's power to regulate and discipline the boundaries of certain social discourses and practices is disappearing. It is worth noting that Redhead is highly critical of much 'interdisciplinary' work that is taking place within the legal academy; for example, when discussing the new 'field' of 'communication and the law', Redhead observes that :

> This is not, though, an exploration in theoretical terms of the transformation of society by electronic technologies, particularly television and cinema, as has been pursued elsewhere. . . . Instead, the field of 'communications and law' represents another flawed attempt to come to terms with a new non-traditional 'black letter law' and crime 'field', but without radically changing the positivist approach which dominates in legal formalism and conventional criminology. (42)

It is clear from this that Redhead enjoys the collapsing of recognizable academic disciplinary boundaries between law and cultural studies, and does not enjoy (or eroticize?) positivist disciplinary conjunctions. Although his celebration of the immanent demise of law may be seen by some as premature – and it undoubtedly risks revisiting the law as a quasi-theological presence – Redhead dances on the grave of legal formalism and positivism in a way which may conveniently be seen as the culmination of a strand of thinking about law that can be traced from Marxism through feminism right through to postmodern theory: 'Welcome to the World of Hyperlegality. Welcome to Accelerated, Post-Literate Culture. Welcome to the New Millenium . . .' (98).

3. Literature and the Possibility of Justice

If it is becoming apparent that theory is, broadly speaking, attempting to show law its own linguistic and discursive commitments, then the field of 'law and literature' would seem to embody the cumulative desire of theory to decentre the law. It can be seen, however, that much law and literature scholarship is unwilling to adopt a radically linguistic stance, and more particularly is unwilling to press the claims of discourse analysis upon the categories and certainties of the law. Largely, it seems, this apparent conservatism is bound up in a certain attitude towards Derrida's preoccupation with ethics. This preoccupation has dominated the law and literature curriculum in recent years, and it is a preoccupation which, rather than waging war upon the totality of the law, seeks rather to redirect law's ethical focus in certain strategic, and by no means necessarily confrontational, ways.

Jacques Derrida has used Bourdieu's concept of 'the force of law' with far greater focus on the play of language than Bourdieu. In *The Gift of Death*, published this year, Derrida continues his discussion of violence and responsibility (developed in, among other things, 'Force of Law: The "Mystical Foundation of Authority"', in Drucilla Cornell, Michel Rosenfeld, David Gray Carlson, eds, *Deconstruction and the Possibility of Justice* (New York, Routledge, 1992), through an analysis of Patocka's *Heretical Essays on the History of Philosophy*. Derrida problematizes conventional, particularly Christian, attitudes towards responsibility, and argues for a need to take into account the difference between theoretical responsibility and practical, including legal, responsibility – 'if only to avoid the arrogance of so many clean consciences': 'We must continually remind ourselves that some part of irresponsibility insinuates itself wherever one demands responsibility without sufficiently conceptualising and thematizing what "responsibility" means: that is to say everywhere' (26). To this extent, the theatre of the law is crucial to the development of a model of responsibility: responsibility consists in responding publicly, both before the other *and* before the law. As he observes in 'Force of Law', 'this freedom or this decision of the just, if it is one, must follow a law or a prescription, a rule' (23). Derrida would agree with Blandine Kriegel's commitment to law as an ethico-political category: 'the principle of public morality is not love, which is proper to familial morality and to faith. It is law.' But this commitment does not deny the ethical nature of law. On Derrida's reading the law itself is an ethical act, consisting of the gift of a responsible, anonymous, donor: the gift 'subjects its receivers, giving itself to them as goodness itself but also as the law' (41). And, it might be added, the law is a gift which, on Derrida's account, is received from death: 'It is from the site of death as the place of my irreplaceability, that is, of my singularity, that I feel called to responsibility. In this sense only a mortal can be responsible' (41).

Because the law has its basis in an ethical act, the fate of the law is bound up with that of philosophy and ethics. Indeed, Derrida continually subverts the strict notion of law as predicated upon its absolute separability from philosophy, narrative and history. So, for example, any request for truth that inspires philosophy and ethics will be made by the law as well; although, as Derrida argues, such a request will not always be met with an answer, other than the brute fact of a foundational violence. However, this sort of aporia, which is so much the concern of postmodernist accounts of law, does not, on Derrida's account, stop the law from serving its purpose. On the contrary, the law will operate so much the better:

> What is thus found at work in everyday discourse, in the exercise of justice, and first and foremost in the axiomatics of private, public, or international law, in the conduct of internal politics, diplomacy, and war, is a lexicon concerning responsibility that can be said to hover vaguely about a concept that is nowhere to be found, even if we can't go so far as to say that it doesn't correspond to any concept at all. (85)

Derrida's conception of law and ethics therefore demands faith (63) and in *The Gift of Death*, as in other writings, Derrida takes a qualitatively different approach to the law than that which characterizes much 'critical theory' writing; the difference can perhaps be summarized as that between postmodernist and deconstructionist jurisprudences. To return to the terms of David Caudill (writing in the area of psychoanalytic jurisprudence), Derrida is attempting to bypass a situation where one must renounce the reality of the law in the 'mode of repression' or the 'mode of liberation': Derrida seems to be suggesting that, indeed, one must renounce the 'reality' of the law – law is fantastic, and its 'original site and occurrence are endowed with the qualities of a fable' ('Before the Law', 209). However, on Derrida's view in *The Gift of Death*, one must also critically embrace law as a discourse of responsibility. It is necessary, but also perilous, to conceive of justice without law. In this way 'repression' and 'liberation' before the law become terms of diminished value within the problematic of Derrida's reconceived double-bind. It is this embrace of the law that has established a more moderate political tenor for the project of law and literature scholarship.

One of the most important books to emerge recently from the 'law and literature' field has been Ian Ward's *Law and Literature: Possibilities and Perspectives*. Where studies in law and literature had established themselves as the product of concerns in literary theory – including, in particular, questions of hermeneutics – Ward pleads against the over-intellectualization of law and literature scholarship. It is a complaint which finds echoes in another landmark in law and literature studies, L. H. La Rue's *Constitutional Law as Fiction: Narrative in the Rhetoric of Authority*. La Rue presses a point no more rarefied or convoluted than that the law is constituted by stories and narrative, persuasive by rhetorical force. However, this familiar proposition is carefully tested against an analysis of early US constitutional cases, and La Rue develops the argument that a sensitivity to legal fictionality (he does not use the word 'discursivity') is also a sensitivity to the law's contingency rather than to its 'destiny', to the possibility of telling different – perhaps worse, perhaps better – stories:

> What story one should tell depends on the background story that one assumes should characterize normal life. Is normal life a world of racial discrimination, or not? I do not wish to reach for the rather easy answer to the question about normality, since the peculiar legal context of the problem is more complicated than that. The more precise question is, What sort of story do we wish to have told in court? (112)

It is a vision of law as discourse which has – if one wants them – quite radical ramifications, and it is a vision which subtly and powerfully redescribes conventional jurisprudence. La Rue's thesis – one might say theory – is an increasingly popular one; Herbert Eastman, for example, endorses this redescription when he emphasizes the strategic value of storytelling in civil rights litigation ('Speaking Truth to Power: The Language of Civil Rights Litigators', *Yale Law Journal* 104.763–879). It is intriguing, however, that La Rue, even while showing law its own discursive nature and its own political possibilities, should pit 'storytelling' against 'theory', as if the two were natural antagonists. He begins by wryly noting that 'even in the writings of Immanuel Kant narrative is "inserted into that blank place where the presumed purely conceptual language of philosophy fails or is missing" ' (15). However, one of La Rue's final pronouncements is that 'the topic of storytelling in law is . . . not the sort of practice about which there can be a theory' (148).

Ian Ward is not so extreme. Whilst arguing for less theoretical debate, he is not anti-intellectual or anti-theory; his procedure rather is one of delimitation, rehearsing those specific areas of theoretical enquiry that are, in his view, proper to the concerns of law and literature studies: the dominance in the law of 'scientific' discourse as against the creative possibilities of metaphor and narrative as a constituent of any text (Rorty); the pervasiveness of rhetoric in legal texts (James Boyd White); Heideggerian, Derridean and de Manian issues of responsibility and ethics (Richard Weisberg's 'poethics', and the work of Robin West); literary theory that is relevant to law students so that they can better understand what a text means; and deconstruction generally (including, for example, the deconstruction of rights discourse).

However, Ward would, it seems, steer law and literature away from debates concerning authorial intent and interpretive (in)determinacy, of the sort which characterized the Gadamer–Derrida debate, and which have been aired more recently between (one the side of Gadamer) Owen Fiss and Ronald Dworkin, and (on the side of Derrida) Stanley Fish. Ward refers to the recent work of Mark Tushnet and Robin West, each of whom see a concern with interpretivism in law and literature studies as distracting attention away from the politics of law. Ward's work, indeed, reveals a scepticism in relation to the value of seeing law as simply discursive. Ward, like Peter Brooks in his discussion of the US Supreme Court cases dealing with victim impact statements, seems continually to operate within the terms of a real–discursive binary, and is unwilling to surrender law to narrative and rhetorical forces.

Ward discusses, with obvious approval, Allan Hutchinson's suggestion that the political model which best complements a preoccupation with law's textuality, without the excesses of textualism, is the Foucauldian idea of 'participatory democracy'. And, moving from politics to philosophy, Ward also seems to endorse Richard Weisberg's advocacy of the reconstructive ethics of Derridean postmodernists such as Drucilla Cornell. Continuing this analysis, Ward outlines the extent to which textualism in law and literature scholarship has revealed the limits of literature's relevance to feminist legal study. Critical feminist lawyers, at least in North America, have been less than committed to the law and literature movement, with Robin West being one notable exception.

Indeed, Ward sounds a note of caution in outlining the scope of law and literature scholarship. Law and literature, he argues, must avoid the fate of the critical legal studies movement, which had, at least in its early phases, the primary ambition of educating law students about the politics of law:

> It has ended, not by reaching any particular goal, or indeed identifying one, but by going round in ever-decreasing circles, using up its dissipating energies in a multitude of various internecine disputes, and in the invention of increasingly pretentious and ultimately useless language which, rather than educating, serves only to mystify and then to alienate all but the most fervent of believers. (22)

All this, it is to be remembered, takes place against a legal culture which, as exemplified by Richard Posner, sees methods of literary theory as inappropriate for the interpretation of legal texts. Indeed, one of the law and literature movement's great virtues has been its awareness of Posner's reductive 'law and economics' approach, and the movement has shown, by and large, great resistance to this mode of thought.

Ward lends his own weight to law and literature scholarship by arguing, in the context of rape law, that literature and language are not threats to feminist legal theory, but are its potential saviour. In other chapters he also draws upon Derridean analyses to show that the modern novel (at least in its Heideggerian explication at the hands of Kafka and Camus and, more recently, Ivan Klima and Umberto Eco) has called for a taking of responsibility. Ward notes that Heidegger and Heideggerians such as Derrida, Arendt or Marcuse have advocated precisely the 'cross-disciplinary' study, or 'Ciceronian unity', which law and literature scholars such as James Boyd White have advocated; and which has been the continuing concern of CLS scholarship, notably through the agency of Roberto Unger and Peter Gabel.

To this extent the law and literature movement has a crucial role to play in the reconfiguration of conventional models of responsibility; however, it should also be recognized that the concern with responsibility and ethics shown by much law and literature scholarship is not, in many cases, very critical, much less radical. Martha Nussbaum's approach to the topic, for example, is resolutely liberal humanist. Although she distances herself from the law and economics approach of (most prominently) Richard Posner, her thesis is by no means at odds with the most doctrinaire legal formalism. In *Poetic Justice: The Literary Imagination and Public Life* she defends 'the literary imagination' as part of public, legal rationality: 'precisely because it seems to me an essential ingredient of an ethical stance that asks us to concern ourselves with the good of other people whose lives are distant from our own. Such an ethical stance will have a large place for rules and formal decision procedures' (xvi). At a theoretical level she is most indebted, it seems, to Aristotle and Kant, and her preferred novels are not those of Kafka or Camus, but Dickens. But Dickens is unexceptional: Nussbaum sees ethical issues which are relevant to legal decision-making as being inherent in the novel as form and genre: 'Indeed, we can say of the mainstream realist novel what Aristotle said of tragic drama: that the very form constructs compassion in readers, positioning them as people who care intensely about the sufferings and bad luck of others, and who identify with them in ways that show possibilities for themselves' (66). On this argument, novels instil in their readers 'the emotion of the judicious spectator' (78). Nussbaum sees Aristotelian ethics as combining with institutional constraints to bring about a complex and superior ideal of judicial neutrality. She is not concerned with ontological, jurisprudential and ethical challenges to this ideal, although at one point she does, rather bafflingly, castigate Stanley Fish for failing to recognize that: 'the law has always based its reasoning on history and social context and has rarely attached importance to establishing an eternal basis for its judgements' (84). Nussbaum concludes by analysing a judgement of Richard Posner's, where he was determining a sexual harassment appeal, and she is gracious enough to observe that, whatever Posner's theoretical faults, as a judge he is possessed of ample quantities of 'literary imagination', as evidenced by his finding for the plaintiff appellant.

4. Limits of the Law: Theory in the Law School

Whatever inroads critical theory and cultural studies may have made into the law, there are countervailing institutional pressures which would see theory colonized by the law, and which raise doubts as to the terms of the relationship between the disciplines. In particular, it is apparent that much of the writing which spans the discourses of law and critical theory is generated from within law schools. The relative conservatism of the law and literature movement, with its distinctive reading of Derrida on ethics and its wavering commitment to law-as-discourse, is the political effect of an institutional allegiance which is owned by the law: for much law and literature scholarship has stayed within the law school. Indeed, the debilitating effect of such an allegiance can be seen in much of what Gary Minda (*Postmodern Legal Movements: Law and Juris-prudence at Century's End*) calls 'the "law and" genre of legal scholarship': 'It is well, therefore, that at least as far as the left is concerned, certain reservations be held regarding the politics of theory and the law. The political and intellectual products of the encounter between theory and the law will not always be provocative or even productive' (78).

It is true that the curricula of most English, American and Australian law schools have liberalized and diversified considerably over the last ten years, and by way of recognizing that law does not exist in isolation from political and social pressures, the traditionally conservative masthead of the law school, the law journal, has been opened up to disciplines other than law. Largely as a result of this trend within the law school, the bulk of writing in the area of law and critical theory is produced within the law school, by lawyers, with a lawyerly audience in mind. Law journals, and sociolegal journals, have proliferated.

However, this fact alone tends to make way for the possibility that in the largely binary relationship between law and theory which is currently being constructed in the law school, law will, by and large, be put forward as the dominant party, the discipline which matters. In Derrida's paraphrase of Kafka: 'The door is physically open, the doorkeeper does not bar the way by force. It is his discourse, rather, that operates at the limit, not to prohibit directly, but to interrupt and defer the passage, to withhold the pass' ('Before the Law'). In a legal context, critical theory gains legitimacy and institutional endorsement by becoming a tool for the 'progressive lawyer', a quasi-political heuristic device that is called upon only selectively. Gary Minda describes the problem in a passage which is worth quoting at some length:

> Arthur Leff was mistaken about the new 'law and' movements, as they were not really radical departures from traditional modes of legal thought at all. Rather, they were novel applications of the same 'good old fashioned lawyer-academics' that characterized much of modern legal scholarship. The 'law and' movements simply shifted the frame of analysis away from 'applying the law to the facts' (the traditional frame) to 'applying the theory to the law.' The same legalistic rhetoric, however, was used in the age-old search for the disciplinary authority of the law. As Pierre Schlag amusingly put it: 'The interdisciplinary travels of traditional legal thought are like a bad European vacation: the substance is

Europe, but the form is McDonald's, Holiday Inn, American Express'. (79)

Stanley Fish has written in some detail about this phenomenon (in, for example, *Doing What Comes Naturally*) and would no doubt see it as something of an inevitability. In his most recent publication, *Professional Correctness: Literary Studies and Political Change*, Fish reiterates the difficulty that a practitioner, including a practitioner of legal studies, must face when attempting to 'do' something which is outside the disciplinary purview – including 'doing theory'. Fish's argument, put simply, is that theory has no necessary practical consequences, because the generation of statements of universal application (theory) is a different thing from practice, including legal practice. It is in the nature of disciplinary practice to be distinctive from doing theory, which stands aside from the rituals of practice: there is, in Derridean terms, 'a critical difference' ('On the Name', 4) So, to take an example in legal context, the practice of judging is one thing and giving accounts or theories of judging is another. Within the disciplinary confines of the law school, the discursive pressures against in-house theoretical writing are immense; writing which cannot be justified internally, cannot be made 'immanently intelligible'. In *Professional Correctness*, Fish elaborates and clarifies some of his earlier arguments which question the possibility of transforming either legal or literary study so that they are more immediately engaged with political or theoretical issues. Fish quotes Ernest Weinrib: 'Nothing is more senseless than to attempt to understand law from a vantage point extrinsic to it' (20). Fish is willing to concede that lawyers and law professors, when they wish to mount political and theoretical commentary, have an advantage over (for example) literary critics because their disciplinary discourse is better connected with established networks of public political theory and communication (52); but Fish would still stand by his contention that when such commentary emerges from the law school, it is no longer legal discourse; and conversely, that recognizably legal discourse cannot be theoretical. Fish states: 'An analysis of contract law that foregrounded its contradictions would be embarrassing to its project only if the goal of that project were to be philosophically consistent. But that is not the goal of any project except for the project of philosophy itself' (102). Whether one shares Fish's interdisciplinary pessimism, there is evidence to suggest that lawyers do have difficulty when working in theoretical terrain. One paradigmatic example of this phenomenon may well be the way in which academic criminologists, often working within law schools, typically acknowledge Foucault in their discovery of the operation of non-juridical power within and between apparently 'legal' institutions. Critical theory is used as a working hypothesis, a starting-point, a framework within which one can conduct empirical research; however, it is a framework which can be interrogated in only the most basic ways.

In the case of Rod Settle's *Police Informers: Negotiation and Power*, for example, Foucauldian paradigms are universally, and unquestioningly, confirmed. In his comprehensive Australian study of the twilight zone which falls between the courts, the police and police informers, Settle takes Foucault's thought as his preferred model and, at the end of his discussion, concludes: 'The most salient feature of the data presented in this study is the extent of informal, largely covert, interaction between police and their sources of information. That observation sits awkwardly with traditional assumptions about the role of operational police posited by much legal doctrine.' In other words, Settle finds that his data support a Foucauldian, non-juridical conception of power at work in the world of police informers. The point is that it is very rare for such writing to argue (for example) that Foucault's theories of non-juridical power are empirically falsifiable, or require development or modification. It is a curious, and I think important, fact that Settle unearths and suppresses much data which might be thought to qualify some of Foucault's claims, and which presents a very premodern, juridical picture of criminal justice. This is a good example of a widespread wariness and hesitation amongst lawyers when the question arises as to whether theory might have to be interrogated or redeployed: the alteration or advancement of theory is, it seems, beyond the proper concern of the legal academic, even when she is apparently confirming or applying those theories. There is comparatively little interest in ways in which legal events can create new paradigms for critical theory.

This is true also of this year's Australian introduction to law, edited by Rosemary Hunter, Richard Ingleby, and Richard Johnstone, *Thinking about Law: Perspectives on the History, Philosophy and Sociology of Law*. This work marks a radical break with other texts that attempt to explain the relationship between legal and non-legal institutions to the extent that it attempts to confront the dichotomies that have traditionally been used to introduce 'the law' to a non-legal audience. The book studiously avoids, for example, the persistent mode of analysis that predicates law in any relationship in which law might participate: law and morality, law and justice, law and freedom, law and custom, law and society. . . . Rather, Hunter et al. encourage their readers to reflect on the way that law is implicated in social and political histories, to reflect on differences between competing legal systems, and upon the shiftless nature of legal doctrine.

Nevertheless, however well Hunter's text connects with current scholarship in the fields of political philosophy, Marxism, feminism and postmodernism, it is unable to show that law has any consequences which might impact upon those modes of thought at a theoretical level. At the level of theory, Hunter's main concern is to consider 'a number of critical theories of law which provide alternative explanations of the function and position of law in (post)modern, (post)liberal states' (86). Again, the ongoing concerns of 'the law' – its 'function' and 'position' – take centre stage; theoretical frameworks are ancillary and, taken in their own right, are in this view unimportant.

Even in the area of queer legal theory, the emerging scholarship seems to delimit itself to a legal audience. For example, Michael Dobber ('Hegemon: Tracing Power through Bodies of Law'), by way of introducing his investigation of some of the jurisprudential and political dimensions of sexual identity, remarks that: 'The work of lawyers is quintessentially . . . language work. The postmodern account of truth has had devastating effects on literary criticism; its consequences for the practice of the law should be no less spectacular' (64–5). The problem seems to be that, for as long as theory must have 'consequences for the practice of law', the results will unfortunately continue to be less than spectacular: theory, in the law school, is still a one-way street. Within even the most 'politicized' and 'theorized' sections of the legal academy – the critical legal studies movement, for example – the challenge has been, for the most part, to find the most satisfactory social theory of law; relatively little attention is paid to the question of law's implications as a discourse for the concerns of social and political theory: gender, sexuality, race, class and so on. Steve Redhead (*Unpopular Cultures: The Birth of Law and Popular Culture*) has said that CLS: 'has to date achieved far more in the way of 'critique' . . . than political programme or strategy, and concentrated largely on undermining, or to use its own coinage 'trashing' traditional positivist-oriented legal scholarship in the academy rather than producing reform outside the law school walls' (18).

Law, it seems, is cast as a novice who must be educated and refined within the walls of its home (law school) before it can be inducted into the wider academic community and taken seriously as a discourse with a self-avowed relevance at a theoretical level. Because law apparently lacks the vocabulary with which to modify the theoretical terrain it is beginning to inhabit, we must, it seems, wait for it to develop, to acquire theoretical sophistication. In the meantime, we should pretend that law is of no consequence outside the law school, which involves pretending that legal discourse does not (for example) produce bodies and texts which might be of interest outside the discipline. It is certainly an achievement that legal discourse is adopting certain analytical frameworks from critical theory, and is beginning to scrutinize its own totalizing ambitions, but if these analytical frameworks are without exception simply being uncritically selected, applied and confirmed – within an academic context (the law school) which is profoundly disconnected with other faculties and departments – then the ramifications of this process for critical theory are nil. There is, apparently, no sense in which theory is being tested and modified in the law school – a problem which, apart from anything else, circumscribes the ability of theory to be taken seriously by the liberal positivist law school establishment.

It should not be forgotten, however, that there is some work emerging from within the discipline of law which seeks to challenge conventional notions of the acceptable uses of theory. For example, Bruce Kercher, a legal academic at Macquarie University in Australia, has written a history of law in Australia – *An Unruly Child* – which draws upon and contributes to ideas of Foucauldian genealogy, governance, cultural studies and postcolonialism. Kercher traces the history of Australian law from first settlement, and develops the argument that in the Australian colonies, law was shaped as much by popular vision as by jurisprudential science. Law was a contested site, between imperial Britain's legalistic arrogance and Australian demands for local expediency.

Kercher's analysis takes on Althusserian characteristics in his preoccupation with the ideological function of law: to ensure that official values become part of received common sense. So, for example, Kercher explains that convicts in the early colony were disciplined as much through grants of property as through physical brutality, and that a complex system of rewards, generous by English standards, ensured that convicts accepted the rule of colonial law: 'that process was much more complex than the simple notion of rules and values being imposed on convicts from above' (30). Similarly, Kercher shows how imperial law depended, for its existence in Australia, upon the often inappropriate political deference of Australian lawyers and upon the naive popular belief in 'British rights'. However, if the law relied upon non-legal motivations, it was also resisted by them at every turn: Kercher cites the example of women using doctrinaire divorce law to rid themselves of unwanted husbands by using 'a degree of play acting' (141). Kercher explains: 'Like female convicts and Aborigines of both sexes, it is inaccurate to cast nineteenth-century wives as passive objects without self-defined rights' (141). There is a contrast which Kercher cumulatively elaborates between legal officialdom and a colonial reality which, he argues, did not admit of accommodation.

Kercher continually suggests a productive model of power at work within ostensible paradigms of legal positivism, even from the very early days of Australian colonization, and he documents a gradual transition towards a disciplinary surveillance which, it seems, was there from the outset – 'there was no sudden jump from punishment of the body to supposedly rational bureaucratic imprisonment' (35). In Kercher's vision, the history of Australian law is actually the history of the defeat of law at the hands of local practice: law moves from being an institution which is totalizing and world-encompassing, and instead gradually becomes the reflection of specific, local concerns of a political and economic nature. The role of law, he reminds us, is subtle, and it is inadequate to see it as no more than an expression of dominant power. If, in Derrida's words, the law 'intolerant of its own history, intervenes as an absolutely emergent order, absolute and detached from any origin' ('Before the Law'), Kercher's work challenges this order.

5. Conclusion

The collision of law and critical theory in 1995 in many ways illustrates the general crisis in Western reason that has been noted across disciplines. This crisis, however, should not be taken as effecting the *disintegration* of the master narrative caught in the theoretical clinch. Law has demonstrated extreme resilience in the face of concerted critique; its rational positivist formation still has real purchase within the terms of our culture.

Indeed the argument has been made several times in this paper: the proper project of theory is not to liberate us from law by somehow demolishing law's edifice, but rather that project is 'simply' to remove or *displace* law as an onto-logical, quasi-theological centre, and to relocate it as one discourse competing with many. Law is a discourse whose importance is now rediscovered as contingent and institutional rather than necessary and universal.

So law as discourse is fragmented and localized rather than coherent and 'rational'. But once law is posited in the terms of discourse, it becomes even more difficult to envisage law's disintegration at the hands of theory. As we have suggested, theory's investment in law-as-discourse is manifold. There is no doubt that the law continues to be able to disqualify or disavow challenges to its identification as a discourse. But in many contexts law can be seen to accept modification or even modify itself, by performing radical re-readings of its own history, and by conducting radical re-readings of competing disciplinary discourses, such as economics or history. In this way, then, the relation between law and critical theory does not have the consistency or coherence of dialectic; it is much more diversified and discontinuous. No matter what its nature, however, the engagement of law and critical theory is now firmly established.

Books Reviewed

Berger, Maurice, Brian Wallis, and Simon Watson. *Constructing Masculinity.* Routledge. pp. 342. pb £14.99. ISBN 0 415 91053 6.

Brown, Wendy. *States of Injury: Power and Freedom in Late Modernity.* Princeton University Press. pp. 202. hb £32.00. ISBN 0 691 02990 3.

Caudill, David S., and Steven Jay Gold, eds. *Radical Philosophy of Law: Contemporary Challenges to Mainstream Legal Theory and Practice.* Humanities Press. pp. 336. pb £15.00. ISBN 0 391 03862 1.

Cornell, Drucilla. *Imaginary Domains.* Routledge. pp. 287. pb £11.99. ISBN 0 415 91160 5.

Delgado, Richard, ed. *Critical Race Theory: The Cutting Edge.* Temple University Press. pp. 592. pb £17.95. ISBN 1 56639 348 5.

Delgado, Richard. *The Roderigo Chronicles: Conversations about Race and America.* New York University Press. pp. 275. hb $35.00. ISBN 0 8147 1863 9.

Derrida, Jacques. *The Gift of Death.* trans. David Wills. University of Chicago Press. pp. 115. hb £15.25. ISBN 0 226 14305 8.

Derrida, Jacques. *On the Name.* trans. Thomas Dutoit. Stanford University Press. pp. 150. pb £10.95. ISBN 0 8047 2555 1.

Eades, Diana ed. *Language in Evidence: Issues Confronting Aboriginal and Multicultural Australia.* University of NSW Press. pp. 289. pb $29.95. ISBN 0 868 40119 6.

Fish, Stanley. *Professional Correctness: Literary Studies and Political Change.* Oxford University Press. pp. 146. hb £17.99. ISBN 0 19 812373 6.

Hunter, Rosemary, Richard Ingleby and Richard Johnstone, eds. *Thinking about Law: Perspectives on the History, Philosophy and Sociology of Law.* Allen and Unwin. pp. 254. pb £16.95. ISBN 1 86373 842 8.

Janikowski, Richard W., and Dragan Milovanovic, eds. *Legality and Illegality: Semiotics, Postmodernism and Law.* P. Lang. pp. 288. ISBN 00 113 28564.

Kercher, Bruce. *An Unruly Child: A History of Law in Australia.* Allen and Unwin. pp. 248. pb $29.95. ISBN 1 86373 891 6.

Kirkby, Diane, ed. *Sex, Power and Justice: Historical Perspectives on Law in Australia.* Oxford University Press. pp. 302. pb £18.99. ISBN 0 19 553734 3.

Kriegel, Blandine. *The State and the Rule of Law.* trans. Marc LePain and Jeffrey Cohen. Princeton University Press. pp. 173. hb £15.95. ISBN 0 691 03291 2.

La Rue, L. H. *Constitutional Law as Fiction: Narrative in the Rhetoric of Authority.* Pennsylvania State University Press. pp. 158. hb $28.50. ISBN 0 271 014067.

Minda, Gary. *Postmodern Legal Movements: Law and Jurisprudence at Century's End.* New York University Press. pp. 350. hb $45.00. ISBN 0 8147 5510 0.

Naffine, Ngaire. *Gender, Crime and Feminism.* Dartmouth. pp. 469. hb $127.95. ISBN 00 112 89524.

Nussbaum, Martha. *Poetic Justice: The Literary Imagination and Public Life.* Beacon Press. pp. 147. hb $20.00. ISBN 0 8070 4108 4.

Redhead, Steve. *Unpopular Cultures: The Birth of Law and Popular Culture.* Manchester University Press. pp. 136. pb £12.99. ISBN 0 7190 3652 6.

Settle, Rod. *Police Informers: Negotiation and Power.* Federation Press. pp. 288. A$35.00. ISBN 1 86287 148 5.

Smart, Carol. *Law, Crime and Sexuality: Essays in Feminism.* Sage. pp. 250. hb $69.95. ISBN 0 8039 8959 8.

Stychin, Carl. *Law's Desire: Sexuality and the Limits of Justice.* Routledge. pp. 186. hb £40.00. ISBN 0 415 11126 9.

Thornton, Margaret, ed. *Public and Private: Feminist Legal Debates.* Oxford University Press. pp. 336. pb £15.99. ISBN 0 19 553662 2.

Walklate, Sandra. *Gender and Crime: An Introduction.* Prentice Hall/Harvester Wheatsheaf. pp. 212. pb £12.50. ISBN 0 13 433459 0.

Ward, Ian. *Law and Literature: Possibilities and Perspectives.* Cambridge University Press. pp. 264. hb £35.00. ISBN 0 521 47474 4.

Williams, Patricia. *The Rooster's Egg.* Harvard University Press. pp. 262. hb $22.00. ISBN 0 674 77942 8.

20

Aboriginal Identity, Art and Culture

MICHELE GROSSMAN and DENISE CUTHBERT

This chapter has five sections: 1. Introduction; 2. Down by Law: Native Title, Land and Loss; 3. Culture and Country: Heritage, Wilderness and the Politics of the Indigenous Sacred and Secret; 4. Author(iz)ing Aboriginalities: Identities, Cultures, Histories, Bodies; 5. Representations: Literature, Art and Media.

1. Introduction

If it is possible to identify an underpinning concern in the substantial array of writings on Aboriginality published in 1995, it lies in the politics of positionality as manifest in the increasingly contested connection of Aboriginal culture to country and the political rights which stem from that connectedness, however it is interpreted. The politics of positionality is also manifest in and through the vexed politics of speaking positions *for* Aboriginal people and the concomitant listening and speaking positions of non-Aboriginal Australians; and it appears too as a signal issue for those discourses involved in and constituted by speaking *about* Aboriginality for a host of commentators, who are themselves variously authorized by institutional, professional and disciplinary knowledges and practices that continue to be subject to opposition across a spectrum of political and critical orthodoxies, both indigenous – and non-indigenous – based.

Also by way of introduction, we find it necessary to comment on our own chronological position, reviewing work published in 1995 from the vantage point of early 1997, given that the intervening period has seen not only a change of government but an ensuing and dramatic change in the ways in which Aboriginal affairs are being conducted by the Australian state. In 1994, Patrick Wolfe ('Nation and MiscegeNation: Discursive Continuity in the Post-Mabo Era', *Social Analysis* 36.93–152) wrote that Aboriginal affairs in Australia were dominated by the political/juridical 'triumvirate' initiated by the Labor governments of Bob Hawke and Paul Keating (1983–96): Mabo and the on-going negotiations authorized by the Native Title Act (1993), the Royal Commission into Aboriginal Deaths in Custody (finally reporting in 1991) and the National Inquiry into the Separation of Aboriginal and Torres Strait Islander Children from their Families (expected to report in 1997), an investigation of the forced removal of Aboriginal children from their families which persisted as government policy in Australia into the late 1960s. As we write, this triumvirate is being dismantled and/or disempowered by the Federal Liberal government of John Howard, elected in a landslide victory in March 1996. In its first twelve months of office, the Howard government has demonstrated an uncompromisingly regressive political will on Aboriginal and Torres Strait Islander affairs: it is currently threatening to extinguish the common-law right of Native Title in the aftermath of the High Court's decision in the Wik case (1996); it has pre-empted the final report and recommendations of the National Inquiry into the Separation of Aboriginal and Torres Strait Islander Children from their Families by announcing that no compensation will be paid to Aboriginal people wrested from their families or to those that had children stolen from them by the state through the assimilationist policies of earlier governments; it has turned a blind eye to the fact that Aboriginal youths and men continue to die in police lock-ups in intolerable numbers; slashed funding to ATSIC (Aboriginal and Torres Strait Islander Commission); and resiled from, if not as yet rejected, the principles and policies of reconciliation which, while flawed from both sides of the table, none the less offered some possibility for just settlements between the Australian state and Australian indigenous peoples. In many respects, history and political events in 1996 and 1997 render many of the debates reviewed below somewhat obsolete. Our comments here should not be construed as an elegiac moment, however, but rather as remarks that signal our sense of the urgent need for engaged scholarship and intellectual work in the field of Aboriginality in Australia to respond to these changed political circumstances. In the following chapter, we endeavour to provide an evaluation of the works published in the context of 1995, but not without reference to the changes which have intervened between publication and the timing of our review.

2. Down by Law: Native Title, Land and Loss

2.1 Responding to Mabo: Interpreting and Extending the Implications of Native Title

The implications, meanings and possible extension of the principle of Native Title as enunciated in both the High Court's Mabo decision (1992) and the Commonwealth Government's Native Title Act (1993) continue to be discussed throughout 1995. A detailed and multidisciplinary survey of the field is provided in the collection of essays edited by J. Finlayson and D. Smith, *Native Title: Emerging Issues for Research, Policy and Practice.* As the editors of the volume point out in their introduction, both the Native Title field and other arenas, such as the Hindmarsh Island Royal Commission (1995) in which the status and significance of Aboriginal culture was a central issue, have cast research, particularly the work of anthropologists, into the public arena and subjected it to (often hostile) scrutiny. Anthropologists and other researchers and professionals working in the Native Title arena are being faced with substantial issues of advocacy, objectivity and practice. The position of the consultant researcher, providing advice to Aboriginal clients (rather than researching Aboriginal subjects) is particularly open to charges of partisanship and, because the consulting process only infrequently leads to publication of research in recognized scholarly journals which may serve as reference points for critics, the issue of probity looms large. While recognizing these problems, many essays in the collection are keen to problematize and deconstruct the divide between 'pure' and 'applied' research and to develop frameworks which can address the needs of the professionals (academic and otherwise) and their indigenous clients. The collection contains eight essays by legal academics, legal practitioners and anthropologists which variously take up the question of *how* and *by whom* Aboriginality is represented in the Native Title claim process. Mary Edmunds, in 'Why Won't We Tell Them What They Want to Hear? Native Title, Politics and the Intransigence of Ethnography' (1–8), takes up the issue of the representation and interpretation of ethnographic 'facts' about Aboriginal culture as provided by 'experts' such as anthropologists in legal evidentiary contexts in which expectations of factual certainty and interpretative stability are at odds with the complexity and discursive instability of these ethnographic knowledges and their interpretation. Moreover, Edmunds argues, such facts and the meanings attached to them shift and change: the facts of Aboriginal culture as they are known to Aboriginal people are translated and interpreted in and through the domain of anthropology and then are subjected to further translation (generally under intense legal and political pressure and contestation) as they become facts of law, policy and administration. Edmunds bases her investigation of these issues on an examination of the Finniss River Land Claim (Northern Land Council, 1981) by uncovering and tracing the meanings attached to ethnographic facts about Aboriginal culture; the claim is of particular interest as it involved incompatible and contested representations by disputing Aboriginal groups.

Other essays in the collection include Bruce Rigsby's comparative study 'Anthropologists, Land Claims and Objectivity: Some Australian and Canadian Cases' (23–38); Ione Rummery's 'The Role of the Anthropologist as Expert Witness' (38–58); 'Representative Politics and the New Wave of Native Title Organizations' (59–74), Diane Smith's critical analysis of the politics of representation in the new wave of Native Title Representative Bodies, of which twenty-one had been determined by the Minister for Aboriginal and Torres Strait Islander Affairs by August 1995; Peter Sutton's examination of forensic anthropology and its deficiencies in 'Forensic Anthropology in Australia: Does it Have a Case to Answer?' (83–100); and Hal Wooten's overview of the position and role of two professional stakeholders, particularly in relation to the position of their indigenous clients, in the Native Title process, 'The End of Dispossession? Anthropologists and Lawyers in the Native Title Process' (101–18).

An extremely useful consideration of Mabo, and an attempt to read its significance in the light of poststructuralist theory, is provided by Paul Patton's 'Post-Structuralism and the Mabo Debate: Difference, Society and Justice' (in Margaret Wilson and Anna Yeatman, eds, *Justice and Identity: Antipodean Practices*, Allen & Unwin, 153–71). Patton examines Mabo and the debates it has generated in the terms provided by Deleuze and Guattari to account for transformative social moments and 'lines of flight' as part of a post-structuralist understanding of society as an unfinished process as distinct from a finished structure. Patton then analyses the variety of responses to Mabo in Australian political, legal and cultural debate, and argues that these may be understood as falling into two broad categories, the assimilationist and the separatist. By way of intervening in and furthering this debate, Patton suggests that poststructuralist theorizations of difference are more important and useful than the category of identity *per se*. Mabo clearly poses an enormous challenge to Australian law and institutions to recognize and accommodate difference and to formulate models of justice, as in the Native Title arena, which are universally accessible but necessarily also differentiated.

Paul Smith in *Mabo: Three Years On – Current Developments in Native Title Law* provides a survey of the field of Native Title law in the three years since the Mabo decision. The overview, published by the Queensland Department of Justice and Attorney-General, is a lawyerly but accessible account containing a summary of the Mabo decision; a summary of the statutory definitions of the key terms 'Native Title', 'Aboriginal' and 'Torres Strait Islander' provided in the 1993 Native Title Act (NTA); a survey and commentary on post-Mabo judgments, with distinctions between common-law Native Title claims and those made under the NTA; a discussion of future developments; a note on the increased role played by mediation under the NTA; and a table showing claims lodged with the National Native Title Tribunal for lands within the boundaries of Queensland as of 31 July 1995.

The sociopolitical responses to the High Court's 1992 Mabo decision are the subject of a large study by Gary D. Myers and Simone Muller, the first part of which appears as *Through the Eyes of the Media (Part 1): A Brief History of the Political and Social Responses to Mabo v Queensland*. The study draws largely from Australian print media, primarily the national daily *The Australian* and the *West Australian*, the daily in the state of Western Australia, which will be subject to more Native Title claims than any other in the Commonwealth. Myers and Muller proceed with a brief note on the Mabo decision and then document via media reportage and comment the initial political responses, particularly at the state and state/Commonwealth levels; the legislative responses in each state and at the Federal level; the responses of the then Federal opposition; of Aboriginal groups and organizations; and of industry, particularly the mining and pastoral sectors. In its conclusion, the study examines the background to the Federal Government's Native Title Act, providing comment on the legislation and comparing it with the Western Australian legislative response, the Land (Titles and Traditional Usage) Act (1993). The study is historical rather than analytical, and has a legal rather than a media/cultural focus; it provides an extensive assembly of media reportage and will prove a valuable resource for media and cultural research in the field.

Ronald Paul Hill surveys the impact of the Mabo decision through the lens of the differing cultural apprehensions of land by Aboriginal and non-Aboriginal Australians in 'Blackfellas and Whitefellas: Aboriginal Land Rights, the *Mabo* Decision, and the Meaning of Land' (*Human Rights Quarterly* 17.303–22). Hill partially bases his argument on in-depth interviews with Aboriginal people conducted in six sites in the Kimberley region; excerpts from many interviews are reproduced by Hill and provide forceful statements on the connections between country and culture, spirituality and Aboriginality.

2.2 Land and Sea Rights Across Cultures: Environmental Law and Native Title

In 'The Water is not Empty: Cross-Cultural Issues in Conceptualising Sea Space' (*Australian Geographer* 26:1.87–96) S. E. Jackson provides an analysis of the differences between the cultural concepts held by Europeans and Australian indigenous cultures which determine the ways in which the sea is seen and understood, valued and used. Drawing on the work of cultural geographers who argue that landscape is not merely the world we see but the way we see it – in other words, a sophisticated construct – Jackson points to the profound ontological differences between Western views of the sea (particularly the firm conceptual distinction made between land and sea) and the views of the sea held by Australian indigenous cultures which do not make elemental distinctions between land and sea (or earth and water) and fully integrate sea spaces, sea events and sea creatures into their cosmologies. Jackson uses this analysis as a vantage point from which to discuss the inadequacies of Western property and marine law to account for and protect the rights, needs and interests of indigenous people in relation to the sea. Jackson published a shorter consideration of this subject with discussion of the extension of the principle of Native Title to sea rights in 'Sea Country: Indigenous People's Sea Rights in Northern Australia' (*Arena Magazine* June–July, 24–7). A further examination of the sea rights of indigenous people under the Native Title Act is provided by Jason Behrendt in 'So Long, and Thanks for All the Fish . . .' (*Alternative Law Journal* 20:1.11–15/*Aboriginal Law Bulletin* 3:72.11–15). Behrendt's particular focus is Aboriginal fishing rights, Commonwealth law – both the Constitution and the Native Title Act – and the conditions under which Native Title in offshore fishing rights may be extinguished and the just terms of compensation payable in such an event.

In 'International Environmental Treaties and the Rights of Indigenous Peoples in Australia' (*Australian Geographer* 26:1.44–50) S. E. Jackson and G. J. Crough provide a descriptive summary of recent developments in international environmental law and their effects on domestic policy as it relates to indigenous peoples. The focus of the paper is not restricted to environmental law but also covers human rights law where it encompasses the land and resources rights of indigenous peoples. The paper considers the implications for Aboriginal and Torres Strait Islander peoples of a raft of international agreements, covenants and other documents including the United Nations Draft Declaration on the Rights of Indigenous Peoples, the Declaration on the Rights of Persons Belonging to National or Ethnic, Religious or Linguistic Minorities, the International Covenant on Civil and Political Rights, and the International Covenant on Economic, Social and Cultural Rights.

2.3 Lore, Law, Language and Land: Aboriginal Culture and Legal Pluralism
Both the Mabo decision and the on-going Australian republican debate have focused attention on the capacity of Australia's Constitution and institutions to serve adequately the interests of all groups within the nation. Mabo, by challenging the legality of the foundation of the Australian state, has also heightened discussion of the imperative for the Australian legal system to recognize and account for its own Eurocentrism. Two perspectives on how the constitution and Australian governmental and social institutions can be reshaped in order to address the rights and needs of indigenous Australians are presented by Noel Pearson and Will Sanders in the discussion paper, *Indigenous Peoples and Reshaping Australian Institutions: Two Perspectives.* A consideration of the relationship between Aboriginal 'lore' and non-Aboriginal 'law' is provided in a brief comment by Aboriginal and Torres Strait Islander Social Justice Commissioner Michael (Mick) Dodson, 'From "Lore" to "Law":

Indigenous Rights and Australian Legal Systems' (*Alternative Law Journal* 20:1.2/*Aboriginal Law Bulletin* 3:72.2) in which Dodson argues that the history of the Australian legal system's recognition of Aboriginal customary lore is poor and one which has enacted great damage on Aboriginal cultures. Dodson also argues that when and where the law does give some cognizance to Aboriginal customary law, it does so only in its own terms, that is, by isolating components of customary lore into categories appropriate to Western law – as in the Native Title arena – even though these categories are not necessarily relevant or even extant in the indigenous context. Herein lies an irony, argues Dodson, for if Native Title is a title based in indigenous law and custom, how can the Australian legal system recognize this title, but fail, in other contexts, to acknowledge the existence of the traditional laws and customs from which it is derived? Dodson concludes with a call for true pluralism at law by which indigenous lore is both recognized and accommodated. A fuller discussion of the paradox outlined by Dodson, whereby Native Title is recognized by common law as arising, in part, out of customary connections with land and lore, while these very customs and lore remain, in other contexts, unrecognized by the Australian legal system, is provided by Garth Nettheim in 'Mabo and Legal Pluralism: The Australian Aboriginal Justice Experience' (Kayleen M. Hazelhurst, ed., *Legal Pluralism and the Colonial Legacy,* Avebury, 103–30). In the course of his argument, which puts the case that the time for tinkering with existing legislation in order to address these issues has passed and the necessity for wholesale legislative review is pressing, Nettheim turns to documents prepared by the International Labour Organisation and the UN Working Group on Indigenous Populations for principles which might inform the development of a legal pluralism in Australia sufficient to accommodate the interests and protect the rights of indigenous and non-indigenous people.

Closely related to the principle of legal pluralism, the principle of cultural relativism in legal systems offers some promise for recognizing the cultural differences of indigenous peoples and other non-Anglo cultural groups within Australia. In 'The Impact of the Doctrine of Cultural Relativism on the Australian Legal System' (*E-Law* 2:1) Sam Garkawe discusses the doctrine of cultural relativism and its validity, the endorsement of cultural relativism in and through international law, and its applicability to Australia by means of discussion of two vexed cultural and legal issues – female circumcision in some Islamic communities and the customary Aboriginal punishment of spearing. Garkawe concludes that the doctrine of cultural relativism offers considerable scope for the accommodation of a range of cultural values and practices within the Australian legal system; however, its effective adoption will require a strong will on the part of judges and legal practitioners, extra time and expense through its reliance on the calling of expert witnesses to attest to cultural value and practice, and also the ongoing cross-cultural education of legal practitioners.

Christine Stafford's 'Colonialism, Indigenous Peoples and the Criminal Justice Systems of Australia and Canada: Some Comparisons' (Kayleen M. Hazelhurst, ed., *Legal Pluralism and the Colonial Legacy,* Avebury, 217–41) offers a critique of the Canadian and Australian legal – and particularly criminal justice – systems based on the principle that both legal systems are active inheritors of colonialist legacies with respect to their treatment of indigenous peoples. In her study, which is generously documented with statistics and, with respect to the Australian context, analysis of the recommendations of the Royal Commission into Aboriginal Deaths in Custody, Stafford uses postcolonial theory, including the work of Fanon, to read the roles of police and prison officers as crucial to a persistent 'gatekeeping' of settler society, creating and maintaining a social order which is deeply divided and characterized by structural violence. The way forward lies in a thorough overhaul of the system and in the provision of access to land, economic self-sufficiency and autonomy for indigenous people.

The question of the relationship between indigenous language and non-indigenous (frequently Western) law is taken up by Fernand de Varennes in 'Indigenous Peoples and Language' (*E-Law* 2:1). De Varennes considers, within the international arena and selected national contexts, the status and recognition of indigenous languages in the law and the implications (flowing from acknowledgment in international law) that indigenous peoples are entitled to preferential treatment in relation to their languages. This, argues de Varennes, stems not from their status as minority groups, but from acknowledgement in international forums and some national jurisdictions that they occupy a unique political and legal niche which justifies preferential treatment that may not necessarily be extended to other minority groups. De Varennes includes discussion of the status of Aboriginal languages in Australian law relative to the recognition accorded to indigenous languages in other national jurisdictions. A more focused study of the recognition afforded to Aboriginal languages in the Australian legal system is provided in a number of essays in the collection, edited by Diana Eades, *Language in Evidence: Issues Confronting Aboriginal and Multicultural Australia*. The collection contains several essays on the practice of forensic linguistics and on the status of languages other than English in the Australian legal system. Essays pertaining directly to Aboriginal languages and Aboriginal English are: Russel Goldflam's 'Silence in Court!: Problems and Prospects in Aboriginal Legal Interpreting' (28–54); Michael Cooke's 'Aboriginal Evidence in the Cross-Cultural Courtroom' (55–96); Michael Walsh's 'Tainted Evidence: Literacy and Traditional Knowledge in an Aboriginal Land Claim' (97–123); and Eades's own consideration of Aboriginal English in 'Aboriginal English on Trial: The Case for Stuart and Condren' (147–74).

2.4 Law and Loss: The Stolen Children

Alongside land and law, another area in which the Australian state is being challenged to account for its conduct with respect to Aboriginal people is that of the forced removal of Aboriginal children from their families. This practice commenced in some areas very early in the century, in 1904 in the Northern Territory, and escalated during the assimilationist decades following 1945; it was an expression of aggressive state paternalism and assimilationist policies which hoped to redeem the 'white bit' of mixed-race children through isolating the 'black bit' from Aboriginal culture (Ian Anderson, 'White Bit, Black Bit', *Republica* [1994]1.113–22) so that the child might be de-Aboriginalized and made fit for a productive role in white Australian society. For girls this meant menial work and domestic service, for boys, rural labour; it frequently also meant sexual and other abuse, prostitution, criminality and incarceration, alcoholism and profound loss. This policy impacted on the lives of thousands of indigenous people and families (see Coral Edwards and Peter Read, eds, *The*

Lost Children, Doubleday Books, 1989). It is a recurrent theme in Aboriginal writing – for example, Glenyse Ward's *Wandering Girl* (Magabala Books, 1988) and Rita Huggins and Jackie Huggins, *Auntie Rita* (Aboriginal Studies Press, 1994) – and other forms of cultural production, such as the songs of Archie Roach, Ruby Hunter and Kev Carmody. Child stealing persisted until 1967 in New South Wales and 1976 in the Northern Territory (Lorna Lippmann, *Generations of Resistance: Mabo and Justice*, 3rd edn, Longman, 1994) and its legacy survives painfully in the lives of individuals who were stolen and communities who lost several generations of children. It is not unusual for families to have had six or seven children stolen from them by the state; harrowing stories circulate about the lengths that Aboriginal women went to in order to keep their children (Jan Pettman, *Living in the Margins: Racism, Sexism and Feminism in Australia*, Allen & Unwin, 1992). In response to long-standing agitation from Aboriginal groups, such as the Aboriginal and Torres Strait Child Care Agencies, for the government to acknowledge, account for and provide compensation for the harm caused by this practice, a Human Rights Commission Inquiry into child stealing was called in 1995.

In 'They Took the Children Away' (*Alternative Law Journal* 20:1.35–6/ *Aboriginal Law Bulletin* 3:72.35–6) Tony Buti reports on the activities of the Aboriginal Legal Service of Western Australia in collecting life histories and testimonials from Aboriginal men and women removed from their families by the state and from parents of stolen children as part of its preparation of a submission to the Federal government for an inquiry into stolen children. Buti includes brief summaries of three of the hundred stories collected to date. He also canvasses some of the legal issues surrounding child removal, noting that forced removal of children arguably constitutes genocide under Article 2 of the United Nations Convention against Genocide and a clear contravention of Paragraph 6 of the Draft Declaration of the Rights of Indigenous Peoples. Buti also suggests that both governments and church groups (who colluded with government policies and practices in child removal) may be found liable for breaching their fiduciary duty to Aboriginal people on this matter; these arguable breaches could open the way for equity actions. The work done by the Aboriginal Legal Service of Western Australia in gathering together the testimonials of stolen children is published in the year under review, *Telling Our Story: A Report of the Aboriginal Legal Service of Western Australia (Inc.) on the Removal of Aboriginal Children from their Families*. The report is essential reading for those working in the field. It comprises an introduction on the relationship between child removal and assimilation policies; a history of Aboriginal child welfare policy and practice in Western Australia; a chapter on the psychological, social, cultural and other effects of removing children from their families; a chapter profiling a series of individual and family case studies; a detailed study of the impact of child removal on one Aboriginal family; and a chapter surveying the legal implications of child removal. A number of pertinent documents are reproduced in appendices. From a social services perspective, a parallel call for national action on the issue of child removal is provided by Nigel D'Souza in 'Call for a National Inquiry into the Removal of Aboriginal Children' (*Impact* 1.8). In 'The Lost Kooris' (*Alternative Law Journal* 20:1.26–8/*Aboriginal Law Bulletin* 3:72.26–8) Kelly Godfrey provides a brief history of Aboriginal child welfare policies in the state of New South Wales as administered by the Aborigines Protection Board established in 1883, which became, in 1940, the Aborigines Welfare Board. The philosophy of the Board was to provide 'protection' for full-blood Aborigines until such time as the race died out, and to assimilate into white society so-called 'half-caste' children by removing them from their families and placing them in missions, state care or with non-Aboriginal families. With the National Inquiry into the Separation of Aboriginal and Torres Strait Islander Children from their Families yet to complete its report, forced child removals and the cultural fragmentation and loss this exacted will remain a topic of importance in the field of Aboriginal studies into the future.

3. Culture and Country: Heritage, Wilderness and the Politics of the Indigenous Sacred and Secret

As we have already suggested above, the national context of 'after Mabo' continues to resonate for cultural critics in 1995. Another area for which the designation 'after Mabo' poses particularly complex issues is that of discursive positionality in relation to the Aboriginal sacred and the Aboriginal secret, particularly in the context of rights and meanings generated through relationship to land, and for which the complex and disturbing controversies initiated in 1995 over the proposed building of a bridge to Hindmarsh Island in South Australia and the competing claims revolving around Aboriginal women's secret business have become emblematic. We will look at Hindmarsh Island in 1996, by which time the affair will have percolated through to a range of publications that attempt both to contextualize and theorize the issues it raises for a number of critical orthodoxies about the contemporary politics of negotiating race, gender, land and the secret/sacred in Australia. Nevertheless, in the range of press reports and editorial comment emergent during 1995 over Hindmarsh (see Chris Kenny, 'Empowerment', *Adelaide Review* June.3–5, 45; Geoffrey Partington, 'Determining Sacred Sites – The Case of the Hindmarsh Island Bridge', *Current Affairs Bulletin* Feb./March.4–11; Roff Smith, 'Disputed Secrets' *Time,* June.5.38–9) it was clear that fundamental issues of who speaks, from where and about where in relation to land and the sacred have been raised to an extent that will not easily subside or be reconciled with prevailing notions of discursive entitlements and ethics.

3.1 *Talking Country, Talking Silences: Competing Paradigms of Aboriginal 'Heritage', the 'Secret' and the 'Sacred'*

Something of the same knotty problematic is already evident in work published during 1995. 'Talking out of place', as Ken Gelder and Jane Jacobs note ('Talking Out of Place: Authorising the Aboriginal Sacred in Postcolonial Australia', *Cultural Studies* 9:1.150–60) suggests both speaking out of turn and simultaneously a situated discourse, a 'talking out of *a* place', that crucially locates indigenous and non-indigenous critics alike in their relationship to intersubjective formations of nationhood, histories and identities in the public sphere. In addition to the work of Gelder and Jacobs, this territory is explored in several pieces dealing with heritage and heritage management, material culture, 'wilderness' and the discourses that both underwrite and impel their circulation in various cultural and institutional domains.

In their thoughtfully argued and theoretically provocative essay, Gelder and

Jacobs examine the range of discursive positions both enabled and disabled in the context of 'after Mabo' as they arise in relation to the Aboriginal sacred and secret. Prior to Mabo (albeit this affords a slightly too convenient 'pre/post' divide), discourses of the Aboriginal sacred and secret were confined largely to the disciplines of anthropology, ethnography and comparative religion, with some permutations filtering through in governmental decrees and statutes where these were required for direct adjudication in relation to land claims across Australian states and territories. Most frequently, the sacredness of Aboriginal sites and land areas depended for their status precisely on the kind of secrecy and silence that made their articulation outside of ceremonial practices a violation of the very principle they were intended to protect, thus disadvantaging Aboriginal peoples for many decades in their efforts to secure sacred sites and land areas against non-indigenous appropriation and destruction. Gelder and Jacobs suggest that the 'after Mabo' moment is, for non-indigenous Australia, one that occasions both pleasure and panic as they anticipate the 'liberation' of the sacred into discourses of the nation at large. For Gelder and Jacobs, the eruption of the Aboriginal 'sacred' and 'secret' into the public domain brings with it a resurgence of fears about the – quite literally – unmanageable nature of Aboriginal peoples and of Aboriginality itself.

How the sacred is negotiated 'outside of itself' between Aboriginal and non-Aboriginal people in the public domain informs the main theoretical thrust of 'Talking Out of Place'. A critical paradigm is supplied in the essay by turning to issues of the performativity of the sacred in the public domain – 'the way it is spoken about, the way it is unspoken about' – which in turn helps illuminate the ways in which the Aboriginal sacred and secret invite but also disarm the constraints of non-indigenous law that seek to contain it yet are unable finally to control and manage it. By definition, the Aboriginal sacred occupies an important border zone as an extra-legal, 'non-fixable' surplus, in which the foundations (legal, geographic, spatial) of European *laws of the land* are continually challenged by the question, 'where *is* the sacred?' The most frequent responses to that question from non-Aboriginal-based institutions and interests – mining, government, pastoral – attempt both to spatialize and authorize fixed areas that allow boundaries to be drawn and temporal limits to be set (for example, the requirement of unbroken or 'continuous' occupation) in which the 'sacred' is held within a rigidly defined zone of sanctuary. Yet as Gelder and Jacobs's discussion of the Coronation Hill claim of the Jawoyn people and the Alice Springs dam controversy for the Arrernte people of the Northern Territory makes clear, such wishfully simplistic 'inside/outside' distinctions bring a range of local, global and regional performances to bear on the spatial/temporal dimensions of the sacred, with resultingly complex affiliations across local/global divides. Perhaps the most telling section of Gelder and Jacobs's paper deals with the issue of strategic disclosure as a tactic now more readily availed by Aboriginal people in the 'after Mabo' moment; for example, the increasing disclosure of women's business to non-Aboriginal environmental feminists during the struggle over the Two Women Dreaming site in Alice Springs points to both the possibilities but also the very serious risks faced by Aboriginal people when 'the sacred spiral[s] out of its locality through the manufacture of sympathy' with people outside the traditional group for whom such knowledge is designated.

Gelder and Jacobs conclude by examining the shifts in the meaning of silences surrounding the Aboriginal sacred, suggesting that they have become multi-layered as a way of dealing with the complex necessities of both disclosure and withholding. Using Paddy Roe's remarks on country and talking in and out of place in Stephen Muecke's *Textual Spaces: Aboriginality and Cultural Studies* (New South Wales University Press, 1992), the authors read Roe's commentary to suggest that the sacred has gone 'underground' in order to accommodate a 'top layer' of permissible discourse in the public domain that is advantageous to Aboriginal people in their efforts to (re)claim land in the theatre of the global, while the 'bottom layer' remains bound to the local, and the secret, despite the accommodations performed in the public sphere. Gelder and Jacobs's hopeful positing of an authentic sacred lying somewhere beneath the surface of the version performed in, and on behalf of, the public sphere invites critique from a number of vantage points, but the authors do gesture in their closing remarks to the risks, both theoretical and more urgently practical, that their interpretive model may entail.

Just how urgent some of those practical considerations are is demonstrated in a brief report by Andrew Chalk appearing in the *Alternative Law Journal* (20:1.34–5/*Aboriginal Law Bulletin* 3:72.34–5). The discovery in 1994 of the largest known Aboriginal burial site in Australia arose (literally) from the depths of Lake Victoria in New South Wales when the waters were lowered from an artificially maintained maximum level to allow work on the lake's regulator. The area is reported by Chalk to be of 'immense significance' for its traditional owners, the Barkandji people. Still under adjudication at the time of Chalk's report, the New South Wales Aboriginal Land Council faced a stand-off in the Land and Environment Court, since a preliminary ruling granted rights to the Murray Darling Basin Commission (MDBC) to continue to artificially maintain water levels in Lake Victoria, despite clear evidence of wind and wave erosion to an area that archaeologists estimate contains between 6,000 and 18,000 burials. Despite some legal protection accorded to 'relics' located on Crown land under the National Parks and Wildlife Act (1974), which have been defined to include Aboriginal remains, the MDBC's application rests on the priority status of an agreement between the Commonwealth and four state governments to 'ensure an equitable allocation' of waters from the Murray Darling rivers system. At the time of Chalk's report, the intention of the MDBC to continue its application to gain 'consent to destroy burials' remained intact, a telling instance of the ways in which 'after Mabo' has by no means always and everywhere had a revisionist impact on non-indigenous approaches to Aboriginal land rights and cultural significance claims.

Issues of discursive positionality also arise in Peter Collins's review of debates surrounding the Wandjina rock paintings in the Kimberley caves of Western Australia (*Revelation Magazine*, 11.56–9). Collins documents the strands of contesting theories – anthropological, archaeological and ethno-geographic – brought to bear on the cultural origins of the Wandjinas and of a proximate group of rock art formations called the 'Bradshaw' figures in the archaeological and anthropological literature, but referred to as 'Kuyon' by the Kamali people of the region. At stake, Collins argues, is the fundamental resistance of some white Australian researchers in these fields to adopt what critics, including Jane Jacobs, Ken Gelder and Stephen Muecke, term a discursive 'listening position', one that elicits rather than effaces the indigenous agency of story and meaning in relation to land. Ultimately, what is being resisted, suggests Collins, is the agency and differential valency of Aboriginal spirituality itself, particularly as it relates to issues of land now under scrutiny as Native Title claims accelerate in quantity and urgency. The effort to desacralize Aboriginal land, however, is at dramatic odds with the reinvestment in the Aboriginal sacred made by successive Australian state and federal governments wishing to promote regional and international tourism by capitalizing on Aboriginal culture and heritage as a marketing device. Collins's review of the Kimberley caves debates, while untheorized, raises interesting points around the contradictions that such disinvestment/reinvestment models in the meanings of indigenous culture and heritage perpetuate as part of a broader struggle for negotiated meanings between Aboriginal and non-Aboriginal peoples in the spheres of cultural production and heritage management.

3.2 The Politics of the Secret: Managing and Mismanaging Material Culture

The politics of how the meanings of culture and country for Aboriginal peoples intersect with those of the secret and the sacred frequently challenges received Western meanings about the definition of what constitutes 'land' and 'country' by extending beyond the overtly land-based into other realms of material culture. These include what have come to be known as sacred/secret objects and artefacts that signify in Aboriginal ceremony and knowledge systems. This domain of Aboriginal culture and country, with particular reference to the cultures of Western and Central Desert peoples, is the subject of an important collection, *The Politics of the Secret*, a monograph in the Oceania series edited by Christopher Anderson. The term which denotes Aboriginal secret/sacral objects is *tjurunga* (also spelled *tjuringa, churinga, chooringa*). A number of the essays in the collection traces the interactions and transactions – and the meanings accorded to these – by which *tjurunga* (objects primarily of wood and stone) were removed from Aboriginal custody and care and placed either in private collections or in the collections of the world's museums, in particular the Museum of South Australia; and, more recently, the negotiations which have seen some of them returned to the descendants of their traditional owners. As a whole the collection of essays works to problematize a number of widely held assumptions in relation to *tjurunga*: for example, that when Aboriginal people parted with *tjurunga* it was always a matter of theft, appropriation or expropriation; and that 'secrets' are static, unchanging and removed from and therefore not influenced by the changing dynamics of sociality and history. Other essays in the volume critically examine the non-Aboriginal preoccupation with *tjurunga* as the key to Aboriginal culture and the problematic complicity of non-Aboriginal collectors in another politics of secrecy, offering critical perspectives on the practices of explorers, missionaries and anthropologists engaged in *tjurunga* collecting.

The essays in the first section of the collection provide contemporary ethnographic accounts of Aboriginal secret business (business being the English word used by Aboriginal people to denote ritual and other cultural practices) with an emphasis on demonstrating the responsiveness of ritual to change. In 'Religious Knowledge and the Politics of Continuity and Change' (15–25) Kingsley Palmer looks at an Aboriginal community on a cattle station in north-west Australia; the community is largely composed of recently arrived immigrant Aboriginal people from desert regions whose ritual life and store of sacra are more robust than those of the Aboriginal people who have lived on the station for a longer period of time. Palmer documents some of the means by which this community adapts its ritual business to account for their new surroundings as well as maintaining links with the country many members have left behind. Palmer utilizes the metaphor of political economy to account for the transfer of religious knowledge within the community, the augmentation of religious knowledge through transfer and exchange, and the way in which ritual business serves as a regulator of community relations.

The essay by Erich Kolig, 'Darrugu – Secret Objects in a Changing World' (27–42), takes up many of the concerns in Palmer's essay through a study of secret business in the Aboriginal community at Fitzroy Crossing in the Kimberley region, in particular the efforts of a number of recently arrived men to endow their new home with a strong religious sense and the impact that this had on the rest of the community. Kolig's work focuses on the role of darrugu, the Womadjeri (Walmatjari) term for tjurunga. The essay documents the resilience of sacral traditions in adapting to new country, changing demography and to new practices, including, following the success of Central Australian dot-style painting on the world art market, the community's involvement in a thriving commercial art scene which involved the translation of many sacral designs to a form appropriate to wide viewing and sale.

The particular challenges posed to the secrecy of Aboriginal sacred business by the success of Aboriginal art, which uses many sacred designs, and the processes by which Aboriginal artists in the new art movement developed a style of painting to accommodate the demands of secrecy are the subject of Dick Kimber's essay, 'Politics of the Secret in Contemporary Western Desert Art' (123–42). Kimber's study provides some historical background to the formation of the community at Papunya, and the traditional and geographical associations of the various groups which make up the community there, explaining the reasons for the differences between Pintupi people and other groups at Papunya. Kimber then provides a selected chronology of events following the arrival of Geoff Bardon in the community and his encouragement of a number of men to take up painting with acrylics on board. The works, which were originally done by way of an education for Bardon in some aspects of men's business, took on different meanings, with significantly different implications for the restricted and privileged knowledges they depicted, when they were later exhibited and sold. Kimber details the ways in which the artists attempted to come to terms with the profound conflict of interest presented by the success of the paintings: initially the problems were addressed by ensuring that the paintings were exhibited and sold at some distance from the communities affected by their depiction of business, but this temporary measure was ultimately replaced by a more mediated response which was to change the way the paintings were produced and the ways in which their knowledges and stories were depicted.

The Aboriginal men, Kimber argues, developed a mode of painting that figuratively alluded to the business which was the ultimate subject of the painting without actually depicting privileged or restricted knowledge. This, suggests Kimber, has some parallels with other Aboriginal discourses which are conducted on two levels: an 'easy' way for the uninitiated – women, children and young men – and the 'hard' or dangerous way for those admitted to knowledge of the particulars of business at hand. The appearance of the paintings has changed over time to accommodate these changes: extensive dotting rather than hatching or the use of arcs, and other modifications such as alluding to *tjurunga* by means of concentric circles rather than their depiction by the traditional motif of an elongated oval with a distinctive in-fill design.

A further group of essays in the collection provides historical accounts of settler knowledge and collecting of *tjurunga*, detailing the exploits of collectors such as T. G. H. Strehlow, F. J. Gillen, Price Maurice and the trooper Ernest Cowle. In 'Secrets of the Arandas: T. G. H. Strehlow and the Course of Revelation' (51–66) John Morton examines the sociological, religious and psychological aspects of secrecy in the life and work of Strehlow, famous for his work with the Arrernte (Aranda) and other Aboriginal peoples. Morton's work focuses on the insoluble contradictions in the life of Strehlow, his mission upbringing providing him with a profound and intimate knowledge of Arrernte culture that conflicted deeply with his inability to view Arrernte culture as creatively transmitted, relegating the Arrernte perpetually to the prison-house of the past. His view of the Arrernte as a 'decadent' or dead culture was confirmed for him by the fact that many *tjurunga* were passed on to him by elders unwilling to entrust them to younger Aboriginal men. These contradictions are read by Morton as reaching their inevitable and paralysing conclusion in the bitter disputes which characterized Strehlow's final years, as he struggled to maintain control over the secrets in his possession. Philip Jones, in 'Objects of Mystery and Concealment: A History of *Tjurunga* Collecting' (67–96), details how the *tjurunga* of Central Australia were 'discovered' by Europeans and how they readily became highly prized and highly symbolic objects. Using the journals and correspondence of collectors, Jones shows how *tjurunga* became incorporated into colonial discourses of primitivism and were inserted into narratives of mystery, concealment and revelation not unlike the narratives of key colonial texts such as the novels of Rider Haggard, in which, characteristically, one artefact or site contains the key to all mythologies. *Tjurunga* were viewed as *the* Casaubon-like key to the mysteries of Aboriginal culture in the belief that their possession and systematic study would unlock those secrets for the possessor, thus substantially distorting the significance of *tjurunga* in their Aboriginal contexts.

The third section of the volume contains essays that examine the processes, politics and meanings of decollecting: the repatriation or return of *tjurunga* to the descendants of their traditional owners. The first essay, 'The Economics of Sacred Art: The Uses of a Secret Collection in the South Australian Museum' (97–107), is by Christopher Anderson, who works on the staff of the museum and has been directly involved in negotiations for the repatriation of artefacts and sacra. Like other contributors to the volume, Anderson chooses to emphasize the variety of ways in which Aboriginal ritual objects left Aboriginal hands. In addition to the outright theft and appropriation of such objects, Anderson contends that Aboriginal people were willing to utilize what he calls the 'social currency' of objects by means of exchanges for goods (tobacco, flour), or in order to obligate recipients, particularly Europeans perceived to be in key positions, against future necessity.

Anderson writes that the pressure for repatriation of indigenous objects in museum collections runs contrary to the very *raison d'être* of museums, which is, simply, to collect and keep things. From the mid-1960s and early 1970s museums worldwide have been under increasing pressure from the traditional owners of materials held in collections. In Australia, the pressure was such that the collections could not be used for any museum purposes as both exhibition of and research on collections were discontinued. Into the 1970s, pressures on museums increased and Aboriginal groups began making claims for the repatriation of their material. Anderson goes on to document the processes of negotiation which took place between the Museum of South Australia, which has the largest collection of Central Australian Aboriginal artefacts in the world, and some of the traditional owners of those materials – the Warlpiri, the Anmatyerre, the Pintupi, the Luritja. In some cases these negotiations have resulted in agreement that the museum retain materials on the understanding that it serves as custodian of artefacts for and on behalf of the traditional owners; where permission is granted by the owners of the material, such collections may again be available for research. In other cases, materials have been returned to communities. Anderson's essay emphasizes the very dynamic view of culture held by the Aboriginal communities with which he has dealt and the transformative effect that this process has had on the museum itself. The negotiations with Aboriginal communities over the return of objects including secret/sacred objects have involved numerous exchanges which further evidence the social currency of material objects and which, at times, have seen the museum taking on new roles in relation to Aboriginal communities. The museum has provided advice to communities on establishing their own museums, cultural centres and keeping places for the holding and, where appropriate, display of repatriated objects. In other cases, communities have negotiated with the museum for its use as a venue for the exhibition and sale of contemporary and non-restricted art and artefacts, with the museum shop also serving as an important outlet for the Anmatyerre's acrylic art.

Sandra Pannell also examines the issue of repatriation in 'The Cool Memories of *Tjurunga*: A Symbolic History of Collecting, Authenticity and the Sacred' (108–22). Pannell's concern in this essay, an expanded and revised version of her 1994 'Mabo and Museums: The Indigenous (Re)Appropriation of Indigenous Things', *Oceania* 65.18–39) is with how objects such as *tjurunga* move in and out of changing systems of meaning. Pannell suggests that this movement entails not merely processes and histories of objectification but of 'objectypification'. Turning to the work of Baudrillard (*For a Critique of the Political Economy of the Sign*, Telos Press, 1981) on exchange and equivalence, Arjun Appadurai (ed., *The Social Life of Things: Commodities in Cultural Perspective*, Cambridge, 1986) on diversion, enclaving and the sacred, and Igor Kopytoff ('The Cultural Biography of Things: Commoditisation as Process' in Appadurai, ibid.), Pannell argues that the urge to commodify, which seeks to produce equivalences between objects and reduce more and more objects to the processes of exchange, needs to be understood in relation to the counter-tendency to mark difference/ambivalence as unique, thereby restricting the commodity phase of the object, or removing it from its usual sphere of exchange, enclaving and essentially decommodifying it. This process goes some way to accounting for the categorization of some objects as sacred by Europeans; as Pannell argues, the 'European valuation of Aboriginal ritual objects as instantiations of the sacred has very little to do with their cultural significance to Aboriginal people and much more to do with our own search for meaning.'

Turning to the work of Durkheim (*The Elementary Forms of Religious Life*, The Free Press, 1915), much of which is based on his understanding of the operation of *tjurunga* in Central Australian Aboriginal societies via the work of Spencer and Gillen, Pannell recalls Evans-Pritchard's wry comment that 'it was Durkheim and not the savage who made society into a god'. In a similar vein, Pannell argues, it is Europeans and not Aboriginal people who turned *tjurunga* into 'sacred' objects. This is not to suggest that *tjurunga* are not highly significant objects to Aboriginal people, or to suggest that only Europeans enjoy the exclusive privilege of bestowing meaning, but rather that the term 'sacred' has a long history of meaning in European consciousness to which the concept of *tjurunga* was assimilated. Further, Pannell argues, while the term 'sacred' has a long genealogy in the West, the memory of the sacred is often forgotten, so that the appellation frequently comes to stand for itself: the sacred quality of an object is assured by its very designation as sacred. Pannell continues that, notwithstanding the ethnographic problems with Durkheim's analysis of Australian totemism, the contention that the totems/*tjurunga* are an abstracted and deified signification of society provides a clue to understanding the meaning of these objects for Europeans. Certainly, it serves to illuminate the practices of missionaries, museums and anthropologists in relation to *tjurunga* – an illumination which serves to connect the sacred with the domain of politics and power, which Durkheim himself failed to do.

Pannell illustrates the point by reference to the missionary practice of removing and destroying *tjurunga* which was seen as a necessary step in the process of converting Aboriginal people to Christianity. The ritual objects were read by Europeans as images of 'false gods' and, in a Durkheimian sense, as images of a false society. Their destruction signified the destruction of Aboriginal society and the requisite preparation for 'civilization' to replace it. Museum practice also affirms the notion that ritual objects are distilled and deified instances of the society which produced them, although the museum collections represented the interests of science rather than those of God. The ethnological core of any self-respecting collection of Aboriginal objects was the collection of ritual or sacred objects. The sacral objects were invariably complemented by a cache of weaponry – spears, clubs, shields – creating a highly gendered construction of Aboriginal society.

The acquisition by museums of key symbols of the society of the 'other' serves, Pannell continues, to resolve the dilemma of radical alterity. The appropriation and incorporation of objects of alterity serve to erase the identity originally signified and to remake new, more familiar identities in radically different contexts. The enclaving and preservation of ritual objects in museums is used by Pannell to illustrate the point. With the aid of technology, museums can revive the transient, transform it into the permanent, and ensure a continuity that did not necessarily pertain in the original context, as with Aboriginal wooden ritual objects such as the boards which are particularly susceptible to weather, termites, dry rot and age. Several writers note in their field observations that no attempt is made by Aboriginal people to preserve such items, which do not survive beyond one generation. By comparison, the museum appears far better equipped to preserve Aboriginal culture: but, as Pannell asks, to what end and by what means?

In a profound irony, many ritual objects, whether received or wrested from Aboriginal control, have enjoyed a status similar to their place in Aboriginal culture in so far as they have continued to have stringent restrictions attached to them. Pannell cites as illustrations of this the vast secret/sacred vault in the South Australian Museum or the extreme protocols of restricted access which obtain in the Strehlow Research Centre. The power of these objects derives not from ritual or mythic knowledge of them but from what Michael Taussig (*The Nervous System*, Routledge, 1992) has called the 'fantasies of the people prohibited', which serve as evidence of the validating power of fetishism. Pannell extends Durkheim's thesis to contend that what accounts for our preoccupation with *tjurunga* is that the ritual objects are held to signify not just the materialization of Aboriginal society *per se* but what that society itself signifies – authenticity. In a world of simulacra, 'when the real is no longer what it used to be' as Baudrillard (*Simulations*, Semiotexte, 1983) contends, the search for the truth lost to us but still to be found in pure, pristine and authentic cultures such as that of the Australian Aborigines redoubles.

Pannell quotes Brian Spooner's work on oriental carpets in which he argues that 'authenticity is our cultural choice' ('Weavers and Dealers: The Authenticity of the Oriental Carpet' in Appadurai, *The Social Life of Things*, op. cit.) and turns her consideration of the meaning of *tjurunga* back to the practice of anthropology itself, contending that 'Aboriginal ritual objects are to anthropologists as oriental carpets are to connoisseurs and collectors.' Pannell then details the means by which anthropology became its own self-fulfilling prophecy, turning *tjurunga* into the totems that Durkheim first imagined them to be. Pannell writes of the perception amongst anthropologists who have worked in Australia that they are somehow more of an anthro-pologist if they have been shown 'sacred objects'. The sighting of the ritual objects in the writings of (mostly) male anthropologists is characterized by Pannell as a 'revelatory act which lays bare the fundamental truths and . . . stamps the individual with the indelible mark of anthropological authenticity'. Thus, those who have been shown the secrets sanctify their own knowledge and status by the continuation of the observance of indigenous restrictions in other contexts and, in so doing, stimulate the fantasies of those prohibited from the secret.

3.3 Nature as Cultural History: Issues in Heritage, Wilderness, Land Management and Eco-Politics

Further considerations of Aboriginal culture in relation to contemporary debates surrounding heritage and environmental management and values are taken up by various publications under a number of (inter)disciplinary dispensations. Isabel McBryde turns her attention in 'Dream the Impossible Dream? Shared Heritage, Shared Values, or Shared Understanding of Disparate Values?' (*Historic Environment* 11:2/3.8–14) to underlying theories of cross-cultural heritage management with particular reference to the difficulties arising from contradictions between the models of 'shared cultures and values' on the one hand, and 'commonalities of concern' on the other. McBryde cites two recent controversies surrounding heritage, land and cultural management in the Mungo Lake area in New South Wales and the Mount William (originally Kulin, after the indigenous inhabitants of the area) greenstone quarry near Lancefield in Victoria.

McBryde deconstructs the model of 'shared cultures and values' by pointing to what she sees as irreconcilable disparities between Aboriginal and European approaches to heritage valuation. Her sense of these disparities is not under-written, it should be noted, by a static or synchronic investment in differential models of Aboriginal and European valency regarding land and heritage, but by a conviction that the archaeological and ethnographic models of heritage valuation are rooted in fundamental structures of Aboriginal dispossession – both material and imaginative – that are embedded in a specific history and discourse, primarily that of social Darwinism. As such, they are more about the value of Aboriginal heritage for 'us' and for grand narratives of Western civilization, she suggests, rather than about the significance of Aboriginal heritage for contemporary indigenous peoples and communities. McBryde poses important questions in her sometimes deceptively simple paper, including the question of how the model of 'shared culture and values' assumes unquestioningly both the nature of 'sharing' and the objects to be shared: what, exactly, is it we are meant to be 'sharing: knowledge? or belief systems? or the values that underpin that knowledge?' She also raises contemporary issues that vex the theory and practice of cross-cultural heritage management in Australia, including the appropriateness of accepting the 'loss of physical heritage' through repatriation and relinquishment to its traditional Aboriginal owners and custodians in cases where 'conservation is counter to traditional mores', and the dynamics of heritage management models that must confront the 'assertion' of heritage values by indigenous people in the absence of a failure to reveal the specifics of their claim where it would countermand the taboo against disclosure in the context of sacred and/or secret cultural business.

McBryde reminds her readers that nineteenth-century ethnography and archaeology regarded Aboriginal culture as so distinct from the 'modern world' that indigenous peoples and cultures were effectively relegated to the status of natural history. A similar point is made about contemporary discourses of wilderness and 'natural' vs. 'cultural' heritage management by Ian McNiven and Lynette Russell in 'Place with a Past: Reconciling Wilderness and the Aboriginal Past in World Heritage Areas' (*Royal Historical Society of Queensland Journal* XV:11.505–19). The National Wilderness Inventory definition of wilderness endorsed by the Australian Heritage Commission consistently refers to the erosion of wilderness by 'European settlement' and defines wilderness proper as a 'location . . . remote from and undisturbed by the influence of *modern technological society*' (McNiven and Russell's emphasis). McNiven and Russell read this to say that the impact on wilderness from 'non-modern' (that is, 'traditionally' oriented indigenous) societies is 'consistent with wilderness values', and they proceed to problematize this view. Given the emphasis on the non-human as a constituent part of contemporary wilderness definitions, there is, for McNiven and Russell, a disturbing alignment of 'traditional' Aboriginal peoples with the natural and the non-human, reminiscent of the pre-1967 referendum view that (as recently as 1966) saw representations of Aborigines during the European contact phase described in government publications as 'in equilibrium with other members of the fauna to which he belonged' [*sic*]. Moreover, McNiven and Russell discern troubling distinctions and hierarchies between 'traditional' Aborigines and their urban counterparts in such discourses, in which indigenous peoples 'with spears, firesticks and stone tools are welcome in wilderness landscapes', but

Aboriginal people leading lives marked as 'modern' by 'motor vehicles, guns and houses' are not. Such alignments of 'wilderness' with the 'pristine environments' of what McNiven and Russell perceive as a corollary of the Eurocentric imaginary of both nature and the indigene as 'other' are 'anathema' in the Australian context of reconciliation efforts between Aboriginal and non-Aboriginal citizens. As their case-studies of the management of wilderness areas in south-west Tasmania and Fraser Island attempt to show, contemporary wilderness and heritage management work, unwittingly or not, to extend and refine imperial notions of *terra nullius* in ways that bear significant traces of neo-colonial nostalgia and a resistance to acknowledging the historical contemporaneity of Aboriginal cultures, identities, and claims for land and partnership in heritage management. The recognition of the Aboriginal past within wilderness areas and the accommodation of this history, argue McNiven and Russell, must necessarily challenge us to rethink the ways in which wilderness is conceptualized and managed; specifically, not merely as a natural resource, but also as cultural heritage.

An attempt to reconceptualize wilderness along the lines proposed by McNiven and Russell is provided by Greg Sargent in 'A Land Needs its People' (*Wilderness News* May/June, 8–9) which details the management of wilderness along environmental and cultural lines on the Cape York Peninsula in far north Queensland. Sargent outlines some of the long-standing tensions between environmental activists and indigenous peoples on issues of conservation and environmental protection. The issue of traditional hunting rights is particularly contentious, with radical environmentalists frequently citing the extinction of megafauna as proof of the environmentally destructive nature of traditional Aboriginal land management practices. Sargent details co-operation between the local Aboriginal community at Starcke and the Cairns Branch of the Wilderness Society in developing management strategies that recognize and protect the extraordinary biodiversity of the area and also the rich land-based cultural traditions of the Aboriginal people, which include hunting and fishing. Sargent concludes by calling for greater recognition from governments and environmentalists of the cultural and social dimensions to wilderness in Australia.

Contested interpretations of nature and conflicts between indigenous and non-indigenous philosophies and practices of land management were issues taken up in the Ecopolitics IX Conference at the Northern Territory University in September 1995, the proceedings and resolutions from which are published in *Ecopolitics IX: Perspectives on Indigenous People's Management of Environment Resources*. The volume contains the texts of twenty-two papers presented at the conference and the texts of statements and resolutions passed by conference delegates. The papers cover a range of indigenous land management issues across the Australasian region (environmental issues in Papua New Guinea, indigenous fishing rights in New Zealand, Melanesian land management practices) with additional contributions from North American delegates. The papers on Australian ecopolitics cover a number of issues: commercial wildlife use and its potential benefits for Aboriginal communities; marine environment issues, including the extension of Native Title to sea and fishing rights; Torres Strait Islander knowledge and management of dugong and turtle; the pastoral and mining industries and the environment; indigenous intellectual property rights and biodiversity.

Marcia Langton's paper, 'Art, Wilderness and *Terra Nullius*' (11–24), provides an historical overview of discourses on Aboriginality, nature and 'wilderness' in Australian culture – discourses that continue to produce a 'double bind' for Aboriginal people and that do not 'permit real Aboriginal people to manage national parks but emphatically require that Aboriginal culture serves as the advertising emblem in international markets of Australia as the wilderness experience in the last great frontier'. Langton draws on and makes reference to a range of cultural representations of Australian Aborigines in contexts which emphasize their authenticity and 'naturalness' and their place in (but not sovereignty over) the Australian wilderness.

Michael (Mick) Dodson, in two separate papers, 'Indigenous People, Social Justice and Rights to the Environment' (25–9) and 'Indigenous Peoples and Intellectual Property Rights' (30–6), canvasses key issues for indigenous peoples in relation to rights to country, the management of country and rights to the resources of country, particularly in terms of traditional knowledge about those resources which Western law has been slow adequately to recognize. The rights of Aboriginal peoples to indigenous biological resources is, Dodson argues, 'indivisible and indistinguishable from other rights'. The issue of indigenous intellectual property rights in biodiversity is the subject of Henrietta Fourmile's paper 'Protecting Indigenous Intellectual Property Rights in Biodiversity' (37–42). Fourmile introduces her paper with the observation that Aboriginal customary law is the longest surviving system for the protection and maintenance of intellectual and cultural property in existence. Indigenous knowledge in and of biodiversity – totemic identification with certain species, the use of flora and fauna for food, medicine and other applications, the avoidance of some toxic species or the special preparation of others to render them non-toxic – all indicate the development of bodies of knowledge and the exercise of usufructuary rights which have not been recognized or protected by Western law. While the principle of Native Title might appear to restore the intellectual property rights of Aboriginal people in plants and wildlife and other rights, such as those to mineral resources on or under the land, statements such as those made by the Queensland Government in 1993 that notwithstanding any consideration of Native Title all such resources remain the property of the Crown indicate that Aborigines and Torres Strait Islanders still face considerable obstacles in this regard. Fourmile goes on to detail some particular examples of conflicts between indigenous people's intellectual property claims and those of groups in the established area of the pharmaceutical industry and the newer, but burgeoning, field of the commercial production of bush tucker (indigenous bush foods). The intellectual property dimension to the relationship between indigenous peoples and biodiversity is also taken up by Jean Christie in 'Biodiversity and Intellectual Property Rights: Implications for Indigenous Peoples' (61–77), with particular attention to biotechnologies, biopiracy, life and human patenting, and the Human Genome and the Human Genome Diversity Projects.

The failure of legislators and policy-makers in the environmental area to account fully for the different meanings applied to land and resources by Aboriginal and non-Aboriginal Australians is highlighted in the study by Marcus Lane and Allan Dale of the deficiencies of the Environmental Impact Assessment process, 'Project Assessment in Australian Indigenous Domains: The Case for Reform' (*Australian Journal of Environmental Management*

2.30–9) By failing to take into consideration the impact on culture and social life in assessing the potential effects of proposed resource development in indigenous domains, the legislative requirements of the Environmental Protection (Impact of Proposals) Act (1974) reveal their monocultural bias and fail to provide adequate protection for Aboriginal communities whose land is subject to development proposals. The authors make a compelling case for legislative reform and for administrative changes, including the provision of cross-cultural education for personnel involved in the assessment process.

Singing the Land, Signing the Land is one of several publications resulting from a collaborative project involving Helen Watson, David Turnbull and Wade Chambers with the Yolgnu community at Yirrkala which sets out systematically to review cross-cultural materials in the curriculum in Deakin University's Social Studies of Science programme. The volume is a catalogue of an exhibition of materials, with extensive commentaries and notes, on the interaction of European and Aboriginal epistemologies of nature, of ways of knowing and being in the natural world. The guiding metaphor of the exhibition is *ganma*: a theory of confluence articulated by Yolgnu people to account for the meeting and mixing of two streams which flow – one from the land, one from the sea – into a mangrove lagoon on Caledon Bay in Arnhem Land. For the Yolgnu, *ganma* holds (in part) that the forces of the streams combine and lead to a deeper understanding and truth. It is an ancient metaphor which has served Yolgnu society well in the past. More recently it has been used by the Yolgnu and those non-Aboriginal people they have chosen to work with them (including Helen Watson as part of the Ganma Research Project at Yirrkala) to apply to the meeting and interaction of Aboriginal and non-Aboriginal cultures. The first exhibit documents the Yolgnu understanding of *ganma*. Other exhibits present rich cross-cultural material on the natural histories and cultural meaning of the crocodile, frequently an object of fear and revulsion to non-Aboriginal Australians, and admiration and reverence to the Yolgnu; on the ways in which Aboriginal and non-Aboriginal people attempt to order and understand the world and represent that understanding in patterns, graphics and schema (maps, paintings of country and songlines, graphs); and on the ways in which Aboriginal and non-Aboriginal people assert ownership and belonging to country, which is neatly juxtaposed in the exhibition's title, the 'singing' and the 'signing' of land and of one's relationship to that land.

In 'The Way of Logic' (*New Scientist* December, 38–41) Margaret Wertheim reports on the work of Helen Verran and the Aboriginal community at Yirrkala and their production of interactive cross-cultural knowledges of the world and ways of living in the world. Quoting French philosopher Bruno Latour's assessment of the Yirrkala project, Wertheim positions Verran's work at the foremost edge of cross-cultural enquiry into philosophies of science, and then goes on to examine what Verran calls the 'machinery of logic' that underpins Yolgnu knowledge systems. The logic which drives Yolgnu knowledge is not based in mathematics, as in Western models, but rather in kinship. The name the Yolgnu give to this kinship-based logic is *gurrutu* and, as Verran's work demonstrates, this should be understood as nothing less than an alternative mathematics. The parallels with Western mathematics are quite explicit. Whereas in Western mathematics, the number ten (derived from counting the fingers of both hands) forms the organizational principle, in *gurrutu* it is the number sixteen, derived from the various relationships encompassed by husband and wife, both sets of grandparents and four sets of great-grandparents. Just as, in Western mathematics, any number can be represented using combinations of the first ten numbers, so can all individuals in Yolgnu society be represented by combinations of the sixteen basic kinship terms. The sixteen kinship terms correspond to sixteen clans, which are divided into two groups of eight, a division which serves as an organizing principle for knowledge as well as society. Wertheim argues that *gurrutu* and its division of the world into two halves – *yirritja* and *dhuwa* – functions for the Yolgnu as science, as a way of apprehending and understanding the world.

3.4 Ta(l)king Culture and Country: The Assimilation of the Aboriginal Sacred and Spiritual by the Non-Indigenous

The publication in 1994 of Marlo Morgan's New Age spiritual travelogue, *Mutant Message Down Under* (HarperCollins), in which the author claims to have travelled through a remote Australian desert with a tribe of Aboriginal people, has sparked considerable controversy as indigenous people and others voiced objections to her representations of Aboriginality and raised serious questions concerning her claims that the book was based on her own experience (Craig Henderson, 'Mutant Messenger' [*Who Weekly* 4 December, 36–40] and Victoria Laurie, 'Another Story Grows in the Telling' [*Bulletin* 26 September, 38]). In the controversy surrounding *Mutant Message* the issue of Aboriginal control over depictions of their culture and questions of the politics (and economics) of representation came to the fore. *Mutant Message*, like LA New Age guru Lyn Andrews's *Crystal Woman* (Warner Books, 1987) and *Teachings Around the Sacred Wheel: Finding the Soul of the Dreamtime* (Harper & Row, 1990) represent the incursions of the New Age movement into the domain of Aboriginal spirituality in moves which simultaneously and very problematically reproduce racist and primitivist stereotypes of indigenous peoples; erase differences between different indigenous cultures; relegate indigenous peoples to the prison-house of a transcendental past and exclude them from the dynamics of history; and by-pass contemporary political struggles for land rights and social justice. As part of a concerted response by (primarily Western Australian) indigenous people to the gross distortions of Aboriginal spirituality in the work of Morgan, the self-styled 'messenger' from Aboriginal Australia, the Dumbartung Aboriginal Corporation published *Bounah Wongee – 'Message Stick': A Report on Mutant Message Down Under*. The report, co-ordinated by Robert Eggington, provides an invaluable record of indigenous responses and resistances to the work of Morgan. Eggington first became aware of Morgan's book in 1990 when the self-published edition (later picked up by HarperCollins) appeared; he undertook collation of Aboriginal responses and opposition to the book and spoke extensively to Aboriginal communities across the territory which Morgan claims to have walked with the lost tribe she dubs the 'real people' to gauge their responses to her egregious depiction of them and their land. These responses are reproduced in the report, as are media reportage of the success of Morgan's book and of Aboriginal criticisms of its fantastic and exploitative appropriations of Aboriginal culture; also included are letters from Aboriginal groups and organizations to HarperCollins protesting at the book's inaccurate and offensive material and requesting that its production and distribution be ceased. The report also includes an anthropological review of the contents of *Mutant Message* which refutes many of its descriptions of Aboriginal ceremony, culture, belief and diet. *Bounah Wongee* is an important intervention in the Aboriginal struggle to maintain control of culture and in resisting a persistently exploitative politics of representation.

The attractiveness of Aboriginal spirituality and connectedness to land to non-Aboriginal Australians characterizes other publications this year. In *The Aboriginal Gift: Spirituality for a Nation*, Eugene Stockton provides an argument for the Aboriginalization of Australian spiritual life. In the first part of the work, Stockton provides an introductory historical and anthropological overview of Aboriginal religious culture, addressing such subjects as traditional Aboriginal spirituality, the connection of Aboriginal spiritual culture to land, the role of ceremony, the degree to which contemporary urban Aboriginal people may be deemed to be Aboriginal, and the degree to which traditional spirituality has persisted in non-traditional settings. In the second part of the book, Stockton moves to a consideration of the Aboriginal spiritual concept and practice of *dadirri*, a nature-oriented asceticism enunciated by the Aboriginal Christian Miriam-Rose Ungunmerr. Stockton argues that by adopting *dadirri* in their worship and liturgy Australians will develop a spirituality more appropriate to this country than the church-based worship of the old world and may experience a deeper connection with place than is currently enjoyed.

Stockton's book represents a significant and characteristic moment in a certain kind of soft reconciliation politics circulating in post-Mabo Australia. There is in Stockton's writing an earnest attempt to account for, respect and learn from Aboriginal culture. This is certainly a welcome change from some past practice by Christians in relation to Aboriginality, but Stockton's argument also highlights the insurmountable problems with the reconciliation model within which he works. The title of his book points to much which is wrong with the model he is using: the term 'gift' is clearly problematic in the context of such a long and on-going history of non-Aboriginal taking from Aboriginal people and, while it is a term used by Ungunmerr herself in talking about *dadirri*, it is difficult, in terms of Stockton's argument, to see just what Aboriginal people themselves are to gain from handing over to 'us' aspects of their spiritual lore and practice. Other questions arise as Stockton continues to extol the benefits to be had from rejuvenating Australian spirituality with the gifts of Aboriginal spirituality: to what extent can transformations in Catholic liturgy be held to represent or even point to greater transformations in the society as a whole, and who will benefit from these unlikely transformations should they take place? As Catholic liturgy expands to stand for the 'spirituality of the nation', so the nation contracts to stand for white (and probably also Christian, even Catholic) Australians.

Stockton appears to be critically unaware of his own moves, continuing to exclude Aboriginality from his conceptual framework even as he attempts most earnestly to include it. It becomes difficult to distinguish his model of reconciliation from assimilation as he argues that 'we' come to terms with history and cultural difference by means of incorporation:

> An integral part of *our* history is the Aboriginal experience *we now make our own*. Through our forerunners in this land we have a taproot running deep into the soil of Australia. They are not an

unfortunate hiccup in our history, on the fringe of the main event. Given the antiquity of Aboriginal presence in Australia, we must acknowledge that by far the greatest number of Australians who ever lived have been Aborigines and that *they deserve a core position in our story*. In *integrating* Aboriginal experience *into our sacred story*, it is proper to seek in it some divine purpose and meaning bearing on our present and future.   (our emphasis)

Stockton also published in the year under review a further consideration of the potential for Aboriginal spirituality to transform Australian mainstream spirituality, 'Minding the Universe: Aboriginal Leads to Australian Spirituality' (*Compass Theological Review* 29.15–24). The potential for *dadirri* to transform and indigenize Australian spirituality is also taken up by Frank Fletcher in 'Australian Spirituality and Mary McKillop' (*Compass Theological Review* 29.1–5) in which the spirituality of McKillop is placed alongside *dadirri* and other Aboriginal concepts such as *murakin* – the capacity to hear voices – in an argument which amounts to a call for the selective incorporation of Aboriginal concepts and practices into Catholicism. Catholic theologians, it seems, now claim the non-earthly and transcendental domains and those of the earth and the earthly. This has very troubling implications for the rights of indigenous people to the land on which their own spiritualities (evidence of which is crucial to their claims) are based. The urge to Aboriginalize Australian spirituality evident in these publications seems rather like a retrospective spiritual justification for dispossession.

A similar set of problems and arguments which amount to apologies for dispossession is presented by David J. Tacey's *Edge of the Sacred: Transformation in Australia*. Tacey, a literary scholar influenced by Carl Jung, depth psychology and James Hillman, offers a vision of the potential for spiritual transformation in Australia along mythopoeic, archetypal and depth-psychological lines. Tacey's popularizing text is troubling for many of the reasons that Stockton's text is, and its wider readership renders more urgent the need for responses to it. Tacey supports a reconciliation agenda, land rights and social justice for Aboriginal people but does so within a framework that remains deeply problematic and that serves, in the end, the interests of white Australians in search of spiritual rejuvenation and a comfort zone enabled by an ersatz mythology of place which ultimately effaces the claims of indigenous people to land and to justice.

In a series of gestures towards universal spirituality, Tacey strenuously eschews the material and the political and posits the 'imaginal' as the only domain in which white and black can be reconciled. 'White' and 'black' are not seen so much as the embodied, lived experiences of men, women and communities through the onslaught of invasion, colonization and their aftermath, but as the clash of archetypes. Via mythopoesis and archetypal consciousness, it is possible not only to by-pass the realities of colonial history and experience but to rewrite them, as Tacey does in this disturbing passage:

> It could well be that, at an archetypal level, white intrusion into the primal round of Aboriginality is a profoundly significant symbolic event. In other words, there could be a meaningful synchronicity to the clash of white and black in Australia.

Although mostly we are aware of the negative side of this intrusion, or invasion, it could prove to be very much more than just political take-over and cultural tragedy. The puncturing of the circle could be seen in a larger sense as the intrusion of a progressive spirit that had to arrive in the Aboriginal psyche in one form or another.

Tacey's idea of the invasion which *had* to happen gives the lie to any ostensible liberalism in the book and reveals its regressive politics (alongside its progressivist teleology) quite clearly. That which is more than mere 'political take-over and cultural tragedy', and which ultimately serves as the end that justifies the unfortunate (but readily dismissible) means of invasion and dispossession is the enlightenment and further liberation of the white Australian male. Now he stands, as Tacey does, at the edge of transformation: he can cross any 'geopsychical barrier' and feel truly at home in the Australian bush (or anywhere else for that matter) and be greeted as a fellow by the likes of Les Murray (or D. H. Lawrence) in the 'free mental space' disallowed by the clamours of the politically correct – Aborigines, women and other 'others'.

The impulse to conscript Aboriginal culture, spirituality and sacred sites to roles in overmythologized romance narratives that privilege non-Aboriginal protagonists and displace Aboriginal subjects from their own cultural domains has a long history in Australian discourses about Aboriginality and in discourses which seek to produce an authentic and authenticating Australianness. The work of Stockton and Tacey indicates the degree to which such discourses persist post-Mabo largely unabated. A provocative critique of these discourses is provided by Barry Hill in his review ('Romancing the Centre', *Australian Book Review* September, 29–31) of James Cowan's *Two Men Dreaming: A Memoir, A Journey* in which he diagnoses in Cowan's work the telltale signs of 'white possessiveness about Aboriginal culture'. *Two Men Dreaming* tells of a 'journey' undertaken by Cowan and a male Pintupi elder, Sunfly Tjuperula. Juxtaposing Cowan's work with that of Fred Myers, *Pintupi Country, Pintupi Self: Sentiment, Place and Politics Among Western Desert Aborigines* (University of California Press, 1986), Hill is most critical of the enthusiastic glosses provided by Cowan on Tjuperula's commentaries on country, culture and spirituality, and of Cowan's efforts to mythologize his own role in relation to Tjuperula and the Aboriginality he represents. Cowan writes: 'Between us we were the last remnant of an ancient order that chose to recognize this great hiddenness inside the serpentine folds of the world. Who but a rain-man and a writer could possibly take hold of these surviving crystals of light and translate them into *kurunba*, spirit[?]' There is, Hill argues, in Cowan's writing an urge to mythologize and universalize, to take over the teachings of the Aboriginal man and to dress them in more poetic, more mythological clothes. Cowan, Hill continues, does not talk about place as the organizing principle of a land-based mythology (as Tjuperula does) but translates this as universalized earth: 'Say earth in the Cowan mode and you might as well say Space or Time or Eternity, for all the good it will do you.' Non-Aboriginal Australia yet stands to learn from Aboriginal knowledges, cosmologies and ontologies. However, the repeated rehearsal of inadequately apprehended and poorly translated wisdoms by non-Aboriginal 'messengers' from Aboriginal Australia, who then attempt to co-opt this wisdom into

Western categories (the romantic, the cosmic, the primitive, the liturgic) without any effort or will to transform the categories themselves, will not realize this project.

A final instance of the conscription of the Aboriginal sacred, in which it is simultaneously asserted and evacuated by non-indigenous Australians within and beyond a frame of fictive narrative practice, occurs in an interview with Margot Nash, the maker of the ominously titled film *Vacant Possession*, by Claire Corbett for *Cinema Papers* (104.18–21). The film deals with the return of a young white woman to the long-since vacated family home located near the historically resonant Botany Bay, and her encounters with issues of personal significance, both past and present, as she reckons up the meanings of 'home' in her life to date.

As writer-director, Nash describes the processes she engaged with in her efforts to produce a cinematic meditation on the meanings of houses, of families and of land circulating in 1950s Australia to the present day. The presence of golden dolphins, an Aboriginal family who figure in the protagonist's past, and an Aboriginal script consultant whom Nash met during the film's production function to authorize her contention that the film 'hints at a different connection that Aboriginal Australians have with the land, a bond not confined to the dream of owning a house'. There are 'things in the film that are to do with the land, to do with a more – how to say it? – spiritual relationship with the land', says Nash, and this diffidently represented spirituality becomes, as so often, a way of critiquing conservative white Australian mores and values by resorting to a version of the romanticized indigene who is held to live in some instructively originary connection to land and to nature.

Notwithstanding Nash's stated desire to 'acknowledge . . . the relationship between indigenous people and colonisers', the meanings of land in this regard are evacuated by Nash's production pragmatics even as they are asserted within the film itself. Referring to the decision to narrate the film from a single point-of-view – that of the young white woman at its centre – this 'turning point' in the script's progress also becomes the occasion for its liberation from any scruples regarding a truly land-based practice of representation: for instance, the film's location is shifted away from the La Perouse area (the site of a historically and culturally significant Aboriginal mission) 'onto the other side of the Bay' and relocated in a 'mythical place that was closer to where Captain Cook landed'. The erasure of La Perouse, which occupies a signal discursive space in the lives and histories of many Aboriginal people in the New South Wales area, as well as the relocation of the film's setting to a 'mythical land' and its production to Kurnell, New South Wales, parallels the disengagement of non-indigenous Australians from the materially enmeshed, rather than purely symbolic, meanings of land and the land-based sacred that many Aboriginal people struggle continuously to assert. The dispossession of land and its meanings for indigenous Australians accomplished by the film's location and production practices, as well as its plot device of 'eavesdropping' to insert Aboriginal perspectives within the film's narrative, makes of *Vacant Possession* (at least in this interview with its maker) a continuity with, rather than intervention in, the problematic of *terra nullius* to which its title so explicitly alludes and allegedly critiques.

4. Author(iz)ing Aboriginalities: Identities, Cultures, Histories, Bodies

A number of pieces by Aboriginal and Torres Strait Islander writers, academics and activists were published in 1995 that deal specifically with identity, history and representation in both personal and collective terms. Working across a range of genres and representational strategies – essays, memoirs, interviews, polemic and critique – Ian Anderson, Martin Nakata, Lionel Fogarty, Sam Watson, Lyall Munro and Stephanie Gilbert write and speak about a range of issues related to their perspectives on indigenous identity-making – and unmaking – in contemporary Australian cultural contexts.

In 'Aboriginal Nation(s)?' (*Asian and Pacific Inscriptions: Identities, Ethnicities, Nationalities*, ed. Suvendrini Perera, special book issue of *Meridian* 14:2.65–82) Ian Anderson provides a cogent and deservedly complex analysis of how Aboriginal identities are layered, performed and how they set in tension competing constructs of family, community, region and nation in the context of contemporary negotiations between Aboriginal communities and the state. The essay as a whole seeks to document and account for how contemporary indigenous identities are informed by the ways in which 'the particular and the general interpenetrate'. Anderson deploys two points of departure for his critique of Aboriginal 'nationhood' and its strategic relationship with forms of Aboriginal 'personhood'. He begins by elaborating the interrelationship between Pallawah Trouwerner people from the Tasmanian islands with Koori people from what is now the Victorian part of mainland Australia in the wake of colonial sealing activities on the Tasmanian coast, as evinced in his own family history, and then he begins again with an analysis of the Melbourne-based 'Koori Inc.' 'scandal' as represented in the pages of Melbourne's *Age* newspaper during 1994. This affair involved sustained charges against prominent Koori community member Alf Bamblett and his family members of protracted nepotism, financial misappropriation and inadequate accounting in the administration of various monies granted by the state to regional and community Aboriginal services and organizations.

The connection between Anderson's adumbration of family history and the vicissitudes of representation in the Bamblett funding controversy is sustained throughout by his interest in exploring the dynamics of the 'tension inherent in the question of pan-Aboriginality'. On the one hand, Anderson argues, pan-Aboriginality and related notions of Aboriginal nationhood are crucial in facilitating the development of Aboriginal structures capable of meeting the state on equal political, financial and rhetorical ground. On the other hand, pan-Aboriginality has the capacity both to affirm but also to contest and undercut the specificities of history, cultural and kinship affiliations and experience that continue to invest Aboriginal community life with structure, meaning and agency at the local level. The 'contours of nationhood', for Anderson, are always and everywhere bounded by the engagement of the local with the national, and by which the investment in kinship relations that form a crucial part of both Aboriginal identity and Aboriginal agency continues to be ameliorated. Much of Anderson's consideration of Aboriginal 'nation(s)' at the strategic level of national interventions is supported by his extraordinarily illuminating account of the ways in which 'pre-colonial classificatory kinship relations' have been transformed by the incursions of colonialism, particularly the mission and reserve systems, 'into the extending kinship forms common in contemporary Victorian Aboriginal communities'. Such contemporary kinship systems, he observes, have increasingly been modified to address and accommodate a complex and multilayered configuration of identities, including the 'mediation of entry' into urban Aboriginal communities by those from outside a local land- and/or family-based system in Victoria, and the vigorous balancing of the obligations and reciprocities involved in kinship relations with the 'equally important value placed on autonomy' for the individual in structures ranging from the family unit through to community and regional levels of relatedness.

Anderson then turns to the impact of self-determination or 'self-management' policies, in place since the 1960s, on the processes of balancing social alliances as a political force with the needs and entitlements conferred by local autonomy within Aboriginal communities. This impact, he suggests, has forged a reconfiguration of disparate 'mobs' into groups that have sustained the balance between social alliance and local autonomy. Such groups constellate around the need to distribute and maximize funding resources for Aboriginal health, legal services, housing and education, areas that are inflected by the state within a national, rather than kinship or local, framework. And 'herein', comments Anderson, 'lies the rub'. Whereas the 'idea of nationhood is, although unstable, an expected outcome of the colonial processes of the late twentieth century', enabling 'a commitment to the development of community when often such communities have been created out of the ongoing dislocation of peoples', its potential as a 'social form' is still based on an Aboriginal notion of personhood that is grounded in the network of 'reciprocal relations', a network for which the ongoing use of generic kinship terms such as 'auntie', 'uncle', 'sister' and 'brother' continues to signify in contemporary community life. Thus the issues raised by the Bamblett episode signify not, as the *Age* would have it, in terms of a 'resurgent Aboriginal tribalism', but more revealingly as the outer limits of the tensions set in train between Aboriginal negotiations of reciprocity, kinship and community with regional and national political imperatives. 'Indigenous identities have been formed at the seam' of colonial economic relations that have at once transformed them internally but also linked them to 'globalising processes' across a range of distinct historical forms.

The final section of Anderson's essay deals with these processes of globalization, their implications for contemporary indigenous identity formations, and the resonance of forms of Aboriginal nationhood within them. Central to Anderson's final remarks here is the need to identify how an Aboriginal political economy that has gained 'some independence from the beneficence of government . . . should articulate with a global capitalism which threatens to undermine the values [of reciprocity, alliance, kinship and autonomy] which the Aboriginal movement has sought to protect'. His essay concludes by looking beyond the national to the global – thinking about 'new political forms which transgress national boundaries in order to ameliorate the impact of globalisation on local indigenous populations', which in turn suggests that the current focus on 'Aboriginal nation(s)?' may be at a 'historical juncture' that will yield new enquiries into 'indications of an imminent global Indigenous'. Anderson's comments on contemporary issues in Aboriginal health, research and community health services, as well as an account of his own background as a medical doctor, writer and cultural critic, appeared in

1995 in an extended and useful transcript of an 'Interview with Ian Anderson, Chief Executive Officer, Victorian Aboriginal Health Service' (*Ulitarra* 8.30–45).

Writing in *Republica* ('Better', 2.61–74), Martin Nakata, a prominent Torres Strait Islander, educationalist and academic, revisits 1993 – the United Nations's 'Year of Indigenous Peoples' – and uses it as an occasion to intervene in the global representations of indigenous peoples, politics and culture authorized by the United Nations's declaration of a discursive space in which such issues might receive international prominence. Eschewing a model of historical *recit* that rehearses perspectives and theories 'grown ritual', Nakata turns to a broad interrogation of the meanings of 'culture' as a more pertinent way of understanding the history of 'what happened' in the history of cultural identity in the Torres Strait Islands since the first 'significant' contact with Europeans' in 1836.

In so doing, Nakata provides a lucid and powerful exposition of the always partialized inscription of the peoples of the Torres Strait Islands by a raft of Western 'experts', whom Nakata argues have during the last 150 years effectively 'silenced territorial boundaries and political affiliations between and among the different tribal groups of the various islands'. Nakata observes that such silencing, and the disruption and remapping of Torres Strait Islander identities that ensued, was achieved by two interrelated strategies: on the one hand, the imposition of a 'collective identity' (symbolized by the collective name of 'Torres Strait Islands' itself) that created great difficulties for the social memory and retention of old boundaries, names and places; and on the other hand, the discursively partialized representation (always disciplinary in the Foucauldian sense) of the peoples of the Torres Strait Islands in nineteenth- and twentieth-century Western scientific, anthropological, ethnographic and religious literature which has produced variously, says Nakata, 'the Linguistic Islander, the Bilingual Islander, the Bicultural Islander, the Multilingual Islander, the Linguistically Diverse Islander, the Historical Islander, and even, in 1988, the Musical Islander'. As Nakata notes, Foucault might describe the Islander as having been 'set up by a "technology of the self" ' which continues to 'legitimate colonial interventions'.

Nakata's particular interest is in 'educational institutions, policies, research, pedagogies and curricula' and the ways these have been in used in the Torres Strait Islander context to designate the peoples of the Islands as invariably 'culturally deficient' and constituted by a condition of 'lack'. Nakata poses the question: 'From whose point of view are these "lacks" inscribed upon us?' Noting the currency of several key 'textual misrepresentations' in circulation since the 1880s and which, Nakata notes, 'continue to be a foundational reference' for contemporary scholars and policy developers 'working on issues to do with the Torres Straits', he moves on to his current project, a cultural critique of the 'educational agenda set for the Islander (alongside the Aborigine . . . through the National Aboriginal and Torres Strait Islander Education Policy (NATSIEP) of 1989'. Central to his critique is his effort to relocate Torres Strait Islanders as the 'subjects of [NATSIEP's] discourse, and not as its object'. In this essay, Nakata mobilizes his own subject status by way of providing a personal history of his family, upbringing, education, and political and cultural development in order to illuminate and contextualize some of the mechanisms by which both the unmaking and the remaking of

Torres Strait Islander identities have been driven during the colonial and neo-colonial periods. One of the most interesting sections of Nakata's discussion in this regard is his analysis of the politics of 'lost and found' in relation to the status of culture as viewed under the gaze of Western 'expert' eyes. An integral component of the 1989 National Education Policy revolves around the construction of contemporary Islanders as the survivors of a 'lost' culture. Nakata points out the ways in which 'lost' not only serves to iterate the construction of Islanders as marked by 'lack', but also the troubling connotations it bears in terms of racist discourses of 'native' incapacity: 'Is it simply the case that we just weren't too good at holding on to our culture . . . innocent savages that we were?' The inaccurate designation of Islander culture as 'lost' obscures the colonial history of its being 'taken from us very aggressively' and discursively positions Western educationalists and others as the 'finders' and redeemers of this 'lost' culture, now suitably analysed and explicated by Western academic scrutiny. As a model of cultural history and dynamics in the Torres Strait Islands, it is for Nakata severely 'limited' and becomes another form of dispossession at the level of culture and education which is recycled for repossession by Torres Strait Islander students primarily as a 'regulatory device' that serves broader regimes of political and cultural management by dominant institutions.

Nakata calls polemically for a more sophisticated understanding of what 'literacy' might entail in contemporary Torres Strait Islander contexts: 'we need', he says, 'as people positioned in the margins, to be *critically* literate, not simply in any liberal sense, but in a political sense'. Quoting Audre Lorde's dictum that it is silence, not difference, that immobilizes the emancipatory projects of marginalized peoples, Nakata concludes: 'I don't think my children should have to celebrate a difference whose very constitution is still framed in terms of lack.' As Lorde says, 'There are many silences to be broken.'

In 'The Sixties' (*Republica* 2.51–9), Lyall Munro writes of growing up as a young Murri in Moree, New South Wales in the 1960s, when 'the "assimilation" idea was taking over from the "mission" idea'. The 1967 referendum giving Aboriginal and Torres Strait Islander people the vote and a range of other federal rights was yet to come, but what did arrive was the Freedom Ride, a busload of Aboriginal and non-Aboriginal university students and activists headed by a young Murri, Charlie Perkins (later to be Secretary of the Federal Department of Aboriginal Affairs under the Hawke Labor Government), that travelled through parts of Australia in the style of the American civil-rights movement some years earlier. The Freedom Riders and their tactics of 'direct confrontation' of the white Moree town fathers, who had entrenched a structure of profound segregation in Moree's municipal amenities, had a permanent impact on Munro's sense of the politically possible that was to stay with him through his conflictual years as a sports scholarship student at De La Salle College, a Catholic secondary school where, despite the lead-up to the referendum and its mooted emancipation of Aborigines, he was referred to continuously as 'Jacky Jacky' at the instigation of the school's Catholic Brothers.

Munro's beautifully rendered account of his experiences as a young Murri man dealing with his developing Aboriginal political consciousness, the 'devastating effect' of his personal and institutional entanglements with Catholicism, and his initial optimism about the struggle for Aboriginal rights generated by the 1967 referendum ends with his return to Moree and his romantic involvement with a young white woman from a prominent Moree family. That family banned Munro from contact with their daughter, and as he says, 'That showed me. Because what everything all boiled down to is this. That it didn't matter what I'd achieved at De La Salle, or what I'd achieved in the town of Moree, I was still just another nigger from the mission. Nothing ever changed, not here, except for my way of thinking, and that changed forever.'

In a brief and pointed essay ('A Postcolonial Experience of Aboriginal Identity', *Cultural Studies* 9:1.145–9), Stephanie Gilbert – an Aboriginal academic based at James Cook University in North Queensland – revisits issues related to how we understand Australian history and Australian indigenous experience and identity through the lens of postcolonial frameworks of analysis. In so doing, Gilbert asks her readers perforce to revisit issues of how, in a putatively 'post'-Mabo political and cultural context, non-indigenous audiences continue to rely on paradigms of 'guilt' and the 'guilt industry' and 'anxiety', in forms both individual and political, to explain away complex issues of colonial history that continue to imbricate Australian indigenous and non-indigenous relations – despite the obvious fact that, as she remarks, 'all Australians are in just as deep'.

Gilbert's particular interest is in a problematizing of the term 'history', which she suggests, drawing on a 1993 conference paper delivered by Christine Morris, employs different valencies when applied to the Aboriginal as opposed to European past. When Aboriginal and Torres Strait Islander people relate their experiences of the past, 'we are told that it is all history and not relevant, but if we talk about the Anzacs or Australia's federation, history becomes incredibly important and relevant'.

Gilbert argues that colonization cannot be considered 'post' in any temporal sense of the term, and points to the ways in which colonization continues to be practised through academic structures of research, data collection and 'expert' status assumed by non-indigenous researchers in search of what Gilbert terms the 'captured communities' of Aboriginal and Torres Strait Islander people who are frequently under-resourced – whether geographically, economically or educationally – to militate against this form of neo-colonial intellectual 'taking' and the loss of control and rights it entails.

She also offers a critique, albeit very brief, of the impact of federally established Aboriginal 'self-management' policies in place since the 1960s, quoting at length from an (as yet) unpublished essay by Aboriginal educational policy analyst Errol West on the 'pauperisation of Aboriginal cultures, will, expectations, capacity and hope' as a consequence of such policies. West sees these policies as window-dressing designed to disguise the failure of successive governments to deal economically or politically with the health, poverty and deaths-in-custody issues facing Aboriginal and Torres Strait Islander communities in every part of the country. The result, concludes Gilbert, is an 'entrenched pain . . . about being Aboriginal' that needs to be acknowledged and faced by non-indigenous Australians (and others) if progress is to be made beyond what the current Australian Prime Minister John Howard (taking a leaf from Australian historian Geoffrey Blainey) has controversially termed 'the black armband view of history'. In some ways, Gilbert's piece, published in 1995, anticipates Howard's comments in 1996. Gilbert concurs that 'the black armband' view of history is problematic, but for different reasons: she suggests that such a paradigm allows white Australia off the hook all too easily by assuming 'guilt' and 'anxiety', which allows problems faced by Aboriginal people as a direct consequence of economic and political policies to be individualized, psychologized and thus dismissed rather than confronted.

The emphasis on positionalities and the processes by which they are authorized, deauthorized and reauthorized continues to be prominent in work concerned explicitly with Aboriginality, identity and discursive strategies of representation at the level of cultural production, particularly in the disciplines of literary and cultural studies. Debates revolving around speaking positions – as well as those of reading, writing and listening – inform a number of key texts produced during 1995, as the title of the collection *Speaking Positions: Aboriginality, Gender and Ethnicity in Australian Cultural Studies*, edited by Penny van Toorn and David English, attests. The essays included in this volume represent an edited selection of papers given at the 1993 conference of the Cultural Studies Association of Australia, and a significant number of them take up the complexities of negotiating contemporary formations of Aboriginality across plural sites of contestation and conditionality. One such site is the urgency for some cultural critics of devising explicitly localized critical frameworks and vocabularies that address 'Aboriginality', 'gender' and 'ethnicity' in ways departing from a reliance on what Jon Stratton and Ien Ang see as the critical hegemony of the 'class/race/gender triad' in British cultural studies. Such a model, contend the editors of *Speaking Positions*, obscures the particularized tensions and possibilities that characterize the territory of Australian engagements with Aboriginal identity, culture, land and language, and potentially disables the efforts of a cross-section of projects intent on critiquing the political and cultural imagination driving contemporary national dialogues on race, culture and difference.

Taken together, most of the essays collected here attempt to elaborate, critique or move beyond the essentialized 'politics of identity' that a substantial portion of earlier work on 'speaking positions' entailed. Of particular interest in this context is David Hollinsworth's important contribution, 'Aboriginal Studies – An Epistemological No Go Zone?' (90–9), which continues a vigorous debate instigated by Patrick Wolfe's 1992 review of Bob Hodge and Vijay Mishra's *Dark Side of the Dream: Australian Literature and the Postcolonial Mind* (Allen & Unwin, 1991). In that review and in a subsequent piece (Wolfe, 1992a: 'Reluctant Invaders', *Meanjin* 51:2.333–8, and Wolfe, 1992b: 'Reply to Bob Hodge and Vijay Mishra', *Meanjin* 51:4.884–8), Wolfe argues that Hodge and Mishra, to the extent that they incorporate Aboriginal history and experience into a unified narrative of Australian postcolonialism *per se*, 'are reproducing the structure of invasion in its assimilationist aspect'. Wolfe's critique of Hodge and Mishra's work is broadened to cover 'a whole emergent industry devoted to the analysis of Aboriginal cultural production', and he concludes that, given the uneven power relations informing 'the production of academic knowledges about Aborigines', non-indigenous academics and other cultural workers need to practice a form of ethical self-censorship, 'speak[ing only] when you're spoken to', in order to avoid filling up the space(s) where the 'other' might speak.

Hollinsworth's carefully argued essay calls for a shift in the paradigm of essentialized, unitary, mutually exclusive 'speaking positions' which are, for him, implicated in Wolfe's exhortation for non-indigenous silence. Such formations, he notes, involve assumptions of 'fixed and transcendental racial categories', relying on what Paul Gilroy ('Problems in Anti-Racist Strategy', London, Runnymede Trust, 1987) sees as a version of 'ethnic absolutism', which in turn produces a 'cultural insiderism' that bears troubling parallels with the 'biological insiderism' of racist discourse. Moreover, Wolfe's approach forestalls precisely the kind of intersubjective dialogue that Aboriginal critics such as Marcia Langton have insisted are necessary if indigenous perspectives and positions are to be taken seriously and engaged with meaningfully in the public sphere. Hollinsworth shrewdly notes that 'non-Aboriginal people who vacate the space' of speaking as exhorted by Wolfe 'risk the patronising implication that, without their silence, Aboriginal voices lack the power to be heard or to persuade'. The theoretical implications of race- or ethnicity-based speaking positions, for Hollinsworth, act as a powerful form of occlusion for both Aboriginal and non-Aboriginal people interested in negotiating the politics of race and representation; he suggests that to refuse to recognize and mobilize the multiple subject positions of indigenous people functions to disable, rather than empower, various political strategies for maintaining indigenous agency in the political and cultural arena. For non-indigenous academics in particular to claim 'innocence by abstinence' from speaking, he suggests, is disingenuous, to say the least. His solution is to reorient the debate away from a 'politics of difference' towards a multipositional 'politics of address', in which the fluidity and intersection of identity categories can be creatively mobilized for political and cultural agendas without falling into the essentialist trap whereby 'the category of Aborigine is . . . invoked but not questioned or historicised'.

Multipositionality and the politics of address are taken up also by Gerhard Fischer in 'Heiner Müller's *Der Auftrag* "Aboriginalised" by Mudrooroo: On Intercultural Dramaturgy and the "Highjacking" of a European Piece of Theatre to Black Australia' (56–72). Fischer recounts a recent history of the genesis and management of the *Mudrooroo/Müller Project*, in which the critic and writer Mudrooroo deploys a Brechtian model of theatre-as-protest to address the politics of republicanism and race through a set of internal and external 'frame' plays. Mudrooroo's project, for Fischer, participates in wider dialogues on what he calls the 'theatre of memory' and the 'theatre of mourning' in which disparate spatial, historical and cultural modalities – 1990s urban Aboriginal life in Sydney and European metropolitan life in Germany, the 1789 French revolution and 1788 invasion/settlement of Australia – are set in productive conflict with one another. The politics of address here begins with schematic reciprocity, as the play-within-a-play seeks an indigenous dialogue with European theatrical forms to rehabilitate connections across historically apposite moments of conquest and liberation, but concludes with a rejection by the Aboriginal players in the frame play of the relevance of Müller's *Der Auftrag* to their own project of protest and proclamation in the lead-up to an imagined confrontation on the politics of the Australian republic in the year 2000. While Fischer's essay will be of greatest relevance to those with a specific interest in Aboriginal theatre and dramaturgy, it also raises broader issues of the limits and possibilities of intercultural adaptation and framing, particularly in the context of what Fischer sees as the 'hegemony' of naturalism in indigenous theatre in Australia, despite recent examples of Aboriginal cultural production that explicitly reject naturalism in favour of symbolist, hyperrealist and pastiche modes of dramaturgical scripting, staging and production (see, for instance, Wesley Enoch and Deborah Mailman, *Seven Stages of Grieving*, Playlab Press, 1996). Despite Fischer's persistent implication that Mudrooroo moves Aboriginal dramaturgy into a new politics of agitation that owes more to postmodern forms of destabilization than Brechtian disruptions of false consciousness, the project appears, in Fischer's own version of it, to fall back on fundamentalist models of identity, Aboriginality and politics rather than engaging in postmodernist forms of interrogating such categories, their constructions and their effects.

Marion Benjamin explores the visual politics of 'reading' positions as part of a broader analysis of the discursive processes involved in colonial and contemporary photographic representations of Aboriginality. In *'Blond Captive: White Feminine Sexuality and the Censorship of Images of Indigenous Australians'* (43–55) Benjamin reminds her readers that the ways in which images speak to their viewers are constituted in large part by their audiences, some of whom may have been explicitly excluded from the photographer's or documentary-maker's frame of production. In many ways, colonial policies of administration regarding the 'management' of Aborigines in nineteenth century Australia were dependent 'on the ways in which they were seen and how they were visible' and, of course, invisible. The photographic gaze – deeply implicated, for Benjamin, with the scientific and medical gazes of European colonialism for which photography served as a signal technology – surveyed Aborigines in a disciplinary fashion, corollary to the surveying and taming of the land, using pictorial documents to justify and reinforce colonial methods of regulation and management of Aboriginal people on reserves, missions and in other institutional contexts. Such regimes of visual management and colonization, however, do not necessarily diminish the value of the photographic record for indigenous Australians, who, as the Koori photographer Leah King-Smith observes, see such images as 'treasures, bearing a storehouse of stories and family history' that symbolize their Aboriginal heritage (King-Smith [1992] quoted in Benjamin).

The politics of vision in nineteenth-century Australia was further complicated by a renegade medical photographer, 'Dr Walker' of Adelaide, who traversed Central Australia in order to document the ravages of venereal disease visited on Aboriginal women by European men. Benjamin's focus here is on the regimes of gender management that simultaneously censored the production and circulation of images of 'sexualized' Aboriginal women – particularly when such images detailed the consequences of such sexual colonization – in the official literature but endorsed traffic in the same images for pornographic consumption by white men. Benjamin is particularly interested in the ways that images of 'white woman' were produced to counterbalance the sexualization of Aboriginal women. Such images, she contends, both addressed pervasive official anxieties about miscegenation but also participated in the promotion of white Australia policies of nation-building by reorienting the white male gaze away from Aboriginal women and toward the 'safety zone' of racially cognate sexual union. Indeed, Dr Walker's photographs themselves were explicitly harnessed to efforts to 'clean up' the Australian Centre by tackling the presence of venereal disease head-on and making it 'safe' for white women to reproduce (in) the colony. Benjamin is particularly attentive in her essay to the intersection between linguistic and visual texts in setting the parameters for photographic meanings, and she focuses intelligently on the absence or purely trace elements of discursive aspects of race and gender – especially where these are seen to disrupt dominant national and administrative agendas – as much as on what and whom are actually addressed by various documents of record regarding Aborigines in nineteenth-century Australia.

The 'Blond Captive' of Benjamin's title refers to a rogue film made in 1932 purporting to provide 'scientific' documentary evidence of a white woman living as the willing 'captive' and consort of an Aboriginal man and his community, much of which was filmed in the then-remote north-west of Australia. The film, which neatly dovetailed a salacious treatment of mis-cegenationist fears and fantasies with equally potent stereotypes of the sexualized male 'savage' and the 'tamed', willing/unwilling white woman, enjoyed considerable commercial success in North America, but was finally banned in Australia for viewing by Aboriginal audiences. The exclusion of Aboriginal viewers from films held to 'riotously arouse' their imaginations was standard practice in post-Federation Australia, as the Royal Commission into the Moving Picture Industry in Australia made clear in their report of 1928. Benjamin sees in such policies a double structure of censorship, one that disenfranchised indigenous peoples not only as the *subjects* of representation but also as *consumers* of certain kinds of cultural production. In this context Benjamin suggests that Koori photographer Leah King-Smith's 1992 exhibition, *Patterns of Connection*, in which King-Smith recomposes original photographs of Victorian Kooris held by the State Library of Victoria, reasserts the power of the audience and the politics of vision and visual interpretation for indigenous communities once deemed 'outside' discursive regimes of cultural production at the levels of both self-representation and consumption.

In addition to Ian Anderson's 'Re-Claiming TRU-GER-NAN-NER: De-Colonising the Symbol' (31–42) (reviewed in *YWCCT* 4) and Stephen Muecke's 'Toward an Aboriginal Philosophy of Place' (167–79), both published prior to 1995 but appearing in this volume, *Speaking Positions* includes 'Does Paper Stay Put? The Politics of Indigenous Literature in Australia and Canada' (73–89) by Adam Shoemaker. Adopting a comparative approach indebted to frameworks of 'Commonwealth' literature in which he simultaneously homogenizes and renders problematic the category of 'indigenous literature' itself – disturbingly reprised throughout the essay as 'Native writing' – Shoemaker attempts to delineate in what he sees as the emergent popularity of indigenous texts some evidence of deeper attitudinal or perceptual shifts toward indigenous culture and writing in contemporary Australian, Canadian and international literary-intellectual trends.

Shoemaker is particularly interested in the process of 'anthologizing' indigenous literatures, which he argues can be harnessed to multiple agendas of indigenous liberation struggles and self-definition on the one hand, and the spawning of a non-indigenous 'Aboriginal' industry within academia and publishing firms on the other. His professed concern is the politics of production of such anthologies and how they signify in the interpretive and political landscape; noting that three 'Canadian white Anglophone males' – J. J. Healy, Terry Goldie and himself – were the first to demonstrate an interest in 'Black themes in literature', Shoemaker seems oblivious to the implication that it is the telling absence of Aboriginal access to the means of literary production and representation in English-language publishing until the 1980s, rather than the supposedly enabling presence of three non-Aboriginal Canadians, that might usefully inform the core of his concerns. Nevertheless, he retails what is by now a tired argument, formerly subscribed to by many practitioners of 'Commonwealth' literary analysis, that it is the deracinated, globally mobile 'outsider' who is best positioned to identify and interpret local trends of cultural production, particularly when they involve emergent voices and forms located beyond the putative 'centres' of national/international formations. Much of the essay is taken up with similarly outmoded ideas concerning oppositionally rendered distinctions between the 'oral' and the 'written', and their significance for commercially viable and culturally sanctioned forms of indigenous writing.

Shoemaker's most provocative claim revolves around his assertion that the 'anthologizing' of indigenous writers and literatures not only reflects but in fact *requires* the prior development of a groundswell of cultural and political significance of which anthologies are the textual manifestation, capitalizing on a cultural movement that is already somehow 'out there'. Such a view is distinctly at odds with other theoretical models of textual production that regard forms like anthologization as strategic interventions in the creation of new spaces for unrepresented and under-represented voices and perspectives in literary culture. Shoemaker posits that the anthologization of indigenous writing is a strategy not so much of the promotion of indigenous cultural production, but rather one of *containment* which seeks to manage a 'phenomenon which is growing so fast it has become threatening'. This makes some sense in relation to the continued problems besetting the positioning of Aboriginal writing in non-Aboriginal collections, for which James Tulip's essentializing and patronizing comments on Aboriginal poetry in his 1995 review of Kevin Hart's *Oxford Book of Religious Verse* (Oxford University Press, 1994) serve as an example (James Tulip, 'Oblique Syntheses', *Southerly* 55:2.179–86; see especially 181–2). Yet Shoemaker's discussion of anthologies clearly centres on collections of exclusively indigenous material. What, or who, is threatened by the exponential growth of anthologies of indigenous writing (of which Shoemaker considerably inflates the impact)? There is no explicit answer here except for an oblique reference to the 'danger' of such work rendering Aboriginal culture 'commercially accessible and fully known' – the danger, perhaps, being to the continued non-indigenous preservation and mystification of what Shoemaker a few paragraphs later calls 'a[n Aboriginal] spirituality which it is not possible to quantify'. Despite the paternalist rumblings that characterize much of this paper, Shoemaker does, in his concluding remarks, enjoin readers to consider the uneven distribution of economic and cultural capital that characterizes the ownership and profit-making of publication ventures for indigenous writers, particularly where material is owned by a community rather than an individual 'author', and to ensure that indigenous writers and cultural workers are co-equal participants in such transactions. Taken together, the essays in *Speaking Positions* comprise an uneven but generally provocative and valuable collection of contemporary cultural perspectives on Aboriginality and positionality.

Beyond this collection, Penny van Toorn ('Mudrooroo and the Power of the Post: Alternative Inscriptions of Aboriginalist Discourse in a Post-

Aboriginalist Age', *Southern Review* 28.121–39) turns to a complex and heavily theorized discussion of the slippage of subject positions and the unfixing of theory as these play out in her reading of several key texts, moments and utterances in the 'Aboriginalist/Aboriginality' debates informing the work of Hollinsworth (reviewed above) and Attwood, Huggins and others (reviewed below; see also our entry for Aboriginal Identity, Art and Culture in *YWCCT* 4). Van Toorn uses Mudrooroo's *Doin Wildcat: A Novel Koori Script* (Hyland House, 1988), his metanarrative account of trying to turn his novel (written as Colin Johnson) *Wildcat Falling* (Angus & Robertson, 1965) into a film, as a point of departure for her investigation of how debates around proponents of 'Aboriginalism' versus 'Aboriginality', essentialist versus constructionist models of indigenous identity, and 'Aboriginality-as-persistence' versus 'Aboriginality-as-resistance' (see Kevin Keefe, 'Aboriginality: Resistance and Persistence', *Australian Aboriginal Studies* [1988]1.67–81) are challenged by what van Toorn calls Mudrooroo's 'tactical propensity' to deploy now essentialism, now constructionism, in his efforts to make strategic interventions in what he views as the hegemony of non-indigenous discourses on Aboriginalities in both theory and in practice. Of most significance in van Toorn's wide-ranging essay is the caution she recommends, following Benita Parry, for cultural critics intent on incorporating an essentially 'progressivist' notion of history – theoretical/critical no less than Aboriginal – in their various methods of disciplinary and interdisciplinary practice. Such a historically 'progressivist' model of critical practice, like that of Aboriginal history, occludes 'questions of ambivalence and cultural difference' in its haste to delineate a configuration of 'developments' that situate 'all articulations of given categories or practices on a single evolutionary timeline'. To operate in this way is to obscure a field of simultaneously contesting articulations of how 'Aboriginality' may, and is, theorized, by whom, and on behalf of whom. Moreover, van Toorn argues passionately that to divide critical articulations of/on identity along an evolutionary axis of 'styles', with some registering as 'outmoded' and others as 'advanced', is unwittingly to 'carry on the work of the old colonial histories that constructed indigenous peoples and their cultures as prior versions of the modern European self'.

Concomitant with issues of speaking positions are the listening positions taken up by those being addressed. In 'Listening But Not Hearing: Voices of Black Women in Feminist Discourse' (*Northern Radius* 3:1.3–5), Leonora Spry, writing from an Australian indigenous feminist perspective, provides a critique of the resistance of white feminists who listen but do not 'hear' the voices of black women. Spry contends that when black women speak, their speech is inserted into one or more of the available categories allowed to them in Western discourses: thus they are heard to speak in 'confessional' mode, as 'victim', as 'success' despite victimization, as 'exotic' or 'erotic' Other. Spry uses the work of Rey Chow and other feminists of colour, and calls for, among other things, a far more thorough interrogation of formations of ethnicity and race constitutive of whiteness than has occurred to date.

The maintenance of Aboriginal culture in contemporary Australian society is the subject of Karl Neuenfeldt's 'The Kyana Corroborree: Cultural Production of Indigenous Ethnogenesis' (*Sociological Inquiry* 65:1.21–46). The article provides an analysis of the 1993 Kyana Corroborree of the Noongah Aborigines of Western Australia as a case-study of the cultural production and cultural politics of ethnogenesis and indigeneity through public performance and celebration. The event, a contemporary celebration of Aboriginal culture, music and dance organized by the Dumbartung Aboriginal Corporation, took place in February 1993 and attracted an estimated crowd of 50,000, which included Aboriginal and non-Aboriginal people. Neuenfeldt draws on a range of contemporary cultural theorists of identity, ethnicity and difference, in particular the work of Stuart Hall ('Old and New Identities, Old and New Ethnicities' in A. King, ed., *Culture, Globalization and the World-System: Contemporary Conditions for the Representation of Identity*, Macmillan, 1991, 41–68) and Werner Sollors, *The Invention of Ethnicity*, Cambridge, 1989) and provides an analysis of the production and performance of contemporary Aboriginality – in particular 'Noongahness' – at and through the corroborree.

Speaking positions in relation to culture, identity and Aboriginality, particularly when they take place within the intersubjective paradigm developed by Marcia Langton ('*Well, I heard it on the radio and I saw it on the television . . .*', Australian Film Commission, 1993), are often shape-shifting in the context of performativity, as they encounter the limits within contemporary discursive formations of what can and cannot be said, not just by whites about indigenous people but by indigenous people about whites and about themselves. Such discursive shape-shifting, and the corollary lacunae it exposes in available ways of speaking (about and within) formations of 'culture', 'Aboriginal' and 'white' are explored in a narrative meditation by Bill Cope in 'The Language of Forgetting: A Short History of the Word' (*Republica* 2.181–206). Cope's chosen landscape is Groote Eylandt (where his uncle, he tells us, served as an Anglican minister thirty years ago) and his text is the impact of white missionary interventions in the area. His position, articulated in terms more speculative than definitive, is that white Australians will continue to be hampered in their efforts to hold up and move beyond their own side of the intersubjective bargain as long as there remains no 'Aboriginal anthropology of whites' that allows a reciprocal knowing of the 'self' as 'other' in the intersubjective domain. Until this occurs, Cope suggests, non-indigenous Australians will remain trapped in a 'history of the white culture of forgetting' which, while explicitly imposed as part of the missionary imperative in Australia for many decades, has involved implicit forms of forgetting for white people as well. His method for coping with such entrapment is for non-indigenous people to 'get out, to allow the renegotiation of words and space', and to contemplate return to the intersubjective space only on the terms of indigenous invitation. Cope's perspective here is similar in some respects to that of Patrick Wolfe's advocacy in 'Reluctant Invaders' (see above) of a white/Aboriginal intersubjective realm in which the non-Aboriginal person 'speaks only when spoken to'.

4.1 Author(iz)ing the Past: Remapping Indigenous Histories

Two important works of historical retrieval of suppressed or marginalized Aboriginal experience and endeavour published this year are Colin Tatz's *The Obstacle Race: Aborigines in Sport* and Robert A. Hall's *Fighters from the Fringe: Aborigines and Torres Strait Islanders Recall the Second World War*. Tatz's work is encyclopaedic in its coverage of the involvement of Aboriginal and Torres Strait Island people in sport in Australia: while the pre-eminence of indigenous athletes in all codes of football and in boxing is well known, Tatz's work brings to light the achievements of indigenous athletes in many other sports, including the participation of indigenous women in broadly based sporting activities such as basketball and netball. Tatz also documents the importance of sport within Aboriginal communities and provides valuable data on communities with the infrastructure to support a variety of sporting activities. A further consideration of racism in Australian sport is provided in Tatz's 'Racism and Sport in Australia' (*Race and Class*, 36:4.43–54). Robert Hall's book *Fighters from the Fringe* provides personal reminiscences of six Aboriginal and Torres Strait Island men and women (Reg Saunders, Oodgeroo Noonuccal, Charles Mene, Leonard Waters, Tom Lowah and Saulo Waia) on their service in, and experiences of, the armed services during World War II. Hall introduces his text, which is augmented by extensive reference to archival and other historical material, with the argument that despite their extensive military service, indigenous Australians are effectively excluded from the mythologizing associated with the figures of the Anzac and Digger in Australian culture; and despite the fact that many indigenous Australians and their non-indigenous supporters hoped that war service would shore up the claims for indigenous people to participate fully in the rights and privileges of citizenship, over twenty years were to elapse after the end of the war before the 1967 referendum granted these rights.

An historical remapping of the rich pastoral district of western Victoria is provided by Ian Clark in *Scars in the Landscape: A Register of Massacre Sites in Western Victoria, 1803–1859*. Clark's harrowing work is the product of painstaking research through archives in New South Wales and Victoria – letters, journals and other documents – and details scores of violent encounters between settlers and the indigenous peoples of the region. Wherever possible Clark provides the names of the Aboriginal dead and survivors as well as the identities of the settlers and their men involved. Clark also reproduces Aboriginal testimonies and reports of evidence given by survivors of the violence, ensuring, wherever possible, that Aboriginal voices are heard. Clark organizes his register chronologically within region and his regionalization of western Victoria corresponds to the organization of territory between the many Koori language groups and clans who traditionally own this country.

The 'history of forgetting' by whites is given extensive consideration by Lyn Riddett in 'Think Again: Communities which Lose their Memory: The Construction of History in Settler Societies' (*Journal of Australian Studies* 44.38–47). Riddett's discussion of memory and forgetting centres on the disjunctive memories, and their (mis)management, of communities composed of Aboriginal and non-Aboriginal peoples in Darwin. Riddett details the contradictions inherent in the digging up of Aboriginal burial sites at Mindil Beach, an internationally recognized Darwin city locale that attracts a great number of tourists year round, as part of an environmental improvement programme mounted by the very local government department charged with responsibility for the 'protection of burial sites'. How this occurred, and its relationship to cultures and practices of memory loss by settler societies in relation to indigenous populations, forms the main focus of Riddett's paper. She also raises and theorizes important issues to do with the gaps that attend the construction of private and public identities by whites in relation to their interaction with Aboriginal people and communities, in which private social memories related to local episodes of Aboriginal history, culture and events are buried, ironically, in public discourses. But Riddett suggests that a concept like 'memory loss', with its emphasis on repression and denial, is too simple a way of understanding the complex negotiations of non-indigenous social memory in relation to indigenous history. She details the ways in which both social amnesia *and* selective social memory converge to define the relationship of white settler memory to the 'other' represented by the Aboriginal presence in that social memory; indeed, she argues, the 'emphasis on the "otherness" of Aborigines is functional in the construction of non-Aboriginal memory' in settler societies such as Australia. Paradoxically, 'constructors of settler history depend on being able to forget in order to remember'. The dangers for Aboriginal people in this scenario, for Riddett, are manifold: the most significant involve the risks of relying on a generation of disappearing elders whose 'thin voices' will increasingly be lost in the absence of preserving and committing those voices to some form of material record; and the risks of leaving the 'work of remembering' in its public historical mode to (non-indigenous) others, in which case the ability to 'think again' about 'settler' history, its omissions, interpretations and constructions, is increasingly threatened.

Henry Reynolds continued his project of revisionary histories of Aboriginal and non-Aboriginal contact on Australian frontiers with a Tasmanian history, *Fate of a Free People: A Radical Re-Examination of the Tasmanian Wars* which, alongside Lyndall Ryan's *The Aboriginal Tasmanians* (University of Queensland Press, 1981), provides a powerful narrative of the black wars on that island. Also published in 1995 is an important collection of essays providing a series of histories of the Aboriginal people under the British Crown. Edited by Ann McGrath, *Contested Ground: Australian Aborigines under the British Crown* contains eight regionalized histories following McGrath's introductory chapter from the national perspective, 'A National Story' (1–54): Heather Goodall writes on New South Wales (55–120); Richard Broome on Victoria (121–67); the Queensland history is jointly written by Henry Reynolds and Dawn May (168–207); Peggy Brock writes on South Australia (208–39); Sandy Toussiant on Western Australia (240–68); Peter Read on the Northern Territory (269–307); there are two essays on the history of the Tasmanian Aboriginal people under British rule, by McGrath (306–37) and by Maykutenner (Vicki Matson-Green) (338–58). The final chapter, by McGrath (359–97), takes up the topic of 'contested ground' in relation to the writing of Aboriginal history and deals with the vexed epistemological questions of who is authorized to speak for whom in Aboriginal history and historiography, and in what terms. This essay is an extremely valuable critical survey of writing on Aboriginal history, by Aboriginal and non-Aboriginal historians and commentators. McGrath raises important metahistorical issues about speaking and authorizing positions, and also provocative questions and possibilities for what constitutes Aboriginal history. As a collection, *Contested Ground* may have been better served by placing McGrath's essay at the beginning rather than at the end, where its careful consideration of the issue of who speaks for whom and how appears as something of an afterthought rather than as an integral and motivating set of principles for the work.

McGrath's final chapter is usefully read alongside two other works published in 1995 which survey the field of Aboriginal history and consider its constitution, methodologies and the cultural politics of the speaking positions which authorize it (and which are authorized through it). The first is Bain Attwood's 'Aboriginal History' (*Australian Journal of Politics and History* 41.33–47). While Attwood's piece was written in 1990 and its discussion is thus less current than McGrath's, it none the less offers valuable contributions to the question of how and by whom the field is constituted. The second piece is Bill Thorpe's 'Frontiers of Discourse: Assessing Revisionist Australian Colonial Contact Historiography' (*Journal of Australian Studies* 46.34–45) in which, as part of his examination of different strands in recent revisionist histories, Thorpe reconsiders the role and influence of Paul Carter's *The Road to Botany Bay: An Exploration of Landscape and History* (University of Chicago Press, 1987). Thorpe's strategy is to pit empirical history against the more theorized, poststructuralist histories that have followed Carter's work or that have been influenced by similar intellectual traditions, namely Francophone poststructuralism. A further consideration of Carter's influential book and the later publication *Living in a New Country* (Faber & Faber, 1992), which is more concerned with language than with history, is provided in Lars Jensen's 'Is There No End to Travelling? Paul Carter in the Linguistic No-Man's-Land' (*Australian Literary Studies* 17:1.88–94). In this study, Jensen returns to the first contact scenarios mapped by Carter and provides analyses of his readings of the European bestowing of names in the (to their eyes new) land.

An assessment of recent Australian historiographical treatments of Aboriginality in the context of charting shifts in leftist, specifically labour history, and feminist historiography is provided by Ann Curthoys in 'Race and Gender in Recent Australian Historiography' (*Journal of Interdisciplinary Gender Studies* 1:1.1–9). Curthoys notes that while women's history has enjoyed a 'rise and rise' in recent years, and Aboriginal history has occupied a fairly central position, especially post-Mabo, there is a sharp difference between the two: women's history has been written by women, while Aboriginal history for the most part continues to be written by non-Aboriginal people. Additionally, where women's history has moved beyond the early retrieval of women's experience and women's stories to challenge the categories of history itself, Aboriginal history yet remains separated from mainstream historiography in a number of key areas. Curthoys cites the writing of labour history as a case in point: despite the research of historians such as Anne McGrath, whose *Born in the Cattle: Aborigines in Cattle Country* (Allen & Unwin, 1987) documents the role of Aboriginal workers in the Australian cattle industry, labour historians continue to exclude Aboriginal labour from their view of the history of Australian labour. Curthoys points to the potential for a more inclusive historiography arising from developments in a number of quarters: the abundance of Aboriginal life-writing, particularly by women; the growing influence of cultural histories; and the efforts by feminist historians to extend their consideration of gender difference to accommodate racial and cultural difference. In this last regard, Curthoys cites the collaborative history *Creating a Nation, 1980–1990* (Penguin, 1994), written by Patricia Grimshaw, Marilyn Lake, Ann McGrath and Marian Quartly, as a model for a more inclusive historiography. Even with the reservation that the treatment of Aboriginal histories by Grimshaw et al. in clusters of chapters at the beginning and end of the work may be construed as a continuation of the device of an Aboriginal frame around the main, non-Aboriginal picture, Curthoys finds in this work a productive strategy for future oppositional historiography. Such a historiography must aim to tell the stories of injustice, exclusions and oppression, but not without acknowledgement of the agency and powers of resistance of those oppressed, whether women or Aboriginal people. Not all historians in Australia shared Curthoys's enthusiasm for *Creating a Nation*, or for historiography which challenges the old orthodoxies (see John Hirst, 'Women and History: A Critique of *Creating a Nation*' [*Quadrant* March, 35–43]).

4.2 Author(iz)ing Bodies: Discourses on Aboriginal Health and Disease

In 'Bodies, Disease and the Problem of Foucault' (*Social Analysis* 37.67–81) Ian Anderson takes up the problem of power/resistance as articulated by Foucault and examines some issues in Koori health. When, in the early 1970s, Koori people established community-controlled health and medical services, asks Anderson, were they complicit in better incorporating themselves within the medical gaze? While these organizations and the services they provided emerged directly out of a struggle for better access for Koori people to biomedical services appropriate to their needs, is this, in Foucault's terms, resistance to or deployment of power?

A critical analysis of the discourses of Aboriginal and Torres Strait Islander health is the subject of Tim Rowse's 'Expert Testimony: How we Talk about Aboriginal Health' (*Arena Magazine* December–January, 32–35). The piece, revised for *Arena*, originally appeared as an appendix to a Federal Government report, *Alcohol Related Violence in Aboriginal and Torres Strait Islander Communities* (1993). Rowse posits and then addresses current anxieties about representing Aboriginality which spill into the area of health and the difficulty faced by policy-makers and practitioners who uneasily struggle for a language in which to talk about the pathological and pathogenic conditions of Aboriginal and Torres Strait Islander life. Rowse traces contemporary anxieties about terminology to the views of Paul Hasluck who, as Minister for Territories from 1951 to 1963, is one of the architects of post-war Aboriginal affairs policies. For Hasluck, the term Aboriginal has inevitable connotations of 'decrepitude' and Aboriginality conjured images of the 'primitive and the insanitary'. For Hasluck, better race relations could be more readily ensured by 'teaching a native personal hygiene' than by attempting to break down prejudice by any other means. Aboriginality is now linked to more positive qualities: community, heritage, spirituality, a special relationship with the earth. In this move, argues Rowse, Marcia Langton's point that positive images are mobilized to drive out negative ones, with the lived reality of indigenous people remaining unrepresented, is pertinent. Moreover, the emphasis on positive Aboriginality and the eschewing of the old stereotypes – the drunk, the dirty, the decrepit – leaves little scope for talking about and acting on the pathogenic conditions of the lives of many Aboriginal and Torres Strait Islander people. Rowse elaborates on these problems in areas such as female mortality rates, rates of HIV/AIDS infection and alcohol-related violence and disease.

The issue of Aboriginality and alcohol consumption is central as it is not only a major contributor to the poor health and high mortality rates in Aboriginal communities, but is also a vexed issue in the politics of representation of Aboriginality in Australia. As well as the image of the drunken Aboriginal being one of the negative stereotypes still in circulation, the consumption of alcohol has been recognized as a subcultural marker of Aboriginality, whereby to be a drinker is an expression of Aboriginality. This view has been documented by anthropological research, but it is contested by others who argue that drinking, far from being an expression of Aboriginality, is a gross distortion of Aboriginal traditions and values. For those concerned with the pathologically high levels of alcohol consumption in some Aboriginal and Islander communities, there are further problems of representation to be faced, for example, the question of how the responsibility for Aboriginal alcoholism is narrativized. Rowse summarizes the conflicting views of a number of commentators and workers in the area. For some the responsibility lies unequivocally with colonization. For others, including the Aboriginal Merv Gibson, the responsibility needs to be shifted to the drinking individual in order that solutions to the problem may be found. As Rowse argues, the Aboriginal attribution of individual Aboriginal responsibility provokes anxiety among pro-Aboriginal intellectuals because it seems to undermine the argument basic to social reformist policies: that indigenous people, as a group, have been treated unjustly and that their present predicaments are a product of that history of injustice. What is needed, continues Rowse, is an appeal to the historical record which can withstand the charges of scapegoating and the denial of Aboriginal agency to produce an active understanding of how colonial domination 'has helped to form contemporary Aboriginal agency as self-destructive'.

On the issue of anxieties in speaking about domestic violence in Aboriginal communities, which accounts for a portion of the intolerably high female mortality rates in the Aboriginal and Islander populations, Rowse revisits the controversy occasioned by the paper published in 1989 on the subject of intra-racial rape by the anthropologist Diane Bell (well known for her influential *Daughters of the Dreaming* [McPhee Gribble, 1983]) and her Aboriginal collaborator Topsy Nelson ('Speaking About Rape is Everyone's Business', *Women's Studies International Forum*, 12:4.403–16). The publication of this paper occasioned a vigorous protest by a group of Aboriginal women, including Jackie Huggins, who, among other things, accused Bell of conscripting Nelson to a white feminist agenda and reinstating the primacy of sexual over racial inequality and discrimination. The controversy highlights many of the problems of representation with which Rowse is concerned. Rowse concludes by way of reference to the work of Jan Pettman ('Gendered Knowledges: Aboriginal Women and the Politics of Feminism' in Bain Attwood and John Arnold, eds, *Power, Knowledge and Aborigines*, La Trobe University Press, 1992, 120–31; and with Helen Meekosha, 'Beyond Category Politics', *Hecate* 1991 XVII:2.75–92), which argues cautiously and conditionally against the kind of cultural relativism which constrains us within 'identity enclosures' and 'category politics'.

Combating alcoholism and substance abuse in indigenous communities and the cultural dimension to these health problems is addressed by Charlotte Wood in 'Spiritual and Sober' (*Connexions* February–March) which canvasses a range of community responses to the problem which have attempted to battle substance abuse and addiction on the 'culture is treatment' model adapted from the Canadian model developed by the Nechi Institute and Poundmakers Lodge. Wood includes profiles of the work being done in a number of communities where attempts at cultural revival and the re-engagement with traditional spirituality have been made in order to tackle alcoholism and other abuse. Graphically confirming Rowse's argument that colonization has produced a contemporary Aboriginal subjectivity which is self-destructive, Wood quotes Yvonne Wroe, who studied at the Nechi Institute and now works in the field in Australia: 'We ourselves are continuing the genocide. We're injecting the stuff, we're swallowing it, we're sniffing it, we're killing ourselves.'

Aboriginal health as a central political issue for contemporary Australia for which only a political solution may be found is the argument of Noel Pearson's 'Aboriginal Health: The Way Forward' (*Arena Magazine* June–July, 20–2). Attempts to remedy the health problems of Aboriginal people which do not address the profound and continuing injustice inflicted on the indigenous races of the nation simply perpetuate those injustices, becoming another version of the 'smoothing the dying pillow' rhetoric and policies of the past. This rhetoric and the policies it produced were and are enabled by a racism which is the most virulent malaise in Australian culture. Aboriginal health can only improve when full political restitution is made to Aboriginal peoples.

A similar argument is mounted by Pat O'Shane in 'The Psychological Impact of White Colonialism on Aboriginal People' (*Australasian Psychiatry* 3:3.149–53) in which she details the on-going psychological impact of dispossession and subsequent policies such as removal to missions, child-stealing and the deeply entrenched racisms of white Australia on the psychological and mental well-being of indigenous Australians. O'Shane writes that in recognizing that the violence and suffering inflicted on her family had also been inflicted on thousands of other indigenous families, the wonder was 'that we weren't all stark, raving mad'.

4.3 Re-Auth(or)izing the Nation: Cathy Freeman and the Aboriginal Flag
The incident in which the Aboriginal athlete Cathy Freeman swathed herself in the Australian national flag and the red, black and gold Aboriginal flag for a victory circuit after taking gold at the Commonwealth Games in Victoria, Canada, in 1994 is read by Wanda Jamrozik in 'Flagging a New Australia' (*Independent Monthly* January, 12–18) as a major watershed in Australian cultural life. Jamrozik is not only concerned with the installation of an Aboriginal woman as national hero, a status never afforded Evonne Cawley (Goolagong), but with a non-ironic vision of the future offered by the image of the dual flags: 'a pure moment of shining, guilt-free nationalism'. Jamrozik's essay naively assembles other instances of reconciliation-in-action in the contemporary Australian cultural scene: the runaway success of Yothu Yindi, the prominence of Ernie Dingo, and (the logic here seems to be because it is okay to feel positive about Aboriginality, it is also okay to feel good about gays and trannies) the success of *Priscilla, Queen of the Desert*.

Ian Anderson responds to Jamrozik in 'Flag of Convenience' (*Independent Monthly* February, 44–5) and asks to be excused from the euphoria of the 'new nationalism'. Anderson finds himself more concerned with the on-going problems faced by Aboriginal people that are glossed over by the 'new tolerance': 'This crisis is about health, access to country and culture, education, housing, and legal rights.' Anderson considers the amount of popular support given to Freeman and writes that while this support registers some positive shifts in attitudes to Aboriginality, underlying this apparent endorsement of Freeman's actions is a depoliticizing of both the Aboriginal flag and Aboriginality by which Freeman and the two flags are held up as comforting images of tolerance and multiculturalism which allow mainstream Australia to overlook its parlous record in relation to indigenous peoples. To forestall the appropriation of the red, black and gold flag as an 'icon of a more inclusive Australian nationalism', Anderson retells the history of its origins and restates its core symbolism of Aboriginal self-determination and sovereignty.

The flag issue is also taken up by Jock Given in 'Red, Black and Gold to Australia: Cathy Freeman and the Flags' (*Media Information Australia* 75.46–56). Given sets his examination of the Freeman incident and the receptions it provoked against other instances of political protests by oppressed racial minority groups at international sporting/media events, namely the black glove protest by Tommie Smith and John Carlos, supported by the white Australian silver-medallist Peter Norman, on the winners' dais after the men's 200-metre final at the Mexico Olympics in 1968, and the intrusion of Aboriginal issues and land rights into the media coverage of the 1982 Commonwealth Games in Brisbane. Given usefully gathers together some of the most significant media coverage of the Freeman event and the responses it generated. He argues that the potency of Freeman's action in Victoria was 'its conscription of international media and public attention not just to a sign – the Aboriginal flag – but its juxtaposition of that sign with the ideas of nation and victory'. Freeman's political symbolism was thus able to be accommodated within the determinedly anti-political thinking of many sports and media commentators. A further profile of Freeman and an assessment of her importance as an iconic figure in Australian sport is provided by Ian Cockerill in 'Cathy Freeman's Dream Run' (*Inside Sport* 38.19–24).

5. Representations: Literature, Art and Media

5.1 Textual Formations: Contemporary Criticism and Aboriginal Writing
Literary formations, both contemporary and historical, dealing with Aboriginal representation and representation of the 'Aboriginal' are the subject of a range of other publications in 1995. A small but useful introductory book is Anne Brewster's *Literary Formations: Post-Colonialism, Nationalism and Globalism*. Brewster's critical project is to examine the ways in which minority voices are interpellated into and transform national formations of identity within an increasingly globalized and unevenly postcolonial context. The minority voices she selects are those of Australian Aboriginal women writers; the migrant/diasporic voices of Australian poet Ania Walwicz and Indo-Anglian writer Bharati Mukherjee; and the ethnically differentiated 'nationalisms' of Singaporean writers Arthur Yap and Philip Jeyaretnam.

The politics of Aboriginal identity and the valency of subject positions are also the focus of several articles that consider, under quite different theoretical dispensations, strategies for representing the self in Sally Morgan's *My Place*. Subhash Jaireth ('The "I" in Sally Morgan's *My Place:* Writing of a Monologised Self', *Westerly* 3.69–78 and 'Who Speaks for Whom? Mikhail Bakhtin and the Idea of Chronotopic Nature of Speaking and Listening', *Imago* 7:3.78–83) and Annabel Cooper ('Talking about *My Place*/My Place: Feminism, Criticism and the Other's Autobiography', *Southern Review*

28.140–53) respectively intervene in a critical debate precipitated in 1992/1993 by the historian Bain Attwood ('Portrait of an Aboriginal as an Artist: Sally Morgan and the Construction of Aboriginality', *Australian Historical Studies* [1992] 99.302–18). Attwood problematizes Aboriginality along post-structuralist lines; given that all identities are cultural constructions, he argues, Morgan's assertion of a 'unitary' Aboriginality and the narrative strategies she uses to represent it become 'inherently problematic', foregrounding what Attwood views as 'the contradiction between Morgan's freedom to choose this identity and her assertion of it as essential'. The arguments mounted by Attwood in this essay earned rejoinders from four historians/cultural critics in a subsequent issue, including the Aboriginal historians Jackie Huggins and Tony Birch as well as Tim Rowse and Isabel Tarrago (Jackie Huggins, 'Always Was Always Will Be', 459–64; Tony Birch, 'Half Caste', 458; Tim Rowse, 'Sally Morgan's Kaftan', 465–8, and Isabel Tarrago, 'Response to Sally Morgan and the Construction of Aboriginality', 469, all in *Australian Historical Studies* 100 [1993]). To some extent, the question of Sally Morgan's narrative authority/ authorization of her Aboriginality became eclipsed by broader questions of Attwood's own authority/authorization to pronounce on 'Aboriginality' given his position as a non-indigenous historian working within acadaemia. In many ways, the debate highlighted the issues raised more recently by David Hollinsworth (reviewed above) concerning the epistemological and cultural 'no go zones' of critical discourses about Aboriginality and the problem of how speaking positions are imbricated in these discourses.

In 'Who Speaks for Whom?' Subhash Jaireth attempts to recontextualize Attwood's concerns about the construction of Aboriginality by reference to Bakhtinian frameworks of chronotopic and monologic discourse. Bakhtin, Jaireth argues, consistently refuses to privilege an 'internal sovereign territory' for the self, and locates the construction and mobilization of the self as a (representable) subject at the boundaries of intersubjective encounters with others. The chronotopic nature of subject formation, in which time and space always both produce and delimit the subject position(s) available to an individual, creates competing subject positions in which both a 'surplus' and a 'deficit' of vision regarding the self are activated chronotopically. Jaireth goes on to explicate (very briefly) the situatedness of such subject formations, in which the positions of 'I-for-myself', 'I-for-the-other' and 'the-other-for-me' vie for authority according to a range of strategic and dialogic exigencies. He concludes that claims for the exclusivity of speaking positions on the part of any one – including indigenous peoples – rely on the model of 'I-for-myself', forcing them into 'an exile . . . creating a mimic self which is cursed by its deficiency of vision'. This argument is extended in 'The "I" in Sally Morgan's *My Place*', in which Jaireth concurs with Attwood's insistence that an essentialized, unitary self is sustained by the narrative strategies of Morgan's text, but analyses this as an instance of Bakhtinian monologism, despite the presence of a range of 'heteroglossic' and 'dialogic' elements apparent in the structure and narratological episodes in the work. Whereas Attwood's analysis argued that 'anthropological discourses' of Aboriginality had encouraged Morgan to develop her own static notions of Aboriginal identity, Jaireth relocates this development within purely textual and narrative terms.

Jaireth's arguments in both essays appear primarily intent on the application of Bakhtinian models of subject formation, for which Morgan's work and

Attwood's critique provide convenient and contemporary examples, and there is little to suggest any broader consideration of problems of Aboriginality, indigenous subject formation or the particularities of literary genres such as autobiography and life-writing that have been mobilized in recent years by Australian indigenous writers for a variety of reasons. Annabel Cooper's 'Talking About *My Place*/My Place' does, however, engage with such concerns. In a carefully argued explication and deconstruction of both Morgan's text and the debates surrounding it, Cooper uses Gayatri Spivak's critique of the 'over-simplified oppressed subject', as formulated by Deleuze and Guattari, to investigate whether it is possible to engage in cultural practices that, in their efforts to restore or make audible the silenced voices of marginalized people, do not resort finally to a critical reinstatement of the 'undivided subject' which 'speaks for itself'. Reviewing earlier commentary on the problems of identity, authority, authenticity and Aboriginality in *My Place*, Cooper discerns in Attwood's critique a problem not so much with 'Aboriginality' but with the genre of autobiography itself as a textual strategy of subject formation. The politics of the text are as much at issue here as are the politics of 'voice' and 'identity', and Cooper reminds us that Rowse's objections to Attwood's reading of the 'person' rather than the 'text' and Muecke's conflation of 'autobiography' with the discourse of 'confession' in his own discussion of *My Place* ('Aboriginal Literature and the Repressive Hypothesis', *Southerly* [1988] 48:4.405–18) participate similarly in a blindness to the possibilities of Aboriginal autobiography not as confession but, in Cooper's terms, as counternarrative. Cooper bases her discussion of Aboriginal autobiography as counternarrative on a substantial body of feminist critique of both autobiography-as-literary-genre and the negotiation of subject positions by those with less privileged access to social and cultural structures of articulation and audience.

Cooper's central intervention in this debate is to pose a reorienting of the terms of the Attwood/Huggins/Rowse/Birch/Muecke debate away from the polarized discussion of 'is she or isn't she' (Aboriginal, essentializing, authorizing and so on) and toward an examination of how *My Place* deals explicitly with the 'cultural politics of being both and neither', with the textual 'Sally Morgan' negotiating simultaneously her Aboriginality *and* her whiteness, and their vexed relational nature in her formulation as a subject. In so doing, *My Place* as counternarrative counters both white Australian but also indigenous Australian assumptions of identity, race and gender, and Cooper (who positions herself explicitly at both the beginning and the conclusion of her essay) asks her readers to think about what this implies for the project of moving beyond Trinh Minh-ha's famous extension of Barthes's dictum on gossip: 'We continue to talk to "us" about "them", as if "we" were transparent and without interest, and as if the construction of "them" were not interdependent with that of "us". How might we do differently?'

Two interviews with Aboriginal writers were also published in 1995. Lionel Fogarty, in conversation with Philip Mead, engages with issues of Aboriginal education and the role he sees his own writing playing in this regard ('Musgrave Park: Lionel Fogarty talks to Philip Mead', *Republica* 2.119–31). Fogarty, a Murri poet, essayist and political activist, is widely regarded as one of the most innovative Aboriginal writers in Australia; in addition to being frequently anthologized, he has written and published several collections of poetry and other writing (*Yoogum Yoogum*, Penguin Books, 1982; *Ngutju*, Murri Coo-ee, Brisbane, 1984; *Jagera*, Murri Coo-ee, Brisbane, 1990) that Philip Mead categorizes as 'Black Australian surrealist writing' and that Fogarty himself terms the engagement with 'the difficulty of divided and conquered language', for which English, the 'most bastardised language in the world', serves simultaneously as medium and object of critique. The interview, besides providing a forum for Fogarty's views on the relationship between culture, politics, writing and Aboriginal identity, includes some very illuminating discussion by Fogarty of his upbringing and education at Cherbourg Mission in Queensland, and also some very painful material related to the death in police custody of his brother Daniel Yock, a case which became a focus of sustained public grief, rage and protest for Murris and non-indigenous activists in Brisbane, and which is dealt with in the play *The Seven Stages of Grieving* by Wesley Enoch and Deborah Mailman of the Brisbane-based Koemba Jdarra Indigenous Performing Arts Company (Playlab Press, 1996). Other interviews with Murri writers published in 1995 include two with Sam Watson, the author of *The Kadaitcha Sung* (Penguin Books, 1990), winner in the Fiction category of the Victorian Premier's Literary Awards in 1992. In an interview conducted by Elizabeth Dean for *Famous Reporter* (11.70–8), Watson talks about the connections between his novel-writing, his role as manager of the Aboriginal Legal Service in Brisbane, and his long record of political activism in Queensland and elsewhere. He comments in this interview on issues related to the politics of address for contemporary Aboriginal writers in relation to cross-cultural audiences. He also talks about forthcoming writing projects, including a novel on women's business which he sees as an important element in efforts to balance the issue of gender perceptions among Aboriginal men who have been raised outside of 'traditional' Aboriginal family structures and knowledge systems, whether as the result of mission or forced removal policies (the 'stolen children' generations) or other circumstances. Watson also speaks to *BLAST* Magazine (27.4–6) about his own writing, the representation of Aboriginal people in non-Aboriginal literature, and the nature of various 'masks' worn by Aboriginal writers in their engagements with literary and publishing endeavours.

5.2 New Readings for Old Texts: The (Im)possibilities of Representation
Issues of positionality have not been confined to assessments of contemporary writers and critics but have spilled over into critical attempts to reposition earlier Australian cultural texts and representations through contemporary theoretical lenses. Kay Schaffer, well known for her study *Women and the Bush: Forces of Desire in the Australian Cultural Tradition* (Cambridge University Press, 1988) in 1995 published an extensive examination of the Eliza Fraser episode, *In the Wake of First Contact: The Eliza Fraser Stories*. As Schaffer herself makes clear, the events which followed the wreck of the *Stirling Castle* in 1836, the deaths of Captain Fraser and some crew, and the 'captivity' of Eliza by a group of Badtjala (Butchulla) people (inhabitants of the island known as Thorgine by its original owners, as Great Sandy Island by English settlers and as Fraser Island after the events of 1836) were neither a first-contact scenario nor an originary moment in the white (English) settlement of Australia or even of the Great Sandy/Wide Bay region of Queensland. None the less the story readily passed into white settler mythology and made its way back to the metropolis of

London largely through the offices of Eliza's entrepreneurial second husband, Captain Green.

The stories of Eliza's period of captivity by the island's inhabitants, her ordeals and dramatic rescue rehearse a number of key colonial tropes of savagery and sexuality, of racial and gender difference. Schaffer's study is an attempt to peel back the layers of accreted narrative and to interrogate the cultural meaning generated by the stories of Eliza since 1836. She assembles and provides detailed readings of a number of Eliza texts including: Fraser's testimony to the Commandant at the Moreton Bay penal settlement; contemporary colonial and metropolitan newspaper reports; Fraser's accounts in the Sydney press; Fraser's substantial renarrativizing of the events after her return to England in 1837; popular broadsheet ballads; North American appropriations of the story in which it is assimilated to the generic conventions of the Indian captivity narrative; John Curtis's history *The Shipwreck of the Stirling Castle* (George Virtue, Ivy Lane, 1838); Michael Alexander's historical account, *Mrs Fraser on the Fatal Shore* (Michael Joseph, 1971); Sidney Nolan's paintings; Patrick White's *A Fringe of Leaves* (Penguin Books, 1976); the flurry of media and other popular reconstructions which accompanied the Tim Burstall (screenplay by David Williamson) film, *A Faithful Narrative of the Capture, Sufferings, and Miraculous Escape of Eliza Fraser* (Hexagon Films, 1974); reworkings of the story beyond Australia such as Michael Ondaatje's long poem *The Man with Seven Toes* (Coach House Press, 1969) and André Brink's novel *An Instant in the Wind* (Fontana, 1983); and several texts which Schaffer calls 'oppositional voices' including Allan Marett's play *Eliza: An English Noh Play* (directed by Richard Emmett and Akira Matsui, Sydney, 1989), the documentary film by Gillian Coote, *Island of Lies* (Ronin Films, 1991) and contemporary Badtjala artist Fiona Foley's series of paintings and installations, *By Land and Sea I Leave Ephemeral Spirit* (1991).

Schaffer provides a very useful analysis of the ways in which constructions of gender difference give shape to the various retellings of the Eliza Fraser story. Also useful, but relying heavily on the work of Gananath Obeyesekere (*The Apotheosis of Captain Cook: European Mythmaking in the Pacific*, Princeton University Press, 1992), is her analysis of the European fear/fascination with cannibalism. While Schaffer is scrupulous in her sustained critique of discourses of alterity from which both Eliza's own voice and the voices of Aboriginal people are excluded, the book disappoints in its failure – with the notable exception of its attention to the work of Foley – to make a genuine space for Badtjala narratives, mythologies and responses. Of course, a feminist project which seeks to critique and dismantle the power relations which silence Eliza herself has some parallels with an anti-colonial project which seeks to restore Aboriginal knowledges of the event and to critique and dismantle the power relations which reduced the Badtjala people to the status of savage props in a white Western drama. But these are not the same tasks: the execution of the former is not the execution of the latter. These issues were brought to the fore at the symposium 'Post-Colonial Fictions: Re-Reading Eliza Fraser and the Shipwreck of the *Stirling Castle*' organized by Schaffer at the University of Adelaide in November 1995 to coincide with the launch of the book. Elder Badtjala women objected to what they claimed was Schaffer's continuation of some unacceptable colonialist practices of scholarship which by-passed Badtjala knowledge and experience and asked the question of who exactly gets to set the agenda in establishing more equal and open dialogue between Aboriginal and non-Aboriginal people. Olga Miller, a Badtjala elder, 'expressed bemusement at the amount of attention Eliza Fraser has received . . . and continues to receive [from Europeans]' when her 'stay with the [Badtjala] people was, after all, of no great importance to them' (Julie Carr, 'Tales of the White Woman' *Meridian* [1996]15:1.76–84).

Katherine Susannah Prichard's 1929 novel *Coonardoo* – which deals in realist fashion with a range of issues including miscegenation, the multiple sites of oppression of Aboriginal women in frontier/outback Australia, and the perils of debased marginality across racial, gender and class boundaries – is the subject of renewed focus in cultural criticism published in 1995. Stephen Muecke, embracing a ficto-critical mode in 'Coonardoo 1993' (*Republica* 2.136–46) and employing the conceit of an extended letter to Trinh T. Minh-ha, posits earlier, intertextual versions of the Coonardoo story from which Prichard might conceivably have drawn, but directs attention to their differences in the representation of Aborigines at the level of narrative. Prichard, he suggests, textually extinguishes Coonardoo at the novel's end and in so doing endorses the pervasive equation he argues her contemporary readership would have made – that 'death is the consequence of miscegenous desires'. Moreover, Prichard's central male protagonist, Hugh, never overcomes his ambivalence about the privileges and also the costs that his male, landed status brings. By contrast, E. L. Grant Watson, a naturalist who in 1914 published a pseudo-scientific tract called 'Out There', offered in his reprise of what Muecke calls the 'miscegenation scene' a kind of ethnographic gaze that purported to reveal the 'truth' of racial interactions in the context of invasion and settlement, but also conferred a kind of agency on the Aboriginal women in his version that, if it withholds narrative power, still enables their survival by the narrative's close. Moreover, Jeffries, the white man at the centre of Watson's tale, represents for Muecke a clear instance, through his subsequent marriage and integration into an Aboriginal 'tribe', of an 'Aboriginal-becoming' that Prichard's version does not at any stage countenance. The comparison of these two versions of 'the Coonardoo story' suggest to Muecke the desirability for a third version – the working title of which provides the name for the essay – a film which, in its operations as a metanarrative, will deal with the impossibility of 'representing Coonardoo at all, either as a *formal* figure, or as a *representative* figure for Aboriginal womanhood' (emphasis in original). Along the way, through a counter-balancing metanarrative of the fictive film's progress in script and production form, Muecke explores important issues: the continuing inability of European men (his fictive film-maker is Parisian) to elucidate their sexual desire for 'other' women in ways that disentangle 'her' from 'them'; the 'liberal white demands for authenticity which preserve *distance* in relation to Aboriginal lives'; and the disruptive (at least to Western postmodernism) demands for authenticity and truth in contemporary representations of historical Aboriginal figures that emanate from indigenous communities concerned less with realism versus poststructuralism and more with what Muecke calls 'local authorized accounts' of particular characters and events.

In raising and problematizing the limits of representation here, Muecke is less concerned to offer a way out of the representational entrapments of speaking positions than with an effort to test the theoretical boundaries of the representable by applying them to contested forms of narrative and other cultural production in relation to matters Aboriginal. The remainder of the essays reviewed here that deal with earlier efforts to engage with 'the Aboriginal question' in Australian culture and society proceed from the premise that representational dilemmas can indeed be resolved by a reorientation of reading strategies. Thus Cath Ellis, in 'A Tragic Convergence: A Reading of Katherine Susannah Prichard's *Coonardoo*' (*Westerly* 2.63–71), offers a critically regressive reading of *Coonardoo* that attempts to link it with Engels's theory of family structures and civilization and with classical models of dramatic tragedy. The novel's status as tragic, she argues, relies on the 'incompatibility' of two models of family structure and kinship that converge but then clash throughout the text. In this case, Prichard's *Coonardoo* is first rehabilitated by Ellis along the lines of acknowledging and foregrounding models of 'difference', but then consigned to the social scrapheap of liberal-humanist models of negotiating 'difference' that fail to recognize the fundamental 'incompatibility' between Aboriginal and European modes of living. This is a profoundly separatist analysis in both the conclusions it draws and the critical methods it employs, and it is interesting – and disturbing – to speculate about its appearance at a time when indigenous/non-indigenous reconciliation is precariously positioned at the forefront of cultural and political agendas in contemporary Australia.

In 'Terra Australis: Landscape as Medium in *Capricornia* and *Poor Fellow My Country*' (*Australian Literary Studies* 17:1.38–48) Lydia Wevers mounts an interesting case for re-reading Xavier Herbert's use of the phrase 'Terra Australis' in the two social realist novels under consideration here in light of the Mabo decision. Both *Capricornia* (1938) and *Poor Fellow My Country* (1975) are set in Australia's Top End, and both deal centrally with the debasement and destruction of Aboriginal society at the hands of colonialist expansion in its economic and cultural dimensions. Herbert's notion of Terra Australis, retailed throughout both novels, now may be taken, suggests Wevers, to represent a 'significantly altered conceptual space' no longer beginning in *terra nullius* and *terra incognita* but 'in Mabo country, a terrain whose distinctiveness' moves away from the binaries of city and bush that govern much earlier critical analysis of Australian fiction in the service of white nationalism and toward a 'more volatile and complex notion of what and whose the landscape might be'. The remainder of Wevers's piece is devoted to a close reading of Herbert's two major works in which she attempts to demonstrate that landscape functions as both 'the material and the medium' through which a cultural geography of meaning is constructed and sustained by Herbert's narrative. Such a geography of meanings, she observes, actually becomes also an anatomy of meanings, in so far as the landscape in the novels, littered with a 'Bakhtinian carnivalesque' of grotesque and fractured bodies, is transformed into a body itself, bleeding, violated and dismembered through the incursions of miners and loggers in the 'clearing days' of expansion in the Northern Territory. While Wevers's terrain remains a reassessment of Herbert's *oeuvre*, her essay is stimulating for readers more generally interested in contemporary cultural mappings of the relations between bodies, landscapes and representation.

Other contributions in the reassessment of Australian literature dealing with Aboriginal representation include Brenton Doecke's 'Challenging History

Making: Realism, Revolution and Utopia in *The Timeless Land'* (*Australian Literary Studies* 17:1.49–57), which argues that Eleanor Dark's 1941 novel dealing with events in 1788 is unusually heterogeneous and intertextual both in its treatment of European colonial versions of invasion/settlement history and in its inclusion of reconstructed Aboriginal points of view (most centrally that of the historical figure Bennilong) which, uncharacteristically for the genre if not for Dark, emphasizes the fulsome reciprocity of the gaze – as well as its 'unbridgeability' – between Aboriginal and white characters in the narrative.

5.3 Representing Australian Indigenous Art and Artists: The Politics of Display
Writing on film and media, the influential Aboriginal academic and activist Marcia Langton observed in *'Well, I heard it on the radio and I saw it on the television . . .'* (Australian Film Commission, 1993) that it is vital for indigenous cultural production to identify 'those points where it is possible to control the means of production and to make our own self-representations'. The link between identifying such points in the landscape of cultural institutional practice, and their implications for performances and practices of Aboriginal identities as a consequence is clearly addressed by the innovations in curatorship, education and representation at the Yiribana Gallery of the Art Gallery of New South Wales, which in 1995 was the focus of three articles documenting this important development in the representation of and access to Aboriginal and Torres Strait Islander art. Opened in 1994, Yiribana – translated as 'this way' from the Eora language of the Sydney area's indigenous inhabitants and custodians – is a permanent display of the largest single-space collection of Aboriginal and Torres Strait Islander art in the world. The story of the Yiribana Gallery's inception and development participates in a larger narrative of the history of discursive struggles over Aboriginal art – its definition, acquisition, circulation and display – that speak directly to paradigmatic shifts in how Aboriginal art is currently viewed by galleries, museums, curators, artists and the public.

In 'The Presentation and Interpretation of Aboriginal and Torres Strait Islander Art: The Yiribana Gallery in Focus' (*Periphery* 23.11–14), Margo Neale, Yiribana's assistant curator, offers an indigenous curatorial perspective on the ways in which the Gallery's architectural design as well as its curatorial rationale work to redress both the definitions and what Neale terms the 'confinement' of indigenous Australian art by previously established 'artificial boundaries of region, time and medium'. One reconfiguration of previous curatorial practice instigated by Yiribana was the decision to abandon the standard grouping of Aboriginal art according to chronology, geography or media (bark painting, ceremonial poles, rarrk [X-ray] techniques and so on) in favour of a series of thematic groupings: *Landmaps, Sorry Business, Land Before Time, Claiming a Space, A Collection Begins, Shimmer* and *Spirits of Place*. As Neale points out, such groupings permit not only an emphasis on diversity and difference in the treatment of such themes across various communities, language groups, periods and media, but also dismantle the persistent divisions between 'traditional' and 'contemporary', 'regional' and 'urban' art that have minimized the dynamics of contemporary Aboriginal art practice across widely contrasting contexts. Neale is an advocate of the notion that contemporary curatorship of Aboriginal art should demonstrate not just diversity, but also the 'continuity of tradition' and 'persistence of Aboriginality', a model that receives discussion in another theoretical context above. Thus the shift toward multifocal exhibition practices highlighting both conjunctions and disjunctions is underwritten, for Neale, by the need to demonstrate the internal 'multiculturalism of Aboriginal society' itself, rather than aligning Aboriginal art with broader national discourses of Australian multiculturalism as a whole.

Neale also offers an extended discussion of curatorial motive in deciding to provide substantial textual support, or 'labels', for the art on display at Yiribana. In addition to the educational functions that Yiribana is intended to serve – and Neale notes the increasing public demand for didacticism and context displays in contemporary exhibitions – the textual accompaniments are intended to disrupt Western aesthetic conventions on the subject of art 'speaking for itself', based on the presumption of a cultural elite well-versed in visual literacy, and to recognize the political and cultural importance of making such work accessible, able to speak to a variety of indigenous and non-indigenous audiences and contexts. Neale's discussion here points usefully to distinctions between cultural translation versus cultural contextualization, suggesting that the translation mode belongs to past treatments of Aboriginal art that considered such work to be largely ethnographic in significance, more appropriately housed in museums than in art galleries. Cultural contextualization, by contrast, is an important modality for the assertion of the specificities of indigenous art in ways considered relevant and appropriate by indigenous artists and communities themselves.

A further consideration in Yiribana's curatorial choices revolved around the need to balance the national contexts in which the Art Gallery of New South Wales operates with the regional and local concerns of Aboriginal artists and communities in New South Wales. This tension between the national and the regional, the 'global' and the 'local', has significant implications for a number of the dilemmas currently faced by cultural institutions across Australia that are endeavouring to deal with the politics of contemporary discourses about representation, culture and identity in relation to Aboriginal and Torres Strait Islander art. In this context, Neale details the ways in which the thematic grouping titled *Claiming a Space* has been used not to endorse a version of pan-Aboriginal aspirations regarding art, space and place in the national framework of discourses about Aboriginality, but to present art which deals with the local experiences of contemporary Aboriginal artists working in urban and provincial *milieux*. As Neale notes, however, the thematic groups are to some extent fluid and permeable, and regional works also appear in the *Landmaps* and other thematic sections of the gallery.

Yiribana also gestures in its design and structure toward an expanded and contextualized concept of how Aboriginal art signifies on its own terms. It contains, in addition to performance spaces, an inner room concerned specifically with women's business from the Yuendumu community of women artists, and to which only women gallery visitors are permitted access. Such recontextualizing of Aboriginal art to respect and alert non-indigenous viewers to the boundaries of what is permitted and not permitted for general public consumption is further accentuated by other 'inside/outside' motifs in the gallery's design that link the gallery's topography to its contents and spatialize some of the themes addressed by the curators.

A final issue raised by Neale is the question of whether a dedicated permanent collection of Aboriginal and Torres Strait Islander art marginalizes such work by hiving it off from an integrated presentation of other aspects of Australian national and regional art collections. Neale contends that marginalization would be a risk if Yiribana were the *only* place that Aboriginal art could be viewed within the Art Gallery of New South Wales as a whole (which it is not), but suggests that the benefits of providing a separate space for Aboriginal art on what Angela Carver ('Claiming a Space: The Yiribana Gallery of Aboriginal Art', *Art and Asia Pacific,* 2:4.42–3) calls 'its own terms' outweigh the potential for marginalization at the level of curatorial and consumer practice.

As Angela Carver notes, Yiribana is an exhibition space that 'operates *for* Aboriginal people . . . and not only *about* them'. The paradigm shift in the politics of representation here carries through into parallel shifts in gallery and museum practice, and a subtext of Carver's article is the difference made by Aboriginal curatorship, as manifested by Daphne Wallace and Margo Neale in the case of Yiribana. Wallace, Carver notes, has been instrumental not just in the movement of curatorial discourses toward a more inclusive and culturally dynamic representation of Aboriginal art, but has also initiated a policy for the 'repatriation of secret-sacred works' to their original owners or their descendants and custodians. Moreover, the indigenous-led design and management of the gallery's exhibition spaces and contents has made it appropriate for inclusion as an element of various 'cultural awareness courses' attended by Native Title judges and lawyers, an excellent example of the ways in which the map of the relationships between land, law, art and politics is being discursively redrawn in contemporary Australia.

The innovations in Yiribana's practices as they relate to prior exhibits and displays of Aboriginal and Torres Strait Islander art touched on by Margo Neale receive more sustained examination in Susan Cochrane's 'Yiribana (This Way): A New direction for the Art Gallery of New South Wales' (*Art Monthly Australia* 79.7–9). Cochrane offers a concise and valuable history of the Art Gallery of New South Wales's Aboriginal collection since the 1950s, drawing attention to some of the main figures behind the Gallery's acquisition and display policies: Tony Tuckson, Margaret Preston, C. P. Mountford and the American–Australian Scientific Expedition to Arnhem Land (AASEAL), which turned over a share of works it collected to the Commonwealth government, which in turn distributed them to state art galleries in the mid-1950s.

Cochrane reminds us that despite the anthropological and scientific intent of such collections to begin with, it was Mountford – an Australian anthropologist – and Tuckson, an artist and Deputy Director of the Art Gallery of New South Wales from 1957, who were most insistent on the aesthetic rather than the ethnographic status of such work, arguing for its housing in galleries rather than museums. Nevertheless, what a number of people have described as the 'crypt-like' storage area in which the Gallery originally housed and displayed its Aboriginal artworks; its sporadic, largely *ad hoc* and at times moribund acquisition practices; and its favouring of Arnhem Land and other Top End art in 'traditional' media by men to the exclusion of women's, contemporary media and urban indigenous artworks persisted in both policy and practice until the 1980s. Despite the ambivalence about aesthetics and ethnography that beset the Gallery's perspectives until this period, however, the first works acquired for what became the permanent collection of the

Gallery – seventeen Pukamani Grave Posts from Bathurst Island and story-barks from Yirrkala in Arnhem Land – were commissioned specifically for acquisition, rather than being stolen, appropriated or purchased from extant works. As such, there was early, if tacit, recognition that a separate cultural as well as commercial economy was required for the circulation and consumption of Aboriginal artworks, some of which dealt with the sacred, the secret and the ceremonial, by non-indigenous viewers.

Cochrane also maps the shifts from the separation and marginalization of Aboriginal art in the 1950s through the integrationist policies of the early 1980s and back to the separation once again of such work as instanced by the current practices of Yiribana. She notes that even at its height, the integrationist moment, as evidenced by the 1981 Australian Perspecta movement, was far from achieving a visibly balanced and inclusive display, particularly when compared to the work of other state galleries around Australia in the same period. The return to a separate space for the exhibition of Aboriginal artwork in the contemporary period has a set of quite different inflections to prior divisions of this kind – in relocating the collection out of the crypt and into the new Yiribana space, it was simultaneously rescued from its vertical subordination in the storage area beneath the Australian Colonial art display of the Art Gallery. Both Cochrane and Carver note that a companion book produced by Margo Neale, *Yiribana: An Introduction to the Aboriginal and Torres Strait Islander Art Collection* (Art Gallery of New South Wales, 1994), provides a valuable contextualization and sourcebook for the collection and the artists and communities represented by it. For readers interested in a brief discussion of particular works within the collection, Susan McCullough provides a selective review in 'An Extraordinary Display of Identity' (*Asian Art News* March/April, 56–9).

The efforts of places like Yiribana to deconstruct pervasive Australian curatorial practices that have homologized Aboriginal art, overemphasized spurious distinctions between the 'traditional' and the 'contemporary', and privileged certain regions and media over others in an effort to capitalize on international market and tourism trends can clearly be read in the context of broader agendas that seek Aboriginal empowerment in relation to the management of culture and identity in the terms set out by Langton above. As such, the success of the Yiribana Gallery, its curators and the Art Gallery of New South Wales is a salutary one. Less sanguine, however, is the resistance offered to such changes when Aboriginal art circulates overseas, where it frequently confronts and is confronted by a range of often formidably internationalized pressures – critical, commercial and cultural – that seek to limit, dismiss or defy contemporary developments in the field.

The vexed area of how indigenous art circulates, signifies and is reproduced in overseas contexts is the subject of both Sonia Harford's 'Post Cologonialism' (*World Art* 1.18–19) and Jo Holder's 'True Colours' (*Art and Asia Pacific* 2:2.115–16). Discourses of authenticity are central to the concerns of each article and the controversies therein detailed, and suggest something of the gap that exists between contemporary interrogations of categories like 'authenticity' and the strength of their continued influence across various regimes of situated cultural and institutional practice. Harford (with additional sourcing from Uta M. Reindl, Tony MacGregor and Sarah Bayliss) deals with the outcry generated by the refusal of Germany's Art Cologne 1994 organizers to accept the work of a group of contemporary Aboriginal artists represented by Gabrielle Pizzi, on the basis that their work was 'folk art', merely imitative of a 'tradition', rather than 'authentic' in the terms of the art fair's organizers. Their decision was reversed following the intervention, among others, of the then-Australian federal arts minister, Michael Lee. But Harford raises a number of theoretical issues that arise from but also exceed the initial response of the Art Cologne 1994 judges. Working primarily with arguments first mooted by Eric Michaels in *Bad Aboriginal Art* (Allen & Unwin, 1994), including the notion that ideas about 'traditional' or 'authentic' Aboriginal cultural production rely on mistaken assumptions about the static nature of such work and the culture that generates it, Harford reminds her readers that 'even Aboriginal art produced before contact with a colonising white population and [with] Western art history, materials, aesthetic theories and belief systems, involved the continued reproduction and re-vivification of pre-ordained designs and meanings'. Moreover, she contends, notions of the 'authenticity' of Aboriginal art are highly dependent on the belief that, where Aboriginal art derives from non-urbanized settings, such work continues to be produced only 'for itself' – in other words, as a direct material constituent bearing non-material traces of the ceremonies and rituals by which it may be contextualized in Aboriginal cultural business.

Yet the history of Aboriginal art production since white contact has on many levels been marked by complex engagements with and subversions of the European art market as well as Western styles and media; the 'authenticity' that the Art Cologne 1994 organizers yearned for, suggests Harford, was never really there to begin with. Where it does exist, it is not for outsiders; such meanings are routinely limited for external consumption by a series of substitutions in visual iconography and technique that continue to maintain a sharp distinction between what is available for Aboriginal versus non-Aboriginal eyes and experience. As Harford and many others have pointed out in other forums, the entire terrain of the urban, the contemporary and the hybrid is excised by the foregrounding of nostalgic desires for a 'lost authenticity' imaginatively repossessed by resort to a reconstruction of the imperial 'primitive'. Perhaps the most telling moment in Harford's article comes when the artist Lin Onus (who has since passed away) relates his puzzlement and frustration at the contradictory views of one of Art Cologne 1994's steering committee members. This man, says Onus, claimed on the one hand that the irruption of 'different' art from 'exotic' places into the Art Fair might potentially dilute or compromise the 'good' (Onus's gloss) art in Cologne; on the other, he suggested that to import the artworks of the 'other' into the Cologne context might somehow damage their meanings and effects, since they would be divorced from the significance of their original locale. It is this last point – the ambivalence about the status of the relationship between art, identity and land, the ambiguity about whose interests it is, finally, that require protection – which alerts observers of these debates to the unsettling and unsettled nature of contemporary discourses on difference, on country, and on power in relation to indigenous art and self-representation.

In contrast to the Cologne experience, Jo Holder's 'True Colours' looks at the more enthusiastic if still vexed uptake of Aboriginal art in London, Liverpool and Leicester during a 1994 travelling exhibition mounted collaboratively by London's Institute of the New International Visual Arts and the Boomalli Aboriginal Artists' Co-operative of Sydney. The exhibition, which also ran on Australia's West Coast and was titled 'True Colours: Aboriginal and Torres Strait Islanders Raise the Flag', is for Holder about (again following Eric Michaels) 'a dissenting voice' in contemporary indigenous Australian art – 'what is it, who's got it, and why museums want it bottled'. Holder's review of the intent and impact of what she sees as a politically confronting exhibition acknowledges what she calls 'an astute recognition of the curatorial achievement of community informed and artist-oriented' Aboriginal-run art galleries in Australia, which the British tour has made available to those beyond Australian borders. Such recognition, however, continues to vie with competing art-world orthodoxies about what constitutes 'real' (let alone 'bad') Aboriginal art, and Holder comments incisively on the juxtaposition of the 'True Colours' exhibition at its London venue with that of the explicitly 'tradition'-oriented exhibition run concurrently by the Hayward Gallery, titled 'Aratjara: Art of the First Australians'. This collection received its first international exposure at the Kunstsammlung Nordrhein-Westfalen art show in Düsseldorf in 1993, and Holder points out that the Düsseldorf fair specifically excluded work included in 'True Colours' on the basis that it was not 'ethnographic' enough (though Holder argues that the real reason for its exclusion was the 'excess', for Düsseldorf, of its political content). The designation of Aboriginal peoples as 'First Australians' in the context of 'Aratjara' resonates not only as a gesture toward the precolonial occupation and sovereignty of Aboriginal and Torres Strait Islander peoples; it also functions to relocate Aboriginal art, however contemporary in production, as belonging collectively to a remote historical past, like that of the First Fleet.

While Holder is understandably more attentive to the visual than the linguistic politics attending the ways in which the in-your-face 'True Colours' exhibit worked 'in the shadow', as she says, of the essentialist and romanticized Hayward showing of 'Aratjara', she returns to issues of language and textual representation in the closing paragraph of her article. In connection with yet another exhibit of contemporary Aboriginal artists held during the 'True Colours' run in London, a review of the London Camerawork Gallery's concurrently displayed show of Brenda Croft and Adrian Piper's *Conference Call* described this collaborative project between two Aboriginal artists as 'a dialogue "about experiences of prejudice resulting from their mixed-race identities"'. We will let Holder have the last word in this instance: 'Sometimes you've just gotta laugh at the authenticity industry.'

Other work on Aboriginal art published in 1995 consists of interviews with indigenous artists and non-indigenous gallery owners and a range of profiles of various artists and exhibits active in Australia during 1994 and 1995. An important interview conducted by Simeon Kronenberg with Gabrielle Pizzi, of Gabrielle Pizzi Gallery in Melbourne (*Art Monthly Australia* 85.7–9), points to the disturbing complicity between major international gallery representatives of indigenous artists and the tropes of authenticity that circulate in the international marketplace. In this interview, Pizzi openly deplores what she considers to be the weakening of the market by the failure of the gallery and art-agency industries to regulate the quantity, 'quality' and venues in which Aboriginal art is displayed and sold. In detailing her own gallery's policy shift away from Central Desert and other varieties of 'traditional' and 'tribal' art, toward the representing and marketing of contemporary urban Aboriginal artists, Pizzi, perhaps unwittingly, demonstrates the industry's capacity to stay one step ahead of international art-market trends, while at the same time creating and managing those trends by virtue of almost instantaneous redefinitions of 'authenticity' in contemporary and hybrid forms – including hybridity at the level of medium, as Pizzi's recent exhibit of photographic and video works by young urban Aboriginal women artists suggests. That a number of politically active, culturally aware and theoretically well-informed young indigenous artists are interested in exhibiting with Pizzi, despite her avowedly self-interested and market-oriented perspectives on the Aboriginal arts scene, suggests something of the complexity of the contemporary Aboriginal art world in relation to its mediation by industry representatives in international contexts, and the absence of easy ways of understanding contemporary political, commercial and cultural developments in this area.

Daphne Wallace is the first full-time Aboriginal arts curator in Australia, currently holding a position as Curator of the Yiribana Gallery at the Art Gallery of New South Wales (see above). In an interview conducted by Kirsten Dunlop published as 'Ground Painting' (*Siglo* [Sandy Bay, Tasmania] 4.43–7), Wallace offers a range of perspectives on the relationship between Aboriginal art and land, focusing particularly on the ways in which varieties of artistic representation of land become a form of discursive practice of Aboriginality in their own right. Her efforts to make sense for non-indigenous readers and audiences of some of the issues involved in the art–land relationship are extraordinarily valuable, and she raises as well pertinent issues of the politics of Aboriginal curatorship and training in Australian community and other arts contexts by highlighting the absence of cross-cultural reciprocity in the curatorial field: when, she asks, is an Aboriginal curator going to select, design and hang a non-Aboriginal exhibit?

In the same issue of *Siglo*, Amanda Beresford (4.47) comments very briefly on the dilemmas facing non-Aboriginal curators of Aboriginal artwork exhibitions, whom she argues are still bound by desires for a 'master narrative' that will allow them to unify a show in curatorial terms. Aboriginal art, by contrast, eludes and exceeds such unifying tropes of meaning and representation, particularly for non-Aboriginal curators who must necessarily remain 'outsiders' to the works and the communities in which they signify. For Aboriginal curators, she notes, discourses surrounding the explication of 'Dreaming' stories and their representation in artworks are marked not so much by multivalent as by polysemous and compounded meanings, dependent on a wide range of positionalities related to clan, gender, language, but all mediated ultimately by Aboriginal curators' situatedness as 'insiders' in cultural terms. Like Wallace, Beresford also anticipates implications in the new generation of Aboriginal curatorship for 'curatorial practice across the board, affecting non-Aboriginal as much as Aboriginal art'. Taken together, Wallace and Beresford's interventions on the subject of extending Aboriginal curatorial practices to encompass Western art and curatorship make for interesting speculation on the continued desire by curators for globally incorporative approaches to curatorship across a diverse range of forms of cultural and art production contexts.

A series of interviews by Julie Copeland with Aboriginal community arts advisors – who play a crucial mediating role between indigenous arts communities and art market agents, buyers and collectors – in Aboriginal communities now strongly associated with art production appears in 'The Land and the Market' (*Art Monthly Australia* 83.4–9). Originally broadcast as part of a series on Australia's ABC Radio National, the edited transcript moves through visits and discussions with arts advisors at Yuendumu, Oenpilli, Delmore Station, Balgo, Arnhem Land and Yirrkala.

In her engaging and theoretically speculative profile of Papunya Tula artist Maxie Tjampitjinpa, who is recognized by the Western art world in part for his trademark stippling or 'flicked dotting' style of work, Vivien Johnson ('Maxie Tjampitjinpa the Minimal Mythologist', *Art + Text* 50.54–9) debunks some of the contemporary myth-making surrounding the identification of Western Desert art as an emerging market in 1970s, which constructed a 'kind of artistic "first contact" experience – as if the painters just walked out of the desert into some remote settlement one day and picked up their brushes'. The truth, as Johnson shows, is far from the myth. Moreover, Tjampitjinpa's development as a painter, which included his training and collaboration with Mick Tjakamarra, is used by Johnson to foreground these artists' attitudes of relative 'indifference to issues of authorship and individual accreditation', which helps to 'derail the devouring of Maxie Tjampitjinpa as a new kind of artist-hero by a contemporary art world that increasingly intersects with the "star-making" operations of the mass media'. Johnson offers an informed history of the vagaries during the 1970s and 1980s of Aboriginal art's struggle to gain a cultural and commercial foothold in the contemporary European art world in defiance of its dismissal as 'folk' or primarily ethnographic art, and considers the issues raised for art interpretation and appreciation by non-indigenous audiences of work that, like Tjampitjinpa's, represents 'country in mind' in ways that bespeak the effort to mobilize what Johnson calls 'the challenge of contemporaneity'.

Ann Brody offers a similar though less theoretically or culturally oriented profile of Ginger Riley Munduwalawala in 'Ginger Riley Munduwalawala: His Own Man' (*Art and Australia* 33:1.70–9), which contextualizes the artist's work in relation to country, to growing up in the Anglican-founded Roper River Mission, and to ancestral stories, practices and dreamings in his mother's Marra country, located in the Limmen Bight region on the western side of the Gulf of Carpentaria and informing the range of artwork that he has produced since the late 1980s.

In an interview conducted by Christopher Chapman with the contemporary artist Gordon Bennett ('A Discussion with Gordon Bennett: The Inland Sea', *Art on View* [National Gallery of Australia] 1.38–41) during his 1994 multimedia 'Inland Sea' exhibit, Bennett comments on the ways in which he has used the binary systems of thought that mark Western thinking about art, culture and identity to subvert and 'disturb the gaze' trained on indigenous art and artists, particularly as that gaze is imbricated in the paradoxical valencies attached to persistent concepts of the 'primitive'. He locates his own work theoretically as an art practice that operates in the 'spaces in between' categories, where permeability and overlap are privileged in favour of discrete divisions between genres, techniques and meanings. In 'Another Kind of Dreaming' (*Campaign* March, 18–21), Deslea R. Judd interviews three gay Koori contemporary artists on issues revolving around the identity politics of being gay, being Koori and being artists who, while strongly Aboriginal-identified, produce art which departs from recognizably Koori themes and techniques. The responses of the interviewees – Luke Close, Brook Andrew and Rea – explore racisms in the gay and artistic communities, homophobia in Aboriginal communities, AIDS and identification with country.

Finally, three works by the Wurundjeri (Victoria) elder Barak (c.1824–1903) acquired by the National Gallery of Victoria receive descriptive and interpretive treatment in Judith Ryan's in-house commentary, 'Barak in the National Gallery of Victoria' (*Gallery* [National Gallery of Victoria] March, 11–12), which focuses as well on the 'silence of the iconography' for the twentieth-century non-Wurundjeri viewer, given the decimation of Wurundjeri clans and languages by the impact of colonialism in Victoria throughout the 1800s.

5.4 Stopping the Rip-Offs: Aboriginal Cultural Production and Intellectual Property Rights

In 'The Carpet Case: Aboriginal Culture Acknowledged in Landmark Decision' (*Periphery* 22.4–6), Terri Janke and Nathan Tyson report and comment on the decision in the Federal Court which awarded damages to Aboriginal artists and the representatives of deceased artists whose works were reproduced without their knowledge or permission. The case, *Milpurrurru & Others v Indofurn Pty Ltd & Others* (known as the Aboriginal Carpet Case), has been heralded by Aboriginal and legal commentators as the cultural equivalent of the High Court's Mabo decision of 1992 in being the first decision to recognize the cultural significance of Aboriginal artwork to the communities from which it originates and to award damages for the cultural harm produced by the inappropriate use of Aboriginal images. Prior to this decision, Aboriginal artists and communities had no redress at law against the exploitation of their cultural heritage. The Copyright Act (1968) is inadequate for dealing with works of Aboriginal art because its emphasis on copyright as a property right vested in individuals fails to recognize Aboriginal customary law, which vests the guardianship of particular themes, images and designs among those with the relevant standing in particular communities.

These issues are also taken up by Colin Golvan in 'Stopping in the Rip Offs – A Response' (*Art and Entertainment Law Review* June, 51–2). The article addresses some issues raised in the Issues Paper released by the Federal government in October 1994, *Stopping the Rip-Offs: Intellectual Property Protection for Aboriginal and Torres Strait Islander Peoples*. Golvan argues that rather than amending the Copyright Act to make it more accommodating of the particular understandings of property and ownership which apply to a consideration of Aboriginal cultural and intellectual property, that the Aboriginal and Torres Strait Islander Heritage Protection Act (1984) might serve as a basis for forging the requisite changes in the legal recognition of indigenous property rights. Golvan further highlights the important educative role performed by the National Indigenous Arts Advocacy Association (NIAAA) in promoting awareness of these issues in Aboriginal and non-Aboriginal communities. However, Golvan points to persistent problems in the marketing of Aboriginal arts and argues for the development of strategies to better support their marketing and the commercial return to communities. Ironically, one of the lessons to be drawn from the Aboriginal Carpet Case is that there is a great potential for a non-infringing market in high-quality, hand-woven carpets bearing appropriate Aboriginal designs. Further comment is provided by Catherine Hawkins in 'Stopping the Rip-Offs' (*Alternative Law Journal* 20:1.7–10/*Aboriginal Law Bulletin* 3:72.7–10).

Stephen Gray takes up the problem of the capacity of Australian law – either through the common law or legislation – to accommodate the interests of Aboriginal artists and Aboriginal cultural production in 'Enlightenment or Dreaming?: Attempting to Reconcile Aboriginal Art and European Law'(*Arts and Entertainment Law Review* April, 18–26). Gray argues that while for some time Anglo-Australian law has been dominated by a rationalist, post-Enlightenment mode of legal process, there are other pre-Enlightenment traditions in the law which work on compromise and the reconciliation of opposites: this 'irrationalist' tradition, while suppressed for centuries, may be turned to as one possible way in which Western law may be reconciled to the interests of Aboriginality, particularly the interests of Aboriginal artists and cultural production in Australia.

In 'Protection of Indigenous Arts and Cultural Expression' (*Copyright Reporter* 12:4.6–8), Gail Fulton reviews the present situation at law with regard to the protection of indigenous cultural production, and canvasses five options for reform: amendments to the Copyright Act; amendments to the Aboriginal and Torres Strait Islander Heritage Protection Act (1984); special legislation: the development of an indigenous authentication mark to be registered under the Trade Marks Act; and administrative and educational action.

5.5 Aboriginality and Media

'No set of nominated individuals exercises the significance outside Australia that Aborigines have done, and continue to do, as a collectivity, via their uptake by forms of social and cultural theorisation dedicated to understanding modernity and its post.' This claim drives the trajectory of Toby Miller's 'Exporting Truth from Aboriginal Australia' (*Media Information Australia* 76.7–17) as he selectively surveys the history of 'white intellectual discourse outside Australia' and its use of Aboriginality as a theoretical trope. Glancing at the intellectual capital for which Aboriginality served as a significant currency in the work of European and American sociocultural writers over the last 150 years – among them Hegel, Marx, Freud, Durkheim, Mauss, Lévi-Strauss and Geertz – Miller turns to an examination of the structures of discursive differentiation that allowed colonists in Australia to be represented as a national identity distinct from their counterparts in Britain via tropes of Aboriginality.

There are oversimplifications in Miller's discussion of how the term 'Australians' came to serve as what he calls a 'master signifier' for white settlers rather than 'Aborigines', including his merely cursory allusion to what the historical record displays in the way of discursive and rhetorical shifts from the late eighteenth century onward. More persuasive is his demonstration of how representations of Aboriginality in the literature of sociology and anthropology were used as a form of 'negative imaging' in the delineation of what constituted modernity and its conditions; while the territory is familiar, Miller's treatment repositions perspectives on it by citing the deployment of such tropes by a range of twentieth-century political and social theorists, who mobilized Aboriginality as a regressive formation that served double-duty as tales of caution and of inspiration regarding the place of modernity in history and in contemporary social life.

Miller also attends to the ways in which 'the disarticulation of the sign from its referent undergoes a fascinating rearticulation in Australian sociology'. Thus, he notes, current Australian undergraduate sociology textbooks draw heavily on Durkheim's theories of the relationship between emotions and morals, without acknowledging how much of this work was 'grounded in [Durkheim's study of] Aboriginal society', so that 'Australian' knowledges are first 'exported' to Europe and then reimported back to Australia minus the 'anchoring' of their original referent in (representations of) Aboriginal culture and society. Miller extends his notion of disarticulation into the contemporary arena by looking at the ways in which Aboriginality has travelled, in white intellectual discourse, from the modern to the postmodern, where Aborigines are colonized discursively once again as contemporary cultural studies seeks 'new fields to conquer', and for which Miller finds the work of Baudrillard and Mauss to serve as exemplars. A crucial role for the construct of 'Aboriginality' in cultural-theoretical discourses of the postmodern, for Miller, is the 'discovery' of Aboriginal agency in the work of Eric Michaels on media and Fred Myers on culture and performativity; ultimately, Miller seems to suggest, their takes on Aboriginal agency seem to locate that agency as being produced in and by the vicissitudes of contemporary theory, rather than grounded independently in Aboriginal knowledges and practices that Western (modern and postmodern) epistemologies have been constrained from acknowledging for a complex range of motives. The work of Faye Ginsburg (reviewed in *YWCCT* 4), by contrast, is cited by Miller as an admirable corrective to such biases, in so far as she relocates her discussions of indigenous media and communication away from the territory of Western preoccupations with the postmodern and toward a politically as well as theoretically engaged interrogation of how Australian Aboriginal media practices are discursively aligned with the interests and practices of indigenous and 'First' peoples in other parts of the world. Thus, for Miller, is the totalizing globalism of postmodernism undercut by the localized network of global interconnections accommodated and authorized in work such as Ginsburg's.

Miller's efforts to return the 'sign' to its 'referent' and critique the disarticulation of Aboriginality from its local and international contexts *qua* indigenous aims, claims and aspirations demonstrate that the postmodern condition in relation to Aboriginality continues to be marked by its appropriation for a variety of intellectual and cultural agendas of the West, but *not* necessarily, as Miller's language sometimes suggests, the universal agency or complicity of Aboriginal people, whether individually or collectively, in doing so.

The field of Aboriginal and Torres Strait Islander media production is the subject of Helen Molnar's 'Indigenous Media Development in Australia: A Product of Struggle and Opposition' (*Cultural Studies* 9:1.169–90). Molnar surveys the development of indigenous media production in Australia with an emphasis on the development of community media associations which, in the face of invariably inadequate funding, were forced to develop innovative means of production, which also frequently represented subversions of mainstream media conventions.

In 'Everyone's Agreed, The *West* is All you Need: Ideology, Media and Aboriginality in Western Australia' (*Media Information Australia* 75.102–22), David S. Trigger provides an analysis of Western Australian media content on issues of race and Aboriginality. The study assembles four sets of data: a content analysis of Aboriginal subjects in Western Australian newspapers (the metropolitan *West Australian* and five rural papers from different regional centres) for the years 1984 and 1988; content analysis of discussions on Aboriginal land rights on Perth talkback radio, 1984 and 1988; Aboriginal criminality on Perth talkback radio, 1990; a survey of public views on issues of race, Aboriginality and criminality in two Perth suburbs, 1990. Trigger finds that the public not only 'mirrors' media representations of Aboriginal people, as in the easy and consistent identification between Aboriginal people (especially youth) and criminality, but that the disproportionate instances of Aboriginal subjects in the media in the years under survey represents the media mirroring deeply held racist views in the West Australian population. This enables the transformation of a low-profile issue into a very high-profile one through 'harnessing' an underlying prejudice against Aboriginal people.

Howard Sercombe's 'The Face of the Criminal is Aboriginal: Representation of Aboriginal Young People in the *West Australian* Newspaper' (*Journal of Australian Studies* 43.76–94) provides a detailed content analysis of articles on young people (aged between 12 and 25) in the *West Australian* between April 1990 and March 1992 – a period that includes one of the moral panic outbreaks in relation to Aboriginal juvenile crime also covered in Trigger's work. In the sample of 2,683 records, references to Aboriginality (410) represent the single largest ethnicity group and it is this subsample which forms the subject of Sercombe's analysis. Sercombe's conclusions are grim: news about Aboriginal youth in the west is crime news and crime news is frequently inflected by racism; the 'criminal' is habitually constructed as having a young Aboriginal face.

The recalcitrance of the mainstream press in failing to take up Aboriginal issues is discussed by Wendy Bacon and Bonita Mason in 'Aboriginal Deaths in Custody: A Dead Issue?' (*Reportage* Autumn, 17–22). The authors focus on the media coverage of the Australian Institute of Criminology's report *Australian Deaths in Custody and Custody-Related Police Operations, 1993–4*. This report is part of an annual series related to the Royal Commission into Aboriginal Deaths in Custody which charged the Institute of Criminology with the role of monitoring and reporting on deaths of Aboriginals and Torres Strait Islanders in custody. Despite the fact that the report contained devastating results for those concerned about the implementation of the recommendations of the Royal Commission, reporting on fourteen custody-related deaths, the highest figure for four years, the media was sluggish in its coverage of the report and discussion of its contents. Many major daily newspapers (including the *Cairns Post*) did not cover the story at all. Where reports were published, they were generally limited and disappointing – many papers, for example, reported in gratuitous detail the physical causes of death but provided no insight into the why the deaths had taken place.

The performance of the media on Aboriginal issues is also the subject of an important article by Rosaleen Smyth, '"White Australia Has a Black Past": Promoting Aboriginal and Torres Strait Islander Land Rights on Television and Radio' (*Historical Journal of Film, Radio and Television*, 15:1.105–23). Smyth covers an enormous amount of material in this survey and analysis of the representation of Aboriginal and Torres Strait Islander issues in the media and, more importantly, of the ways in which these issues have been actively promoted by means of indigenous production, non-indigenous production of programmes (particularly documentaries) with Aboriginal content, and by the manipulation of the media by indigenous groups and individuals through the staging of events expressly to secure media coverage. Smyth bases her study on a wide range of materials, including broadcast material (for which her study is a useful resource for those wishing to pursue work in the area), policy and legislation, and critical appraisals of the discourses on Aboriginality in Australia media.

Books Reviewed

Aboriginal Legal Service of Western Australia. *Telling Our Story: A Report on the Removal of Aboriginal Children from their Families in Western Australia.* Aboriginal Legal Service of Western Australia. pp. xi + 247. A$20.00. No ISBN.

Anderson, Christopher. *The Politics of the Secret.* Oceania Publications (Oceania Monograph Series, No. 45), University of Sydney. pp. 142. A$35.00. ISSN 1030 6412. ISBN 0 86758 990 6.

Brewster, Anne. *Literary Formations: Post-Colonialism, Nationalism and Globalism.* Melbourne University Press. pp. viii + 152. A$14.95. ISBN 0 522 84534 7.

Clark, Ian. *Scars in the Landscape: A Register of Massacre Sites in Western Victoria, 1803–1859.* Aboriginal Studies Press. (Australian Institute of Aboriginal and Torres Strait Islander Report Series) pp. x + 199. A$20.00. ISBN 0 85575 281 5. ISSN 1038 2372.

Cowan, James. *Two Men Dreaming: A Memoir, A Journey.* Brandl & Schlesinger. pp. 354. A$29.95. ISBN 0 646 23925 2.

Eades, Diana, ed. *Language in Evidence: Issues Confronting Aboriginal and Multicultural Australia.* University of New South Wales Press. pp. xiv + 289. A$29.95. ISBN 0 86840 119 6.

Eggington, Robert, and the Dumbartung Aboriginal Corporation. *Bounah Wongee – 'Message Stick': A Report on* Mutant Message Down Under. Dumbartung Aboriginal Corporation (Waterford, WA) pp. 90. A$20.00. No ISBN.

Finlayson, J., and D. Smith eds. *Native Title: Emerging Issues for Research, Policy and Practice.* Centre for Aboriginal Economic Policy Research, Australian National University, Canberra. Research Monograph No. 10. pp. xxii + 128. A$20.00. ISBN 0 7315 2319 9.

Hall, Robert A. *Fighters from the Fringe: Aborigines and Torres Strait Islanders Recall the Second World War.* Aboriginal Studies Press. pp. viii + 218. A$27.95. ISBN 0 85575 286 6.

Hazelhurst, Kayleen M. ed., *Legal Pluralism and the Colonial Legacy: Indigenous Experiences of Justice in Canada, Australia and New Zealand.* Avebury. pp. xxxv + 273. ISBN 1 8579 2078 1.

McGrath, Ann. *Contested Ground: Australian Aborigines under the British Crown.* Allen & Unwin. pp. xxxi + 415. A$29.95. ISBN 1 86373 646 8.

Myers, Gary D., and Simone C. Muller. *Through the Eyes of the Media (Part 1): A Brief History of the Political and Social Responses to 'Mabo V Queensland'.* Murdoch University Environmental Law & Policy Centre. pp. ii + 126. A$10.00. ISBN 0 86905 399 X.

Northern Land Council. *Ecopolitics IX: Environment and Conservation: Conference Papers and Resolutions.* Northern Land Council. pp. 168. A$20.00. ISBN 0 9596377 8 8.

Pearson, N., and W. Sanders. *Indigenous Peoples and Reshaping Australian Institutions: Two Perspectives.* Centre for Aboriginal Economic Policy Research. pp. ii + 18. A$6.00. ISSN 1036 1774. ISBN 0 7315 1776 8.

Reynolds, Henry. *Fate of a Free People: A Radical Re-Examination of the Tasmanian Wars.* Penguin Books. pp. xii + 257. A$19.95. ISBN 0 14 024322 4.

Schaffer, Kay. *In the Wake of First Contact: The Eliza Fraser Stories.* Cambridge University Press. pp. xvi + 320. A$34.95. ISBN 0 521 49920 8.

Smith, Paul. *Mabo: Three Years On – Current Developments in Native Title Law.* Queensland Department of Justice and Attorney-General. pp. 69. A$16.95. ISBN 0 7242 6520 1.

Stockton, Eugene. *The Aboriginal Gift: Spirituality for a Nation.* Millennium Books. pp. 208. A$19.95. ISBN 1 86429 026 9.

Tacey, David J. *Edge of the Sacred: Transformation in Australia.* HarperCollins. pp. xvi + 224. A$19.95. ISBN 1 86371 408 1.

Tatz, Colin. *The Obstacle Race: Aborigines in Sport.* New South Wales University Press. pp. xiv + 408. A$39.95. ISBN 0 86840 349 0.

van Toorn, Penny, and David English, eds. *Speaking Positions: Aboriginality, Gender and Ethnicity in Australian Cultural Studies.* Department of Humanities, Victoria University of Technology. pp. vi + 226. A$22.95. ISBN 1 86272 461 X.

Watson, Helen, and David Wade Chambers. *Singing the Land, Signing the Land.* Deakin University Press. pp. vi + 66. A$25.00. ISBN 0 7300 0696 4.

Wilson, Margaret, and Anna Yeatman. *Justice and Identity: Antipodean Practices.* Allen & Unwin. pp. xvi + 223. A$29.95. ISBN 1 86373 889 4.

21

Australian Pacific Cultural Theory

HILARY ERICKSEN, SOPHIE GEBHARDT, CHRIS HEALY and
DANIEL V. S. PALMER

This chapter has four sections: 1. Interpretations/Embodied; 2. Policy and
Beyond; 3. Visual Cultures; 4. Postcolonial?

Wuwekeniga-Wrunjeri/Bunnarong.
Ngun: Rak Mak MakMarranunggu paegu.
Wuwa ngany-Kurrintyu.
Marrany ngany-ga: Marranunggu, Marrithiel, Dek tyerrety.
Ngany tyangawitya-Makali ngany, tyabuty ngany.

This country is Wrunjeri and Bunnarong.
I am a woman of the White Eagle Marranunggu camp.
Country I am of is Kurrintyu
Languages mine are: Marranunggu, Marrithiel, Dek tyerrety.
I listen to my grandmother's and my grandfather's languages.
> Linda Ford (Paiyi) in Deborah Rose, Linda Ford and
> Nancy Daiyi, 'The Way We are (Working in Flux)',
> Greenwood et al. eds, *Work in Flux* (10)

> In Oceania we have a space so immense that the mile and metres
> of our personal experience can scarcely encompass it, so aged in
> time that the minutes of our days and the years of our lives can
> make no sensible measures of it. We have called that space for
> about 150 years Oceania. Like all imposed names, Oceania has
> had its seasons of fashion.
>> Greg Dening, 'Deep Narratives in Cultural Encounters',
>> Greenwood et al., eds, *Work in Flux* (74)

The cultural theory with which we are concerned here emerges between the
grounded particularity of Linda Ford speaking-in-place and the enormity
which Greg Dening tries to think in terms of deep narratives. If this theory is to
be held together by space – 'Australian and Pacific' – it is less the hyper-real
place of Europe speaking the generality of humanity in philosophy than a
tactical chronotope, which is necessarily multilingual. Here we will propose
writing out of Australia and the Pacific as a trajectory from theory at its most

universal to the possibilities of and for postcolonialism: another journey, perhaps from Oceania to the White Eagle Marranunggu camp.

1. Interpretations/Embodied

Interpretations is a series published by Melbourne University Press and edited by Ken Ruthven which aims to 'provide clearly written and up-to-date introductions to recent theories and critical practices in the humanities and social sciences'. Of the three titles which appeared under this imprint in 1995, Niall Lucy's *Debating Derrida* is perhaps the most ambitious. The book takes as its task to 'encourage people to read the work of Algerian-born French philosopher Jacques Derrida' (preface) by focusing on three intellectual debates in which Derrida has been a player. In this sense it introduces us to Derrida in debate. The first of the debates arose from the responses of Anne McClintock and Rob Nixon to an essay which Derrida published as a catalogue essay to accompany a 1983 art exhibition dedicated to a free South Africa, and in Derrida's 'reply' in the same issue of *Critical Inquiry*. Lucy's use of this debate revolves around Derrida's statement that 'there is nothing outside the text'. By elaborating upon the misunderstandings which have surrounded this proposition, Lucy makes the obvious but important case for Derrida's 'text' as not mere form to be distinguished from the 'real world' of racism, the 'politics' of South Africa or ethical 'responsibilities'. Similar procedures are mobilized in Lucy's subsequent discussion of Derrida's debates with John R. Serle over 'writing' and with Michel Foucault over 'reason'. The Derridas who are introduced in Lucy's book are, in the end, remarkably professional in their attention to the protocols of scholarly activity while, at the same time, available to and for politics.

In the second of 1995's *Interpretations* offerings, *Theories of Desire*, Patrick Fuery provides a consideration of the role of desire in some works of French critical theory. Outlining the place of desire in the work of these writers, Fuery sets out to map desire's contours, while remaining firmly anchored in Lacan's conception of desire as 'the metonymic lack constitutive of subjectivity itself'. Along the way, he presents us with the central tenets of Lacan's theory of desire, and the origins of the untranslatable term *jouissance*, a central poststructuralist metaphor for transgression, and discusses Derrida's use of *différance*. *A Lover's Discourse* is dealt with at some length, while the final chapter is focused on Hélène Cixous, Luce Irigaray and Julia Kristeva who, as the 'end point' of the book, occupy a privileged position. The notable omission in this account of desire is the collaborative work of Gilles Deleuze and Félix Guattari, who only appear as one of a series of quotations that make up the text's 'conclusion'. This is disappointing though hardly surprising given Fuery's obvious attachment to Lacan.

Unlike Fuery, Anne Cranny-Francis's *The Body in the Text*, another of the *Interpretations* series, explores the many ways in which material embodiment has been featured in recent critical theory, fiction and popular cinema. More interested in Michel Foucault and everyday lived experience than psycho-analytic theory, she analyses the social constitution of specific embodied subjectivities within networks of discursive practices. Rehearsing the broad conceptual debates, including the feminist reconceptualizations of writers like

Judith Butler, her first move considers efforts towards dismantling the mind–body dualism of Western thinking, thereby undermining traditional conceptions of desire as lack. She also considers the bodily articulations of race, ethnicity and class – especially in the work of Homi Bhabha and Marcel Mauss. Finally she examines how the theme of the technological body figures in popular texts such as *Blade Runner* and the *Terminator* series. Donna Haraway's now famous figure of the 'cyborg' (the *cy*bernetic–*org*anic body) as 'our late twentieth century ontology' receives brief explication here, and desire returns, cybernetically, in the utopian metaphor of the network. With its abundance of well-picked examples, this work contextualizes some of the most important and current theoretical issues surrounding the body with the introductory reader in mind.

Elizabeth Grosz – one of the writers featured in *The Body in the Text* – is committed to theorizing the body with an openly radical agenda, as the subtitle of her collection of essays *Space, Time and Perversion: The Politics of Bodies* suggests. Perhaps Australia's best-known feminist philosopher, this work can be read as a companion piece to her popular *Volatile Bodies: Toward a Corporeal Feminism* (1994). Once again, she is interested in themes connected by feminism and the body, where desire figures as the specific product of sexed bodies. Here, however, she extends her philosophical ideas about the body into cultural analysis. *Sex, Time and Perversion* is divided into three thematically linked sections. The first, 'Bodies and Knowledges', deals with the sexual specificity of knowing. The second, 'Space, Time, and Bodies', focuses on questions of space and its accompanying arts – architecture, urban planning and geography – in the form of a series of meditations on their relationship to subjectivity, corporeality and thought. In the third section, 'Perverse Desire', Grosz explores the possibilities of thinking sexuality, sexual desire, 'otherwise' (predominantly, but not solely, lesbian). Following Foucault, she argues that the preferred social body is a strictly regulated and controlled one. In rethinking the body and 'undomesticating' desire, she argues, the ways in which we understand subjectivity and its lived relations are themselves transformed. The general movement in these essays is away from psychoanalytic discourses to a discourse of exteriority and inscription, broadly from Freud to Deleuze. However, as Grosz explains, these essays can be read more productively as a series of temporary subversive illuminations than as a position.

Grosz is also co-editor, with Elspeth Probyn, of the collection *Sexy Bodies: The Strange Carnalities of Feminism*. As its title suggests, bodies and sexualities are celebrated here precisely for all that is 'fundamentally strange' about them, a strangeness which might inspire new ways of thinking. Contributors to this volume include Grosz, Probyn, Barbara Creed, Mary Fallon, Anna Gibbs, Melissa Hardie and Sue Best. The *production* of sexualities and not their description unites the essays, and the result is a collection that re-dresses bodies which have thus far appeared as 'unmarked, unsexed, and definitely unsexy' bodies. As the cover art, though not the title, make clear, this is a feminist project. All the contributors are women and most write about and out of lesbian and queer sexualities, with the exception of Grosz's 'Animal Sex', which explores the work of Roger Callois and Alphonso Lingis. The sexiness of bodies here is thought in terms of movements, productions, transitions, modes of transportation and metamorphosis – in short, in terms of Deleuzian inspired becoming. The eros of writing both theory and fiction is also emphasized. In the more libidinous prose there are moments when the capacity of the postmodern body for self-determination seems just a bit too romantic.

Queer appears in a different register in the special issue of *Media International Australia* (78), *Queer Media* (*Media International Australia* 77 was the first issue of the renamed *Media Information Australia*). This special issue draws together writings on representation, reception, policy and new sites of communication technology to discuss the ways in which queerness is both figured and policed in the media industry. Rebecca Huntley (5–12) discusses the current swing towards conservatism in the censorship office, and argues that the vague rhetoric that guides decision-making will lead to increasingly censorious legislation. Ralph McLean and Robert Schubert pit mainstream media's resort to 'scandal' against the enabling possibilities of the Internet and electronic bulletin boards in negotiating sexual difference and the politics of representation. Importantly, this special issue of *MIA* brings debates on media, society and sexual politics to a broad audience, and for the same reason the issue would have benefited from a more rigorous introductory framework through which to conceptualize 'queer'.

A sobering collection edited by Paul A. Komesaroff entitled *Troubled Bodies: Critical Perspectives on Postmodernism, Medical Ethics and the Body* explores the medical construction of the body. Medicine is viewed here as a practice of ethics, since in its discursive generation, the body – the 'object' of medical discourse – becomes a complex site for ethical negotiation. Ethics is broadly understood here in terms of Alasdair MacIntyre's influential work *After Virtue*, where he argues that ethical thinking requires a connection between the individual and society. But, and in addition to Foucault, the essays also reveal the influence of the phenomenological philosophies of Merleau-Ponty and Levinas in adopting the view of the body as *the* source of meaning, our internal horizon of knowledge and the perspective we bring to bear on the world. Some of the essays engage in a dialogue with the more abstract field of bioethics, some question its underlying assumptions, but in all the essays embodied experience is foregrounded alongside key instances in which the body 'appears' in contemporary medical discourses: transplant surgery, abortion, reproductive and life-prolonging technologies. Placing medical ethics in a broad framework of philosophical and cultural analysis, this is an excellent and thought-provoking foray into this fascinating field.

Anne E. Becker's *Body, Self and Society: The View from Fiji* is a sensitive ethnographic enquiry into the relationship of embodied experience to the social context of selfhood. Her study into an apparent obsession with body shape in Fiji – exhibited in an exceptional monitoring of bodies – argues that Fijians are not 'self-reflexive about their bodily habitus'. Rather, body morphology in Fiji is 'a primary lexicon of social processes: it is a matter of social, not personal, concern'. Central to Becker's study is the Fijian ethos of 'social relatedness' – well established in ethnographic literature – and the corresponding belief that among Pacific Island societies the self is conceived less as an individuated body than as a locus of shared social relationships. Becker extends this research by describing the complicated relationship between self, body and society in the representative microcontext of a village in Fiji (Nahigatoka). Her argument challenges the Western assumption of bodily experience as personally authored and circumscribed by a governing agent (the mind/self). While obviously very different in approach from theorists of the body such as Foucault, Butler or Grosz, this study exemplifies and amplifies their argument that bodies are discursively and historically produced within specific cultures. Specifically, it argues that embodied experience is necessarily contingent on how the self is situated in a relational matrix.

Edited by Debbora Battaglia, *Rhetorics of Self-Making* is a collection of anthropological writings on the cultural fashioning of selfhood. Through studies of a number of empirical instances this volume illustrates the exchanges between cultural ritual and often unconscious 'self-action'; the problem-atization of the experience and the conceptualization of self in postmodernity; and the fallacy of binary rhetorics in thinking the Western and non-Western subject. In 'Production Values' (121–38) Faye Ginsburg examines the effect of television on remote Aboriginal communities. Given the importance of knowledge and communication management in Aboriginal culture, she argues that mass forms of technology can be co-opted and repositioned as a strategy for shaping cultural futures. Ginsburg notes the importance of the late Eric Michaels's work in this field, but for those who have read Michaels this essay offers little more. By contrast, Fred Myers's 'Representing Culture: The Production of Discourse(s) for Aboriginal Acrylic Art' (George E. Marcus and Fred R. Myers, eds, *The Traffic in Culture: Refiguring Art and Anthropology*) has produced a very rich study of other technologies of representation in relation to Aboriginal people. Despite being a reprint of a 1991 article and isolated from the local nuances of the Aboriginal art markets, this essay holds up well.

Transitions: New Australian Feminisms, is a broad interdisciplinary reflec-tion on the influence of feminist theory on cultural analysis in Australia. Edited by Barbara Caine and Rosemary Pringle, this collection includes contributions by Ien Ang, Zoë Sofia, Sophie Watson and Anna Yeatman, united only by their self-reflexive approach to rethinking previous positions. Almost every category of feminist theory – including 'woman', 'patriarchy', 'oppression' and 'feminism' itself – is problematized or disaggregated in this introduction to some new directions in current Australian feminist scholarship. For example, Ang argues in 'I'm a Feminist But . . . "Other" Women and Postnational Feminism' that feminism is reductive when, acting like nation, it exhibits a homogenizing desire for the inclusion of multicultural voices in a predefined space. She writes of her particular ambivalence as a non-Western woman critic and the problem of constructing an 'Asian' voice in Australian feminism. Critical of feminist theory that seeks to universalize female experience – with its typically white, Western, middle-class assumptions – she considers the difficulties involved in thinking a more complex politics of difference. Eventually she calls for a more modest project of feminism that seeks dialogue without a premature sense of unity, adopting a politics of *partiality* rather than of inclusion.

Ron W. Connell's *Masculinities* is an attempt at rethinking gender relations through an examination of masculinity. This particular study represents a comprehensive introduction to this new field of knowledge. Avoiding any simplistic model of masculinity by denying the possibility of a single explanatory science such as psychoanalysis, he argues that masculinity is a multiple concept that can only be understood in specific social contexts. Connell theorizes gender as a social practice that is irreducible to bodies but nevertheless constantly refers to bodies and what bodies do. He introduces the useful idea of 'hegemonic masculinity' to designate a currently accepted configuration of gender practice that maintains the dominance of heterosexual men. The book includes a section of case-studies – sensitive to the intersection of class, but not, unfortunately, of ethnicity – as well as briefly tracing the historical development of modern Western masculinities. Finally, he critiques certain forms of masculinity politics that have appeared in the wake of contemporary feminism. While it is easy to be suspicious of the current popularity of men's studies, this is a well-informed and balanced account of a field that is certain to be crucial for future studies of gender relations. Connell has been working on the sociology of gender relations for years, and, unlike some work in this area, he writes with a sustained commitment to the goals of both women's and gay liberation.

2. Policy and Beyond

Public Voices, Private Interests is formed and informed by cultural policy studies. Edited by Jennifer Craik, Julie James Bailey and Albert Moran, this collection traces the economic, political and historical terrain that has shaped Australia's print and broadcast media through the 1980s and into the 1990s. The editors argue that the deregulation of the 1980s, with its repositioning of viewers as consumers, has not led to the self-regulating media marketplace. It has instead attenuated any notion of public interest and led to the marginalization of the desires of many media consumers (see, in particular, Jo Hawke's 'Privatising the Public interest', 33–50).

In his contribution to this collection Errol Hodge considers the rise of the Australian Broadcasting Corporation's international television broadcasting (through what is now Television Australia) as both a response to expanding media technologies and desires, and as a challenge to its antecedent, Radio Australia. Hodge is concerned that the editorial and journalistic integrity that Radio Australia fought hard for in over fifty years of operation cannot be credibly maintained by Television Australia. This essay is a shorter version of the final chapter of his *Radio Wars: Truth, Propaganda and the Struggle for Radio Australia*, where Hodge details the past of the station that began transmitting to the Asia-Pacific region in 1939 largely as a mouthpiece of government. This is a dense book, full of scholarly detail as well as anecdote, and whose ultimate richness lies in the author's ability to deliver a clear history of the politics of internal struggle that finally led to Radio Australia's independent, factual commentary and its editorial strength. *Radio Wars* highlights the construction and use of propaganda, and contextualizes the station's early short-wave external services agenda and strategies alongside those of the BBC World Service and Voice of America. Hodge raises important questions regarding issues of censorship, foreign policy and journalistic ethics in news production. A more practical and pragmatic account of cultural policy is to be found in *The Cultural Policy Handbook*, by David Crogan and Colin Mercer, which is an excellent introduction to the field in Australia.

Cultural policy studies is also central to *MIA* 76. This issue takes as a point of departure the coalescence of culture and economics in the rhetoric and strategies of cultural policy in the 1990s. While culture and economics were once antithetical concepts, this issue illustrates that the 'export of culture' has become a preoccupation of both the producers and administrators of culture.

Issue editor Jock Given claims that the reorientation implicit in current policy shifts takes three forms: it is geographical in its sedimentation of Asia-Pacific relations; it is technological with new modes of communication giving rise to diversified forms of cultural exchange; and it is an ideological reorientation, with economics figuring strongly in the production and circulation of culture.

Cultural policy studies has an institutional base in Australia in the Institute for Cultural Policy Studies (now part of a larger National Key Centre in Cultural and Media Policy across three Brisbane campuses). Under the directorship of Tony Bennett, the Institute has involved a number of eloquent cultural theorists, including John Frow, whose *Cultural Studies and Cultural Value* seeks to examine some of the central tenets of the 'discipline' of cultural studies, 'to understand the changed conditions of cultural production and consumption in the post-modern world', and, specifically, 'to know why, under what conditions, and on what basis' one can 'continue to make and apply judgements of value within this disrupted and uncertain universe of value'. Drawing on and critiquing the work of Pierre Bourdieu, Michel de Certeau, Stuart Hall and Ernesto Laclau, among others, Frow is concerned with 'the organisation of cultural value in the advanced capitalist world', and the now familiar relationship between knowledge and power. Central to this analysis is an extended critique of the notion of the 'popular', which he sees as central to the cultural studies enterprise. Frow complicates Bourdieu's link between class and culture with the mediations of mass education and media, and introduces the notion of 'regimes of value': 'a semiotic institution generating evaluative regularities under certain conditions of use, and in which empirical audiences or communities may be more or less imbricated'. Finally, and by way of addressing 'us' directly as his 'silent reader', Frow identifies the 'knowledge class': an historically specific designation of those possessing or using cultural capital, who play the crucial role in the mediation of the cultural field. The book's reception in Australia included a notorious review by John Hartley, who parodically attacked the book in the *UTS Review* for reinforcing an elite form of self-reflexive address. Nothwithstanding this review, the book's indisputable asset is its lucid exposition of dense theoretical material.

A very different account of cultural studies emerges in Peter Goodall's *High Culture, Popular Culture: The Long Debate* which is concerned with historicizing the long and ongoing debate over 'culture' – locating the term's aesthetic and anthropological origins – and the role these conceptions have played in disciplinary formation within the humanities, particularly in the formation of English and cultural studies. There is, Goodall suggests, a certain Oedipal structure to the relation between English and cultural studies, with the struggle for ascendancy revolving around the understanding, use and analysis of culture. Goodall wants to move beyond the hermeneutic schism that determines this antipathy and bring some notion of aesthetics to the current practice of cultural studies. He believes that it is a dependency on 'contemporary' studies and on an undifferentiated populism in what counts for culture that may ultimately lead to a disciplinary crisis.

The echoic title of Tony Bennett's *The Birth of the Museum: History, Politics, Theory* foregrounds a Foucauldian affiliation that would be misleading if taken literally. The Foucault put to use in the book's introduction is less the author of the early studies and more the 'later' theorist of governmentality; not the philosopher of spectacular punishment or the archaeologist of order, but the historian concerned with the conduct of self and the positivity of constraint. Then, a more European-influenced and slightly later cultural studies which is politically committed but less textual and more attentive to cultural practices and technologies, collectivities and histories; it is more concerned with seemingly universal categories – modernity, the subject and power; it is methodologically resourceful. Finally there is a cultural policy (cultural) studies. Here the cultural critic has been replaced by the cultural scientist, who is 'clear-eyed' about cultural politics and concerned primarily with techniques of person formation. The cultural scientist is interested in how citizens and their conduct are produced through mechanical strategies and the assemblage of technologies which constitute culture; and, ultimately, with how it is possible to intervene in programmes of cultural management; how to make cultural policy.

The Birth of the Museum is announced as the first in what is promised to be a series from Routledge under the rubric *Culture: Policies and Politics*, a series committed to 'a fuller and clearer policy calculus in cultural studies' that will 'help to promote a significant transformation in the political ambit and orientation of cultural studies and related fields'. It is a challenging beginning. Those concerned with the histories of museums will find much to enjoy and reflect upon in *The Birth of the Museum*. Those concerned with cultural policy studies might consider how this account of the museum (and accounts of other cultural institutions) might be extended to consider not only the question of programmes, which dominate Bennett's consideration, but also, as he notes, how the birthing of the museum and the use of museums might be thought of together. Those who are anxious about cultural policy studies as an instrumental and restricted form of cultural studies should read *The Birth of the Museum* for the subtlety of its scholarship, the productiveness of its curiosity, and its open and pluralist orientation.

Perhaps the most important publication in cultural theory during 1995 came in the form of the first issue of the *UTS Review* Subtitled 'Cultural Studies and New Writing'. Under the editorship of Meaghan Morris and Stephen Muecke the journal aims to provide 'an international space for academic and creative writing on culture to receive serious attention and critical discussion in Australia'. They describe the outlook of the journal as regional, and explicitly position it as a response to the shrinking spaces available to those who write outside of the parochial hegemony of US publishing. The first issue, thematically entitled 'Intellectuals and Communities', features essays presented as papers to the fourth annual Cultural Studies Association of Australia Conference by Rey Chow, Bruce Robbins, Philip Morrissey, Ghassan Hage and Ruth Barcan as well as an outstanding selection of reviews.

3. Visual Cultures

Rey Chow's *Primitive Passions: Visuality, Sexuality, Ethnography and Contemporary Chinese Cinema* is a compelling theorization of the confluence of Chinese modernity, modes of self-inscription and postcolonial politics. Chow's grounding in literary studies is clear in her explication of Chinese modernity and the turn to visual technologies, although this is a complex interdisciplinary work that draws its material and conclusions from various sources. In her critique of contemporary Chinese cinema, Chow questions the ways in which visuality (a meeting of the aesthetic and cultural) is constructed under non-Western production and – given film's tendency towards commodification and Western consumption – towards what ends it operates. In this discussion of 'first' and 'third world' transferences, she proposes that Chinese cinema is ultimately a form of 'postmodern *self*-writing' – a technology for recording 'the people' – and that it simultaneously provides a space where intercultural translation may take place. Reading the process and effects of translation through the work of Benjamin and Derrida, Chow argues, with a rare blend of elegance and authority, that Chinese cinema is 'a form of *intercultural* translation in the postcolonial age' (xi). If there is some sense of betrayal in this ethnographic exchange, she writes, 'translators pay their debt by bringing fame to the ethnic culture' (202).

Kiss Me Deadly: Feminism and Cinema for the Moment has its origin in a 1991 conference on film and feminist theory. As with all collections there is a certain eclecticism to this book, but it is the recurrent trope of temporality that draws these essays into some proximity. This is suggested by the book's title, and editor Laleen Jayamanne is quick to point out that, as it is conceived of here, 'moment' is an 'elastic notion . . . which can sustain a sense of multiple durations, memory, and incommensurable temporalities' (2). Indeed this temporal trope marks its place variously – in reference, for example, to Ruiz's 'cinematic moment', Deleuze's 'time-image' or Walter Benjamin's 'involuntary memory', but it also emerges at a more formal discursive level. These essays derive from what Jayamanne cites as the third moment of feminist film criticism. Neither blind to discursive heritage nor enslaved to it, these essays signal the urgency of 'passing time' and paradigms, and respond by rethinking the relation between women, cinema and modes of theorization. These readings of films as diverse as those of Bigelow, Kluge, Roeg, Campion, Akerman, Bresson and Moffatt are primarily informed by the writings of Deleuze and Guattari and Walter Benjamin, although the writers use this work in consistently innovative ways. There is commitment in this volume, which is most explicitly claimed in Melissa McMahon's 'Fourth Person Singular' (126–46), to theoretical frameworks that operate alongside cinema rather than against it. Jayamanne claims that these authors work towards a rigour in which cinematic pleasure is not the casualty of critical exegesis.

The Error of My Ways collects essays written by Brisbane critic Edward Colless between 1981 and 1984. Colless's writing begins with a consideration of the Australian art movement best known as Popism in the early 1980s. In attempting to write his way out of Hebdige and Barthes, he is increasingly drawn to enacting a kind of critical practice perhaps best described as poetic performance. In these often beautiful essays Colless casts a loving eye over various artists and contemporary art practices, tourism, the museum and cinema, returning again and again to the phenomenology of the sign. While he often seems to eschew the apparatus of theory, these essays are strikingly coherent in their theoretical concern: to write occasions, exhibitions, commissions, moments while travelling as necessarily failing to mark the occasion despite relentlessly trying to evoke 'substance'. This book raises the question of what kinds of theory, or perhaps what kinds of theoretical discourses, can arise from the ruins of twentieth-century art criticism.

4. Postcolonial?

Australian culture is often, and often uncritically, described as postcolonial. This term intersects uncomfortably with older notions of nationalism and the newer formations of globalism. Postcolonial literatures and postcolonial theory have, to date, intervened in national literary and academic canons in order to expose their blindness to 'otherness'; this has resulted in an increased circulation of texts by indigenous and migrant writers in educational institutions, but has not by implication produced a 'postcolonial culture'.

Southern Review 28.3, 'Framing (Post-Colonial) Cultures', edited by David Birch and the Central Queensland University Committee of Southern Review, deals with the crucial question of the relationship between cultural criticism and cultural policy, specifically in terms of the formation of a 'postcolonial' culture in Australia. Stuart Cunningham's foreword to this special issue frames the debate within a history of cultural criticism as 'anti-statist oppositionism' and the need for critical attention to the policies formed around notions of postcoloniality in government and related institutions. This shift in cultural studies towards policy studies reflects not a turn towards the production of 'cultural technicians' and away from the critical force of cultural theory, but rather a recognition of the complex and mutual relationship between the two. Underpinning most of the articles in the issue is the question: what is postcolonial culture, and what might it look like? This obviously refers to the ways a 'postcolonial' culture is 'framed' within national culture at large, and necessarily, if not inevitably, intervenes in questions of policy.

In '"Being Post-Colonial": Culture, Policy and Government' (Southern Review 28.3.273–82) Paul Washington argues that postcoloniality is both a concern with a Western representational economy (and its critique) and the effect of relations of governmentality. Postcoloniality can only be achieved, he maintains, when 'the government rationalities identified in policy studies and those critiqued within post-colonial criticism are brought to a point of convergence, where the things of everyday life appear disposed in accordance with the conditions of "being post colonial"' (275). It is precisely such attention by cultural theorists to the details of 'progressive' cultural policies that informs what a postcolonial culture might be. The recent government and economic emphasis on Australia's place in Asia both imaginatively and practically transforms ideas of nation and culture for the 'cultural citizen'. Yet, as M. Garbutcheon Singh and Helen Miller argue, in 'Mimicry as a Tactic for Engaging Cultural Policy: Australian Studies of Asia' (Southern Review 28.3.303–14), embedded in this renegotiation of geographic ties via cultural policy are nationalist and colonial tendencies. Not least in that Australia's move toward Asia, whilst couched in cultural and geographic terms, is predominantly driven by the reshaping of global economic orders. Singh and Miller use Bhabha's concept of mimicry to show how, in relation to the material used in teaching Asian studies in Australian schools, ambivalences and contradictions in the policy can be appropriated as critique of that policy. In the process the neo-colonialist representations of Asia, as like Australia and therefore 'naturally' a part of it, are exposed.

This issue of Southern Review responds to a crucial and growing concern with the ways 'postcolonial' has come to stand for a perceptible stasis in cultural life, where 'difference' is emptied of critical force and 'progressive' cultural policy replaces material conditions as the source and site of social change. The articles all point to the need for a repoliticization of the post-colonial that, in Stephen Muecke's words, 'can only be properly achieved in relation to the original inhabitants whose occupancy of the country was never properly acknowledged by the invaders . . . a postcolonial political situation might be said to exist only when the Aboriginal peoples achieve recognition, compensation and political autonomy' (quoted in *Southern Review* 28.3. 273–4). A related project of triangulating Australia, Aboriginality and the Asia Pacific is found in *Asian and Pacific Inscriptions: Identities, Ethnicities, Nationalities* edited by Suvendrini Perera.

In *Literary Formations: Post-Colonialism, Nationalism, Globalism,* Anne Brewster argues for a more subtle and nuanced deployment of the term 'postcolonial' – one that avows the discontinuities of its articulation within the global reconfiguration of power, its convergences and divergences with theories of postmodernism, and examines the effectivity of reinscriptions and re-formations of the national for specific marginalized subjects. Central to Brewster's argument are the ways nationalism is reiterated and persists in 'minority' literatures, as a way of redefining the dominant culture from the periphery. She contests that theories of the postcolonial and/or the global are both enabling and constraining in their attempts to 'identify' the indigenous or ethnic subject in history and of the text. Postcolonialism, she suggests, has avoided questions of an enabling and transformative nationalism because the concept is seen to be embedded in the imperial project; however, this cannot account for the ways diasporic writers, such as Bharati Mukerjee in the United States, reinvent and redefine nationalism from the position of the immigrant.

Similarly, Brewster takes up the growing critique of postcoloniality as solely the condition of diasporic intellectuals, whose relation to the flow of global capital is explicit. Thus she argues, it is contradictory, and indeed lacking in critical force, to describe as postcolonial those who remain subject to colonial institutions of power, such as Aboriginals in Australia. In her examination of Aboriginal women's autobiographies Brewster comes to the conclusion that 'the term "post-colonial" is unhelpful when talking about Aboriginal constituencies' (76); most significantly when the categories of gender and class cut across that of race, and when the narratives are articulated within the process of decolonization rather than a condition of postcoloniality. By arguing for the political force of such narratives, Brewster resists the aestheticizing and depoliticizing effect on indigenous texts when they are appropriated and commodified for a dominant 'national culture'.

The intricate historical connections, and now apparent disjunctures, between 'Aboriginality', autobiography and gender are the subject of Annabel Cooper's article 'Talking about *My Place*/My Place: Feminism, Criticism and the Other's Autobiography' (*Southern Review* 28.2.140–53). Cooper's work participates in the ongoing intellectual and political struggles around the category of Aboriginality, notions of identity and self-representation. Her article examines a specific moment of scholarly response to the 'self-representation of othered groups' (141) in a reading of the debates generated by Sally Morgan's *My Place*.

Cooper rigorously exposes the assumptions of critics such as Bain Attwood, Stephen Muecke and Eric Michaels, around the function and construction of the genre of autobiography as expression, confession or 'truth'. She argues that while ostensibly undoing the implied subject (and object) of auto-biography, in an effort to foreground its naturalizing and essentializing claims, these critics unself-consciously participate in a fixed concept of the genre, and contribute to the devaluation of autobiography as a critical literary mode. This, she implies, is a gendered response which cannot include 'other' accounts of autobiography: as a social construction (rather than merely individual) that enables previously marginalized subjects a place for articulation; as a self-reflexive production that is consistently aware of its mediated status; as a historical text. The critics she discusses, in concentrating on the assumption that autobiography claims to speak the 'pure truth about a romantic subject' (146), mask the text's constructedness within specific historical and cultural conditions.

In *My Place,* Cooper discovers that those moments when the textual 'Sally' questions her Aboriginal status are moments of uncertainty rather than unreflexive claims to an identity on the grounds of genetic inheritance. Similarly she suggests that the critic's condemnation of Morgan, on the grounds that she claims Aboriginality on the basis of genetic inheritance, fails to see how integral the fact of genetics was/is to the social construction of race. Miscegenation is central to Morgan's and 'Sally's' struggle with identifying Aboriginality. Cooper maintains that the text resists any notion of 'pure' Aboriginality – in fact is about the impossibility of this. Thus, the criticisms of Morgan's book collapse, or at least foreground their own preoccupations with a notion of real or 'true' Aboriginality.

Cooper concludes with a return to feminist scholarship in the field of autobiography, drawing on work around the writing of African-American women by Elizabeth Fox-Genovese and Regenia Gagnier. These scholars reject the search for the 'truth' of the subject of autobiography and address textuality as central. The notion of 'experience' can be conceived, not as foundational, but as discursive; as part of identity production and as always political. What is finally missing, then, from the critics of Morgan's text is a sense of their own implication in the quest for a referential 'truth' against which they can test and/or refute Morgan's claims. Cooper thus argues for the historicization of both reader and writer, to avoid an interpretive practice which claims to 'know' better than the text what that 'truth' might be.

Us Mob: History, Culture, Struggle: An Introduction to Indigenous Australia by Mudrooroo is a series of 'lectures' ranging from the spiritual and tribal histories of Australia's indigenous people, to contemporary issues of health, education, the commodification of Aboriginal culture, land rights and reconciliation. Mudrooroo challenges the hegemony of white Australian history, and indeed the existence of the postcolonial, by rewriting indigenous history from the position of the traditionally excluded. Positioning his work within 'Aboriginal Studies', Mudrooroo is at once contributing to the discipline's growth, as part of what he calls a 'healing process', and suspicious of the appropriative capacity of the dominant institutions. Thus he speaks from the position of 'Us Mob', reversing the usual us/them dichotomy, and subtlety engaging the white reader in a play of inclusion/exclusion that foregrounds the way colonial history 'objectified', if not erased, the indigenous subject.

Throughout the text Mudrooroo emphasizes the 'our' of 'our culture', 'our health' and so on. This draws attention to the ways indigenous people are consistently repositioned as 'other' in the official languages of policy and politics; even, perhaps, in the academic debates around 'aboriginality' and authenticity. A crucial point in his retelling of Aboriginal history is that the concept of 'Aboriginal Australians' constructs a totality which obliterates the heterogeneity of Australia's indigenous people. It is, Mudrooroo suggests, an imaginary totality which can only ever be strategically useful for those it has come to represent: its history is one of containment and violence that constructed the diverse population of indigenous Australians as a homogenous 'other'.

In the present 'Aboriginal' refers to an equally diverse community, whose demand for representation relies on the term, and yet are always in a skewed, if not antagonistic, relation to its genealogy. In emphasizing the plurality of subject positions and material conditions experienced by Australia's indigenous people, Mudrooroo makes a significant contribution to his avowed project, as Aboriginal writer, to 'give his people a history'.

At the same time Mudrooroo is, as many critics have asserted, difficult to place in relation to the debates around the possibility of constructing an anti-hegemonic 'Aboriginal' history. He moves between essentials and anti-essentialist positions in a way that refuses the full authority of either. In 'Mudrooroo and the Power of the Post: Alternative Inscriptions of Aboriginalist Discourse in a Post-Aboriginalist Age' (*Southern Review* 28.2.121–39) Penny van Toorn explores the problematic practice of writing Aboriginal history when 'history' itself is 'deeply implicated in the colonial project' (121). Van Toorn reads Mudrooroo's novelistic rewritings of history as inscribing the dual and potentially theoretically contradictory agenda of postcolonial discourse.

In a reading of *Doin' Wildcat* van Toorn argues that Mudrooroo negotiates between two ambivalent theoretical positions: one she calls the 'commonsense' approach which relies on binary categories, a mimetic theory of representation; the other, a constructivist approach, which deconstructs the former and undoes essentialist assumptions about identity, language and history. To disclaim all popular and/or traditional essentializing discourses as outmoded and oppressive cannot account for the interventionary power of writing such as Mudrooroo's. Van Toorn's reading raises questions of ambivalence and cultural difference that cannot be contained within a chronology of the 'new' and the 'old', and her critique undermines the fashionable tendency to disavow the political usefulness of categories of the authentic.

As much recent scholarship around subject-formation and identity politics has revealed, the conjunctions and disjunctions between race, gender, class and nationality are not easily articulated. It is not enough to recite this now familiar mantra without examining the implications of the differences contained in each position, and indeed in their multiple combinations. In *Speaking Positions: Aboriginality, Gender and Ethnicity in Australian Cultural Studies*, edited by Penny van Toorn and David English, a vastly diverse collection of critical studies around the construction of cultural identity is brought together under the rubric of 'speaking' and 'positionality'. Both these terms foreground the performative and transitive nature of both political identity and articulations of self.

As a way of departing from the race/class/gender triad that 'dominates British cultural studies' (2) the collection focuses on the specificities of

'Aboriginality', 'ethnicity' and 'gender' as they are informed by the cultural and historical geography of Australia. *Speaking Positions* emphasizes the differences between experiences and articulations of marginality dependent upon cultural contexts, and in this way contributes to a growing sense of an Australian cultural studies that simultaneously reflects the complexity of fixing its project within any uncritically defined national boundary. Thus the collection ranges from Catherine Driscoll's exploration of representations of 'The Girl' as homoerotic virgin in adolescent women's magazines (188–97) to Stephen Muecke's formulation of an Aboriginal practice of place that is post-Oedipal and takes on the anti-representational implications of Deleuze's notion of becoming (167–79). In 'Who Should Speak for Whom? African Women and Western Feminism' (100–29) Sekai Nzenza argues that, as a diasporic African woman moving in academic circles, although she is consistently assured of commonality as gendered woman, she is also the subject of a colonizing gaze that objectifies her difference. She suggests that in speaking back she deconstructs her status as 'other' and enables a critical and theoretical, as well as practical, dialogue to emerge.

While these brief descriptions indicate the range of *Speaking Positions'* engagement with critical theory, such inclusiveness is never without its problems: it is the paradox of 'naming' the margin in the process of dismantling such identifications. Van Toorn and English acknowledge their complicity in a process which places marginal subjects in an anomalous relation to the dominant culture. However, in emphasizing the history of the concept of a 'speaking position', from that which is fixed, essential and monolithic, to the 'shifting', 'plural' (3) and contextual, they also emphasize the strategic and fluid nature of the terms that form the lexicon of their collection.

Cultural Studies 9.1, edited by Tony Bennett and Valda Blundell, focuses on the struggles of 'First Peoples' in New Zealand, Australia and Canada. Whilst recognizing that each of these countries has a specific colonial history, and specific responses to the formations of the postcolonial and the global, the issue locates similarities in the cultural politics of indigenous populations and the cultural policies that result. Thus, the articles both represent the inherent differences between countries traditionally (and now contentiously) characterized as 'white settler societies', and the convergences in patterns of indigenous struggle.

One such convergence is the demand by indigenous people for degrees of cultural autonomy, and the connections between this demand and land-rights movements. A number of the articles trace the histories of questions of indigenous land ownership and the varied responses in cultural policy regarding cultural ownership. Thus debates about the custodianship of indigenous artefacts and remains, categories of the sacred, and indigenous knowledge have been foregrounded in aspects of national life.

Ken Gelder and Jane M. Jacobs's article ' "Talking out of Place": Authorising the Aboriginal Sacred in Post-Colonial Culture' (150–60) argues that post-Mabo concepts of nation are inseparable from an Aboriginal sacred. They explore the way the sacred is negotiated in the public domain, significantly in the ways the sacred is figured not solely as about Aboriginal claims on land, but as it impinges on a non-Aboriginal self-consciousness of historical and national self. Mabo, the writers suggest, simultaneously mobilized residual racisms and romantic and sympathetic alignments with the dispossessed of Australia's colonial past. This is not to say, however, that the category of the sacred as a way of channelling land-claims has been without constraints: in many cases the sacred has been constructed as an illegitimate and/or ill-specific demand for land that threatens non-Aboriginal stakes in mining and farming. Conversely, its appropriation by the law has stood in the way of land claims not based on the sacred. Gelder and Jacobs suggest that in order for the sacred to resist or escape 'predatory appropriation' it needs to be rendered 'hidden for all to see'; a double encoding of the sacred as authorized and authorizable, while always located elsewhere.

In 'Broaching Fiction: A Short Theoretical Appreciation of William Ferguson's *Nanya*' Simon During traces the conditions of emergence of Aboriginal fictionality. He locates this emergence of Ferguson's story, written in 1930 and republished in an anthology in 1990, as it is seen to broach or transgress the line between 'Dreaming narratives' and Western fiction. This reflects a historical moment, according to During, when assimilationist policies were dominant and rejection of traditional 'native' culture was a condition of becoming a citizen. Thus Ferguson's narrative is directed towards a readership 'for whom Dreaming narratives are no longer true' (167) and thus become fiction. But this does not eradicate Aboriginal difference in the process; the Aboriginal heroine Ada, while taking on 'white' culture, marries an Aboriginal. In this narrative twist During traces a politics of cultural and political autonomy that Ferguson, writing in the assimilationist 1930s, was unable to imagine. A more conventional account of colonialism and literature emerges in Robert Dixon's *Writing the Colonial Adventure: Race, Gender and Nation in Anglo-Australian Popular Fiction, 1875–1914*, which explores the ways an imperialist ideology was promulgated through popular fiction, both British and Australian, in the period from the 1870s until World War I. The fiction of this time is of particular interest to Dixon as it reflects a historical shift from perceiving British domination as colonial to 'imperial'.

During's brief and evocative study of fiction, Aboriginality and the globalization of a genre he calls 'magic realism' contrasts sharply with Helen Molnar's examination of indigenous media in 'Indigenous Media Development in Australia: A Product of Struggle and Opposition' (*Cultural Studies* 9.1.167–90). Molnar's is a comprehensive and detailed history of the production of Aboriginal media in Australia and the inadequate government response to what has become a critical site for indigenous cultural expression and political articulation. Molnar's article responds to the demand within cultural studies for critique of cultural policy, a theme which underwrites much of the 'First Peoples' issue.

If there is one final set of debates emerging from the Pacific that threatens to recast cultural theory it is that emerging from cultural and historical anthropology. Two American anthropologists, Gananath Obeyesekere and Marshall Sahlins, have recently conducted a book-length debate on the status of Cook for Hawaiians. Europeans, argues Obeyesekere in *The Apotheosis of Captain Cook: European Mythmaking in the Pacific*, were myth-makers when it came to Cook, a case he demonstrates by revisiting aspects of Bernard Smith's work on Cook's posthumous reputation in Europe. Obeyesekere's real interest is in suggesting that this European vision of Cook was subsequently back-projected onto the 'natives' of the Pacific, enabling historians, biographers and

Marshall Sahlins to claim that in 1778–79 Hawaiians really thought Cook was the god Lono. Hawaiians were not so stupid, says Obeyesekere. They, like all humanity, were and are possessed of a 'practical rationality' which enabled them to recognize Cook for what he was, a man from elsewhere who wielded power. What really happened, says Obeyesekere, was that Cook was installed as a chief and that after his death he was deified in the same way in which Hawaiian chiefs were normally deified. Only after the colonization of Hawaii was more fully realized did the European influences of missionaries and others plant the notion of Cook as Lono, thus influencing some Hawaiians to mistakenly identify this as an indigenous belief. Although Obeyesekere describes his book as one part of a larger project in which he will analyse Cook as a Prospero/Kurtz figure of and for Western culture, the principle focus of his attack is Sahlins's argument that for Hawaiians, Cook was Lono.

Sahlins's reply in *How Natives Really Think* is both focused and wide-ranging. First, Sahlins sets out to make a detailed empirical case for the actuality that 'in word and deed, Hawaiians received Cook as a return of Lono' (2). Not that Cook was Lono, but that because of an historical encounter which involved a vast array of coincidences and communications, of cultural exchange and violence, of sex and ceremony, of recognition and misrecognition, of strangeness and familiarity, Cook was understood and incorporated by Hawaiians as an historical metaphor for a mythical reality. In the process, *The Apotheosis of Captain Cook* emerges as 'a veritable manual of sophistical and historiographical fallacies' (191). The broader argument which Sahlins makes is that Obeyesekere's work is a form of ethnohistory which, although it proclaims itself as anti-imperialist, relies on a crude 'pop nativism' which homogenizes all 'natives' as both alike (and hence accessible to other 'natives') and possessed of (and by?) rationality. The West and their white academic spokesman meanwhile view the world, especially the historical world, through an eye rheumy with the veil of ideology, a gaze which continually represents the violence of colonialism. For Sahlins, this misrecognition of actual violence is achieved by simple inversion of 'the West and the Rest', an inversion which although masquerading as subaltern resistance, in fact effects symbolic violence against 'natives'. This debate offers important resources for any project in cultural theory.

Books Reviewed

Battaglia, Debbora, ed. *Rhetorics of Self-Making*. University of California Press. pp. 160. pb A$26.50. ISBN 0 520 08799 2.

Becker, Anne E. *Body, Self and Society: The View from Fiji*. University of Pennsylvania Press. pp. 206. hb £32.95. ISBN 0 8122 3180 5.

Bennett, Tony. *The Birth of the Museum: History, Politics, Theory*. Routledge. pp. 320. pb A$39.95. ISBN 0 415 05388 9.

Brewster, Anne. *Literary Formations: Post-Colonialism, Nationalism, Globalism*. Interpretations. Melbourne University Press. pp. 160. pb A$14.95. ISBN 0 522 84534 7.

Caine, Barbara, and Rosemary Pringle. *Transitions: New Australian Feminisms*. Allen & Unwin. pp. 243. pb A$ 24.95. ISBN 1 86373 776 6.

Chow, Rey. *Primitive Passions: Visuality, Sexuality, Ethnography, and*

Contemporary Chinese Cinema. Columbia University Press. pp. 252. pb A$31.50. ISBN 0 231 07683 5.

Colless, Edward. *The Error of My Ways: Selected Writing 1981–1984.* Institute of Modern Art. pp. 234. pb A$19.95. ISBN 1 875792 16 3.

Connell, Ron W. *Masculinities.* Allen & Unwin. pp. 295. pb A$24.95. ISBN 1 86373 825 8.

Craik, Jennifer, Julie James Bailey and Albert Moran, eds. *Public Voices, Private Interests.* Allen & Unwin. pp. 192. pb A$29.95. ISBN 1 86373 628 X.

Cranny-Francis, Anne. *The Body in the Text.* Interpretations. Melbourne University Press. pp. 144. pb A$14.95. ISBN 0 522 84575 4.

Crogan, David, and Colin Mercer. *The Cultural Policy Handbook.* Allen & Unwin. pp. 192. pb A$29.95. ISBN 1 86373 894 0.

Dixon, Robert. *Writing the Colonial Adventure: Race, Gender and Nation in Anglo-Australian Popular Fiction, 1875–1914.* Cambridge University Press. pp. 228. hb A$90, pb A$29.95. ISBN 0 521 48190 2, 0 521 48439 1.

Frow, John. *Cultural Studies and Cultural Value.* Oxford University Press. pp. 190. hb A$90, pb A$26.95. ISBN 0 19 871127 1, 0 19 871128 X.

Fuery, Patrick. *Theories of Desire.* Melbourne University Press. pp. 107. pb A$14.95. ISBN 0 522 84620 3.

Goodall, Peter. *High Culture, Popular Culture: The Long Debate.* Allen & Unwin. pp. 224. pb A$27.95. ISBN 1 86373 833 9.

Greenwood, Emma, Klaus Neumann and Andrew Sartori, eds. *Work in Flux.* History Department, University of Melbourne. pp. 242. pb. A$12.00. ISBN 0 7325 1255 7.

Grosz, Elizabeth. *Space, Time and Perversion: The Politics of Bodies.* Allen & Unwin. pp. 288. pb A$27.95. ISBN 1 86373 953 X.

Grosz, Elizabeth, and Elspeth Probyn, eds. *Sexy Bodies: The Strange Carnalities of Feminism.* Routledge. pp. 303. pb A$32.95. ISBN 0 415 09803 3.

Hodge, Errol. *Radio Wars: Truth, Propaganda and the Struggle for Radio Australia.* Cambridge University Press. pp. 324. hb A$75, pb A$29.95. ISBN 0 521 47380 2, 0 521 47927 4.

Jayamanne, Laleen. *Kiss Me Deadly: Feminism and Cinema for the Moment.* Power Publications. pp. 285. pb A$14.95. ISBN 0 909 95226 4.

Komesaroff, Paul A., ed. *Troubled Bodies: Critical Perspectives on Postmodernism, Medical Ethics, and the Body.* Melbourne University Press. pp. 256. pb A$29.95. ISBN 0 522 84684 X.

Lucy, Niall. *Debating Derrida.* Interpretations. Melbourne University Press. pp. 128. pb A$14.95. ISBN 0 522 84625 4.

Marcus, George E., and Fred R. Myers, eds. *The Traffic in Culture: Refiguring Art and Anthropology.* University of California Press. pp. 380, pb $17.95. ISBN 0 520 08847 6.

Mudrooroo. *Us Mob: History, Culture, Struggle: An Introduction to Indigenous Australia.* Angus & Robertson. pp. 242. pb A$17.95. ISBN 0 207 18818 1.

Obeyesekere, Gananath. *The Apotheosis of Captain Cook: European Mythmaking in the Pacific.* Princeton University Press. pp. 249. hb A$45.00. ISBN 0 691 05680 3

Perera, Suvendrini, ed. *Asian and Pacific Inscriptions: Identities, Ethnicities, Nationalities.* A special book issue of *Meridian: The La Trobe English Review.* vol. 14 no. 2. pp. 254. pb A$30. ISBN 1 86446 065 2.

Sahlins, Marshall. *How Natives Really Think: About Captain Cook, For*

Example. The University of Chicago Press. pp. 318. $24.95. ISBN 0 226 73368 8

van Toorn, Penny, and David English, eds. *Speaking Positions: Aboriginality, Gender and Ethnicity in Australian Cultural Studies*. Humanities, Victoria University of Technology. pp. 226. pb A$22.95. ISBN 1 86272 461 X.

Index